THE EMERALD MODEM

Also by Richard Leviton

Seven Steps to Better Vision

The Imagination of Pentecost: Rudolf Steiner and Contemporary Spirituality

Brain Builders! A Lifelong Guide to Sharper Thinking, Better Memory,
    and an Age-Proof Mind

Weddings by Design: A Guide to Non-Traditional Ceremonies

Looking for Arthur: A Once and Future Travelogue

Physician: Medicine and the Unsuspected Battle for Human Freedom

The Healthy Living Space: 70 Practical Ways to Detoxify the Body and Home

What's Beyond That Star: A Chronicle of Geomythic Adventure

The Galaxy on Earth: A Traveler's Guide to the Planet's Visionary Geography

THE
EMERALD MODEM

A User's Guide to Earth's Interactive Energy Body

RICHARD LEVITON

HAMPTON ROADS
PUBLISHING COMPANY, INC.

Cover design by Steve Amarillo
Cover photograph © 2004 NASA, all rights reserved. Use of this
NASA image does not implicitly or explicitly imply endorsement of
this product or the information contained herein.
Interior illustrations © 2003 Anne L. Dunn Louque

Hampton Roads Publishing Company, Inc.
1125 Stoney Ridge Road
Charlottesville, VA 22902

434-296-2772
fax: 434-296-5096
e-mail: hrpc@hrpub.com
www.hrpub.com

If you are unable to order this book from your local
bookseller, you may order directly from the publisher.
Call 1-800-766-8009, toll-free.

Library of Congress Cataloging-in-Publication Data

Leviton, Richard.
  Emerald modem : a user's guide to earth's interactive energy body /
Richard Leviton.
     p. cm.
  Includes bibliographical references and index.
  ISBN 1-57174-245-X (alk. paper)
  1. Sacred space. 2. Mythology. 3. Occultism. I. Title.
  BL580.L46 2004
  133.3'33--dc22
                                        2004000739

ISBN 1-57174-245-X

10 9 8 7 6 5 4 3 2 1

Printed on acid-free paper in the United States

Dedication

To the Supreme Being,
for thinking it all up, and for having the nerve to go through with it.

Table of Contents

Introduction
What Is the Earth's Interactive Energy Body?
A New View of the Human, Earth, and Galaxy

This book is an offering towards an answer to a question I have long pondered: *What is my true relationship to the Earth?*

The prevailing culture of our contemporary Western postindustrial societies does not encourage the raising of this question. Maybe it never occurs to the arbiters and controllers of modern thought and inquiry. Yet anthropological evidence suggests it was once a paramount concern of pretechnological tribal cultures, some of which, like the American Hopi and Australian aborigines, still retain threads of understanding of this relationship.

Ecological movements encourage us to respect Nature's biodiversity and to stop polluting our Mother Earth. James Lovelock's Gaia Hypothesis suggested the planet has an impressive self-regulating mechanism. Deep Ecology advocates counsel us to "think like a mountain" and include all sentient beings in any discussion about the environment. Eco-friendly products, eco-tourism, and the Green political movement have focused public attention on the impact of consumer choices on a fragile global ecosystem.

These approaches are laudable and important, but I am after a deeper, spiritual affinity, which has been virtually erased from Western cultural awareness for centuries. I think we desperately need to resuscitate and enlarge it, to guarantee our survival. Environmentalism teaches us we are embedded in a natural ecosystem. This view posits two things: humans and the physical world. In *The Emerald Modem* I describe an environmentalism that posits only one thing: humanity and the planet as an interdependent singularity.

The basis of our true relationship with the Earth is not shared physiological and biochemical processes, but interlinked consciousness.

Western science does not yet even credit human consciousness as more than a by-product of physical brain processes, so to propose that the Earth as a planet has consciousness is, to conventional thinking, preposterous. Yet it's true. *The Emerald Modem* will show you how to enter into the planet's consciousness.

Where does this interlinked consciousness between humans and planet take place? In the

Earth's energy body. Think of this as the planetary equivalent of the human aura, said by psychics to consist of seven layers and to include many features, such as chakras, channels, and nodes, for the conduction of energy—or shall we say, different qualities of consciousness. In essence, our human energy body is much like the planet's, if not identical, and both are based on a cosmic original. This correspondence makes it possible for us to interact efficiently with the Earth and be interlinked through consciousness with it.

The Earth's energy body is complex and has many features. I describe 85 in this book, but most likely there are many more. But this fact alone should definitively overturn our parochial notion that the Earth is a third rate minor planet stuck inconsequentially out on the farther edges of the galaxy and that we, its human inhabitants, are similarly of less than major significance on it.

Rather, the classical assumption that the Earth is at the center of the universe and that everything revolves around it, if not literally true, is certainly geomantically so. The physical Earth is at the center of the cosmos *because* the cosmos is present all around it as its energy body and its 85 + features. It's like the planet is enwombed in a hologram or virtual reality matrix of the galaxy.

I call this energy body with the cosmos in it the Earth's *visionary geography* because it is a realm of visions and psychic experiences of the planet's numinous essence. I also call the planet's energy body the *Galaxy on Earth* because much of the galaxy is virtually present all around us through the planet's array of sacred sites. I further call it *Heaven on Earth* because much of the contents of the spiritual worlds—temples, planes, dimensions, denizens—are similarly present. Perhaps closer to our present-day consensus reality is the term *planet of sacred sites*.

So the Earth is at the center of the cosmos, and we humans are major players in its life,

health, and destiny. In fact, we, too, are at the center of the universe, and through our consciousness we hold the planet's life in our hands.

Truly, the fate of the world rests with us. When we interact with the Earth's energy body through its diversity of sacred sites and their subtle but potent cosmic connections, we contribute to the planet's well-being. In fact, we're supposed to; as I explain later in the book, the Earth is a designer planet specifically created and fashioned for regular human-planet interaction through its visionary geography accessed through its many thousands of holy sites.

The 85 different geomantic features discussed in *The Emerald Modem* are arrayed around us in a hierarchy, based on their order in creation and their function in the planet's energy body. They are "organs" in the Earth's body and the means for uplifting human awareness. They are directly correlated with equivalent structures of consciousness in our own constitution and with that of the cosmos. The clues for this connection are all around us, but we routinely ignore them. I will take you through these 85 features in a kind of organic, hierarchical, experiential order, illuminating them with myths and direct psychic experiences to present a plausible model of Earth, human, and galaxy.

This is of more than intellectual interest. It is not an exaggeration to say the well-being of the Earth *depends* on our understanding the pattern and interacting appropriately with it. Think of this as a subtler kind of proactive environmentalism, as the spiritual underpinning of deep ecology. The fate of the planet does rest in our hands—or consciousness. Why? It's a theological matter.

It has to do with our Judeo-Christian theology of light and matter, of how the Light "fell" into matter and how we "lost" Eden and how matter needs to be redeemed, and whose fault it all was. A very large beneficent angelic being is awaiting our understanding of the Earth's visionary geography so he may rejoin the Supreme Being, his Father. Those in the angelic realm call him the Lord of Light; we call him Lucifer, which means the Light-Bearer, but we usually forget that part and regard him as humanity's scapegoat. It's *his* fault, we assume.

Maybe, and maybe not, but what's important is that we must come to terms with this "scapegoat" if we want to endure on this planet. At present, the Lord of Light occupies humanity's collective Shadow, the parts we never look at. The problem is, we have to because all of Earth's visionary geography is his benevolent, God-commissioned endowment to us. Later I explain how all 85 features are aspects of a single cosmic jewel called an Emerald, a six-sided, double-terminated lovely green Emerald bigger than the entire planet and placed around it as a kind of master energy field. This is the key that operates this planet of sacred sites, this Heaven on Earth. I call it the Emerald modem.

Each human has one, and the planet has one, and there is one more.

The Emerald modem has an owner. It belongs to the Light-Bearer. And to use the Emerald modem, we must execute a "handshake" across the platforms, us with him, with the planet as witness and beneficiary. That's the basic set-up. To use the Emerald modem we must redeem humanity's Shadow called Lucifer.

This may sound shocking, yet it has biblical precedent. Paradise is said to have two trees. One is the Tree of Life, "which is so huge, that it would take a man five hundred years to traverse a distance equal to the diameter of the trunk, and no less vast is the space shaded by its crown of branches."[1]

The other is the Tree of the Knowledge of Good and Evil. Later in the book I explain how Lucifer *is* this dualistic tree, yet the Tree of Life is also Lucifer's, for it is the Emerald. Here's the key part: It's said that the Tree of the Knowledge of Good and Evil forms a hedge about the much vaster Tree of Life. This means to get to the paradisal inner tree, you must pass through the outer hedge, or dualistic tree. To achieve paradisal conditions on Earth, you have to breach the outer hedge.

So *The Emerald Modem* presents a new view of the relationship of humans to our host planet. To some, this may confirm long-held suspicions and secreted intuitions; to others, the details of this relationship may seem shocking, incredible, or unbelievable. Either way, it's information that requires action. Once we know this, we need to start acting on it, interacting with the planet, awakening its energy nodes, remembering our origins, redeeming Lucifer.

This new view is eminently practical: I present many tables listing locations of sacred sites around the planet where you may best experience certain aspects of this relationship. I explain how many of the world's oldest myths contain valuable clues to this unsuspected visionary world all around us. I give you the means for accessing this *corroborable* reality, just as they were given to me, just as they are meant to be given to everyone who wishes it.

At first it didn't seem corroborable to me. Twenty years ago it was foreign, unsuspected, and unlikely for me. I didn't realize, then, my planetary context. Why should I? It wasn't expected, and the question never arose. I meditated, practiced organic gardening, and recycled my paper, tins, and plastics; I was kind to animals, had a dog, and liked to wander through the Massachusetts woods.

Then I moved to England and discovered the planet.

The stone circles fascinated me. The evident antiquity of many sites intrigued me. The enigmas of the Celtic myths beguiled me. I occupied myself for a year researching the permutations of the King Arthur myth and its baffling relationship with certain locations in the British Isles. I found myself looking for the real King Arthur, for the origin and inner meaning of a myth that was so intimately rooted in the British countryside and psyche as to be inseparable and inextinguishable. King Arthur after all, was the *once and future* king, and so was his myth of Camalate and his Knights of the Holy Grail. The subject deeply engaged me, but it was still an affair outside me.

Then a door opened up and I got handed a marvelous invitation. How would you like to be a present-day Grail Knight and discover some of the secrets the Arthurian Knights knew about life, themselves, and the landscape? Step through the door. I did. If I were an anthropologist, my colleagues would have said of me that I went native, succumbed to the elements, and forgot I was a Westerner. I offer you the same invitation, and the same door, in *The Emerald Modem.*

I went through that open door and started to see what the Grail Knights and initiates of old saw, and in seeing, I began to change. I realized that seeing itself is a kind of initiation, a permission to transform. My mentors dispatched me to various specific locations in the Somerset landscape, at all hours of the night and day. I sat on hills and valleys and rocks in sunlight, moonlight, rain, snow, and fog and had visions. I started to see another landscape behind the apparent landscape, an apparitional landscape with stars, planets, galaxies, angels, spirits of Nature, mythic deities, divinity.

I was completely unprepared for this, yet I felt entirely at home with it.

Remarkably, looking back on it, I was never nonplussed by the wild stuff I had gotten myself into. Talking with angels every day. Visiting Celestial Cities. Following gnomes down miles-long tunnels. Beholding the Grail. Cradling the Earth inside a brilliant pinprick of light at the center of my body. Understanding that sacred sites and a human body were identical in essence, both suffused with celestial light, awareness, and purpose. Realizing that at one level I was the same as the planet, an equivalent form, and that both of us had an intimate relationship with the galaxy.

I had never thought much about the galaxy. I looked at the stars now and then, daydreamed about the Milky Way, and went back inside to watch TV. I had never thought it was possible to experience the galaxy, yet there I was, experiencing it. I had visionary "trips" to the Pleiades, the Great Bear, and Sirius. I saw constellations twinkling in the Somerset landscape. I sailed down celestial rivers such as the Ganges and the Nile. I communed with the Dog of Canis Major, the gods' guardian of the dwelling of all the stars. I found myself living inside the myths of the world as if they were scripts for inner adventures. Not surprisingly, I was speechless for a little while and needed to catch my breath. I never once thought I was crazy. Why should I? Quite the opposite. I believed I was finally getting grounded in something real. But it would take me 20 years to make sense of it. That sense is embodied in *The Emerald Modem.*

Even with its length and apparent complexity, the model presented here of *experienceable* interconnections among the human, Earth, and galaxy is just a beginning. My sense of it is provisional and no doubt still quite fragmentary. I describe 85 different subtle features in the planetary landscape. These features are various types of inner plane temples and visionary contexts, and each has multiple copies, some numbering in the many thousands. These are "places" you can go for mystical experiences, *and* they are features of the Earth's energy body, organs, and systems and functional aspects of its inner anatomy and physiology.

Wonderfully, whatever you do at such a place benefits you *and* the entire planet. That is why I use the word *interactive:* It describes the reciprocity of the link between us and the planet. Send Earth a rose, She'll send you a dozen.

Regrettably, almost all of the 85 types of sites are initially invisible to conventional sight. Yet they are visible to the psychic eye, and psychic cognition can be trained. Even so, you can usefully interact with any of these sites today without, technically, seeing what you're doing. Your *intent* to interact for the benefit of yourself and the planet is all that's required. You're invited.

The best part of this situation is that ultimately its reality is provable. You can, if you wish, experience something like what I describe throughout this book. The flavor of your experiences and visionary pictures will no doubt be different, but sufficiently close to what I've described for you to be confident that I have not made it up. Of course, in the final analysis, it is all made up, this fabulous planet of apparitional, visionary geography. But its maker is a fabricator without parallel, as you may gather from my dedication.

What does it all add up to? An introduction to the planet's spiritual life: how it affects you, how you are expected to help sustain it. Expected? Let's say it's part of the admission price to human life on Earth. It's expected, but we've forgotten.

But what's a modem got to do with the Earth? Nothing. It's a metaphor. A modem is how we connect to the Internet. It dials up and our computer is online for as long as we want to stay there. We're connected. The 85 features of the Earth's spiritual or energy body comprise a mechanism like a modem. They are organs and arteries, ganglia and cells in a living modem. We have one; the Earth has one. The Emerald modem is how we get online with the myriad websites of the galaxy.

The Earth was designed to make this modem function possible. So were we. The revelatory fun house of the galaxy is waiting for us to dial up again.

Part One

What Is the Emerald Modem?

1 The Earth As a Designer Planet
Let's Find a New Relationship with the Earth, Our Home Planet

Western culture encourages us to assume the Earth is a freak of nature, a global accident that somehow defeated the forces of blind chaos and evolved on its own, with no master plan, no orchestration, no divine intervention, and probably no purpose. It's just here; it's matter, we're stuck with it, it has its advantages, so let's get on with our lives and not worry about it.

Our prevailing scientific model is materialistic, mechanistic, three-dimensional, nonspiritual. The spiritual worlds have no place in science or objective modeling of the physical world. From the viewpoint of science, these subtler worlds do not exist.

Therefore, we tend to forget about the Earth; we pollute it, exploit it, neglect it, and sometimes fear it. We worry about natural disasters and then resume being oblivious to it, our environment, treating it like an inanimate source of wealth.

By and large, the Earth for most of us has not much more than an abstract reality, if we even think about it. In fact, our cultural appreciation for the Earth as our home in the galaxy is so low that it is now officially correct in book editing to always put the name Earth in the lower case, as earth. We do not even respect the planet enough to capitalize its name, even though products, slogans, religions, philosophies, deities, other planets are capitalized. This may seem a trivial point, but it represents the nadir of our awareness of the Earth as a being.

What if the opposite of the prevailing scientific view is the truth about our Earth? What if our home planet turns out to be a *designed* planet, the result of divine intervention and nurturance facilitated for our highest future potential?

For most ancient cultures, the world possessed a vertical dimension, reaching up from the material aspects into the higher worlds. Through this vertical dimension, metaphysical energies and truths poured into the waking human world like water, "saturating it with meaning."[2]

For the ancients, the illuminating presence of the gods was acknowledged in both the upper and lower worlds, giving both meaning and purpose. In fact, "ancient consciousness felt itself to be surrounded by an inner world." The landscape in which they lived and built their temples had a "non-subjective, inner dimension" to it and continuously transmitted transcendent values to the mundane realm. Important aspects of the cosmos existed "entirely inwardly" and were the source of the physical, manifest world.[3]

For the ancients, the internal world existed

around them and invited their participation. "It is an imaginative vision that *sees through* the physical landscape into its interiority."[4] In other words, the spiritual world existed around them in the subtle aspects of their own physical world, in the landscape. Perhaps this is what the Gnostic Gospel of Thomas meant when it declared: "The Kingdom of God the Father is spread upon the Earth and men do not see it."

Since the 1970s we have seen a steadily expanding effort to redefine the human being along spiritual and energy terms to replace the conventional view of the human as a machine that emits consciousness. Today some circles in Western culture are prepared to say consciousness precedes and survives the body and therefore is its creator or parent. Many have taken up spiritual practices that operate on this assumption of the primacy of consciousness. The leading edge of this trend has mapped out some energy aspects of this consciousness field that parents the physical body, and we increasingly hear discussions of meridians, the aura, and chakras. But for the most part, these practices do not put the planet in the equation. We may meditate *on* the ground, *on* the Earth, but not *with* it.

Such a complex, multiaspected human organism with biological and spiritual components and a vast range of potential consciousness cannot be an accident. A consensus is forming that the human being must be a *designed* organism. This of course implies a designer and a purpose.

What if we could make the same case for the planet and demonstrate that the Earth has meridians, an aura, chakras, and many other features indicative of a spiritual constitution? What if we could build a persuasive case for the possibility that the Earth is a designed planet? Would we then be prepared to expand our limited concept of the planet? Would we then meditate *with* the Earth?

Why the Earth Is Relevant to Human Spiritual Evolution

Most indigenous peoples have tended to regard their landscape and tribal territories, and by extension, the Earth, as sacred and worthy of veneration. European cultures retain a residual appreciation for their ancestors' greater understanding of the Earth's sacredness by preserving a few ancient megalithic structures, as well as old churches and cathedrals.

More recently, the advent and increasing popularity of what is called sacred-sites tourism and ecotourism have acquainted many Westerners with this different perception of the landscape and planet. At least one traveler has made it a lifetime career, noting in 2002 that in the past 18 years he had visited and photographed 1,000 "holy and magical places" in 80 countries.[5]

People in diverse fields of interest all share the same concern: What makes a specific place holy? How can I relate meaningfully to the planet on which I live? How can I form and experience an emotional bond with Earth?

People are searching for ways to relate to the Earth, with Christ, without Christ, as feminists, as pagans, as scholars, as geographers, with ecological awareness or new-age awareness, as geometers or mystics, as healers or magicians, as tourists or priests—everyone is searching for a bridge into the Earth's visionary terrain.[6]

Some sites have become virtual household names, such as Stonehenge, the Pyramids of Giza, Silbury Hill, Easter Island, Machu Picchu; others have accrued a kind of new-age cult status as places of high and desirable strangeness, such as Sedona, Glastonbury, Mount Shasta; still others draw tourists by the millions as they have done for centuries, such as Rome, Mecca, Lourdes, Santiago de Compostela; new sites are emerging, as if for a new era and spiritual agenda, such as Medjugorje in

Bosnia and Conyers, Georgia, both for their claims of Virgin Mary apparitions; and some locales, long forgotten or hidden from the world, are coming back into public awareness, such as Lhasa, Tiahuanaco (in Bolivia), or Great Zimbabwe.

Still others, like Eleusis, a dozen miles from Athens, had their day (reputedly two thousand years of continuous operation) as preeminent Mystery initiation centers, then lapsed into a seemingly permanent inactivity. The annual celebration of the Eleusinian Mysteries, which dealt with the enigmas and beatitudes of an experiential knowledge of the after-death state, were inseparably bound up with the nature of Greek existence and were thought to hold all of Greece together. When Eleusis closed, classical Greece ended.[7]

We've learned that certain sites are inherently holy and numinous and have been recognized as such for millennia by the peoples living there. Sanctuaries, shrines, pyramids, stone circles, chapels, pagodas, cathedrals, even ancient cities have been built at these sites and over time have become the focus of pilgrimages and ritualized activities from the worshipping of specific gods to seeking their guidance through oracles. Every country has its own sacred sites; in many instances, certain sites seemed to have held empires together; and the tally of the planet's total number of holy sites keeps growing.

In India's vast epic poem, the *Mahabharata,* a chapter called "The Tour of the Sacred Fords" describes the preferred pilgrimage route for spiritual aspirants. Dozens of holy sites, or "sacred fords," are described, as well as the types of experiences and benefits one is likely to garner there and the various deities and celestial beings one is likely to encounter. To the ancient Hindu mind, a sacred ford (called a *tirtha*) is a place where one can cross the "river" between the physical and spiritual worlds and ascend into the glories of spirit.

Here are some of the typical benefits one may expect to accrue from visiting a sacred ford,

according to the *Mahabharata:* become steeped in all fields of knowledge; enter auspicious worlds; rescue and purify one's family lineage for seven generations; lose half one's evil; be freed from all one's sins; go to the heavenly world; attain the world of the seers; find much (spiritual) gold; partake of beauty; gain the incomparable benefit of innumerable sacrifices, austerities, and 12-year vows; attain to inexhaustible worlds; shine like a moon; attain the world of Brahma (the Creator god) "on a lotus-colored wagon."[8]

The abundance of sacred sites and the extent of the megalithic ruins still scattered across the global landscape has led some theorists, notably British Earth Mysteries expert John Michell, to speculate as to their overall original purpose. Only now, with the advent of global communications, can we begin to appreciate "the vast ruin" within which we live, he says. Based on the extant megalithic structures, we can start to imagine what the landscape must have looked like—how it must have *functioned*—millennia ago when all the sacred sites and their stone structures were intact and in operation, he says.

"A great scientific instrument lies sprawled over the entire surface of the globe." For Michell, the "vast scale of prehistoric engineering" is not yet generally recognized, even though the ruins of "the old system of spiritual engineering" are still visible. He suggests that all of the Earth's megalithic structures—the stone circles, earthworks, buildings of giant stones, standing stones, pyramids, barrows—once constituted a "celestial pattern" upon the ancient landscape, a series of interconnected, closely linked centers "engaged in the same scientific programme." What program? Michell proposes it had to do with monitoring and managing the flow of terrestrial magnetism across the landscape for the purpose of ensuring crop fertility and the well-being of people and all of nature.[9]

Through Michell's analysis, first offered in 1969 then updated in 1983, we gain the sense that what we think of today as the world's grab bag of sacred sites might originally have been part of a single vast pattern, engaged in fulfilling a large purpose, and perhaps accomplishing this through means we barely understand and perhaps do not yet even suspect.

Mention terms like "pattern" and "purpose," and you introduce the idea of design and intention. It's sufficiently widely recognized today that sacred sites have a varying degree of spiritual charge or numinosity. But the next threshold in thinking is whether the *totality* of sacred sites comprises a global pattern. Michell suggested they did.

Another pioneering British expert in Earth Mysteries, Nigel Pennick, pointed out in 1979 that geomancy is the science of "putting human habitats and activities into harmony with the visible and invisible world around us," an approach that was once appreciated throughout all cultures.

Those cultures understood the land to be "an awesome living complex" of power points and archetypal patterns; they understood the "concurrence of outward form and inner purpose" and knew where to find "special places where the mind can expand into new levels of consciousness," Pennick says. Further, the world was seen as a continuum, in which "all acts, natural and supernatural, conscious and unconscious, were linked in a subtle manner, one with the next." It entailed a "multi-level hierarchy of cross-reinforcing rituals" with the purpose of maintaining the cosmic order on Earth and keeping the planet in harmony.[10]

Mention terms like "invisible world," "inner purpose," "supernatural," and "unconscious," and you get the sense of the possible cognitive scale of the setup. Clearly, the Earth's array of sacred sites implies connections with the greater world, the macrocosm, and this highlights the necessary and important human responsibility in maintaining this relationship.

As a Tibetan spiritual teacher wrote in the mid-1800s about his pilgrimage through eastern Tibet, "These sites are considered the principal sacred places because each features a primordial, naturally appearing celestial palace in which resides an assembly of emanated deities." In his view, pilgrimage undertaken after proper meditative preparation was a key to successful Tantric practice and enlightenment *because* the outer world of sacred sites mirrored the inner world of the human Tantric or energy body, with corresponding channels and sites.[11]

In my previous book, *The Galaxy on Earth: A Traveler's Guide to the Planet's Visionary Geography* (Hampton Roads, 2002), I proposed that the numerous holy sites around the planet could be classified into different types, or geomantic structures, according to their function. That function is two-way: It regulates the connection of the site to the galaxy, and it regulates the site's relationship with humans who interface with it. The context is the entire planet, appreciated as a single organism; all the sites are necessary, interconnected parts in a unified operating system.

Finding out which type of structure a given site represents calls for clairvoyant vision, because the outer physical aspect is not always indicative of the inner energy one. A stone circle may not outwardly look like a Sun temple, or Mithraeum, even though "inside" its energy configuration does. By "inside" I mean the subtle spiritual temple accessed through the physical site. You might think of this relationship as a jewel (the spiritual energy configuration) and its setting (the geomantic structure, or physical aspects of the site). In this analogy, the wearer of the rings is the Earth, and She has a lot of rings.

Here is another way to approach the matter. Acupuncture says the body is threaded with at least 14 lines of energy called meridians, a bit like a subway system. The subway "stops" are treatment points into which acupuncturists insert needles. You can't see these acupoints, at least not with ordinary seeing, yet when the needles are inserted, you get healing results. Energy moves; stagnation dissipates; your bodily and mental condition improves.

These acupuncture treatment points are the body's version of the planet's sacred sites. Insert some focused human consciousness at a geomantic site, and energy starts to move in the global body. Just as traditional Chinese medicine (and Taoism, its philosophical roots) gives evocative names to this array of body points (such as Shining Sea, Gate of Abundance, Front Valley), so can we apply equally descriptive terms to distinguish one type of Earth point from another, such as Mithraeum, Avalon, and Underworld Entrance, discussed below.

At this point we could say the *pattern* of Earth's sacred sites is that there are many different types of structures, found in generous multiples across the global landscape, whose *purpose* is to form the Earth's energy body, auric field, or visionary geography. The Earth's sites have aspects visible and invisible (except to clairvoyance); energy passes through them, wells up in them, and can be distributed from them to the land, and the whole organism of the Earth as an energy entity can be healed, refreshed, supported, and nourished through this system.

Another example from Chinese medicine may help us understand the pattern and purpose of the Earth's sacred sites. One of the oldest concepts in Chinese medicine, the ten Celestial Stems and 12 Terrestrial Branches, holds that the body's energy meridians have correspondences, both seasonal and astrological, with large-scale energy cycles of the Earth and the planets of the solar system. The *Wu* stem, for example, corresponds to the element of earth (as in solidity, not the planet), a male-tending type of expression (yang), and the planet Saturn.

The point here is that the human's rhythms of mind and body are wired into larger planetary and extraplanetary influences and cycles. These models, says acupuncture theory, are "abstract definitions of how man interacts with Heaven and Earth." The ten Stems chart the interactions of yin and yang energies and how their cycles influence the seasons and the growth of living things.

The energies of Heaven, Man, and Earth "interact to form the true Chi," our fundamental starting reservoir of life force vitality, derived prenatally from our parents, from the "breathing of Heaven," and from the life force (chi) of food and water on Earth, "mixing together."[12]

A Taoist expert puts it this way: "Without leaving the earth, people can ascend into heaven" because "man's body is a universe and the universe is not beyond this body." The Taoists divide the human form into three sections: The head is Heaven, the abdomen is Earth, and the rest of the torso is the universe. Each section has ten heavenly stem energies and 12 earthly branch energies "for their communication with the energies of heaven and earth."[13]

This model of Stems and Branches links the human with the Earth *and* the cosmos, thereby extending the application of the geomantic pattern to this larger scale. You could say the Galaxy on Earth template is an application of the Stems and Branches theory to the planet to suggest ways in which humans and Earth are part of a broader pattern of rhythms and cycles and operating under the impetus of a grander goal than you'd conventionally suspect.

Implications and Opportunities in Living within the Galaxy on Earth

I call the planet's variety of sacred sites the Galaxy on Earth, not in reference to my previous book's title, but because of the origin and function of the sites. They represent different aspects of the galaxy—the higher spiritual worlds, the solar system, the brightest stars, the realms of angels and ascended humans, sentient beings from other star systems, the structures of Heaven, the conditions of existence before and after human life—as imprinted in the planet's energy field.

My previous book described 41 geomantic structures, discussed how they worked and interacted at 56 different holy sites, and showed the ways they affect human consciousness. As my research continues, the number of geomantic structures is now 85, and growing (see table 1-1). I have visited all of these in psychic vision; in many cases, I briefly present the mythic resume for such sites when they have been described in any of the world's myths. This is to show you that though my descriptions and model may be modern in tone, I am investigating a reality much visited by psychics in the deep past when the myths were "made."

Let's look at some of these effects.

A Grail Castle facilitates deep cosmic memory of states of existence before this planet, the solar system, or even the universe existed.

A Dome enables you to experience the energy and essence of an individual star postulated as a god or large-magnitude sentient being.

By walking a Tree of Life, you can experience the hierarchy of energies, dimensions, and states of awareness said to encompass four worlds and 40 aspects.

A Landscape Zodiac enables you to walk across a physical landscape and through the energy imprints of numerous constellations described by astrology as comprising the human horoscope.

At a Mount Olympus, you can meet any of the 14 Ray Masters from the Great Bear, better known in Western culture as the Greek gods of Olympus.

A Cosmic Egg gives you information about what reality was like before Heaven and Earth were separated, before the "Fall" of Man into incarnation.

A Gnome Egg is a portal into the world of the elemental spirits of earth, the element of solidity, substance, and matter as handled by the nature spirits popularly called gnomes.

At a Golden Egg, you can birth the Christ Consciousness as the divine child within.

In a Three Star Temple, you can integrate the energies of the angelic, elemental, and human in one body.

This partial listing should give you an idea— an exciting one, I trust—of possibilities. It also suggests three things. First, you can conduct your spiritual journey on the Earth, out in the landscape. Second, somebody *thought all this up*, organized the 85 different types of features so they would relate to human consciousness. Third, somebody also realized it would be useful to humans that all these features deriving from the spiritual worlds be presented as interactive holographic realities—as real as the original.

One premise of the Galaxy on Earth model is that arrayed across the Earth's surface, in its esoteric energy field, are structures, temples, locales, or agencies found in the spiritual worlds. The system is a way of grounding Heaven on Earth and enabling Earth to ascend to Heaven.

It will be useful to take a moment to define four terms: geomantic, geomantic structure, geomythic, and visionary geography.

Geomantic: Literally the term means "to divine Ge," the verb *divine* meaning "to figure out," and *Ge,* or *Gaia,* understood here to mean the planet Earth—as the classical Greeks called it, *Ge Meter,* Earth Mother, the Mother of all, giver of wealth. Geomancy in this book means the study of the energy body of the planet in all its intricacies; this is the divination of Gaia, figuring out Her esoteric energy configurations, which include lines of energy and alignments, stone structures that enhance that effect, and the practice of interacting with that matrix. By appropriately interfacing with Earth's geomantic structures, you help to

Table 1-1: An Inventory of 85 Galaxy on Earth Features

(Presented in order of their treatment in this book)

Feature	Number on Earth	Feature	Number on Earth
Hyperborean Time Library	456	Zeus Face	12
Lemurian Information Crystal	46,221,000	Control Bubble	238
Sipapuni (Entrances to Earth's interior)	360	Prana Distributor	288
Grail Castle	144	Mount Olympus	108
Dragon, Primary (Midgard Serpent)	1	Ray Master Sanctuary	1,080
Dragon, Major	13	Arc of Expanding Consciousness	174,060
Dragon, Minor	1,053	Pointer's Ball	174,060
Dragon Egg	33,232,930,569,601 (49×49^7)	Avalon	144
		Golden Apple	47
Naga Celestial City	144	Griffin Gold Reserve	47
Jewel of Michael	24,441	Garden of Eden	26
Soma Temple	144	Tree of Life (Yggdrasil)	1
Dome	1,746	Valhalla	108
Dome Cap	83,808	Seat of Christ Consciousness	3
Planetary Umbilicus	1	Cosmic Egg	48
Tree of Life	2,856	Silver Egg	1,080
Labyrinth	108	Sphinx	1,080
Chakra Template	26^{26}	Round Table	1,080
Crown of the Ancient of Days	12	Golden Egg	666
Palladium	60	Gnome Egg	10,660
White Lily	indeterminate	Earth Circle	indeterminate
Three-Star Temple	144,000	Sylph Doorway	1,746[9]
Oroboros Line	15	Camalate Center	26
Vibrating Stone	12	Ixion's Wheel	360
Albion Plate	12	Mithraeum	144
Albion Plate Emerald	12	Time Portal	45
Original Landmass Egregor	9	Interdimensional Portal	60,600
Landmass Subdivision Egregor	72	Heavenly Caves	360
Universe Dome	12	Albion, Primary	1
Dhruva Anchor Point	12	Albion, Major	12

Feature	Number on Earth	Feature	Number on Earth
Albion, Minor	432	Mobile Shambhalic Focus	1
Landscape Zodiac	432	Epiphany Focus	6,004
Zodiac Dome	432	Stone Circle	1,746
Landscape Zodiac Amplifier	360	Stone Row	1,746
Perpetual Choirs (*Cyfangan*)	3	Single Standing Stone (*Menhir*)	2,430
Chakras	36,097	Light Corrective Center	1,080
Major Nodal Points (Primary Earth chakras)	9	Cyclopean City	6,300
Energy Focusing Nodes (Minor Earth chakras)	72	Barrow	not available
		Underworld Entrance	1,746
Planetary Energy Receptor	3	Energy Funnel (Avenue of trees)	2,864,000,224
Albion Celestial Body Lights	613		
Albion Viewing Chamber	36	Lucifer Binding Site	3,496
Shambhala Doorway	1,080	Stargate, stars	1,080
Golden Pillar	228,964	Stargate, constellations	2,200,000

render the planet divine; you acknowledge its essential spiritual nature.

Geomantic structure: This one is based on an understanding of the local energy configuration and uses, placement, design, and building materials to amplify the inherent disposition of that site to elevate consciousness. A stone circle such as Stonehenge is a geomantic structure, as is Sacsaywaman, the partially ruined cyclopean stone emplacement in Cuzco, Peru. You could think of a geomantic structure as an earthworks temple designed to interact with the esoteric landscape. A geomantic structure is usually positioned at the spot where a subtle, spiritual feature can be accessed. For example, at Montsegur in France, a craggy treeless mountain peak in the French Pyrenees, the ruins of a former stone castle mark the spot where a Grail Castle exists above the peak in the subtle realm. When the physical castle was extant, the occupants—thirteenth-century spiritual seekers called Cathars—could use the physical site as a platform to enter the spiritual one. In this book, I use the term "geomantic structure" interchangeably in denoting a physical or energy structure. The giant stones of Stonehenge or Sacsaywaman ground an energy configuration that produces effects on consciousness that complement the effects the stone structure has on its own.

Geomythic: This term means "the myth in the landscape," or, even more briefly, "the Earth myth." The reality of key myths from various cultures and myth systems is found in the actual geomantic landscape. The more clearly a myth is referenced to a specific locality (e.g., the god Apollo slew the dragon Python at Delphi on Mount Parnassus), the more it embodies a geomythic reality. That means the myth actually happened at *this* place and should be taken almost literally as a clue to the site's geomantic nature. The qualification is that you need to be subtle and clairvoyant in interpreting these old, intact myths; the plane of reality in which their actions took place is not our everyday world, but parallel to it.

Visionary geography: This term is meant to evoke the entire Galaxy on Earth template imprinted on the surface of the planet, including geomantic and geomythic features. It is the landscape as seen through clairvoyant eyes, in which realities and dimensions overlap and the spiritual temple and energy configuration are seen to coincide with the physical aspects of a site. It is a terrain in which myths are real and living, in which the mythic is the vocabulary of being for that realm. It is the dimension of sacred sites, both their physical and geomythic aspects, taken as a special layer of planetary "skin." Some writers use the term "planetary grid" to indicate all the subtle-energy aspects of the Earth's mythic body expressed in essentially geometric terms. The planetary grid approach models the planet's energy pattern as a series of lines and solid shapes, with sacred sites being formed at the intersections of lines, globe-encircling rings, and the vertices of the geometric shapes.

The planetary grid description reveals, according to two commentators, "not only an ancient global mapping system but a universal energy code" changing our view of the world as a dead empty place into one "bursting with an unending froth of full bubbles of living energy."[14] This implies "an intelligent geometric pattern into which, theoretically, the Earth and its energies are organized, and possibly in which the ubiquitous ancient megalithic sites are also positioned." The geometric pattern of the planetary grid is "energetic in nature" and "organized into a precise web."[15]

These four essential terms—geomantic, geomantic structure, geomythic, and visionary geography—should evoke a sense of relatedness between humans and landscape, and they should suggest a spiritual source of the myths that describe these connections. Perhaps in addition to "spiritual," I

should say "galactic," for these myths have galactic affairs as their frame of reference. They are myths about star gods, transhuman heroes, vast energy processes, the majestic affairs of angels, the arcane activities of nature spirits, the taming of formidable celestial beings such as dragons, the sublime plans of the Creator, and the travails and epiphanies of humans interacting with it all.

The Galaxy on Earth Is a Template of the Spiritual Worlds

I mentioned above that the Earth's geomantic structures represent holograms of places, temples, or locales in the spiritual worlds and that they afford us, while living in a body, useful interactions with these features that otherwise we would not encounter until after death, if even then. Here are a few examples of aspects of the spiritual worlds found on the Earth.

One of the most conspicuous and perhaps most practical is the Underworld Entrance, of which there are 1,746 replicas around the planet. Depending on how you look at this, the Underworld Entrance is a doorway into the Underworld, known in Greek myths as Hades, or the place itself, including the doorway. Earth contains 1,746 doorways into Hades, or 1,746 holograms of Hades—it amounts to the same thing.

I say hologram because it has the quality of a virtual reality interactive environment. Whether the Hades you access through an Underworld Entrance on the Earth (such as at Cumae, near Naples, Italy) is the same Hades you encounter when you die or is a copy of it is probably a moot point. It will seem like the real thing, and it will enable you to conduct your business with efficiency. Depending on your mind's ability to make pictures (to decode higher frequency realities into something that looks familiar), you may see the oft-described Gates of the

Underworld, the Three Judges of the Dead, and possibly a glimpse of the Garden of Eden.

Psychics and mystics throughout history and among all cultures assure us that the after-death experience will entail something along these lines. What those who have a near-death experience (NDE) commonly report as the viewing of one's current lifetime as if watching a movie—along with the sense of remorse or elation in response to events portrayed—may be a contemporary way of referring to the activities of the Three Judges of the Dead. In fact, if you have sustained an NDE, accessing an Underworld Entrance could be helpful for integrating the transbodily experiences of the NDE.

How about a jaunt into a paradisal realm? Celtic myth has its Avalon, the Isle of Apples, presided over by Morgan le Fay and her eight sisters; for the Greeks this locale was called the Garden of the Hesperides, where the goddess Hera's golden apple trees bloomed in an orchard guarded by a dragon. Among the delights of this paradisal realm are soft sweet music that lulls humans to sleep and golden apples whose luscious juice produces visions and ecstatic insights into the higher worlds. Golden apples are the fruits of spiritual wisdom and accomplishment and are highly desired by the wise, the myths tell us. Here you may also encounter the Gandharvas (celestial musicians) and Apsaras (celestial dancing maidens) of Hindu legend, and the god Apollo's Nine Muses of Greek myth. Avalon is a place you can visit by accessing any of 144 sites around the planet. Each will conduct you to the same place and afford you the opportunity to experience the music, the apples, and the paradisal quality of this realm, which is an aspect of the astral plane.

Maybe a visit to the Sun god's cave? I call this kind of temple a Mithraeum after the Roman name for caves, both real and artificial, in which the Bull of the Sun was ritually slain by Mithras the solar hero. (In terms of this book, the Mithraeum is a spiritual or subtle energy configuration, not an actual cave or physical temple.) The myth about the Bull of the Sun is actually about the origin and dispensation of cosmic time, here portrayed metaphorically as bull's blood. The myth also evokes a sense of the Sun as a liquid essence, like pourable gold; there is also its necessary role in the cosmos. You'll find, working in the Mithraeum, figures out of myth and legend that perhaps you thought were fancies somebody made up. But there they are, cosmic beings as real, or more real, than you.

My point here is simple: The Mithraeum is a place or function in the spiritual worlds that has to do with modifying and dispensing a primordial energy and consciousness source. Multiple copies of this temple are distributed around the planet. A human accessing this temple produces two benefits: It allows some of the energy of this feature to flow into the physical world, and it allows the person making the interface to *reconnect* with another part of one's celestial self, to *remember* another aspect of one's true nature as a being of the universe. This statement is true for all the Galaxy on Earth features.

This may sound a little grandiose, but actually it gets at the heart of the concepts of visionary geography.[16] It is a *template*, an *imprint*, an *impression* created elsewhere and applied to our planet for the benefit of the Earth, ourselves, and all of nature. The Galaxy on Earth is the total *pattern* created by this multiplicity of holy sites and their inner spiritual temples, the jewels and their settings, the acupoints and meridians.

That total pattern, the planet's visionary geography, is a multilayered hologram containing some of the stars and constellations of our galaxy, many of the temples and locales of the spiritual worlds, and access to many of the higher beings and their activities.

Interesting, but why is this so? Because it's a mirror, as in the axiom "As above, so below, and in the middle, too." Most metaphysical and spiritual traditions teach that the human being is made in God's image—or embodies all the aspects of the greater world, the macrocosm. The human in this model is the little world, the microcosm. (This correspondence, for example, makes astrology possible.)

The Galaxy on Earth model invites one more player into this correspondence: the Earth. The Earth is the *middle, too* part of this equation. It too is a microcosmic expression of the greater world, the galaxy and its life. You could say the Earth has been created in God's image, just as we are. The place where you find all this embodiment is in the planet's visionary geography.

That the Earth has the same spiritual template as we have means we can feel at home as beings of the cosmos living in bodies on a physical planet. The Galaxy on Earth template enables us to feel at home in the world. Its starting premise is that humans are originally and ultimately spiritual beings.[17]

There should be no reason to feel stranded in a foreign world, an alien dimension—in godawful *matter,* as some people secretly think of it—because all around us we can see where we came from and who we are. It's all done with mirrors—mirrors that are the planet's thousands of sacred sites in all their wonderful variety (see table 1-2 for a summary of principles).

The Name of the Design— Restoring Albion's Starry Wheels

Earlier, I brought up the idea of pattern with respect to the planet's holy sites. Earth Mysteries theorists such as Michell and Pennick suggest that originally the Earth's sacred sites were linked with one another, and the pattern these sites created had to do with spiritual engineering. This is a good and solid foundation for the explanation I propose, but now let's expand our concept of possibilities. What is the largest possible pattern the Earth's sites might be expressing? Think of the myriad stars in the night sky. What if these billions of stars are part of a vast pattern? Say these billions of stars are atoms in a body, points of light in an immense shape, the holographic interference pattern between original and image. What would it look like?

Jewish mystical tradition, or Qabala, calls it Adam Kadmon, God's idea of perfect existence expressed as a human being made of light. Adam Kadmon, explains Gershom Scholem, a highly regarded explainer of Jewish mysticism, is "the first being which emanated from the light . . . the 'primordial man' . . . a first configuration of the divine light." Adam Kadmon is a cosmic being that contains all the universes, galaxies, solar systems, and planets in "himself"; "his" spiritual station is higher than the highest angels.

This figure was the first great soul, concentrating the power of the universes and "the entire soul substance of mankind . . . [in] his vast cosmic structure." Adam Kadmon is "the mystical structure of God as He reveals Himself." His enormous size, which filled the multiverse, was later reduced to create Adam, the first human being and the archetype for the human soul.[18] ("Adam," though it sounds like a male's name, is a code expressing a mathematical matrix with symbolic, spiritual significance and has no gender reference.)

Not only the Judaic mystical tradition recognizes this celestial being. The Hindus know it as Purusha or Prajapati; the Chinese as P'an Ku; the Norse myths as Ymir; the classical Greeks as Macroanthropos; the ancient Persian mystics as Gayomart. Throughout these different perceptions, one aspect is consistently acknowledged: The world originated as a dismemberment of this vast being; the various realms of creation derive from its body, sacrificed and carved up to generate reality.

Table 1-2: 25 Principles of the Galaxy on Earth

1. Holy sites are distributed uniformly across the planet and exist in many forms, each with different effects on consciousness.

2. The sacred is a place where the real unveils itself and the holy irrupts into human life, such that this act opens communication between the cosmic planes and Earth.

3. Holy sites have something to do with us, allowing us to look into a cosmic mirror, in which the "face" reflected back is an ancient face made of stars.

4. Visionary geography denotes the hierophantic, geomythic, geomantic landscape—a planet of holy sites. It is a landscape of visions, purposeful and relevant to humans; it pertains to consciousness, the structures and processes of the galaxy, and the reason we and the planet are here.

5. The underlying "energy" encountered at holy sites is not Earth energy, but cosmic energy, the energy and consciousness of stars.

6. The Earth is a miniature galaxy, brimming with stars and pulsating with lines of connection. Everything in the galactic and celestial worlds is here on Earth as part of its visionary geography. The Earth was purposefully designed this way.

7. Earth's visionary geography was here *before* the Earth was. It's the planet's mold, the armature, the plan, the organizing field out of which the planet emerged.

8. The Galaxy on Earth is a mirror of the spiritual organization of the human, a magnificent planetary mirror. It's us, projected outside to make a world around us.

9. Five fundamental shapes, described by geometry as Platonic Solids, are central to the design feature of the visionary geography.

10. Many basic functions described by mathematics are operative in the Earth's visionary geography, such as pi, phi, and e.

11. The structures, contents, beings, and processes of the galaxy are found in the human.

12. The key principle is *As above, so below, and in the middle, too.* The middle is planet Earth, and it, too, is templated with the same galactic imprint as the human.

13. The Galaxy on Earth is here so we will feel at home on the planet, our home away from home, so we won't feel exiled and alone and forget our celestial roots.

14. Remembering the Self is what the Earth's visionary geography facilitates for us.

15. The Earth maintains us as physical beings, but we must maintain "Her" spiritually by looking after Her holy sites and infusing them with our spiritual essence.

16. We have something the planet needs: the Blazing Star at the center of our being, given to us by the angelic realm.

17. Any person can, if they wish, interact with this visionary geography for their benefit and the planet's using this Blazing Star as a guide.

18. Your quest to wake up and gain spiritual insight is enhanced at the holy sites.

19. As you search for yourself in the visionary landscape, you simultaneously contribute to the planet's healing and awakening as a being in the solar system.

20. Planetary detoxification is one of the benefits to the Earth from responsible sacred-sites tourism and questing.

Table 1-2 *(continued)*

21. Contributions to maintaining the Earth's energy body require interaction among humans, angels, and elemental spirits of nature.

22. You can refine your spiritual quest according to the 85 different types of geomantic features at the Earth's many thousands of holy sites.

23. Myths and legends provide invaluable clues as to a site's possible geomantic significance, function, and history and its effects on consciousness.

24. Myths are door-openers, living keys to an esoteric understanding of the landscape.

25. The paradoxical truth of myths is that you should take them almost literally, but not as necessarily happening in our three-dimensional reality.

"The primordial giant Purusha (the 'Man') is represented at once as cosmic totality and as an androgynous being," comments religious historian Mircea Eliade. Creation begins with the cosmic sacrifice of this god's body, such that, for example, the sky came from his head, the Earth from his feet, the Moon from his consciousness, the wind from his breath, the Sun from his gaze. The parallels to this myth illustrate "a cosmogony of an archaic type: creation by the sacrifice of an anthropomorphic divine being."[19]

Adam Kadmon is a grand, primordial figure of the human made of stars and expressed at the highest level of creation. What does that have to do with the Earth's sacred sites? The Earth's visionary geography is defined as the Galaxy on Earth template, and Adam Kadmon has an expression in this template, where "he" is known as Albion—A Light Being in Our Neighborhood.

Albion on the Earth is the mirror image, the unawakened terrestrial version, of Adam Kadmon in the spiritual worlds. The largest pattern the totality of Earth's sacred sites expresses is the figure of Albion. Think of the thousands of sites as points of light—stars, if you like—that together create the virtual image of Albion laid upon the planet, like a human draped on his back over a large beach ball, or like a human in a round shape, a *rotundum*. In classical thought, the soul was seen as round, and the *rotundum* was another name for the World Soul. The whole man was the round element, but this was understood to be the Original Man, the Anthropos. The total man is "as big as the world, like an Anthropos," C. G. Jung wrote, adding that this "indescribable totality of the psychic or spiritual man" is "compounded of consciousness as well as of the indeterminable extent of the unconscious."[20]

How this works is too big an idea to explain here. This book will show how the entire planet and its visionary geography is Albion's body. But for now: Who's Albion?

The English mystic poet William Blake (1757–1827) left us a magnificent poem about the Earth's visionary geography and its spiritual destiny, called *Jerusalem: The Emanation of the Giant Albion.* Blake wrote it between 1804 and 1820. It's one of those cases, as with James Joyce's *Finnegans Wake,* where everybody says the guy was a genius, but hardly anybody reads it because it doesn't make much sense without some kind of decoding primer. Blake is one of the few in the West to use the name Albion the way Hindus use Purusha, to indicate the primogenitive, sacrificial, total human archetype.[21]

In *Jerusalem,* Blake was talking about the geomantic and geomythic terrain of England, and especially about the spiritual disposition of holy sites around London. Blake presents Albion as the prototypical human, the collectivity of human consciousness over time. He is a forlorn figure. Albion is the name of the design, the designer's logo imprinted on the back pocket of our planet. Originally, Albion was "the Angel of my Presence" and the "mildest Son of Eden," according to the "Divine Voice."

Blake writes: "You have a tradition, that Man anciently contain'd in his mighty limbs all things in Heaven & Earth: this you received from the Druids. But now the Starry Heavens are fled from the mighty limbs of Albion." This is a key insight, both that the "Starry Heavens" have fled Albion's limbs and that they were ever there. That they were ever there is a deep mystery of visionary geography. But first let's focus on the image of this giant in the landscape.[22]

Albion, as the Earth's virtual image of Adam Kadmon, is in fact found templated, big and small, in the Earth's energy body in many places, his limbs ranging in geomythic size from a few hundred yards to hundreds of miles.[23]

The Starry Heavens that once graced but have now fled the mighty limbs of Albion are his awareness of, and participation in, what Blake called the "Divine Vision"—what I call the Galaxy on Earth, the Heavens on Earth. In geomantic terms, this means the Earth's visionary geography. The Starry Heavens have fled Albion's mighty arms and legs because we have forgotten the mysteries of our global landscape. We have forgotten the axiom *As above, so below, and in the middle, too.* We don't see the majestic star patterns in the landscape.

So Albion lives "in gloomy majesty and deepest night," bereft of and alienated from the divine vision. Hurled down to Earth from eternity, "Albion is himself shrunk to a narrow rock in the midst of the sea," miserable in his "long & cold repose," groaning "in the deep slumbers of Death upon his Rock," exclaiming "Hope is banish'd from me." In a dark and unknown night, wrote Blake, "outstretch'd his Giant beauty on the ground in pain & tears."[24]

For us today, the divine vision is darkened, and in our secret interior we do often feel as if we are alone, forlorn, and in pain on a barren rock on the edge of a cold sea. The pain of having lost the divine vision is what turned Klingsor, once an applicant to be a Knight of the Holy Grail with the rest of the Grail Brothers, into the black magician and chief enemy of Amfortas, Lord of the Grail Castle, in Richard Wagner's opera *Parsifal.* Klingsor strove to join the Grail fraternity but was rejected on account of his impurities, so, "lacking strength to slay the sins that were within him," he turned against it, Wagner wrote. Klingsor stole the "holy spear" that created Amfortas's seemingly incurable wound, and could cure it, and hid it in his enchanted castle of wizardry and necromancy in the lonely, heathen valley where he traps and ruins unsuspecting young Grail Knights "with wicked lust and hellish torments," using the holy spear to wound the holy knighthood.[25]

However, Blake's vision of Albion's ultimate destiny is not pessimistic, but apocalyptic in a positive sense. One day the Starry Wheels will return to Albion, his limbs rippling with the Starry Heavens again, his vision of the spiritual worlds reawakened. "When all Albion's injuries shall cease, and when we shall/Embrace him, tenfold bright, rising from his tomb in immortality," Blake prophesied in *Jerusalem.*

But how do we get there?

A third figure is central to the plot, connecting Adam Kadmon above with its mirror image Albion below. That third figure, the subject of chapter 11, is the Lord of Light, the Light Bearer, the living *embodiment* of Adam Kadmon and the soul of Albion, who is his unawakened reflection. The Light Bearer is the phenomenal, visible reality of Adam Kadmon and Albion, the reason things are *visible* at all outside the most exalted reach of Heaven.

We can—and will—awaken Earth's Albions (445 expressions in all, subsumed into a singular one) when we address the Lord of Light, our connection between Earth and Heaven and the source of the Emerald modem. We can address the Lord of Light by working his pattern on the Earth, the differentiated visionary geography of sacred sites that is the spiritual essence of this designer planet. An excellent way to get started on this grand Earth-transforming project is to remember *how* and *why* this designer planet got here.

2 The View from Inside the Blue Room
The 2.7 Million Year Project

Here are some details from a psychic snapshot of a moment long ago: Somewhere deep in Siberia is a large pale-blue room with crystal walls. The walls are translucent, shimmering. The room is very bright by today's standards. There are many people there—including many beings who do not seem to be human—and they all have red and gold light around their heads. To the extent that they are clothed, they appear to wear red and gold. Some are dressed in green, and on their heads is a device like a spiral tube or perhaps what the Celts later would call a torc. Somehow these devices will help them remember something important in the far future.

A large crystalline table shaped like the Greek letter π (pi), perhaps 12 feet long and waist high, stands in the center, and on its sides tower three archangels. The table is intensely bright, and it's only intermittently a table; it continually blinks into another, indescribable form. This "table" was brought here from the heavenly realm; it is the interdimensional energy matrix for the creative interactions of the archangels Uriel,[26] Raphael,[27] and Michael.[28] There are in fact many angels present.

Placed upon the crystalline pi-table are the five Platonic Solids and the 13 Archimedean Solids, 18 different geometric shapes made into handheld models. Some are simple like a cube and pyramid, some more complicated geodesic solids. Each is made of a different mineral, and together they represent the different energy matrices of the Earth as seen over its future lifetime, for this is a moment very early in its life.

Each of these geometric shapes has its own energy, its own rate and style of vibration, its own emitted light. People place them one after the next over a projected hologram of the Earth above the pi-table, to see how each resonates, which best stores and transmits the energy.

Looked at more carefully, the "table" resembles a vertical column with three vertical sections; each is an archangel. It's as if they are standing elbow to elbow inside a pole of light that is turning clockwise like a tornado in slow motion. The Earth's energy grid, and perhaps the planet itself, is inside this archangelic tornado, as if sucked into the whirling vortex; more likely the higher dimensional spin of these three archangels working in unison has enveloped the planet. It's hard to determine exactly what is occurring because what they're doing is in the sixth dimension.

In general terms, this confluence of these three archangels (out of a possible 18) energizes the Earth's energy body, invoking the spiritual essences of the various Heavens each archangel represents and imprinting them upon the planet. The vortex they've made is a workshop for the Blue Room team; they can try out different energy combinations as delivered by the geodesic solids. It's as if the archangelic matrix creates a living thought of the planet expressed in multiple dimensions.

Their whirlwind comprises the realities of primal fire, air or spirit, and earth as matter and substance. It is both an imprimatur of divine assignment and a promise to the Earth's future. It's the breath of the Holy Spirit blowing like cleansing fire through the vastness of space designated to be the home for matter, substance, and Earth, preparing the space for the creation and manifestation of a planet. The combined energies of these three archangels create a fiery current that burns through the space the planet Earth occupies and the planet itself.

Among the beings in the Blue Room is a man with a brilliant red light or star in his lower back, at the sacrum. This red star is an energy transmission that brings a creative impulse into the inner and outer natures of this man, simultaneously with the planet by working through one of the geodesic solids on the crystal table. Somehow this man with the red star at his sacrum transmitted an impulse from it through one of the geometric shapes on the pi-table and, through it, into the Earth itself. He harnessed the creative energies of the beings assembled in the Blue Room and transmitted them into one of the Platonic Solids for future use.

Another man juggles a Slinky of light behind his head, and each time the Slinky rises, it's transformed into a different geometric shape of light, one after another, like an alphabet. This is the being who originally brought or summoned the Oroboros dragon impulse to encircle the planet, that Earth-encircling dragon the Pelasgian Greeks called Ophion summoned up from the North Wind, Boreas, who coiled seven times around Eurynome, the Mother of All Things, a universal egg in the form of a planet. The man is juggling the Slinky forms of light because he is practicing or perhaps demonstrating how that visualization of energy works. Even the angels don't remember his name.

The time is unbelievably early in the life of Earth, long before the epochs of Atlantis and Lemuria. This is a snapshot of the time when the Hyperboreans first established a working space more or less in the physical plane within the Earth's crust. The Hyperboreans were wanderers, though their origin is lost in time. They originally were resident in the Pleiades (a name from the Greek *plein,* which means to "sail or wander").[29] This was their latest assignment, back then.

Each of the beings in the Blue Room—also present were representatives from other stars— had a task in relation to the Earth's energy matrix, what I call the planet's visionary geography. Each had the possibility of completing an inner and outer circuit within the energy matrix, matching the awakening and illumination of an energy dynamic within their own consciousness with a corresponding one on the planet.

How long it would take for those tasks to be completed was indeterminate, but it would be reckoned in billions of years. How long these planet energizers would be in and out of the Blue Room was easier to quantify: 2.7 million years for the setup of the Earth's energy and geomythic terrain.

Certain Hyperboreans and Elohim, that family of mid-ranking angels who accomplished so much of the early groundwork for the Earth's visionary geography, were sent to Earth by the Being the angels reverently refer to as "the Most High Architect of Supreme Existence" to lay down certain energy matrices over the surface of the Earth so that it could support biological beings with an energy organization capable of producing exalted states of consciousness by means of auric layers and chakras.

Think about this. It means the Earth was designed so as to make higher human consciousness states possible, an intention that in itself provides clues for the purpose of human incarnation: to be ever more aware and awake. It also means in a parallel sense the planet itself could become a sentient being in the solar system and galaxy, capable of higher consciousness states, largely made possible by the attainment of these states by Her resident humans.

The Blue Room is the answer to how the Galaxy on Earth got here. It's hard to describe the Blue Room accurately in physical or even form-based terms, because inherently it is multidimensional. After all, what is the state of mind of a Hyperborean, or any of the others working in the Blue Room? What is reality for them? Certainly it is not reducible to familiar three-dimensional terms. Even so, as a three-dimensional metaphor, I can say that the Blue Room was like an engineering team's field office.

Say you work for a multinational, multibillion-dollar engineering firm, and your team is posted to a Third-World country to build something big. You bring your equipment, the team of engineers, the whole hard-hatted entourage needed to complete the project. You know you'll be there for years. You have your designs and flow charts—but it all has to be worked out in real life. You'll have to be flexible. The Blue Room project was like this, only now you're building a planet.

You came here with the complete engineering blueprint for a planet, the inventory of 85 key energy features to be installed or accounted for so as to make those higher human consciousness states one day possible.[30] It's not like you brought everything in a big truck, or even in a spaceship. Yet.

The 10,660 Gnome Eggs were created in distant star systems and were transported here for the purpose of unfolding possibilities in relation to angelic-human and human, angelic, and elemental interactions. As for the gnomes—they arrived here by other means.

But how do you transport a Cosmic Egg? A lot of these features will be visualized into place. When the Elohim "visualize" a Cosmic Egg into place, it's there, and will be for as long as the planet lasts. A few features, like the landscape zodiacs and the globe-encircling energy lines, are part of the inherent anatomy of the Earth; others, like the domes and the Cyclopean Cities, will be brought or built on site. The stargates will be assembled here, for example, the Blue Room planners knew.

Those Cities—elegant, elephantine structures made of massive stones, ten to 30 tons each in some cases, placed together without mortar or evident joinings yet perfectly fitted, and fitted to last for millions of years until humans eventually tear them down—you'd think it would take the Elohim a very long time to build 6,300 of them. But it won't. These guys are master engineers, efficient builders.

Even though the Elohim will take on the form of 18-foot-tall giants, there will be no heavy lifting because there will be no need. With a snap of the Elohim's fingers, the stones will jump into their preassigned places, fitted, joined, placed perfectly. That's the mark of their efficiency. No effort. The shapes of the Cyclopean Cities are already created in the etheric field of the Earth, so it's just a matter of telling the stones to match their preexisting group energy configuration, and they do. It's as if the energy structure pulls the physical stones into their rightful place, and, as heavy and dense as they are, they do not resist.

Everyone on the team has access to the entire blueprint. It's done with hologram projections. You can study the Earth and its projected 85-plus energy features in all angles, dimensions, and perspectives; you can extrapolate it forward in time, moving it fast or slow; you can factor in astrological and astronomical cycles; you have three- and four-dimensional star maps projected as holograms. You can zoom in on the local details, or you can take the big picture. You can see the effect of planetary magnetospheres, sunspot activity, and lunar influences on the global pattern; you can experiment with the differing probable effects on matter and consciousness by changing the ratio and order of the geodesic solids.

You can calculate the planet's capacity to carry multiple expressions of each of the 85 features from the cosmic light pattern library of building blocks for consciousness. This part is exciting, because you hold in your hands, so to speak, the full design parameters, the maximum load-bearing limits, for Earth.

The specific number present of all the features (refer to table 1-1 in chapter 1) is, metaphorically, the planet's DNA makeup, what will make this planet Earth and not Venus, Mars, or Jupiter, give it this density level and not another, allow it to evolve to approximately this. It's all specified and planned.

If you were to design and outfit another planet and you wanted to have conditions for consciousness more or less equivalent to Earth's, you would use these design parameters to do it. In fact, that's probably what the Blue Room team did, why they proceeded with confidence, because they had applied these limits elsewhere and had a fair idea what to expect, and when.

But in the Blue Room, you can experiment with different sequencings: What if we activate this feature first, rather than these three—what effect can we expect? In some respects, it's a planetary version of Hermann Hesse's cerebral Glass Bead Game, a study in permutations. "The Glass Bead Game is thus a mode of playing with the total contents and values of our culture," wrote Hesse. It plays with them the way an artist uses his colors, such that "on all this immense body of intellectual values the Glass Bead Game player plays like an organist on an organ." It's an organ whose foot pedals and manuals "range over the entire intellectual cosmos; its stops are almost beyond number." The Game, ultimately, was a form of music-making and an exercise in mathematics, uniting symbols and formulas in a universal language of unlimited combinations.[31]

Except in the Blue Room, that intellectual cosmos is a residue of past accomplishments on other planets in other galaxies, notably the Andromeda spiral galaxy, and future possibilities here. Except all those in the Blue Room are prodigies of the game. But not, mind you, the game's creator. The plans for the planet came from the top, from the Architect, thought up, commissioned, and handed over to the Blue Room team.

Not only is the Blue Room the place of planning and execution of Earth's energy design, but it is in many respects the place where myths were created. Perhaps I should say, the place where the things happened that we now regard (and disregard) as myths. Contemplating the Blue Room you can sense what mythographer Karl Kerenyi called "the mood of the timeless wilds of original mythmaking."[32]

Was it really a blue room? Yes and no. The predominant color was a pale sky blue, but that might have been the radiational effect of the crystal walls. Some say that shade of blue is the color of the etheric world and of the essential eggshell outer membrane of the human aura, so maybe the Blue Room wasn't quite in the physical realm as we think of it today. Maybe it flickered somewhat between the etheric and the physical. The people in the Blue Room, even though they look solid, fleshed out, human, probably were in some state between spirit and matter. The angels clearly were in light bodies.

The "building" resembles a pale blue sphere or egg perhaps 300 feet tall set partially into the ground. Inside are many tiers, a bit like a university library with study cubicles and workstations. Each Blue Room team designed its own holographic workshop. Sit down, push a few buttons or perhaps just mentally pronounce a command, and there is the entire Earth and its light pattern features before you, an interactive hologram. You can spin it, invert it, focus down on any of its many layers or dimensions; model the interfacing effects of energy grid and geophysiology, meteorology, vulcanism—anything you're interested in. Others can instantly see your results through their own holograms.

For later, when the humans on this planet start playing out the dialectic of free will and blind compulsion, you can model outcomes, alternatives, positive and negative scenarios. You can study the interaction and effects of solar and galactic events and energy tides, weather, the Earth's energy lines, its geodesic solids, and visionary terrain on social events, politics, economics, health, and of course levels of awareness.

The key matter is sequencing, timing, and maturation. You have to turn things on in the right order, like an 85-stage multidimensional rebooting of a very complex computer. The physical aspects of the Earth have to congeal. Remember, you are growing a planet; it's still *in utero*, except the womb is the energy grid, the geomythic terrain you're working on, the light pattern armature out of which the physical Earth will be manifested. You can't rush things.

So while, technically, the Blue Room team could "visualize," unpack, and install the many features in a fairly short time, it can only do a little at a time. Some 2.7 million years will elapse after the Blue Room team first arrives until the planet is ready for occupancy of any kind.

By the time the first phase of the job is over, you've seen every inch of the planet; you know the location of every one of the domes, stargates, eggs, portals, and the rest.

Towards the end of that long stretch of waiting, you can step out the "front door" of the Blue Room and have a look around at the virginal Earth. It is an arresting prospect. No people or animals yet, but there are trees and plants. They've been here since Polaria, the Time of

Plants and before the grid. Can you imagine the Earth today with nobody on it? Before anything started? When it was all promise and possibility? Pristine, immaculate, silent, factory-fresh?

Standing outside the Blue Room, on the land, you note that many of the Earth's physical features are still coming into manifestation, still settling into physicality, but what is most beautiful is the interface between matter and light. Both realms are apparent. You see how the prototypes of the light pattern library created, influenced, or even summoned up physical shapes in the landscape. How the domes called up the mountains from inside the Earth. How the Oroboros Lines delicately hold the planet together in an energy basket.

Or take the terrestrial star maps, which later we'll call landscape zodiacs. Miniature light forms of the galaxy, zodiacal theme parks, constellation merry-go-rounds—the star forms have summoned matching shapes out of the soft clay. You can see the constellations sculpted out of the land, each a face fresh awoken from sleep, seeking its image in the looking glass above and beholding a scintillation, awaiting the human recognition and its gesture of Love from Above that will justify its existence, bringing it online and in service.

Start Your Recall of Planetary History at Two Types of Information Libraries

Two geomantic features can now facilitate deep recall of past planetary events all these eons after the activities of the Blue Room were concluded. The first is called a Hyperborean Time Library; the second a Lemurian Information Crystal.

The Hyperborean Time Library (there are 456 on the Earth) is an archival center for events and

Table 2-1: Hyperborean Time Libraries and Lemurian Information Crystals		
Feature	Planetary Total	Selected Locations
Hyperborean Time Libraries	456	Ferral's Plantation, Tetford, Lincolnshire, England
		Crewkerne Church, Crewkerne, Somerset, England
		Burrowbridge Mump, Burrowbridge, Somerset, England
Lemurian Information Crystals	46,221,000	Ilmandalen Valley, Rondvassbu, Rondane Mountains, Norway
		Holy Thorn, Wearyall Hill, Glastonbury, Somerset, England
		Ponter's Ball [sic], Glastonbury, Somerset, England
		Dundon Beacon, Compton Dundon, Somerset, England

conditions in Hyperborean days on Earth and an experiential portal, at least psychically, to that time. I first discovered this feature in the course of taking a long afternoon walk in Lincolnshire, England. I was just outside Tetford, a newly discovered and opened geomantic site with many features (see *The Galaxy on Earth*, pages 475–480). Off the side of the road was a lovely, soft crescent curve of green, a rounded bowl of a hill girded with beeches. The place had a "magical" pull to it, grabbing my attention at once. (It is known locally as Ferral's Plantation.)

The Library itself is a large crystalline torus, a mathematically described shape that is like a smoke ring in which the ribbed walls of the tube are constantly cycling in and out of the shape. The torus is perhaps 100 feet in diameter.

You access the Library by standing at the still, hollow center of the cycling torus where information from multiple sources is simultaneously downloaded into your being bodies. If, hypothetically, we say the torus has 100 ribs that are constantly cycling in and out, you are exposed to 100 information inputs at once.

The Lemurian Information Crystals are far more plentiful, there being 46,221,000 planted around the planet. They are not equally distrib-

uted across the symmetrical geometrical divisions of the Earth's surface (called Albion Plates, explained later in the book). Rather they are distributed on the spiral patterns generated by energy features called domes as they generate dome caps (see chapter 5). Domes are energy canopies representing stars, usually positioned over mountains; dome caps are smaller versions of the same; the overall pattern of domes and dome caps resembles a mature sunflower head in which spiral lines are implicit in the distribution of seeds. The Lemurian Information Crystals can be conceived as lying on these implicit spiral lines.

Obviously, the Lemuria part of this feature derives from the defunct continent in the Pacific called Lemuria.[33] The key point is that conditions in human consciousness were far different in the Lemurian epoch from what we experience today, and perhaps so different that it is nearly impossible to conceive what they might have been like. Attunement with a Lemurian Information Crystal is one way to gain direct though initially highly strange information on those earlier conditions. Consider them archival records, entire libraries of information, deposited prolifically across the land surface of the planet (see table 2-1).

The feature may appear as a giant vertical clear quartz crystal perhaps 100 feet high and 50 feet across, perhaps much bigger. I saw one in Norway that size, but the Holy Thorn on Wearyall Hill in Glastonbury marks one that initially appears not much bigger than a human; however, on the inside, it is actually about one-fifth the size of the hill. It is a complex crystalline form with a cubic base out of which rise dozens of icicle-shaped vertical shafts.

Inside the Crystal at Wearyall Hill is like liquid light, a matrix of pure creativity. An angel librarian is there and directs me to the geomancy section. The experience is like standing in a shower, a tight vertical column or cylinder in which the shower acts like a fourth-dimensional pictographic imprinting tube. Information is showered upon me like water; it enters my space as energy or picture-symbols, or perhaps the light language antecedent to that. These symbols or pictures—they are like hieroglyphics—get imprinted on my etheric body as on a cylinder for later downloading.

In Lemurian times there was a different cognitive basis for memory storage and retrieval based on different structures of consciousness, more of a dreamlike picture-symbol consciousness, as Rudolf Steiner said the Lemurians had. The information I accessed deals with Earth-celestial interactions, but many other topics could be accessed, for I pulled only one drawer in the card catalog of this library.

The Lemurian Information Crystal represents energy storage from a past time, but it is also information in a different form. It is energy at another level waiting for people to download and assimilate. Bear in mind, the information is very dense, and your initial contact with it may be disorienting as it is registered by your subtle bodies, that is, the subtler aspects of your auric field.

As my mentors the Ofanim (see below) note, "It is necessary for the times that have already been and for those that are to come that this information and energy be available for those who need to access it." To do so, practice Sufi twirling, the Ofanim suggest. Stand with your right arm extended, hand upwards, and your left hand extended, hand downwards, then turn clockwise very slowly for a few minutes. You will need to do this frequently, increasing the time allotted until you start "downloading" consciously.

Why Was There a Need for the Planet Earth?

You might reasonably wonder why was there an Earth at all? Who needed it? What's wrong with Venus that we couldn't live there? The answer is Maldek. You can see the remains of that planet in the asteroid belt between Mars and Jupiter. It blew up long before the Blue Room team started getting the Earth ready as its replacement planet.

Some years ago two British friends and I dreamed of Maldek's demise. Impatience caused it. On Maldek, the planet's physical and energy aspects were united through a grid system based on hydrogen. What we would call power plants on Earth were situated deliberately at the key energy nodes in the planet's grid matrix. Here we would call those nodes the sacred sites. Think of power plants at Stonehenge, Giza, Easter Island. The physical power that ran everything on Maldek was hydrogen, and the plants processed and distributed hydrogen the way our plants produce electricity.[34]

On Maldek, hydrogen production was no secret. The government was a spiritually informed one, combining technology and geomancy for the public welfare. What was kept secret was the seduction of the hydrogen plant engineers. There the plant engineers were also grid engineers, what we would call geomancers. They were psychic and capable in the occult arts; they were aware of the interface of subtle and gross energy at these grid nodes.

That planet's physical and spiritual life was held together by these hydrogen plants. On Maldek, the etheric and physical levels of reality were not separated by human obliviousness. The etheric "bled through" into the physical, and the hydrogen plants grounded this.

A time came when the grid engineers working in the hydrogen plants around the planet started to get impatient with the pace of things on Maldek. It was too slow. The pace of consciousness was stultifying. Maybe it was merely a few engineers at first, perhaps too smart for their own good, too evolved, too subtle to be comfortable with the saturnine rate of evolution.

An idea came to them. This is the key part of the seduction and disaster.

They thought about moving the planet into a faster orbit. That required, according to Bode's Law, actually moving the planet to another zone in the solar system that permits this. Bode's Law describes the numerical and necessary distances of planets from a sun in a solar system.[35] (Of course they had their own name for that necessity then.) How to move a planet? Certain alien intelligences, listening in on the thought processes of the impatient Maldekian grid engineers, came forward and offered to help. Their consultations became frequent. The grid engineers thought they were getting professional advice, but they were being had by the aliens, who wanted conscious life eliminated from the planet. With every visit, they more deeply infiltrated the Maldek hydrogen grid installation with their energy and occult machinations.

In the dream, I saw a murky beige sludge emanate from the aliens into the power plants. Their energy was incompatible with what the Maldek system produced. Eventually, the hydrogen global grid system got destabilized. The planet wobbled and exploded.

A new but comparable planet was required for the Maldekians to continue their evolution. You can't cook up a suitable planet for human conscious evolution overnight. That's where the 2.7 million years came in. The Maldekians had to wait a bit for the Blue Room team to get Earth ready.

The Earth is thus both a designer planet and a replacement planet.

So does that mean all humans on Earth are descendants of Maldek? No. The Maldekian is only one of many incarnational soul streams that use Earth as home. According to the Ofanim, the planet Earth has a greater diversity of soul origins for its humans than any other known planet. Call it Planet Melting Pot.

Earth is cosmopolitan on a galactic level, entertaining a greater range of souls at a wider range of evolutionary levels than anywhere else in the universe. It's like one classroom with students ranging from kindergarten to the postgraduate level. Those are a lot of diverse energies to service and harmonize, which is partly why the grid will have so many different geomythic features and, from the viewpoint of the Blue Room, why it will take so long for this impressive experiment to come to fruition. Naturally, as it does so over the eons, it will attract a great deal of attention and visits from other star systems, from those seeking to help, to watch, to hinder. Today, all the parts have been in place for many ages of humanity, and we have passed from knowing to forgetting to obliviousness about the system.

Who Were the Hyperboreans?

That explains why there is a planet Earth. Now who were the original players in its implementation? Some of the original members of the Blue Room were Hyperboreans, a name found in classical Greek sources. Essentially, the Hyperboreans were Pleiadians, the "wandering ones," who went on assignment among the planets. Astronomically, the Pleiades is a star cluster of seven fairly distinct stars and an estimated 300 associated stars. From somewhere amidst this congeries of stars came the Hyperboreans. Their involvement with the Earth has spanned its entire life and continues today.

From the Greek sources we get a picture of the Hyperboreans after the Blue Room, when they lived on the planet for a while. Herodotus, writing in the fifth century B.C., relates third-hand information that beyond an already remote land lived a one-eyed race called the Arimaspians, beyond them was the land of the "gold-guarding griffins," and beyond that the Hyperboreans. Sacred objects tied in bundles of wheat straw were regularly shipped from Hyperborea to Delos (a Greek island), and Herodotus mentions a Hyperborean named Abaris who "carried an arrow all the way around the world without eating anything."[36]

Apollodorus in the second century B.C. said that the legendary Gardens of the Hesperides and the golden apple trees tended by Atlas were "among the Hyperboreans."[37] The Greek lyric poet Pindar, writing in the fifth century B.C., said the hero Perseus had been at the feasts of the "People beyond the North."

The Hyperboreans feasted and celebrated most of the time, Pindar wrote, and their constant praising of "their God" was Apollo's "chief delight" and possibly the reason he spent time there. The Muse never leaves that land, and constant is the sound of harping, flutes trilling, and young women dancing. The Hyperboreans bind their hair with bay leaves of gold, they are glad all the time, never get sick or infirm with age as their bodies are holy. They live without effort or conflict "and do not trouble the stern scales of Nemesis."[38]

Classical scholars have pieced together more of the Hyperborean picture. After Apollo's birth, he flew with his team of celestial swans to Hyperborea where he stayed until he was ready to make his ceremonial debut at Delphi. Apollo would come to Hyperborea every 19 years (alternately, it's said he spent his winters there), and his visits were based on large-scale Moon cycles and on when the stars returned to their original places.[39] In the nights between the spring equinox and the summer rising of the Pleiades, he would sing hymns, play his lyre, and dance through the night. The sacred objects used to venerate Apollo at Delos came from here, and his mother, Leto, was said to have been born in Hyperborea, hence Apollo's close ties to this distant land.

The Hyperboreans were a people of happy temperament and civilized customs, and they spent much of their time in their sacred groves, playing music. Supposedly, the elderly, when they decided they were finished with incarnation, jumped to their death from a high cliff, their heads garlanded with flowers.

The oracle of Delphi may have been founded originally by a Hyperborean named Olen, said Pausanias. He wrote that "Olen and the remote Northerners" founded the oracle of Apollo, and that it was Olen who first "prophesied and first sang the hexameter" at Delphi.[40] Pliny said that for six months of the year in Hyperborea, it is all one long day, then for the next six months, it is all one long night. Their climate was blissful and pleasant, they lived mainly in groves and the woods where they worshipped their gods, but at night they slept in caves.

Diodorus of Siculus, a classical historian of the first century B.C. from Sicily, in a comparatively voluble account of the Hyperboreans, tells us that on the "island" of Hyperborea is "a magnificent sacred precinct of Apollo and a notable [spherical] temple" and at least one Hyperborean city was dedicated to Apollo.

On account of Leto's birth in Hyperborea, all the residents there were known as priests of Apollo, her divine son, and "daily they praise this god continuously in song and honor him exceedingly." Most Hyperboreans played the cithara (a stringed instrument) and continuously sang hymns of praise to Apollo, glorifying his deeds.[41]

The kings and supervisors of the sacred precincts were called Boreades, as they were descendants of Boreas, or the North Wind, after whom the land was originally named. Hyperborea was understood by the Greeks, who were ever wondering exactly where it was, as "a blessed land beyond the reach of Boreas, the god of winter and of the hurricane."[42] That area may well have included Scandinavia, the British Isles, Greenland, Iceland, and the Arctic. The Greeks never found Hyperborea because they asked the wrong question: not where but when? Their folktales of Abaris, Hyperochus, Laodocus, Olen, Arges, and Opis were well-preserved memories from an antique time, long before their advent.

After human life on Earth started, the Hyperboreans remained present for a while. Their era became known as Hyperborea, as did their residency. Hyperborea was for a while a world culture enveloping the planet, with its culture centered first in Lemuria (in the Pacific Ocean), then Atlantis (in the Atlantic), on landmasses now underwater, their existence disbelieved in by historians. The epicenter of the Hyperborean civilization was the British Isles, which is why Blake said so presciently, "All things Begin & End in Albion's Ancient Druid Rocky Shore." From stone circles to crop circles.

Key Planet Builders—Merlin, the Ofanim, and the Elohim

A unique planetary builder present in the Blue Room, known by many names, is Merlin. Much later in the Earth's history, Merlin will become known as King Arthur's magus, the creator of the celebrated Round Table, the architect of Camalate, possessor of the 13 Treasures of Britain (a panoply of magical tools). He is credited by at least one source with having moved Stonehenge twice, from Southeast Africa to Mount Killaraus in Northern Ireland then to Salisbury Plain in England.

But Merlin has been around since the beginning of the Earth; in fact, according to the Welsh *Triads,* the first of three ancient names for the British Isles (which is to say Hyperborea) was named after him: Myrddin's Precinct. That was before the island was taken or settled; the next name was Island of Honey, used after the first inhabitation, and the third, after the island was conquered by Aedd the Great, was the Island of Prydein, later known as Britain. Myrddin's Precinct aptly described the Earth in the early days of the Blue Room presence.

Merlin was a land mover, a continent evoker, a cleanser of vast territories, and a prodigious prophet. You can see this in his various guises: the Polynesian demi-god Maui; the Irish Hound of Chulainn, Cuchulainn; the Scottish mystic of Iona, Saint Columba (Columcille); the Buddhist missionary Padmasambhava, who prepared Tibet for Buddhism; the Apostle of Christ, John the Revealer, Patmosian author of Revelation; the Greek master hero and demi-god Heracles.

In his 12 labors as Heracles, Merlin mastered various primordial energies and grounded them on the Earth for the benefit of the energy grid. His role, as he saw it, was as a purifier of sites, ridding places of ferocious chthonic and autochthonous energies, beasts, and monsters. "I wore my useless life out clearing monsters from your woods and seas and where are you now?" Heracles laments about the Greeks as he faces his own death by poisoning.[43]

The Greeks portrayed Merlin as Heracles as a brutish subduer of all the forces opposed to civilization, using his invincible body as his weapon to order the chaos. "He belongs to a world of limitless space" which is "inhabited by forces of inhuman savagery"; Heracles is "a figure of crushing strength."[44] Geomantically, he is preparing the landscape for human habitation, mastering the primordial energies, regulating them, putting them in their place.[45]

But his name, correctly written, holds the secret of his activity, his commission from on high: *Mer-Line*. Merlin is the line to the Mother, the Mer, the Sea, the vast ocean of cosmic consciousness. Merlin is our link to the fathomless sea of awareness, the Mother's love.[46]

Think of the Sea as the unconscious or greater consciousness of Man. Merlin is the umbilical connection between every human and the Mother, the Mother's Line from Heaven to Earth, from above to below, from Her to you, the pure fire of compassion, the warmth and caring of the Mother for her "children." Love from Above is conveyed from the Mother and the angelic realm via the Mer-Line to us. Merlin is the line by which, through a clear point of light, you may reach more consciousness, more awareness, and more love, state the Ofanim.[47]

The influences of the Ofanim and the clear point of light just mentioned reach us through the Mer-Line. The Ofanim have a long-standing working relationship with Merlin, as with the members of the Blue Room. The Ofanim are what we would call a family of angels, known in Greek angelologies as the Thrones. Their name is derived from the Hebrew root word, *ofan*, which means "wheels."[48]

It's not that they look like wheels; they look like angels, or more precisely, they look like whatever suits them, including, among many possible examples of cultural images, the much beloved Hindu elephant god Ganesh, progeny of Shiva and Parvati. Another is the Hindu image of Garuda, known as Vishnu's Mount and Wings-of-Speech, the great bird celestial encharged with transporting the god Vishnu all over the universe. The wheels connotation is meaningful in the con-

text of the Ofanim's functions, one of which is to provide motion to the Throne of God, known as the Merkabah.

Not a great deal has been written about the Ofanim in conventional angelologies. They are either relatively unknown or mysterious, or perhaps, paradoxically, because they are ubiquitous, they get overlooked. One account says the Ofanim are "full of eyes and wings."[49]

Much of the information in this book comes from my conversations and experiences with the Ofanim over the course of 20 years. It's been a bit like a postgraduate program in a subject that does not yet have its own curriculum in a field not yet recognized. The Ofanim's "brief" with the Supreme Being with respect to us has been to clarify human interactions with the Earth's energy body and to illuminate aspects of planetary history relevant to understanding that relationship. That, and to facilitate direct training experiences, as when they introduced several colleagues and myself in 1990 to the Blue Room or, rather, reminded us of its existence, bringing us in spirit form to that place to facilitate our memory.

I can offer a few factual statements about the Ofanim: Their fundamental manifestation is as a tiny pinprick of brilliant light, a Blazing Star. When they manifest as angels, they appear as a minimum of six, but these six have a total of 40,310,784 possible manifestations. The Ofanim oversee 18,723,488,640 galaxies, communicating with a few individuals here and there, assuming appropriate cultural forms and images to help this out, and clarifying energy and structural aspects of planets.

Somewhat whimsically, they refer to their activity as cosmic dentistry. They see themselves, metaphorically, as toothpaste and the toothbrush, making the stars "brighter than bright," cleaning out the "dark crevices" in galaxies and conscious life forms, and "trying to get rid of the decay so that we may all become One again in the brightness of the star we are."

The Ofanim are approximately 30 billion years old. "Most of the other angel families are youngsters and have lived less time," they comment. "We have been around since the Beginning, when the Architect of All That Is brought us into being."[50] They don't come from this place, but it acts as an aperture for their energy to enter into our galaxy: the star Vega in Lyra, the constellation of the Harp; Vega is the fifth brightest star in our galaxy. As for their extreme brightness, the Ofanim note: "We are brighter than the brightest star. As you have measurements in light intensity, we are brighter than those."[51]

The Ofanim, Merlin, and the Hyperboreans performed many geomantic tasks together. For the most part, the installation of megalithic structures was handled by the Elohim, another family of angels who played a pivotal role in Blue Room planning and grid installation. Confusingly, most Bibles translate God as Elohim, leading us to equate the two, but in the original Hebrew, and in any correct angelology, the Elohim are plural. In fact, there is an astonishing number of them: 1,746 to the ninth, or 155 septillion, spread out over the same 18 billion galaxies as the Ofanim.

The Elohim are the worker angels. As the mythic Giants,[52] they created and installed most of the Earth's megalithic structures; they built the Avebury stone circle; they created Silbury Hill; they were the prime architects of Mexico's Teotihuacan.[53]

On a few occasions I have had the opportunity to interview the Elohim. "We refer to ourselves as a group with a collective view that has transcended your physical world but has still karmic debts to certain of humanity and the planetary body called Earth," they said once. During one epoch, three Elohim manifested themselves as the 14 planetary logoi, or all-encompassing spirits of the planets of this solar system, two per planet.

The Greeks called them Titans. They had a good reason for being giants.

"The Elohim came to form, materialized as a direct consequence of the Plan that was formed by the Cosmic Masters of Destiny. We were giants as one aspect of a Being manifestation projected by us. We were most vulnerable in a situation of animal level manifestation. Our consciousness was not attuned to any form of bestiality or the procreation prevalent on this planet at that time. Size was our only protection. We were very big." The Elohim were among the prime "genetic engineers" of the human race on Earth, infusing their consciousness into many of the animals, "and out of this, with some mistakes, we derived the present form you know as Man."

According to the Ofanim, "The Elohim have been very helpful and continue to be so." In a sense, their function as prime creators of form is embodied in their name. The Al or El in Elohim is the essence of creation. "It is the in-drawn breath, the birthing of something, the point of light, the Star, the essence of Mind, the forgiveness in forgave. The Elohim are the forms of AL, the projections, entities, or forms that are acceptable to conscious perception of this essence." The Elohim are implicit in Albion, one of the forms of AL.

It is possible to investigate a little of this firsthand. At energy nodes around the planet, you can access memories of some of the Elohim's genetic engineering activities. One such place is Burrowbridge Mump in England, a small grassy hill about ten miles from Glastonbury in Somerset. You can access aspects of their dimensional reality by sitting on the Mump and "tuning in." There is a link between the esoteric aspects of the Mump's energy field and the Elohim's sphere of activity.

One time I looked at the Elohim and saw a dark blue crystalline domain, a realm of holy existence. Imagine that the entirety of their manifestation package is expressed as a multifaceted blue crystal, a dimension of reality inhabited and energized by a Holy Name of God. It's not that you would necessarily hear these syllables intoned in Hebrew. Rather you would be inside the reality field they create; you would experience the results of that perpetual intoning of the Name.

This vast field of blue crystalline facets is the seedbed or reservoir of the energies of *AL*, prime creative energies. When the Elohim wish to act, it's as if a certain number of the facets join together to form a prototypal human face, a focus of attention. This Elohim face can contain a species, planet, solar system, or galaxy. For the Elohim, to think it is to create it.

When they became giants they merely turned themselves inside out so that the blue stone field was inside them as a creative matrix. Their composite creative face was inside them like programming. It was easy for them to create with stone, lay out circles, build megalithic citadels, summon stone out of the ethers. It was just a denser version of what they dealt with all the time in the subtler realms of reality: stone. This bit is very interesting, but I have to digress for a moment to Polynesian legend for the point to make sense.

Polynesian myth says that in the earliest days on Earth the sky was so low it pressed down on the Earth, requiring men to crawl around on their hands and knees. The sky ceiling was so low they couldn't stand up, and it was made of stone.

"The sky of blue rock was in those days covered with sharp nobbles." The Polynesian myths also say of a later day, when the stone sky was lifted off the Earth, that "Haehae is the gateway in the sky's hard blue rock through which the sun emerges each morning." The Polynesians also say that after the gods were created, the "Highest One" birthed the rocks, and "the high rocks married the earth rocks producing the earth."[54]

How can the sky be a stone? Alchemists call this the *prima materia*, the first matter, out of which forms are created. Stone is an image of density; what is densifying is the *prima materia*, which we might also call primordial etheric sub-

stance, the stuff of Earth when we think of Earth as all cosmic space outside of Heaven.

So the Elohim, as world creators, work with stone, or *prima materia*, all the time. It's the familiar clay on their potter's wheel. They wrap their attention around some *prima materia* and create whatever they intend. Humans, planets, planetary spheres are birthed within the Elohim attention field. As the last stage, they set a golden Sun to burn inside the stone. Out of the Elohim's blue stone matrix come the progeny of *AL*.[55]

Of considerable interest to the unfolding of the Emerald modem as the primary design archetype and means of using it is the fact that in the Western Mystery tradition the Elohim are called the Lords of the heavenly sphere of Venus. This will become apparent later in the chapter when we discuss the Jerusalem archetype.

The Fallback Position: *Sipapuni*—360 Hollow Earth Emergence Points

The planet designers prepared a fallback, contingency plan for the topside Earth humanity experiment—another version inside the planet.

In case you've ever wondered what the Hopi, Zuni, and Pawnee of the American Southwest mean when they state earnestly that they "emerged" from inside the Earth at an earlier age of the planet, there is now a plausible explanation. They did so literally out of one of the 360 doorways that connect the Earth as we know it on the planet's surface with another civilization as we don't know it inside the Earth.

The Hopis say their *sipapuni*, or Place of Emergence, was the Grand Canyon, and they define *sipapuni* as "the hole in the sky above the Lower (Third) World through which the people emerged into the Upper (Fourth) World."[56] The hole in the "sky" from our point of view would be

Table 2-2: *Sipapuni,* **Entrances into the Hollow Earth**

Planetary Total: 360

Selected Locations:
Mount Balsam Cone, Waynesville, North Carolina, U.S.
Salt Cave, Grand Canyon, Arizona, U.S.
Hessdalen, Norway, Arctic Circle, North Pole
Kluskap's Cave, Cape Dauphin, Cape Breton, Nova Scotia, Canada
Truckee, California, U.S.
Frijoles Canyon, Bandelier, U.S. National Monument, New Mexico, U.S.

Equivalent Names: Place of Emergence, Door into the World beneath the Earth

the surface of the Earth, under our feet, which for them would be the "roof." The underground Hopi ceremonial center called a kiva has a symbolic *sipapuni* to remind them of their Emergence and their connection with the interior of the Earth (see table 2-2).

The Zuni of New Mexico have a similar emergence story. All humans and animals were originally created deep inside the Earth, in the first of four "cave-wombs." The "all-sacred master" Poshaiyankya, a divine human hero, traversed the next three cave-wombs to explore the surface of the Earth on behalf of all created beings and found it was a vast island, wet and unstable. Eventually, the rest of his people traversed the cave-wombs to emerge. They climbed up a great ladder created by growing, twisting plants in the first cave-womb. The second cave-womb was called *K'olin tehuli* (the umbilical womb or Place of Gestation); the third was *Awisho tehuli* (the vaginal womb, or Place of Sex-Generation); the fourth was *Tepahaian tehuli* (the ultimate-uncoverable, Womb of Parturition). Each successive cave-womb was larger and brighter. At last they emerged into the great upper world called *Tek'ohaian ulahnane,* the

World of Disseminated Light and Knowledge, the World of Seeing.[57]

Other Native American peoples have similar emergence myths. The Mi'kmaq (Micmac) Indians of Cape Breton in Nova Scotia, Canada, maintain that there is a cave into the "World beneath the Earth" accessed on Kelly's Mountain at Cape Dauphin. The cave is considered sacred by the Mi'kmaq who say one day their god will return to Cape Breton through this same portal from the inner Earth. Two other doors into the interior Earth are said to be in Cape Breton as well.[58]

According to the Ofanim, there is even today a parallel human civilization within the Earth. Its population is miniscule compared to ours, a mere 17,000, but they are humans in bodies like us. These come and go into our world, and sometimes, as legend and folklore and the disbelieved claims of certain adventurers hold, people from our world venture down into theirs.

What's the reason for two parallel civilizations? First, they may be topographically parallel, but the one inside the Earth is, in the angelic view, more spiritually advanced and "at a higher state of evolution" than the one on the surface.

Second, it is for the "self-protection of the being of the Earth, if anything happens on Her surface" that compromises either the viability of the planet or its human evolutionary project. Those living inside the Earth are the planet's fallback plan, or maybe it's the reverse, and we're the fallback.

The inner Earth has an energy grid (the geometric, bare-bones aspect of the Earth's visionary geography) that relates to the one on and above the planet's surface, like lines of energy converging within. It appears to be interdependent with the one aboveground.

Those living inside may be more spiritually advanced, and also more technologically advanced. Apparently, UFOs come from both outside and inside the Earth. Sites around the Earth which are well known for UFO sightings often are actual entrances into the hollow interior. Others you may happen upon. Mount Balsam Cone in the Blue Ridge Mountains near Waynesville, North Carolina, is one. There I observed in vision a UFO base inside the mountain. At the time I did not realize it was more likely deep underneath the mountain and that the cone was the top hatch out of the interior base.[59]

The Cube of Space—Earth's Ten-Dimensional Cosmomythic Body

Now that we have a provisional idea of who was in the Blue Room in the early days of the Earth, the next thing to ask is, what were their blueprints? What master plan for the planet were they using to create the Earth's visionary geography? There is a paradox here, of course. Whatever description we settle on here will be a reduction of a multidimensional reality into three-dimensional terms. Even so, that is our basis for understanding even the first thing about the Earth's energy body. So we look for useful metaphors, analogies, and descriptive systems. These include myth

(discussed earlier), Qabala, and geometry, predominantly, among others.

These descriptive tools imply a cosmogony, which is to say, the creation and unfoldment of a cosmos, or in the language of this book, the precipitation of a Galaxy on Earth template.

Using these tools we'll see how the different and multiple reality layers of Earth's visionary geography came into being and how we can interact with them for the mutual benefit of human culture and the planet. We'll use these descriptive tools to move through the layers of Earth's visionary geography in practical, experiential ways.

The first and perhaps most important observation we can make is that our reality is contained within a cube.

The Qabalistic tradition talks of a Cube of Space. A classical arcane text of Qabala, the *Sefer Yetzirah*, states that in the beginning the Supreme Being (Yah) "sealed" space in six directions, creating the six surfaces of a cube (see figure 2-1). That means the Supreme Being marked off a specific quantity of Space in which creation would happen. This created a ten-dimensional reality. Four spheres of light, called Sefirot, were on the inside of this spatial cube, and six more were on the outside.

What can we say about the cube? It has six faces, eight vertices (or corners), and 12 edges. The cube is a "limiting" agent that defines and fixes the formless void into a contained space; it offers "fixation and limits for divine expression."[60] The cube is "the subtle container of the higher cosmic worlds and defines both the process of divine emanation and of spiritual return."[61] The cube "represents fully developed Man in his relationship to the Universe."[62] The cube represents a map of the cosmos, the coordinates of space, and "the soul purified of all imperfections."[63]

The cube is one of the Platonic Solids,[64] five unique polyhedra that fulfil specific shape requirements.[65] They look the same when viewed from any vertex or corner point; every edge is identical; their faces comprise the same regular shape; as regular polygons, all sides and angles are equal; they exhibit perfect symmetry. Each Solid has been associated with one of the primary elements or building blocks of matter: water, fire, air, ether, or (the cube) earth. As such, the cube is usually taken as symbolic of material existence, the element earth.

Why need we be concerned with Platonic Solids? They are implicit in the Earth's energy body, and they are part of the structure of the galaxy, universe, and reality. God geometrizes, the philosophers say, and one way God does this is through the generation and interaction of these five cosmic volumes. "The first manifestations of the universe are geometric," and the first 92 natural atoms of the periodic table, from hydrogen to uranium, have geometric shapes.[66]

God geometrizing means the use of these essential forms and numbers (the mathematical aspects of these figures) to order the primordial chaos on a higher plane so as to produce the five elements on the lower planes.[67] The forms and numbers of these cosmic volumes then "act as the interface between the higher and lower realms" and through their interactions with their analogous elements have "the power to shape the material world."[68] The Earth's energy body or "grid" is an elegant nest of these five regular polyhedra.

The cube was the primordial creative space for the generation of Adam Kadmon, the Anthropos or First Human on an archetypal

level. Qabalists say, metaphorically, that Adam Kadmon, made of four Sefirot (primordial vessels of Light), stands upright inside this cube facing East, his head and feet each touching a Sefira (singular of Sefirot), his gaze fixed on another one, his back to still another, each arm extended and pointing towards two more spheres of light.

The subsequent human being, a microcosm and copy of Adam Kadmon (us) was thereby introduced into an inner space defined by ten dimensions. "Thus everybody lives inside an enclosed and bounded cube locking inner space in a package."[69] Qabalists call this residence the Cube of Space.

In this model, the universe is described as a function of the ten Sefirot (see table 2-3), a hierarchy of spheres of primordial light. In practical terms, the Sefirot are the same as the ten directions of sealed Space. These are boundaries, realms, or dimensional layers, expressing the inner life of the Supreme Being. They are the products of

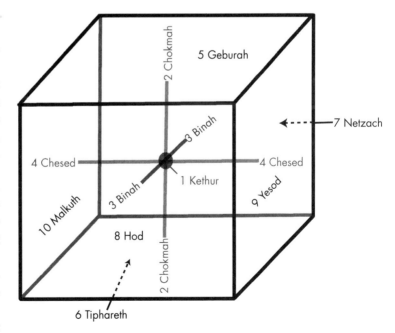

Figure 2-1. Mapping the Ten Sefirot onto the Cube of Space

Table 2-3: The Sefirot: A Ten-Dimensional Model of Reality

According to Qabala, when Yah sealed Space, this created the ten Sefirot and the Cube of Space with Adam Kadmon, the Primordial Human, inside.

Inside the Cube

1st Sefira	Kether	center-point of cube	
2nd Sefira	Chokmah	vertical axis	
3rd Sefira	Binah	East-West horizontal axis	
4th Sefira	Chesed	South-North axis	

Outside the Cube

5th Sefira	Geburah	Adam Kadmon's head	top of cube
6th Sefira	Tiphareth	Adam Kadmon's feet	bottom of cube
7th Sefira	Netzach	His gaze	East
8th Sefira	Hod	His back	West
9th Sefira	Yesod	His right arm extended	South
10th Sefira	Malkuth	His left arm extended	North

Summary Meanings of the Sefirot

Kether	Crown, First Principal, Primal Glory, Ancient of Days
Chokmah	Wisdom, Supernal Father, Splendor of Unity
Binah	Understanding, Intelligence, Supernal Mother, Marah, the Great Sea
Chesed	Mercy, Receptive Intelligence, Love, Jupiter
Geburah	Strength, Power, Severity, Justice, the Scourge, Mars
Tiphareth	Beauty, Lesser Countenance, the Son, Adam, Heart, Sun
Netzach	Victory, Lasting Endurance, Occult Intelligence, Rose, Venus
Hod	Glory, Majesty, Vision of Splendor, Mercury
Yesod	Foundation, Universe's Machinery, Astral Light, Moon
Malkuth	Earth, Kingdom, Crowned Woman, the Bride, Virgin, the Gate

what Qabala calls His Ten Holy Names, ten fundamental utterances and attributes.

They are the "foundations" for a ten-dimensional universe, "energy structures" that funnel, filter, and step down the original Endless Light in stages, like a cascading waterfall in which water (light, consciousness) flows downward, spilling over nine basins before it reaches the ground.[70]

God generated a light that was too overwhelmingly brilliant for our physical world; it had to be stepped down in nine stages, each successive stage being a more dilute version of the original Endless Light. The Sefirot are simultaneously aspects of the Supreme Being and Adam Kadmon (hence, humanity) and the world itself.[71] They are the ten creative "words," the agencies and instruments of creation.

Qabala further proposes that the ten Sefirot exist in Four Worlds, giving us from a certain viewpoint 40 dimensions, not ten. The Four Worlds concept is central to the Emerald modem model, so let's review it briefly. Think of it as four different playing fields in which the same game is played, except that in each successive field, the game is either more rarified and abstract or more densified and specific, depending on your direction of movement, up or down the cascade.

Qabala calls these Four Worlds Atziluth,[72] Beriah,[73] Yezirah,[74] and Assiyah,[75] moving from subtlest to grossest. Each Sefira has a projection in each of the Four Worlds, which means reality is the result of a four-stage process of manifestation, an escalator of 40 steps.[76]

One way to get a fix on Qabala's model of the Four Worlds is through Greek mythology. The classical Greeks said Earth (Ge) was divided into three realms. Zeus was the god of the Sky; Poseidon, Lord of the Sea; and Hades, Ruler of the Underworld. The common assumption is that these are the three physical zones of our physical Earth, but they are not. They are the first three Worlds, all subtler than our material planet. Zeus is Lord of Atziluth;[77] Poseidon is Lord of Beriah;[78] and Hades is Lord of Yezirah.[79]

The Language on the Tip of Adam Kadmon's Tongue

The *Sefer Yezirah* states, "With 32 mystical paths of Wisdom engraved Yah." Ten of these mystical paths are the Sefirot just discussed; the other 22 are the letters of the Hebrew alphabet, which Judaic mysticism and Qabala regard as prime living generative agents used by the Supreme Being to create reality. The letters represent basic forces of nature and are derived from "flows of light" between the Sefirot. The ten Sefirot have "flows of spiritual matter" between them, flowing through what Qabalists sometimes call "pipes" (*tzinorot*). There are 22 such pipes, from which are derived Hebrew's 22 letters.[80]

According to Qabalist Carlo Suares, the 22 letters of the Hebrew alphabet (called the Autiot) are ideograms, each embodying one aspect or structure of cosmic energy. The letters are energy forms in a sacred creative language, "archetypes preexistent to any articulate language." The letters are the "workmen" that make the ten Sefirot function; they are transformers of the Endless Light into materialization. Each letter, Suares says, is the "name of a cosmic energy acting both outside of us and within us"; each letter unites us with the energy it describes. The letters are "apertures" through which we can glimpse the presence of living cosmic forces, of independent cosmic life.[81]

The Judaic assumption is that "the Torah or Teaching existed before Creation and that God consulted it before bringing the Universe into being."[82]

It is counterintuitive to conceive of a language as having independent cosmic life, as comprising animate energy structures of the higher mind, but Rab Hamnuna the Venerable relates that when the Holy One (the Supreme Being, or Yah) was about to make the world, all the letters petitioned Him one by one to be the first one to be used. This means the Autiot was with the Supreme Being before Creation happened. It is said to have been circulating like a living wreath of fire letters around the Holy One's head. As God announced His plan to create reality, the letters "descended from the terrible and august crown of God whereon they were engraved with a pen of flaming fire."[83]

It's intriguing to note here that one contemporary Qabalist explains that the 22 Hebrew letters naturally and perhaps necessarily map on to the 22 components (the center, three interior dimensions, six faces, 12 edges) of the Cube of Space, making a cube of letters that describes humanity's spiritual path.[84]

Jerusalem As the Cosmic Archetype for the Earth's Visionary Geography

It's important to keep in mind that the Cube of Space is made of ten spheres of light and 22 living-generative letters of creation, with us inside it all.

Qabala and geometry are key elements in the blueprints for Earth's visionary geography, but what is the *big* picture? What does it all add up to?

It adds up to the city of Jerusalem as the celestial archetype and fulfillment of the Earth's visionary geography. By Jerusalem I refer not to the city in Israel nor to the First and Second Temple of Solomon built on Mount Moriah. I refer to the archetype, the higher dimensional blueprint, from which these temples derived. The spiritual, archetypal Jerusalem is the Cube of Space.

Jerusalem is what Earth Mysteries expert John Michell calls the "heavenly city as eternal standard" whose plan represents the "complete order of the universe." It is the cosmic temple, the ideal city, embodying the canon of number and proportion, described by mystics and philosophers including Plato, who said it was a pattern set in the heavens and that those who wanted to see it could do so and establish its pattern "in their own hearts."[85]

Saint John the Divine's magisterial vision in Revelation set the stage for this early messianic clairvoyance in Judea. John saw the holy city of New Jerusalem "coming down from God out of heaven, as beautiful as a bride all dressed for her husband." In this heavenly city come to Earth, God will live among humans, John foretold (Revelation 21:1-29),[86] and the original Jerusalem

from the infancy of Earth would be refreshed, updated by the New Jerusalem of the future.[87]

John the Evangelist did not say where the new temple would be placed.[88]

In the Old Testament, the city's name appears 656 times, almost always as *Yerushalem*, a shorter form of *Yerushalayim*, which is usually translated as "to found" (*yarah*, or *yeru*) "peace" (*shalom, shalem*, or *shalayim*)—Foundation of Peace.[89] Jerusalem will be "the place where later God will show (*yir'eh*), or make known on earth, the fullness and perfection (*shalem*) of what is above."[90]

There is another possible etymology for Jerusalem. Here *Salem* refers to the Evening and Morning Star, and *Jeru* to "foundation." Isaiah (14:12) refers to "O Helel, son of Shahar," which is usually interpreted as "O shining one, Son of the Dawn." Shahar was the Babylonian god of the Dawn; Helel was his son, the morning star; and Shahar's twin brother was Shalem. Thus Jerusalem means "the foundation of the Morning (Shahar) and Evening (Shalem) Star."[91]

Astronomically, that star is Venus, giving us the cosmic archetype of Jerusalem as the Foundation of Venus, Morning and Evening Star.

You Already Have the Keys to the Jerusalem Temple

With this foundation laid, I offer three observations about Jerusalem as a cosmic archetype. First, it is the Cube of Space turned inside out. Second, it is the Emerald, the Heart within the Heart, the inner heart chakra in the human. Third, it is the master structure for the Earth grid, so the Earth already exists within it.

In the Cube of Space, the ten Sefirot are represented, four on the inside, six on the outside. Chesed, Binah, Chokmah, and Kether are inside; Malkuth, Yesod, Hod, Netzach, Tiphareth, and Geburah are outside the Cube. In the Jerusalem archetype, the Cube is turned inside out. Chesed, Binah, Chokmah, and Kether are outside the Cube, while the other six are inside. The Cube itself has changed; it is now a six-sided double-terminated green crystal.

Picture a transparent cube that consists only of its structural lines, a skeletal cube. Look at it from one of the vertices or corners. You will see a hexagram consisting of six equilateral triangles. You are in effect looking up from the bottom of a hexagonal (six-sided) figure, as if you were standing underneath a skyscraper, beneath the basement, but able to see through its structure to the top, many stories above you.

This figure has six sides, it's Emerald green, and it's double-terminated, meaning it comes to a point at the top and bottom. You might think of this hexagonal crystal as a higher dimensional expression of the cube, produced by rotating the cube 45 degrees diagonally. This is Jerusalem.

The Jerusalem archetype exists within the energy field of every human. It is an esoteric aspect of the heart chakra, the Heart within the Heart. The outer heart chakra is called Anahata, is traditionally depicted as having 12 petals, and is located approximately under the left nipple. The inner heart chakra is called the Ananda-kanda and has eight petals; it is situated under the right nipple. If you picture two interlocking circles (called a *vesica piscis*) and place them against your chest, the left circle is the Anahata, the right is the Ananda-kanda, and the almond-shaped space in the middle is the Heart within the Heart.

The Heart within the Heart, midway between the outer and inner heart chakras, is called the Emerald because that best describes its color, and (appropriately, given that it is the esoteric aspect of the heart chakra) there is very little written about it, at least in obvious outward terms.

The Indian sage Ramana Maharshi called it the *Hridayam,* the seat and source of consciousness, identical with the Self, "the very Core of

one's being, the Center, without which there is nothing whatsoever." The *Hridayam* is that which attracts everything into itself; it is the place where the "Ultimate Divine" dwells in each human. Light originates here then flows upwards to the crown chakra and down to the other energy centers.

The *Hridayam* is not an organ nor does it correspond with one. It is pure consciousness beyond space and time, transcending the Mind. The Heart is the Self, Ramana Maharshi says; the Heart, which is pure consciousness, includes everything; it is indivisible.[92]

While the Heart within the Heart doesn't correspond with an organ, it does have a bodily reference point. It is a tiny doorway in the electromagnetic field of the heart, two inches long, situated on the right side of the sternum starting at the third rib. Picture a double-terminated, two-inch-long Emerald crystal positioned vertically and you give yourself a point of access to this arcane Heart. It is a miniaturized Jerusalem the Ofanim call the Emerald. Here are some of the comments the Ofanim have offered over the years on the Emerald:

"The Emerald was dropped into Man's biophysical organism at that point when the human form was brought into matter by the Lord of Light. This was the time known as the Fall. The Lord of Light was the one closest to the Lord of Absolute, Infinite Love and Light, His Holiness Extreme in Excelsius. The Lord of Light wished to experience something that none of us had even thought possible. He achieved a part of the Plan and is most blessed amongst angels for his part in the whole."

The Ofanim note that originally the Emerald existed in between two spheres of light, or Sefirot, on Qabala's Tree of Life model. When it was placed in the human energy field, it was simultaneously moved into Chesed, the fourth Sefira from the top of the Tree. So the installation of the Emerald within humankind signaled a momentous change in the structure of cosmic energy.

The Emerald is the container of vast supernal light on an order incomprehensible to conventional cognition. "Were you to be exposed to the source of love and light within the Emerald, you would lose your sense of space-time continuity. The light that it contains is beyond any description. The experience of it is beyond any description. The nature that you become after experiencing that is beyond what you refer to as the experiencer."

The approach to the Emerald is slow, gentle, and by degrees.

"The Emerald has six sides. Each side is an aspect of the truth of yourself. One side is understanding; the others are knowledge, compassion, intuition, peace, and bliss. Each side has to be balanced. Each side when penetrated removes the Emerald's outer layer and reveals the light within. Each person may approach the Emerald from a different side. The Emerald and its light are available to you relative to your readiness and openness to be able to approach it from a side. So the Heart within the Heart is approached differently, dependent on your differing characteristics."

Appropriately, Qabalists refer to the Cube of Space as the Luminous Cube, the Cube which illuminates, and the Cube of Ayn Soph Aur (the highest Light). Working with the Emerald, the Ofanim explain, puts you in potential contact with the Lord of Light because ultimately the Emerald is his. Our individual Emerald is a copy of his original. My Emerald, your Emerald, everyone's Emerald—we are already, inalterably connected. It is as if all humans are born with an identical modem link. So this puts you in spiritual proximity to all other humans similarly approaching their Emerald.

"When a person begins to awaken aspects of the Lord of Light within themselves, the Emerald starts to glow. It is a positive aspect of the Lord of Light awakening in the One. It is also when a human begins to awaken to other humans, when the love in you meets the love in someone else, then the Emerald awakens. It is the access point where that which in you is love is in love with that in others which is love. When two Emeralds open synchronously, there is spontaneous transmission of love from heart to heart." (The love connection with the Emerald will be treated in chapter 3.) "There is intensively but one Emerald. When all those who have Emeralds awaken spontaneously at the same moment in time and space, then the Lord of Light will be united again with the Father."

This is what John the Evangelist meant in Revelation when he referred to the 144,000 standing with the Lamb of God (Christ) on Mount Zion (Jerusalem), each with the Name of God (clairvoyant cognition) inscribed on their foreheads (brow chakra, the seat of psychic insight). Four angels, standing at the four corners of the Earth, hold back the four winds of the Apocalypse while a fifth angel puts the "seal of the living God" on the foreheads of the 144,000 "servants of God" to protect them against the coming destructive onslaught.[93]

At one level, these 144,000 Emeralds are *nadis,* or discrete energy channels in the body;[94] at another level, they are possibilities or probabilities within the biophysical base of certain humans for activation within the Heart of the Heart; at still another level, they are points within the Earth's geomagnetic field.

This brings me to my third point. The Earth's visionary geographic body exists *within* the Emerald. The highest expression of the Platonic Solids in the context of the Earth's energy body is the Cube, or more precisely, the Cube of Space turned inside out as the Jerusalem archetype or Emerald. This is the ultimate structure designed, implemented, and built in the Blue Room; the Cube of Space is the totality of the planet's geomantic body; we carry it within us as the Emerald, and this same Emerald or Cube of Space is the structure of reality.

Here's the equation: The Cube of Space is the Jerusalem Temple, and that is the Emerald, the inner heart chakra, and that's the Emerald modem, in us and around the Earth.

The amended Hermetic axiom describes this: *As above, so below, and in the middle, too. As above* is the Lord of Light's original Emerald; *so below* is the Emerald within the human as the inner Heart chakra; *and in the middle, too* is the planet Earth inside the vibratory field of this same Emerald. The Emerald modem involves the linkup and use of these three expressions of the Emerald.

Throughout the planet's visionary geography are copies of this Emerald. There is a prime Emerald for the planet, located near Oaxaca, Mexico, and placed there by the Lord of Light in the earliest days of Earth. There are secondary Emeralds in the 12 equal divisions of the Earth's surface called Albion plates; and there are tertiary Emeralds within the terrestrial star maps called landscape zodiacs. All of these Emeralds are holograms of the one original Emerald.

In a sense—it may seem magical to our modern sensibilities unfamiliar with the protocols of geomancy—all these Emeralds have been visualized by geomancers from their own Emeralds at various times in the Earth's history. In other words, since you have one, you can project an energy imprint of your Emerald into the landscape as the Blue Room team did; this projection enables you to interact with a particular geomantic site and its other energy features, and it enables future visitors to this site to do the same.

If you find an Emerald projected into the geomythic landscape, you can enter it. The Harmonic Convergence, for example, took place inside the Lord of Light's Emerald. Potentially, everyone on Earth could have shown up inside that Emerald during those August days. Many did,

though they remained unaware of what their higher being bodies were doing, or where.[95]

Inside the Emerald you'll find some surprises. King Arthur's legendary Round Table, for one. The Holy Grail, for another. Merlin's baffling Glass House. In fact, the Emerald is the initiation chamber in which the Christed Initiation in the Buddha Body takes place. This is a new form of geomythically based initiation that the angelic world is supporting based on the Christ Mysteries. Under the supervision of the Archangel Michael, it brings forward the revelation of the Mystery of Golgotha—Rudolf Steiner's evocative phrase—into our time.

In a somewhat disarming sense, the initiation has very little to do with the dogmas of either Christianity or Buddhism, but it does pertain to the spiritual realities embodied and demonstrated by their two prime teachers. It takes as a premise our "As above, so below, and in the middle, too" axiom as it involves and benefits the three realms; and it's an inner experience—a kind of inner temple building—that proceeds by degrees and repetitions. You don't have it once, but maybe a dozen times, until it's real for you, and assimilated, and living.

If you could sneak a view of the Jerusalem archetype, what would it look like? Or, put differently, how did the Blue Room team see this blueprint?

To some extent, the brow chakra's psychic picture-making process will track John's description of the Celestial City. Jerusalem will appear to be a vast walled city. On Easter 1985, I saw it over Glastonbury Tor—local tradition says it's the site of the New Jerusalem—like a golden cathedral city with spires, gates, and high walls. On another occasion, it appeared to me as a huge stone city set solitary in a desert in a dim olive-hued landscape.

Paradoxically, one's ability to perceive it is dependent on the likelihood or imminence of the 144,000 Emeralds opening because it is the shared cognition that makes Jerusalem cognizable, that makes it real. Certainly, it's real there, in the higher spiritual worlds; but for us in bodies to sense its reality, many of us need to be looking at it—be in it—at the same time. It's that 144,000 thing again.

Jerusalem is not so much a fixed structure or astral temple as it is a shared, cocreated reality. When you're in it, you cannot actually see it. Jerusalem is a shared state of mind or state of awareness. When sufficient members of the 12 Tribes[96] are aligned in their Emeralds, it electrifies the Earth's array of geodesic solids to birth the hexagonal Emerald or Cube of Space. Again, it's paradoxical: The Cube is already there; what's birthed is our new awareness of it.

In simpler terms, we might picture it this way: Opening 144,000 Emeralds acts like a magic wand that morphs the prevailing geometric face of the Earth grid into the Emerald. To generate the Emerald, you need to tilt the Cube of Space 45 degrees, and this is the magic of the collective focus on the Emeralds.

So here is a way of conceiving of the Jerusalem archetype. In many respects it is a cosmogram of the three parts of the Heart chakra, only inverted. What is most recessed in the human chakra hierarchy, the Heart within the Heart, or Emerald, is most prominent in the Jerusalem Temple archetype.

The eight petals of the Ananda-kanda here assume a structural support role, as a kind of foundation for the citadel of the Anahata and Emerald.[97] Geometrically, the octahedron (eight-sided polyhedron) is implicit in the Cube of Space. If you connect the center of each of the six faces of the Cube with every other face, it forms three squares, each on a different plane. This composite form is an octahedron (a Platonic Solid of eight equal triangles),[98] and this form, though unfamiliar to us at present, is a representation of the Buddha Body.[99]

The Cube of Space presents four Sefirot as inside the box, and six outside. The fourth Sefirot,

Chesed, is the interface between what is inside and what is outside in the Cube of Space. It is like a swinging door. In the Cube of Space, it is the threshold between the three higher Sefirot and the six lower ones.[100]

In the Jerusalem archetype, the Cube turned inside out, Chesed acts as the highest Sefirot, the top of the Tree of Life, as the three Sefirot beyond it are too rarified to be active players in the unfolding of tangible existence. In the Jerusalem archetype, Chesed is inside the Emerald, and the lower six Sefirot are the crossbeams of the hexagon of the Emerald.[101]

The Jerusalem archetype is a reality creation matrix. It contains the ten primordial vessels of Light (the 40 Sefirot in Four Worlds) and the 22 prime generative agencies for creation. Qabalists say the names of myriad stars come from a vast number of permutations possible with 22 letters in different combinations. Every star in the universe has a name, a generative signature or invocation,[102] and everything has been spoken into existence through the Cube of Space.

Jerusalem is a kind of energy scaffolding connecting our physical planet with its higher dimensional origins and "parents." It's also the *purpose* or goal of the Earth's visionary geography. The goal of becoming aware of the Earth's multilayered cosmic terrain is to reconstruct this Jerusalem temple as an experiential reality and *to use it* to dial up the cosmos.

The Jerusalem archetype, the Cube of Space, the Heart within the Heart—this is the Emerald modem. And the modem should be on.

Part two of this book will take us through the components of the Jerusalem infrastructure. We'll study each of its many aspects—the 85 features of the Earth's visionary geography thus far identified—and see how they are part of Jerusalem.

We will rebuild it, within and without, as above, so below, and in the middle, too, enabling humans and planet to benefit from the reawakened cognition. To see it is to make it real, and when it's real for us, we can use the Emerald modem to link up with whomever we wish, wherever we choose, across the planet, solar system, galaxy, and beyond.

To use the Emerald modem is in effect to redeem ourselves and the planet. The fate of the world sits in our chest.

The Jerusalem temple is not easily seen from the outside. It is something collectively created, experienced from the inside. When you're in it, this helps to manifest it in the world, even though that manifestation may defeat easy perception. It is an alignment, an influence, a presence, a knowing, but only "visible" to higher dimensional sight. Obviously John's vision of the New Jerusalem was a clairvoyant one, just as the Blue Room team members were working with clairvoyantly obtained blueprints. The Jerusalem archetype was the epitome of the Blue Room engineering diagrams, the master plan.

Even so, the Emerald can help us see the Jerusalem archetype.

When you look through the Emerald, from one corner to the other, and your perception settles at a midpoint, your eyes are creating the green bridge between one cube corner and its opposite. It's a green bridge because you can walk across it into the center of the Emerald, into the outskirts of Jerusalem.

In a sense you have turned physical reality inside out. You are now in the part that links the two ends, Heaven and Earth. You are in the space between realms, where you may reaffirm your intentions of incarnation. Not only for this life, but for any life here, for all of them, and especially for the first one—why you came here.

You can participate in the fused focus, the human with 288,000 eyes. Inside the Emerald is the opposite of an oubliette, a dungeon with an opening only at the top. (In many respects, much of our time on Earth is like time spent in an oubliette. We forget everything, even that we're in an oubliette. Our body is like an oubliette, the crown chakra seemingly the only opening in the darkness. But when the crown remembers, it illuminates the Emerald, and its light dispels the oubliette.) The Emerald is a positive oubliette, an oubliette turned inside out, a place of deep remembering, refocusing, reconnecting. It is the pivot between Earth and Heaven, humanity and God, the modem link.

In summary: The Cube of Space (Emerald, Jerusalem, inner heart chakra) is inside us, the Earth (with its visionary geography) and galaxy (with its spiritual worlds) are inside it, and it comes from the crown of the Lord of Light.

In chapter 11, we'll learn more about the Lord of Light, but for now, let's see how the 85 features of the Earth's visionary geography work as part of the Emerald.

Part Two

Building the Emerald Modem—
Jerusalem on Earth

3 The Once and Future Grail Castle
Reclaiming the Vast Riches of Memory

In part one, we gained an idea of what the Emerald modem is and why it's here. Now in part two, we examine its components in detail and see how it was built and how we can rebuild it in ourselves and around us in the world. Of course, to say "rebuild" is not quite accurate. It's already there, in us and around us, but our coming into awareness of it can be like building it anew.

The Emerald modem's components are at least 85 different energy structures, inner plane temples, or megalithic-geomantic installations, situated across the globe with reference to what we call holy or sacred sites. These are structures such as Grail Castles, Cosmic Eggs, landscape zodiacs, domes, stone circles, labyrinths, stargates, and many other features both known and unknown to myth and folklore—or, more likely, once known, then long forgotten. In rebuilding the Emerald modem in our awareness we also reacquaint ourselves with many of the cognitive riches that mythic memory has held in trust for us.

The Earth's energy body is not "built" as straightforwardly as, say, a motor, whose construction can be described in a series of numbered steps. Although my sequencing of energy structures in the next eight chapters suggests a hierarchical and linear order to the components, the situation is more complex, more multidimensional, more *organic* than that. I've assigned them according to the order and function of the chakras in the human, presuming that the human microcosmic version mirrors the planetary and cosmic original.

The order of the 85 Emerald modem components as presented here tracks a certain primacy of orientation and use, yet you can also enter the system anywhere. From our conventional framework of linear cause and effect, the situation is fluid, even paradoxical, and that's that.

These 85 features represent the elements of the Earth's energy anatomy, its geomythic *body*. Think of human organs and systems: Which is the most important? Which comes first? Which is created first? To an extent you can answer this with some precision, yet when the human body is complete and you're walking around in the world, all the systems are interconnected, interdependent, and hard to separate one from another. It's like that with the Earth's anatomy. Not only is its geomythic body inextricably a single system, but so is its physiology, how it functions. So we must proceed knowing we are describing momentarily isolated parts in an organic, unified whole.

Another fascinating discovery is that the world's myths, when pieced together, accurately describe this global organic, multidimensional body and show us how to interact with it to benefit ourselves and the planet. When you decode the myths geomantically you get an operator's manual for the Earth. That's because the myths, when linked together in the right order, also describe a *process* that equally involves human consciousness and planetary reality—as the front and back of the same hand. The myths recounted throughout this book equally describe aspects of your spiritual reality *and* the planet's energy construction.

Remember, then, that these 85 elements of Earth's geomythic anatomy are also part of the essential human being when you factor in all our bodies—physical, subtle, and very subtle. Ultimately, we are describing a bodily terrain that exists on the planetary and human level; both are copies of the galactic model, itself copied from an antecedent prototype. It has to be this way because as we saw in part one, the Emerald modem is inside us, outside us, and is the essence of the relationship between the Earth as a planet and the galaxy, and the Earth (as cosmic space) and Heaven (as the source of light).

So with this in mind, we will tour these 85 features to get a provisional understanding of how the parts got here, fit together, work, and comprise the Emerald modem. We will track them in a sequence that has provisional relevance. Even better, we'll see how we can use them to open a direct connection between ourselves as individual humans and the galaxy and the numerous aspects of the spiritual realms the Emerald modem contains. Remember, the fundamental fact of the system, of the Emerald modem, is it's *interactive*.

We start with the Grail Castle because it is about remembering, and reclaiming deep memory is both the beginning and end of our using the Emerald modem. But it's a process that takes a little time. We remember by degrees.

Remember what? What we stand to remember through accessing the Grail Castle is the history of the cosmos, consciousness, and creation and the recollection of a state of existence before there was an Earth or even a thought of the human as we know ourselves on this planet.

The Wounded Fisher King of the Grail Castle in the Wasteland

Anfortas, the Wounded Fisher King, sits invalided in his Grail Castle in the midst of the Wasteland of Logres. The landscape is blighted and infertile; his people are not flourishing; and he's miserable. Every day the Holy Grail is borne in procession before him, unveiled for his examination, then covered and stowed in a back room in Castle Carbonek. The Grail Maidens are in charge of this procession, but even they know it's a pointless spectacle. He possesses the world's preeminent healing miracle, the Holy Grail, but he can't heal himself.

Land and king languish in a rotten enchantment. Logres is the name of his country, but it's also a state of mind, a condition of loss.[103] The king can't get up off his couch for the wound in his groin. He can't walk; he can't sleep; and he can't heal. It has been that way ever since he wounded himself with that sword. The Perilous Stroke, the legend makers call it. One slip of the sword and he's an invalid for life. Some say he should have left the sword alone; it was too formidable even for him, though he is a king. For was it not once the property of the giant Goliath, then David the giant slayer, then his son Solomon, who sent it to Logres on the Ship of Time?

Now Klingsor has it—not that he knows how to use it properly either. His having it keeps it from Anfortas and closes the door on any possibility of his healing, for only this sword can heal what was wounded by this sword. And there's not a chance in hell that Anfortas can do it himself.

After all, his very name, Anfortas, belies his condition: It means infirm, unwell, unhealed.

As to whether Parsifal will ever return and do the job properly, who can say? Parsifal made it to Castle Carbonek (the Grail Castle), and that's better than most Grail Knights, but he was too green to know what question to ask, what to do there. The moment passed, and he was summarily spun out of the Grail Castle and the castle vanished.

The Grail Castle has a queer way of turning away all potential visitors and peremptorily ejecting those who behave poorly or say the wrong thing or don't say the right thing. That's why the Celts called it *Caer Sidi,* the Spinning Castle. Hard to find, very hard to get into, even harder to stay in once you get there.

That is the streamlined version of the Grail Castle story. It is an essential element of the King Arthur mythos, and since the advent of Christianity two thousand years ago, the Grail has been understood to be the chalice of the Last Supper, which collected some drops of Christ's blood at the Crucifixion on Golgotha and was brought to Glastonbury, England, for safe and secret keeping. As for the Grail Castle itself, most people, especially scholars, dismiss it as a convenient physical prop for what was essentially a spiritual allegory.

While Christianity sought to incorporate the Grail story as part of the Mystery of Christ, the myth never entered the mainstream of Christian belief. Rather, it remained troubling and numinous on the fringes of understanding. Although it is genuinely a Christ Mystery, as we'll see (though not in an exoteric sense that would please or even interest mainstream Christianity), the Grail, Grail Castle, and Wounded Fisher King saga have much older, deeper roots than this.[104]

Go far back into the mists of ancient myth and there is no mention of woundedness, infirmity, or an inability to be healed. There is a Grail King, but he's not wounded; he's rich. For this is part of the mystery of the Fisher King: Originally he is rich, only later is he wounded. What happened?

Let's start with the basics: The Grail Castle is a real place, and you can visit it. The Fisher King is a real being, and you can interact with him. The Grail is a real object, and you already have it. It's just a matter of understanding *where.*

Early in my years of research, I gathered this bit of orientation from the Ofanim about the Grail Castle: "The Grail Castle does not exist anywhere on Earth in the sense you know it. What is present is the etheric double of something in a different time and space, mirrored here for a purpose. These castles above various sacred hills are etheric doubles of this place, brought here and placed as buildings, as etheric temples, for the evolution of the planet and its soul beings. Their purpose is yet to be fulfilled.

"A very small number of humans in the past had access to the particular level of consciousness necessary to perceive these castles in the etheric realm. Access was made from the etheric castles on Earth to the actuality in another dimension, but this has not occurred since Atlantean days. Access will become more available, and this will be firmly established in a short period of time."

The Ofanim added that there are 144 replicas of the Grail Castle around the planet (see table 3-1). Few are remembered as Grail Castles; some are remembered as something else; and the rest are forgotten entirely.

What about the Fisher King? How did he go from being rich to injured? "The Fisher King rules over the deep past and the deep memories of the soul. The Fisher King is an aspect of consciousness in relation to the deep past. The Fisher King has to do with different doorways in the soul and the relation to the deep past. His wounds are that in him which does not remember, contained in the root chakra at the base of the spine. Conscious energy there is not manifest and cannot be brought to the crown chakra," the Ofanim state.

Table 3-1: Grail Castles

Planetary Total: 144

Selected Locations:

Montsegur, French Pyrenees, France	Acropolis, Athens, Greece
Horncastle, Lincolnshire, England	Mount Temehani, Raiatea, French Polynesia
Alcatraz Island, San Francisco Bay, California, U.S.	Mount Damavand, Iran
	Mount Parnassus, Greece
Bayreuth, Germany	Hamdon Hill, Montacute, Somerset, England
Dome of the Rock, Jerusalem, Israel	Mount Ararat, Armenia
Montserrat, Spain	Mauna Kea, Hawaii, U.S.
Mycenae, Greece	Isle of Grassholm (or Gwales), Wales
Mount Hood, Portland, Oregon, U.S.	Island of Hlesey (Lessoe or Läsö), Cattegat, Norway
Chalice Hill, Glastonbury, Somerset, England	Eridu, Abu Shahrain, Iraq
Castle Rigg, Keswick, Lake District, England	Babylon, near Baghdad, Iraq
	Acoma, New Mexico, U.S.

Equivalent Mythic Names: Castle Carbonek; *Caer Sidi,* the Revolving, Spinning Castle; Sarras; *Munsalvaesche,* Mount of Salvation; Celestial City of Lanka, Lord Kubera's palace in the North on Mount Trikuta; Boat of the Vedas; Enki's Sea-House, *E-engurra;* Noah's Ark; Aegir's palace on the Island of Hlesey; Scuabtinne; Yima's *var;* Emerald Rock; Ibex of the *Abzu;* the Ship of Time

Equivalent Names for the Grail King: Anfortas; the Wounded Fisher King; Oedipus; Tantalos; Kubera; the Rich Fisher King; Mnemosyne (Memory); Manu Satyavrata; Matsya-avatara (Vishnu); Oannes; Enki-Ea; Deucalion; Ziusudra-Utnapishtim; Nu; Poseidon; Aegir; Mannannan Mac Lir; Varuna; Logos; Christ; Yima

"Injury has closed down the access to the root energy that would reveal the soul's purpose and nature, its level of development, and the individual's present ability to penetrate that veil. The healing energy is released through a passage through these doorways related to the development of the soul life."

The pain of *not remembering* is intense, and it can be catastrophic.

We may think of all this as an intriguing symbolic story from the past that has no relevance to us today. That would be wrong. *You* are the Wounded Fisher King. So are your mother, father, brother, sister, children, friends—the entire planet. Each of us is the Wounded Fisher King. All

of humanity is, too. In fact, all of humanity over the history of our habitation of Earth is the Fisher King. We as biological humans are amnesiac.

Lama Anagarika Govinda, the monk-scholar of Tibetan Buddhism, presciently observed that today's human is "torn and tortured," oblivious of his infinite past and his future "because he has lost the connection with his timeless being," like a man suffering from incurable amnesia. This amnesia deprives us of the continuity of consciousness over many lifetimes and makes us unable to "act consistently in accordance with [our] true nature."[105]

We've forgotten we were looking for the fabled Castle Carbonek, home of the Grail. Yet

Castle Carbonek (also spelled Corbenic) is a joke hidden in plain view: It means carbonic, as in *carbon*, the human body as a castle made of carbon. Castle Carbonek is the Grail Knight's exploration of his own *inner* temple out in the landscape.

Think of it: We do not remember. We cannot remember. We don't even remember we *could* remember. We don't remember that much of our earlier years in this lifetime. What of the lifetimes before that? What of the states of existence before we ever had a human life? What of the times before the Earth existed? Before humanity ever incarnated for the first time?

Why is it important we remember any of this? Because, not remembering, we don't know why we are here, why we exist, why there is consciousness at all, or reality. Why so many stars. How things got here. Where it all is going.

Since we can't recall the continuity of consciousness, we abuse one another and the planet.

Of course, Western culture, and increasingly, world culture, has schooled us in the "reasonable" limits to recall. There is nothing to remember past early childhood, it firmly tells us. So there is nothing to remember in the first place. We've taken the Wounded Fisher King to a new threshold of denial.

Because we are unconscious of our spiritual purpose, our root and crown chakras remain unconnected, and we are immobilized on the couch in the Grail Castle. We are spiritual invalids.

Not knowing, we cannot move. Knowing, the energy flows up and down and up and down in continuous circuit, and we unite Earth with Heaven, root chakra with crown chakra, and manifest the miracle of awareness that the human being was originally intended to be. Then we're using the Emerald modem, and then we are the *Rich* Fisher King, rich in deep memory.

He's the *king* because he is in command of all the memories of the soul, the vast continuum of experiences, insights, and knowledge of the earliest days of the cosmos and his own involvement in it. He has awakened from his own spiritual wasteland of "slavery, exile, oblivion, ignorance, drunkenness, sleep" and has reclaimed his original "freedom, the original home, memory, knowledge, untroubled radiance, wakefulness."[106] He has remembered his previous pure state before incarnation.

Years after his (somewhat humiliating) neophyte's visit to the Grail Castle, Parsifal makes it back and stands before the Wounded Fisher King again. *What ails thee?* he asks. At last, the right question. Selfless compassionate inquiry on another's behalf. Except not quite. The correct question is this: "Whom does the Grail serve?" The Fisher King answers, "It serves you." Based on the Grail texts, you would expect the Grail King to say it serves him. He doesn't. It serves *you*. "You and I are one," he adds. You are confronting an older part of yourself.

This is an archetypal experience. If you make it into the Grail Castle, you will probably experience something along these lines. Parsifal is a symbolic figure for one who *pierces the veil* of the worlds and perceives the Castle. He (and she) is also the Grail Knight specially equipped with something to *pierce the veil* of the King's not remembering, the scar tissue in the wounded root chakra.

First and Subsequent Visits to the Grail Castle— Welcome to Sarras

You don't have to travel too far to find a Grail Castle. See table 3-1 for a list of a few of their locations. Know that if you go in search of a Grail Castle experience, you will be facilitated by the Ofanim, provided your intentions are pure. There is an old saying that the Grail will not serve the impure. Your perceptions of the Grail Castle will gain in sophistication over time and repeated visits. Any of the 144 Grail Castle replicas will do, as they are all copies of the same original. Think of them as 144 doors opening into the same place.

The first time I visited a Grail Castle I was in Glastonbury, England, sitting on Chalice Hill, the softer, rounder, feminine hill next to the enigmatic, much-visited Tor. I didn't know there was a Grail Castle *above* it until I had already left it and started wondering what that experience was all about. You experience the Grail Castle as above a given physical location because that is the way your mind interprets and positions the data of a subtler dimension. It's higher, above the physical, and until recently, very hard to see.

Sometimes the locale's name itself belies this seeming spatial differentiation: *Horn*castle, as in the horn up to the castle; or Castle *Rigg*, the rigging up to the castle. You climb psychically into the Grail Castle. Let's not overlook the obvious either: Chalice Hill, the elevated residency of the Grail chalice.

I entered a large hall, the kind you would expect a king to have. The Fisher King was seated at the far end, on a throne, under a rotunda. He looked like my high school biology teacher. He wore a crown, but he looked crabby, forlorn. I offered him my Grail bowl. I changed a light in the ceiling. I stood next to him and watched the Grail Maidens. Eventually, I wasn't there any more but was merely on Chalice Hill being prodded by cows.

On another occasion, I entered the Grail Castle through the door at Mount Hood, near Portland, Oregon. The castle appeared to me, as if I were seeing it from overhead, as an equal-armed cross, with a golden rotunda at the end of each arm and a larger rotunda with a sky-blue roof in the center of the cross. In all, it was a Grail temple with five chambers, big enough to accommodate thousands of Grail Knights. Each of the chambers was overlit by an archangel, as if by floodlights. A vast golden Grail chalice occupied the central rotunda, and at some point I immersed myself in the pure waters of this vessel.

I entered the Grail Castle through Montsegur in the Pyrenees of France. Montsegur, an old Cathar stronghold, has a legend about its being the site of a Grail Castle and is remembered by some writers, notably the thirteenth-century Wolfram von Eschenbach, author of *Parzival*, as *Munsalvaesche*, the Mount of Salvation. The Papacy considered the Cathars to be dangerous heretics and burned them out of Montsegur in 1244 A.D. But the Grail Castle is still there, above the peak, open for business 24/7.

The Montsegur Grail Castle is guarded by a dragon; so is the Chalice Hill one, for that matter. In a sense, the castle is inside the dragon because you enter through the dragon's mouth. The castle's interior presents itself as the inside of the coiled dragon and has a spiral shape. The Fisher King's throne, a pale eggshell blue, gives him an excellent view of the Grail, effulgent, almost too bright and golden to see, like sculpted dry ice emitting an intense golden mist. The mist clears, but the scene shifts to an apricot-tinted amphitheater. Numerous healthy looking men and women walk around, laurels on their heads. It looks like a scene from classical Greece, the way we might imagine it.

The Cathars at Montsegur kept this Grail door open for the continuous, uplifting two-way flow between Grail Castle and human world—Sarras and Logres, in the old words. Initiates throughout the Pyrenees had only to position themselves at a holy site in the vicinity and they could access the Montsegur Grail Castle by a kind of etheric subway system. The Cathars did not need to do anything else, geomantically, other than just to keep the door open. The fact that they had been inside the Grail Castle was sufficient and had a positive impact throughout the area.

On another occasion, I entered through the door above Mount Temehani on Raiatea, one of the Tahitian islands in French Polynesia. Raiatea was once regarded as the holiest Polynesian precinct, and its temples were visited by many. When the mist cleared, I saw a small, stone-lined pool set high in the mountains, surrounded by lovely slender white birches. Perhaps they were Grail Maidens in disguise. I immersed myself in this pool of heavenly dew in a self-administered baptism.

I deepened this sense of deep recall through my Grail Castle experience at Alcatraz Island in San Francisco Bay. How ironic that government authorities would erect first a military garrison then a prison on this isolated rock, surrounded by treacherous currents—under a Grail Castle. What better way to block access to a higher spiritual reality than with a jail. But mythic reality will have its own, and the legendary Birdman of Alcatraz was a kind of Grail Knight manqué, unconsciously seeking flight upwards with his birds. And perhaps he was a Wounded Fisher King figure, too, so close to a paradisal place of total remembering and spiritual fulfillment yet unable to ascend, his wings clipped and his legs almost literally in chains.

Somehow I managed to get myself a considerable distance above Alcatraz so that I was looking down on it at a 45-degree angle. I saw a miniature spiral galaxy with a flat silvery disk and a golden mound in its center. It looked like a spaceship and a traveling galaxy with an intensely golden sun at its core. I flew down into the sun and encountered what I would describe as a Shepherd of the Sun.

He gestured to a series of vertical golden rectangles each perhaps five feet high. I walked through one and onto a causeway high above the ground. At the end of this elevated walkway was a small beehive chamber 20 feet across, its walls made of golden pentagons. On the surface of

each was a written script. The figures or letters seemed written in living fire; within the letters were angels—Seraphim, I think, as they tend to manifest as living fire—whose essence was the living fire script. They seemed to exude liquid fire into a golden phosphorescent puddle at my feet that quivered like mercury. I daubed some on my crown chakra, and it burst into golden flames.

Once you've made a physical connection with a Grail castle site, you can revisit from a distance. Your being bodies remember the way. In fact, technically, once you've visited even one replica, you can access them all from a distance. You just need to know where they are. I revisited the Chalice Hill Grail Castle several times. On one occasion I saw that pool of heavenly dew again. This time, instead of immersing myself for a baptism, I dove in headfirst. I had figured out it was a dimensional portal cloaked as a mountain pool. I emerged outside a tall white-stoned wall on a small hill overlooking a vast desert plain. Out on the plain was a huge stone-walled city; the walls were formidable, perhaps 40 feet high.

I stood outside the wall, looking for a way in. I sensed a city full of bright, happy people inside. I asked the Ofanim for a lift over the top, and they obliged. It was intensely emerald inside the city, a bit like Frank Baum's emerald City of Oz. In fact, I briefly saw the jeweled crown atop a vast being; one of the jewels was an Emerald. The emeraldness of the city had a morning freshness to it, like the first moments of pure wakefulness, as if one were conducted from sleep to waking while participating in the awareness of the highest angels. The city was pervaded by a sense of eternal consciousness, a present and unending moment.

I later learned this place is called *Sarras*. It's referred to obliquely in the Grail sagas as a place to which the Grail or Grail Knights were taken, but generally the nature of this place is left vague in the accounts.[107] According to the Ofanim, Sarras is the name of the place that Grail Knights use to ground their individual experience of the Grail.[108]

But what about that well or pool in the mountains? I take that as the waters of memory known to the Greeks as Mnemosyne, Goddess of Memory and mother by Zeus of the Nine Muses, the goddesses of the fine arts, music, literature, poetry, inspiration, and generally of all artistic and intellectual pursuits.[109] In Mnemosyne and her Nine Muses you have the qualities of memory, water, flowingness, patronage of the arts, artistic creativity, inspired eloquence, deep transcendent knowledge. You have also the suggestion of a being of high spiritual stature: She is not the Fisher King, but rather more of a guardian of the lineage, perhaps an overseer of the Grail process.

All of this gains relevance later in this chapter under the discussion of the Fisher King, the Sea, and Kings of the Watery Deep. But for now, what process?

The process of the Grail is that of deep remembering. But it also involves synthesis. The Grail as a bowl is the unitive function in consciousness, the pre-Fall condition of unified consciousness, free of separation, differentiation, and duality; all the signs of the zodiac are unified, welded together as a golden chalice.

But the Grail is a hollow, receptive space, intended to contain something. The Waters of Life, some myths say; the blood of Christ, say others. That something is the process of individuation, the vast congeries of life experiences and insights one gains over the long haul of multiple incarnations, as selfhood on the way to the Self. All the things you pick up in your eons as a Grail Knight trudging through the Grail fields. Put it all in your bowl and cook it, alchemically. The process of individuation is expressed as the overflowing of the bowl with water—the muchness of the experiences as a separate self, seeking unification.

It is paradoxical. You end up with the one *and* the two, unified and individualized, both God

and yourself, or yourself now transparent to God. The Grail legend is the synthesis of these two processes in consciousness, the unitive and individuative processes, the nondual and the dual—both, inclusively.

You might wonder why the Grail has to come into the picture at all. Isn't that a concept from a limited mythic vocabulary, of interest mostly to the Celts and early Christians? What if I don't care about either? As I understand it, the Grail and the other symbolic structures and devices reported in this book are part of the archetypal mythic structure of the Earth. Touch them and you're touching something that was put there purposefully at the beginning of the Earth to be a continuing revelation and mirror for consciousness of its celestial origins and nature.

Think of it metaphorically as the Tower of Babel. Once there was a unified, singular symbolic system and descriptive language that linked human consciousness with the energy and spiritual structures of the planet and cosmos. Then the tower got blown to pieces, and these pieces of the full picture got scattered across the planet. They are now resident, somewhat enigmatically—certainly out of context—in dozens of mythic traditions and cultural memories. Rather than struggle to interpret the individual pieces, I prefer to see how they once fit (and can fit again) in that singular symbolic edifice, the metaphorical Tower of Babel of unified spiritual vision.

The Grail, then, is one such symbolic structure or description. Call it a bowl, dish, chalice, or cauldron; call it the cup of the Christian mysteries or the beer stein of the inebriating gods, the essence is the same. It's something you'll need as you make your connection with the Earth and galaxy.

Traversing the galaxy on Earth necessarily leads you into the Grail mystery, which will organize and process your experiences. Nearly all of the many geomantic features you will encounter are implicit in the Grail. It is the first and last thing, which is why Parsifal had two trips to the Grail Castle.

The Grail is a process whereby, over a long stretch of time, you blend the individualized with the unified. The Grail Castle is the place where you do this, or at least get training, or inspiration, and at the end of that long day, confirmation from colleagues. But how did the Grail Castle get here, duplicated and positioned around the Earth? Who created it in the first place? Who built it? And where?

As to where, the best bets are the Andromeda Galaxy or the Pleiades in our galaxy. As you'll see later in the book, "we" came from Andromeda a long time ago; more recently, the Pleiades has been a big player in Earth affairs.

As for the builder, in the Grail stories that credit (or name) usually goes to Titurel, Anfortas's father or grandfather. In one Grail text attributed to a German named Albrecht von Scharffenberg (circa 1270 A.D.) and called *Der Jüngere Titurel,* Titurel, at age 50, is told by an angel that the rest of his life will be dedicated to preserving the Grail and that, with the help of his friends, he should build a castle as a hallows for the Grail in the Forest of Salvation and upon a solitary peak called *Munsalvaesche.* Before this assignment, the Grail had lacked a proper home; it had been sustained by angelic hands, which held it above the mountain.[110]

Hindu myth says the architect of the gods' celestial residences is Visvakarman (or Tvastr). He was the lordly progenitor of the crafts, creator of the thousands of crafts, carpenter to the 30 Gods, "greatest of craftsmen, he created all the ornaments and fashioned the divine chariots of the Gods."[111] Visvakarman is the divine architect of the universe, the creative power that welds Heaven and Earth together. He built Kubera's golden city of Lanka on Mount Trikuta. So maybe Visvakarman built the Grail Castle.

I had another Grail Castle visit. This time I arrived on top of a mountain, though it resembled a peak more in the spiritual world than in the physical one. There was a large white archway into which were set at least a dozen glittering jewels. On the other side of the archway, which was also an entrance, were numerous spuming fountains, lush statuary of elephant gods, copious bouquets of flowers that seemed made of light, and other signs of astonishing opulence. Everything was made of gold. When I heard that single word, *Lanka,* I knew where I was. The Rich Fisher King's palace. Kubera's place.

Discovering the Celestial Affluence of the Rich Fisher King

Kubera, the Lord of Riches, lives in the North in his Celestial City called Lanka, the Hindu myths tell us. Lanka is a golden city set atop Mount Trikuta; it extends for 800 miles; it's constructed of gold, has innumerable golden palaces, is studded with gems, and it was built by Visvakarman long ago.[112]

Legend has it that the wind god Vayu originally tore off the top of Mount Meru, the planet's preeminent city of the gods and cosmic mountain, and tossed it into the ocean where it became Lanka atop Mount Trikuta. This is apt, because Lanka is one of what Vedic tradition calls the Eight Celestial Cities constellated around Mount Meru. Lord Kubera and the other seven gods in their respective Celestial Cities are *Lokapalas,* Guardians of the Eight Directions of Space and World Protectors; they are the arms (fingers, palms, lower and upper arms) of the Cosmic Person called Purusha (also called Adam Kadmon, Ymir, Pan Ku). We'll meet these other seven later in the book.

Lanka "comprised a large number of shining buildings supported by pillars of ivory, gold, and crystal. The palace was astonishing to behold and highly pleasing to the mind," the *Mahabharata* tells us. The palace had a magnificent central stairway of gold, all the walls were thickly set with gems whose luster illuminated the palace; the citadel resounded with delightful music, scents filled the air, and there were fountains and ponds encircled by flowers of every possible description.[113] Kubera's hall is "lustrously white," 100 leagues long and 70 wide; luminous like the moon, it floats in the sky like a mountain peak— "the celestial hall seems as though fastened to the sky."[114]

Kubera is in charge of the world's wealth and treasures. He has a remarkable celestial chariot called the *Pushpaka*: It is like a city of the gods floating in the air, emitting celestial music and delightful fragrances, shining like the midday sun. Kubera's half-brother, the ten-headed demon Ravanna, stole the Pushpaka as well as forcibly occupied Lanka and abducted the god Rama's beautiful wife, Sita, occasioning a great battle, which Ravanna lost. It's all recounted in glorious exaggeration in the Hindu epic the *Ramayana*, and I'll tease out its significance to the Grail Quest at the end of this chapter.

The Vedic imagination paints a well-fleshed picture of Kubera. He is *Ratna-garbha* (Jewel-belly or Womb of Jewels), *Dhana-pati* (Lord of Wealth), and *Iccha-vasu* (Wealth-at-Will). He's a corpulent white dwarf with a bulging belly, and his body is covered in rich ornaments. He has a jewel hoard beyond belief and owns all the gold, silver, and jewels of the Earth. He is richer than rich. But what is he *really* rich in?

Kubera's vast riches are spiritual wealth, treasures of knowledge and wisdom—the riches of cosmic intelligence and *memory*. He remembers. This means knowledge of the stars, the jewels of the Earth, in which "Earth" is understood to

mean the vast cosmos of vacated space and "jewels" are the glorious star-intelligences whose rich awareness is crystalline clear.

Fat, jolly, wealthy Kubera is a happy image of the Fisher King before he was wounded. Kubera is an image of the Fisher King's true and original self. His knowledge surrounds him like an environment, and everything is at arm's reach. This gives us an idea of Kubera's riches. But what about the fish? Why is the Grail King called the Rich *Fisher* King?

Why the Rich Fisher King Is the Lord of the Watery Deeps

We find a vivid answer to this puzzle in an old Puranic myth about Vishnu that reveals much of the original intent of the Grail myth. One day a spiritual lawgiver and child of the thousand-rayed Sun named *Manu Satyavrata* found a small fish called Saphari who asked him for protection. The fish told Manu that a terrific deluge was coming that would drown all creatures—save Manu, provided he helped the fish. Manu agreed and found a suitable receptacle for the fish.

First he tried a pitcher, then a well, then the Ganges River. The fish kept outgrowing the vessel, and Manu had to find a larger one, and then a still larger one. Soon the fish was too big even for the ocean. Eventually, when the fish grew to be one million *yojanas* long, or about eight million miles, Manu understood he was dealing with a god, specifically, Vishnu.[115]

The fish, whose celestial name was *Matsya-avatara*, which was Vishnu's first of ten major incarnations, told Manu to build a ship and to put on it all the sages, plants, animals, and seeds of life from everywhere for safekeeping against the flood waters. The fish helped Manu build the boat, fashioning it out of the assemblage of all the gods so as to protect the assemblage of great living souls. Alternately, the Puranas say that a group of all the gods collaborated in building the boat so as to rescue the great aggregate of all creatures.

This seagoing vessel would be known as the Boat of the Vedas because it would house the sacred teachings known as the Vedas as well as the Puranas and other documents of spiritual science. The boat would also contain the Moon (Soma), Sun (Surya), the *Lokapalas,* Brahma, Vishnu, the holy river Narmada, the great sage Markendeya, and other august personages. All of this would be protected in Manu's ark during the interval of destruction in which the entire world would become a single ocean. The fish told Manu he would be in the boat for a complete Night of Brahma, then the waters would recede.

I will proclaim the Vedas to you at the beginning of creation, the fish announced to Manu, and taught him all the spiritual principles necessary for guiding a new humanity after the Flood. These principles included understanding of the doctrine of the Self and the Immensity. The Puranas report that the demon Hayagriva had stolen the Vedas from Brahma, which had flowed from his lips while he slept during an earlier period of world dissolution; now the wakeful Brahma was restoring the wisdom teachings to their rightful possessors, humanity, by way of their progenitor and benefactor, Manu.

The fish attached the ship's bow to its horn and used the great primordial serpent Sesa-Ananta as a rope to tug the ark across the top of the deluge waters. The god Vishnu "appeared again distinctly on the vast ocean in the form of a fish, blazing like gold, extending a million leagues, with one stupendous horn." During that Night of Brahma, the fish conveyed to Manu "an infinite mystery to be concealed within the breast of Satyavrata." Sitting in his Boat of the Vedas with the saints and gods, he heard the "principle of soul, the Eternal Being, proclaimed by the preserving power [Vishnu]."[116]

The boat sailed to the northern mountain, the Puranas tell us, and the northern slope of that mountain where it beached became known as Manu's Descent. Manu, equipped with all the divine knowledge of the Vedas and direct instruction from Vishnu the Pervader in the form of *Matsya-avatara,* the fish, became the all-knowing wise king for the start of a new age of humanity. This new Eon would be called *Satya Yuga,* the epoch of Truth, the Golden Age, a *manvantara* over which Manu Satyavrata would preside as spiritual king and benevolent regent. A *manvantara* is 306,720,000 years, or one-fourteenth part of a Day of Brahma in the Vedic time model. "A *manvantara* is a period of a Manu, and a Manu is the mythical progenitor of the world in his period, a kind of secondary creator who exercises the functions of a regent of the world throughout his *manvantara.*"[117]

In the Vedic time model, Brahma, the universal creator, lives for 100 years, but these are Brahma years, not human. One Day of Brahma (also called a Kalpa), for example, lasts 4,320,000,000 human years. Multiply this by 360 days and nights, then that by 100 years, and you get Brahma's age: 15.5 trillion days. But that's only one installment in an endless cycle of Days and Nights of Brahma. When Brahma's 100 years are up, there is a dissolution of everything created, a long restful pause while he floats asleep on the cosmic sea, then it begins again.

Similarly there are periods of dissolution at the end of each *manvantara.* Life ceases in the world, and the Manus and the gods ascend to a higher sphere of existence to remain for a period so as to preserve life. In effect they climb aboard the Boat of the Vedas to ride out the wild time of world dissolution mythically described as the Deluge. Then the next *manvantara* begins, and all the gods and seeds of life get unpacked from the ark and life is restored to the world.

When the world begins again with a new Eon, out pour the 33,333 gods from the Boat of the Vedas, the *Mahabharata* tells us, the same ones emerging in the same order each time, though perhaps with new names. "Thus, without beginning and without end, rolls the wheel of existence around in this world, causing origin and destruction, beginningless and endless."[118]

In Vishnu's incarnation as *Matsya-avatara* we have perhaps the archetype of the Rich Fisher King image. He is rich and whole. His riches are what he seeks to protect from the destruction of the Deluge. Vishnu entrusts all the esoteric secrets and wisdom teachings of spiritual science to the Boat of the Vedas and instructs humanity's forthcoming benefactor, the Sun-child *Manu Satyavrata*, in all aspects of this knowledge.

In effect, he stows in the ark for safekeeping the full panoply of cosmic intelligence—all that can be known of the origin, purpose, dynamics, and future of the created world, of cosmic Earth.

So Vishnu in his fish form is the Rich Fisher King, and *Manu Satyavrata* is also the Rich Fisher King, or the Grail Keeper, in a more "terrestrial" guise. The Grail is the repository of the knowledge of Vishnu; we could say the Grail *is* the Boat of the Vedas. Similarly, the Grail Castle is the Boat as well.

The Rich Fisher King's True Element—the Deep Seas of Consciousness

If the fish that makes the Grail King the Rich Fisher King is Vishnu in his first incarnation as *Matsya-avatara*, then what, in this scale of things, is the water?

According to one interpreter of the Puranic texts, the size of the fish—eight million miles long—suggests that it was swimming in a cosmic sea. The Earth that was inundated with floodwaters, says one commentator, was the plane of the ecliptic (the apparent path of the Sun through the zodiacal divisions of space); its illuminated

region extends for hundreds of millions of miles out to the orbit of Saturn. "This would provide swimming room for the divine fish."[119]

In this interpretation, then, the water is the vast illuminated space of our solar system.

Let's propose that the Deluge water, on top of which floated the Boat of the Vedas and in which swam the divine fish, represents the Sea of Consciousness. This would be the vibratory ocean of the etheric world, the undulatory ethers of all vibratory frequencies, what the Greeks termed Oceanos and his 3,000 Oceanids, each a stream of consciousness. The watery deeps are Earth (not the planet but cosmic space) as the cosmic etheric realm, what some cultures call the Abyss, primeval sea, chaos, *tehom*, or *apsu*.

Water equals consciousness. We need to keep this in mind as we encounter the different descriptions of Rich Fisher Kings and their habitats below. It isn't water that's meant, even though the terms water, sea, and ocean are used. Water is a symbol for consciousness.

A Deluge would mean the flooding of all space-time with undifferentiated consciousness. Such an event would seem chaotic and destructive to rational consciousness. It seems like chaos because it is *so much* consciousness that it overwhelms and dissolves all separate identities and structures of consciousness at all levels of creation. We might also usefully think of the Deluge or the cosmic sea as the entire electromagnetic spectrum of light, remembering that what we take to be "visible" light, and thus our apparent physical world, is only a small portion.

The Flood, then, is an inundation of matter-based space-time by supergalactic consciousness. To flood the Earth is to inundate the entire created and filled space of the galaxy (that gigantic space for cosmic matter called Ge, Gaia, or Earth) with primordial consciousness (pure ether, original vibratory substance, pleromatic water, which is to say, drops of pure God awareness from the

Pleroma of Heaven). The flooded world or primordial waters is the cosmos in its undifferentiated, unitive state, when it's blazing light everywhere.

Except for the Boat of the Vedas, or Matsya the divine fish, or the Grail Castle. There the seeds of all life are maintained against the apocalypse of total forgetting during the Flood. There the records and wisdom of the previous pre-Deluge existence are kept, along with all the laws, principles, and incantations. The Grail Castle or Boat of the Vedas is an ark that will float *atop* the flood waters and *preserve* the cosmic intelligence until the next cycle of time. There it floats in the highest strata of the etheric sea just under the roof of Heaven, preserving knowledge for the next cycle of creation.

Qabala has an analogy for this seemingly endless cycle of Flood and world renewal. It's called the Vacated Space. Originally God filled all of space; there was no place where God was not; hence there was no room for creation, because for it to be creation, by definition, it had to be distinguishable from God. So God withdrew from a portion of existence, and this empty area became the Vacated Space. Creation would take place there. This is dry land in the cosmos from which the flood waters of God have retreated, like low tide; high tide means God fills in the Vacated Space, terminating it as a distinguishable space in reality.

So here is the cycle of creating an empty space, filling it with life, then flooding it at the archetypal, if not ultimate level. It's an analogical description applicable at any level of expression, too, from the cosmos to a landscape zodiac.

The cycles of time described by the Vedas would describe a kind of cosmic pulse, an in-breath and out-breath, an endless pulsing of manifestation and dissolution, differentiation and unification of consciousness.

We find some elucidation through the Sumerian understanding of *apsu*. The watery *apsu* (or *abzu*) was understood to be the realm and home of the wise god Enki, also known as Ea

by the Akkadians. Enki is the Lord of the *Apsu*. Enki had lived in the *apsu*, a subterranean freshwater or sweetwater ocean which lay beneath the Earth, since before humanity was created. The Sumerians construed the *apsu* as a sublime otherworld dimension, but one above or higher than the Underworld. Enki's chief cult center was at Eridu in what is now Iraq and was called *E-abzu*, "Abzu House," or *E-engurra*. It was a Grail Castle.

Similarly, Babylon on the Euphrates River, some 150 miles northwest of Eridu in Iraq, was built on the *bab-apsu* and was known as the "Gate of *Apsu*," indicating the presence of a Grail Castle at that site. In Jerusalem, the Dome of the Rock on Mount Moriah (or Temple Mount, site of a Grail Castle) is founded upon a prodigious stone, an oblong rock outcropping that measures 56 by 42 feet and is said to cap the outpouring of the *tehom*, or watery deeps below.

Tehom refers to the primordial waters of chaos that preceded the creation and forever threaten to overwhelm the created world. The word means an abyss, such as a surging mass of subterranean water, or to make an uproar, or waters in violent commotion or waves in turbid violence, making a great noise. *Tehom* implies the deep, as in the principal sea or underground water source, and fountains of the great deep, and it implies chaos, mystery, depth, and power.

In a larger sense, *tehom* signifies the watery precreation abyss, the primordial substance from which God created the world. This primeval water, if not stemmed, would erupt from apertures in the land and flood the entire Earth. The Biblical Flood is understood to have been produced by an "uncorking" of the *tehom*, the waters from deep below.

Ea, the presiding deity of the *apsu* or *tehom*, was regarded as one of the great gods of Mesopotamia, based on his numerous positive epithets: He is a water-god, Lord of the Spring, Lord of Wisdom, King of the Watery Deep, Owner or

King of the River, Image Fashioner.[120] As Enki, this god is praised as *nudimmud,* "[the one] who creates," while *nagbu,* a qualifying term for Enki, means "source, groundwater." He is the Lord of the Earth, having organized all the aspects of the Earth (in the cosmic sense) according to plan. His prime symbols included a goat-fish, tortoise, ram-headed staff, a ship, and a vessel with overflowing water.[121] He was in charge of the divine order of things and the gods who kept the cosmic laws in place.[122]

Enki was typically pictured as a seated god with a long beard, wearing a cap with many horns, a long pleated robe, and with streams of water flowing from his arms to the ground. He was another guise for the Rich Fisher King.

Enki had a boat called the Ibex of the *Abzu*; he makes the life-giving rain fall; he is the promoter of fertility; he keeps the countryside green with lush vegetation; he fixes the boundaries of the cities; he appoints the Sun-god Utu to be in charge of things. He builds his sea-house of silver and lapis lazuli like sparkling light at Eridu, the oldest city in Sumeria. "Then Enki *raises* the city Eridu *from the abyss* and makes it *float* over the water like a lofty mountain."[123] The Sumerian text says that he raised up Eridu from the Earth like a mountain.

This is an excellent topographical description of the placement of Grail Castles *above* well-defined sacred sites (in this case, the extant mound of Abu-Shahrain in Iraq) as an indicator that the Grail Castle resides in a subtler, higher dimension, even above the energy feature (a dome) that makes a site holy.

Variations on a Theme— Multiple Rich Fisher Kings in Their Sea Palaces

We have *Manu Satyavrata* in his Boat of the Vedas, containing all the secrets of the ages, being towed by the huge fish. We have the sublime Enki with his 100 divine laws in his sea-house in the mysterious *Abzu*. These are equivalent images for the Rich Fisher King in his element, the Sea of Consciousness, secure in his castle, boat, or ark *above* the Deluge waters—ever remembering.

We can find further equivalent expressions of the Rich Fisher King in world Flood myths, notably as the biblical Noah and the Ark. We may consider Noah to be the same as *Manu Satyavrata* and his Ark to be the Boat of the Vedas, or at least the principle of a Manu for a new *manvantara* of human time. Here is a geomantic clue: If a myth is *site-specific* about *where* the sole Flood survivor and his boat *landed*, it's likely there is a Grail Castle there and that this figure is a renewed Rich Fisher King expression for that new time.[124] Other cultural examples of the Rich Fisher King include Nu (Egyptian), Poseidon (Greek), Aegir (Norse), Mannanan Mac Lir (Irish), Varuna (Vedic), and Utnapishtim (Babylonian), each of which reveals more of the archetype.

The Norse mythic formulation of Aegir, their Lord of the Sea, retains some of the original features of the Rich Fisher King archetype. His name derives from *Eagor,* which means "the Sea" in Old Norwegian. Aegir and Ran had nine daughters called the "waves of the sea" or "billow-maidens." Each of these represented one aspect of the ocean, "one moment of the epiphany of the sea."[125] In Aegir's nine daughters of the waves we have a Norse formulation of the function of the Grail Maiden, whom we encountered earlier with Anfortas.[126]

The Ofanim explain it this way: "The Grail Maiden is the intuitive aspect freely available to penetrate by access to the astral realm into the soul lessons learned by the soul up to the present time. Meeting the Grail Maiden brings you intuitive insight and wisdom pertinent to the soul's journey up to that point."

So Aegir's nine daughters are different nuances of the Grail Maiden function, aids to the soul in attaining the vast, total, and festive cosmic memory the gods enjoy every time they visit Aegir and have a draught from his five-mile-deep mead kettle. It's festive because there is no not-knowing, no forgetting, and thus no possibility of being wounded and miserable.

Let's look at Varuna for a moment. One of the earliest Vedic gods, his name apparently derives from the root *vr*, which means "to cover" or "encompass," which is consistent with his function as lord of light and darkness, supreme ruler of the physical and spiritual world, and upholder of *rta,* the divine laws. Varuna is associated with celestial order, the cycles and regular movements of stellar bodies, with rainfall, as well as with justice, law, and order. He is Lord of *Rta.*

The Son of Aditi, or infinity, Varuna rules the entire world with *rta* (equivalent to Enki's 100 divine laws, or *mes,* as well as the secrets of the Vedas). He measured out the extent of the Earth, settled all its worlds, and established the ordinances by which they operate. He is the king of the universe and all the stars, having fixed them in their locations; he possesses all the secrets of creation, all secret things, the truth and untruth of everything, and he foresees the destinies of all creatures and humans. Those who drown come to him.

In effect, Varuna is an earlier, more broadly conceived version of Vishnu, so that the Vedic mythic imagination has given us two descriptions of the Rich Fisher King: Vishnu as the gigantic divine fish; and Varuna, as Lord of the Sea and upholder of the celestial laws.

There are two important principles here. First, the Rich Fisher King is the retrieved celestial knowledge itself, the food of deep, unbroken memory that sustains the Grail Knights and gods. Second, the Rich Fisher King must struggle to keep the Vedic revelations secure against universal forces even more primal than himself and thus dangerous to the world order.

Vishnu as the Rich Fisher King is the sacrifice, the divine substance devoured because he is the fish itself. Ultimately all the epithets of the Fisher King flow into this singular image of the Grail King as a fish. It also alerts us to another, more familiar, identity: The Rich Fisher King is the Christ, known to the Greeks as *Ichthys,* or "Fish."

The inexhaustible food from the cauldron, the gods' joyous mead, the boar's meat that never runs out, the horse sacrifice, the jeweled riches of Lanka, the secrets of the Vedas, the celestial laws of *rta* or the *mes*—all are expressions of Christ Consciousness, or what the Greek philosophers called the Logos.[127]

Vishnu the Pervader is the sacrifice because he is the big fish swimming in the depths of the cosmic sea. The Christ is the Pervader because he is the space between all the stars; the Christ (Vishnu) sustains and preserves all cosmic space, holding it together as a kind of cosmic glue. The Christ remembers it all.

The Christ is the connection between all things and thus the *knowledge* of that which is connected as well as the full participation by awareness in all that is connected. This approaches the process of total cosmic recall and what you can have from a Grail Castle. To have this knowledge requires one to be senior to the network, older than all the star gods, a trait consistently attributed to the Rich Fisher King as Sea *Lord.* The Rich Fisher King is above the Sea of Consciousness just as the Grail Castle is not located in any of the seven chakras but is antecedent or transcendent to them.

The Christ as portrayed in his various guises as sea god is among the oldest beings and possesses the full recall of previous eons. This recall is a consumable "food." He is the divine fish, the devourable sacrifice. It's all a meal for the Grail Knight who in effect eats the Rich Fisher King. The more you eat of the fish, the more cosmic your awareness grows, just like Vishnu as the little fish that became eight million miles long. Inside the Boat of the Vedas, feasting on Christ Consciousness, your awareness spans eons, days, hours, weeks, years of Brahma; you feast on all the seeds of life, all the secrets of the Self and Immensity. You drink the refreshing waters of Mnemosyne, remembering everything you as a soul ever experienced.

What happens when you have completely consumed the fish that is the Rich Fisher King? You become the Rich Fisher King. You are healed. You are now one of the happy gods sitting festively about the cauldron, enjoying another draught of the full consciousness of the history of the universe. This is why Parsifal visited the Grail Castle twice. The first visit was—like this chapter—introductory, hearing about the fish for the first time; the second, later visit is when you want the fish of remembering more than anything else in life.

The Christ is the single fish swimming in the great sea of consciousness, the immense Self that is both separate and unified, two and one, the individuated and the unitive consciousness. Of course the cauldron restores life to the dead: Deep cosmic memory is regenerative for consciousness that is dead to its own past, quickening the soul that has forgotten its origin. The fish, symbol of fertility and wisdom and natural denizen of water, is hidden in the ocean's depth, possessing sacred powers of the deep. But it is also fantastically mobile, capable of swimming anywhere in the ocean, pervading the sea everywhere with its mobile fluidic presence.

The cosmic waters symbolize the foundations of the world. They exist *prior* to creation and, like Noah's Ark, contain "the potentiality of all forms in their unbroken unity." The waters *precede* forms and *uphold* subsequent creation, which is why Vishnu (the Hindu version of Christ) is also called the Sustainer. Life and real-ity are concentrated in this one cosmic substance out of which all other forms proceed.

The Fisher King is the one who can reel in the fish and eat it, that is, plumb the psychic depths of his own total existence over time and hook the Self and consume its knowledge and wisdom. Paradoxically, the Fisher King is also the fish, or Self, that is hooked, just as Vishnu is the personified sacrifice.

The core of the Fisher King myth is about attaining knowledge of the Self and the Immensity from which we humans came. The knowledge of the Vedas is a big fish dinner. It is nourishment for the soul by way of deep and total memory. Christ as the fish is the Vedas, the contents of the Ark, the full cosmic memory, the knowledge of the Self, the experience of the Immensity, Christ Consciousness.

And when *you* eat, *the planet* eats. The Ark is unloaded, the Secrets of the Vedas unpacked, the *rta*, *me*s, Dharma, laws, distributed.

The Grail Castle, Boat of the Vedas, Enki's sea-house, Kubera's bejeweled Lanka, the Rich Fisher King, the cauldron, the Holy Grail—it all coalesces into a consumable big eight million-mile-long fish, *Matsya-avatara*—Vishnu/Christ.

The Body Mythological—the Castle Carbonek That You Live In

All of this is a description of a spiritual process inside *your* body, the Castle Carbonek, the mythological Grail Castle. It's only mythological until you realize where the "myth" exists in you and why it's there.

The Grail Castle is your body and auric field, but we could also say it is the heart chakra. The Holy Grail itself is *in* the Emerald, that secret place *in you* between the outer (Anahata) and inner (Ananda-kanda) heart chakra. You see then that the human body is the ultimate mythic terrain, the source of the Mysteries, the playing field of the Grail Quest.

The variety of descriptions of the Grail Castle as boat, ark, and palace and of the Rich Fisher King as Kubera, Enki, Nu, Poseidon, Mannanan mac Lir, Aegir, Varuna, Vishnu, and Christ sharpen our focus on where the Grail action is taking place within us. The overlapping images of the Rich Fisher King also give us a look at the end result of the Grail process.

Chapter 2 showed that the geomythic terrain of the planet is organized so as to reflect our inner spiritual realities. There is an outer Castle Carbonek (the 144 Grail Castles situated above holy sites) *because* there is one inside us. The Earth's geomythic terrain is a projection of spiritual realities within the human. And there is an outer and inner one because there is an original one in the spiritual worlds, the Grail Castle archetype as a fundamental structure neither inside nor outside the celestial realms. The Grail Castle myth pertains simultaneously to human and planet. It is an organic, living, reciprocal arrangement: Our deep memory, accessed, heals the Earth's wounds.

Our inner spiritual reality is laid out around us as an outer interior space. It's easier, at first, to enter an exteriorized, projected Grail Castle out in the landscape than to climb into a two-inch-long vertical electromagnetic doorway known as the Emerald on the right side of your sternum. Yet it's the same place. You can interact with the one outside you to gain access to the one inside you. When you access the Grail Castle and the Holy Grail, both you and the planet benefit, as both you and planet get connected to the spiritual original.

Let's consider this on a *palpable* level. Find your third rib on the right side of the sternum; measure two inches down and about an inch across. That's where the Emerald is in your body, and how big it is. It's an electromagnetic doorway, an esoteric middle ground in between the outer and inner aspects of your heart chakra. The whole Grail mythos is in this little energy doorway in your chest.

This is *where* this myth takes place in you, and me, and every other human. This groundedness in the body mythological is what guarantees its reality and relevance. It is your passkey to interact with the planet mythological, so to speak—with the Earth's visionary geography encoded with temples, structures, and spiritual presences so as to *mirror* your own makeup. These are the "instrumentalities provided by the godhead for his [terrestrial mankind] redemption."[128] Everything we have forgotten and need for our "redemption" is *right here*: in the human body and surrounding us as the planet's visionary geography. We need go nowhere to have it.

The identification of the Emerald as the site of the Grail and of Sarras is attested to in Iranian mysticism. It's an exalted, highly mystical depiction of the same place and process we've been visiting.

The gods told Yima, a dazzlingly beautiful mortal, to prepare a *var*, or cave sanctuary, on Mount Damavand in Iran to preserve the seeds of life against the coming Deluge. The *var* would house those beings that were the most beautiful and gracious so as to be saved from the certain death the flooding of the world would occasion.

"This *var* or paradise of Yima is like a walled city, with houses, storerooms, and ramparts," explains Henry Corbin, a preeminent interpreter of Iranian mysticism. "It has a gate and luminescent windows *which themselves secrete an inner light* within, for it is illuminated both by uncreated and created lights." The couples in the *var* produce one male child and one female child every 40 years; this select population comprises beings of light and "truly beings of the beyond" living in a shadowless, unchanging paradise.[129]

The *var* is surrounded by "the Climate of the Soul, the Earth of Light, Hurqalya." *Hurqalya* is an Iranian mystical term that denotes in part the lush, fertile, rich lands surrounding the *var*; it is the perpetually green environment in which the Rich Fisher King lives and which his spiritual accomplishments generate. It is a celestial realm of Light existing outside Heaven yet vibrationally above the Earth. It is an exalted domain within Earth's visionary geography. Incidentally, Yima's *var*, like the heavenly Jerusalem, is a perfect square.

It is the opposite of the Wounded King's Wasteland, the King's environment before the fall into nonremembering. It is what you *and* the Earth receive on the completion of the Grail Quest—your new level of being.

Yima is the "Man of Light" possessed of the "knowledge that is self-consciousness." He is rich in the pure light of morning knowledge, "having attained the abode which secretes its own light," which the Iranian mystics called the Emerald Rock.[130] The Iranian Yima is an expression of the successful, Christed Grail Knight and the healed Fisher King, giving us an idea of both the attainment of the Grail Quest and something of its aftermath, that is, life in Sarras.

Why the Fisher King Battles the Beast of the Primeval Sea

The final thread we need to tie up here is why the Rich Fisher King is sometimes at odds with a beast of the primeval sea, such as Sesa-Ananta, Tiamat, or Hayagriva. Why has this abyssal creature stolen the secret teachings (the Vedas), forcefully occupied the Grail Castle (Ravanna at Lanka), or in more recent versions, abducted a beautiful celestial female?

In the *Ramayana*, Sita, a woman of celestial parentage, is abducted by Ravanna, the ten-headed demon. Sita is the consort-wife of Rama,

one of Vishnu's ten major incarnations. She is described as shining like pale gold; she is the cause of the universe and its primordial energy, the Upanishads declare. She is in fact an expression of Laksmi or Sri, the white goddess of beauty who emerged when the gods churned the Ocean of Milk (another name for the Sea of Consciousness) at the beginning of creation.

She has in fact appeared with Vishnu in all his incarnations as his consort. "The power of the all-pervading Preserver, Vishnu, is represented as the power of multiplicity or goddess of fortune."[131] Hence Laksmi, Sri, Sita is also called Fortune, "She of the Hundred Thousands." She is Vishnu's Fortune in its thousands of guises, giving us another insight into the fabulous jeweled riches of Kubera's Lanka or the source of the Fisher King's spiritual wealth.

The story line of the *Ramayana* is almost identical to that of Homer's *Iliad*.[132] The same story is repeated in the Celtic myths about Arthurian Glastonbury in England. King Arthur's beautiful wife, Guinivere (the Sita-Helen figure: her Welsh name, *Gwenhwyfar,* means, approximately, "the White One," as in, a celestial being), is abducted by King Melwas (also called Meleagaunce), Lord of the Summer Country, and held inside Glastonbury Tor (or perhaps Chalice Hill), until she is rescued by either Arthur himself (the Menelaus figure) or his chief knight, Lancelot. As mentioned, there is a Grail Castle at Chalice Hill in Glastonbury.

To make sense of this big myth, we need to look at its earliest expression, in which the energy dynamics are the purest.

When Vishnu made his descent into the world as the eight-million-mile-long fish, he used Sesa-Ananta to tow the Boat of the Vedas. When the world dissolves in between eons and cycles of manifestation, Vishnu sleeps upon the coiled length of this great cosmic serpent, who represents the residue of the previous eon of life (hence his name, the Remainder). But Ananta on its own means "the Endless or Infinite One" because he always remains to support the Earth as a cosmic space for creation and to be the foundation for Vishnu.

The key thing to observe here is the lack of enmity, friction, or opposition: Vishnu and Sesa-Ananta are clearly colleagues, allies, fellow gods with a celestial job to do. Later this relationship gains tension and difficulty, and the Grail King has to struggle against the cosmic dragon for possession of the secret wisdom teachings, his consort, his celestial residence, or a hallowed spiritual object such as Anfortas's lance.

The next chapter deals with the cosmic and terrestrial dragon, but it's important here because it points to another energy relationship within the human form and the geomantic landscape. The subject and location of the cosmic serpent illuminate the Wounded Fisher King situation—in fact, the location of his wound: the root chakra.

In the relations between the Rich Fisher King and the dragon or sea monster, either ally or opponent, we are observing energy relations between the heart and root chakras. We are also dealing, geomantically and cosmically, with relations between two Celestial Cities: Kubera's Lanka and another one called Naga City or Raksovati, discussed in chapter 4. (As with the Grail Castle, there are 144 copies of Naga City in the Earth's visionary geography. There are also 1,067 dragons upon the Earth.)

Remember, the Fisher King's wound is that the energy cannot flow from his root center up through the five chakras to his crown so that he can know. The blockage of this flow is in the root

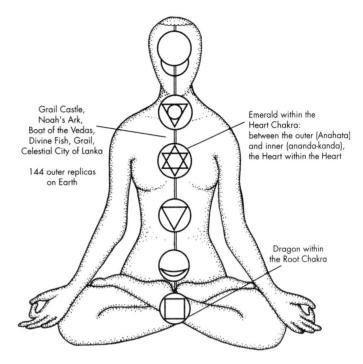

Grail Castle, Noah's Ark, Boat of the Vedas, Divine Fish, Grail, Celestial City of Lanka

144 outer replicas on Earth

Emerald within the Heart Chakra: between the outer (Anahata) and inner (ananda-kanda), the Heart within the Heart

Dragon within the Root Chakra

Figure 3-1. The Grail King and the Dragon of the Abyssal Sea

chakra, the well-known location of the primordial life-force energy called kundalini, which the ancient Vedic yogi-philosophers also likened to a beautiful goddess, the radiant Goddess Kundalini.

"By Her radiance it is that the whole of this Universe and this Cauldron is illumined," the yogic texts state of the Goddess Kundalini. "It is She who maintains all the beings of the world by means of inspiration and expiration, and shines in the cavity of the root (*Mula*) Lotus like a chain of brilliant lights."[133] Yogis describe kundalini in the human body as like a sleeping serpent coiled three-and-a-half times at the base of the spine; when awakened, kundalini rises up and flows upward through the chakras to the crown, illuminating the body and being.

As the *Mahabharata* vividly describes it, long ago the gods churned the Ocean of Milk, and ten beings, creatures, and objects essential for life emerged. One being was the white goddess, Sri, described above as Vishnu's fortune and power, the cause of the universe and its primordial energy. Sri, as the Goddess Kundalini, emerges from the undifferentiated primordial waters or Ocean of Milk and becomes the consort of the King of the Heart, the Grail King in his secret castle in the innermost part of the heart chakra (see figure 3-1).

Sri is a beautiful revelation and a world-transforming power, but the Ocean of Milk and its prime denizen, the cosmic dragon, keep trying to pull her back to her place of origin. Myths remember this pull as the abduction of the Fisher King's consort or as the stealing of the Vedic secrets of creation, for Sri is both the energy and the means. More properly, we should say the cosmic waters exist *inside* Sesa-Ananta. When the lands are parched and all creation dying for lack of moisture, the Hindu god Indra "slays" Vrtra, another name for the cosmic dragon, who had been holding back the waters. Slaying Vrtra and churning the Ocean of Milk are equivalent mythic acts.

The Rich Fisher King is Sri's divinely appointed consort *because* only he can wield kundalini energy responsibly, to create, heal, and nurture. Contemplate this majestic image: Vishnu or Christ as the Rich Fisher King, the representation of the Immense Self from outside Time and the cycles of creation and incarnation, the perfect balance of individuation and unitive consciousness, abiding joyously, festively, in the secret chamber of the heart chakra. He is the first to arrive for the world party of human incarnation, and the last to leave the previous gala. What more judicious position from which to wield the fundamental creative powers? What better model for us to study so as to claim this mastery?

Here we might usefully think of kundalini (as the energy aspect of the Goddess) in terms of the sacred spear that Klingsor stole from Anfortas and which Anfortas misused, precipitating the Perilous Stroke that incapacitated him. Or as the Sword of David, which he wrested from the giant Goliath, an Elohim in mythic disguise, and which his son, Solomon, dispatched across time and space on the Ship of Time (yet another Ark image) to King Arthur's Camalate and the prepared, Christed knight Galahad, who would use it to heal the Fisher King.[134]

In this version of the myth, David's sword (Goliath's sword) dispatched in the Ship of Time is the same as the secrets of the Vedas in the Boat of the Vedas. The sword is merely a condensed image of all the knowledge of the Vedas.

The variously named Rich Fisher King, because "he" is the Christ Consciousness, can wield the kundalini sword (his rightful consort, the Goddess Kundalini) without injury to himself and others for the betterment of all. So can the Christed Grail Knight, such as Parsifal or Galahad, which is why the Grail legends credit them with having healed the Fisher King's grievous wound. He can waken the sleeping dragon and release the healing waters, flooding the parched wasted landscape of Logres with a surfeit of pure consciousness.

You could say somebody "stole" the King's goddess, or you could say his access to "her" is blocked. In either case, he's wounded, his richness diminished.

From the viewpoint of an unfolding cosmic creation, the dragon or kundalini is the first thing created; the root chakra, paradoxically, is the first chakra created, the one closest to God. From the viewpoint of the Grail Knight transiting the Earth's visionary geography dedicated to a process of remembering and healing the Wounded Fisher King, the dragon is the last thing encountered. Here is where the creative energy is released to heal the wound.

How to waken the dragon, release the primordial waters, and free the beautiful Goddess Sri, inside us in the body mythological and outside, geomantically, in the planet's visionary terrain, is the subject of the next chapter.

4 The Primordial Dragon Upholds the World
Life in the Celestial City of Bhogavati

So what does a dragon *look* like? I've seen a few of the planet's dragons; of course, bear in mind, "see" in this context is at best a reduction of a fantastically complex energy feature into something approachable in human cognitive terms—a plausible image.

Preliminary Glimpses of the Dragon—a Few Photo Opportunities

Let's take the dragon at Silbury Hill in Wiltshire, England. It's one of the planet's 13 primary ones (explained below), and to some extent, the odd cone-shaped hill across the fields from Avebury was built there long ago to mark the spot for the dragon. To me, the Silbury dragon is a bronze-gold mass of coils, its face the living mask of a Sun-god, open-mouthed, fierce, adamant, spikey rays enhaloing its huge head. "I contain Avalon," it told me, meaning inside its girth is the astral plane, the Gnostic's lower astral light—Avalon, the fabled paradisal, pleasure realm of the Celts.

How about *Nidhoggr,* the Norse dragon that gnaws at the roots of Yggdrasil, the spectacular Tree of Life belonging to the high Norse god Odin?

You'll find the actual and geomantically real *Nidhoggr* (and the Tree) at an obscure place called Rondablikk in the Rondane Mountains in south-central Norway. I saw this big fellow recently.

This dragon is some six miles across, one of the planet's original 13; its name in Old Norwegian means "the one striking full of hatred." It's spherical but also like a crowned abstracted human face or a vast celestial face looming open-mouthed over the assembly of the many gods who gather every day to hold court at Urd's Well at Yggdrasil's base, as the Norse myths say. It's open-mouthed because there are worlds inside *Nidhoggr;* its mouth is the portal.

The dragon at Tintagel on the rocky promontory of western Cornwall in England, said to be the birthplace of King Arthur and today a windswept Celtic ruins popular among tourists, is a huge golden sphere several miles across, like a mammoth balloon barely roped down to the headland and facing out to sea. Picture a golden sphere onto which has been glued a golden seahorse, its body gracefully arcing the full girth of the sphere, its tail touching its head. On the sphere are hundreds of little golden pockmarks, like the indentations on a golf ball. These are the one thousand crowns of Sesa-Ananta, each vibrating continuously like a struck bell or a Tibetan crystal bowl.

Then there's the Midgard Serpent—*Midgard-sormr,* meaning "world serpent"—living in the primeval ocean, encircling the planet, tail in its mouth, like a precious jewel in the center of a circular clasp. Also known as *Jormungandr,* it is mostly head. Its circularity is implied, but the entire Earth is inside its single oroboric coil.

Jormungandr looks like a wrathful but protective deity. It has an exaggerated, somewhat puffed out face, a huge nose and mouth—it resembles a caricature of a generic human. Its eyes are jewels, its body is golden, and its overall ambiance is at best ambivalent. Its name in Old Norwegian means, not surprisingly, "huge monster," but a similar name, *Jormungrundr* is an old poetic Norwegian name for the Earth and means "mighty ground," and *Jormunr* means "the mighty one." So perhaps "mighty, Earthground monster" might be apt. These correlations are fitting because in some respects, the Midgard Serpent and Earth are functionally the same, and it is Earth's prime dragon, first among 1067.

Dragons on Four Tiers—the Midgard Serpent, the 13, and Their Progeny

The Earth presents us with four levels of dragons for our interaction. First, the Midgard Serpent, wrapped around the planet, its head and tail at Mount Meru in the deep South Pacific. Second, this *Ur*-dragon has 13 primary understudies, or major dragons, located mainly in the Northern Hemisphere. Third, these 13 each have 81 offspring, or minor dragons, or 1,053 in total. Fourth, there are 49 times 49^7 dragon eggs (33 trillion) distributed across the planet, one for each sentient being over the life cycle of Earth (see table 4-1).

The archetype of these four dragons is Sesa-Ananta, the Endless One of Hindu myth, described below, but on the level of the galaxy, the prototype for Earth is the constellation—or should we say, celestial being—called Draco. This constellation of 24 major stars is positioned close to Polaris, the current Pole Star (at the handle of the Little Dipper or Ursa Minor) at the "top" of the galaxy. Based on star maps, you couldn't say Draco coils around Polaris, but its lower torso and the latter part of its tail frame the Pole Star in a three-sided square.

The Earth's 13 major dragons are primarily the concern of the Ray Masters and highly initiated humans. These dragons have already been "slain," that is, their energies have already been released into the world and continue to be released. More within our likely sphere of activity are the 1,053 minor dragons and their 33 trillion dragon eggs distributed across the planet.

The 1,053 dragons were originally placed in the Earth's visionary terrain as eggs located within the 83,808 energy enclosures called dome caps. These are the ends of long unwinding spiral energy currents originating in even larger energy canopies called domes (see chapter 5) positioned over 1,746 sites, usually mountains, around the world.

The minor dragons were placed as eggs at the larger dome caps where they remained as seed potentials until some "dragon slayer" came along and activated them, freeing the energy (the primordial "waters" in microcosm) to flow into the Earth's energy matrix and the local landscape configurations.

Often the minor dragons were positioned at dome caps so as to be guardians for the geomantic temples. You can see this in the Greek story of the dragon Ladon (see below) who guarded the golden apple trees of the Hesperides. The image of Saint George and other dragon slayers defeating a monstrous dragon is actually about their competently *taming* the dragon to enable safe and

Table 4-1: Dragons

Planetary Total: 1 (primary), 13 (major), 1,053 (minor) = 1067

Location (Primary): Head in the South Pacific Ocean, near New Zealand's south island's east coast: *Jormungandr* or *Midgardsormr*

Selected Locations (Major):

Rondablikk, Rondane Mountains, Norway: *Nidhoggr*

Uluru, Alice Springs, Australia: *Ngaljod*

Serpent Mound, Locust Grove, Ohio, U.S.: *Tokchi'l* (Guardian of the East)

Fajada Butte, Chaco Canyon, New Mexico, U.S.

Grand Canyon, Arizona, U.S.

Silbury Hill, Wiltshire, England

Dragon Hill, The Ridgeway, Wiltshire, England

Glastonbury Tor, Glastonbury, Somerset, England

Delphi, Mount Parnassus, Greece: *Python*

Tintagel, Cornwall, England

Mount Damavand, Iran: *Ladon*

Lake Tahoe, California, U.S.

Selected Locations (Minor) *and Their Names, Where Available:*

Thebes, Greece: *Dragon of Ares*

Colchis, River Phasis Valley, Vani, Republic of Georgia

Lahaina, Maui, Hawaii, U.S.: *Kihawahine*

Walmsgate, near Tetford, Lincolnshire, England

Korochinsk Mountains, near Kiev, Ukraine: *Gorynchishche* or *Goryshche*

Spooner Valley, Lake Tahoe, Nevada, U.S.

Aller, near Langport, Somerset, England: *Aller Dragon*

Tronfjell, Throne Mountain, near Roros, Norway

Mount Kinabalu, Borneo: *Kinabalu*

Tarascon, River Rhone/Durance confluence, France: *Tarasque*

Wormhill/Wormstall, Baslow, Derbyshire, England

Burley Beacon, Burley, Hampshire, England: *Bisterne Dragon*

Dinas Emrys, Snowdonia Mountain, Wales: 2 dragons

Putsham Hill, Kilve, Somerset, England: *Old Ben*

Castle Neroche/Ratch, Somerset, England

Shonk's Moat, Peppsall Field, Brent Pelham, Hertfordshire, England

Mount Pilatus, Wilser, Switzerland: *Wilser Dragon*

Kapenga, New Zealand: *Hotu-puku taniwha*

Lhasa, Tibet, Underneath Lu Gyalpo Palace of Serpent King, Potala

Belvedere, Tiburon, California, U.S.

Olampali State Park, Route 101, Marin County, California, U.S.

Bell Rock, Sedona, Arizona, U.S.

Mont-Saint-Michel, Normandy, France

Cumae, Naples, Italy

Hill Cumorah, Palymra, New York, U.S.

Mount Kailash, Tibet

Uturoa, Raiatea, French Polynesia: *Long Jaw*

Gorge of River Sill, Innsbruck, Austria

Lindwurmgrube/Goritsschitzen, Klagenfurt, Austria: *Lindwurm Dragon*

Knotlow Hill, Wormhill, Derbyshire, England

Linton Hill, Wormistone, Roxburgh/Borders, Wales: *Linton Worm*

Tuckasegee River, near Bryson City, North Carolina, U.S.: *Uktena*

Cohutta Mountains, Cohutta Wilderness, Cisco/McCaysville, Georgia, U.S.: *Ustu'tli*

Brand, Vorarlberg, Austria

Ukisima Pool, Yamashiro, near Kyoto; Japan: *Ogoncho*

Table 4-1: Dragons *(continued)*

Rondablikk, Rondane Mountains, Norway: *Graback*

Rondablikk, Rondane Mountains, Norway: *Goin*

Rondablikk, Rondane Mountains, Norway: *Svafnir*

Rondablikk, Rondane Mountains, Norway: *Grafvolluth*

Rondablikk, Rondane Mountains, Norway: *Ofnir*

Rondablikk, Rondane Mountains, Norway: *Moin*

Rondablikk, Rondane Mountains, Norway: *Grafvitnir*

Draguignan/Beaucaire, France: *Drac*

Nevsehir, Cappadocia region, Turkey ("slain" by St. George)

Silene, Libya ("slain" by St. George)

Heiligenberg (Holy Mountain), Heidelberg, Germany

Lough Derg, Ireland: *Caoranach*

Lake Manasarovar, Mount Kailsh, Tibet

Mount Moro, Japan (*Ryuketsu-jinja*, Dragon-cave shrine)

Individual dragon eggs: $49 \times 49^7 =$ 33,232,930,569,601

Selected Dragon Names: Fafnir of Gnita-Heath; Rainbow Serpent; *Ngaljod; Nidhoggr II; Kihawahine; Hotu-puku taniwha;* Long Jaw; Bisterne Dragon; *Tarasque;* Dragon of Ares; Python; *Smok Wawelski;* Old Ben; *Uktena; Kinabulu;* Ladon of the Garden of the Hesperides; Kur or Tiamat; Vrtra; Sesa-Ananta; Svarbhanu; Rahu and Ketu; Draco; Apep/Apophis; *Tokchi'l* (Guardian of the East); Huracan (Caribbean); *Aido Hwedo* (Dahomey); *Bida* (West Africa); *Ogoncho* (Japanese); *Goryshche* (Russian); *Caoranach* (Ireland)

---

supportive entrance to the inner sanctum that the dragon guards.

Then you have the 33 trillion dragon eggs. Where do you find these individually designated dragon eggs? Probably fairly close to their mother. In the Russian dragon-slaying tale, Goryshche, after her reprieve from the *bogatyr* Dobrynya, gave birth to progeny that remained close by in the Sorochinsk Mountains. She agreed not to destroy Kiev if Dobrynya left her baby dragons (eggs) intact. I have found numerous dragon eggs at an obscure site called Walmsgate in Lincolnshire, England, which is the site of one of the 1,053 minor dragons, as in Gate of the Worm (Walm, an old Celtic name for dragons).

Numerous dragon eggs are said to reside in the River Neckar which flows by the city of Heidelberg in Germany. Local myth attests that once people collected these eggs, hatched them, and raised the dragons to be house protectors.[135] Fittingly, *Heiligenberg*, or Holy Mountain, across

the river from Heidelberg, is the site of one of the minor dragons; there is also a Saint Michael's Basilica on the mountain, further supporting the dragon suspicion.[136] Saint Michael, or his original, the Archangel Michael, is regarded as a dragon slayer.

"Within each dragon egg is a seed of something to be transformed through the cooperation of the elemental, human, and angelic kingdoms," the Ofanim explain. "When this trinity of forces comes together at a dragon egg, then the force latent there can be diffused within a center of a section of the Earth grid matrix for the unfoldment of consciousness within the elemental and human kingdoms, depending on the energy aspect present in each dragon egg."

According to the Ofanim, you have to unfold and assimilate the seven aspects of seven levels of the dragon egg, or 49 aspects in all. You could also think of this in terms of seven aspects of seven chakras; the number of petals in the first six chakras is 50. The complete human unifies and embodies the whole, being the fiftieth.

The dragon egg and its dynamics mirror our own inner energy dynamics, described as the archetypal dragon within each of us, the Goddess Kundalini. This coiled inner serpent is a miniaturization of the outer one. "She" has four beautiful arms, her eyes are brilliant red, her overall appearance is "resplendent" with the light of many suns. Her "shining snake-like form" coils three-and-a-half times around the base of the central energy channel called sushumna, along which the first six chakras are vertically arrayed. Her luster is like a flash of strong lightning, and she is the carrier of "the ever-pure Intelligence."

The Goddess Kundalini, also called Shakti, is the energy of the Pervader, Vishnu. She is "immaculate, glowing like molten gold." She looks like a snake, "asleep illumined by her own light" or standing, like a serpent at the center of the world. She is the deity of Speech (Vac-devi) and the Seed of the universe.[137]

Kundalini's sweet incessant murmur is like "the indistinct hum of swarms of love-mad bees." She is also the receptacle of that "continuous stream of ambrosia" that flows downward from the "Eternal Bliss," the Tantric texts tell us. "By Her radiance it is that the whole of this Universe and this Cauldron is illumined."[138]

This statement and its references to heavenly ambrosia, Kundalini's radiance, and the cauldron will gain vivid relevance a little later when we discuss the Churning of the Ocean of Milk.

Further, whoever meditates on the Goddess Kundalini with her luster of ten million suns becomes the Lord of Speech and an adept in all types of learning. He becomes free of all diseases, his innermost spirit becomes ever-glad, and he serves the world and the gods by way of his "deep and musical words."[139] The element of profound, creative, even musical speech will also assume its

rightful significance below when we discuss the results of "dragon-slaying."

Clearly, the benefits of dragon "slaying" are much more interesting than the legends suggest. Thus only highly developed humans can interact with the minor landscape dragons; they need that development to handle the strong energies involved. The rest of us are invited to interact with individual dragon eggs, ideally with one or more. "A complete person has assimilated the energy from at least one dragon egg and thereby effected the energy matrix, which in turn effects all dragon eggs and their existence in matter," the Ofanim say.

To work on even one dragon egg benefits the local geomantic setup. The Ofanim note that when a person can "activate a realization within oneself of the human dragon," this simultaneously (due to the dragon egg's location in the grid matrix) allows the celestial light to flow through the ley lines associated with it. These are the energy conduits, both straight and spiral, connecting the domes to domes and the dome caps to the domes (explained later in the book).

To activate or even interact with the outer dragon, you have to confront your inner one. It's an inner and outer allegory. A good way to practice this is with the dragon egg with your name on it.

If you've demonized the primal life force energy called kundalini and spent your life denying it or pretending it doesn't exist, don't try to encounter a dragon. There is no need to fight, battle, or slay the dragon; there probably never was, but certainly in the imminent Aquarian Age, that approach is entirely inappropriate on a personal and geomantic level. Don't think of fighting; think of transmutation, assimilation, cooperation.

Here is how *not* to deal with a dragon in the landscape. It's the example of Beowulf, the medieval Danish hero who died from his dragon wounds. The dragon is not named, but it is characterized as the worm, the terrible guardian, the dreadful visitor ready for combat. The worm lives in a cave beneath stone cliffs, but it is also called a barrow and earth-hall, suggesting it was a geomantic fortress of some type. The dreadful worm of course sits on a fabulous jewel hoard. He is its "barrow-ward" and "hoard-guard."

Beowulf and his companion engage the dragon in battle. The *Beowulf* poet says the worm has a savage heart and exhales "death-fire" and "war-flames" such that when his "hot-war-steam" flows out of his mouth, the Earth resounds. The worm is angry, a "terrible malice-filled foe, shining with surging flames," it hates men, they are its enemies, and the worm's fire advances in waves upon those its opponents.

Beowulf slew the dragon, but not before the worm cut him. Its poison caused Beowulf to burn and swell, and soon he died. Beowulf, the "war-king" who had survived every combat and dangerous battle and deed of courage, lost this one. His redoubtable sword broke, and the dragon poisoned him to death.[140] Beowulf wasn't prepared for the dragon, so he couldn't have its treasures.

You see a better outcome in this experience in the West African tale of the dragon Bida as recounted in the *Epic of the Dausi.* Lagarre, the youngest son of King Dinga, sought the secret of kingship on his father's behalf. He flew on a vulture into heaven to collect the royal drum called Tabele, then he went out into the desert and banged the drum. Suddenly a city of domes and date palms rose out of the sand, completely encircled by the dragon Bida. Lagarre promised the dragon-guard the sacrifice of one virgin girl every year in exchange for his access to the ancient city of Wagadoo. Once a year thereafter Bida flew over Wagadoo and spewed gold over it such that its streets were paved in gold. Three generations of kings reigned pacifically in Wagadoo when one year Bida's lover, Mamadi Sefe Dakote, also called Mamadi of the Silent Sword, cut off the dragon's head, which then flew on its own off to the Gold Coast.[141]

In the Nordic myth of Sigurd the dragon slayer, Fafnir the dragon presides over *Gnita-heid,* which means "Glittering Heath." Fafnir (in Old Norwegian, "the Embracer"), the son of the dwarf-king Hreidmar, changed himself into a dragon to protect a fabulous gold hoard.

There is no known place more rich in gold than Fafnir's lair, Sigurd learns, although Fafnir is an ill-natured dragon of considerable size and ferocity and blows poison around in all directions. In fact, he is the "most evil serpent and lies now upon this hoard," we read in *The Saga of the Volsungs,* a thirteenth-century Icelandic rendition of the Sigurd story.[142] Sigurd's sword, Gram, is better forged than Beowulf's and doesn't break. He slays Fafnir and drinks his heart blood. Then he gets a treasure potentially greater even than the enormous gold hoard.

As the dragon blood touches his tongue, Sigurd becomes immediately clairvoyant and can understand the speech of the birds. Although the *Volsung* poet qualifies this by saying these are "nuthatches," the "birds" in question are more likely angels, and access to them is the dragon's wisdom. In Sigurd's experience, we get more of the full picture of encountering the dragon: His hero's sword doesn't fail him, he defeats the dragon, gets the gold, *and* reaps the additional benefit of the dragon's wisdom, which is clairvoyance. He is the Lord of Speech.

So who takes care of the 13 dragons and the world-encircling one?

Greek myth records an amusing story about how Draco became a constellation. It was during the Titanomachy, the tumultuous ten-year war for dominion of the world between the Titans and the Olympian gods. The dragon sided with the old gods, the Titans. Seeing this, Pallas Athena, an Olympian, seized Draco by its long tail and hurled it off the Earth. As the dragon sailed through the great void of Heaven it became twisted in knots; then it struck the dome of the stars (the "roof" of the galaxy) and became entangled in it due to the rotation of the celestial sphere. Before Draco could disentangle itself and unkink the knots, it froze to the spot, owing to the extreme cold of the place.

I called this myth amusing because it doesn't hold up against the profounder perception of Sesa-Ananta in the *Mahabharata*. Yet it offers a clue.[143]

It is unlikely that Pallas Athena hurled Draco anywhere. He preceded her on the scene, being after all the remainder and residue from the past cycle of creation. To say Pallas Athena was an Olympian is a code for identifying her as one of the Ray Masters from the Great Bear or what the Hindus called the ancient *rishis*, august sages who survived the previous cycles of universal existence and were among the first of the gods to reappear on the galactic scene.

It is the 14 Ray Masters or *rishis* from Ursa Major who handle and ground the 13 dragons.

The *rishis* (from *rsi*, which means "to see") are the seers who *see* the divine laws and reveal them to humanity and also express them in creative acts. The *rishis* are often presented as human sages, but they are "eternal powers who appear every time a new revelation is needed." The Vedic texts usually spoke of seven *rishis*, though they sometimes referred to ten or 12, or assigned "wives" to the principal seven (giving us 14), but they were consistent in attributing the *rishis'* residence to the seven stars of the Great Bear. The *rishis* keep the world stable by performing rituals and reciting hymns three times every day.[144]

In brief, the 14 Ray Masters pertain to the energies of the constellation of Ursa Major (the seven-starred Big Dipper in the Great Bear, adjacent to Draco) and its role in the galaxy as the provider of the seven major and seven minor colors, rays, cosmic principles, or consciousness streams necessary for human conscious evolution.

Each Ray Master is in charge of one such consciousness-evolution ray. Many of the world's primary pantheons of active gods involve the Ray Masters. Among the Olympians, Apollo, Hephaistos, Aphrodite, Artemis, and Pallas Athena are Ray Masters in Attic disguise.

The Ray Masters (including Pallas Athena) use the dragons to seed and ground their energies on the physical Earth. So while to say Athena "hurled" Draco up to the top of the celestial vault is misleading, the inference of her direct involvement *with* Draco is right on point. But what does this mean?

Think of the electromagnetic spectrum of light as the Rainbow Serpent, as described in Australian aboriginal myth. He contains the complete range of possible light frequencies from radio waves to infrared to ultraviolet to gamma rays, and all the gradations of awareness associated with these. The Rainbow Serpent is "the first cosmological model for the spectral order of universal energy." It represents "the original appearance of creative energy in the Dreamtime," which we can construe as "the preformative spiritual order of the universe"—the fresh moment when Vishnu awakens and Brahma recreates the world.[145]

In a sense, the 14 Ray Masters each own a color slice of the Rainbow Serpent: Apollo claims the pale blue, Hephaistos the scarlet, Aphrodite the pink. The Ray Masters "bleed" these energies into the world by "slaying" the dragon, but there is no slaying, no bloodletting. Draco as the Rainbow Serpent embodies the essential color codes of creation and consciousness; the Ray Masters help move these differentiations of the pure blinding white astral light into the world. To use the language of the physics of light, the white light (the dragon's essence) gets diffracted into the rainbow spectrum (the Ray Masters).

We might think of the Ray Masters as rivers of colored light, flowing continuously out of

Draco into collecting pools and from these into the world. In other words, they channel the diffracted chromatic energies of the dragon from the *Muladhara*, root chakra, through the Ocean of Milk, second chakra, into the solar plexus for distribution into the world. Appropriately, out of the 700 or so nerve cords of the sympathetic spinal system, as modeled by classical Tantric-yogic physiology, the 14 most important have their connection with the *sushumna* or *Merudanda* (the central energy conduit running vertically through all the chakras—Mount Meru in the body) at the solar plexus, although they service various different parts and regions of the body. The Tantras also tell us that of the 72,000 or more *nadis* in the body, there are 14 principal ones.[146]

These 14 nerve cords are the bodily equivalent (and work space) of the Ray Masters. Clearly the Ray masters are "hard wired" to the spiritual-physical human constitution and the Earth.

The Ray Masters also handle the primary, planet-encircling dragon, the Midgard Serpent, the worm oroboros, its head and tail conjoined invisibly in the South Pacific. It's called Midgard because in Norse myth, *Midgardr* was the part of the world assigned to humans—in Old England, *Middangeard*, "dwelling place in the middle." The gods (*Aesir*) lived in Asgard, the giants (*Jotunns*) lived in Utgard, and the humans lived in the middle. Midgard had a protective wall erected around it, made from the eyebrows of Ymir, the sacrificial original human-giant from whose body the entire world was created.

There isn't much for humans to do with respect to interacting with the Midgard Serpent. This is in the hands of the Ray Masters, the Ofanim, the Archangel Michael, and other celestial superintendents of our planet. "Oroboros, the world dragon, has many eggs over the Earth," the Ofanim note. "They hatch. The dragon is about to shed its skin. The Earth will cleanse herself."

What do the gods actually *do* to a planetary dragon on our behalf? We get some sense of their activities in the big myths of dragon-slaying. Take the case of Indra and Vrtra. Indra is the Hindu chief of the gods (equivalent to the Greek Zeus or Norse Thor), and Vrtra is the cosmic dragon who held back the waters needed by the world. Even his name reflected his resistance: *Vrtra* derives from the root *vr*, which means "to hold back" or "restrain." Vrtra is a gigantic dragon who withholds the waters in the dark hollow of the mountains.

Vrtra was considered a demon of drought, on account of his refusal to let the waters go. "His cavernous maw drank up the sky; his tongue licked the stars of the [Great] Bear." He covered the worlds with darkness, and his yawn, exposing his "huge, terribly fanged-mouth," caused all who saw him to flee to the ten directions.[147]

Indra, ruler of heaven, wielder of the thunderbolt, and giver of the rain, was the god who forced Vrtra to release the waters into the world. Indra sheared off one of Vrtra's arms with his hundred-jointed bolt, split open Vrtra's belly with his *vajra* or thunderbolt, and forcibly cut off his enemy's head, which was as big as a mountain. Finally, the fecundating waters flowed into the world "like bellowing cows," as the Rg Veda put it.

Slaying the dragon "constitutes the preliminary condition for the cosmogony." Using the *vajra*, Indra "puts an end to the immobility, or even the 'virtuality,' symbolized by the dragon's mode of being."[148] Now the world can begin. Returning to the yogic model of the human, the primal waters held back by Vrtra are released into the world (the chakras) by way of the 72,000 *nadis*, the thousands of tiny riverlets for the flow of life-force energy or prana from the root chakra (see below).[149]

I mentioned that the Ray Masters use the dragons to ground their own energies into the planet. Here is a vivid image of the flow of that cosmic water.

Goryshche was a 12-headed dragon who lived in a network of caves in the foothills of the Sorochinsk Mountains near Kiev in the Ukraine. She had captured many Russians for food and held them in her warren. Dobrynya Nikitich, a *bogatyr*, a Knight of Holy Russia, in his first encounter with the dragon, cuts off all her heads save one and strikes a deal with her; she will no longer plague Russia and she keeps her head.

In a variant version of the story, Goryshche breaks the deal, flies into Kiev, and abducts the princess. This time Dobrynya slays the dragon and her offspring after a three-day battle. The dragon's blood is so copious it forms a noxious lake that the Earth will not absorb. Dobrynya calls on Earth and demands She swallow the dragon's blood. At once a chasm opens up and the blood is drained away into the Earth.[150]

The key part here is the *blood* draining into the Earth. This is the life-renewing cosmic *waters* flowing into the planet from the activated dragons. In the mythic equation, dragon's blood equals cosmic waters equals *consciousness*.

Discerning the Secret Identity of the Cosmic Dragon, the Endless One

Now let's take a cosmic view of the dragon, seeing it in its true home.

The vast Hindu epic, the *Mahabharata*, has a scene involving the primordial dragon that is remarkable for two reasons. First, it takes for granted the existence of this dragon—it's called the "firstborn of the first among the Snakes"—an idea bafflingly mythic to our modern sensibilities. Second, this Snake-dragon, called Sesa-Ananta, is commissioned by Brahma, the Creator God, to uphold the Earth and be a primary support for existence.

Sesa, the firstborn among the innumerable Snakes, whose numbers had grown into the tens

of millions and whose ranks were powerful and unassailable, was practicing his austerities on Mount Gandhamadana in the Himalayas, the *Mahabharata* tells us. (It would be wise here to think of these mountains as existing in the celestial worlds, not the ones we know on Earth.) Sesa, even though he is a Snake, is described as a human, and his austerities are judged to be "awesome" by the witnessing gods. He regards his Snake brothers as "slow of wit" and prone to constant quarreling; his aspiration is to shed his Snake "carcass," be something finer, and no longer consort with his brothers.

Brahma grants Sesa a boon. He will hold the world steady. The wide Earth, with its forest, mountains, oceans, and settlements has "rocked unsteadily." Sesa will now encompass them and hold the world steady.

Sesa would go underneath the Earth, pass through a chasm, and there find the best place from which to hold "Goddess Earth on his head, encompassing all around the felly [outer circle of a wheel] of the ocean." Sesa alone, Greatest of Snakes and the God of Law, will lend support to this Earth, Brahma tells him, "encircling her entire with endless coils . . . holding good Earth up at the bidding of Brahma."[151]

Let's look more closely at Sesa's mythic resume. The name *Sesa* means "Remainder," meaning he embodies or contains the residues of the past cycle of creation, from an earlier life (and universe) of Brahma, after that sphere of existence had been incinerated by his fiery breath. Sesa is also the residue after the present world was extruded and shaped out of the cosmic abyssal waters in which he resides; he is (and he contains) the world's *prima materia*, the original undifferentiated state of the cosmos and the stuff everything is made from.

Sesa's vast coils, some commentators say, symbolize the "endless revolutions of Time," and perhaps his own eternal existence, because when vast world cycles end, Sesa remains. He is the remainder of "unmanifested divine power," of residual demiurgic potential.[152]

Sesa as the Remainder represents "the nonevolved form of Nature (*prakrti*), the totality of the causal stage of consciousness, the eternity of time's endless revolutions." When a cycle of creation is terminated, it cannot entirely cease to be, and "there must remain in subtle form the germ of all that has been and will be so that the world may rise again." This subtle germ of past and future creations, of destroyed and yet-to-be generated universes, is Sesa.[153]

Sesa is the thousand-headed cosmic serpent, sometimes called *Naga,* as the prototype for a generic Hindu term for Snake gods, and *Ananta,* which means "Endless or Infinite One." One reason he's called Endless is that he is wrapped oroborically around the Earth, both the cosmic and planetary forms. But he's also shown with the Earth on his head, like a crown, and wearing a white garland consisting of the gods, humans, and demons. Sesa lives in *Mani-Mandapa,* "Jewel Palace," his hood is *Mani-dvipa,* "Jewel Island," and he is ruler of the Lower Region called Patala where he is known as Vasuki, King of the Nagas.

The myths say that Sesa's head sustains the Earth and supports the celestial spheres and their inhabitants. In between cycles of creation, Vishnu, the world preserver, sustainer, and source of its cohesion, reclines in a state of inactivity on the coiled form of the sleeping Sesa on the primeval World Ocean. Then Vishnu is known as *Ananta-Shayana,* "Sleeping on Ananta."

In traditional depictions, Vishnu reclines on Sesa's chest; Sesa, clothed in royal purple or dark blue and wearing a necklace of white pearls, shades the god's head with a canopy made of hundreds of his heads. At the end of the present cycle of world life when the gods decree time is up, Sesa will "vomit the blazing fire of destruction," an inflammable poison originally manifested when the Ocean of Milk was churned, which will burn up the world.

Let's take stock of an important fact. We've established that the chakras and their contents in the Earth's visionary geography correspond to the human chakras inside our energy field, and that both correspond to the much larger version in the galaxy, and that to an original cosmic model. However, in going from the celestial to the bodily model, the order of the chakras is *reversed,* just as it would be seen in a mirror.

From the celestial viewpoint, for Brahma starting to regenerate the world, the root chakra with its primordial dragon is the *first* energy center to be created. It's the oldest and most fundamental, hence *Muladhara*'s name, which means "foundation, starting point." It's the cosmic chakra *closest* to God, the home of the Goddess Kundalini and her ultimate expression as Sesa-Ananta.

From the *Muladhara,* Brahma builds *downwards* ever deeper into the levels of manifestation, culminating at the crown chakra, a realm, from Brahma's viewpoint, the closest to Earth, the furthest penetration into the realm of cosmic Earth, that is, the cosmic space designated for all frequencies of matter. It's like the Tarot image of the Hanged Man, a celestial figure hanging upside down, one leg tied to a tree, his head nearly touching the ground. God *starts* with Sesa.

But from the embodied human viewpoint, the root chakra is merely the first step in the ladder by which we climb *upwards* to the crown chakra. There is even an assumption that, putting aside the fact that the root chakra is the home of kundalini, it's a fairly low-rent proposition and the higher chakras are more spiritually desirable residences for our awareness. Yet the Supreme Being builds the universe from the dragon (root chakra) downwards to the crown. We return to the Supreme Being by climbing from the root chakra up to the crown. As the cliché has it, it's all done with mirrors (see figure 4-1).

The beauty of the system is that the Earth's visionary geography is the fulcrum between the two mirror images. We can become aware of the dragon within us in our root chakra and its cosmic mirror image by encountering it as a geomantic presence in the Earth's landscape. That encounter *in the middle* puts us in contact with the other two versions, above and below. We encounter the dragon, then, for our mutual benefit—ours and the Earth's.[154]

So by encountering the dragon in the Earth's landscape we get to experience this first phase of cosmic generation, and that leads to a key point. The cosmogony, the essential stages in the unfoldment of reality, is replicated in the 85-plus features of the Earth's visionary geography *and* in each of us. That means we can experience the cosmogony within ourselves out in the landscape.

Why the Dragon Is Spherical—Mysteries of Pi, Phi, and the 231 Gates

An interesting variation on the Sigurd-Fafnir's blood motif is in the rationale for the Olympian god Apollo slaying Python, the dragon at Delphi. It was competition. Python, a legitimate son of Gaia, was capable of pronouncing oracles, but that was Apollo's (presumed) rightful domain, so Python had to go.

That's the outer husk of the story. In actual fact, Apollo activated Python's oracular abilities on behalf of Delphi, the Pythia, the oracular priestesses who would preside at that site for centuries, and for any people who came in contact with the dragon's oracular-generating energies.

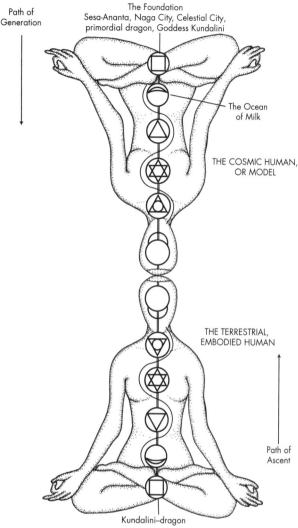

Figure 4-1. The Dragon at Both Ends, the Cosmic and Human

Remember, the dragon, as the Goddess Kundalini-Shakti, is also *Vac-devi*, the deity of Speech. But before we can account for this, we must see why the dragon is spherical.

Qabala has a useful analogy to explain this. In the beginning, before anything existed or was created, the Supreme Being removed "Himself" from a portion of Reality so that there would be room for creation. If He didn't, then nothing could be created because there would be no empty space for it as His presence filled everything and everywhere. The concept is called *Tsimtsum*, which means concentration, contraction, withdrawal, and retreat—the Vacated Space.

God retreats away from a point; He shrinks Himself. "God was compelled to make room for the world by, as it were, abandoning a region within Himself," explains Qabala scholar Gershom Scholem, "a kind of mystical primordial space from which He withdrew in order to return to it in the act of creation and revelation."[155] In a sense, God went into voluntary exile from a part of this primordial space He once occupied. Leaving it, He limited it.

The now empty space from which the Supreme Being retreated became known as the Vacated Space. It was a sphere. Everything would subsequently happen inside that sphere. This would be Ezekiel's many-eyed, Hayyoth-filled wheel of the Chariot of Yahweh and the treasure-filled, gold-encrusted dragon's cave. It would be the space in which all of Earth's visionary geography was templated.

Why a sphere? So pi could exist. The mathematical principle of pi (π) is the diameter ever in search of its circumference; technically, pi is the ratio of a circle's circumference to its diameter, or the circumference divided by the diameter. Less abstractly, let's say it's the consciousness created within the Vacated Space eternally seeking to know its creator, to find the limits, to reach the periphery of the sphere to which God has retreated. Pi reminds us the sphere exists, *proves* it exists. In a sense, it's an oroboric quest for the created, limited, and finite (the diameter) to dissolve back into God (the circumference) by knowing it.

This knowing is never to be completed; hence pi is an irrational number: 3.141592653589793238. . . . Or it seems the knowing is not to be completed *because* pi is irrational and endless, goes on forever without repeating itself.[156]

Pi is "one of the most fundamental constants in mathematics," explains a mathematician. Irrational numbers are much more abundant than rational ones and "float in a sea of irrationality."[157]

Pi is the math expression for Sesa-Ananta.

Pi expresses the primordial stasis, the immobility of the cosmic waters held captive by Vrtra in the Night of Brahma. It signifies the inertia and basic resistance that prevent the world from starting. Pi may be a transcendental, irrational, endless, and ultimately unknowable number, but it is interior, unmoving; it does not represent a dynamic, unfolding, evolving state. Phi does.

Phi is a letter from the Greek alphabet that looks like a sword passing vertically through an egg. This is a perfectly apt image, as phi is what happens when Indra slays Vrtra with his *vajra* thunderbolt or sword. Vrtra's immobility and inertia are broken, and the deeply desired waters flow out into the world. And they flow out in expanding spiral coils, presumably of infinite extension.

Mathematically, phi is what you get when you divide a line unequally, at a ratio of 1:1.6. It's expressed as 1.6180339887498948. . . . It is an irrational, unending, nonrepeating decimal expansion; in 1996, a mathematician used his computer to calculate phi to 10 million decimal points. Phi is what you get when you stick a sword into pi, or the sleeping dragon. Awakening, it becomes phi.

Phi is also the basis for the generation of the Golden Mean spiral, an expression of dynamic unfoldment and provably one of the prime design bases for most things in Nature, from Platonic Solids to plants to galaxies as well as music, architecture, and the human body.[158]

Let's say that in the image of Indra "killing" the dragon with his *vajra*, thereby freeing the waters to flow into the world, we see how pi becomes phi. A sword passes through it (pi, Sesa-Ananta, Vrtra), activating it, initiating the spiral.

The Vacated Space (pi, Sesa-Ananta, Vrtra), static, eternal, infinitely full, unknowable, is stimulated by the celestial electric charge of the thunderbolt (vajra, sword) and starts to move, to unfold (phi). The dragon stirs, quickens. Vrtra bleeds God-essence into the world. The cosmogony begins.

Yet Vrtra is a paradox: She is oroboric *and* coiled spirally. In the dialectic of Vrtra as the immobile, resistant, static reservoir of the primal Waters (her oroboric form) and as the coiled, unraveling, moving serpent (her spiral form) we see the relationship between pi and phi. Vrtra encircles the Earth, eating its tail, *and* its massive coils spiral out endlessly from their point of origin.[159]

How come its blood enables one to hear the language of the birds? How come when Sigurd drank Fafnir's blood he became clairvoyant? Will we if we repeat this act?

All these apparently disparate mythic or mystic allegations are accounted for by the mechanics of what Qabala calls the 231 Gates.

God contracted Himself and retreated from a portion of reality, thereby creating the Vacated Space, a sphere. Take the 22 letters of Hebrew and arrange them on the circumference of a sphere, the edge of the Vacated Space. Make all the possible two-letter combinations by connecting the letters with straight lines across the sphere; you get 231 two-letter combinations. The resulting shape is a complex geometric matrix of many crisscrossing lines called the 231 Gates.

Qabalistic tradition holds that God—the Ancient of Days in Judaic terms, equivalent to Brahma, whose age is reckoned in vast numbers of years—used the combinations of the 22 "elements" to make Heaven and Earth. Through these 22 letters (or energy forms or energy agents), He created "the soul of all creation and everything else that was ever to be created." At every "gate" in the circumference of the sphere there is a two-letter combination, "and through these gates the creative power goes out into the universe."[160]

This is merely an abstract way of referring to the waters of Vrtra, Fafnir's dragon blood, a dragon egg, the world-creating potency of the Kundalini, the prodigy of speech.

Creation took place through these 231 Gates as they are "what remained in the Vacated Space that preceded creation." The *Sefer Yetzirah*, a primary Qabalistic text, states that God placed the 22 "foundation letters" in a circle "like a wall with 231 Gates" and that this circle "oscillates back and forth." Already we can sense the coiled, writhing dragon within this otherwise abstract image.[161]

Appropriately, the word for circle in this usage is Galgal, which also means sphere or cycle; the cycle, or Galgal, is one of three aspects of kingship and dominates time. It connotes the cycle of events in the world, all cyclic motion, and the function of the King over Time. This evokes the image of the ever-moving Nagas and their time cycles contained by Sesa-Ananta (see below).

Think of the Vacated Space or the 231 Gates as the dragon's cave. It is a womb (or sphere or Galgal) filled with world-generating energies that sound like a rushing army, the sea, a swarm of mad bees, or the voice of the Almighty: "The voice of Your thunder was in the sphere [Galgal]," states Psalms 77:19. An equation: The dragon's cave is the 231 Gates is the Goddess Kundalini. The dragon's gold, its jewel hoard, is the array of world-generating spoken letters and the accompanying clairvoyance you get from immersing yourself in this Space.

Let's picture this on a global scale with our four tiers of dragons. On each dragon level, there is the same spiritual architecture. The Ray Masters, already having mastered their own and many other dragons, work with the Midgard Serpent to activate and deploy its 231 Gates on behalf of the planet. They do the same for the Midgard Serpent's 13 progeny, releasing a beneficial word-flood of energies across the Earth and through its geomantic network.

Sufficiently developed (and prepared) embodied humans work with the 1,053 dragons and in consultation with the Ray Masters to release these word-floods from this tier of dragons, slaying their local dragons, as legends will recount. Then humans desiring a geomantically contexted initiation experience "slay" their own dragons by finding then hatching a predesignated dragon egg. Ideally, the planet is continually fecundated by these regular dragon floods. Earth resounds with the incessant roars of dragons, or love-mad humming bees.

The Sovereign Lady, the revered supreme Paramesvari, Goddess Kundalini, who "holds within Herself the mystery of creation," has been awakened. By her radiance the universe is illumined and eternal consciousness quickened, for she is the World consciousness, the source from which comes all sound or energy, as ideas or speech, "the mightiest manifestation of creative power in the human body"—and planet, solar system, and galaxy.[162]

She, as Sesa-Ananta, will generate the planets out of her inexhaustible sound matrix within the dragon's cave of the 231 Gates. The 50 petals surrounding the first six chakras, each corresponding to a letter in the Sanskrit alphabet, come from her, the yogic texts tell us. In many respects, the Sanskrit alphabet and the chakras are identical, or in a mother-offspring relationship, the petals being the vibratory field that generates and maintains the planet.

These 50 letters are the same energies or sound-powers that will generate and sustain the seven classical "planets" (Sun, Moon, Mars, Venus, Mercury, Jupiter, Saturn) whose microcosmic expression is the human chakras.[163] By planets, though, I mean planetary spheres or realms (or seven of Qabala's Sefirot) and not the physical planets known to astronomy. Dealing with these 50 energies is your task in working with your own dragon egg.

The planetary spheres produced by the 50 Sanskrit letters are also sound matrices made of mantras, or sacred sound utterances that use Sanskrit letters. Tantric texts tell us that each petal has a spiritual being, called a Devata, in attendance; in fact, the mantra is the Devata's body. The entire human body (as well as the solar system, dragon, and galaxy) is a mantra, or a composite of mantras resounding with what the Western esoteric tradition calls the Music of the Spheres. The same dragon energy produces these letters manifesting as mantras as well as the subtle and gross universe, and they also vitalize, regulate, and control all activities in those realms.

What a spectacle: Life-fertilizing and consciousness-quickening kundalini flows through the many layers, realms, and geomantic structures of the Earth's energy body. It flows upwards through the six chakras and their planetary expressions, and downwards again, linking them all in a continuous oroboric circuit. The entire global body is "watered" with this fundamental energy. The stimulated ("slain") Sesa-Ananta and all her manifestations and progeny thus provide the root support, the inexhaustible reservoir of creative energy for all conscious evolution and developments in the world.

There is another remarkable aspect to the dragon mythos to contemplate. Think of the familiar biblical image of our "Fall," the Serpent under the Tree of Life in the Garden of Eden tempting Eve with the apple. The Judeo-Christian tradition teaches us this is a bad moment, but is it?

In light of our discoveries about dragons and kundalini, why not reframe this symbolic image and say the serpent itself is the gift of kundalini to humanity? Every human comes equipped with a miniature Sesa-Ananta and its creative energies in the root chakra. Each of us has the same world-generating potency—the Goddess Kundalini—to work with what Brahma and Vishnu used when they recreated the world after the Night of Brahma.

The Nagas in Their Celestial City Called Bhogavati, City of Pleasures

Sesa rules over the Nagas. Nagas are usually understood as serpents, dragons, or snakes, but their name suggests "the ever-moving," which some scholars interpret as the ever-moving cycles of time. They are often depicted as half-human, half-serpent, with human heads; they wear jewels, crowns, and large earrings, are handsome, courageous, and dangerous, have two, three, seven, or ten heads, tusks full of poison, and they vary in color, being blue, red, or white.

They are gigantic, powerful, prosperous, towering like mountaintops, one or two leagues long and wide (a league is about three miles), "protean, ubiquitous, venomous with a virulent poison that burned like a blazing fire." One "wondrous" Naga called Taksaka flew through the sky like a "lotus-colored streak that parted the hair of heaven." At a holy rite called the Session of the Snakes, hundreds of thousands of Nagas were sacrificed to the flames; in fact, the number of sons, grandsons, and further Naga progeny was beyond count.[164]

The Nagas dwell in their own realm called Naga-loka (alternately Patala or Niraya, with seven levels), said to be an immense voluptuary domain packed with palaces, towers, residences, and pleasure gardens. It is a Celestial City, in fact, sometimes called Bhogavati, which means "City of Pleasures" and "Full of Treasures." The *Mahabharata* said of one residence of human heroes that "that grand city shone as Bhogavati with its Snakes."[165]

We encounter our second

Celestial City in the context of the dragon. I call it Naga City, although it is also known as Bhogavati and Raksovati, even Wagadoo. While it is associated with Sesa-Ananta, it is not always located at a dragon site, and there is a fair amount of confusion in the Hindu texts as to its identity and character. You could say a Naga City is where the dragons come from and where the prime cosmic dragon Sesa-Ananta, the Endless, still resides, awaiting your visit (see table 4-2 for a few site listings).

The place is said to be located in the cosmic Southwest, one of the eight directional divisions of cosmic space in each of which resides a Celestial City. The Puranas state that this is the city of the "great-souled Nirrti" named Raksovati and that it is entirely inhabited by Raksasas who worship her. Nirrti is described as a black goddess who signifies dissolution, misery, corruption, evil, old age, and decay and whose vile offspring include death, fear, and terror. Nirrti—her name means "misfortune"—is the Goddess of Misery; her sons are the Nairrta ("evil omens") and Raksasa (demons).

As Hindu mythic imagination presents them, the Raksasas are free-ranging demons and shape-shifting malevolent spirits who can assume the forms of dogs, birds of prey, dwarves, husbands, and lovers—generally, they could take on any conceivable shape. They like to interrupt rituals, sacrifices, and sacred events and tend to disturb pilgrims at holy sites.

Ravanna, the fearsome ten-headed demon who abducted Rama's consort, Sita, and occupied Kubera's Lanka and stole his celestial chariot, the bejeweled Pushpaka, was a Raksasa; he was also their king. Raksasas can be charming and handsome

Table 4-2: Naga Cities

Planetary Total: 144

Selected Locations:

Croagh Patrick, Ireland

Mount Damavand, Iran

Lake Manasarovar at Mount Kailash, Tibet

Lake Tahoe, California

Kashmir, India

Equivalent Names: Raksovati; Bhogavati; Patala; Arabot; Seventh Heaven; Wagadoo or ugly and revolting; they are said to wander about at night, terrifying all they encounter, to haunt cemeteries; known as harmers and destroyers, they can be yellow, blue, or green in appearance.

Seemingly inconsistent with all this is the claim that Brahma created the Raksasas from his foot to be guardians of the precious original waters on Earth. So perhaps like church gargoyles, they are fearsome as part of their job, to scare away the really unwholesome types who would corrupt the primal waters.

While I do not dispute the attributions of the Raksasas, I propose that their association with the Celestial City in the Southwest is mistaken and that it comes from the same widespread cross-cultural resistance to the reality and opportunity of kundalini and the true nature of Sesa-Ananta and the dragons that has kept Judeo-Christian culture in suppression and near ignorance of it all. In fact, my research suggests that the Celestial City of Raksovati-Nirrti is not a demonic realm but, in fact, is the opposite, the highest, purest celestial realm, what Judeo-Christian angelology calls the Seventh Heaven, or Arabot.

First let's understand what the Hindu texts say about the Naga's "city" called Patala. The Puranas explain that there are seven Patalas, or netherworlds, associated with the Nagas. Probably the attribution of netherworld to Patala is due to the continuing cognitive error (or fear) that the Nagas are Snake-gods, a kind of fearsome astral version of terrestrial snakes. Nagas as snakes evoke the undulatory, oscillatory aspect of the dragon and the "serpents of wisdom" aspect of Kundalini.

Each of the seven Patalas is 10,000 leagues deep, each with its own regent, so the total depth of Patala is 70,000 leagues. Sesa-Ananta lies coiled at the base of this 70,000-league-high realm, its king, his thousand heads illuminating the space and his great bulk bearing the entire

realm like a chaplet on his crown. Patala is studded with radiant, lustrous jewels; during the day, sunbeams diffuse light, not heat, and at night, moonbeams are luminous but not cold. It is always feast time in Patala, and the Nagas, Danavas, Daityas, and other denizens make merry with delicious food and drink and forget the passage of time.

The Patalas are basically a pleasure realm, one of aesthetic delights and ambient beauty. This is hardly a demonic realm. The august sage Narada once said of Patala that it was better than Heaven or Indra's paradise, in fact, that it was a realm of luxury and sensual pleasures. Colors associated with Patala (its "soil") are white, black, purple, or yellow, but overall Patala is golden. Its capital, as mentioned earlier, is Bhogavati.

We must keep clearly in mind Patala's cosmic location and place in the sequence of cosmogonic generation. It is at the top, not the bottom, of Earth, and it was the first thing Brahma and Vishnu used when they started the World again, which means Sesa-Ananta's Patala lies the closest to Brahma of all eight Celestial Cities.

Let's look at three geomantically placed Naga Cities around the Earth, out of the planet's 144: Croagh Patrick in Ireland; Mount Damavand in Iran; Lake Manasarovar at Mount Kailash in Tibet.[166] Keep in mind that in examining the exterior features of a Naga City we are also observing the archetype of our human root chakra projected out into the Earth's visionary landscape.

Croagh Patrick is a mountain 2,510 feet high, off Ireland's west coast. Named after Saint Patrick, Croagh Patrick is regarded as Ireland's holy mountain and is the site of an annual pilgrimage. Irish myths say that in 441 A.D., during Lent, Saint Patrick drove all the snakes, serpents, and demons from Ireland, starting with those resident at Croagh Patrick. He rang a silver bell, after which the serpents turned into crows and flew away.

But the myths also say, a bit confusingly, that the snakes didn't turn into crows but returned to their source, the Devil's mother, called Coara (or Corra, "Female Friend"), who had the form of a great bird. She was known as the Great Swallower, having swallowed a guileless harper who played music near her den; she was also the chieftainess of a flock of demonic birds who assaulted Saint Patrick during his geomantic exorcism of the mountain. But she was also Caoranach, a water serpent who tried to beguile the steadfast Patrick, and failed. He chased her off the mountain to a lake 70 miles away, called Lough Derg, where he killed the mother of all demons and turned the waters red with her spilled blood.

The Irish myth is garbled, and the lines of the Naga City resumé are blurred and distorted. We can see the demonization of Sesa-Ananta's realm so common to myths around the world in which the Nagas get downgraded to demonic forms (like the Raksasas). In the confusion of Coara as somehow both the Great Swallower (dragon) and great bird (Garuda), we can discern the essentials of the Naga-Ofanim relationship.

While there is no dragon at Croagh Patrick, Sesa-Ananta's presence is implicit. The seven levels of Patala are there coiled dragonlike within or around the mountain, and Sesa-Ananta is there by implication. Saint Patrick was a Ray Master in one of his cultural guises; his task at this mountain was to release some of the energies and consciousness of Patala into the Irish landscape, to let some Seventh Heaven awareness trickle into Irish ground.

He didn't drive the Snakes (Nagas) out of Ireland; he grounded their geomantic presence in Ireland. They didn't turn into birds; their cousins, the Ofanim, were on hand in their bird form as Garuda to bring the consciousness of the no-Time, eternal realm into the first stages of the Time domain. Saint Patrick didn't slay a dragon at Lough Derg; he activated one, turning the tables,

so to speak, by swallowing (assimilating) the energies of a miniature Great Swallower.

Matters are also confused at Iran's great holy peak, Mount Damavand, an extinct volcano which stands 18,603 feet above the Iranian desert near Tehran. Mount Damavand has many geomantic features: Grail Castle, Cosmic Egg, Soma Temple, Golden Apple, Dragon, Lucifer Binding Site, and Naga City. Regarding the last two, Persian myth has unfortunately blended their aspects together.

A demonic three-headed being, variously called Bevarasp, Azidahaka, Azdahak, Dahak, and Zahak, is forcibly chained and bound to the rocks on the top of Mount Damavand as punishment. The culture hero who chained Zahak is called, variously, Faridu, Fredun, Faridun, or Thraetona. Zahak will remain there exposed to the harsh sunlight until the end of time. This is obviously a code story for a Lucifer Binding Site, but it is potentially easy to mistake it for a Naga City, especially as there is one at the same place.

You have to come in the back door on the Bevarasp story to discern the Naga City, but there are three giveaway clues. First, there is the Simurgh, the Bird of Marvel in Persian myth which built its nest of ebony and sandalwood on Mount Damavand in the earliest days of creation when the mountain's peak touched the stars and had never been visited by humans. The Simurgh perched in the limbs of the *haoma* tree, the Persian equivalent of Soma (see the next chapter). The Persian myth recounts the Simurgh, but this is actually Garuda who is the Ofanim in one of their guises.

The Angel Sraosha (the Archangel Michael) resides on the summit of the mountain of mystic initiation, Alburz (another very old name for Mount Damavand). Sraosha is in charge of initiation, takes the souls of the dead to Paradise, and is the staunch supporter of Ahura-Mazda, the prime Persian Sun-god (their Vishnu-Christ equivalent). Sraosha helps the faithful destroy demons and their father, the destructive spirit called Ahriman who promotes lies, by instilling in his charges obedience to the divine word.

A sword is involved, only it's a *gurz*. Thraetona, the designated dragon slayer, wields a cow-headed mace called a *gurz* to overcome Dahak. Here's where the attributions about Lucifer Binding Site and Naga City are muddled. If you're Indra or Thraetona, you don't use a *vajra* or *gurz* against Lucifer—you chain him to the rocks—but you do use it to activate a dragon.

The presence of a Naga City and a dragon at Mount Damavand is implied by these three clues, but the dragon is not named. I propose that its name was Ladon, the dragon made famous by Herakles' eleventh labor, collecting a golden apple from the Garden of the Hesperides. The perpetually watchful Ladon lay coiled around the golden apple tree as its guardian. He had one hundred heads and spoke many languages.

Herakles (another guise of Merlin, one of Earth's prime geomancers who did most of his work long before the advent of humanity here) gained his three golden apples by subterfuge. He offered to hold the world on his shoulders for a few moments while Atlas fetched the apples for him. Meanwhile Herakles "killed" Ladon with an arrow then gave the world back to Atlas and left the Hesperides. Only a Ray Master or a free-agent geomancer such as Herakles-Merlin could activate one of the 13 original planetary dragons. At Mount Damavand, then, you have a Naga City and its original context, one of the 13 major dragons.

Our third example of a Naga City is set at the base of Tibet's monumental holy peak, Mount Kailash, which towers 22,028 feet in the southern Trans-Himalayan Range 800 miles northwest of Lhasa. About 20 miles from the base of Kailash is Lake Manasarovar, said to have been created by Brahma as an extension of his Immense Mind. Its name means Lake of Manas (Mind).

Brahma created the lake as a place where his holy sons could cleanse themselves after venerating Shiva and his consort Parvati on Kailash. The lake, which sits at 14,950 feet and is 200 square miles in surface area, is also known as *Tso Mapham*, "The Undefeated" or "The Lake of the Invincible Forces of the Buddhas or Victors." Next to it is another lake called *Rakshas Tal*, the "Lake of the Flesh-Eating Demons [Raksasas]" and *Langag Tso*, which means "Lake of the Dark Deities." Other mythic allegations suggest that the two lakes may once have been connected, if not the same lake, thus separating into two opposed realms qualities that were once singular.

Textual evidence for a Naga City here comes from a Hindu legend that the King of the Nagas resided in the lake and that the Nagas sustained themselves with the fruit of the huge jambu tree that grew in the lake's center. The jambu tree's fruit is the source of a life-giving elixir; the fruit exudes gold drops that infuse the entire lake, transmuting it into an elixir of immortality. This part of the world was anciently known to myth as Jambudvipa, or "Rose-apple Tree Land."

Geomythically speaking, at Lake Manasarovar we have the Tree of Life rooted in the Lake of Supreme Consciousness. This is geomythic code for a dragon, a Naga City, and a Soma City. The Tantric texts on the Goddess Kundalini say that she lies coiled about the Merudanda and receives the stream of ambrosia from the Moon chakra above, also known as Soma, the drink of immortality. Soma is the subject of the next chapter, but for here we can say it is the substance or source of unbroken, immortal consciousness, and we could rightfully characterize a Soma Temple as a Lake of Supreme Consciousness.

Insofar as there is also one of the 1,053 minor dragons at Lake Manasarovar, we have an elegant and balanced geomantic setup: a dragon enjoying drops of liquid immortality from a Soma Temple surrounded by its rightful courtiers within the

Naga City, continuously emanating the exalted consciousness of the Seventh Heaven into the lake.

The most confusing thing about the Nagas is their description as Snakes. The *Mahabharata* calls these beings Snakes, but most of the characteristics attributed to the Nagas do not correspond to snakes or serpents literally, but only analogically, in that they are undulatory.

The Nagas appear (to me) as beings with human or angelic heads, a complex crown apparatus, and a snakelike torso that undulates as if a current runs through it. The Nagas are surrounded by a bubble of pale gold. As the current wriggles up the torso, it illuminates the head then radiates out through the bubble, brightening it. The bubble, in fact, has layers and is the radiational field for the 49 aspects of the awakened dragon egg. In effect, the Nagas are the awakened, enlivened 33 trillion dragon eggs floating like undulatory bubbles in the Sea of Consciousness surrounding Sesa-Ananta who is like a vast island of total, unbroken, endless awareness. On a cosmic level, the dragon eggs (Nagas) are seeds of the myriads of stars; on a human body level, they are seeds of cells.

The Nagas are the germs of awakening awareness, the larval stage of star gods. They are the archetype of the awakened 50-part dragon egg of awareness.

Another intriguing nuance to the ever-moving aspect of the Nagas is to be found within the body's esoteric physiology, as described by yoga. The root chakra is the source of a minimum of 72,000 *nadis*; some texts say 300,000 and even 350,000. These tiny conduits or fine streams for prana or basic life force that flows from the *Muladhara* chakra permeate the body like veins in a leaf.

"Could we see them, the body would present the appearance of those maps which delineate the various ocean currents."[167] The term *Muladhara* is apt: It is the root (*Mula*) of the *nadi* network and the support (*Adhara*) of the chakras, and as the kundalini center, it is a "blind spring" that modifies energies passing through it and "a fountain of formidable and diversified streams of power."[168]

The word *nadi* derives from the root, *nad*, which means motion, so we could reasonably say the *nadis* are an active expression of the ever-moving ones, the Nagas, out of which and through which the life principle—the yogic texts call it the solar and lunar currents—moves throughout the body (and universe and planet). The *nadis* (Nagas) facilitate the movement of the cosmic serpent's essence (kundalini) from the Ocean of Milk out into the world (the chakras).

The Bodily Truth of Why the Cosmic Dragon Swallows Its Own Tail

Garuda in Hindu myth is said to be the Eater of Snakes. I asked the Ofanim about this. They had already told me one of their manifestations was as Garuda, the fabulous bird. Picture Garuda as a living pointillist painting, a vast bird of light composed of 40.3 million angels or miniature birds just like itself. Garuda is the Eater of Snakes because "Garuda swallows awareness as humans awaken. Garuda's function is to eat awareness. The awakening of that awareness is the snake."

Sesa's tail is in his mouth: That's the meaning of oroboros—the end is in the beginning. The Norse myths about the Midgard Serpent tell us this graphically in their version of Sesa. The great god Odin (equivalent to Brahma) cast the Midgard Serpent into the "deep sea which surrounds the whole world, and it grew so large that it now lies in the middle of the ocean round the earth, biting its own tail," wrote Snorri Sturluson in his twelfth-century *Prose Edda*.[169]

Let's see where this myth of Sesa-Ananta sits in the body. If you would, stand up and gently bend forward as far as you can towards your knees. Don't strain, but see how far you can bring your head down to your knees. People who practice hatha yoga a lot can probably do this. As far as you get, without straining, visualize your body going the rest of the way so that your head is between your knees. The knees, however, aren't the focus here. Your groin is. Essentially, in this posture you have the top of your head close to the base of your spine. You have made an oroboric loop of your physical body.

The crown chakra, called *Sahasrara* (Thousand-petaled) which sits on and just above the top of your head, is said to have 1,000 petals or vibrational wings. The root chakra, called *Muladhara* (Foundation), occupies your anal area to the base of the spine; it has four petals, its primary iconographic shape is a square, and it represents the element of earth.

"This foundation chakra is the root of all growth and awareness of the divinity of man," and of course it is the "home" of the Goddess Kundalini, expressed as a coiled serpent. When the kundalini energy rises from the root to the crown (the goal of yoga), "the illusion of 'individual self' is dissolved" and the yogi becomes "one with the cosmic principles that govern the entire universe within the body."[170]

In the Vedic image of Sesa-Ananta as a cosmic serpent with 1,000 heads, we have the oroboric meeting of the crown chakra of 1,000 petals and the root chakra.

It's not comfortable for most of us to bend over with our head between our knees and thus put our crown chakra in proximity to our root center, nor is it practical as erect-standing humans. However, this is the bodily truth of the myth. The crown and root chakra are sundered parts of an original unity in which cosmic serpent and innumerable Nagas intermingle as part of *one*

expression. The foundation and the crown are meant to be in the same place, that is, given the nature of the human body, energetically connected—nested.

And Garuda? As you bend over, become aware of a spot just above your belly button. Become aware of a tiny pinprick of blazing light at that spot. That's Garuda—the Ofanim—in his primary manifestation as a pinpoint of brilliant light. That's Garuda in his preflight form, even in his pre-Wheel, pre-angelic expression. But think about it: More or less, Garuda as the Blazing Star is in about the center of this oroboric loop. The idea of proximity I'm trying to convey will be more apparent when we look at how this myth sits in the planetary body.

This next image is hard to describe in writing, and it involves some elements of the Earth's visionary geography that won't be explained fully until later in this or subsequent chapters.

Picture the Earth as the familiar blue-white planet hanging beautifully in space. On one "side" of this sphere is a point of brilliant light, a Blazing Star, just as we have at our midriff. This planetary site is a 28-acre stone circle in Wiltshire, England, called Avebury. This is where the Ofanim live in the planet, where they buried their light in Earth. Think of this as Garuda's nest on Earth.

At another site directly on the other "side" of the planet are the head and tail of the Midgard Serpent as it encircles the globe. This is off the southeastern coast of New Zealand (South Island) at a seemingly mythic (and physically invisible) location called Mount Meru, the archetypal cosmic mountain and home of the 33 million Hindu gods. Here the crown and root meet oroborically: Sesa-Ananta's 1,000 heads and the innumerable Nagas, like two clasped hands. The crown has swallowed the tail so that the tail is inside the serpent's head, effectively putting both ends in the same place.

Now pretend that the planet is transparent like glass and that from a position in space you can look through either of these sites straight through to the other. I say "straight through" for these two sites are directly aligned, on an implicit axis. Looking in either direction, you will see the point of light at the center of Sesa at Mount Meru.

You will see the Ofanim's planetary point of brilliant light at Avebury at the center of the great wheel of Sesa-Ananta and the innumerable Nagas. This is Garuda eating, attacking, devouring the Snakes; this is Garuda nested within Sesa-Ananta. Even better, this is Garuda, Wings of Speech, as fleet as light, as fast as thought, and free beyond time, moving in and out of the oroboric connection of crown and root, fertilizing the cosmic serpent with the wisdom of the Vedas.

The presence of the Ofanim as a Blazing Star amidst the spherically coiled rings of Sesa-Ananta explains one of the minor intriguing mysteries of dragons—why dragons sometimes are seen to possess diamonds or pearls: It's a Star.

Jewels of Michael—Meeting Places for the Archangel Michael above Holy Sites

Earlier we encountered the Angel Sraosha on the summit of the mountain of mystic initiation. The Archangel Michael, who is centrally concerned with Earth site activations and the infusion of Christ Consciousness on Earth, has his own dedicated site called a Jewel of Michael, of which there are 24,441 on Earth.

You will typically find this feature at a holy site already noted for an appearance, either one time or

Table 4-3: Jewels of Michael
Planetary Total: 24,441
Selected Locations:
The Tor, Glastonbury, England
Mont-Saint-Michel, France
Wu-Ta'i Shan, China
Other Names for the Jewel:
Michaelion
Other Names for Michael:
Manjusri (Buddhist)

recurring, of the Archangel Michael. Bear in mind, not all cultures acknowledge him in this guise so you need to be sensitive to cultural nuances of description. To Buddhists, he is Manjusri. Like the Grail Castle, the Jewel is above the physical aspects of the site, which is often a mountain (see table 4-3 for a listing of some sites).

At Mont-Saint-Michel, in France, for example, the Jewel of Michael appears several hundred yards above the Mount summit. Archangel Michael appears to be standing on the summit, towering hundreds of feet high, holding in his hands a crystal that is both white and green. Inside, it may appear as a circular room of blazing white light with dozens of crystalline pillars along the periphery, overlit in green. Alternatively, you could say you are inside a dome made of Michael's celestial form; this dome or globe narrows at the base to form an eye that surveys the world below. We could think of the Jewel of Michael as a portable Seventh Heaven, as Michael's Arabot (Seventh Heaven) miniaturized and edited for travel.

This is a meeting place for humans with Michael, and a kind of higher sanctuary of Grail Knights (spiritual aspirants he is tutoring). The Jewel is a means for Michael's epiphany in our world, for the regular downflow of his energy into our midst. Insofar as Michael is the chief of all 18 archangels for the next 123 years (his 268-year reign began in 1879) with respect to Earth evolution and the planet's visionary terrain and all other galactic matters, too, access to a Jewel of Michael could afford one a valuable immersion in aspects of what Rudolf Steiner called Michaelic cosmic intelligence and the Michaelic initiation.

Michael is also involved with the grounding of the Mystery of Golgotha, the transmission of the Christ experience to human conscious evolution, so anyone desiring to deepen that long-term initiation experience can benefit here.

As the Ofanim note, "The Archangel Michael is the vehicle through which the integration of the major streams of spiritual energy come to Earth at this point in time. They come from the Buddha and the Christ to bring the Cosmic Christ to the Earth. In this work, we are the direct means through which the facilitation of the awareness of the Christ could happen in this time."

5 Lustrous Soma
The Moon God's Immortality of Consciousness

I start this chapter with two Hindu myths about Soma, the substance of immortality, the life-sustaining nectar of the legendary Fountain of Youth.

The gods wanted the elixir of immortality, or Soma, and realized they would have to churn the Ocean of Milk to get it. With the help of Sesa-Ananta, they uprooted the vast celestial mountain called Mandara and used it as the churning staff. They got Akupara, King of the Tortoises, to lend his thick back to be the foundation for the churning stick, although the myths also say the tortoise was Vishnu in his second major descent or incarnation as Kurma in the earliest days of the world. And they enlisted the Snake Vasuki to be the twirling rope for the churning stick, although other myths say Vasuki was another name for Sesa.

What was the Ocean of Milk? The "treasury of the waters," the *Mahabharata* says, the cosmic sea (of Light) upon which Sesa-Ananta had floated for eons and, as it turned out, now the repository of some 15 precious objects, deities, and beings needed for the next stages of world creation.

While Mount Mandara was being driven around, churning the Ocean, all the trees and plants on its slopes tumbled into the Ocean. They caught fire and flamed terrifically. The copious juices and resins from all this burning plant mat-ter flowed into the water. "And with the milk of these juices that had the power of the Elixir, and with the exudation of the molten gold, the Gods attained immortality."[171] All drank their fill of the precious *amrita*, Soma, or nectar of immortality.

Now that they had the Soma, the gods wanted to keep it from Svarbhanu, a giant dragon, probably yet another form of Sesa-Ananta. The *Mahabharata* says a Danava called Rahu took the guise of a god and began to consume the Soma. Just as the Soma had reached Rahu's throat, Vishnu cut off his diademed head, using his magnificent *Sudarsana,* or golden discus. Ever after, there was a dreadful feud between Rahu and the Sun and Moon, as a result of which Rahu regularly swallows them both (astronomically in the form of the monthly new moon and lunar and solar eclipses).

Another version of the story says that the gods cut Svarbhanu (also called "Radiance of Soma") in two; his head was called Rahu and his tail was called Ketu. In Vedic astrology these became known as the North (or ascending) and South (or descending) Nodes of the Moon.[172] Ketu, who drives a chariot with eight green horses, is understood to be the tail of the original whole cosmic serpent who at a higher level is still intact. "Outwardly they began to function as Rahu and Ketu, but together they continued to represent the great cyclic law of manifestation that sustains the universe."[173] So Svarbhanu, the whole cosmic dragon, gets cut in two and becomes two beings, Rahu, the Dragon's Head, and Ketu, the Dragon's Tail. Neither got any of the Soma because the gods prevented it.

Here's the second myth about Soma: The time is the moment just before the universe was created. Two figures appear, the Father, Prajapati, and his virgin daughter. Prajapati, an active aspect of Brahma, is the lord of procreation and propagation, sacrificially creating all living creatures out of his own essence. The first living creatures he formed were the 33 principal Hindu gods, although these are also construed as Prajapati's 33 daughters.

The Father starts making love to his daughter, then stops, withdraws, because somebody has shot an arrow into him. It is Rudra, the Wild Archer, later known as Shiva. A little of the Father's seed dribbles down to Earth to a place known as the *vastu,* the place of sacrifice. The place is also called the Lake of Sperm, the Lake of Prajapati's Seed, and the Lake of Fire. Rudra-Shiva becomes *Vastospati,* the guardian of this dwelling and the sacred order, the house of stars, which is mythic code for saying the entire cosmos and its myriad stars.

Bear in mind, this is a big myth, a story about the cosmogony; it's not about sex or rape or any other physical details. Rudra was defending the integrity of the Uncreate, the original homogeneous, unitive totality before it got differentiated into created forms, gods, and realms. The Uncreate was the Absolute, the unruptured, self-contained, "pre-existential" wholeness, the "pre-conscious totality," the state inaccessible to the senses beyond words, neither being nor nonbeing—"the transcendental integrity before the beginning of things."[174] Rudra was trying to *stop* Prajapati from rupturing this unitive state, and he

almost did, but some of Prajapati's semen fell to Earth and formed the *vastu* or cosmic dwelling for all the stars.

Let's look more closely at the players. It turns out this is a star myth. Rudra is the star Sirius, located in the neck of Canis Major, the Greater Dog. The Hindus call this constellation *Mrgavyadha,* the Hunter of the Antelope. Prajapati, the father of all creatures and lord of generation, is the constellation *Mrga* (to the ancient Hindus, an antelope) and, to Western astronomers, Orion, the Great Hunter. Prajapati's virgin daughter, Rohini, is Aldebaran, in the eye of the constellation of Taurus the Bull. Rohini as the Bull would be the first container for time-based creation.

To simplify: Rudra (Sirius) fired an arrow at Prajapati (Orion); some of his seed (Soma) leaked out into the *vastu* (cosmos) as a house of stars. The star Sirius became Vastospati, the Guardian of the Dwelling.

Rudra is blamed for the failure to prevent Soma from leaking into the lower worlds. On the other hand, maybe his task was to *allow* Soma to descend from the Uncreate into the realm of Time and contingency, into the great *vastu* of stars. Rudra-Sirius as Vastospati, the guardian, will later be called the Hound of Heaven Canis Major, and his dwelling known as the thousand-gated House of Varuna, Rudra's father. Watcher of the House, he will be perennially on duty.

Inside the Soma Temple with the Immortal Star Gods

Lake of Sperm? Vastu? Prajapati's seed from the Uncreate? King Soma? These seemingly abstract references actually refer to consciousness.

To start with, let's remember that all further developments in creation take place within the primordial Vacated Space, that vast but finite sphere whose diameter perpetually seeks knowledge of its ultimate limit. Second, all further developments, technically, exist *within* Sesa-Ananta. The cosmic dragon is after all the Rainbow Serpent, repository of the entire electromagnetic spectrum of visible light, of all things *seeable* within Earth.

On an anatomical level, when the gods churned the Ocean of Milk, they did so inside Sesa-Ananta's cosmos-sized body, probing the full extent of the space designated for creation, as it were, reaching down through the *Muladhara*, or first chakra used by Brahma and Vishnu, to the inchoate, the second through seventh

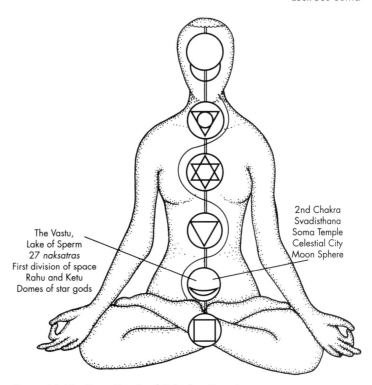

The Vastu,
Lake of Sperm
27 *naksatras*
First division of space
Rahu and Ketu
Domes of star gods

2nd Chakra
Svadisthana
Soma Temple
Celestial City
Moon Sphere

Figure 5-1. The Soma Temple of Unbroken Consciousness

chakras. Those 15 treasuries of the Ocean that they discovered while churning the Ocean of Milk were energy aspects of those next six chakras. Remember, from Brahma's viewpoint, the *Svadisthana*, or second sacral chakra, comes *next* in the cosmogony after the root center is activated, which is to say, after Sesa-Ananta or Vrtra is "slain" and its copious original waters released.

Within the human form, this chakra corresponds to the genitals and procreative function; traditionally, the Moon is indirectly associated with this energy center, as the element assigned to the Svadisthana is water and the Moon rules its tides. This chakra has six vibratory fields or petals surrounding it, each with its own Sanskrit letter and sound. The *Svadisthana* is so named because it is the "dwelling place of the Self."[175] (See figure 5-1.)

We must also remember that this chakra represents the second planetary sphere to be extrap-

olated from the cosmic dragon. This *planetary sphere* is called the Moon, but this does *not* refer to the physical celestial body that we call the Moon. Think of it rather as a dimension of the cosmos, a sphere that bounds a realm of existence and that exists within the larger bounded sphere of the first planetary sphere, that of Sesa-Ananta. We should also keep in mind that it exists in mirrored form, in our own human bodies, as well as in the Earth's landscape.

In Tantric depictions of this energy center, Vishnu, lord of preservation, is shown four-armed, holding a conch shell, his *Sudarsana* discus, a metal club (or mace), and a pink lotus. His consort, Rakini Shakti, is two-headed, representing the split energy in this chakra and the requirement of balancing one's attention on the world within and without. The inside of this chakra is said to be a "white, shining, watery region" in the

Table 5-1: Soma Temples

Planetary Total: 144

Selected Locations:

Barbury Castle, The Ridgeway, Wiltshire, England

Warden Hill, Bag Enderby, Lincolnshire, UK

Lake Manasarovar, Mount Kailash, Tibet

Ur, Iraq

Harran, Syria

Hermopolis, Egypt (Thoth as Moon God)

Afrasiab, Samarkand, Uzbekistan

Banaras, India

Hardwar, India

Allahabad, India

Nasik, India

Ujjain, India

Equivalent Names: Moon Temple; *Ekisnugal* at Ur; Celestial City of Kantimati; Audumla (Norse primeval cow); Prajapati's (Orion) Seed; *Hoama* Tree (Persian); Mead Vat; *amrita;* ambrosia; Fountain of Youth; Nectar of the Gods; Behemoth

shape of an upturned half moon; this watery region is "luminously white."[176] It's the Ocean of Milk, in other words.

Soma, preeminent product of the Ocean of Milk, is said to be the *amrita* or ambrosia stored in the mystic vessel of the Moon out of which the gods drink every month to maintain their immortality. Soma frees one from death; it is the substance of immortality. King Soma, the Moon God, is among the gods he who is *awake*; he is a god who is an edible substance "and hence the most material; he is perfect wakefulness, and hence the most immaterial, the nearest to the elusive flow of consciousness."[177]

Soma is the "eye that watches the multiple expanse of the wakefulness in which it is immersed." Soma is the unbroken continuity of awareness. "Without the soma, nothing in the world could shine, nothing shone in the mind, nothing emanated sense."[178]

As a deity, King Soma is the son of Atri (Detachment), a mind-born son of Brahma the Creator. The Vedas tell us Atri was a holy seer who practiced *tapas* (a special form of fire austerity) for 3,000 divine years until his body turned to Soma, the substance of immortal consciousness. It flowed out of his eyes into the ten directions of cosmic space, illuminating all regions of space with the cool rays of the Moon and impregnating the ten goddesses who supervised those spatial divisions. Thus Atri nourished the world with his own substance (Soma).[179]

The Vastu, Lake of Sperm, and the cosmogony's second chakra or stage has been templated across the planet in the form of Soma Temples. There are 144 of these geomantic structures around the Earth (see table 5-1); the Soma Temple is the third of our eight Celestial Cities. This City is also known as Kantimati, the City of Isana in the Northeast, or Yasovati, and is associated with Isana, an aspect of Rudra-Shiva.

I first visited a Soma Temple at Barbury Castle on the Ridgeway in Wiltshire, England, a few miles from the huge stone circle of Avebury. Barbury Castle has never had a physical structure corresponding to a castle; it is an oval hill-fort, a ditch and ring structure enclosing about 11 acres of flat grassland. It sits on the high ridge overlooking a fair expanse of Wiltshire.

Inside the "Castle" I stand under a domed roof made of apricot-colored squares through which it seems faces are gently pressing as if it were a membrane of thinly stretched skin. This is the "hive of the Immortals," a voice says. Thousands of faces look down from this tortoise-shelled roof, but their features are vaguely defined; it is as if they are looking in from another, rarefied dimension. In a sense, it is like looking up at the geometrically apportioned top shell of a turtle—the Vedic Kurma perhaps.

Before me on the floor of the "Castle" is a small circular pool filled with a bright white liquid. It is thick, gooey, viscous, like liquid astral substance, like ichor, the blood of the gods, or the exudate of the dragon Sesa-Ananta. It is Soma, the divine substance. I sample the Soma and immediately start ascending to the turtle-backed roof where I pass through its glassy membrane into the realm of the Immortals. The Soma is the ticket to that realm, and you get the Soma by going to a Soma Temple.

In this dimension it is as if I have entered a tightly packed space full of multicolored points of light, crystalline, laid close together in a space that resembles a walnut shell yet is larger than the universe. It is as if the space in which these myriad points of colored light exist has been intricately and minutely and *geometrically* apportioned into a grid, like a turtle's back, or the way a jeweler would inlay many gems in a single setting.

As I survey the space, it resembles a large open white sphere studded with jewels. I examine an orange one: "Inside" it is a face or a point of consciousness, a face for a solar logos, the spirit of awareness within a sun. The Soma Temple ceiling is a gallery of sun faces, of stars, but all these star-faces have their eyes on the Soma. They all want a drink, and they eye it hungrily.

My second Soma Temple visit was at Warden Hill, near Tetford in Lincolnshire, England. The Ofanim had requested I visit this Soma Temple on behalf of the blue dragon on Bluestone Heath Road, which was supporting eight stargates (see chapter 11) and was parched from a long-term lack of nourishment. Warden Hill is a lovely but nondescript bare green hill amidst farmland.

The Ofanim said this dragon has a very long tongue that it had extended in search (so far, fruitless) of life-sustaining Soma. The Soma Temple at Warden Hill was in fact only a few miles away, but it required human assistance, in cooperation with the gnomes, to get the Soma to the dragon.

This time I saw an interior temple space with a high rotunda, the star gods peering down from the ceiling, the vat of precious Soma in the center of the floor, and a giant attendant deity towering some several hundred feet and presiding over the Soma Temple. Presumably this is King Soma, the Moon God. The Soma vat sent up many reflections or beams of light to the eyes of the star gods; it was as if their eyes were tongues that lapped up the light. There was a clear sense of adoration; if they had had bodies, the gods would have been prostrate before the Soma, thankful for every drop.

At this point I realized the Vedic myth about the gods preventing Svarbhanu (or its head, Rahu) from drinking the Soma was backwards. The dragon is the sacrificial *source* of the Soma for the gods; Soma is Sesa-Ananta's precious ichor, and the gods depend on it for their continued existence. In fact, Soma is the source of their existence.

If anything, they should be alarmed that the dragon might prevent them from drinking the Soma and thus cause them to lose their immortality and fall asleep to their origin in the Uncreate of Prajapati. For the star gods, the Soma is a taste of the consciousness of unbroken awareness.

They are shown who they are *before* they were individual stars. They adore the substance, those precious drops (Prajapati's seed) from the Pleroma or Uncreate (Orion) allowed to trickle down into their created world. The Soma vat that I described is an expression of the Lake of Fire or Sperm, the *vastu* into which Prajapati's seed of the Uncreate fell after Rudra-Sirius shot him. Think of it as the cosmos before it had any stars in it, a sphere or Ocean of burning light (or milk).

The dragon does not drink the Soma; all it needs is to see its reflection in the mirror of the Soma vat to be reminded that Soma is its own true, original essence. The Soma rays refresh its identity. Soma is the original unbroken state of consciousness, the Uncreate Light, the immortality of consciousness before it dribbled (due to Rudra's arrow) into the differentiation of myriad star gods.

The star gods drink the Soma because it is a profounder state of consciousness. Soma is the dragon's blood. The gods lean over the vat to be bathed in a state of consciousness *prior* to their existence. Sesa-Ananta, denizen of the *Muladhara* root chakra, is *older* than the star gods in the Ocean of Milk in the second (*Svadisthana*) chakra, and *senior* to them.[180]

It may not be entirely obvious, but descriptions of Soma as the Fountain of Youth are metaphysical. They are not unreal, but they pertain not to the physical body, but to consciousness. Soma is the state of consciousness before it ever fell into differentiation. This is long before the differentiation of the Uncreate into individual human selves.

Soma as a state of unbroken, homogeneous consciousness does not and cannot die. It is immortal, and vigorous with the light of a new Day of Brahma. It is also ours for the asking.[181]

You visit a Soma Temple to be reminded of what this state is like. It may, paradoxically, be beyond your ability to digest, but it will start a process by way of resonance whereby the part in you that is Soma will start to awaken and dribble into your waking and dream consciousness, gradually transforming your personality into a miniature lake of fire and *vastu*, the created space for your own inner microcosm.

Soma, King of Space, His 27 Wives, and the Mystery of the 33 Gods

An important marriage takes place in King Soma's Moon sphere. Brahma orchestrated the wedding of Soma to the 27 daughters of Daksa (Ritual Skill).[182] These 27 daughters are called

naksatras and astrologically refer to the 27 asterisms or mansions that Vedic astrology assigns to the Moon. The *naksatras,* says the *Mahabharata,* are the "faithful wives" of the Moon who are "appointed to the procession of Time," and as the lunar mansions they "regulate" the world's life.[183]

The vast 360-degree sphere of the Vacated Space got divided into 27 equal divisions, each 13.333333 degrees wide. (All the sphere's space is not quite accounted for as 27 wives occupying this many degrees comes to 359.99999 degrees.) This 13.33-degree division of space is born out by actual star latitudes as measured by astronomers; the average gap between *naksatras* is 13.33 degrees, while the maximum gap is 22 degrees and the minimum eight degrees.[184]

This is the first division of the Vacated Space into smaller spaces. The Vedic myths say King Soma visits his wives regularly, residing with each for a day, giving us the Vedic sidereal month of 27.32166 days (how long it takes for the physical Moon to circle the physical Earth once).[185] With the marriage of King Soma to the 27 *naksatras* we witness the distribution of unitive consciousness throughout the first divisions of cosmic space.

Who are the *naksatras?* Vedic astrology characterizes them as stars or constellations, each "fronting" a 13.33-degree division of cosmic space, like the head of a large family, and forming the basis of the lunar zodiac. Rohini, Prajapati's virgin daughter, identified with Aldebaran above, the Eye of Taurus, is a *naksatra. Krrtika,* the Vedic name for the constellation Pleiades in Taurus or its brightest star, Alcyone, is another. *Mrgasiras* (or simply *Mrga,* "Deer's Head") is a third, which in Vedic astronomy (confusingly) is *Al Nath,* a star in Taurus, although in the Soma myth it is the constellation Orion, Prajapati's body.

Even though the 27 *naksatras* are the basis of the 27-day Vedic lunar month, we must not think of them in terms of time. They are purely a *spatial* division of the Vacated Space; each is one twenty-seventh of the whole. The 27 *naksatras* represent the fundamental *division* of the sphere (Ocean of Milk) into spatial units. Each *naksatra* is married to King Soma, which means each partakes of Soma's essence—unbroken, immortal consciousness. But it's more than a marriage. In the cosmogony, the *naksatras* are the first 27 stars *born* of the dribbling of Soma into the Vacated Space.

The *naksatras* are the star gods on the inside roof of the Soma Temple. They are the first to drink of an essence that predates their own existence; or we could say they are the first 27 celestial beings who are both differentiated into different forms (the physical stars being their outer forms) *and* still participate in the sublime unitive state of continuous, unsundered, undying consciousness. As "wives" to King Soma, Lord of Constellations, we could see the *naksatras* as the *mothers* of all the constellations and stars yet to appear in the total space allotted to Soma.

We might think of them as Regents of Space, space holders for the myriad star gods that later would fill out the 27 wedges, taking their predesignated spot in this vast but finite star grid. All 27 faces contemplate King Soma from the periphery into the center of the sphere of space, or it is one face with 27 expressions. Vishnu's consort Sri emerged out of the Ocean of Milk as the beautiful white goddess of a multiplicity of forms in Time. We could think of the 27 *naksatras* as 27 aspects of Sri.

The intriguing question to ask is why 27 and not some other number? One possible answer is so the mathematical function of *e,* logarithmic expansion, could be possible, for $e = 2.71828182845908. \ldots$, which is rounded off to 2.72. The number is irrational, which means it has no calculable end and is shown by a nonterminating and nonrepeating decimal. The number is a mathematical constant, the natural base of logarithms ("ratio numbers").[186]

The number *e,* known as Napier's Constant, governs logarithmic expansion of growth—the exponential expansion of an additive series towards infinity. The figure expresses the *limit* in a sequence of numbers, specifically $(1 + 1/n)n$th power as n tends to approach infinity. In fact, the essence of *e* is that it defines the limit process, and mathematical analysis has confirmed that "no matter how large n is, the values of $(1 + 1/n)n$th power will settle somewhere around the number 2.71828."[187]

Philosophically, we could say the number *e,* as the expression of the limit process to the expansion of a series of numbers, represents the limits of Sri's powers of multiplicity within the galaxy. Sri or Laksmi is She-of-the-Hundred-Thousands, meaning she has the power of multiplicity, of producing myriad heads or *spaces* for heads, which we could translate as meaning preassigned points for star gods as differentiated aspects of unitive consciousness.

The existence of *e* as the limit process of logarithmic expansion answers a simple question: How *big* and multilayered can the galaxy get and still be viable? In what *increments* can it multiply itself and still be congruent and integrated?

On a terrestrial level, *e* appears to have a fundamental role in the measurements of key geomantic structures such as domes (discussed below), zodiacs (see chapter 9), and stone circles (chapter 10). Their sizes were originally given in terms of *e* by way of a different name: the megalithic yard (MY), discovered and demonstrated by English archeoastronomer Alexander Thom in the 1970s in his study of 200 stone circles in the British Isles and France. He calculated the megalithic yard to be 2.720 feet +/- 0.003 feet.[188]

Let's combine some images now. We may think of the 27 *naksatras* as the first divisions of primal space into wedge-shaped allotments, each inundated with Soma. The *naksatras* are the first expression of Sri's power of multiplicity: first one (as Sri-Laksmi), then 27 (as *naksatras*); this expansion is ruled by and *is* the mathematical constant *e*, the base of natural logarithms. In other words, e = Sri's powers of multiplicity and regulates or limits it. The *naksatras* are a personification of *e*, but by this I don't mean in any way to detract from their reality. As Regents of Space they *are* the mathematical function *e* in action. Thus in the Vacated Space a mathematical *function* is now incarnate and active.

What is the biggest number they can expand into galactically? Recall that in chapter 4, I presented the number of fourth-level dragon eggs as 33 trillion. The actual number, based on 49 times 49 to the seventh power, is 33,232,930,569,601. That number refers to individual dragon eggs on the planet Earth allotted to individual humans and other creatures of high sentience in or out of bodies. That's the *below* number, for Earth; but what does the *above* number refer to?

Let's focus on the number 33 for a moment. We already see it in the division of 360 degrees by 27, which yields 13.333333. We see it again in the gematria (number decodement of Hebrew letters) of *Galgal* (GLGL), the Hebrew for "sphere," which is 3333. *Galgal*, to review our chapter 4 references, is the circle of the 231 Gates of the dragon, the womb of Binah, the cycle of Time. There is also (mentioned earlier) the fact of Prajapati's 33 daughters as presented to Soma. In Western esoterica, we find the number 33 embedded in the Magic Square of the Moon, a number table based on the number nine for the Moon; it includes 81 numbers in nine rows, each line totaling 369, and the entire square being *3321*.

In Vedic lore, we see it in reference to the 33 Gods. It is thus the number of the gods, although this number gets exponentially expanded to 330,000,000 and is understood to be the number of all possible aspects of manifestation. The sacred circle of all the gods, the complete pantheon, comprised 330 million deities, the Vedas said. The *Mahabharata* also cites the number of gods as 36,333, based on the somewhat odd yet precise formula of 33,000, 3300, and 33. So clearly, 33 is a number worth keeping an eye on.

Returning to the 33 trillion dragon eggs, on the galactic level or even the level of the cosmogonic archetype that templates galaxies of this type, let's postulate the eggs are star eggs, to put it metaphorically. On the Earth, the intent is for each of us to work with at least one dragon egg and assimilate its 49 aspects, completing the egg and embodying all its aspects as the fiftieth. We hatch ourselves and emerge as a star-infused radiant human.

On a galactic level, let's construe 33 trillion dragon eggs along similar lines, opportunities for celestial beings to hatch themselves and emerge, literally, as stars in the galaxy. Think of the physical aspects of stars as we think we know them as the radiant aura of sublime celestial beings—star gods, the 33, 330 million, or 33 trillion, depending on which number we credit with accuracy. It's possible that the Vedic 330 million is in error, having perhaps been distorted over time, and the correct number is 33 trillion, which was provided recently by the Ofanim in reference to the number of terrestrial dragon eggs.

If so, then we have 33 trillion egg slots within the star grid created by the division of the 360 degrees into 27 *naksatra* wedges. That puts 1.2 trillion (1,230,849,280,355.5925) cosmic dragon eggs or star gods into each of the 27 wedges in space over which a *naksatra* or primary star presides. So we have potentially 33 trillion slots within the finite vastness of the Soma-inundated Vacated Space for differentiated star gods, each a hatched cosmic dragon egg.

This plenitude of star beings would constitute the Ocean of Milk, an almost blinding sea of starlight, with stars packed in so close that it would be sheer uniform light.

Gandharvas, Apsaras, and the Emergence of the Celestial and Earthly Domes

Krsanu, the Vedas tell us, was the chief Gandharva, the archer who shot Prajapati, and guardian of Soma. It's the Rudra-Shiva story again, with a twist: Krsanu is a Gandharva, a different order of being. Krsanu and his Gandharvas then protected the elixir of immortality and inspiration from misuse, misappropriation, or squandering. Their abode is beyond the star gods and precedes their creation; they guard the state *between* the Uncreate and creation.

Let's say this means they guard the *lines* of connection that link the created, differentiated stars and their source, Soma, the elixir of unbroken, unitive, deathless consciousness. The Gandharvas protect the "borderland between the state of integrity as it was before creation and its loss in creation."[189]

The term *Gandharva* means "the macrocosm, 'the primeval universal life-force enveloped in the cosmic shell.'" They revealed the secrets of Heaven, including the method of preparing the Soma, and the divine Truth to the rest of creation, and they are connected with Vac, the goddess of speech.[190] Gandharvas are the celestial harmonies, skilled in dance, instrumental music, song, and in keeping musical time. Myths show them as musicians and singers, playing the *vina*, and as teachers of musical knowledge.[191]

Radiant beings, angels of song, the Gandharvas sing sweetly on the holy mountains (Meru, Mandara, Gandhamadana, and others), feed on the fragrances of herbs, may appear with horses' heads as the Kimnaras (celestial musicians), and play delightful music for their wives, the celestial nymphs called Apsaras.

The Apsaras are singers and dancers, manifested during the churning of the Ocean of Milk. Their collective name means "essence of the waters," "moving in the waters or between the waters," or "water stream." Apsara also comes from *apsu rasa*, which means "the essence of the ocean-water produced at the churning." It may yet also derive from *ap-saras*, to denote water spirits, aqueous women, and celestial nymphs, the feminine counterpart to the Gandharvas, the celestial men, who are together the "husband of the waters."[192]

Colloquially, the Apsaras are referred to as "gods' girls," as they delight and enchant the entire pantheon of gods, but they are also called "Indra's girls," as troops of them accompany the chief god.[193] Like the Gandharvas, they appear to have sprung from Vac; their chief is sometimes named as Urvasi or Rambha, a water nymph of unsurpassed beauty.[194] They are overloaded with gems, garlands, necklaces, golden girdles, and anklets, which "tinkle as they welcome saints to heaven" with their music of *vina, vallaki, muraja*, and bells.[195] The Vedas say that 60 *crores* of Apsaras originally appeared during the churning of the Ocean of Milk. That's 600 million Apsaras.[196]

Gandharvas and Apsaras are the key to what happens to the 33 trillion cosmic dragon eggs. The thing that happens to them *up there* also happens *down here*. The Gandharvas and Apsaras sing and dance the star gods into being.

Let's recall from the previous chapter that the seven planetary spheres and their vibratory petals arise in a column out of Sesa-Ananta. This sequence of petals is actually a series of mantric syllables expressed as the Sanskrit alphabet; these surround or perhaps create the chakras. There are 48 vibratory petals or sustaining energy fields around the first five chakras and a final two from the sixth chakra, giving us a column of 50 mantric vibrations.

The cosmic dragon eggs get organized similarly. Clusters of 48 array themselves in a precisely defined geometric pattern based on the

Golden Mean (phi) and, surprisingly, resemble the head of a mature sunflower.[197]

In the sunflower, you can trace out spiral lines in between the petals, and 21 of these spin to the right, and 34 to the left, generating a dynamic phi-based pattern of 55 spirals. The numbers 21, 34, and 55 are part of the Fibonacci sequence of Golden Mean progression numbers. The petals are thus placed in reference to the spiral lines. In the creation of stars, which for now let's think of as the galactic version of the sunflower petals, seven spirals are taken away, to leave 48. There are also only 48 spiral lines linking all the petals, or in this case, dragon eggs. The number 48 is not a Fibonacci sequence number, but, as mentioned, it is a key number in the chakra sequence. It's as if the creator gods wanted to have the best of two fundamental design principles.

In terms of our metaphor, let's think of the 48 petals made of 48 cosmic dragon eggs as the Apsaras, dancing gracefully to the music of the Gandharvas. Some Apsaras turn to the right, others spin to the left—it is a whirling dance. Let's remember Rahu and Ketu, the head and tail of the bifurcated Svarbhanu, the dragon the gods sliced in two. Rahu and Ketu represent the introduction of the fundamental dichotomy in creation, the principle of polarity, phi in motion.

Again, metaphorically, we could say in our galactic sunflower image, 21 lines spin right and 34 spin left to match the dynamics of Rahu and Ketu, but since this is the mirror image of the planetary sunflower, we have to reverse the numbers: 21 lines spin left (for Ketu, the tail) and 34 spin right (Rahu, the head). In other words, the polarized nature of Svarbhanu, cut into a head, Rahu, and tail, Ketu, now determines the nature of all phenomena in this and all subsequent lower realms. They shall be polarized, twofold, dichotomous, left and right.[198]

In the human body version of this original template, we find this polarized condition in the way two of the three primary energy circuits criss-cross through the chakras on their way up the chakra column from root to brow. These are the *ida* and *pingala* energy channels that intertwine like snakes up the central energy channel parallel to the spine.

In this polarity, *ida* carries the Moon current, *pingala* the Sun; they pass through each of the first five chakras, imparting this basic duality to the energy centers. In this human cosmophysiology, *pingala* the Sun starts its rise on the left, *ida* the Moon on the right of the *Muladhara*, root center. After rising and intertwining through five chakras, they meet and blend in the sixth chakra. On the way "up," they sound the 48 petals or mantric syllables that surround the chakras so that the journey is like a mantra recitation, a song, if you like, with 48 voices.

When the 48 syllables sound—remember here they are 48 dragon eggs—they generate a dynamic, living pattern, a sonogram based on the Golden Mean, as the Apsaras dance to the left and right in accordance with Rahu and Ketu. When they reach the brow chakra, or the forty-ninth mantric sound, the pattern nears completion. Rahu and Ketu themselves join the dance, completing it at 50, in the brow center.

Thus the two archetypes of the dualistic nature of the Apsaras' dance join the dance themselves and complete the pattern—a dynamic, Golden Mean–based totality. A completed, hatched, awakened, and quickened cosmic dragon egg pulsating, radiant with all 50 parts alive. The Apsaras have birthed a star.

This concept is difficult to get across in its galactic level of expression. Let's switch to how it manifests in the Earth's visionary terrain.

Across the surface of the Earth is a network of energy enclosures resembling half-globes. These range in size from a few to dozens of miles in diameter and, being half-circles, naturally, they are correspondingly high. They are variously colored, though mainly translucent shades of gold, orange, and lilac, and they appear to throb with radiant energy. They are mostly situated over mountains, especially old and new volcanos, and resemble halos.[199] (See table 5-2 for a partial listing.)

Here's the key point: Most of the planet's sacred sites, and certainly all its holy mountains, are created and sustained by domes and their subsidiary dome caps.

Each dome emits particular patterns of dome energy to other domes in the form of straight energy lines. In effect, all 1,746 domes are connected in a web of straight-running, oscillating dome lines. These patterns, and the locations of the domes, were predetermined before the domes arrived on Earth so that they settled down onto their assigned places in this planetary dome matrix. The dome lines are pulsating lines of energy that oscillate in intensity at various times during the calendar year.

Each of these energy globes has a subsidiary network of smaller energy globes connected to the central globe by spiral lines of light. The central energy globes are connected one to the other by straight lines of light. Of the primary energy globes (domes), there are 1,746 across the Earth; of the subsidiary globes (dome caps), 83,808. (Each of the 1,746 globes can generate up to 48 subsidiary ones.)[200] Nearly every place on Earth is within reasonable distance of one of these energy canopies. Seen from above, the Earth's skin seems to be pockmarked with hundreds of complex sunflower heads of light.

The domes, both the major and the subsidiary energy canopies (dome caps), are largely what make planetary sites sacred, charged, numinous—and once universally regarded as the homes of the gods on Earth. Originally, all the domes measured 33 miles in diameter, though now they tend to be smaller; dome cap diameters vary from one-half mile to nine miles.

The domes correspond to, and energetically

represent, the 1,746 brightest stars in our galaxy, those most relevant to *our* style of human conscious evolution *here*. By style, I mean the parameters for the evolution of consciousness within human bodies set for *this* planet back in the Blue Room.

On a practical level, this means you can encounter domes (and interact with them) for the major, high magnitude, and mythically loaded stars such as Sirius, Canopus, Arcturus, Pleiades, Aldebaran, Vega, Capella, Alpha Centauri, Regulus, Antares, and many others. Even more exciting for the mystically minded, you can have visitations with the star gods through these domes over mountains.

Take Orion, the constellation of the Hunter in Western star myths, and Prajapati, Lord of Progeny, in Vedic star lore. Go to Mount Palomar, in Southern California, near San Diego, and you can sit inside the dome for Alnilam (from *Al Nitham,* for "String of Pearls"), epsilon Orionis, the middle star in the Belt.

Surveying the vista in 360 degrees from this peak, know that 48 smaller peaks, hills, and other locations are canopied with a dome cap anywhere from 900 yards to nine miles wide. If you were sitting at one of these dome caps, you could psychically find your way back by the energy lines to Mount Palomar, the host and mother dome. It's as if you are sitting in the center of a vast landscape sunflower of light, made of 48 radiant spheres connected to a central very brilliant and larger one. In many respects, the 48 plus one is the entire dome.

Imagine you were observing our Earth from space, far enough away so as to see the planet as a blue-white globe as in the NASA photos. Imagine the planet is transparent. Sparkling all over its surface are 1,746 lights. By a trick of your eyes or a different way of looking, you find many of these points of light are connected and form images: Orion, the Great Hunter; Ursa Major, the

Table 5-2: Domes

Planetary Total: 1,746

Selected Locations:

Machu Picchu, Peru

Montserrat, Spain

Mount Bugarach-Rennes-le-Chateau, France

Dome of the Rock, Jerusalem, Israel

Mount Ida, Crete, Greece

Easter Island, Chile

Montsegur, France

Cathedral Rock, Sedona, Arizona, U.S.

Banaras, India

Bayreuth, Germany

Mount Vesuvius, Naples, Italy

Mycenae, Greece

Troy, Turkey

Mount Vesuvius, Naples, Italy

Tenochtitlan, Mexico City, Mexico

Chalice Hill, Glastonbury, England

Dornach, Switzerland

Afrasiab, Samarkand, Uzbekistan

Acropolis, Athens, Greece

Iona Island, Scotland

Santiago de Compostela, Spain

Grand Jer Mountain-Lourdes, France

Externsteine/Grotenburg, Detmold, Germany

Mount Haleakala, Maui, Hawaii, U.S.

Wawel Hill, Cracow, Poland

Jasna Gora, Czestochowa, Poland

Wilson Mountain, Sedona, Arizona, U.S.

Wu Tai Shan, China

Mount Fuji, Japan

Abydos, Egypt

Mont-Royal, Montreal, Quebec, Canada

Schnebly Hill, Sedona, Arizona, U.S.

Cerro Gordo, Teotihuacan, Mexico

Beckery, Glastonbury, England

Mount Kailash, Tibet

Chichen Itza, Mexico

Mount Etna, Sicily, Italy

Hardwar, India

Mount Temahani, Raiatea, Society Islands

Boynton Canyon, Sedona, Arizona, U.S.

Mount Damavand, Iran

Uluru, Alice Springs, Australia

Mount Holyoke, Hadley, Massachusetts, U.S.

Clingman's Dome, Tennessee, U.S.

Croagh Patrick, Ireland

Tetford, England

Juozapines Hill, near Vilnius, Lithuania

Hill of Tara, Ireland

Carnac, France

Glastonbury Tor, Glastonbury, England

Cusco, Peru

Citamparam, India

Delphi, Greece

Brown's Hill, Monticello, Charlottesville, Virginia, U.S.

Mount Kithairon-Thebes, Greece

Hill Cumorah, Palmyra, New York, U.S.

Mount Shasta, California, U.S.

Mount Hood, near Eugene, Oregon, U.S.

Tintagel, Cornwall, England

Mount Warning, Queensland, Australia

Arunachala, Tiruvanamalai, India

Adam's Peak, Sri Lanka

Monte Alban, near Oaxaca, Mexico

Mount Rainier, Washington, U.S.

Mount Ararat, Armenia, Turkey

Mount Sinai, Egypt

Mount Chimborazo, Ecuador

Mount Kilimanjaro, Kenya

Mount Kenya, Kenya

Mont Blanc, French Alps, France

Steep Hill, Lincoln, England

Mount Balsam Cone, near Waynesville, North Carolina, U.S.

Mount Mitchell, North Carolina, U.S.

Mount Tamalpais, Mill Valley, California, U.S.

Table 5-2: Domes (continued)

Beacon Hill, Boston, Massachusetts, U.S.	Jay Peak, Vermont, U.S.	Dunkery Beacon, Dunster, Somerset, England
Bunker Hill, Boston, Massachusetts, U.S.	Mount Diablo, Lafayette, California, U.S.	Okehampton Tor, Dartmoor, England
Mount Washington, New Hampshire, U.S.	Mount Orford, near Foster, Quebec, Canada	Chartres, France
Mount Wachusett, near Worcester, Massachusetts, U.S.	Mount Sutton, near Foster, Quebec, Canada	Hagia Sophia Basilica, Istanbul, Turkey
Mount Pisgah, Westhampton, Massachusetts, U.S.	Mount Glen, near Foster, Quebec, Canada	Mount Palomar, near San Diego, California, U.S.
Owl's Head Mountain, Lake Memphremagog, Quebec, Canada	Mount Gregory, Quebec, Canada	Swannanoa, Waynesboro, Virginia, U.S.
Hawley, Massachusetts, U.S.	Burrowbridge Mump, Somerset, England	Mount Rose, California
	Cader Idris, Dolgellau, Wales	Mount Wallac, California

Great Bear; Canis Major, the Greater Dog; and many others.

We are now in a position to contemplate a fascinating mirror image. Above, at the galactic level, we have 48 dragon eggs, or Apsaras, dancing in a group according to the left-right dualistic beat of Rahu and Ketu, so as to collectively generate a new totality, a star of 50 parts. Below, at the planetary level, we have a star as a dome generating 48 subsidiary dome caps that constellate around the mother dome according to the Golden Mean. Above, 48 Apsaras surrounding and sustaining a star god; below, 48 dome caps arrayed heliacally around a dome that represents a star god.[201]

But who's the piper? It's the Gandharvas, of course, all 1,746 of them. There are actually a great many more Gandharvas than this. Their number is 1,746 to the ninth power, which comes to approximately 155 septillion.[202] It turns out that the Gandharvas, who have been called "angels of song," are an angelic family in mythic disguise, the Elohim.

Why 1,746? That's the total number of different *aspects* the Gandharvas as Elohim can manifest. But they can make a *lot* of copies of these aspects.

On a practical level, this means that, in the generation of the star gods, by hatching the 33 trillion dragon eggs, there will be 1,746 different types of stars; there will be that many different tones at which stars will manifest and be sustained by the perpetual Gandharva music. We could also think of this perhaps in terms of a stellar spectral scale based on a limit of 1,746 gradations. That comes to about 396 million stars for each of the 1,746 aspects.[203]

As we know, the Gandharvas, through their chief, Krsanu, are credited with being Brahma-appointed protectors of the precious Soma, the elixir of immortality that all the star gods want. The Gandharvas guard the Soma, which is to say they *regulate* the relationship between the Uncreate (source of Soma) and its expression in the created world as stars that are fed with Soma. The Gandharvas through their "music" maintain the *lines* of connection, the feed lines between

Soma and its recipients, the 691.4 billion stars in a galaxy. The Gandharvas or Elohim direct the *continuous* flow of Soma (or as light, refract it) into 1,746 primary gradations, each an aspect of their total being.

The Gandharvas then keep the created stars in perpetual connection with their higher source, Soma, the essence of unitive, undifferentiated consciousness. The birth of each star after all is a first step into individuation, a fall from unity, a sundering of fullness, a diffraction of Light into rays of light, paralleling (and antedating) our own human incarnation as individual beings.

The 33 trillion dragon eggs that hatch to become stars are then assigned a vibratory place in one of these 1,746 gradations, the Gandharva's dance tunes. In the mirror image of this arrangement, on Earth, we get 1,746 domes over our mountains, one for each of the Elohim's aspects expressed as a type of star.

Within the geomantic structure of the Earth domes, we get a recapitulation of the Rahu-Ketu and *ida-pingala* polarity. We also get an explanation for how the dome can generate 48 dome caps yet express its totality as 50.

Each of the domes on the Earth has a dual cord at its top connecting it to a central location also on the Earth. It's a crude image, but let's see the dome as a lampshade with a bright bulb in the center. Atop the lampshade is the cord, which consists of two strands of "wire" that connect to an outlet to get electrical power to run the light. In domes, the dual cord consists of a silver and a gold line of light that interweave heliacally across the planet to the "electrical" socket at a central place of connection. That place is Avebury, a 28-acre stone circle and encircling ditch (and thriving village with tourist facilities) 90 miles west of London and 20 miles south of Stonehenge, just outside Marlborough in Wiltshire, England. Avebury is the site of Earth's master dome, which measures 27,210 MY, or 14.017272 miles wide.

All domes have an interwoven gold and silver cord leading from their top to Avebury, where they are grounded and receive their "electricity." Within the dome structure this duality plays out also, as the silver and gold lines generate their share, determined by the Golden Mean, of dome caps. The gold and silver cords act like Rahu and Ketu, the dragon's head and tail, emitting the primary polarity that structures the dome complex. The cords also represent the *ida* and *pingala* energy circuits that interweave through the first five chakras.

The 48 dome caps are organized according to a vibratory chakra petal hierarchy mirroring the way they are arrayed around the first five chakras in the human. In other words, the first five chakras and their 48 vibratory fields or petals are implicit in the dome's array of 48 dome caps. Even though, looking at a dome or the array of 48 Apsaras dancing round a star god, they do not appear to be in a vertical, hierarchical sequence as in the chakra columns, their sequential relationship is implied, but it is expressed laterally.

If the Gandharvas are the angelic family called Elohim, then who are the Apsaras in the angelic hierarchy? They are the Hashmallim.[204]

Here are a few impressions of the Hashmallim in action.[205] Inside one dome I saw a series of circular wells of golden fire; each was a dome cap. Inside a single dome cap, I saw a multitude of flaming humans, on fire but not burning up—perhaps, rather, made of perpetual fire.

Collectively, the Hashmallim in a dome resemble a lovely fiery field of waving wheat or tall grass swaying in a solar breeze from the dome. Each blade is a golden fire stalk, and they are all packed closely together. Fittingly, in biblical lore, it's said that the River Dinur (Fiery River) was created out of the sweat of the Hashmallim who perspire copiously (and presumably it's beads of fire, not water) because they carry God's Throne, and it is heavy.

At one dome, I saw the Hashmallim flowing down from the star represented by the dome as a radiant shower of light all the way to the ground. They formed a stained glass window effect inside the dome, representing four dozen points of refraction. They impressed me as being like shepherds of the sun, the sun being the specific star the dome represented. The Hashmallim are also the *glory* of the individual star god, like the aureole that surrounds the saint's body, as represented in Christian art, and that radiates light—as in the Latin *gloria,* meaning "splendor" or "glorification."

I also saw the Hashmallim as horse riders. There was a single massive burgundy-hued rider on a celestial horse filling the sky, with starlight in his eyes. Surrounding him like an aureole of glory were 48 similar but smaller riders. These were the 48 princes of the star who was the principal burgundy-hued rider. These 48 were the fiery strands of the star's glory, the threads of his aura, the field of burning, galloping glory enveloping him—the angels of the dome caps.

Equivalently, I saw these 48 horses and riders as the team that pulls the splendid chariot of the star god, kingly, august, blazingly bright. It looked as if the celestial charioteer were storming prodigiously out of Heaven directly towards Earth accompanied by his fiercely majestic 48 outriders, the Hashmallim fishnet of fire beings delivering the starlight to Earth like a torrent of fiery rain.

Obviously, I am building an impressionistic case for the proposition that stars are evolved celestial beings and not merely big balls of gases and fire.[206] Persian Shi'ite gnosticism speaks of celestial beings and Imams in terms of "domes," according to Islamic scholar Henry Corbin. This spiritual tradition also speaks of theophanies (the periodic manifestations and descriptions of God) as domes.

Domes, Corbin says, are *spatial* not temporal images, in keeping with our discussion of Soma, the *naksatras,* and all else in this realm as pertain-

ing to the archetype of space. Appropriately, the Dome of the Rock in Jerusalem, which has a dome along the lines I've described here, is called *Qubbat as-Sakrah,* telling us in code that the architectural dome is topped by an energy dome.

The Shi'ite nuance on domes seems to refer in part to a sphere of spiritual influence delivered from on high, from the spiritual worlds. It's based on an original epiphany or manifestation of light (perhaps the time of influence for a specific star) in the cosmos and/or on Earth that then "curves around on itself into a cycle, or dome." The passage of influence from one dome to the next is due to "the initiative of a single transcendental Light, whose modes of Manifestation take on the form of domes."[207]

Corbin cites a Persian mystical tale in which an Islamic saint beholds the Lord looking down on him from the heights of space. "He was underneath a red dome, built from a unique pearl, whose light shone from the East to the West," the saint said. This particular color, says Corbin, was the "aura around the theophanic vision of the Imam."[208]

The planetary domes have a preset time for operation; over the life of the planet, they periodically come on and off, in accordance with celestial and planetary events and influences providing, as it were, selective and transient theophanies of individual star gods and their train.

Domes—a Dazzling Intimation of the Vault of Heaven in the Landscape

What does it feel like to be inside a dome? Something like the exaltation you can sometimes experience in one of the old, classically designed churches. Take the Hagia Sophia in Istanbul, Turkey, first constructed in the 530s A.D. by Emperor Constantine, then redone in 537 by the

Emperor Justinian who wanted to outdo Solomon's Jerusalem temple in architectural majesty.

The Hagia Sophia is considered "the only true domed basilica in Christian architecture." The dome, 100 feet in diameter and supported by 104 slim marble columns, looks down upon a vast open central space for worshipers with 40 windows piercing the base of the walls. "The effect is one of lightness and buoyancy, not massiveness or heaviness." The Hagia Sophia, whose name means "Holy Wisdom," is "intended to inspire awe."[209]

As one recent visitor to Hagia Sophia remarked, "No other building is so successful in transporting one to the threshold of another world, or so dazzlingly intimates the imminence of the transcendent under a dome that blazes like the vault of Heaven." Its walls are not barriers of stone, defining an interior sacred space against a profane outer world, but "passages into a higher reality."[210]

It is a reasonable assumption that the architectural style of the domed ceiling as used in churches, cathedrals, and mosques derives from early psychic perceptions of the energy canopies over holy sites. To get a sense of what an energy dome is like, visit a domed church such as Hagia Sophia or Saint Paul's Cathedral in London. What you feel or psychically sense there will be a clue to what the experience inside the energy dome might be like.

When the energy domes were "physically" here, it wasn't as if you could walk up to one and tap on its hull like a visiting spherical spaceship, even though one would reasonably mistake a dome for an extraterrestrial spaceship. In a sense they were. They traveled faster than the so-called speed of light, which means they existed spatially in between what we call spirit and matter, in the fourth dimension.

Here's how the Ofanim explain it: "The domes are light impressions, radiating and vibrating at various wavelengths reciprocally all over the planet. Sound is an aspect of the reciprocal vibration and wavelength of the type of light that

the domes are. They made the etheric structure of the Earth what it is by imposing a conscious matrix upon the planet to make it a place for possible human or conscious-being evolution. They were used to create a Paradise on Earth.[211] After the domes departed, they left impressions on the Earth's surface, an oscillating pattern which will persist until the Earth ceases to exist or until they are reaffirmed by another dome visit."

You're standing in a dark closet. It is so dark you can't see anything. Suddenly someone flashes a 500-watt light bulb in your eyes, then turns it off. You will continue to see that bright light for some time, even though, technically, it is not physically before your eyes. It's like that with the domes. They "came" to Earth three times, stayed a while, and left; the Ofanim say they will come a fourth time, in the foreseeable future. I call these visits the Dome Presences.

In the first Dome Presence, there were no humans on the planet. In the second Dome Presence, there was primitive life. In the third, there were some humans who could see them clearly and interacted with the visitors. Egyptian myth recalls this third Dome Presence as the *Zep Tepi,* the First Time or First Occasion, when the *Neters* or gods lived on Earth and more or less walked among the humans, or at least among a few of the more highly developed ones.

Zep Tepi was Blue Room time, the mythic Golden Age, the momentous time when spiritual archetypes were first unfolded into physical reality. "The First Time is both an era so long ago that it existed before time as we know it came into being, and a dimension of existence ontologically prior to that in which events occur in mundane time."[212] How long ago? About 18 million years.[213]

The first time the domes came to seed and energize a preset pattern. The second confirmed it and gave it an amplification. The third time was to activate it and hang around to answer questions. In the *Zep Tepi,* as the Egyptians remembered it, the gods lived on Earth and imparted their wisdom to humans.

The Elohim were the "e" in the *wise domes,* meaning, they fielded the questions, made the instructions, directed the quest, and did the heavy lifting. When the Elohim left and the energetic residues of the domes remained, we still remembered them in the slightly truncated word, as the source of *wisdom.*

The Elohim set up most of the original geomantic and megalithic structures around the Earth—the stone circles, stone rows, giant single stones, the odd hills such as Silbury and the Tor, stone cities, henge and rings, Avebury.

You can sense the Elohim at Avebury, even today, millions of years after they created and placed the stones. The huge sarsen stones were not quarried; they were summoned out of the ethers into their bizarre molten shapes. They still look only partially congealed, not definitively in matter yet. There were originally 72 big standing stones arranged on the inside edge of the deep ditch that encircles Avebury. Most of these big stones are gone now (only 27 are left, and some weigh up to 40 tons), but their energetic residues, their etheric forms, persist and are still active. Avebury still works.[214]

It is where the planet plugs into the galaxy. It's Earth's umbilicus to the stars. Two stars, specifically: Sirius in Canis Major (the Greater Dog) and Canopus in Carina (the Ship's Keel), a part of Argo Navis (the Ship Argo). These are the two brightest stars in our galaxy, and our planet's "father" and "mother" stars, respectively. Canopus (alpha Carinae) is a Southern Hemisphere star, 30 times the size of our sun and at least 400 light years from Earth. Sirius (alpha Canis Majoris) is only 1.8 times the size of our sun and much closer to Earth than Canopus at 8.7 light years. It has the greatest apparent brightness of any star in our galaxy.

A gold cord of light connects the top of the Avebury dome, the planet's master dome, with Sirius, while a silver cord connects it to Canopus.

These two light lines come into Avebury in a double helix form of solar and lunar currents just the way the *pingala* and *ida* circuits interweave helically around the central channel, the *sushumna* parallel to the spine. Every dome on the planet mimics this double helix connection, such that an intertwining silver and gold cord connects the top of each dome with the master one at Avebury.

Thus all 1,746 domes are "wired" to Avebury and, indirectly, to Sirius and Canopus. Each dome is in some aspects a miniature Avebury. Further, there is a dome for Sirius at Carnac in Brittany, France, and for Canopus at the island of Iona off the west coast of Scotland. These ground the energies of the two stars for Earth in coordination with Avebury.

I will be returning to Avebury throughout this book to comment on different aspects. It's important to remember here that this is the planetary site for Earth's Blazing Star. Through its Star, Earth connects to Sirius and Canopus, and through ours, we are connected interiorly to them as well.

Sirius and Canopus have another connection with the planet, through the eight Celestial Cities, each with a specific star overseer. These eight pertain to the esoteric meaning of Camalate (in myth, King Arthur's residence) and the eight-petaled inner heart chakra, *Ananda-kanda* (see table 5-3). I call them the eight Stars of Camalate, and we will continue to meet them in the next chapters.

These two topics come later, but for now I will say that the Grail Castle (the *Ananda-kanda* chakra) is overseen by Canopus, the Naga City in the *Muladhara* root chakra by Orion, and the Soma Temple in the sacral *Svadisthana* chakra by Sirius. That alone accounts for three Celestial Cities, each of which resides in us and in the Earth.

This means that these eight stars (or in some cases, constellations) are associated with the eight human chakras. For planets, we have Saturn/Cronos associated with the root chakra

Table 5-3: The 8 Stars of Camalate—Their Chakra, Planetary Sphere, and Celestial City Affiliations

Star	Chakra	Planetary Sphere	Celestial City
Canopus	*Ananda-kanda,* inner heart	None	Lanka-Grail Castle
Orion	1st, *Muladhara,* root	Saturn-Cronos	Raksovati-Naga
Sirius	2nd, *Svadisthana,* sacral	Moon	Kantimati-Soma
Great Bear	3rd, *Manipura,* solar plexus	Jupiter-Brhaspati	Amaravati-Mount Olympus
Cygnus	4th, *Anahata,* heart	Venus	Gandhavati-Avalon
Pleiades	5th, *Visuddha,* throat	Sun	Tejovati-Mithraeum
Cepheus	6th, *Ajna,* brow	Mercury	Sukavati-Shambhala
Arcturus	7th, *Sahasrara,* crown	Mars	Samyamani, Underworld

and the Moon with the sacral center. The *Ananda-kanda* does not have a direct planetary sphere influence. I use these terms to denote planetary *spheres* or reality *dimensions,* not the physical planets of our solar system.[215]

Here are aspects of a visionary tableaux you can observe at Avebury: It's as if the 28 acres of Avebury were a dance floor. Blue-throated, diamond-crowned Shiva is dancing, flamboyantly pirouetting. Shiva is Nataraja, Lord of Dancers, and his dance is the *Ananda tandava* by which he demonstrates to the assembled gods, in the golden hall of Citamparam or Tillai at the center of the universe, his awesome supreme reality, his creative *maya* or world-generating powers of illusion, the five aspects of his cosmic activity.[216]

He has a dance partner too: Sita, his wife, or perhaps Parvati, his second wife. (Probably they were the same celestial goddess, each expressing different aspects.) Their dance is wild, improbable, profound, like a mingling of fire and water without either losing anything of its essence. Ganesh, the elephant-headed god and offspring of Shiva and Parvati, sits at their feet as they dance. You find Ganesh at Avebury because Ganesh is the Ofanim, whose Blazing Star for Earth fills all of Avebury like water in a circular swimming pool.

Shiva is like a musical clef in a piece of music, with the Gandharvas the notes arrayed around him in concentric circles, as the choir that shapes the field through sound. For this is the *vastu,* the star-creating factory floor, and Shiva and his Gandharvas and Apsaras are birthing stars by the thousands with their music, shaping drops of Soma into star gods, enlivening them with music.

Avebury as Earth's master dome is in effect the parent of the other domes, each a star on Earth, and Shiva's wild musical dance is conveyed instantly through the gold and silver wires to these 1,746 star gods arrayed around the planet. Shiva remains at Avebury as *Vastospati,* Guardian of the House of the Dwelling with its thousand gates, as the Hound of Heaven, protector of cosmic order and rhythm, with Earth's Blazing Star (Ganesh) at his feet.[217]

Trees of Life—Walking the Four Worlds in the Linga

The Qabalists call the *vastu* the Vacated Space. Avebury is a miniature *vastu* for our planet. Into the Vacated Space comes an original line of light, a straight, thin line of light tentatively penetrating the vast Vacated Space. This line, the *Kav,* also called the *yosher* (straight line), passes only halfway through the sphere and stops at the center—a radius of light. If it became a diameter and bisected the circle, then God would have filled the Vacated Space again with the Infinite Light, canceling His own withdrawal. For the worlds to manifest, the *Kav* can only pass through at most one-half of the Vacated Space.

The *Kav* is a "ray of light from the infinite into the void . . . a single narrow conduit through which the 'waters' of the supernal light of the Infinite spread and are drawn to the worlds that are in the empty space in that void." God withdrew its Light from the Vacated Space so there would be room for creation; now God sends an exploratory line of light back into the Vacated Space, the empty open space when the Infinite Light withdrew from its midpoint. God sends light in "a measured and quantified way" through "a pipe from the edge of the Infinite" into the domain of the finite; it will be the ultimate source of all linear aspects of the finite worlds generated in the Vacated Space.[218]

Importantly, the *Kav* contains the Sefirot, the vessels of Light that comprise the Tree of Life, and thus the planetary spheres, for Sefirot and planets are equivalent.[219] The *Kav* ensheaths the seven planetary spheres.

We find the same concept of the *Kav* in the Hindu description of Shiva's linga. This is his severed flaming phallus, which is full of seeds on fire. It is a pillar with a rounded top. When it originally fell from Heaven, it burned everything and destroyed everything moving and unmoving. It pervades all of Space and is so vast that neither Brahma nor Vishnu could discern the beginning or end of its "burning immensity," which seemed to expand alarmingly into infinity.

This "incredible flaming light," Brahma and Vishnu realized, was a tremendous revelation of the reality of Shiva, "of that fire *linga* of him who is the light and destruction of the universe." It is the impregnating light of Heaven, the quickening of matter with spirit, the fertilization of the primal waters with original infinite light, and it is also the "counter thrust of the ascending, flaming phallic pillar."[220] Like the *Kav,* the linga unites Emanator with emanated.[221] The *Kav* = the *linga.*

You can experience the "seeds" of creation within the *Kav* or Shiva's linga through a geomantic feature called the Tree of Life (see table 5-4). Also known as a Jacob's Ladder, this feature is like a rope ladder unrolled on the ground, with four major divisions and numerous colored knots on which you stand for a time.

The geomantic Tree of Life is a concentrated Mystery temple that includes the 40 Sefirot as

---

Table 5-4: Trees of Life

Planetary Total: 2,856 (238 copies per Albion Plate)

Selected Locations:

Acropolis, Athens, Greece

Avebury, England (Ridgeway)

Chichen Itza, Mexico

Tetford, England (Little London, Dev Aura)

Tetford, England (Blue Ridge Heath)

Glastonbury, England

Hill Cumorah, Palmyra, New York, U.S.

Jasna Gora, Czestochowa, Poland

Montserrat, Spain

Sedona, Arizona, U.S.

Teotihuacan, Mexico

Troy, Turkey

Santiago de Compostela, Spain (St. James's Way)

The Lawn, University of Virginia, Charlottesville, Virginia

Equivalent Names: Jacob's Ladder

expressed in the Four Worlds as described by Qabala (refer to chapters 1 and 2). That means the basic ten Sefirot, or spheres of light, are presented four times, in successively denser levels of expression, which is to say, levels closer to physical, manifest reality. You climb up or down the horizontal dimensional ladder for an experience of ascending into ever more rarefied spiritual worlds or experiencing the descent of the Supreme Being's thought for existence through four levels of expression.

Essentially you are inside the *Kav* or Shiva's pillar when you walk through a Tree of Life temple. All of the worlds and stages of unfolding light that constitute Shiva's revelation of absolute reality to Brahma and Vishnu are in this. The *Kav* contains the seven planetary spheres, which is to say, the seven chakras at their archetypal level of expression. It contains myriad stars and their 40 dimensional homes as the Sefirot. To the extent that you can expand your perception to take in some of this as you interact with a landscape Tree of Life, you are walking in this cosmic wonderland of primal creative manifestation.

The size of these Trees of Life can vary a great deal, though they remain eminently *experienceable* at any size. There are relatively small ones at certain highly visited locations, such as the Lawn at Thomas Jefferson's original Academikal Village, now the University of Virginia at Charlottesville, the grounds of the Acropolis in Athens, and the half-acre snippet of Paradise in Glastonbury, England, called Chalice Well Gardens. There are much bigger expressions in the 80-mile Ridgeway, an ancient walking path in Wiltshire, England, and in the favorite of Christian pilgrims, the Camino de Santiago, Saint James's Road of the Stars that stretches 500 miles across the north of Spain.

How are the Sefirot arrayed in the landscape Tree of Life? Technically, the 40 Sefirot within the *Kav* are arrayed in a straight line, one sphere after the next through the Four Worlds. This is how the earliest Qabalists modeled the descent of energy, as a straight-running lightning bolt; it is also, the Ofanim state, more or less in accordance with how things are in reality.[222] Qabalists describe the descent of light down the *Kav* as a Lightning Flash or Flaming Sword.[223]

In several of the landscape Trees of Life I have observed, which were placed in publicly accessible places such as parks or college quadrangles, the Sefirot appear to be arrayed in the more familiar three-pillared form for easier human-Sefirot interaction.

The Trees are meant to be in public places so that, ideally, parks, gardens, or meditative sites are designed to co-occupy the site or to build their features over it but be compatible with the energetic template to maximize the possibility of a visitor's immersion in the higher energies offered by this feature.

The Tree is suitable as a practice place for attunement with the hierarchical descent or ascent of formative cosmic energies and their angelic counterparts. It works well as a training ground for the Christed Initiation in the Buddha Body, affording introductory exposures to the Fisher King. As the Ofanim note, "Their geomantic function is to offer the possibility of the perfected human to interface with the being of the Earth through the Four Worlds."

Labyrinths—Meandering Pathways through the Ancient of Days's Brain

When it comes to labyrinths, you get the chance to walk through the Tree of Life or *Kav* in a highly unconventional way, sideways, backwards and forwards, zigzagging seemingly erratically through the Four Worlds as if in flagrant disregard for the orderly descent of energies and light. The intent, of course, is to give you a chance to experience and integrate the energies by way of a different, apparently distorted, immersion in them.

I say "apparently" distorted, but it really is not. The labyrinth template—an energetic overlay on the landscape upon which physical labyrinths of various materials were modeled—is meant to be the experiential *counterpart* to the Tree of Life, giving you another way to experience the *Kav* in a blended but nonsequential way.

You can see the demarcations in the *Kav* in the abstracted central axis across which the labyrinth's folds crisscross. This central axis is the straight line of light that was the original Tree of Life, and it is the reference point and center for the labyrinth's meandering way. Some labyrinths (Cretan type) feature seven convolutions or concentric circles; others have 11 (Chartres Cathedral type) with a twelfth circle as the labyrinth's center and a total of 34 turnings.

Geometrically, the unicursal labyrinth is described as a straight line with horizontal branches on either side marking where the convolutions intersect the median. Unicursal means there is only one path into the center and out again. Geometrically speaking, in a unicursal labyrinth you walk a path without intersections: that continually switches back and forth; that completely fills up an interior space but does so by running in the most circuitous manner; that repeatedly leads you past the goal, or center; that finally lands you at the center; that leads you out of the center as the only possible route through the maze.

Seen from above or as an abstract diagram, it resembles or suggests the convolutions of the human brain. Labyrinth experts attest to the mental benefits one gets from walking a labyrinth, such as balancing the two cerebral hemispheres. Walking a physical labyrinth (such as the famous one on the floor of Chartres Cathedral in France)

is a "symbol of integration, individuation, of the concentration of all essential layers, aspects, and levels of meaning of a human existence." It symbolizes a "process of maturation" in which the numerous fragmented parts of oneself—think of the 40 Sefirot here—are knit into one centered, unified being, a life in the center.[224]

In terms of geomantic labyrinths (energy templates in the landscape that preexist its physical manifestation), there are nine types, with 12 of each type distributed evenly across the planet's surface, or 108 in all. One type is the Cretan labyrinth. Scholars have never satisfactorily figured out where it actually was; they tend to settle for locating it somewhere in Knossos. They can't find it because it was never a physical labyrinth, and it is far bigger than they ever imagined.

The Cretan labyrinth consists of a circular matrix some ten miles in diameter, made of eight overlapping dome caps that converge at or surround Mount Ida. Mount Ida (elevation 8,058 feet), also known as Mount Idhi or Psiloritis, is one of three principal peaks on the island of Crete, although it is the highest. Two neighboring domed mountains, Lefka Ori and Mount Dicte, supply some of the dome caps; the rest are from Mount Ida. The energy feature is oriented east-west, with its center facing the east.

In a sense, Mount Ida is the Minotaur at the heart of the labyrinth. Walking this labyrinth obviously is not an afternoon's recreation, but a matter of preparation, physical stamina, psychic penetration, and readiness for a major initiation experience. In a larger context, the Cretan labyrinth (and the 11 others of this type elsewhere on Earth) is a key to the mind, the human, and the local and the planetary landscape.

It is the mental body or "thinking brain" of a huge landscape figure that covers much of Europe, from Greece to Scandinavia, a figure which Greek myth fittingly remembers as Europa, variously described as a white maiden or a white

---

Table 5-5: Labyrinths

Planetary Total: 108 (9 types, 12 copies of each, distributed uniformly)

Selected Locations:

Mount Ida, Crete, Greece: Minotaur type	Schnebly Hill, Sedona, Arizona, U.S.	Monticello, Charlottesville, Virginia, U.S.
Clingman's Dome, Tennessee, U.S.: Hall of Records type	The Tor, Glastonbury, England	Crnica Hill-Krizevach Hill, Medjugorje, Bosnia: Hall of Records type
Chichen Itza, Mexico	Chartres Cathedral, Chartres, France	
Machu Picchu, Peru	The Plantation, Fiji: Minotaur type	Ben Bulben, Drumcliff, Ireland: Hall of Records type
Cerro Gordo, Teotihuacan, Mexico	Addis Ababa, Ethiopia: Minotaur type	
Easter Island, Chile		

Equivalent Names: Troy Town, Caerdroia, Cretan Spiral, Walls of Troy, Prison of the Minotaur, House of Daedalus

---

bull (Zeus in disguise) who mated with her. Europa is one of Earth's 12 astrological egregors (a vast landscape angel and Zeus manifestation), which I describe later in the book. (See table 5-5 for listings of some labyrinths.)

I call this type of formation a Minotaur Labyrinth because the Minotaur ("The Bull of Minos") represents the culminative experience you get after traversing this type of labyrinth. The Minotaur Asterius, the "monster" with a bull's head and human torso from the neck down, dwells at the center of the Cretan labyrinth. Theseus, the Greek hero, is credited with "slaying" the Minotaur, but I propose that what really happened is that Theseus *assimilated* the potential experience of this labyrinth and *became* the Minotaur, not a monster or defect of nature, but a human whose higher head chakras and consciousness have been touched, suffused with the God-aspect, Zeus in his white bull form. You thread the Minotaur labyrinth, and potentially your consciousness is immersed in divinity and the mind of Zeus (Shiva also has a white bull aspect).

Another type of labyrinth is located under the major domes on Earth. This kind maps the correspondences between the human brain and Earth's neural pathways. I call this type of formation a Hall of Records Labyrinth, as a way of describing the potential experience awaiting one who encounters its energies.

Here are some impressions of this type of labyrinth: Clingman's Dome, a mountain in Tennessee, has a dome, and inside the dome is the labyrinth. At first glance, the mountain seemed hollow, carved out, empty, then I became aware of a periphery of 24 golden doors guarded by formidable astral beings.

The Cherokee called them the White Bears or *yanus* who lived in their "townhouses" in the mountain, which they protected against intruders. The Cherokee say the *yanus* were once human and could revert to that form if they wished. According to the Ofanim, the Cherokee "knew how to enter and connect with the past and future by entering the labyrinth."

On the other side of the golden doors a long ramp led down to what at first seemed a vast pool of yellow water. Then I realized it was the energy field of the labyrinth. You walk this kind of labyrinth in your visionary body or in whatever form you can project your awareness into the matrix. Otherwise it essentially resembles a unicursal labyrinth. The Minotaur is different, however. Here it is a Hall of Records. It may at first glimpse resemble an elegant Greek edifice, perhaps the Parthenon in its glory. Probably it is closer to the perception of a multitude of vertical energy filaments deriving from stars, planets, galaxies, and possibly universes above.

Each filament is like a hollow tube in which you can stand to receive the information. In this respect it is somewhat like the Hyperborean Time Libraries and the Lemurian Information Crystals (see chapter 1). It is a Hall of Records in the sense that it records stellar and universal influences and light codings transmitted to this labyrinth and its connections with other geomantic features over the duration of the existence of the planet. You stand in the filaments as if in a chromatic shower as your body gets drenched (imprinted) in the data stream.[225]

Chakra Templates—the Paradisal Realm of the Forest of Bliss

I mentioned above that the domes made it possible for paradisal conditions to exist on the Earth. One of the ways they did this is through the chakra template. The major domes were able to generate a great number of these energy features, so that the seven prime chakras each had seven expressions, and the entirety of the feature then made the fiftieth part. In practical terms, you could walk through a sequence of chakras in the land, attuning your own with those templated in the energy field of an area.[226]

In some respects, we can accurately conceive of a landscape chakra template as a horizontal, topographical sequencing of the seven chakras

with seven subsidiary energy centers for each. Some chakra templates identified in urban areas stretch only a few blocks;[227] others may be longer, such as the one on Iona, an island in the Scottish Hebrides, which is the size of the island, 1.5 miles long by three miles wide (see table 5-6). Chakra templates, incidentally, are different from landscape chakras, which are expressed individually and are part of larger geomantic figures called Albions, explained in chapter 10.

The numbers involved with chakra templates are staggering. There are 26^{26} of these, some 2.6 octillion (2.6 followed by 26 zeroes) produced by 1,080 of the domes. How can there be so many, and why?

As usual, the fabulous deep mythic memory of India gives us a clue. The ancient spiritual city in India variously known as Kashi, Varanasi, and Banaras was once known as *Anandavana*, the Forest of Bliss. *Ananda* means bliss, and it is an epithet or quality of consciousness attributed to Shiva who resided in Banaras. In an old text, Shiva is quoted as saying, "My *lingas* are everywhere there, like little sprouts arisen out of sheer bliss. Thus it is called the Forest of Bliss." As one scholar comments: "A forest with Shiva *lingas* as thick as the fresh sprouts of spring: This is the vision of the sacred city as the Forest of Bliss, the Anandavana or Anandakanana."[228]

In Banaras you meet a *linga* at every step you take, and there is not a place even as big as a

---

Table 5-6: Chakra Templates

Planetary Total: 26^{26} = 2.6 octillion

Selected Locations:

Iona, Scotland, British Isles

Banaras, India

Swannanoa, Waynesboro, Virginia, U.S.

Equivalent Names: Anandavana, Forest of Bliss, Shiva *lingas*

sesame seed that does not sprout a *linga* there, local spiritual allegation has it. Local legend says there are 100,000 *lingas* in Banaras, that the city is made of these subtle *lingas;* the River Ganges is said to contain six million.

In another old text, Shiva tells his consort, Parvati, that there are "uncounted *lingas*" in the Forest of Bliss. Some are of a material nature, the rest of a subtle, spiritual quality. Many are "self-born," established by gods and sages. Any of them can cause liberation and bestow yogic achievement. "One time I counted a hundred billion of them," Shiva declares, adding there might be even more present, established by his devotees after the day he counted them.[229]

One hundred billion *lingas*—certainly that is heading in the direction of the very big number of *lingas* the Banaras dome could theoretically generate: 260 septillion (2.6 octillion divided by 1,080).

Thus Banaras gives us an excellent example of a dome-generated chakra template and how it has been remembered in myth as Shiva's Forest of Bliss. For the bliss element is central here, the clue to the potential paradise on Earth the domes brought. Even if some of the *lingas* are, as Shiva stated in that same text, "broken down by the ravages of time," they are still to be worshipped, still spiritually potent and numinous with the presence and consciousness of Shiva.

Each *linga* is a chakra column or hierarchy of 50 vibratory stages; each is the path that Shakti-Kundalini lying in the root chakra takes to rejoin her consort, Shiva, in the crown chakra in bliss. That's how Tantric kundalini yoga describes it, and it is a useful description for us here. We should think of the Shiva *lingas* or chakra templates as a totality comprised of 50 parts, and that totality by its own nature is and bestows bliss and creates a paradise called the Forest of Bliss.

Initially when the 1,080 domes capable of producing chakra templates came to Earth, the landscape within their aegis was seeded with these 260

septillion sprouts of bliss, and perhaps they germinated, sprouted, and flourished at once and without effort, being reaffirmed and nourished by contact with awakened humans, sages, saints, and the living gods among them. In this sense, each of the 1,080 domes could rightly be called *Anandavana,* Forest of Bliss, for each was floriated with revelations of Shiva in every direction. We could say the planet has 1,080 precincts known as Forests of Bliss, in each of which a major dome generates up to 260 septillion chakra templates of all sizes.

But how can we conceive of such an abundance of chakras in a relatively small area? Think in terms of fractals, such as you see demonstrated in the fjords of Norway's coastline. Each smaller section of a land outcropping copies the form of the larger one of which it is a part; ever smaller sections repeat the same form. It's like an ever-finer hall of mirrors, a valley of echoes that almost never stops sounding. With the geomantic chakra template, you have a large primary one and then a vast but finite series of repetitions of this within every layer of it.

Each of the seven primary chakras repeats the pattern of seven; so do the 48 dome caps; and each sublayer of seven itself has a subsidiary level of another seven; and they do it in accordance with a logarithmic table of expansion.

The point of course is to reveal Shiva as being present *everywhere,* that all of reality, the landscape, air, elements, molecules, atoms, bear the stamp of Yahweh's (Shiva's) name, are his revelation, a hierophany of searing light.

The Head of Osiris—the Crown of the Ancient of Days and the Palladium

So where does Kether, the Sefira of the Crown, come into geomantic play? We have seen that it is excluded from the chakra templates and labyrinths, though it is implicit in the Four Worlds hierarchy of the Trees of Life. There are two geomantic features in which the energies of this exalted level are expressed.

The myths about a god's severed head and its placement in the landscape are vivid and consistent across several cultures. The Egyptians say when Seth cut up Osiris into 14 pieces, the head was buried at Abydos where it remains. Appropriately, one of Osiris' epithets was Lord of Eternity whose form is hidden.[230]

Hindu myth says Brahma originally had five heads; with his fifth, he desired to watch his daughter Savitri from all angles. Then Shiva chopped it off, turned it into his begging bowl, and couldn't let go of it as it inexplicably stuck to the nail of his left thumb until it finally spontaneously dropped off in Banaras, India, at a site thereafter called Kapalamochana Tirtha, "Where the Skull Fell."

In the Welsh myth, Bendigeidfran, or Bran the Blessed, was a prodigy, bigger than mountains, and a great host. At one point he ordered his head to be cut off and to be carried from Wales to Gwynfryn, the White Mount, in London (the future site of Saint Paul's Cathedral), and buried with its face towards France to protect the British Isles against invasion.[231]

Norse myth says the elder gods called the Vanir cut off the head of the wise Aesir, Mimir (of the younger gods), and sent it back to Odin, the king of the gods. It became a talking head and the source of Odin's wisdom and secret information about arcane doings in the celestial world. Norse myth also says Odin buried Mimir's Head under the roots of Yggdrasil, the World Tree, at a site afterwards called Mimir's Well, and went there regularly to consult the Head.

The Greeks offer us a startling different take on the Ancient of Days. They called "him" collectively the Gorgons. There were three Gorgons: Stheno (Strength), Euryale (Wide-Leaping), and Medusa (Ruler of Queen). These three sisters lay in the far West of the world by the shore of Ocean's stream; this was Greek mythic code for saying at the most exalted rim of the manifest world.

An early accounting had the Gorgons as beautiful women with golden wings, so beautiful that they put Pallas Athena (an Olympian goddess and Ray Master) into such a jealousy that she caused them to become ugly. They were often described as having hideous round faces, serpents in their hair—or their heads and torsos were girdled in serpents—mighty boars' tusks, terrible grins, snub noses, beards, lolling tongues, wildly staring eyes, horses' hindquarters, and brazen hands. Their gaze could turn humans instantly to stone.

Two of the Gorgons, daughters of the Sea, were immortal, but Medusa was not. She was slain by Athena's protégé, Perseus, who brought the goddess Medusa's snake-entwined head, her eyes veiled to keep Perseus from being turned to stone by its fell gaze. Athena set the severed head at the center of her breastplate or shield, the aegis, but the old myths also say she buried the head under the marketplace in Athens, the city named in her honor. Later masks of the Gorgon Medusa were placed around Athens to ward off evil spirits, and one was said to be carved on a rock face of the Acropolis and known as a gorgoneion.

The key part of this myth is Gorgon Medusa's head and what it could do. It was terrifying and petrifying and it could protect its host citadel. But how? Of course the Head is terrifying and its gaze can turn you to stone, for haven't the mystics throughout time consistently told us that to look upon the Supreme Being is either impossible or certain death because the vision will kill the ego?

Qabala offers some elucidation here. The Ancient of Days is a metaphor for the Supreme Being's presence in the Sefira of Kether at the top of the Tree. Kether is called the Hidden

> ### Table 5-7: Crowns of the Ancient of Days
>
> *Planetary Total:* 12, equally divided per Albion Plate
>
> *Selected Locations:*
>
> | | | |
> |---|---|---|
> | Golgotha, Jerusalem, Israel (Hill of Skulls) | England (Head of Bran the Blessed) | Sacsaywaman, Cusco, Peru (Head of the Puma) |
> | Shadwell, Hansen's Mountain, Charlottesville, Virginia, U.S. | Banaras, India (Brahma's Fifth Head) | Sodorp Church, Vinstra, Norway (Mimir's Well) |
> | *Gwynfryn*, The White Mount, Primrose Hill, London, | Abydos, Egypt (Head of Osiris) | Mount Ida, Turkey (near Troy: Zeus' solitary temple) |
>
> *Equivalent Names:* Vast Countenance, White Head, *Kapalamochana Tirtha* (Where the Skull Fell), Osireon, Mimir's Head, *Gwynfryn*, Head of Bendigeid Bran (Bran the Blessed), *Urddawl Ben* (Venerable Head), Brahma's Fifth Head, Speckled Head, *Hlidskjalf*, Odin's Throne in *Valaskjalf* (his hall), Mimir's Well, Hill of Skulls

Intelligence because it is the Light that supplies the power of comprehension of the First principle. It is the primal glory which essence no created being can fully attain. Some of its epithets include Concealed of the Concealed, Primordial Point, the Most High, the Vast Countenance, the White Head. Kether is the sphere in which you merge with God; because it was the first thing manifested, so it is the last to return to in the spiritual ascent.

Qabalists also say that "White are his garments and His appearance is the likeness of a Face vast and terrible." The brightness of His skull illumines 40,000 superior worlds, and within his skull are 13,000 myriad worlds. The vastness of His countenance shines into 370 myriads of worlds, and the Face itself has 13 carved sides. Were the Ancient of Days to close His eyes for a moment, all reality would cease; therefore, the eyes are never shut, and it is considered bountiful because it establishes and guards all created things.[232] Qabalists in fact have devoted many pages of vivid description to the symbolic minutiae of the Face.[233]

"Imagine a great head arising from the depths of a calm sea until it completely covers the space above the horizon. Then see the image of this vast countenance reflected in the waters."[234] That was similar to how I first saw the Head, though I did so before I encountered that description. It was, surprisingly, in the Rotunda on the Lawn of the campus of the University of Virginia at Charlottesville. This is the oldest part of the university that was established by Thomas Jefferson in the 1820s. In the same place as the physical Rotunda there is a rotunda of light, but it is inverted such that it appears as a shallow concave bowl with uprising pillars arching like beams of light to form a majestic crown.

In the center of this concavity sits a white marble face of a generic human, looking upwards. You can only see it in profile. It suggests a bejeweled head. Light flashes out in all directions as sharp rays from its eyes. These rays penetrate in all directions, into every one of the 360 degrees in a circle. The face is plastic, mobile, protean; it forms anew at every fresh angle you view it from, a mobile face continuously transfiguring itself, tracking, illuminating everything.[235]

Technically, this Head was not one of the 12

but one of the 60 Heads. The 12 Crowns of the Ancient of Days are large versions of the Head; the 60 Palladium,[236] as I call them, are smaller versions of the same, distributed uniformly around the Earth, five per Albion Plate.[237] (See tables 5-7 and 5-8.)

Why go to a Crown of the Ancient of Days or a Palladium? To get a little boost in your communications with the Supreme Being, or to start a dialogue.

White Lilies in the Field of Earth and the Light of Three-Star Temples

Suppose you pursue this quest for communication with the Above through the Earth's visionary terrain and you establish close, regular contact. Suppose you start to see that this visionary geography is in fact an outward reflection of your inner spiritual constitution, and a virtual presence of the spiritual worlds as well.

You realize, as the Buddhists say, that "the sacred is rooted in the primordial ground of our being" and that the "changeless, enlightened essence of life is primordial liberation," even at the atomic level. You appreciate that everything around you, the world, the geomantic temples, participates in this "ultimate self, or the mind of awakening, or the ever-excellent mind" which is continuously present, always there, the "naturally luminous mind" that abides "free from the impurity of habitual, distorted appearances." All of us are "equal masters in the palace of essential wisdom," have the same complete wakefulness as all the Buddhas and gods.[238]

I borrow this Buddhist vocabulary to evoke the idea that ultimately the Earth's diversified energy body exists so as to facilitate our awakening from the deep, distorted sleep of our misunderstood physical incarnation on Earth. When we start to wake up amidst the planet's spiritual geomantic terrain, a provision has been made by its designers for a feedback loop to begin between us and it. A lily starts to form where we abide and becomes a permanent addition to the Earth's visionary geography. There is no limit to how many lilies might appear.

To conceive of this feature, you need to think big and casually. The geomantic lily is like the botanical flower, only much larger, of light, and created spontaneously by purified human consciousness. The Buddha was said to sprout white lotus blossoms from the soles of his feet wherever he walked in India after his enlightenment at Bodh Gaya, so perhaps the white lily and white lotus are equivalent flower images.

The geomantic lily appears spontaneously as a result of persons purifying their consciousness

---

Table 5-8: Palladiums

Planetary Total: 60 (equally divided, 5 per Albion Plate)

Selected Locations:

Rotunda, The Lawn, University of Virginia, Charlottesville, Virginia, U.S.	Forradh, Hill of Tara, (near Dublin), Ireland	Dunkery Beacon, Somerset, England
Troy, Turkey	Harlech, Wales	
	Gwales, Wales	

Equivalent Names: Gorgoneion, Gorgon Medusa, Miniature Crown of the Ancient of Days

Table 5-9: Three-Star Temples		
Planetary Total: 144,000		
Selected Locations:		
Morningside Park, Knoxville, Tennessee, U.S.	Sacred Grove, Hill Cumorah, Palmyra, New York, U.S.	National Monument, Los Alamos, New Mexico, U.S.
Taj Mahal, Agra, India	Monsignor Patrick Smith Park, Santa Fe, New Mexico, U.S.	Swannanoa, Waynesboro, Virginia, U.S.
Santiago de Compostela, Spain		
	Frijoles Canyon, Bandelier	Truckee, California

over time at a site and from having conscious, voluntary interaction with the angelic realm, allowing it, as it were, to live and ground within the human realm and world through this sustained contact. The lily is white, pure, open, and receptive; it receives higher spiritual light, shapes it into a suitable container, and reflects it back to those in its presence.[239]

Fittingly, there is a white lily underlying the grounds of the Saint Joseph Oratory and Basilica of Notre Dame in Mont Royal Park in Montreal, Quebec, in Canada, in large part due to the long-term residence there of an unofficial Catholic saint named Brother Andre. You find another at Arunachala, the solitary 2500-foot-tall mountain in South India at whose base Ramana Maharshi, the Hindu sage, resided for many years. There is another underlying a two-acre garden and retreat center in Tetford, England, called Dev Aura which has been dedicated to color, healing, and angelic contact for almost 20 years.

Some years before I understood what this feature was, I saw a field of such lilies in a vision. It was from a time long ago, possibly Hyperborea. There were numerous lovely lily-type flowers in a field and angelic beings floating in them. In fact, it seemed that the angelic form was the same as the lily, or that it fit perfectly into the flower mold of the lily so that the angelic consciousness and the lily form were the same. I experienced that melding as well, settling into a lily, noting a few

companions nearby, and felt it a paradisal time upon the Earth.

Another feature designed to help humans attune to the angelic world is called a Three-Star Temple. The design is simple: Over a rectangular stretch of land, often less than a mile long, three stars are present at the interface between the ethers and physical ground. The first is the Earth Star; the second is the Incarnational Star; the third is the Soul Star. These names come from the Ofanim, who first introduced me to this feature at a public park in Knoxville, Tennessee.

To understand this setup, you first need to know that it's based on an angelic visualization provided by the Ofanim. Visualize a brilliant pinprick of light just above your belly button and a little bit inside. This is the Incarnational Star. Visualize a second star just like this one, perhaps ten feet under your body and in the ground; this is the Earth Star. Visualize a third star about ten feet above your head; this is the Soul Star. The three stars are aspects of the Ofanim. In the Three-Star Temple, this vertical alignment is laid out horizontally so that you start with the Soul Star.

The Morningside Park in Knoxville is appropriately physically divided into three distinct sections, each corresponding to one of these geomantic stars. You stand within the landscape expression of the Soul Star and tune into the Soul Star above your head. That puts them in resonance and in effect in the same place.

Then you move to the second, middle star, the Incarnational Star at your belly. Here you may have the odd impression that somehow you have grown to be 200 feet tall and are an exceptionally well-attuned spiritual individual. You may feel the entire site (in this case, a green park surrounded by trees) and the other two stars have melted into this central star. You are experiencing the presence of the archangelic overseer of this Three-Star Temple.

There are 18 different, named archangels in existence, and each is responsible for 8,000 Three-Star Temples, as there are 144,000 on the planet. The archangel at Knoxville is Sandalphon (see table 5-9 for a few locations).

At the third point, the Earth Star, don't be surprised if you sense or perceive a great deal of nature spirit activity. This is their proper place. Their job is to ground the blended angelic and human star energies into an assimilable form for the Earth. The Earth Star site in this temple is like a soup pot for this.

The point of this temple is to enable the human to blend the angelic, human, and elemental (nature spirits) energies through the vehicle of three stars becoming one. These temples were seeded at the inception of the planet then brought to life over time through human, angelic, and elemental interaction so that people could experience and deepen their awareness of the necessary interaction and blended energies of these three realms.

I say necessary because for any real geomantic work, activation, or site-opening to occur, you need the simultaneous presence and participation of these three realms. Consider it a pun on our key phrase, *As above* (angelic), *so below* (elemental), *and in the middle, too* (human). The function of this Temple, the Ofanim note, "is to bring to a point of balance a human initiate's development with the Oversoul [represented by the archangel] and their purpose, and to bring spiritual clarity into the field of individuals."

Obviously, any purposeful human interaction with a Three-Star Temple benefits the landscape and local geomantic configuration as well as the elemental kingdom. For them it is like a great lunch. The elemental spirits (gnomes, sylphs, salamanders, undines) cannot "digest" angelic light and consciousness directly; these energies have to be transduced, passed through the human field first for the elementals to be able to benefit. Then they take the nourishing light and distribute it throughout the local landscape for which they are responsible; through this, all of natural life, botanical and animal, benefits from the infusion.

6 With the Olympian Gods in Their City of Jewels
Ray Masters of the Great Bear

September 29 marks a spiritual holiday still observed in the British Isles and in a few scattered places: Michaelmas. It is properly pronounced with four syllables—*my-kay-el-mass*—and it is dedicated to the Archangel Michael. On Michaelmas 2002 I saw the Archangel Michael holding the Earth like a rug, using his sword like a broom handle to pound the year's dirt out of the Earth's body. In the planet's case, it was the year's accumulation of foreign and literally alien energies that rose from the planetary "rug" as clouds of smoke, mist, and milky-white plumes.

At the same time the 14 Ray Masters were scouring the planet, each beating a one-twelfth division of the planet's surface as if it were a rug. These divisions had a geometrical shape, like pentagons. Both Michael and the Ray Masters were cleansing the prominent energy lines that encircle the Earth.

But the Earth they were beating like a dirty rug was not quite the lovely blue-white orb we're used to seeing from the NASA photographs. This Earth was a geometric one, made of pentagons and triangles and pulsating lines of differently colored light that completely encircled the globe like oroboric snakes and crisscrossed these pentagonal divisions of the Earth's surface. All of it looked as if made of glass, but the glass was smudged and smeared. Yet the effect of Michael's

sword beating upon the glass or rug and of the Ray Masters doing the same with their swords upon the lesser divisions of the planet cleaned the "glass" and brought a light into the "rug," and it all began to look fresh again.

The Great Planetary Cleansing of Michaelmas

Think of it as a planetary housecleaning. During the year, the Earth's energy body, or what I've been calling its visionary terrain and sacred geography, gets toxic with the exudates of human thoughts and negativities as well as the deliberately introduced negative thoughts and control energies of various alien beings with their agendas. In many cases, these agendas run contrary to the best interests of humans and our possibilities of wakeful, freely undertaken evolution in consciousness, and they run counter to the hopes and encouragements of the angelic world and their sponsors. So the planet needs an annual detoxification, and Michaelmas is the day set aside for that global housecleaning.

Michaelmas is a good day for Earth's energy body and all its numinous sites, and for all who care about both. According to the Ofanim, on this day, "Michael blesses the Earth with his sword to cleanse and shift the energy. He connects the major grid lines and tries to flush through any negative blockages. As the Moon is physically farther away from the Earth at this time than any other time in the year, Michael chose this date. The energy of all living matter responds to this and changes its nature at this point. Also the energy matrix of the Earth changes in polarity at Michaelmas due to this phenomenon.

"Michael is the harbinger of the Holy Spirit moving through the Earth's grid," the Ofanim state. "He brings the Supramundane Light to the subtle body of Gaia, and he is working with Gaia empowered to diversify manifestations by the Supreme Being on the Earth. As we have mentioned, Michael rules the development of consciousness within the Earth at this time, and he supports all human activities that lead to the furtherance of the Michaelic energies and mission on the planet."

One of my first occasions in which I witnessed the Michaelic cleansing of the grid was on Eagle Mountain in the Prescelly region of Wales. It is a mostly bare, moor-like, slow-rising hill, spotted erratically with huge boulders, a few trees, and on that day lots of fog. I felt like a journalist called in to cover a major event because clearly big things were going on here.

I saw a vast starwheel, a round table of millions of glinting stars overlaid on the landscape. Numerous angels stood along its perimeter fanning flames while the Archangel Michael, tall, majestic, with sword and shield, sparked the central hub of this huge star wheel with his sword, wielding it like a thunderbolt.

The wheel started to turn, and I realized it was not one wheel, but many, perhaps hundreds, even thousands, across the Earth, perhaps the solar system and galaxy as well, that were now slowly and freshly turning as if after a period of stagnation. It seemed perhaps they had reversed the spin direction, as in calisthenics or yoga, in which you bend to the right then balance it by bending to the left.

As the wheels turned, great plumes of grey smoke rose up from them, like trapped noxious gases finally getting released. I sensed their flavor: They were of fear, guilt, anger, rage, hatred, confusion, grief, pain, doubt, negativity. The angels on the edge of the star wheel fanned these toxic grey mists and moved them out to sea. This was a global event, I realized; it was not limited to Prescelly; star wheels and other geomantic structures around the Earth were being similarly cleansed and detoxified under the direction of the Archangel Michael. And everywhere, like a drone, a sustained hum, came the words over and over: *O Michael, uplift us now.*

"This is the awakening of the energy transmutation in the landscape under Michael's direction," the Ofanim told me, "and another step towards the awakening of the Michaelic stream within humanity." Michaelmas is a great opportunity for humans to voluntarily move closer to Michael and his mission. "The Michael Festival," Rudolf Steiner wrote in 1923, "must be linked with a great and sustaining inner experience of man, with that inner force which summons him to develop self-consciousness out of Nature-consciousness through the strength of his thoughts, the strength of his will. . . ."[240]

After all, support of the development of human consciousness is the whole point of the Earth energy grid and the angelic interaction with it and humanity. Michaelmas each year is a chance, should we wish to use it, to take one step forward towards this awakening and flowering of awareness.[241]

From one viewpoint, it was a grim, intimidating sight, this global angel-facilitated cleansing of a year's worth of human emotional and psychic dross. From another, it was a joyous event, festive, invigorating, like a happy Mass the great J. S. Bach might have written especially for William

Blake. For it was more than a religious event; it was stripped of all religious connotations; it was an event far larger than the cognitive and theological conventions of religion could encompass. It was a glorious Mass for Michael sung by the angelic choirs in observance of this great day of global cleansing.

"The Ray Masters Are Coming to See Us by Train!"

This whimsical expression came to me in a dream one night in France. A few of us were at the long stone rows of Carnac in Brittany on the occasion of the Epiphany, January 6, a time when the Christ sends some attention to a preselected geomantic site on the Earth and keeps it there for a week. The Ray Masters are usually on hand for events of this magnitude for Earth. From my dream, I also remembered that the Ray Masters were coming embodied to a house where a dozen of us lived—us being, presumably, friends of the Ofanim.

The dream was mostly true, though not literally. The 14 Ray Masters of the Great Bear, colleagues of the Christ and the Ofanim, did not take human form that week, but we did feel their presence keenly at Carnac. As the Ofanim quipped, "the White Brotherhood gathers within your consciousness." They had been gathering for some time, actually, most conspicuously since one night in Tetford, England, a little village in Lincolnshire of high geomantic importance, when they wired the dome. (It was one of the planet's first domes to get "wired" to the Great Bear. Since then, many of the other domes have been wired.)

Fourteen figures in all appeared, and some I saw more clearly than others. "Through your consciousness, we have as best as possible earthed the standard 14 rays into the dome overhead, and

at least you have now a rudimentary understanding of these rays," the Ofanim told us when it was over.

"All domes, to be fully activated and active again, must be similarly wired to the 14 rays of the Great Bear [see table 6-1]. These rays have to be anchored by a grid engineer and facilitated by us and by a certain amount of sympathetic resonance of others. However, we would never activate them all as this would be a negative effect, like eating too much chocolate pudding."

I mentioned that the Ray Masters were "coming by train" to see us. If they were coming by train, then Bifrost, their rainbow bridge connecting Asgard with Midgard, or Middle Earth—our physical world—was their private rail car.

The Ray Masters have had many guises and names; they have appeared in many cultures at different times, as gods and human heroes, and have been remembered in different, sometimes confusing ways. My initial impressions of them were simplistic psychically. Read the Buddhist descriptions of deities and you get a grander, possibly more accurate, picture of them: amazing *bodhisattvas* floating in bubbles of light, seated amidst dozens of opulent lotus blossoms, with conches, *vajras*, flowers, and all manner of magical and celestial devices enhaloing them as part of their fantastic epiphany. Or they ride around in golden celestial chariots blazing with light, parking them for a while in the sky above the field of human events, observing developments.

The Greeks knew them as some of the Olympian gods; the ancient Hindus as the seven seers or rishis *(Rsi);* the Norse as the Aesir of Gladsheim at Asgard; the Sumerians as Enlil with his seven gods at Ekur (Mountain House) in Nippur; and the Iranians remembered them as the Seven *Abdals*.[242] The nineteenth-century Theosophists called them the great Masters or Chiefs of the Himalayas, as some at that time (El Morya, Kuthumi, Djwhal Khul) were more or less in bodily

Table 6-1: Color Affiliations and Selected Identities of the 14 Ray Masters

1. *Pale sky-blue:* Apollo, El Morya, Arjuna

2. *Orange, pale gold:* Artemis, Kybele, Kuthumi, John the Baptist, St. Francis of Assisi, Maitreya Buddha, Diana, Durga, Sekhmet, Cernunnos, Cynthia, Diktynna, Virgin Mary

3. *Pink:* Aphrodite, Lady Nada (Sound), Mary Magdalene, St. Joan of Arc, St. Bridgit, Brigit, Brigantia, Narada, Virgin Mary, Freyja, Ishtar-Astarte, Helen of Troy, Hathor

4. *Pale green:* Hilarion, St. Joseph (Jesus' father)

5. *Violet:* Serapis Bey, White Flame

6. *Scarlet, deep red:* Jesus, Subhuti, Santanda, Sanandana, Hephaistos, Goibniu, Wayland the Smith, Mithras, Freyr

7. *Lilac, pale purple:* St. Germaine, Prince Rakosky, Francis Bacon, William Shakespeare, Herakhan Baba

8. *Magenta/blue violet:* Pallas Athena, Valkyrie Brunnhilde

9. *Rich, dark blue:* Kali, Persephone, Virgin Mary

10. *Deep yellow:* Lao Tzu, St. Patrick

11. *Pale yellow:* Kwan Yin, Virgin Mary, Tibetan Green and White Tara

12. *Gold:* Lady Portia, Benjamin Franklin

13. *Purple/indigo:* Mahachohan the Teacher

14. *Emerald green:* Djwhal Khul the Tibetan

Note: The Virgin Mary in her apparitional form is often a composite of four Ray Masters taking a female valence and expressing four complementary aspects.

form for a while and had interaction with H. P. Blavatsky and her colleagues. They are "the eyes through which the Beyond looks at the world."[243]

In the Vedic perception, the rishis are mysterious beings closely associated with the origins of humanity and knowledge, or cosmic intelligence. They are eternal powers who manifest in successive ages. The Ray Masters are credited with authoring the Vedic hymns and are understood by Hindu mystics to be the embodiments of the various fundamental laws and principles of the universe and the basic "energies" that create and sustain life. The Vedas tell us that the seven rishis live *in* the seven major stars of the Great Bear or in some sense they *are* those stars, as each star is given a rishi's name in ancient Vedic star charts.

The Olympian gods, as any reader of Homer knows well, often sponsored human heroes (and fathered them in many cases), such as grey-eyed Pallas Athena, Hope of Soldiers, who unremittingly championed the cunning Odysseus. But sometimes it seemed their "help" was meddling, as when Aphrodite bribed the gullible Paris, son of Troy's King Priam, to pick her as the most beautiful of goddesses in exchange for the "right" to abduct Helen, Menelaus's wife, an ill-considered act that precipitated the ten-year Trojan War.

The Ray Masters are of course still active in human affairs, most notably in recent years in the acceleration of Marian apparitions, that is, appearances of the Virgin Mary in what seems to be a body of light. Often these apparitions are manifestations of several of the Ray Masters together, blending to present a composite image of what the Ofanim call "the compassionate goddess." These include Aphrodite, Kwan Yin, Durga (Artemis), and Kali (Persephone).

Two other Ray Masters (Saint Germaine and Lady Portia) are directly involved with the reopening of the domes and the Archangel Michael's Earth grid cleansing and activation work. Saint Germaine's lilac ray imparts an energy of transmutation, while Lady Portia's golden ray is one of compassion and mercy that brings discriminative wisdom into the transmutation. "Both aid your conscious development and harmonious development," the Ofanim note.

Anchoring the Great Bear with Oroboros Lines and Vibrating Stones

The relationship between the Ray Masters, the Great Bear, and zodiacal energies is demonstrated in a fundamental design feature of the planet's energy body, a series of 15 broad highways of light and consciousness that encircle the globe. I call them Oroboros Lines, because they "eat" their own tail after circling the planet. Each varies in intensity and in width from four feet to several hundred yards, most notably at major geomantic nodal points, such as domes, dome caps, dome lines, or intersections with other Oroboros Lines.

Twelve of these lines correspond to the 12 zodiacal constellations described in Western astrology; the other three correspond to the *pingala, ida,* and *sushumna* energy circuits as described in Tantric physiology. The *pingala* (solar, gold, positive) and *ida* (lunar, silver, negative) Oroboros Lines enter the Earth together, intertwined, at Avebury in England, deriving from the stars Sirius (*pingala*) and Canopus (*ida*).

The third line, the planetary *sushumna,* is neutral, originating in the star Polaris (the Pole Star in the Little Dipper) and grounding in the planet at Mount Meru in the South Pacific, southeast of New Zealand. Its corresponding dome is at Hardwar, India, while the domes for Sirius and Canopus are at Carnac, France, and Iona, Scotland, respectively.

A fairly well known example of an Oroboros Line—that is, among dowsers and Earth Mysteries enthusiasts—is the so-called Saint Michael Ley Line

in England, a straight energy track running about 380 miles from southwest Cornwall at Michael's Mount (at 62 degrees east of north) to northeast Suffolk at Bury Saint Edmunds. Along the way it is speckled with numerous churches dedicated to the Archangel Michael and megalithic sites. Then the dowsers claim it stops at the English Channel. It doesn't stop, of course, but continues around the planet, returning to its point of origin, Avebury.

Another Oroboros Line passes through Carnac in Brittany, a site with many important geomantic features. At an earlier time in Earth's geomantic history, this line (and the other 11) had an "archangelic governor" (the Ofanim's term; in this case, the Archangel Raphael), which gave the line an auric glow of golden light.

The Oroboros Lines each carry a different quality of vibration and celestial consciousness. Their colors tend to be primarily gold, but some are lilac. Visualize the Earth as a transparent sphere with 15 great circles of light encircling it; these light circles make a geometric form with 62 points of intersection among the lines and 120 equal-sized triangles formed by the crisscrossing of the lines. Both the Sirius and Canopus lines intersect and are connected with the other 13 Oroboros Lines at specific points.

You have, for example, a Scorpio Oroboros Line; it is connected to all the others and is intersected by the Sirius, Canopus, and Polaris lines, affording a blend of four energies. This energy quality is in continuous circulation around the Earth, feeding numerous geomantic nodes along its way.

Further, this matrix of 15 lines has direct relationships with the five Platonic Solids that comprise the planet's "body" at another level. I'll come back to the matter of the Solids later, but for now we need to remember that they are five precise geometric shapes with a total of 50 facets, which correspond to the five elements of matter (earth, air, water, fire, ether). All five are "nested" in a complicated geometric form that is an aspect of the Earth's energy-body armature, as in the windings of iron around a motor.[244]

What happens when the planetary "motor" turns? The Earth's environmental structure and film of organic life are maintained and nourished. The Oroboros Lines are the planet's primary energy tracks; after the birth of a biological being—a planet is one such, though a large one— the primary energy lines determine the nature of its environment and growth. An alternate metaphor to use to describe the grid is to call it Earth's cosmic placenta.

The connection with the Great Bear is straightforward: The lines come from the seven stars of the Big Dipper, each grounding at a specific point on the planet. There are seven stars, 14 rays, and 15 Oroboros Lines. Each of the Great Bear's seven stars generates two rays and has two Ray Masters; that's 14. *Three* of the Oroboros Lines are not concerned with zodiacal suns; *that's 12.* Originally, only 12 Ray Masters were grounded on Earth; two Ray Masters, Nada and Mahachohan, were implicit in another ray, like assistants. There's your zodiacal 12 Oroboros lines.

Picture 12 gossamer filaments of light coming out of the seven stars of the Great Bear and tying in to different places on the Earth. At each place where a Great Bear filament grounds, there was once a small conical stone. It is a physical stone, but the energy field surrounding it is much larger. The stone and its aura anchor the Great Bear light line. Glastonbury in England, Delphi in Greece, and Mecca in Saudi Arabia each anchor a Great Bear line. They do so with an actual physical rocklike object called a Vibrating Stone.[245]

The stones are small, about two feet high, and conical. They were set to anchor the incoming lines of light from the Great Bear; after the lines were grounded, they would circle the globe and return to the stone from the opposite direction.

The one at Delphi was called the omphalos; the one at Mecca, the *al-hajar al-aswad;* the one at Glastonbury, the egg stone. The Delphi stone is no longer extant; the Mecca one is housed in the big black cube called the Ka-aba but is said to be in pieces; the one at Glastonbury resides unremarked, ignored, by the Abbott's Kitchen at Glastonbury Abbey. Its original location was about a mile away, at a still obscure geomantic site of high importance called Beckery.

Islamic legend explains that the Mecca stone was originally a white stone delivered to Earth by God or the Archangel Gabriel—a meteorite. Its ultimate origin was as a white sapphire in the Garden of Eden; it turned black when menstruating women touched it, or due to humanity's sins. The Black Stone, as it's called, or *al-hajar al-aswad,* is now in seven pieces, having cracked into first three, then seven, in 684 A.D. in a fire. It was said to have been an ovoid stone, 15 inches high, 11 inches across, set in a silver casing about four feet off the ground in the southeast corner of the Ka-aba.[246]

The origin of the Vibrating Stones is tied to their purpose. They come from the Andromeda galaxy, one of 35 galaxies in what astronomers call the Local Group. Of the 35 described galaxies in the Local Group, the Andromeda galaxy, M31, is the brightest in what astronomers dub "a remarkably dull corner of the Universe."

Why is the Andromeda galaxy important to the Earth? Because one of the many cosmic threads that led to the possibility of human incarnation on Earth at this point originated in Andromeda. Even though we do not remember this—and it would seem, in a linear sense, to be so vastly long ago that it is of no consequence— the memory of the Andromedan antecedent "thread" is outside of planetary time and always available for conscious recall.

The Vibrating Stones were brought from Andromeda "as part of the heritage of human consciousness on Earth and to be transceivers for your stellar inheritance, or the totality of the human collective," the Ofanim explain.[247]

When all the Vibrating Stones were extant and in their designated positions, they were energized and activated by those whom the Ofanim refer to as the "Cosmic Chaplains," who were positioned around the planet in the domes for the benefit of all living beings here.

Each stone had its specific time of activity—they were cyclically timed—but they resonated in harmony and with one another, "matter vibrating in synchronicity." The Ofanim explain: "They were synchronously resonating in reciprocal maintenance with one another and thus fed the Earth. The Earth reciprocally maintained the relationship of interdependence. Each of the 12 Vibrating Stones resonated at a particular frequency in sympathetic harmony with the astrological constellations. The most relevant point is the *relationship*. The Earth is an active force, as well as a receptive one. Each celestial, terrestrial, and lunar body is in sympathetic resonance, one with the other, traveling at tremendous speed through infinite space."[248]

So what has happened to the system in recent millennia now that nearly all the stones either have disappeared or are not in their places? "It is like taking a satellite dish away from its position in relation to the wiring for reception," say the Ofanim. "If the features were moved, then the wiring in some instances is no longer intact. At one point the Oroboros Lines were connected through light filaments to the 12 stones. The planet is not suffering especially from this break in the connection. Now it is rather like a combination of a memory and something that is actualized by the being of the Earth as She develops. The Stones still serve a residual purpose, to remind humanity of its stellar origins."

In other words, the original sites still perform the grounding of Oroboros Lines and the Great Bear connections even though the physical stones

are no longer in place. The planet has *remembered* the connection, or perhaps its entrainment with it was so deeply implanted that it has incorporated that imposition into itself and can now run automatically with that original alignment. So the nourishing currents of the Great Bear are still in continuous circulation around the Earth.

You could stand at Delphi at the approximate place of the omphalos stone and still experience the Oroboros Line linkup. This mystical geomantic perception was encoded in Greek myth, which said Zeus sent two eagles from the ends of the Earth to find the planet's exact center. Their flights and beaks converged at Delphi precisely over the omphalos stone. Later a statue of two eagles was said to stand near the stone as a reminder of the world-encircling energy line whose oroboric path was tracked by the two eagles.[249]

What might you experience by standing where a Vibrating Stone once stood or psychically tuning in to one from a distance? I did both. I have touched the Glastonbury egg stone, and I drew on that tactile memory to enhance my own "tuning" in to the stone from a distance.

Its energy field was a bright yellow, and as I entered it my attention was immediately shifted to a desert. A bearded, turbaned *sheikh* indicated a tentlike enclosure in the desert encampment. Inside, a Vibrating Stone rested on a waist-high pedestal. But it was more than a conical, ovoid stone; it was a god's head, a living presence. I saw the other 11 stones through this one as if they were all, holographically, inside this single one—the Ofanim's "sympathetic resonance." I understood that the stones were judged to be too potent for common, casual viewing or interaction, so they were kept secluded and guarded.

This stone seemed like a bead on a thread, which perhaps was the Oroboros Line passing through it. It resembled an open lion's mouth, swallowing the oroboric current, retaining it in its god's body, transmitting it like food to the other

11 stones, equally open-mouthed. At the same time, the stone lion seemed to spit out the rushing energy current. When it was time for a given stone to be energized (its geomantic role amplified) in accordance with astronomical and astrological cycles and alignments, the stone would "swallow" the Oroboros Line and generate a wide field of influence around it.

The field of influence was like that produced when you drop a pebble in a still pond. Concentric ripples proliferate. The stone would then be overshadowed by a seemingly full-bodied expression or manifestation of the god, presumably the star god of the prevailing astrological constellation—say, Leo, for example, perhaps represented by its brightest star, Regulus. Then it seemed to rise and expand majestically from out of the stone into which it had compressed itself, leaving but the deity's head as a sigil of its presence there.

Then the stone would pulsate and emit sounds, vibrations—maybe music of a kind. When a stone became active, it was lit from within, like the white sapphires described in the Garden of Eden (and Mecca's Black Stone). This sound would be a food for the planet and its organic life, representing one of the basic vibrations that underlie and help to cohere matter, that made the ethers a creative womb for planetary life. Remember, the Oroboros Lines together maintain the organic film of life on Earth. Viewed in a time-lapse photography way, you could see during a year the 12 stones blinking on and off around the planet like fireflies.

Large-Scale Beings in the Windows of the Planet's Landscape

There is another aspect to the 12 Vibrating Stones. They are each a doorway to the same place. Each of these stones opens into Jerusalem, so as an alternate esoteric name, I call them Jerusalem Gates. As I said earlier, this is not the city in Israel, but the "heavenly" Jerusalem, the cosmic design archetype of the Emerald and Cube of Space.

Jerusalem of course has 12 gates. On a global geomantic level, each of the grounding points for an Oroboros Line is a gate into Jerusalem, which is the entire Earth at a more rarified level of expression. It's worth recalling that God's chief archangel, *Helel ben Shahar,* Son of the Dawn, "walked in Eden amid blazing jewels, his body a-fire" with carnelian, topaz, emerald, diamond, beryl, onyx, jasper, carbuncle, and sapphire, "all set in purest gold."[250]

Why should a Vibrating Stone be a Jerusalem Gate? It's the correlations with the astrological constellations. Each Oroboros Line circulates an astrological energy, such as Libra, Taurus, Sagittarius; each Stone grounds that Line and the solar energy from the constellation. The planet's 12 Vibrating Stones and their solar-astrological correlates are a global *hoshen mishpat,* or priestly breastplate. The high priest of Israel wore a breastplate comprising 12 jewels, each representing a Tribe of Israel and by extension a constellation. The Tribe of Judah, for example, was linked with the constellation Leo.[251]

Here's how the breastplate describes a geomantic fact of the planet. Energetically its surface is divided into 12 equal geometric sections, each a five-sided pentagon I call an Albion Plate. These 12 geometric "faces" or plates comprise the Platonic Solid called a dodecahedron, a polyhedron of 12 equal faces, the Platonic Solid that pertains to ether.

The Albion reference will be explained in chapter 10, but here we can say the Plate represents the first major fractalized subset within the Earth's multilayered geomantic matrix. Each Albion Plate repeats most of the design features of the entire planet and, with some exceptions, contains the same amounts of geomantic features as the other Plates.

In addition to the interpretations given to the matter of the 12 Tribes by orthodox Judaism, there is a geomantic aspect as well. The 12 Tribes also refer to the 12 Albion Plates and the disposition of 12 original human soul groups across the global landmass of Earth in its earliest days of human settlement. Originally, there was a Virgo Albion Plate, a Leo Albion Plate, and so forth, in accordance with these fundamental soul group dispositions. Thus the 12 Tribes were manifestations of the people of each of the Albion Plates.

Though there has been much intermingling of the Tribes over the life of the Earth, and now each Tribe has aspects of each other, originally a primary soul root was grounded for the planet in certain indigenous tribes that had their origin within each of these Albion Plates and maintained the original genetic coding.

Each Albion Plate is subject to a prevailing astrological influence for a period of 2,100 years, the same cycle as an astrological Age. This means one Albion Plate will be primarily influenced by Aries for two millennia, while another is under the "eye" of Aquarius, and another under Capricorn. Today the Albion Plate encompassing the British Isles and France is under a Virgo influence; the Plate over north-central Europe and part of the Mideast is Aquarius; the U.S. East Coast is under Scorpio; while the Northwest U.S. is under Taurus, and the Southwest—extending into Peru—is under Leo.

During these 2,100 years, the geomantic features within the Leo Albion Plate will have a Leo *flavor*. Think of it this way: A generic human being without memories (software), but with the essential humanness (hardware), lives in Germany for ten years. He gets imprinted with German-ness. Then he is relocated to Italy; the German slate is wiped clean, and he is now imprinted with the qualities of Italian-ness. Everything is experienced through this Italian *filter*. It's a rough analogy for how an astrological imprinting or sustained influence works on an Albion Plate.

If the 12 Albion Plates were glass windows, there would be at least two prominent painted designs upon them. You would see the sigil of the specific Tribe of Israel (a permanent imprint) and the glyph of the astrological constellation or perhaps an imprint of the entire constellation or its composite figure (a transient imprint). Think of these two imprints as programming rather than a literal image on a glass plate window, which is itself only a metaphorical description.

There was also a thirteenth Tribe kept independent to influence and balance the other 12 in a positive, wholesome way. This thirteenth Tribe was not affiliated with any of the 12 Albion Plates nor did it originate nor was it seeded on the Earth as the other 12 were. This independent tribe came from elsewhere and has already been introduced earlier as the Hyperboreans (Pleiadians).

There is another link between all this and Jerusalem. The Lord of Light's crown (see chapter 11) had 13 blazing jewels, including an Emerald. Alternatively, he is said to wear a crown studded with 13 Emeralds. Either way, these jewels correspond to the 13 Tribes and the 12 Albion Plates, and they are on their way back to his crown in a glorious gesture of restitution or, as Qabala puts it, *Tikkun*, the fixing of the broken world.

Each Emerald ended up with the egregor (explained below), a guardian of each Tribe and its Albion Plate and, according to the Ofanim, now needs "reconciling within the Lord of Light's crown as the Emerald opens within the Heart of Man." Some of the Emeralds from the Albion Plates are almost back in place and activated, and the Lord of Light at this point in time has a part of his crown reassembled.

"As a small percentage of humans begin journeying towards the Heart energy center, so part of the crown is reassembled," the Ofanim say. "The 13 Tribes and the 13 Emeralds need to be opened so that the crown is complete; then the Lord of Light resumes his position in relation to God."

Obviously there is much in this last concept that needs explanation. First, each Albion Plate has a primary Emerald planted somewhere within its domain. This single Emerald represents, holographically, the Emerald for a Tribe and one of the jewels or Emeralds of the crown. Let's consider two of them.

The Emerald for the Albion Plate that occupies part of the East Coast of North America is grounded at Palmyra, New York, the home of Mormonism and the founding visions of Joseph Smith. The Emerald for the Albion Plate encompassing the British Isles is at the Hill of Tara near Dublin, Ireland; this is the ancient seat of the Irish kings and was known as the site of the *Lia Fail*, the Stone of Destiny and Knowledge, brought by the gods called Tuatha de Danann from their magical city of Falias in the earliest days of the Earth.

Outwardly, the opening and activation of these two Emeralds do not depend on the efforts of the Mormons or Irish; they are better thought of as caretakers. Input from humans anywhere, within the extent of an Albion Plate, from any religious or spiritual affiliation can usefully influence the activation of the Albion Plate Emerald. The delivery of this input does not even require you to be present physically at the Emerald site. It's the Ofanim's sympathetic resonance again—thoughts in sympathy travel fast.

I mentioned a strange term above, egregor. This is from the Greek, *egregoros,* and means "Watcher or Guardian." When the Earth was designed, provision was made for nine landmasses now known collectively as Pangaia.[252] These nine would each be "topped" and bounded by an Albion Plate and correspond to a Tribe; the other three would be underwater and not used.

Each of these original landmasses was assigned a landscape angel called an egregor. In a sense, this egregor was an angelic being, neutral and receptive, to process and hold the life experiences of the Tribe living within its aegis. It is like the thoughtform of a human collective that grew over time, a potential based on varying energetic possibilities.

"Humans collectively contribute to what is there in potential, and the interaction between the energetic possibilities and humans brings the egregor into being," the Ofanim state.

While the Earth's landmasses have drifted a good deal over the course of planetary life, the Albion Plates are essentially intact, and so are the nine landmass egregors. They are still processing the experiences of the Tribes and the subsidiary landscape angels. Their purpose is to process the landscape angel's positive and negative experiences. The landscape angel is an egregor that is an accumulation of various entities—a lesser level of an egregor.

It's a matter of delegation. Egregors have smaller egregors that have smaller egregors until you get very small egregors; the smaller egregors are landscape angels. "There are too many landscape angels for us to count," the Ofanim comment. "There are billions. Some are little landscape angels, some medium size, some are big landscape angels, and some very big landscape angels. A small suburban garden, for example, can have a landscape angel."

In addition to the primary nine egregors guarding the nine original landmasses of Pangaia, 72 subsidiary egregors watch over the significant divisions of these landmasses. Over time these 72 have assumed a shape or form appropriate to the landmass they oversee and its quality of consciousness, symbolically expressed. Norway's egregor, for example, is a moose; America's is the eagle; Russia's a star; France's the rooster or cock; England's the matron Britannia with her spear. Here is a simple and obvious example. Ireland's egregor is called Eriu, after whom the country was named, Eriu-land.[253] Anciently, Eriu was a queen among the Tuatha de Danann, the old gods of Ireland. In one of the Irish myths, as Ireland was about to be attacked and inhabited by the Milesians, Eriu declared to their leader, "Grant me one wish, then: let this land be named after me."[254]

Qabala teaches that there are 72 national "angelic regents," assigned one per country or ethnic group. Each nation has an angel set over it as a spiritual leader, and these terrestrial angels oversee public affairs and the doings of princes and magistrates.[255] "The office of a Watcher is to protect from outside pressures a region or ethnic group assigned to its care." Further, a given group of persons (those being protected) is "'tied' to a certain area of jurisdiction." That area of jurisdiction may be a country, state, or city.[256]

You may have observed that there are 81 egregors for Earth in all. This number, in addition to being a "nine" number, so typical of most quantities of geomantic features on Earth, is also the same number as the minor dragons. In chapter 4, I explained that each of the 13 principal dragons can generate 81 minor dragons. The number 81 for egregors is a sideways clue and link with the dragons. It turns out the dragon is the defender of the egregor. This means at least 81 of the 1,053 minor dragons defends a landmass egregor.

Why would an egregor, an astral being of angelic derivative, need to be defended by a dragon? Because the 81 egregors cast a reflection onto the Earth which reshapes itself to match the form of that landmass's egregor. So you have the astral egregor above and the landscape geomantic egregor below.

The landscape expression of the egregor will tend to be an especially numinous district, perhaps traditionally reserved as sanctified land for ritualistic purposes, or sometimes benignly neglected but indirectly protected. The landscape egregor is a mystery temple for a nation's or people's collective experiences and expressions over a vast time, a semiphysical repository of the more subtly manifest astral egregor overshadowing it.

Here are two examples to clarify the point. A possible landmass egregor for one of the nine original landmasses of Pangaia was proposed in 1977 by clairvoyant researcher J. J. Hurtak, although he didn't call it an egregor.

He published a map of North and Central America showing an astral dove overlaid with its beak in the Galapagos Islands, its head from New Orleans to Guatemala City; its body covered all of the continental United States, its wings swept up into Alaska and Newfoundland, and its tail rested over Manitoba, Canada. Hurtak stated that the Dove as a geomantic body or landscape overlay had been "seeded" with galactic knowledge 20 million years ago by the Great White Brotherhood and was in the process of being opened and activated.[257]

The possible landscape tie-down for the United States eagle egregor was identified and interacted with in a provisional way in the early 1990s by a small group on the basis of Masonic and Native American legends and suggestions. The U.S. egregor was proposed to be overlaid on a portion of the Pennsylvania landscape. According to one theory, an original color soils map of one-third of Pennsylvania reveals the figure of an eastward-facing eagle.

On this point the Ofanim comment: "It is a national figure representing the Logos of the nation, that is, the Word in the landscape. It has correspondences with the constellation Aquila [an eagle], but they are not the same. It is the character of a country, teacher and predator. It is the eye that sees far and the heart that embraces all. But it is prone to deception. It needs harmony and truth. The biggest form of deception is self-deception. What is needed is self-perception, and then the eye that sees far functions from the heart."

There are several ways we can look at the 72 egregors. The folk-ness of a people—their *German*-ness, *Italian*-ness—over time flows into the egregor. The egregor is the perpetual reservoir of those folk experiences, taking shape in accordance with the evolution of psyche and landscape under its aegis. Its memory is as old as the creation of the landmass on which this folk now reside, and it retains the impressions of all other folk who earlier inhabited that same landscape. It is the soul of the folk.[258] For the implication of the *fact* of the 72 egregors is that the psyche of a folk is tied intimately to *its* landscape and that landscape and folk evolve interactively.

It isn't that the egregor of Norway, for example, is truly a large astral moose who casts a geomantic reflection somewhere on Norwegian land; rather, the quality of the psyche-landscape interaction over time has generated this symbolically apt form. We might think of the 72 egregors as a landscape-folk expression of the 72 Names of God, in this case, as 72 variations on the possible outcome of a long-term evolutionary interaction between psyche (a specific soul group or folk soul) and landscape (mountainous, deciduous, desert).[259]

How Polaris Supports the World on His Shoulders

Let's return to the Albion Plates. Each of these is topped by an enormous light canopy, what I call a Universe Dome. It's like a star dome, only much bigger, and does not represent a specific individual star. Picture the Earth as having 12 equal-sized pentagonal facets, or Albion Plates. For convenience, picture these as glass windows. On top of each window is a half-globe. I call it a Universe Dome because its quality is akin to what Qabala calls *Ain Sof*, the formless state of light before manifestation, even before Kether, the First Crown or Sefira.

This is abstract territory, but Qabala describes three qualities (or one composite quality) of existence above, beyond, or before the Tree of Life, the Four Worlds, and the 40 Sefirot. *Ain* is absolute nothing, a zero, a void beyond existence. *Ain Sof* means endless, the "Absolute All" to *Ain's* "Absolute Nothing." God as transcendent is *Ain;* God as immanent is *Ain Sof. Ain Sof Awr* is the "Endless Light of Will" that is "omniscient throughout Absolute All." Qabalists call these three principles the hidden roots, or *Zahzahot,* the three Hidden Splendors.[260]

You might think of these three Hidden Splendors as the aura of the Ancient of Days, the arcane halo around His head, the Prime Crown. The Ofanim call the Hidden Splendors the Black Bowling Ball. It sounds whimsical, but it is a helpful construct through which to approach this otherwise recondite matter. Actually, it might have been I who first called this "thing" the Black Bowling Ball (and they didn't object), mainly because to my untutored mind, it resembled one. The Ofanim call it the stable sphere of consciousness, the black void, the black sphere. Not surprisingly, they explained it in terms of a riddle:

"When you know the black sphere, there will be no more questions. It is the memory of all questions. It relates to your purpose, your life, and your existence, here, now, on a moment-to-moment basis. Knowing the black sphere of stable consciousness will take you beyond all questions, all answers, all concepts, all form, all emptiness, all ideas or notions of self-nature, beyond the beyond. It is what you are. It is what you are not. The black ball is the ultimate question, and within that is the ultimate answer. It is beyond space and time, beyond concepts, beyond formlessness." See what I mean about the riddle?

The key point here is that the Universe Dome is akin to the Black Bowling Ball, as if this explains anything. Let's say that out of the emptiness of the black sphere of stable consciousness, the Hidden Splendors rolling towards the Earth, comes the abundance of geomantic forms that comprise Earth's visionary geography.

"These big domes are big, and their function is big," the Ofanim state. "This is a multidimensional energy matrix projection comprising many levels of energy, form, and information." The Universe Dome is like a grand circus tent under which all the geomantic features in the various levels or dimensions in the Albion Plate have their life, including the star domes and their dome caps.

But the Black Bowling Ball expressed as a Universe Dome has another feature: a point of light, a blazing star, a pinprick of brilliant light at its center. It's the Ofanim again. "We come in the black sphere of stable consciousness. We roll it towards you. We are the point of light at the center of the sphere." There's another, perhaps more familiar name for this point of light at the center of the galaxy: Polaris, or as the Vedas knew it, Dhruva, the Immovable, the Motionless.

Astronomically, Polaris is the star at the tail of the Little Bear (Ursa Minor) or the handle of the Little Dipper. Experientially, Polaris is the pinprick of light at the center of the sphere. It is the galactic expression of the Blazing Star.

Dhruva is the fixed, firm, constant Pole Star, as the Vedas put it, the *grahadhara*, the Pivot of the Planets around which the Heavens spin. It's the navel of the Earth (Greeks), the Stake (Laplanders), the Iron Peg (Turks), the Great Imperial Ruler of Heaven (Chinese), the Nail (Syrians), and the Northern Axle, Spindle, or Pin (Arabic).[261]

Hindu myths tell us that Dhruva was the son of King Uttanapada (the constellation Ursa Minor), who in turn was born of Svayambhuva Manu, the Manu of the present age and progenitor of humanity, Lawgiver Son-of-the-Self-born. Dhruva left his father's palace indignant at age five and practiced austerities by the River Yamuna. After five months of intense practice, Dhruva attained full concentration on Vishnu who left Vaikuntha to appear before Dhruva. Seeing Vishnu, Dhruva became absorbed in the love of God.[262]

Dhruva told Vishnu his aspiration was to know how to praise the high god and to attain the highest position; it was not a matter of sovereignty above the gods, stars, and planets, but one of proximity to Vishnu. The god appointed Dhruva to be the Pole Star, as an eternal example to all people of the heights that steadfastness to Vishnu devotion could attain. Dhruva would also sustain all the stars. He would be the highest devotee of Vishnu among the stars, the exemplar of perfect purity of mind and devotion setting the standard for all the star gods.

It is spiritually appropriate that the pivot star, the one that sustains all others and around which all revolve, would be the one closest to Vishnu (Christ). One way of reading this star myth is that Dhruva (Polaris) is the doorway from the galaxy stars to the cosmic Christ (Vishnu). But it's a swinging doorway: you can pass through it to Vishnu, and Vishnu can pass through it to you.[263]

It is also told of Dhruva that as a prince he had a special virtue which alarmed the gods. He could stand on one leg for a month or longer, never moving. For this reason, the gods decreed that all the stars and planets would turn around him. Dhruva then ascended to the highest pole in the universe, to the exalted seat of Vishnu around which the stars would wander forever. He would be like "the upright axle of the corn mill circled without end by the laboring oxen," the Bhagavata Purana states.[264] The seven stars of the Great Bear (Ursa Major) are sometimes called the Seven Oxen, even in Western star lore.[265]

The Bhagavata Purana further explains that the chariots of the nine planets are fastened to Dhruva by "aerial cords" and that the orbs of all the planets, 27 *naksatras,* and stars "are attached to Dhruva and travel accordingly in their proper orbits, being kept in their places by their respective bands of air." All the stars and planets revolve around Dhruva until *akalpa-antam,* the end of creation. "Dhruva literally means 'fixed' in Sanskrit, and thus precession [of the equinoxes] is not recognized in the [text called] Bhagavatam."[266]

To picture Polaris and the Universe Dome, it's helpful to see it as a complete globe set halfway into the Earth. In terms of their active aspects, star domes are primarily half a sphere, rising as a canopy over the ground. The Universe Domes penetrate the Earth to the same distance as they rise above the ground. Here it gets a little confusing: Polaris as the Blazing Star in the Universe Dome is mostly at ground level, yet it can be experienced as above and below and in the middle, too.

You can experience this firsthand at a place called the Eight Riding Tree on Burley Hill, an estate in Oakham in Rutland, England. The Eight Riding Tree is a quaint old English term for the convergence of eight different equestrian trails in the middle of a wood marked by a small wooden tower. If you stand there and tune in to your own Blazing Star, you may become aware of a vast column of light, a hollow illuminated pillar lined with glass rising up many miles and seemingly disappearing in the darkness of space. You could ascend this tube if you wish, but in a funny way just standing there attuned to your Star is the same as ascending the tube. You would find yourself at the top only in the same place.

Technically, it's connecting with the inside top of the Universe Dome just as it is anchoring that top to the ground where you stand. I call this feature a Dhruva Anchor Point.[267] The planet has 12, one for each Albion Plate. It is the umbilicus for each Albion Plate. Think of it as the pivot point around which the cosmogonic structure of the Albion Plate revolves. The Universe Dome thus recapitulates the cosmogonic structure, at the level of both the galaxy and the entire planet.

The tube or column of light is the umbilical connection for a very large geomantic feature called an Albion, which is a large version of yourself, made of Earth and light, supine upon the landscape. It is reminiscent of the long lotus stalk arising from Vishnu's navel as he sleeps on Sesa-Ananta. In this case, the stalk arises from Albion's belly, rising to the inside top of the Universe Dome.

It's important to remember that when we discuss Albion Plates we are dealing with a level of the Earth's visionary body one step down from the global, singular planetary level. We are at the level of first fractal. The Earth as a whole has its umbilical connection at Avebury that anchors two primary Oroboros Lines. The third is anchored at Mount Meru, the primordial holy mountain of the gods, located at the opposite point on the planet from Avebury. There the light from Polaris comes in, is anchored for the planet, then distributed.

In the Albion Plates, the Polaris light comes into Earth at 12 locations, each at the approximate center (if not geographic, then energetic[268]) of an Albion Plate. That light flows in like a celestial river, the original Ganges River said to flow through Shiva's hair down to Mount Meru and then down to Earth. The Polaris Oroboros Line is the Ganges River of light after which the terrestrial river of water in India was named.

The planet's star dome for Polaris, as mentioned earlier, is at Hardwar, India. It's name is a valuable clue: Hardwar means "Gate of the Lord," from *Dwar*, which means "gate" and *Har*, which means Shiva, and *Hari,* for Vishnu. The Brahmakund, or Brahma's Basin, at Hardwar is an actual pool in the Ganges, so named because long ago Brahma came here to greet the River Ganges as it flowed down from Heaven to this spot. So this is the gate for the incoming, grounding river flow, the sluice gates that allow the celestial current of the Ganges (Polaris) to flow into the planet's grid arteries.

The prime Ganges current flows into Mount Meru as the Polaris line; and it flows into the Polaris star dome at Hardwar in India; but it also flows into each of the 12 Dhruva Anchor Points in the first level of fractalization or duplication.

The flow of the celestial Ganges into a Dhruva Anchor Point can be perceived as a hollow, illuminated glass-lined tube. The Greeks personified it and called it the Titan Atlas, the giant deity who held the world on his shoulders. His name meant "He who carries" or "He who endures," or perhaps it should have meant, "He who has superstrong shoulders to uphold the world's weight." Originally, Atlas was conceived to be the guardian of the pillar of Heaven; later he became associated with that pillar and the two seemed to merge into one.[269]

As at Burley Hill, at the Externsteine (a stone formation in Germany) you can look up the Irminsul (a psychically perceived column) as if through a vast hollow column of light, straight up and into Polaris. Doing so, you may get a fresh insight into the meaning of the old myths that said long ago that a great spiritual hero lifted the heavy sky off Mother Earth so humans could stand up and life could flourish on the ground. That hero remained in place, keeping the realms separate, or he put a pole there instead. The Polynesians tell of Tane, the Forest-God, lifting up the sky, Rangi, off of his wife, Papa, the Earth, and keeping him suspended high above the ground. Equivalently, the Greeks tell of Atlas.

Let's equate that huge pillar with Atlas, who is or became a gigantic pillar. The surprising discovery is that he's upside down. If you're standing under the Universe Dome and at the Dhruva Anchor Point, you may notice Atlas's feet are planted at the inside top of the dome and his head is just grazing the ground. In fact, his head is splayed out a great distance in all directions like a vast water fountain, and the Ganges is spuming out of his head.

Yes, Atlas supports the world, but the world is down here, on Earth. The Universe Dome, we must remember, is essentially a void, a black empty sphere. Polaris is the first pinprick of light in the galaxy, the first glimmerings of a world.

Atlas brings Polaris and allows it to gush out of his head like a swollen celestial river, the Polaris current, to inundate the world.

It's probably more accurate to say Atlas provides for the world, rather than supports it, manifesting the world out of his head. In fact, it is probably more accurate—certainly more mythologically elegant—to think of the Vedic Dhruva, the Greek Atlas, and the unconfirmed god Irmin as the same being. The important point, though, is that this pillar is a direct line to Polaris and the Christ.

Just as the Hindu star myth told us that the young Dhruva attained his ecstatic encounter with Vishnu, so the Dhruva Anchor Point can conduct us to it as well. Or looking at it from the opposite end, the cosmic Christ can enter the world and be grounded at the Dhruva Anchor Point. Appropriately, at Hardwar, next to the Brahmakund is the *Hariki-Pairi*, or "Hari's Foot," believed to be a footprint left by Vishnu (Hari is an epithet) when he "visited" Hardwar long ago.

Zeus Faces—Higher Geomantic Mysteries of the Chief of the Gods

Another and comparatively sublime geomantic feature is found at the level of the 12 Albion Plates. I call these Zeus Faces. They are 12 symbolic forms of Zeus, the great chief of the Olympian gods, which have been imprinted on and above the landscapes. Of course when I refer to Zeus, I include (or imply) his other mythic counterparts, Seth, Yahweh, Thor, Enlil, and Shiva (in his executive aspect as Indra).

If you read the resumes of these chief gods carefully, you will find most are associated with an animal or occasionally assume an animal form, such as Zeus and the white bull. The Greeks record that Zeus was besotted by a woman called Europa. Zeus assumed the form of a handsome bull of dazzling whiteness, whose horns were like crescent moons. He lay submissively, coyly at Europa's feet, hoping to win her affections. It worked. She climbed on to his back, and he strode off into the sea with her and swam all the way to Crete from a place in today's Syria.

To decode the geomantic reference of this charming myth you have to read it backwards, as if in a mirror. Europa is the young continent we know as Europe, and the white bull is Zeus's immanence in it. A large overlay of Zeus in his white bull form occupies much of central Europe from Crete through Italy, the Slavic countries, Switzerland, and Germany, tracking the former sites of high prevalence for the ancient Mithraic cult of the slain cosmic bull.

The story of Zeus and Europa is a geomyth. (There are, presumably, 11 others, one for each Albion Plate, although I haven't found them all, nor do the Faces look the same.) The one for the Virgo Albion Plate, overlaying the British Isles and France, comes from ancient Welsh legend.

Culhwch wanted to marry Olwen, the daughter of Ysbaddaden, chief of the giants. The latter would grant the proposal only if Culhwch performed a couple dozen heroic feats, mostly impossible, including getting the comb and razor suitable for shaving the giant's tough beard from between the ears of a great and formidable boar called Twrch Trwyth. The boar had once been a king but had been transformed into the swine shape by God for his sins, although it is also said Twrch Trwyth was the son of Torc Triath, king of the boars and the original divine boar.

Culhwch enlisted King Arthur and his court (in a pre-English expression of that myth) to get the boar for him. Arthur and his entourage chased the boar from Ireland through Wales and Cornwall. The Welsh myth specifies numerous sites where Arthur specifically engaged the boar. They finally overcame him in western Cornwall and got the bristles, their prime objective.[270]

In the Welsh adventure tale of chasing Twrch Trwyth, the boar gets all the screen time, while the originating god figure (Ysbaddaden chief-giant) is in the deep background. He is a king who sinned and was punished by God. Nonetheless, the story is a geomyth of the Albion Plate overlaying the British Isles and a clear description of the form of its Zeus Face: a great boar. The sites where Arthur fought the boar can be interpreted as key landscape energy centers within this huge geomythic figure.

The myth also gives us orientation: Arthur was after the comb and razors between the boar's ears and finally got them in southwestern Cornwall. That tells us where the geomythic figure's landscape head chakras are; its root center is where the chase began, in Ireland. The rest of its energy centers lie in between.

Does Zeus really have animal forms? No. Do the large landscape figures under an Albion Plate truly depict a god in specific animal form? Not precisely. The animal shapes are metaphors to convey aspects of the numinous presence and potency of Zeus whose attention fills the world in 12 places.[271] As metaphors, they suggest some aspects of Zeus: he—and let's remember we are referring to an energy-consciousness working through Sirius—is a strong, mighty, invincible, unlimited generative force that can seem ferocious and raging to the unprepared, promiscuous and lewd to the puritanical, and a delightful coy lover to the mystical; he is a source of dazzling light that nourishes, invigorates, protects, sustains, preserves, creates, fertilizes, even destroys, as appropriate throughout the world.

What's the purpose of the Zeus Faces? To give the Albion Plates an infusion of the higher mind, a geomantic mental body. In a sense, these imprints on the windows of the Albion Plates are idea precursors or mental parents of the 12 signs of the star wheel of the zodiac, which comes later.

From our terrestrial human vantage point, the true contours of the Zeus Face are too exalted to condense into an accurate impression. The animal shapes have metaphorical accuracy and help to ground something that does not directly correspond to physical concepts. The animal shapes and attributions vary somewhat per Albion Plate depending on the cultures that arose under their influence, the astrological filtering of that Albion Plate, and the Tribe and landmass egregor identifications.

The point of it all is to demonstrate the immanence of God in our physical world through His executive representative, the variously named chief of the gods, Zeus, Thor, Enlil, Seth, Yahweh, and the others, through their 12 Albion Plate manifestations. There the Supreme Being is, beaming pacifically or frowning ferociously (depending on our filters), through the energy skin of our world, inviting us to walk all over His face, aware or oblivious, interacting or ignoring His presence. Our choice.

In fact, it's useful to realize that the existence of the Earth's visionary geography means that the spiritual world and God are immanent in our material world and bodies despite our disbelief.

Two geomantic features regulate how much the Zeus Face radiates into the Earth's visionary geography and our physical realm. The first is called a Control Bubble, of which globally there are 238, distributed more or less equally per Albion Plate. The master Control Bubble is at Avebury in Wiltshire; the Control Bubbles in each Albion Plate are distributed somewhat in accordance with the distribution of major stars by way of their domes within an Albion Plate. Think of the Control Bubble as a control room that regulates the inflow of cosmic energies.

I first saw a Control Bubble at what seemed to me a highly unlikely location, behind a building on the campus of the University of Virginia. Later as I understood the associated geomantic features in the Charlottesville, Virginia, area (former home of Thomas Jefferson), it made sense.

The Bubble appeared as a beehive globular cell or spherical greenhouse. Numerous glass panes lined the walls of the Bubble, with smaller panes within those. I realized I was perceiving a hologram of all the geomantic features within the Albion Plate, which meant it existed and operated at several different levels of geomantic reality, just as do the actual features "out" in the Earth's grid.

The central control room seemed to have four large driver's wheels, or perhaps the wheels used on ships for steering. In this case they were for adjusting the mixture of energies flowing through the Albion Plate. There were dozens of smaller wheels and knobs on the walls. A brown-robed man was working the controls, taking instructions from elsewhere by way of a headset; it reminded me of an airline cockpit. I realized I was "seeing" a crude analogy for the function of a Control Bubble. There were no wheels or knobs, but how else do you represent the concept that the mixture of angelic and elemental energies is regulated through this Control Bubble by angelic workers? Perhaps it is closer to the otherworldly reality to say the angelic operator would merely touch one of the glass panes to make a change in the mixture. The entirety of the glass panes formed a kind of composite stained glass figure that included the Zeus Face and a translucent generic human figure called Albion (see chapter 10), which embodied it all.

Father and Son, Zeus Face and Albion, embodied the totality of geomantic features in this spherical control station. It was as if they were both spherically expressed, if you can imagine a face (or bull, boar, or goat) and a generic human curved around the 360 degrees of a gravity-free iridescent soap bubble.

The Zeus Face has 156 openings, places where the Supreme Being through His executive aspect of Zeus can "inhale" humans into that exalted realm. There are exhalation points, too. I call these Prana Distributors. There are 288 of these globally, distributed 24 per Albion Plate.

We find some context for this feature in the Qabalistic descriptions of the archetypal human, in which context they are called the 288 Sparks or Lights. "These 288 Sparks are the total of four quantities of 72 Sparks that fell from above," explains Rabbi Moses C. Luzzatto.[272] It's not an easy concept to explain, as it involves abstruse Qabalistic discussions on the permutations of the Divine Name, *YHVH*. This is the abbreviation of the unpronounceable Name of God, shortened to *Yod He Vod He*, or Jehovah-Yahweh, in brief. The "four quantities of 72 Sparks" are variations on the Divine Name, specifically, 72, 63, 45, and 52.

Rabbi Luzzatto explains that just as when a human dies, some spirit remains in his body, called "heat of the bones," to be sustained until the time of Resurrection, so too when the Kings of Edom (the original, defective humans—refer to chapter 11) descended and were made manifest, "a small amount of spiritual power was left in them" to sustain them during the gap between their emanation and the correction or "emendation" of the world. The power of spirit left in the human body and Kings of Edom is the 288 Sparks.

The function of the 288 Sparks is a bit easier to understand when we examine their geomantic application. Distributed equally across the Earth at points of intersections of grid matrices, the 288 Sparks are Prana Distributors. They distribute life force (cosmic qi, orgone) to the planet through its arterial network of energy lines and internal (geomantic) "organs."

Metaphorically, let's say the Prana Distributors are places where Zeus gently breathes spiritual life and vitality into the Earth's visionary geography.

So what does a Prana Distributor look like? I have seen one in the Rondane Mountains of south central Norway, near Rondablikk. It is in a remote mountain valley, unlikely to be visited often by people, yet visible from a well-used walking trail. I saw another above the town of Crestone, Colorado,

on a slope at 9,000 feet. It looks like a spherical pockmarked crystal, a big clear glass marble perhaps 100 feet in diameter. It's not something you enter, like a Lemurian Information Crystal; this device emits energy and consciousness. You would go to a Prana Distributor for a psychic and life-force invigoration and refreshment.

It's like a huge negative ion generator, pumping out revivifying, invigorating, and uplifting negatively charged ions which are the beneficial, health-promoting type such as you get at a waterfall, the oceanside, or after an electric storm. The device contains a spark of the original, unfallen, pure light before the Sefirot were shattered when the Light pulsed through them and was too much for them to contain, and, alternatively, when the Seven Kings of Edom (an expression of the seven Sefirot) were still viable creations and antecedents of the present-day human.

Standing in the proximity of a Prana Distributor you taste the freshness, the shocking vitality of the original Lights. They are colored lights in the planetary body of the singular Albion. Using another image, they are beautiful roses, open and fragrant, distributed uniformly across the surface of the Earth.

Welcome to the Halls of the Olympian Gods

Zeus may be running rampant in his bull and boar forms across the Albion Plates, mating with the continents and filling the planet with cosmic prana, but he also has more genteel offices in 108 locations around the Earth. The Greeks called this feature Mount Olympus, indicating both the actual mountain (Greece's tallest mountain) and the legendary, otherworldly halls of Zeus and the Olympian gods.

The gods have their "eternal dwelling" in the "fastness" of Olympus, wrote Homer. No wind blows there, no rain falls, no snowflakes drift; nothing errant comes to "stain that heaven, so calm, so vaporless, the world of light."[273] All the gods, including Zeus who views the wide world, sit in golden chairs; when they leave Olympus to visit the world of humans, they travel in chariots.

The Sumerian seat of the high god, though scantily sketched, is similar. Enlil, "Great Mountain," "King of the Foreign Lands," "Lord Air," and wild bull, presided in E-kur (Mountain House) in Nippur in Sumer (today's Iraq). E-kur was the "mooring rope" of Heaven, and nearby stood the physical ziggurat called *Dur-an-ki* (Bond of Heaven and Earth) to reinforce that geomantic function.

At the E-kur Enlil exercised his divine authority over the august assembly of Sumerian gods (Annunaki) and over all of Sumer, described in a Sumerian tablet as "a great land . . . filled with steadfast light, dispensing from sunrise to sunset the divine laws to (all) the people."[274]

The Sumerians described Enlil's E-kur as "the lapis-lazuli house, the lofty dwelling place, awe-inspiring/Its awe and dread are next to heaven." E-kur, high mountain, the "pure place," rises on the "dais of plenty." It is the shrine in which dwells the father, the Great Mountain, whose "lifted eye scans the lands" and who "sits broadly on the white dais" in Nippur, itself "beautiful within and without," like Heaven. Rituals done there were as "everlasting" as the Earth.[275]

Enlil's Norse counterpart, Thor, presided over Asgard, the home of the Aesir, the equivalent of the Olympians. Odin, the high god, has his hall, *Valaskjalf*, roofed in silver and his high seat, *Hlidskjalf* (roughly "Observation Point" or "Guard Tower") in Asgard; Thor has his Valhalla, the Hall of the Slain; and the 12 Aesir have their Gladsheim ("Bright Home" or "Joy Home"). Pure gold inside and out, Gladsheim was judged the largest and best dwelling on Earth. The Aesir goddesses had their own temple called Vingolf (Friendly House).

A specific mountain correlate is not given in the Norse myths; however, this is more than compensated for by an important element the Norse myths do remember: Bifrost, the Rainbow Bridge into Asgard guarded by the giant Heimdall who lives at Himinbjorg, the Hill or Castle of Heaven, at its gate. He keeps his mighty horn Gjallarhorn by him to blow on the fateful day that the Frost Giants of Jotunheim breach the bridge and ride into Asgard to overthrow the gods.

Bifrost (or Asbru, "Aesir-Bridge") means roughly "quivering roadway," "swaying road to Heaven," or perhaps "the fleetingly glimpsed rainbow." It leads from Midgard (Middle-Earth, the inhabited human realm) to Asgard, the godly realm, and is under Heimdall's unwavering supervision.[276] The Bridge of the Aesir flames with fire, and every day the Aesir ride over Bifrost to hold their court of justice at the Spring of Urd beneath Yggdrasil, the great World Tree linking all the realms of creation, according to the Norse poets.

Heimdall ("He who illuminates the world") resides at Himinbjorg ("Mount of Heaven") at the bridgehead at the end of the Bridge of Aesir or its beginning in Midgard. He is the great and holy White God, the White As, birthed by nine maiden sisters, daughters of the sea-king, Aegir. His teeth are of gold, so he is called Goldtooth; his sword is Hofud (Man-head), his horse, Gulltoppr (Golden Mane). Some say he is the father of the gods and of all humankind.

He is the gods' warden, guarding entrance to their bridge. He can see a hundred leagues in any direction and needs almost no sleep; his hearing is so keen he can hear the grass growing in the fields; a single blast of his trumpet can be heard throughout all the worlds. On the Day of Reckoning, Ragnarok or Twilight of the Gods (the biblical Armageddon), he will sound his trumpet to alert the Aesir of their doom.

The Sumerian equivalent of Heimdall was called Humbaba. Enlil commissioned Humbaba to guard the Cedar Forest, also known as Pine Mountain and Land of the Living, which was the *musab ilani,* the dwelling place of the gods, a country residence perhaps for the gods of the E-kur or simply another aspect of it. Humbaba is charged with keeping the Pine Forest safe, to be a terror to all people in the performance of his duty.

Humbaba's face resembles coiled intestines; his utterance is fire; his voice itself is a flood-weapon called *abubu*; his breath is death. His hearing is super-acute: He can hear movements in the forest 60 leagues away. He is a giant who wears seven cloaks or is protected by seven layers of terrifying radiance called *melam*, a word which meant the brilliant visible glamour emitted by gods and worn like a garment or crown. The *melam* was a numinous exudation, a light emission of great, terrifying, and awe-inspiring holiness; the word also indicated the effect of this light on humans who beheld it.[277]

The Sumerian hero-quester Gilgamesh journeys to Pine Forest to win fame for himself and to pledge his fealty to the gods. Humbaba is "ferocious," Gilgamesh said, like "a charging wild bull which pierces/He shouts only once, but fills one with terror/The guardian of the forests will shout."[278] Gilgamesh ends up decapitating the fierce Humbaba, but he pays for the trespass later as Enlil fashions the seven-layered *melam* into a revenge agent to torment Gilgamesh.

So who was this terrifying guardian Humbaba-Heimdall, whose hearing was acute, whose breath was destroying fire, and whose shout or trumpet blast was heard everywhere? Western scholars seem at a loss to equate Heimdall with other known and characterized mythic figures and regard him as an anomaly. He isn't, though. Try the Archangel Gabriel. The match is excellent. Gabriel ("God Is My Strength") presides over Paradise as chief of the angelic guards; he sits on the left-hand side of God and has 140 pairs of wings and a sharp scythe.

Even more on point is the attribution to the Archangel Gabriel of being the Trumpeter of the Last Judgment (the biblical equivalent of Ragnarok) as well as the Divine Herald and the Voice of God (symbolized by the trumpet). Gabriel's primary colors are silver and white (Heimdall as the White's).

Decoding the myth of Heimdall and Humbaba, we can state that the Archangel Gabriel assists the Great Bear and its Ray Masters in their geomantic work on the Earth. Gabriel guards Bifrost, the quivering rainbow-hued entrance into Asgard, but in a condensed expression, we could say Bifrost is Asgard, its rainbow hues the energies of the 14 Ray Masters.

The variously named Asgard, Mount Olympus, and Pine Forest is the fourth of our eight Celestial Cities about the cosmic center, Mount Meru. This one is called Amaravati ("Abode of the Immortals" or "Full of Ambrosia"), capital of Indra's paradise, Svarga. This beautiful godly city lies on an eminent mountain to the east of Mount Meru, the Hindu Puranas explain, and it is "replete with splendors." Thousands of deities, musicians, and dancers worship Indra of the thousand eyes with which he views the entire universe.[279] "This exalted spot, difficult to attain even for these gods, is the dwelling place of those virtuous ones, versed in the Vedas, whose aim is making sacrifice and oblation."[280]

His Sunlike golden chariot is called *Jaitraratha*, Car of Victory, and is drawn by one thousand (or ten thousand) steeds both gold and peacock colored. It descends to Earth with a clap of thunder and the searing brilliance of lightning, yet Indra's celestial musicians fill the air around the chariot with dulcet tones. Indra delights in hospitality, and whoever dies in battle becomes Indra's guest; slain warriors are not called "the dead" but "guests" of Indra (equivalent to the Einherjar of Thor's Valhalla). When ruling, he relies on

---

Table 6-2: Mount Olympus, Home of the Ray Masters

Planetary Total: 108

Selected Locations:

Uluru, Alice Springs, Australia	Jungfrau Mountain, Switzerland	Salfords, near London, England
The Tor, Glastonbury, Somerset, England	Rhinefall, near Schafthause, border of Germany-Switzerland	Cedar Forest/Pine Mountain (Sumeria), Iraq
Heliopolis, Egypt	Hambledon Wood, Rutland Water, England	Nippur (Enlil's city, Sumeria), Iraq
Hills of Heaven, near Roros, Norway	Mount Tom, Westhampton, Massachusetts, U.S.	Hill of Tara, near Dublin, Ireland
Mount Mouatahuhuura, Bora Bora, French Polynesia	Tetford, Lincolnshire, England	Tintagel, Cornwall, England
Cathedral Rocks, Sedona, Arizona, U.S.	Sphinx, Great Pyramid, Giza, Cairo, Egypt	Middle Falls, Letchworth State Park, Castile, New York, U.S.
Brown's Hill, opposite Monticello, Charlottesville, Virginia, U.S.	Mount Phicium, Thebes, Greece	Mount Takachiho, near Ebino, Miyazaki Prefecture, Japan
Ham Hill, Somerset, England	Mount Kailash, Tibet	Mount Shasta, California, U.S.
Machu Picchu, Peru	Mount Parnassus, Delphi, Greece	Pyramid Lake, Nevada, U.S.
Tulum, Guatemala	Palm Beach, Florida, U.S.	Frijoles Canyon, Bandelier National Monument, Los Alamos, New Mexico, U.S.
Assisi, Italy	Holy Mountain, Mount Athos, Greece	

Equivalent Names: Gladsheim at Asgard (Thor); Amaravati (Abode of the Immortals), *Devapura* (City of the Gods), and *Pusabhasa* (Sun-Splendour), all Indra's; Cedar Forest/Pine Mountain; *Ekur* (Enlil's "Mountain House"); Crystal City; Roïyat; City of Gems; *Ynis Witrin,* Glass Mountain

Names for the Connecting Bridge: Asbru, Bifrost, Floating Bridge of Heaven, Iris

Names for the Bridge Guardian: Heimdall, Humbaba, Ozume

Brhaspati ("the Great Father"; the Western Jupiter as planet) to guide his councils of the gods.[281] Even though the Vedic texts assert it requires great austerities and spiritual accomplishments to visit Indra's paradisal world, the designers of the Earth's visionary terrain made provisions for those of us lacking in such high credentials. We can visit aspects of the Celestial City of Amaravati.

Imprinted in the planet are 108 replicas of Zeus's Mount Olympus, or perhaps I should say there are 108 doorways or portals to a single expression of the Ray Masters's home and the Great Bear's presence on this planet (see table 6-2).

A British inner explorer named Stephen Jenkins, author of *The Undiscovered Country: Adventures into Other Dimensions* (Neville Spearman, 1977) first introduced me to them in 1985. Jenkins told me he had visited a strange city of the future called Roïyat through a portal at Goring-on-Thames near London. His was a visionary, not bodily, visit; he went several times and was escorted by a city representative, but the chief fact he learned was that Roïyat existed far in the future and seemed to consist of tall sleek buildings of glass or crystal.

My early visits to Jenkins's Roïyat tended to correspond to his description. On one occasion below me sat a beehive of light cells that formed a domed roof perhaps several hundred yards across. A lilac pillar of light about 100 feet wide rose straight up from this glass-ceilinged greenhouse and passed into space. That's Ray Master Saint Germaine's ray color, and as soon as I saw the pillar I saw him.

Another time I accessed Roïyat through the Cathedral Rocks area in Sedona, Arizona. A four-sided silver pyramid perhaps one-quarter-mile wide occupied the astral space of the Cathedral Rocks. Its sides opened and folded down, revealing a squarish crystalline matrix like a city of gems, like a crystal city.

The ancient name for Glastonbury's anomalous hill called the Tor was *Ynys Witrin*, Welsh for "The Glassy Isle" or Glass Mountain. In Welsh lore this was the water-girded fortress of glass presided over by nine maidens. Glastonbury Tor is one of the 108 Mount Olympus portals; the Welsh saw a glass mountain, while we saw a crystal city.

The site seemed filled with perhaps a million humans. The more I looked at it, the more the crystalline matrix resembled the vast spherical roof of a greenhouse whose glasslike surface was divided into sections, looking like a city of gems.

Inside the "greenhouse" or "crystal city" was an open central chamber surrounded by tall white pillars. Each pillar had a different color and opened into a corridor that spiraled away to the left from the central chamber, terminating in a smaller chamber. This room seemed to be an information storage area or hall of records in which information is retained in variously colored hollow crystal shanks deposited in round shelves in the wall.

Around this time the Ofanim clarified our nascent perceptions and our fairly crude formulations from Jenkins's Roïyat, our "crystal city."

"The Light City, or crystal city, as you call it, exists in the future and is not yet in manifestation. It is an aspect of Shambhala [see chapter 9] and pertains to the Great Bear, with two rays from each of the seven stars in the Big Dipper. We place its date of future manifestation on Earth at around 3,000 A.D. It is possibly both a new dimension and a new realm for humans today, but it is an unknown aspect because humanity has not evolved enough yet."

As for the crystal shank, that was "a solidified precipitation of consciousness from another time frame," needed to be brought into our present time to stimulate another geomantic feature called a Silver Egg (see chapter 7).

I developed a more functionally descriptive model of the Mount Olympus feature in subsequent visits. Here is one way of construing it based on the setup at Monticello, Thomas Jefferson's home in Charlottesville, Virginia.

First you encounter Heimdall at the foot of the bridge. To me, he resembled a giant Hindu deity standing in a whorl of fire a few hundred feet tall. (You may see Heimdall in his guise as the Archangel Gabriel.) The "crystal city" of the Ray Masters appears as an elegant building of white marble shaped like a 14-leaf clover. Inside is a large open central chamber from which 14 equal sections or wedges open up. A statue of a deity stands at the entrance to each section; each "statue" represents a Ray Master. The section behind it represents the Ray Master's domain in the created worlds.

Let's take the example of Saint Germaine. As you contemplate or attune to his statue, it flushes lilac and the virtual presence of the Ray Master appears. His entire section appears lilac as well. That section encompasses all the nodes on Earth and elsewhere in the created worlds where he is active. This means, given your clairvoyance, you could access and possibly visit many of those planetary (and from our point of view extraterrestrial) Saint Germaine points of activity. Through his lilac section, Saint Germaine imparts his quality or theme of consciousness—his *ray,* for which he is responsible.

You may find it easier to access some Ray Masters than others. That will be due to your prior karmic affiliation with one of them or more generally your soul affiliation with a ray and its mission for consciousness. Some people may find, by remembering or direct psychic insight, that they are on a path, albeit at a higher level not always available to daytime consciousness, of initiation to do with one or two Ray Masters. You will naturally gravitate towards their ray sections of the Mount Olympus should you visit. In fact, if you know your ray affiliation, this will help you perceive this geomantic feature and interact with it. Even knowing your strong, consistent preference for a color can be helpful.[282]

To get a more vivid sense of this inner-plane working relationship some people have with the Ray Masters consider the experience of Homer's Odysseus. If you read the *Odyssey* you will notice that Pallas Athena (Ray Master No. 8) is Odysseus's unwavering sponsor and helper, always petitioning his case to Zeus, her father, always finding ways to help him on his journey home. Why?

Think of this marvellous story as a chronicle of geomantic initiation. Odysseus travels throughout the eastern European temple, matching his consciousness with the geomantic structures—helping to open them while confirming their energies in his own energy field—under the auspices of his initiation director, Pallas Athena.[283]

When all the Ray Masters stand at the head of their sections, inhabiting and enlivening their statuesque representations, then you could say the gods of Olympus are assembled in the heavenly halls of Zeus who may manifest as a brilliant ball or undefined mass of blinding light. Let's switch names for a minute.

Osiris (the Egyptian Zeus) had his body cut into 14 pieces. These "pieces" are the 14 Ray Masters, the seven major divisions of light and their subtleties. Osiris's body was put in a lead casket or coffin and dumped in the Nile. Geomantically, that means the energies of the 14 Ray Masters flow from Mount Olympus into the world at Charlottesville, through its varied geomantic features, and beyond. The "Nile River" in this geomantic setup is an Oroboros Line that passes through Charlottesville and has to do with a landscape zodiac present there.

I mentioned earlier that the Mount Olympus feature resembled a crystal city or city of gems. This is apt, for it corresponds to the *Manipura* or solar plexus chakra. *Manipura* means "City of Gems" because it is "lustrous like a gem." This is the home of the Ray Masters, in us and the planet (see figure 6-1).

Appropriately, in the organization of the human energy system, of the 700 nerve cords of the sympathetic nervous system in Tantric esoteric physiology, 14 are of the greatest importance and have their connection through the solar plexus center. We might think of these nerve cords as the Ray Masters within us, even stretching it a little, as the Rainbow Bridge inside us.[284]

The *Manipura* is the third energy center not just in us, but in the organization of energy in the Earth's energy body. We are now in the domain of the third planetary sphere (again working downward into full incarnation from the Supreme Being's viewpoint) and under the influence of Jupiter (the Roman Zeus) or Brhaspati (his Sanskrit-Hindu name).

Brhaspati is the Great-Master and teacher of the gods in Hindu myth. He is Lord of Prayers and the celestial priest of the gods, the lord of beneficent wisdom and the growth and expansion of the universe. He is Lord of Assemblies, King of Elders, Wielder of the Thunderbolt who brought light to Earth. After he worshipped Shiva for 1,000 years, Shiva made him the planet Jupiter or put him in charge of it. In Vedic astrology Brhaspati is the name of the planet Jupiter, and in the *The Emerald Modem,* he is Zeus, presiding over the third planetary sphere as well as in his Indra form over the Celestial City of Amaravati.

Keep in mind that all of this is both inside you and around you when you sit in the landscape at a Mount Olympus feature. The spiritual archetype of your solar plexus chakra has been projected outward into the subtle landscape as a visionary temple awaiting your interaction, and at the same time, you can align your bodily solar plexus chakra with the landscape expression of its archetype so that inside and outside expressions of it, in your experience, become one again.

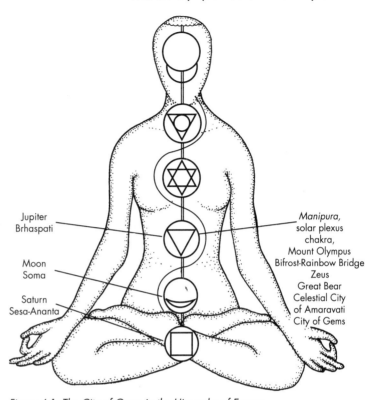

Figure 6-1. The City of Gems in the Hierarchy of Energy

Sanctuaries and Installations of the Gods of the Great Bear

Each Ray Master is also present in the Earth's visionary geography by way of specially dedicated temples or sanctuaries exclusive to them. In a sense, it's like taking, for example, Saint Germaine's "wedge" or section in Mount Olympus, the Lilac Room, and manifesting this as a separate temple on Earth. This site would be exclusive for Saint Germaine's activities and meetings.

I call this feature a Ray Master Sanctuary, of which there are 1,080 on the planet. In our time 443 are open and activated, and they are not equally divided among the 14 Ray Masters. The other 667 are not "open" at this time because there is not enough human interest, cooperation, and potential for interaction with the Great White Brotherhood and their representatives and specialists, the Ray Masters, to warrant or energetically sustain the full infusion of 1,080. Even so, Ray Masters, in addition to presenting themselves through a series of Sanctuaries, are each also capable of 1,746,000 manifestations, which means, functionally, they can be in that many places at the same time.

Presuming these are divided equally among the 14 Ray Masters, that means each Olympian has about 77 Sanctuaries. That is for the current

139

Table 6-3: Ray Master Sanctuaries

Planetary Total: 1,080

Selected Locations:

Ephesus, Turkey: Artemis, Ray 2

Mont-Royal, Montreal, Quebec, Canada: Hilarion, Ray 4

Newgrange, Ireland: Apollo, Ray 1

Thebes, Greece: Cadmus/ St. Germaine, Ray 7

Acropolis, Athens, Greece: Pallas Athena, Ray 8

Jasna Gora, Czestochowa, Poland: Virgin Mary, Ray 3

Rennes-le-Chateau, France: St. Germaine, Ray 7

Eleusis, Greece: Demeter, Ray 5

Delphi, Mount Parnassus, Greece: Apollo, Ray 1

Cynthian Temple, Cynthos Hill, Delos, Greece: Artemis, Ray 2

Temple of Apollo, Corinth, Greece: Apollo, Ray 1

Lourdes, Grotto of Masabielle, France: Kwan Yin, Ray 11

Dendera, Egypt: Hathor, Ray 3

Equivalent Names: Artemision; Cadmeia; Marian Apparition Site; House of Oenghus; Well of Segais; Parthenon

---

time period, however; the number varies with epochs. In our present time, 31 Ray Master Sanctuaries per Ray Master are active. The purpose of the Sanctuaries is to anchor the energies of the Great Bear on Earth, as well as the specific ray differentiation of each Ray Master. This means some sites that have been Ray Master Sanctuaries may be temporarily inactive today.

You can easily find evidence of these in different cultures and mythic attributions: the Artemision in Ephesus, Turkey, a temple dedicated to Artemis; the Parthenon in Athens, dedicated to Pallas Athena; the Cadmeia at Thebes, Greece, dedicated to Cadmus; the temple at Dendera, Egypt, dedicated to Hathor (Aphrodite). (See table 6-3.) In many cases, sites dedicated to or hallowed by apparitions of the Virgin Mary, such as Lourdes, France, and Jasna Gora, Czestochowa, Poland, are also Ray Master Sanctuaries.

Sometimes, the Ray Master Sanctuary is slightly veiled by other attributions. Megalithic Newgrange, near Dublin, Ireland, was dedicated to the Irish god Oenghus and called, among other names, the House of Oenghus; that was the Irish

name for Apollo, Ray Master No. 1; Mont-Royal in Montreal, Quebec, in Canada, is a Ray Master Sanctuary for Hilarion, Ray Master No. 4, who appeared to Brother Andre, a saintlike Catholic man living there, as Saint Joseph, father of Jesus, at the site dedicated to him, the Saint Joseph Oratory.

The Ray Master Sanctuary allows Ray Masters to channel their specific ray quality into an area and to be available for visitation by the sensitive. What does a Sanctuary look like? You could conceive of it as a tall, very narrow rectangle or slit pillar that acts as a doorway between worlds. On the other side (the inside, as we see it) of the slit is the Ray Master's domain, which may appear as a spherical dimension, perhaps a globular amphitheater with living images of all the Ray Master's incarnations, a kind of holographic resume.

You could potentially see evidence of all the Ray Master's guises, mythic representations, deeds, places of activity, and other Sanctuaries. Experientially, you are *in* the ray of this Ray Master; all of Lourdes in this sense is *inside* the manifestation body of the Virgin Mary. All of

Lourdes is her Sanctuary. Let's not forget that we are also inside a ray that is part of the totality of the energy-consciousness input of Ursa Major, a constellation of key importance for Earth. Similarly, all 500 acres of Le Parc du Mont-Royal in Montreal are the domain of Ray Master Hilarion; if you are in the park, you are *in* Hilarion's ray. If you sit in the Saint Joseph Oratory, you simultaneously sit in Hilarion's baptismal font.

In some cases, the architectural and iconographical aspects of a physical temple dedicated to a Ray Master help us understand some of the qualities of that Ray Master as filtered through a specific culture. Consider Egypt's Hathor. The significant temple at Dendera is dedicated to Hathor, known there as *Ta-ynt-netert,* "She of the goddess-pillar." In fact, numerous pillars were crowned with four-sided Hathor capitals in this temple; Dendera was a Hathor cult center, and Hathor, or Ray Master No. 3 (pink), was the Greek Aphrodite, Love Goddess.[285]

The layout of the temple and the evident progression of initiates and priests through it shows it was designed with worship of Hathor in mind; in fact, temple art depicts the ritual of the pharaoh's initial dedication of the temple to Hathor and his subsequent regular visits with her. At this Hathor temple, the physical aspects of the architecture dovetail with the geomantic features, affording an easy and profitable interchange between the realms. Further, the temple architecture would conduct you into the state of mind appropriate for contacting or experiencing the resident Ray Master.

The Ray Masters occasionally install geomantic features across the planet. Ray Master Apollo created something the Ofanim call an Arc of Expanding Consciousness and placed 174,060 of them on Earth. This feature describes a parabolic curve across the landscape from a point of origination to one of grounding. The length may vary, but the first one I encountered and trained in was about eight miles long, curving from Glastonbury Tor, the top part, to a field named Lugshorn in the village of Compton Dundon, the bottom or grounding part of the arc. Experientially, it resembles a walled corridor curving along the ground, but those walls are perhaps 100 feet tall. You walk, ideally, from Lugshorn to the Tor through this corridor and experience alterations in consciousness.

In an uncanny way, it suggests what the biblical account of Moses parting the waters of the Red Sea might have been like. You feel you are walking through the sea on dry ground with walls of withheld water on your right and left. But the water is not water as we know it; rather, it is the substance of our conventional space-time physical reality—the Red Sea—now parted. You walk through this corridor outside your normal sense of time and space and self-identity. It is an etheric bridge that links one reality with another.

I call it a unitive consciousness corridor, for it schools you in a serial way in the quality of unified consciousness. Theoretically, it can put you in the state of mind, according to the Ofanim, of "pre-Babylonian separation and confusion of tongues" that existed over the whole of Earth—unitary consciousness: awareness of oneself as simultaneously co-present with and aware of all other points of awareness and location on the planet and beyond.

The Arc enables you to move from the personal, or individuation level, to the collective, or unitive level, through a combination of grace and precipitation. Whose grace? Apollo's. Precipitation? That means shaking loose insights, obstacles, cobwebs, and shadow contents from your psyche as you walk through the Arc. The grace is that you are able to do this and are supported by Love from Above through Apollo (Ray Master No. 1) in expanding and developing your singular consciousness into a distributed global one through your journey in the corridor.

Table 6-4: Arcs of Expanding Consciousness

Planetary Total: 174,060

Selected Locations:

Glastonbury, Somerset, England	Acropolis, Athens, Greece	Sedona, Arizona, U.S.
Ashlawn, near Monticello, Charlottesville, Virginia, U.S.	Hill Cumorah, Palmyra, New York, U.S.	Teotihuacan, Mexico
Castle Rigg, Keswick, Lake District, England	Mount Holyoke, Hadley, Massachusetts, U.S.	Rennes-le-Chateau, France
	Newgrange, Ireland	Mycenae, Greece
		Kercado Tumulus, Carnac, France

Equivalent Names: Red Sea, Unitive Consciousness Corridor

At some point in our planet's life, Apollo extrapolated 174,060 of these parabolic curves of consciousness into the landscape, which comes to 14,505 per Albion Plate. On a technical level, the intersections of ley line energy (straight lines from domes, spiral lines from dome caps, and Oroboric lines passing through) between Glastonbury Tor and Lugshorn create and describe the parabola, or Arc.

Perhaps an accessible way to think about this feature—certainly it's poetically apt—is in terms of Apollo's arrows. One of this god's primary attributes is that he is a consummate archer, always seen with a bow and quiver of arrows. Think of Apollo shooting off an arrow that goes eight miles; it will describe a parabola. The parabola of Apollo's arrow is a metaphor for the Arc of Expanding Consciousness.

Why Apollo of all the Ray Masters? He's in charge of oracular insight and speech, divination, prophecy, bardic inspiration, music, medicine; he is the sponsor of the Nine Muses, the goddesses who inspire the fine arts; he is the patron of the lyre, lute, and archery; he is the golden-haired god of light. One of his proteges was Cassandra, the Trojan psychic whom nobody heeded; one of his sons was Asclepius, physician-god, father of medicine and the arts of healing.

And the arrow? The arrow symbolizes the light of supreme power, the Sun's rays, swiftness, lightning intuition, keen, quick perception, mental alertness, an instantaneous flash of light, a release from gravity, throwing off earthbound limitations and conventions, psychic penetration into other realms, the straight ascent to the celestial world. Walking through Apollo's Arc of Expanding Consciousness is like a quick flight on a loosed arrow; the arrow is your bridge into another reality, Apollo's (see table 6-4).

In most cases, the Arc of Expanding Consciousness is accompanied by a complementary installation called a Pointer's Ball. The name derives from a vestigial earthworks in Glastonbury and a misspelled place name for it: Ponter's Ball.[286] The Ball is within the parabolic curve, though close to one end, less than two miles from the Tor. There are 174,060 Pointer's Balls on Earth, 14,505 per Albion Plate (see table 6-5).

It is a Pointer's Ball because through this feature you can point to another space-time dimension. In one sense it is a point of access for coming and going from other dimensions of reality; in another sense, it is a point through which you can clearly see across the dimensions. It looks like a ball, a very large crystal sphere or egg of light, perhaps 100 feet in diameter.

The first time I encountered this feature at Glastonbury I saw a ribbon of men and women emerge from the translucent Ball as if from another world. Nimuë, one of the names for the Celtic deity called the Lady of the Lake, was supervising the transit of these hundreds of humans from another time and place. Perhaps this was the legendary crystal cave into which the Lady of the Lake "seduced" Merlin, as reported in the Arthurian stories. Certainly it would be a seductive pleasure to come and go at will between multiple worlds.

Who were the people? "These were the Grail Knights whom Nimuë instructed in Avalon and guided through their initiation into the astral realm over which she is in charge," the Ofanim explained later. "The Lady of the Lake is a figure of authority, the guardian of the astral realms from the lowest astral rubbish to the highest astral orders. Nimuë was one of three aspects of that Lady." The Lake was a Celtic metaphor for the astral realm. We could usefully think of these multiple nodes as little streams that flow into the Lake.

The Pointer's Ball is a rabbit hole into the astral world, of which Avalon is one of the more euphonious euphemisms. Lewis Carroll's Alice falling through the rabbit hole into Wonderland was passing through a Pointer's Ball. In *Field of Dreams,* the baseball diamond that Ray Kinsella improbably carved out of his cornfield for the living to interact with the unfulfilled dead was the reopening of a Pointer's Ball. The Pointer's Ball is also that "crack between the worlds" through which Carlos Castaneda was always falling, jumping, or getting pushed.[287]

Castaneda also called them gateways to the "second attention," which would be our field of dreams in the astral realm. In my visits to Glastonbury's Pointer's Ball, I consistently was aware of myself as being in at least two places at the same time: in my physical body, meditating under a drizzling sky, and in my light body, interacting with Nimuë, pulling a sword out of a crystal tree in bright sunlight, moving in and out of her Egg, and even flying around above the ground, and not affected by the rain.

Another time, the Pointer's Ball looked like a vertical vagina, or a plastic change purse with an open slit in the middle. This was at Ashlawn, the former home of U.S. President James Monroe, two miles from Jefferson's Monticello. Amusingly, Mrs. Monroe was said to have complained of ghosts and spectral presences in her house. Of course she would: The house coinhabits the

---

Table 6-5: Pointer's Balls

Planetary Total: 174,060

Selected Locations:

Glastonbury, Somerset, England	Hill Cumorah, Palmyra, New York, U.S.	Rennes-le-Chateau, France
Ashlawn, near Monticello, Charlottesville, Virginia, U.S.	Mount Holyoke, Hadley, Massachusetts, U.S.	Mycenae, Greece
Castle Rigg, Keswick, Lake District, England	Newgrange, Ireland	Kercado tumulus, Carnac, France
Acropolis, Athens, Greece	Sedona, Arizona, U.S.	Calendar I, South Royalton, Vermont, U.S.
	Teotihuacan, Mexico	

Equivalent Names: The Lady of the Lake's Crystal Cave; Rabbit Holes; Cracks in the World

location of that Pointer's Ball. People would be coming and going all the time through the crack between the worlds in her parlor.

You pass through the slit in the change purse (or walk into the Egg), and you enter a completely foreign terrain. To me, it was a vast plain filled with small white forms and numerous thin, brownish pillars; these might be the Pointer's Balls seen from the other side. It was like a train station, but instead of trains, there were "emanation doorways" into other realms. Our physical Earth was only one of many possible destinations.

Seemingly, souls could walk through from door to door, and from their point of view, it would be like walking through a brightly lit corridor (our physical plane) between rooms (other Pointer's Balls) in a big house (the astral world). One time while meditating at Castle Rigg, a stone circle in the Lake District of England, I saw beings coming and going through a Pointer's Ball in the circle. Extra stones had been arranged on the inside periphery of a portion of the circle to form a square; I saw alien beings—not humans as I recognize them—coming in and out of the stone circle as nonchalantly as if the Ball were a swinging door.

Some of the ancient megalithic barrows and tumuli (artificial mounds or aboveground caves, with earth piled over several standing stones and a lintel) are situated at Pointer's Balls. A tumulus called Kercado in the massive stone alignments of Carnac, France, is one such barrow marking a Ball. Inside the tumulus were eight flat vertical standing stones along the walls. Energetically, they were an eight-spoked interdimensional wheel or dimension selector. Each stone was a doorway to another world or reality; it was a way out of *here*.

The geomantic impact of the tumulus seems to facilitate a clairvoyance or perhaps it inducts you into your dream body or loosens the hold of your etheric body on your physical. Perhaps it was originally intended to be a sensory deprivation chamber to free psychic attention from the physical.[288]

The Arc of Expanding Consciousness and Pointer's Ball can be used together or separately. For example, when used jointly, you can walk the corridor of unitive consciousness as psychic preparation for entering the dimensional shift of the Ball. The corridor consolidates your focus, expands your awareness, inducts you into the fourth dimension, so that you are ready to pass through the multidimensional access portal of the Ball where you can choose among many astral realities within the fourth dimension.

Put differently, you walk along the corridor in the fast lane outside of three-dimensional worldly traffic; you're moving outside of time, perhaps parallel to it; then once you are at psychic acceleration speed, you hit a node (Pointer's Ball) and exit the system.[289]

When the Pointer's Ball is used separately, you can, for example, be part of a group assembled at the different stages of the Arc for group meditation.

While exploring the Arc in Glastonbury, I had visual impressions of King Arthur's Grail Knights arrayed on perhaps a dozen different nodes on the Arc on Michaelmas. The Archangel Michael stood on Glastonbury Tor and transmitted celestial energy through the Arc; the knights in their stations grounded it, enabling the Arc to get flushed with Michaelic energy in this annual geomantic housecleaning. I had impressions, too, of other groups of knights and initiates doing the same or related geomantic activities there much further back in time.

7 The Celestial City of the Heart
Golden Apples, the Garden of Eden, and Avalon

The Norse gods in Asgard may be eternal and puissant, but they are vulnerable to a grievous decline if they run out of golden apples. The goddess Idun ("the Rejuvenating One") guards the orchard of golden apple trees that the gods depend on to stay young, strong, and healthy. She lives in a golden house in the orchard with her husband, Bragi, the Norse god of poetry, and she never leaves her precious trees. She's the Queen of the golden apples.

Her trees grow in Asgard but produce apples only under her direction, and only she can pick those glorious, shining fruits, which she does every morning for the gods, leaving them in a basket. Every day the Aesir consume Idun's golden apples as an antidote to aging. This daily routine will continue this way until Ragnarok, the End of Days.

Once the trickster god Loki and the giant Thjazi abducted Idun, so that the gods were deprived of their apples and started to decline. "The Aesir, however, were much dismayed at Idun's disappearance, and they soon grew old and grey-haired," wrote Snorri Sturluson, the twelfth century Icelandic compiler of Norse myths.[290] Idun was eventually returned to Asgard and the Aesir's well-ordered youthful life continued. But why did they *need* the golden apples?

For the Greeks, the golden apples belonged to their chief Olympian goddess, Hera, consort to Zeus. Her orchard of golden apple trees was situated in the far West, in the Blessed Land at the far edge of the Earth, tended by the Hesperides, daughters of the Titan Atlas. They were also called the Daughters of the Evening, referring to the sunset direction and their alternate parentage from Hesperos (Vesperus), who became the Evening Star, or Venus.

A hundred-headed dragon named Ladon lay perpetually coiled at the foot of the trees, guarding the fruits which had been Gaia's gift to Hera upon her wedding with Zeus. Atlas holds up the world, his feet in the garden. The seven Hesperides sisters—Aegle, Erythea, Arethusa, Hestia, Hespera, Hesperusa, Hespereia—spend their time in pleasant recreation and song. Perhaps not surprisingly, the Garden of the Hesperides has been compared to the biblical Garden of Eden.

In Heracles's eleventh labor, on behalf of Eurystheus, king of Mycenae, he had to collect the golden apples of the Hesperides by tricking Atlas and overpowering Ladon. The golden apples did not make Heracles or Eurystheus immortal, as they did the gods, so why did Heracles *have* to get them?

Avalon and *Emain Ablach*—the Island Paradise of Golden Apples

For the Celts, that question was too self-evident even to ask. Only a fool would not want a golden apple, a celestial fruit precious beyond calculation.

A mysterious woman appears one day before the Irish hero Bran mac Febail bearing a silver branch with white blossoms and golden apples. She beckons him to follow her to *Emain Ablach* ("Fortress of Apples"), a paradisal island filled with immortal women and golden apple trees. The locale was sometimes called the Isle of Women, Land of Promise, Land of Youth, or *Cruithin na Cuan,* after its queen who lived there in a fabulous palace.

One early morning at Tara, Ireland's ancient capital, Cormac mac Airt walks the ramparts of the earthworks and meets an unknown warrior carrying a branch with three golden apples. The branch, when shaken, emits a marvelous, seductive music that lulls one into a trancelike sleep. Cormac keeps the apple, but only in exchange for performing three wishes for the stranger.

On another day in ancient Ireland, Connla walks on the Hill of Uisnech (in the country's center) and meets an unknown but lovely woman in rich garments. She tells him about a beautiful otherworldly paradise called *Tir na mBeo* ("the Land of the Living"). She invites him to visit and leaves him a golden apple; that is all the food he eats for the next month, although the apple never diminishes even with his eating it.[291]

After his disastrous battle with his bastard son, Mordred, at the Hill of Camlann, the dying Celtic King Arthur was ferried by his sister, Morgan, and two other women to Avalon, the undying Apple Land and Celtic Elysium, also known as *Insula Avallonis* and *Ynys Avallach* (Welsh for "Isle of Apples"). Morgan le Fay ruled Avalon with her nine sisters, the *fays* or fairies of Avalon, says Celtic myth.

I confess when I first lived in Glastonbury, England, I became obsessed with golden apples. Were there *really* such things? Why golden? Why apples? Later I realized I was trying to penetrate a deep symbol and very old mystery. You can't do that in a weekend, or even a decade. I probably still do not fully understand the apple image, though I have seen a few of them in Avalon.

First, there *are* golden apples, and Avalon *is* truly a land of apple trees. Second, the name is the entrance password: *Avalon,* when chanted wakefully for ten or 15 minutes, actually conducts you into the realm it names. You can get there without this mantric passkey, but it facilitates your entrance. Third, the place is indeed lovely, all it's been reputed to be. I first accessed Avalon on the slopes of the Tor in Glastonbury, England, a town said in Celtic myth and new-age folklore to be the heart of and doorway to Avalon.

You pass the dragon guardian at the base of the Tor—he's one of the original 13 planetary dragons—and enter Apple Land. Even though the Tor's slopes are fairly steep, somehow in its Avalon dimension, the orchard seems broad and expansive and on mostly level ground. Apple trees in full, lovely white blossom escort the winding (astral) path up the Tor.[292] Each golden apple is like a living radiant sun in apple form; you don't "eat" them so much as assimilate their contents by entering their information field, for the "fruit" is knowledge, cosmic intelligence, the answers to Mysteries.

Inside the golden apple is a space like a tall arching chamber. In a sense, the apple is a temple of wisdom that you enter and absorb from within. I encountered a large golden head, hollow like a hot air balloon, with a small golden circle on a pedestal at its base. You stand on this and the golden head settles down over your head like a corona. In a sense, the apple eats you.

Perhaps this is how the information transfer is accomplished, for it seemed the head was transmitting energy to my consciousness by way of golden pulsations. It filled my head nearly to bursting, and I found myself shifted or "translated," as the Grail Knights used to say, to another dimension about which I cannot report anything at present. Perhaps the golden apple is an induction or attunement device; its "juice" puts you in resonance with the Celestial City "higher" up the mountain, that is, up the frequency scale of awareness.

Each apple is a "stroke of wisdom," a "fruit of insight," the Ofanim note. "The apple is the ultimate symbol. The apple is from the ultimate divine inspiration of the creative divine source. It is for us the closest image of the Earth." The apple shape, seen as a hologram, is the same form as the Earth's energy body as an entirety and works as a light receptor, the Ofanim say. The essential form of the Archangel Sandalphon, who adjusts the spin, rotation, and axis of the Earth, most closely resembles "the essence structure" of an apple, the Ofanim add.

The fruits of spiritual practice in certain cultures are often called apples of insight, the Ofanim say. "These apples are fruits sometimes gained at an inner astral plane. Yet they are keys that can sometimes corrupt the practice of true spirituality, as shown in the stories of the Gardens of Eden and the Hesperides."

In the Garden of Eden experience Adam and Eve tasted the golden apple and gained self-consciousness. They perceived their "nakedness" and stepped into their "clothes," which were their subtle and manifestation bodies. They became *aware* of their divine source and of themselves by eating the apple.

The Hesperides allegory showed Heracles realizing his innate wisdom, which is always pure, always golden, by claiming the golden apple. "To take the apple meant he realized his innate nature," the Ofanim explain. "It was not necessary to remove it from the tree to realize it. Each person who approaches the tree has a different possibility depending on their primary patterning."

Sometimes you can stay too long with the golden apples.

In the sixth century A.D. Welsh poem *Merddin's Avallenau,* Merlin luxuriates in an orchard of 81 golden apple trees, all guarded by one maiden named Olwedd. "The delicious apple tree, with blossoms of pure white and wide-spreading branches, produces sweet apples, for those who can digest them," Merlin reflects. Yet he realizes he may be too comfortable, too spiritually intoxicated in this apple paradise: "I am become a wild distracted object, no longer greeted by the brethren of my order, nor covered with my habit."[293]

The Teutonic myth of Tannhäuser gives us the same story with more information on his beguiler. Tannhäuser is the thirteenth-century *Minnesinger* (lyric poet and minstrel) who travels to the Horselberg in Thuringia, Germany, between Eisenach and Gotha. On the mountain's northwest flank he discovers a cavern called the Horselloch, the Cave of Venus (or Orsel). From inside he hears the roar of flowing water. Folk belief held that deep inside the mountain was the Venusberg, a Temple of Venus, a sybaritic palace of love goddess delights.

Tannhäuser passed through the cavern and saw a glimmering white female figure beckoning him to enter deeper. It was Venus. Once in the Venusberg, Tannhäuser was enveloped in lovely music, surrounded by dancing nymphs who scattered rose petals. He stayed there seven years and only left when he finally called on the Virgin Mary to break Venus's pagan spell.

There is no mention of golden apples in the Venusberg, but the general atmosphere is consistent with the blandishments of Avalon and its

---

Table 7-1: Avalon—The Celestial City of Gandhavati

Planetary Total: 144

Selected Locations:

Glastonbury Tor, Glastonbury, Somerset, England	Navan Fort, Armagh, County Ulster, Northern Ireland	Delphi, Mount Parnassus, Greece
Monticello, Charlottesville, Virginia, U.S.	Mount Temahani, Raiatea, Society Islands, French Polynesia	Mount Kailash, Tibet
Mycenae, Greece	Horselberg (the Venusberg), Germany	Mount Helicon, Boeotia, Greece
Troy, Turkey		Phlambouro, Mount Pieria, Pierian range, Macedonia, Greece
Teach Cormaic, Hill of Tara, Ireland	Montserrat, Spain	
	Cumae, Naples, Italy	

Equivalent Names: Temple of the Golden Apple; the Floating Island of Aeolia; Venusberg; *Mouseion* (a shrine dedicated to the Muses); Gardens of the Hesperides; Wonderland; *Emain Ablach;* Land of the Living; Land of Women; Land of Youth; *Insula Avallonis; Ynys Avallach; Monte della Sibilla;* Field of *A'aru,* Field of Reeds

---

guises. One might be tempted to think the Venusberg is a Ray Master Sanctuary dedicated to the Ray Master Aphrodite (the Greek Venus), but it is not so. The *Venus* in Venusberg is a clue rather to the planetary or celestial sphere operative and not the Ray Master. If anyone, the "Venus" in Tannhäuser's Venusberg would be more akin to the Celtic Nimuë or Vivienne, the Lady of the Lake of Avalon.[294]

The myth of a pagan love goddess's subterranean mountain grotto of delights and treasures was widespread throughout Europe, even if, over time, the goddess became demonized into a baleful witch who consorted with demons. Similar stories to Tannhäuser's were attributed to Mount Pilatus in Switzerland, the Wartburg in Germany, Mount Vettore in Italy, and the Tor in Glastonbury, England.

Tannhäuser in the Venusberg, Merlin in the Avallenau, Heracles in the Hesperides, the wandering Italians in *Monte della Sibilla*—these are folkloric expressions of the encounter with Avalon, the fifth of our eight Celestial Cities.

In Vedic lore, what the Celts called Avalon was known as the Celestial City of Gandhavati, presided over by Lord Vayu, the god of wind and movement. Even his name connotes this, derived from the root *va* for "blow." He is the god of the seven winds and their bodily correlates, the seven *pranas* or breaths; his attributes include purification, speed, strength, and the bearing of perfumed aromas. He is constantly in motion, blowing in all directions.

His city is situated in the Northwest with respect to Mount Meru, and on the Earth there are 144 doorways into it (see table 7-1). Vayu's city is the realm of inspiration, the movement of the cosmic breath and universal spirit, of the substance and essence of speech. Vayu rules over a realm intermediate between Earth and Sky (Heaven)—the astral realm—the Celtic Avalon.[295]

His Greek counterpart is Aiolos (Aeolus), who is in charge of the eight winds.[296] His name means "the mobile" and "the many colored." His domain was known as the Floating Island of Aeolia, girded with "huge ramparts of indestructible bronze and sheer rock cliffs" rising up from the sea, as Homer wrote. Aiolos had 12 children "in the lusty prime of youth," forever enjoying the delights of the feast in Aiolos's halls that "echo round to the low moan of blowing pipes." Odysseus spent a month with him in his "splendid palace" enjoying Aiolos's entertainments; when it was time to depart, Aiolos gave the cunning wayfarer a bag containing the eight winds to use in dead calms.[297]

Even though they are not overtly associated with Aiolos, Aeolia is the dimension of the Nine Muses of classical Greek myth, the inspirers of high art. These are the Greek equivalent of the Celtic tableau of Morgan le Fay and her nine sisters of Avalon, daughters of King Avalloch of the Summer Country. In Greek myth, the Muses are the daughters of Zeus and the Titan Mnemosyne (Memory), but they are under the leadership of the Ray Master Apollo. Their haunts included Mount Helicon near Ascra, Pieria near (the physical) Mount Olympus, and Mount Parnassus, on whose slopes is the oracular site Delphi.

The names and specialties of the Nine Muses are consistent with the various folk legends cited earlier of the "pagan" court of Venus.[298] The Muses were said to dance and sing with and for Apollo and other deities at various Olympian festivals. Hesiod said they danced on "the great god-haunted" Mount Helicon, a peak in central Greece (elevation 5,741 feet), their hands joined in lovely dances such that "their pounding feet awaken desire."[299]

The classical poets tell us the Muses, born "addicted" to song, would pass through the night, wrapped in clouds, only their "wondrously beautiful voices audible," in procession to Mount Olympus. "The black earth echoed with their hymns, and lovely was the tread of their feet as they went to their father." When the Muses sang, rivers, stars, everything stood still, and Mount Helicon began "in its rapture to grow up to heaven," intoxicated by their luscious songs.[300]

Let's pause for a moment and consider where we are in terms of chakras. With the Celestial City of Gandhavati and its mythic variations we are in the *Anahata*, or fourth energy center, the outer heart chakra of 12 petals. We'll find that much of its qualities and iconography are consistent with the myths of Avalon.

The name *Anahata* means "not stricken," and refers to sounds and music produced without striking a palpable instrument. Mythically, we could say Avalon is filled with lovely music, the songs and dances of the Nine Muses, who emit music from their very nature and do not require actual playable instruments to generate pleasing sounds. The Wind God's association here (Vayu or Aiolos) is apt because to the outer heart chakra is assigned the element of air, or movement.

The fleet-footed, joyous quality of Avalon is represented by the deer or antelope; this animal signifies purity, innocence, perpetual inspiration, sensitivity, a leaping joy of the heart, the susceptibility to mirages or reflections, and a predilection for sounds. "The deer is said to die for pure sound. The love of inner sounds, *anahata nada,* is the love of the fourth-chakra person."[301] The *Anahata*'s ruling planet, in conventional assignments, is Venus, with which I agree.

In the Tantric iconography of the *Anahata*, Venus, the "pagan" goddess of the Venusberg, is represented by the four-headed Kakini Shakti. Her skin is rose-colored; she sits on a pink lotus wearing a sky-blue sari; she inspires music, poetry, and art, as a one-goddess version of the Nine Muses; happy and exalted, she is the focus of *bhakti,* the energy of devotion, the positive, uplifting view of what is elsewhere described as luring seductiveness. Kakini holds a sword (discernment), shield (protection), skull (detachment), and trident (balance).

A second goddess is portrayed in the *Anahata,* too. She is Kundalini Shakti, presented as a beautiful goddess seated in a lotus position.

She wears a white sari—the dazzling whiteness of the alluring Venus before the Venusberg—and she's presented as serene, self-focused, virginal, matronly—the Virgin Mother. Seated in her lotus, she is *anahata nada,* the cosmic sound that is heard within, the unstricken, ubiquitous "white noise" of the cosmos, the *AUM,* the seed of all sounds (the Hindu equivalent of the Western *Word* and the Hebraic *YHVH*).[302]

The constellation assigned for this Celestial City of the heart is Cygnus the Swan. One of the star stories told of this constellation is particularly relevant to several geomantic features described below. Zeus took a fancy to Leda, the wife of King Tyndareus of Sparta. He seduced her one night while she was bathing by turning himself into a male swan of dazzling, iridescent whiteness and swam coyly up to the bathing Leda.

She fell for it, and Zeus impregnated her with Helen (the beautiful immortal woman who "caused" the Trojan War) and Pollux (one half of the *Dioskuri,* the Heavenly Twins or "Zeus Boys" of Castor and Pollux [or Polydeuces]). The especially relevant part here is that Helen and Pollux (with Castor) were born in an *egg.* The Greek myths complicate things a bit by saying that on that same night Leda slept with her actual husband, who fathered Castor and Clytemnestra, both mortals. Some versions of the story have Leda laying two eggs, one with the two immortals, the other with the two mortals.

In the Venusberg, Avalon, the Muses on Mount Helicon, Aiolos's daughters, we have images of the Celestial City of the heart, Gandhavati.

What It Takes to Reach for a Golden Apple

These different characterizations of Avalon, *Emain Ablach,* the Venusberg, the Sibyl's Mountain, and Gandhavati give us a fair idea of the terrain of the Garden of the Hesperides. Let's not forget the golden apples that grow there. In a sense, acquiring a bite of the apple is the goal of the quest to get there. The singing, dancing maidens of Venus are of course an aesthetic attraction, but the wisdom in that golden apple, the actual "juice" of insight, is even more attractive.

They are golden for a good symbolic reason. Gold represents that most refined of metals, precious, solar, eternal, and incorruptible. It denotes royalty, even divinity, as the gods' bodies were said to be of pure gold. Gold is the product of the Great Work of the alchemical transformation of lead; in Chinese and Indian philosophical thinking, gold was the base element in elixirs of immortality; and as the Ofanim noted above, gold is (among the angels) equated with knowledge.

Heracles had to travel considerably to collect a golden apple from the Hesperidean orchards because there are very few on the Earth. Only 47. Avalon may have many orchards of lovely white-blossomed trees with golden apples, but they're not all true golden apples. Only 47 Avalons contain an authentic golden apple. "Two thirds have illusions that are not true golden apples," the Ofanim say. The existence of illusory golden apples as deceptive yet alluring simulacra of the authentic thing is part of the enchantment of this realm. Some are real, some are fake—you have to discern which is which.

The authentic golden apple represents wisdom that is implicit, requiring penetration, digestion, and assimilation. But there is another feature involving gold that represents the counterpart, wisdom that is explicit, more accessible, applicable to hand. I call these Griffin Gold Reserves, of which there are 47 (see table 7-2).

Herodotus alluded to the "gold-guarding griffins" that live near the Hyperboreans. To the geomantically minded, this is a valuable clue. One time I encountered a griffin at a site near Avebury and visited his "lair" in a landscape feature called the Sanctuary. I threaded my way into his chamber, which was filled with living gold. There is a similar repository of Hyperborean gold at the base of Glastonbury Tor, and another at the Treasury of Atreus, a *tholos* tomb at Mycenae in Greece, the ancestral seat of the ill-fated House of Atreus that included Agamemnon and Clytemnestra.

Homer declared that Mycenae was rich in gold, but that site's gold treasury is a vat of living solar light, the incorruptible knowledge of the Hyperboreans. The famous Lion Gate at Mycenae, a marvel of megalithic engineering, is an open secret and clue to the griffins guarding the gold; a griffin after all is a winged lion.[303]

Why should a griffin guard the Hyperboreans' gold? Let's remember that the Hyperboreans in actuality were the galactically wandering Pleiadians. The House of Atreus, according to Greek myth, is Pleiadian (though scholars never take this literally), Atreus being the grandson in the original Pleiadian lineage of that family.[304] And the griffin is an astral being that derives from the Pleiades.[305] At the Lion Gate at Mycenae, one can behold two majestic astral griffins twice the height of the stone lintel, guarding the gold reserve in the Treasury of Atreus.

Even though I call this geomantic feature a Griffin Gold Reserve, it is not quite the case that when you enter it you will find a great heap of pure gold. You may see it this way as I first did, and that would be symbolically apt, but there is another, possibly more subtle way. The Glastonbury Tor Griffin Gold Reserve appeared to me as a golden rotunda perhaps 200 feet in diameter.[306] The griffin stands before the rotunda, twice its height, guarding the gold. Inside at the center of the rotunda on a large, broad pedestal is the gold; it seems to resemble a gorgeously golden sun. You immerse yourself in this sun during your visit.

But in many respects the griffin is not only the guardian of the gold, it is also your mentor in

Table 7-2: Griffin Gold Reserves
Planetary Total: 47
Selected Locations:
The Sanctuary, near Avebury, Wiltshire, England
Treasury of Atreus, Mycenae, Greece
Sacsaywayman, Cusco, Peru
The Tor, Glastonbury, Somerset, England
Equivalent Names: Treasury of Atreus

acquiring the Hyperborean-Pleiadian wisdom the gold signifies. This gold, or wisdom, is not something you plunder in a day or even a year. The griffin trains you in the mechanics of consciousness whereby you can acquire it, that is, make it part of yourself, wear it exteriorly, metaphorically speaking, as armbands, belts, breastplates, and helmets. Over time, the griffin puts you in resonance, in an absorptive stance, with the Pleiadian knowledge; it's a slow-motion induction and initiation, a long luncheon feast with the Hyperboreans.

The knowledge you get at the Griffin Gold Reserve is *explicit,* as the Ofanim noted, in that things are stated in definite, almost doctrinal form; nothing is left unsaid or implied in the presentation of the teachings; it is something you *learn.* With golden apples, where the knowledge is *implicit,* all doctrinal matters are not stated; some are left unsaid, insinuated, and implied; it is something you *embody.* Of course, both types of knowledge are desirable.

The griffin is your mentor, feeding you droplets of the Hyperborean gold as part of your tutorial in Pleiadian wisdom; but the juice of the golden apple gets absorbed by your system and distributed throughout so that you cannot see it or even say for sure what it is; it's innate, not exteriorized. In a sense, it is a *shape*-imprinting your soul sustains; your energy bodies are "stamped" with the energy signature of the apple itself, which, as I'll demonstrate below, is a dynamic process that encodes further geomantic mysteries and revelations.

With the golden apple, your reaching for it—as Heracles does in the myth—is an allegory for the conscious recognition of that which is *already* within you, implicit in your being, the innate wisdom of being, the knowledge of the gods. The golden apple in this sense is the mirror for you of that recognition, that reaching of understanding. The Earth was given 47 such mirrors for this process. Innate wisdom is precious and hard to obtain, so there are precious few mirrors for it.

Much inner refinement and self-honing are required for you to be able to reach for the apple, to be awake at this level of being where you are aware *that* you know and of *what* you know and of yourself having this awareness. You are aware that you are aware, and you are aware of your awareness. It's a self-reflexive process, like the cycling of a torus, where the inside cycles up to become the outside then cycles inside again. Seen from the right angle, this cycling torus of self-awareness is an apple, a dynamic process of self-consciousness whose perpetual cycling movements physically resemble an apple.

Geomantically, the mythic tableau is constant. A dragon guards the orchard of the golden apple trees. More specifically, in the case of Glastonbury, the vast dragon coiled around the Tor and beyond (one of the 13 original Earth dragons) guards the one authentic golden apple of Glastonbury, just as its colleague, Ladon, guards the one real golden apple of the Hesperides.

The dragon, whose body extends several miles in all directions from the Tor, is the pedestal upon which the golden apple sits. You might think of the single authentic golden apple of this Avalon as sitting perhaps on the crown of the dragon, or, picturing it as a coiled being, in the centermost coil. In effect, all of Avalon—Appleland, the Isle of Apples—is inside this apple. You make it past the dragon and you enter Avalon and the golden apple. No need to slay or even fight the dragon; recognition and assimilation are all that's required.

This is the same situation, by the way, as the biblical tableau of the Garden of Eden. A tree, a fruit, a serpent—however, the biblical version is distorted.

A Taste of the Garden of Eden—in Real Time, Today

The biblical version presents the golden apple guardian as a tempter and deceiver, as an infernal being (a serpent: Satan) who precipitates the downfall of Adam and Eve. He tempts Eve to eat the apple, and that wrecks the paradisal life for her and Adam. I propose that the more accurate presentation of this allegory, based on its multiple geomantic copies in the Earth's visionary geography, is that the dragon (not a serpent, not Satan either) represents kundalini, the primal energy of the first chakra, that enables one (the Adam-Eve within us) to wake up, see the world and ourselves, an acquisition of awareness of selfhood represented by eating the golden apple.

The apple induces self-awareness; the dragon gives you the necessary running start in consciousness to make that profound turning about in the seat of consciousness to look wakefully at yourself once you reach Avalon. There is a dragon guarding each authentic golden apple because you need its energies to be able to reach for the apple, to claim the innate wisdom and self-consciousness that eating the apple induces, and to sustain that new waking state.

You enter Avalon first, which is both the general astral plane (the court of Venus, the *Lake* of the Lady) and the specific Celestial City within it, Gandhavati. Then in conjunction with the arousing of kundalini (assimilating the dragon guardian), you "eat" the golden apple, that is, you recognize your innate wisdom. You wake up and become self-conscious of your existence.

But Avalon is a doorway to a more specialized realm, a culmination and perfection. If you are coming into *incarnation* from God, Avalon is a pivotal place, a swinging doorway; if you are using the Earth's visionary terrain to retrace your steps and *remember*, Avalon is also pivotal. It's the door to the inner heart.

This is self-consciousness on a much more exalted level than we normally think of it while inhabiting our bodies in the physical world. This is Edenic self-consciousness. We are on the threshhold of the fabled, long-missed Eden.

You see before and behind you, above and below, to the left and right, and in the middle too—across the realms. Your cognition is global, universal. You—on the level of a freshly created androgynous soul—embody the perfected male and female poles of human consciousness and being. You embody it (implicit wisdom) and you know it (explicit wisdom). You are now in the Garden of Eden, for the paradox (due to the biblical distortion) is that you eat the golden apple to get *into* Eden. The apple is your ticket of *admission* to, not expulsion from Eden.

Here is the remarkable thing: Eden is a state of mind, a consciousness, perpetually available and reclaimable, and it is a geomantically templated experienceable place on the Earth.

In archetypal terms, the Ofanim explain, "Eden is a primary patterning from the Architect of All That Is, the Mother Father God. It is the potential for unified existence, male and female as one in unitive harmony. Adam and Eve are the seeds of the perfected man and woman in potential. Eden is like an empty space in which the Creation can unfold."

Yet Eden does exist on the Earth. "Aspects of it exist at 26 different places," say the Ofanim. "There are several duplicates of several parts, but there are 26 parts in total." Together they comprise the Earth Eden, and all the Edens are unified, yet each had its own time of expression and amplification, somewhat like a circle of blinking lights timed to illuminate serially.

"Each Eden emanated a unified field of consciousness," the Ofanim add. Yet there was one place where the primary patterning for the 26 Edens was implanted and still holds the original intention and picture. That is the Rondane Mountains of south-central Norway focused at a hamlet called Rondablikk.

Rondane is Earth's primary *Ananda-kanda*, or inner heart chakra. "The *Ananda-kanda*," the Ofanim note, "is a root to the Garden of Eden, and Eden is an analogy for the potential of what the Mother-Father God seeded here at Rondablikk and on the Earth. To repeat, one of the primary patternings for the Garden of Eden as created upon Earth is in Norway."

The Rondane Garden of Eden attracts a lot of extraterrestrial interest, according to the Ofanim. Most of it is good. "Many beings from many dimensions, both material and nonmaterial, are attracted to what is here. There are lifesaving benefits to what is here, like life particles that give conscious life its life. It is like filling the cup with benefits. Thus many are aware of this. The UFOs come here to the Earth's *Ananda-kanda*, for what is existent as a primary focus point from an original creation fashioned by the Creator of All That Is."

There are three other Eden templates in the Rondane Mountains, three in Saudi Arabia, and others in Jordan, Turkey, China, and Tahiti (see table 7-3). That's 12 Edens still extant. Fourteen have been lost due to massive landmass changes, presumably of Lemuria and Atlantis. With respect to the four Eden templates still extant in Norway, the Ofanim state, "If there are several parts close together, this arrangement amplifies each part."

The Ofanim further note that in all the known galaxies—their range of supervision includes

Table 7-3: Garden of Eden Templates

Planetary Total: 26; 12 still extant; 14 lost to land changes (unknown = to me)

Selected Locations:

Rondablikk, Rondane Mountains, Norway

Unknown locations (3), Rondane Mountains, Norway

Mecca, Saudi Arabia

Unknown locations (2), Saudi Arabia

Unknown locations (2), Jordan

Konya, Turkey

Unknown location, near Yangtze River, China

Papeete, Tahiti, French Polynesia: probably Mount Orohena

Equivalent Names: Hvergelmir (Bubbling Cauldron)

18,723,488,640 galaxies—there are only six patternings for the Garden of Eden. One of those six is on our Earth. Only five other planets amidst more than 18 billion galaxies have the Eden template.

If there are only six physically manifested Gardens of Eden in 18 billion galaxies, it should not surprise us that this would attract a vast array of different souls to Earth, all wishing to experience the Edenic feature as best they can.[307]

The four Eden templates in the Rondane Mountains exist within the additional geomantic context of this area being the planet's prime *Ananda-kanda* chakra. I say "prime" because, as we'll appreciate later in the discussion of planetary chakras, these Earth centers are hierarchical and exist at multiple levels. All the chakras, including the *Ananda-kanda*, are expressed at the singular global level, at the Albion Plate level (12 copies), and within Landscape Zodiacs (432).

If the "myth" of Eden is true, then what about the Fall? In the early days of my association with the Ofanim, they frequently mentioned that they remembered us (I had two colleagues in this relationship) as we were *before the Fall*. After some years of this enigmatic reference, I got them to clarify it. "When we refer to knowing you before the Fall, we mean before you came into physical manifestation. That was when the Lord of Light on a commission from the Arch Architect Most Precious on High, the Mother-Father God, made his first step towards matter. This is described by some as the Fall."

Before the Fall means before the Emerald; after the Fall means after the Emerald. As the Emerald signifies the possibility of independent cognition, selfhood, and the possibility of a conscious return to unitive consciousness, humanity "fell" once it was given the opportunity to return voluntarily. In other words, it was not a fall at all, but an invitation. Before the Emerald was given to humanity and the Lord of Light took a step towards matter, committing himself for the duration of the human experiment on Earth, we lived in unitive consciousness, undifferentiated as visible, biological individuals, either male or female.

In a sense there were two Edens, or two aspects to our living in it. The first was the pre-differentiated state, before the Fall, in unitive consciousness. This Eden would be in the astral world. The second Eden was on Earth, with humans embodied and bearing Emeralds. And we had something additional: kundalini. The Dragon. Christianity's serpent in the garden. Except it was (and is) a God-given privilege to have the powers of the gods in a body.

How is kundalini the gods' powers? Consider what it can do. Tantric yoga talks of *siddhis* or attainments. These are seemingly magical physical and energetic or mental abilities that arise as a result of mastering kundalini. Traditionally, spiritual teachers counsel against dwelling at the level of acquiring *siddhis* as it can be seductive or dangerous and threaten one's spiritual evolution.[308]

One can easily imagine how the possibility of

mastering all these physical and psychic powers would be highly seductive. God said in effect: Here's kundalini, here's free will, here are lovely individual bodies capable of the full range of celestial consciousness—let's see what you make of it all. It easily could, and probably did, lead to excess—and that excess might have been damaging to others and the planet. Prodigious powers of mind and body, when wielded by spiritually immature souls in a context of freedom of will, can easily lead to evil, even abominable acts of selfishness and disregard for others.

Whatever the transgression, the Supreme Being evidently decided things had gone too far. "The emanation of the unified field from the Edens was interfered with by the Supreme Being, the Architect of All That Is, because that correction was necessary for the Plan to unfold," the Ofanim note. "This was to do with the forces of self-awareness and good and evil. Human beings moved away from their divinity and abused power in Atlantean times. Therefore humanity had to be redressed."

It's not quite the same thing as the Christian theory of original sin, but we latter-day humans still bear the taint of the excesses of our forebears. The taint is not a mark of transgression, but a limitation. The Supreme Being, it seems, turned the knob down a few notches on our immediate possibilities.

"There are many means of programming human consciousness," the Ofanim state. "Most of what is programmed in your present time is called negative causation programming. It has to do with redressing an imbalance in the human psyche. This is why you can't remember who you were before the Fall. You are at this period of time at a disadvantage in relation to your conscious capabilities, but we suggest you are as limitless as ever."

Provisions were made for our second chance. "The Architect of human and cosmic destiny, concerned with the soul evolution of all humans to remembrance of their divine origin and its reunification, has in mind a plan to bring about perfect balance once again." A fair share of that plan is the opportunity to remember our divine origin and achieve the reunification with our source by interacting appropriately with the Earth's visionary geography.

Think of it as *interactive* sacred geography. We reassemble our celestial selves through interacting with their varied but interlinked expressions as the Earth's body of sacred sites. The Earth's geomythic grid is like a phone line kept open, a modem still linking your "computer" or consciousness to the macrocosmic original of Earth's visionary terrain. The way back to Eden is always open, because our modem is still connected.[309]

Life in Ygg's Tree, and How to Get There on Odin's Horse

The *Ananda-kanda* at Rondane is the Earth's singular inner heart chakra, and it has three elements, in accordance with Tantric iconographic descriptions: the *Kalpa* (or *Kalpataru*) or wish-fulfilling tree,[310] the jeweled altar, and eight vibratory petals. Yogic descriptions say this chakra is a red lotus of eight petals with its head turned upward towards the *Anahata*, or outer heart chakra, and that the jeweled altar is "surmounted by an awning and decorated by flags and the like, which is the place of mental worship."[311]

Let's take the *Kalpataru* tree first. This is the archetypal Tree of Life, and it has a singular geomantic expression. There is one place on the Earth where this tree is geomantically manifest. Its trunk is 4.5 miles wide, at Rondablikk; its roots extend for 15 miles in all directions; it penetrates the Earth for a distance of 150 miles and ascends 200 miles into the atmosphere. The Norse called it Yggdrasil, Odin's Steed, and their mythographers left us a vivid description of it.

Yggdrasil is Old Norwegian for "Ygg's Horse," Ygg being Odin, chief of the gods. It is the monumental Tree of Life, the World Tree, the Tree of the Universe, said to be an ash, that like a ladder connects the three worlds as labeled in Norse myth: Utgard, Mitgard, and Asgard, the realm of the giants, humans, and gods, respectively. Odin resides at the top of the tree.

At its base lies coiled Nidhoggr, one of the 13 original world dragons, and around it seven further named minor dragons gnaw at the tree's roots. There are three springs at the base of the tree, namely, Urd's Well, Mimir's Well, and Hvergelmir. Every day the gods of Asgard ride over Bifrost to hold their council at Urd's Well *(Urdarbrunnr);* Thor (the Norse Zeus) regularly visits Mimir's Well *(Mimisbrunnr)* for inspiration and guidance; Hvergelmir is a bubbling cauldron in Niflheim (the realm of the Frost Giants), home of Nidhoggr, and source of the Elivagar rivers which flow into the primeval chasm, Ginnungagap, the cosmic void before the creation of the world and in which creation occurred.[312]

Let's decode some of this imagery. Mimir's Well is one of the 12 Crowns of the Ancient of Days, the Well comprising Mimir's Head. Hvergelmir is the Norse name for the Garden of Eden, of which four aspects are at Rondane.[313] Urd's Well is a feature we have not yet encountered or described in this book. The Norse say Urd's Well is also the Well of Fate because the three Norns (Urd, Verdandi, and Skuld), who weave the destiny of all humans and see (and represent) the past, present, and future, live by this well and daily water the tree.[314] The Asgard hold their courts of justice at Urd's Well.

Endless Feasting in Valhalla with the Slain Warriors of Odin

Geomantically, Urd's Well is what Tantra labels the jeweled altar. There is a secluded mountain valley called Rondvassbu, a few miles

overland from Rondablikk. The easiest way to reach it, though, is along a three-mile trail that departs from a dirt parking lot in the hamlet of Mysuseter. Rondvassbu consists of a long, narrow lake called Rondvatnet surrounded by foliage-clad but treeless high hills and a park ranger station with, wonderfully, a small restaurant.

When you sensitize yourself to your geomantic surroundings at Rondvassbu, sitting at the far southern end of Rondvatnet, you become aware that you are surrounded by eyes—deities' eyes, human eyes, friendly eyes. In fact, you realize you are at the center of a vast amphitheater of spiritual presences, gods and post-humans. The "jeweled altar" is the spiritual Hierarchy within the subtle realms symbolized by a packed amphitheater of spiritual beings. The "jeweled" part refers to the different consciousness frequencies of these gods, and the "altar" indicates the dedicated intent of the space, as a ritualistic space.

I must digress momentarily into other mythic names and descriptions to make this clear. In the stories of King Arthur, the decisive act in his coming into his kingship was pulling out the sword from the stone. Only the rightful king of Britain could do so, his mentor, Merlin, declared.[315] I experienced this event at a site near Glastonbury called Ivy Thorn Hill and at Rondvassbu.

The "stone" is the otherwordly, nonphysical realm in which the spiritual hierarchy resides. The "sword" is the penetrative ability of consciousness to see into that world, remain awake, and withdraw the "sword" (focused cognition) so as to be able to use it in this world—to be guided by angelic observations. Both Ivy Thorn Hill and Rondvassbu are Sword in the Stone sites, jeweled altars. Other valid and equally descriptive names for this geomantic feature would be Stone of Heaven, Eye of Venus, the Cave of the Heart, for we must remember that all this is within the *inner* heart chakra, the inmost cave of this center.

You psychically penetrate the "stone" of the

altar and *see* the assembly of higher spiritual presences in the englobing amphitheater, and you present your own sword for validation, hallowing, and "sharpening" by an august spiritual being, unnamed at present, who stands there regally, his sword upraised, and a formidable "female" presence, also unidentified. With her is seemingly the entirety of the angelic and post-human hierarchy, certainly all those spirits concerned with human incarnation on Earth and the fate and destiny of both.

You look around the amphitheater—it's more of a vast sports stadium or coliseum—and behold thousands of crystalline facets of all hues, each condensable, should you fine-tune your psychic attention, into the semblance of a spiritual being. For a moment you see the thousands of spirits raise their swords in concert with the (unnamed) august celestial being raising his; then they all turn about and face out into the world, their swords still upraised.

This tableau instructs us that the inner heart is flexible: It can look even more deeply within and upwards to the Supreme Being at the "top" of Yggdrasil and direct its praises and petitions to that domain, and it can look outwards, into the world—*our* world, the physical realm of the incarnate—and send its regards, energies, inspiration, and guidance into the geomantic Earth.

You go to a jeweled altar site to participate in the Sword in the Stone event—initiation, recognition, validation, confirmation, and baptism in the spirit all in one. You see into the spiritual worlds, you penetrate the stone with your sword, and you see the hierarchy penetrating you with their swords. And remember: This august tableau at Rondvassbu and the other jeweled altar sites is but a mirror to the energetic reality within you, and a reminder: All of Heaven is within you. It is not outside, but inside, and you *already* have it all.

Geomythically, when the Norse myths say that the gods of Asgard ride across Bifrost every day to assemble at Urd's Well to take counsel, this means the Ray Masters of *Manipura*, the third chakra and City of Gems, ride "up" to the fourth chakra, *Anahata*, and into its innermost coliseum, the *Ananda-kanda*, to take counsel with the spiritual hierarchy accessible and/or assembled there. The Ray Masters after all, are a small "away" team on assignment across the Earth; they need to meet regularly with the entire panoply of gods and world planners.

The Norse offer us another name for what I have described as a vast assembly of gods and post-humans in an englobing coliseum. Norse myth refers to the *Einherjar* ("those who fight alone" or "belonging to an army") who feast continually in Odin's Valhalla, the paradisal halls for the slain. The *Einherjar* are slain but noble warriors brought to Valhalla after their death by the Valkyries. Odin's Valhalla (from the Old Norwegian, *Valholl*, "Hall of the Slain," from *valr*, "those slain on the battlefield" and *holl*, "hall") has 540 gates through each of which 800 *Einherjar* can march at once (giving us a total of 432,000 *Einherjar*).

During the day, the *Einherjar* practice their feats of war, jousting, and combat, and they may even "die" again; at night, restored, they drink mead brewed from the milk of Heidrun, Thor's goat, and eat meat from the constantly renewed boar, *Sæhrimnir*. Every night Valkyries (all female; Snorri Sturluson names them all) bring the *Einherjar* their ale, a tableau highly reminiscent of the variously described sybaritic court of Venus, Sibyl, or Morgan in Apple-land.

The Valkyries, in addition to waiting table at Valhalla, collect the souls of slain warriors from the battlefield, as their name suggests. (It is Old Norwegian for *Valkyrjar*, from *valr*, "the corpses lying on the battlefield" and *kjosa*, "to choose"—thus, the Valkyries are "those who choose the slain.") The Norse considered them supernatural female warriors who fulfilled Odin's wishes by

---

Table 7-4: Valhalla—The Hall of the Slain

Planetary Total: 108

Selected Locations:

Rondvassbu, near Kvam, Rondane Mountains, Norway

Ivy Thorn Hill, near Glastonbury, Somerset, England

Da Derga's Hostel, County Dublin, Ireland

St. Paul's Cathedral, Ludgate Hill, London, England

Brugh na Boinne, Newgrange, near Dublin, Ireland

Brugh Da Choca, Breenmore Hill, Athlone, County Westmeath, Ireland

Holyfell Hill, Iceland

Monticello, Charlottesville, Virginia, U.S.

Equivalent Names: Urd's Well; Jeweled Altar; Assembly of the Great White Brotherhood or Great White Lodge; Hostel, *Bruiden* or Brugh

---

sometimes interfering with the course of battle so as to lead the preferred slain heroes to Valhalla. Usually nine in number, they were also known as *Odins meyar,* "Odin's girls," and *oskmeyjar,* "Wish-girls," those who fulfill Odin's wishes.

Thus in the Celtic and European versions of Avalon as a somewhat decadent Venusian court of pleasures we have a later, distorted, and certainly incomplete picture of the Valhalla and its Valkyries. However, Avalon and Valhalla are not the same, and the number of their geomantic expressions is different. Norse myth places Valhalla as within Asgard, and in close proximity to *Gladsheimr,* the Hall of the Ray Masters. If Avalon is the geomantic expression of the outer heart chakra, then Valhalla is the form of the inner.

The Norse give us this vivid image of 432,000 *Einherjar* battling and feasting perpetually within Valhalla, awaiting Ragnarok to assist Odin in his defense of the world against its fated entropic dismemberment. However, it would be mistaken to understand this myth to be referring to physically slain militaristic Vikings.

Rather, let's construe the *Einherjar* as *spiritual* "warriors," those on a spiritual path who succeeded in "slaying" (transmuting and transforming) their ego and body-based identity, fully waking up,

remembering and claiming their divinity, embodying it, and definitively passing out of the human incarnational cycle. They have slain themselves and the cognitive limitations of body-based self-definition, and they have birthed the divine within in the form of the golden Christ Child, the Higher Self in the form of the golden child or newborn Christ Consciousness born in the cave of the heart. I will return to this idea below.

What is the boar they feast on? It is the Eucharist of perpetual Christ Consciousness.

Think of the *Einherjar* as graduates from humanity, the ascended ones. Some traditions call them the Great White Brotherhood or Great White Lodge.

This is understood to be a spiritual world conclave of human adepts and masters who preserve the purity of the world's wisdom teachings. A group of soul-minds dwelling in the etheric world, they earned their membership by living "long and arduous incarnations" on Earth and other planets and achieved their spiritual advancement after "much stern self-discipline, self-denial, and consistent self-development, until they transcend[ed] humans in all avenues of life."[316] Only the self-slain can dwell and work in Valhalla as Odin's *Einherjar.*

To behold 432,000 of them in Valhalla would justify the impression of being in the center of an englobing coliseum of the spiritual hierarchy, of being surrounded by myriad kind, regarding eyes. Remember, this "coliseum" of *Einherjar* is both inside you and outside in the Earth. The jeweled altar in *your* inner heart chakra is the meeting hall of the Great White Brotherhood, the undying *Einherjar* sworn in spiritual fealty to Odin, or God. When you visit a geomantically templated Valhalla, then the inherent structure of your *Ananda-kanda* is projected outside for you as an interactive temple.

Valhalla and its variants in other myths are a geomantic feature (see table 7-4), a portal into the conclave of the Great White Brotherhood. This is Odin's assembled *Einherjar*, before whom, and with whom, you perform the Sword in the Stone rite, penetrating the Stone of Heaven and being penetrated by them, all under the auspices of the as yet two unidentified spiritual presences.

In Balder's *Breidablikk*—in the Seat of Christ Consciousness

These two are Balder and his mother, Frigg, effectively, the chiefs of the Great White Lodge; certainly the focus of its rituals and adoration.

Balder in Norse myth is Odin's second son. He is the best, wisest, brightest, most eloquent, sweetest-spoken, most merciful, and friendliest of the Aesir, or assembly of Norse gods. Once he pronounces a judgment, it cannot be altered or unsaid. Everyone praises him; his appearance is almost unbearably bright and beautiful, such light and splendor radiate from him. He resides in *Breidablikk* ("the Far-Shining One"), a heavenly palace free of taint and impurity.

The name Balder has no definitive etymology, but a variant, *Bældæg* (Old English for "the shining day") might be another form of the name Balder, especially as Snorri Sturluson says

"Beldeg, whom we call Baldr." *Bældæg* could thus be a form of Balder derived from the Old English *bealdor*, which means "Lord, Christ." This is good because Balder is the Christ.

His mother is Frigg, Odin's "wife," Mrs. God, the divine Mother. She lives at *Fensalir* (Marsh Halls), a magnificent dwelling. Her prime role in the Norse saga of Balder is to extract an oath from all living creatures that they will not harm Balder. Everyone agrees, except mistletoe; later, this plant will cause Balder's death, and Balder will be the first immortal god to die.

Insofar as Odin is the Norse name for the Supreme Being, Frigg is the *Mother* aspect of what the Ofanim refer to as the Mother-Father God. The situation is like what C. G. Jung said of the relationship and common nature between Yahweh and Shekinah (Sophia), His self-reflection: "They are originally one, a single hermaphroditic being, an archetype of the greatest universality."[317]

Fittingly, Frigg is the only goddess privileged to sit on Odin's throne, *Hlidskjalf*, next to her "husband," Mr. God. She wears snow-white or sometimes all-dark garments and has heron plumes in her headdress and a ring of keys from her waist. She is sometimes (though mistakenly) equated with the Germanic Holda, often mentioned in the (German) context of mistress of Avalon.[318]

So who better to head the Great White Brotherhood than God's Son? Of course that sounds rather theological, so let's put it another way. Balder-Christ is the focus of the Mysteries and of the attainments of the *Einherjar* who know and have mastered the truth of *Not I, but the Christ in me.* Not the lower self, but the higher one; not the individual ego, but God's ego, the Self; not my will, but God's will. That is certainly a death; that can feel like being slain, a crucifixion of the self. It's the Hall of the Slain because the *Einherjar* have affirmed this radical inner turning about in the seat of consciousness expressed as *Not I, but the Christ in me.*

In Norse myth, poets have the Aesir struck dumb and Odin declare that Balder's death was the "worst thing" that ever happened to humans or gods. Of course you have to read through this, turn it around, to get the true meaning. Odin commissioned Balder to "die" into and from the world of humans. He had the full support of the Aesir, some of whom (the Ray Masters) were incarnate as the Apostles during the Christ's presence on Earth through the Ray Master Jesus.

Every Earth-like planet (and its residents) receives the Christed initiation—Balder's death—once during its vast physical history. In fact, the Christed initiation is the Mystery initiation available through the *Ananda-kanda* at Rondane and through any of its subsidiary geomantic expressions. You penetrate the Stone of Heaven (the jeweled altar: Valhalla) with your sword, stand amidst the *Einherjar* (the Great White Brotherhood), and participate in the rapture and adoration in the presence of Balder, the Christ.

The Christ (Balder) is the focus of the Brotherhood, just as the boar (*Sæhrimnir*) is the focus of Valhalla: It's perpetual unity in Christ Consciousness.

Balder's Breidablikk has a geomantic expression in three places on Earth. The Ofanim call this feature the Seat of the Son of the Father, but I prefer Seat of Christ Consciousness. "It's where the Christ energy rests for three Albion Plates."

One Seat is at Lom, a 90-minute drive from Rondablikk, and on the edge of the Jotunheim Mountains in south-central Norway. The others are at Beckery in Glastonbury, England, and the Church of the Holy Sepulchre in Jerusalem.

You may find that the energies of Lom are too intense, too bright, for you to discern anything.[319] That was my experience. I knew the place was geomantically hot, but I couldn't see anything. Once I drove ten miles away, back towards Rondablikk, my cognition cleared. After all, Balder was said to be the brightest and most beautiful of the gods, which would mean for mortals, virtually impossible to look upon close up.

A giant throne sits in the center of three concentric rings. The throne seems made of pearl, as in the Pearl of Great Price. Where Lom is physically, there is the throne, or Seat of the Son of the Father. This throne is seemingly empty. Again the paradox: What does the Christ look like?

Not the Ray Master Jesus. But the Christ, Balder. The paradox, and it may seem appallingly bold at first until you think about it, is that *the face of the Christ is your own.* You are what the Christ looks like. Any of the *Einherjar* are what the face of Christ is like. The face of anyone who has gone through the Christed initiation, digested, and embodied it is what it looks like.

The Christ Throne turns slowly, facing all the degrees in a circle, one by one. This throne is the grounded expression of Odin's *Hlidskjalf.* Literally. Odin's is at the top of a 200-mile-high tree; the Son's Seat is here at ground level.

Picture a slowly rotating throne the size of a mountain made of the Pearl of Great Price, this condensation of precious insight and spiritual presence making a constant infusion of Christ light into the Earth's visionary terrain.[320] Think of this feature as a perpetual epiphany, a continual showing forth of the light.

We get more of an idea of the geomantic intent of this feature by studying its expression through the Church of the Holy Sepulchre in Jerusalem. The present church, built in 1810, the fifth on the site (the first was built in 335 A.D.), is believed to be situated over the rock cave in which the crucified Christ was buried and from which he rose and ascended.

Amusingly, in light of the consistent Venus associations with geomantic aspects of the outer and inner heart chakra, before the Christians rediscovered this site, the Roman Emperor Hadrian had erected a Temple of Venus on this site, which also encompasses the presumed site of the Crucifixion, the Hill of Golgotha (Place of Skulls). Geomantically, this is highly significant, for the Jerusalem Golgotha is one of the 12 Crowns of the Ancient of Days. To have a Seat of the Son of Christ Consciousness there as well is a rich blend. Father and Son, Odin and Balder, accessible in the same place.

Let's step back and take a global view of this feature. In his teachings, the Christ said, I am the way to the Father and nobody goes to the Father except through me. The Seats provide the *means* to go through the Christ to the Father, from Balder to Odin. The Seats were on Earth from the beginning, long before the Christ was physically manifest on Earth roughly 2,000 years ago in his enactment of the Mystery of Golgotha.[321]

Before the Christ came physically to Earth through Ray Master Jesus, the three Seats of the Son of the Father were continuously infusing the Earth's visionary terrain with the Christ essence. It was a way of preparing the planet, well in advance of the Christ event, to be able to assimilate the ontologically radical energies.

The Seats are not so much something you see, as presences you experience. In a sense, all of us who wish it occupy the Christ throne, not out of some mistaken grandiosity, but so as to be *absorbed* into it. You enter Balder's *Breidablikk* and undergo a numinous, transpersonal experience probably similar in nature to the mysteries of the biblical Upper Room.[322]

Among other geomantic benefits they provide, the seats facilitate the hatching of the Golden and Silver Eggs (described below) that birth the old and new Christ on the planet in multiple expressions. The Egyptians knew the Christ as Horus, the Elder and Younger, the falcon-god with a left and right eye, each with a divinely appointed purpose. The Egyptians also often depicted the infant Horus as seated on the lap of his mother, Isis, whose hieroglyph was a throne.[323] But in Horus and Isis here is the same

tableau, merely mythically translated into Egyptian, of Balder and, Frigg, Christ and the Mother aspect of the Mother-Father God.

Thus *Breidablikk*, as Balder's residence, is also Frigg's (Isis's) throne, the Mother aspect of the Mother-Father God merging seamlessly with Her progeny. The infant Horus on Isis's lap, their proximity and intimacy, as mother and child, bespeaks the truth of the Christ being the way to the Father. You go from the Son (Christ, Balder, Horus) to the Mother (Mary, Frigg, Isis) to the Father (God, Odin, Osiris).

Now let's consider *where* this happens. The Earth has three such Seats. The one at Lom, Norway, is situated within the Earth's primary *Ananda-kanda*, inner heart chakra, at the base of the planet's sole expression of Yggdrasil, and in proximity to four of the original Edenic patternings including the primary one.

We have another Seat at Glastonbury, England. Here the Seat is situated within the Earth's primary *Anahata*, outer heart chakra. At Jerusalem, the Seat is found at the site of a Crown of the Ancient of Days, at the Hill of Skulls, one of the 12 places on Earth where the Head of Brahma is buried. All three sites have many additional important geomantic features. At the Jerusalem site, however, you have the Seat, the *preparation* for the Christ Mystery, precisely at the place where that incarnation was physically enacted, *fulfilled,* and grounded forever, the alpha and omega point of this intention.

The Seat of Christ Consciousness is the inversion of Odin's Throne, also accessible here in the Rondanes at the top of Yggdrasil, the Tree of Life. The Tree of course is the *kalpataru,* the wish-fulfilling tree of Tantric description, but it is also Odin's Steed, which has eight legs. Odin's horse is called Sleipnir ("Slipper; Sliding One"). It has eight legs because like Mount Meru, Yggdrasil is surrounded by the eight Celestial Cities. Each of the eight is templated in the greater landscape around the Tree at Rondablikk—within the farthest reach of its branches, as the *Ananda-kanda's* eight petals.

Yggdrasil, the World Tree, or Ygg's Horse, links the three realms of Utgard, Midgard, and Asgard. It connects *Nidhoggr* at its base with Odin in *Hlidskjalf* at its top. The Tree is the connection, the fluidity, the possibility of easy movement between the realms. This fleet-footedness is charmingly symbolized in the squirrel Ratatosk, who constantly scampers up and down Yggdrasil, carrying messages and insults from *Nidhoggr* to Odin's eagle atop the Tree.

Just think of how effortlessly, even acrobatically, a squirrel runs up, down, and around a tree. Both horse and squirrel vividly suggest fast, sure, strong movement, the ability to transit the Tree from roots to crown, to go straight from Rondablikk to *Hlidskjalf*. The inner heart chakra is the fast lane to the presence of the Supreme Being. You can bypass the intervening chakras and go straight and fast to the top, if you wish.

Odin's Throne can be accessed at the Sodorp church in Vinstra, a Norwegian town a little less than 15 miles from Rondablikk. The branches of Yggdrasil reach out that far and overhang the old wooden stave church. I was with a colleague at this site, meditating one afternoon, when the Ofanim facilitated our quick delivery to Odin's *Hlidskjalf*. It felt as if we were flying up the tree, or perhaps inside it, arriving seconds later in Odin's Throne room. What is it like? Of course, this is the part where I wish I could take better photographs.

You find yourself in a vast interior space, like a majestic open hall of pearl. The 24 Elders are in attendance. The 24 letters of the *Autiot*, the Hebrew alphabet, circle and weave like a flaming torus about the Throne. Innumerable tiers of angels surround the throne, which is empty. Except it's not.

Except what does God look like anyway? I don't know. It's easier to construe a voice. There was a Voice and it spoke. Single words, partial sentences, a little. Behind the Throne is the *Guf* where thousands of souls await incarnation; Hebrew religious dogma describes this as a finite, therefore exhaustible, repository of human souls capable of or permitted to enter human incarnation.

You get a strong sense of omniscience, as if there are eyes that can see into all directions, into all of the 360 degrees in a circle and in 360 to the 360th power of refinement. The Norse myths say that from his high seat Odin All-Father observes all the worlds and their doings. You think you're looking at the Throne from one angle and there it is, but it faces every last permutation of a degree, all directions simultaneously, and thoroughly. Nothing is missed. You know you are on top of the world, at the crest of the tree, and the entirety of Creation and all the manifested worlds are situated below you. When you return to ground level and physical reality, the light is as if refreshed, reborn, *new*.

Hatching the Cosmic Egg in the Great Stream of Oceanos

The classical Romans had an expression, "From eggs to apples," referring to the natural sequence of foods in a meal. You start with eggs, finish with apples. This is geomantically apt, though with an inversion, for we are about to find an apple *inside* a Cosmic Egg and inside the apple a Golden and a Silver Egg.

Many myths from around the world say the world started inside an egg. The Hindus in the *Chandogya Upanishad* explain that in the beginning the world was nonbeing but turned itself into an egg, lay that way for a year, then split asunder. The top half of the eggshell was gold, the lower half silver. The silver became the Lower World, the Earth, while the gold became the

Upper World, Heaven; but the entirety of Heaven and Earth emerged out of both halves.[324]

The Hindu prime god Brahma gestated in the Cosmic Egg or *Hiranyagarbha,* the golden germ or embryo. Sometimes this primal egg is referred to as *Brahmananda,* or Egg *(anda)* of Brahma. The *Hiranyagarbha* is conceived of as a germ, a point, a cosmic seed, a golden seed, that gradually unfolds and expands through the seven planes of existence, eventually generating the seven planets. In the Western Mystery tradition, it's known as the "grain of mustard seed," tiniest of seeds from which the universal tree grew.

In fact, the name Brahma may derive from the root *brih,* which means to expand, grow, and fructify "and stands for the spiritual evolving energy-consciousness of any cosmic unit such as a solar system, which is properly called an Egg of Brahma."[325] The *Hiranyagarbha* is also called the golden child or golden germ, or the one born from a golden womb, *Bala Brahma* (Child Brahma). This is a radiant child with four heads and four arms, King of the Immortals, "resplendent like the young Sun, who has four lustrous arms, and the wealth of whose lotus-face is fourfold."[326]

That's the conceptual basis of the Cosmic Egg. But what's the experiential? I first encountered a geomantic Cosmic Egg at a place near Kingweston, outside Glastonbury, England, called Worley Hill. I had occasion to visit the hill at least six times one autumn as part of a series of assignments from the Ofanim who were introducing me to the Earth's visionary terrain and training me within it.

Seen from a mile away, the egg looked like a huge translucent oblong egg of light bigger than the wooded hill. That would have made the egg perhaps 750 feet tall. In a sense, Worley Hill was set within the egg, yet the egg stood on its own in an overlapping spatial dimension. My assignment was to meditate by a nearly dried up streambed called Magotty-Pagotty—a name straight out of Tolkien—in Copley Wood, at the base of the hill, and search for the Cosmic Egg. As an aid in collecting the Cosmic Egg, I visualized the golden Grail as residing in my heart chakra.

I hadn't seen the egg over Worley from a distance yet, and at the end of the first day on the Cosmic Egg hunt, when I looked back at Worley from a distance, I laughed to realize I had been inside the Cosmic Egg all day. Of course I hadn't found it. Inside that one maybe, but there was another one to find.

In the next days, I would experience Magotty-Pagotty, that diminutive half-trickle of water, flowing through my heart chakra and igniting a white seed I hadn't known was in there. The Ofanim called it "the seed of the immutable flame of love." The goal was to find it and get it to burn; the flame was all.

I was, after all, dealing with a cosmic mystery and only gradually understood what was happening. No doubt in its day Magotty-Pagotty was a formidable stream, but that didn't matter. It was the physical equivalent of an energy stream passing through Copley Wood, a *big* stream of light passing through the Grail bowl visualized in my heart, igniting the seed.

Later the Ofanim gave me a clue: Magotty-Pagotty is a corruption of *Mahati-Prahati,* which is a translation from Sanskrit that means "the Great Stream." Think of it as an infinite stream of unending consciousness, the great flowing forwards, the river of cosmic wisdom, the flowing together of all the mysteries of being since the beginning of existence. The Greeks called it Oceanos, the primordial stream said to encircle the World at its outermost edges. As long as we're with this egg metaphor, we might think of this as the egg's albumen, if slightly runny.

So the Great Stream flowed through the Grail chalice in my heart chakra as I sat before Magotty-Pagotty and lit the seed. It flamed fiercely white, burning. "The Grail has at its center the seed of the flame of immutable love," the Ofanim told me. "The stream Magotty-Pagotty fills the Grail with light to kindle the seed of the immutable flame. The setup is represented inside and out." The Egg is the *Hiranyagarbha.*

This seed of the flame of immutable light is a Cosmic Egg, perhaps the original. I went about with this fiercely burning white flame in my heart chakra for a week or two until it was time to return to Worley Hill. I sat in a grassy dell with my back to a stout oak tree. I was surrounded by nature spirits, gnomes, the Ofanim, and other spiritual beings I knew as colleagues—my support staff.

When I first saw the egg this day from a distance, a huge spiritual being whom I assumed was the Archangel Michael flared behind, above, and within this egg, his flaming sword held upright while the Ofanim flew in seven tiers around the translucent egg. Then I saw the same thing but smaller, before me.

As I concentrated on the flaming seed inside me, it swelled to twice my body size with me inside it. It formed a membrane of white fire around me, a flaming egg, a cocoon of fire, a *whorl,* just like the hill, which was also now solely a white egg. The Archangel Michael touched the membrane of my eggshell with his sword, and my auric cocoon flashed even whiter, even more on fire. Inside my chest, a luminous membrane like an eggshell now protectively enveloped the flaming seed. Three Cosmic Eggs: the flaming seed in the Grail, the flaming auric cocoon around me, and the whorl of light in and above Worley Hill.

Weeks later, I was at another megalithic site outside Glastonbury called Burrowbridge Mump, a grassy hill with the ruins of a church on top. An invisible hand thrust a sword down from Heaven into my heart chakra and cleaved my chest in two, as if it were soft clay, revealing a golden child seated awake, radiant, and vital on a bed of rose petals. I had birthed the golden child within.

I hadn't realized at Worley Hill that I wasn't so much after the Cosmic Egg as the golden embryo, the *Hiranyagarbha,* inside it, the egg yolk, so to speak. The whole process, I later understood, was to create the conditions that made it possible to birth this golden child (*Bala Brahma*) from within the heart chakra's flaming seed. After all, in a physical egg, the eggshell and albumen serve to support and protect the precious yolk of potential new life in the center. Geomantically, the Cosmic Egg serves the same purpose in terms of human initiation.

This is a big concept, so let's recap. Earlier we considered the tableau of Frigg and her divine son, Balder, and equivalently, of Isis and the infant Horus. In essence, both are the same as Mary, Mother of God, and the Christ infant, and all three are the Mother aspect of the Mother-Father god. Think of Balder's *Breidablikk* as the Cosmic Egg. Think of Balder as the golden child, as Odin's son. Balder is also *Bala Brahma,* the creator god Brahma rebirthed as a golden child.

To mention *Bala Brahma* as the golden child is to say *Bala Brahma* is the *son* of Brahma, God's son or divine child, which brings us back to Christ in all his mythic guises, such as Balder, Horus, Dionysus. In a sense, the Christ *is* the *Hiranyagarbha;* he is certainly generated out of this golden embryo. The purpose of the Cosmic Egg is to provide the context in which to birth him.

Where is the equivalent of the Cosmic Egg in the human constitution? Mystics and psychics have described the auric envelope surrounding the physical body as egglike in shape. The oval circle of light around the body is often called an aureole, glory, mandorla (shaped like an almond), or auric egg.[327]

The human is a universe, and "his physical personality is a golden embryo suspended within the brilliant shell of his auric sheaths." As the Macrocosmic Egg is the universe and its presumed borders—"'the brilliant *chiton*' or 'the cloud,'" as the ancient Greeks called it—"the Microcosmic Egg is the human aura."[328]

We sleep in our egg, embedded in multiple invisible worlds until we start to wake up and precipitate the golden germ to recreate the ego along cosmic lines. When we break the Cosmic Egg, we shatter the personality and release our spiritual nature, the golden embryo, "into that Universal being from which it originally emanated."[329] Carlos Castaneda wrote that when a clairvoyant sees a human it is as a field of energy like a "luminous egg" or an "egglike cocoon."[330]

Chinese myths tell us that the primordial Cosmic Egg containing all the polarities in undifferentiated and unmanifested form generated P'an Ku, the original giant of creation containing the entirety of existence within his vast form. He broke out of the egg and separated Heaven and Earth; each day for 18,000 years, he grew ten feet taller, which meant the sky was lifted another ten feet off the Earth. In the end, Heaven and Earth were separated by 30,000 miles.

During those 18,000 years, P'an Ku chiseled out all the planet's physical features, the mountains, rivers, valleys, and oceans; he generated the stars and planets from out of his body and the constellations from his beard.

When he died, his skull became the vault of the sky, his breath the wind, his voice the thunder; his flesh became the soil, his blood the rivers, his bones and marrow became the precious gems, metals, and rocks; herbs and trees were formed out of his skin and teeth; his perspiration became the rain; and the fleas in his hair became humans, although it's also said humans were made from the insects crawling across his body. Everything that is, is P'an Ku.[331]

The same story is told in Norse mythology of Ymir,[332] the first of the immortals and primeval father of the Frost Giants, and in the Vedic tradition with Purusha,[333] the Primal Man, a cosmic giant with 1,000 heads, feet, and eyes, whom the gods sacrificed to create the universe.

Here's the relevance: *You* are P'an Ku. You are Ymir. You are Purusha. You are a colossus. The entire Earth and all its visionary terrain is in you. So is the galaxy. You birth it all out of your cosmic, luminous egg.

All of Heaven and Earth, all the polarities of existence, are in you. All of creation tumbles out of you when the egg hatches. As above, so below, and in the middle, too. You are a player. That's the point of Earth's galactically referenced geomancy. *You* make it tick. You're the world. "Symbolically, Purusha lives in the heart of every individual and Purusha fills the cosmos."[334]

This is not an invitation to grandiosity. It's just a reminder that we've been given a second chance at Eden, but this time without the excesses. Here we are, with Balder in *Breidablikk*, potentially Balder ourselves, potentially able to see and be one with his Mother-Father, Frigg-Odin, the unfathomably vast. But just how big is Odin, is God, Ymir, P'an Ku? Qabalists use the phrase *Shi'ur Komah* to refer to the mystical extent and shape of the Godhead, to God's size.

Moses was on Mount Sinai when he had a stupendous vision of God. The Supreme Being, biblical sources say, opened the Seven Heavens and revealed Himself to Moses, in His beauty, glory, and shape, with His crown, upon His throne, and presented Moses with the Torah and the "Ten Commandments," which most Qabalists understand to mean a revelation of the ten Sefirot.

Ezekiel started his Chariot or *Merkabah* vision through the realms of Heaven while standing on the banks of the River Chebar near Babylon, now in today's Iraq. In fact, his revelation was of the Chariot or *Merkabah* and all its aspects—in effect, he witnessed a Cosmic Egg.

Ezekiel's most sublime revelation, Qabalists say, was the *Shi'ur Komah*. This was the measurement of the Body, the size and extent of God's

---

Table 7-5: Cosmic Eggs

Planetary Total: 48

Selected Locations:

Uffington Castle, Dragon Hill, Wiltshire, England	Dome of the Rock, Jerusalem, Israel	Banaras, India (at the Durga Kund)
Worley Hill, Kingweston, Somerset, England	Mount Pisgah, Westhampton, Massachusetts, U.S.	Heliopolis, near today's Cairo, Egypt
Mount Sinai, Egypt	Mormon Temple Square, Salt Lake City, Utah, U.S.	Idaean Cave, Mount Ida, Crete, Greece
Mount Damavand, Iran		
Steep Hill, Lincoln, England		

Equivalent Names: Brahmananda, Egg of Brahma, *Hiranyagarbha,* Mundane Egg, Universal Egg, Orphic Egg, auric egg, *Shi'ur Komah, Merkabah,* Mount Qaf, cosmic mountain, world mountain, world navel

---

universal body expressed as the Primal Man. It's the same as measuring the size of the Egg of Brahma. Qabalists, incidentally, state that God's height is 7,008,000,000 miles.[335]

Certainly this gives us another version of P'an Ku's phenomenal growth spurt of ten feet daily for 18,000 years and it illustrates the vastness of Primal Man who occupies all the space inside the Cosmic Egg and who contains all the worlds, dimensions, planetary spheres, Sefiroth, stars, planets, and all creatures.

What is the significance of these "monstrous length measurements," as Qabalist scholar Gershom Scholem queries. "God's holy majesty takes on flesh and blood, as it were, in these enormous numerical relationships."[336]

Moses and Ezekiel had their visions by way of starting at a Cosmic Egg positioned in the geomantic landscape. The Earth has 48 such eggs. Worley Hill in Kingweston, England, is a Cosmic Egg (see table 7-5). Cosmic eggs exist at the Dome of the Rock, at Ezekiel's River Chebar visionary site near Babylon, and Moses's Mount Sinai. What does a Cosmic Egg do for the Earth?

According to the Ofanim, in most cases, Cosmic Eggs were originally positioned at the root

chakra of a landscape zodiac or at a place that serves to stabilize that star map on a local landscape (see chapter 9 for zodiacs). A landscape zodiac is an interactive partial expression of variable diameter of the constellations across a landscape; it is a geomantic star map. At Worley Hill, for example, the Cosmic Egg is near the entrance to the Glastonbury zodiac, and the Great Stream of Magotty-Pagotty flows close to that entrance. The egg at Jerusalem is also on the edge of a landscape zodiac just outside the old city gates.

The Cosmic Egg was once sometimes referred to as an Orphic Egg, after Orpheus, the god of the Underworld, or lower astral plane. Orpheus was one of the Nefilim, another angelic family that, like the Elohim, had occasion to enter human biological form. "The Orphic Egg, therefore, is an egg with a seed that is elementally Earth-related, either to do with landscape activations, Earth energy grid activations, or Earth feature amplifications," the Ofanim note.

What does a Cosmic Egg do for us? If we have the clairvoyance of a Moses or Ezekiel, potentially we can have a spectacular vision of the Seven Heavens. Maybe we can glimpse even a little of it. Immersion in the energy field of the Cosmic Egg gives us the chance to find the seed already planted deep within the heart chakra and to ignite it by exposing it to the Great Stream. We can experience a little of the predifferentiated state, of conditions before the world, galaxy, and universe were manifested into hierarchies and polarities. We can experience *Breidablikk* and Balder with Odin-Frigg in the background.

I know. This sounds abstract and remote from practical concerns. Who cares about experiencing Balder in the twenty-first century? How does it help my life?

What I'm referring to in using these mythic names and places is one of the essential mystery initiations in probably all wisdom traditions on Earth. The birth of the new human from within the old one. A turning about in the deepest seat of consciousness. A metanoia, a profound change of mind. The creation of the Philosopher's Stone, the expression of alchemy's *filius macrocosmi* (son of the macrocosm), the emergence of the immortal inner Man. The Higher Self.

The experience of the Higher Self, the immortal "son" of the Mother-Father God is expressed as the divine child within. This figure, in accordance with Jungian depth psychology, "at its highest level and fullest meaning is, or may equal, the Anthropos or 'Christ within' of the Gnostics, the Son of Man figure of the Biblical prophets, ultimately the Son of God."[337] The process of birthing this inner divine child has been at the core of mystery initiations and a continuous stream of spiritual development all the way back to Egypt (which acknowledged two Christlike Horuses, the Elder and the Younger), if not earlier.

A Reign of Golden and Silver Eggs Across the Earth

The Egyptians spoke of two Horuses, the Younger and the Elder, and the Vedas say the Cosmic Egg split into gold and silver halves. These two halves are eggs in themselves, geomantically placed around the Earth. I call these the Golden Eggs and Silver Eggs, and they pertain to the divine child or Christ within.

The Golden Eggs, of which there are 666 equally distributed across the Earth, pertain to the Younger Horus, the newborn Christ child.[338] The Silver Eggs, with a planetary total of 1,080, pertain to the Elder Horus, the eternal Christ as Son of God (Balder as son of Odin-Frigg).[339]

Let's start with the Silver Eggs, which birth the Elder Horus. Horus, the son of Osiris and Isis, was the falcon-headed Egyptian god. At Heliopolis he was known as *Harakhtes,* "Horus of the Horizon"; at Edfu, as Horus the *Behdetite,* the celestial falcon god or hawk-winged Sun disk.[340]

Horus was the Face of Heaven and has two eyes. His right eye is white, the Sun, the left is black, the Moon. Both Sun and Moon are Eyes of Horus, part of a cosmic face that protectively overlooked ancient Egypt. Hence another epithet: Horus of the Two Eyes, the White Eye (Sun) and the Black Eye (Moon). Once Horus lost his left Moon eye in a battle with Seth, but Thoth restored it, calling it the *wedjat* (or *wadjet* or *udjat*), "the Hale One."[341]

The Horus mythology is complicated, but generally Horus the Elder (the left, Black Eye, *wedjat,* Moon, called *Heru-Ur*) is associated with Thoth, god of wisdom, while Horus the Younger (the right, White Eye, Sun, called *Heru-pa-khart*) is associated with Ra the Sun god. The relevance is that the two Horus Eyes represent the total of 1,746 eggs.[342] The White Eye signifies the 666 Golden Eggs of the Younger Horus; the Black Eye the 1,080 Silver Eggs of the Elder Horus.

Why the falcon imagery? To indicate the farseeing aspect, the mobility in the air element (Zeus's sphere, the domain of the air element, *Alef,* primordial spirit). "The falcon image is the inner teacher who sees all aspects of a situation

Table 7-6: Silver Egg, the Left Eye of Horus

Planetary Total: 1,080

Selected Locations:

Store Solukletten, Rondane National Park, Norway	Tetford, Lincolnshire, England	Glastonbury Tor, Glastonbury, England
Chapel of the Holy Cross, Sedona, Arizona, U.S.	Edfu, Egypt	Mount Sipylos (classical Magnesia), near Izmir, Turkey
Cheops Pyramid, Giza Plateau, near Cairo, Egypt	Cadmeia, Thebes, Greece Mount Cithairon, Greece	

Equivalent Names: Heru-Ur, Horus the Elder; Polydeuces (Pollux), the Immortal Twin; *wedjat;* Black Eye, Moon Eye

from *above* as Love from Above," explain the Ofanim. "The silver child, which is the inner aspect of the falcon, is also the other aspect of the golden child. When the silver and gold aspects come together, then the all-seeing aspect arises."

The falcon, as a predatory bird, signifies the ability of the fleet-winged Horus (Christ Light) to disarm, "kill," or transmute the enemies of illumination.

How does this work at the geomantic level? Not all the 1,080 Silver Eggs have been hatched (see table 7-6). For those that have, you may encounter Horus as a fully fledged silver hawk of considerable size; for those that have not, you may perceive a vast Silver Egg as if brooding on its own future hatching.

It is up to us, Grail Knights of Earth's visionary terrain, to hatch the Horus eggs; however, this is something you should consider undertaking only in the context of an invitation from the angelic realm, a certain amount of inner preparation, and the assurance of on-site angelic support and cooperation. All eggs at this level of expression do not have the same gestation time; some may not be slated for hatching for hundreds of years from now, others, for next week.

I worked on the hatching of a Silver Egg during two weeks in January 1992 in Sedona, Arizona. To hatch a Silver Egg and release the Elder Horus, one thing you need is a little glass shank from the Celestial City of Mount Olympus. As I explained in a previous chapter, this "shank" is consolidated, condensed wisdom from the future (as the Ray Master's city exists in our future, at 3000 A.D.). You get the shank, place it in the egg, the egg hatches, and there's the falcon-headed Horus.[343]

What can you do with a geomantically expressed Elder Horus? You can use his *wedjat*, his restored Black Eye. As with many myths, you have to read it backwards, or inverted. Contrary to exoteric myth, Seth was not Horus's enemy, but an expression of Osiris, the equivalent of the Greek Zeus, and thus if anything Horus's father. Seth did not destroy Horus's left eye, rather, he gave it to his son so that Horus could see him. The *wedjat* is the Eye of Horus that looks upon the Father and His mysteries.

The Elder Horus with his *wedjat* that sees Seth, his sublime Father, is the guardian and psychopomp to the eternal, greater Mysteries. When a Horus is hatched and geomantically birthed (grounded, opened, activated) in a terrestrial landscape, this makes the inner temple of wisdom available to humans. He inducts us into the old, eternal mysteries. As Dionysus, he initiates us in the sublimities of the "vine," the divine intoxication. He shows us the vast antecedents to human life, planetary creation, galactic life. He opens the doors of the Mystery temple and supervises our gradual initiation. He is the Elder because he is before Earth and human creation; he flies outside our space-time to arcane and time-free realms. He does not enter human or physical incarnation; rather he takes us to that undying point *before* either happened, *outside* their context.

Horus the Elder conducts you to the Celestial City of the Ray Masters, source of the futuristic knowledge by which he was activated in our present. Horus does more: he conducts us to any or all of the eight Celestial Cities constellated around Mount Meru, the cosmic mountain. He flies us into the spiritually recondite realm of the *Ananda-kanda*, domain of the eight petals that encircle the cosmic mountain that towers up in its midst. He provides us the map of the esoteric territory, the escorts, the introductions, the teaching.

Jousting with the Sphinx on the Seraphim's Round Table

It is not the easiest thing in the world to enter a Silver Egg domain. Nor is it safe, cognitively speaking. You may be torn to shreds, devoured, annihilated. The Greek tragic hero Oedipus became the rightful king of Thebes by overcoming the sphinx, by answering its riddle. The sphinx had been trained by the Nine Muses in the art of riddles and put a seemingly unanswerable riddle to every supplicant who came before it seeking entry to the Silver Egg domain beyond. For the sphinx, described by the Greeks as having a female upper torso, a dog's lower torso, bird wings, snake tail, and lion paws, was the vigilant guardian of the temple. The sphinx would eat

those who failed the riddle, hence she was called Devourer.

Only the prepared could—and *should*—enter the Silver Egg domain, for it is a very dangerous place. Only the truly human could pass through, for that was Oedipus's answer to the sphinx's perennial question: a human. The sphinx guarded the temple and protected the unprepared by testing their humanness. What creature on Earth goes four-footed, two-footed, and three-footed under the same name so that its speed is slowest when it uses the most feet?

A human. A baby crawls on all fours and moves the slowest, an adult stands on two legs, the infirm elderly uses a cane, thus making three feet. It was a test of self-awareness: Are you human by knowing you are human, the sphinx asked, which was really, are you aware you are aware, and are you aware of your awareness in the context of being in a human form? This is another way of testing the initiate's awareness (and the assimilation of that awareness) of his celestial origin, consciousness capable of being one with God, yet individualized.

Similarly, you find a sphinx—the Great Sphinx of the Giza plateau—guarding the entry to the Cheops pyramid, site of a Silver Egg. This is the famously enigmatic crouching lion with human-like face. Similarly, I have seen a sphinx on a small mountain called Vesle Solukletten acting as vigilant sentinel for entry into the Silver Egg of Horus the Elder at a twin-peaked mountain next to it, called Store Solukletten in Rondane National Park in Norway, site of the Earth's primary *Ananda-kanda* inner heart chakra. There are 1,080 sphinxes in the Earth's geomantic matrix, one for each Silver Egg.

In a sense, the sphinx is an aspect of Horus the Elder. Egyptian hieroglyphs tell us that one form that Heru-Ur took was as a lion with the head of a hawk, wearing the crowns of the South and North. At Sekhem, Egypt, one of Heru-Ur's most important shrines, the Elder Horus was worshipped exclusively in his lion form. We also learn that when faced with his enemies, Heru-Behutet (Horus of Edfu) transformed himself into a lion with a human face and was crowned with the triple crown. His paws were like flint knives, his anger was of a lion roused in his lair, he rent his enemies in pieces and tore out their tongues, "and their blood flowed on the ridges of the land in this place."[344]

It is surprising but exciting to connect this attribution with something attributed to the mysteries of Dionysus, the Greek version of the Elder Horus. His worshipers were described as wine-intoxicated, god-crazed women called Maenads (*Mainadai*, "frenzied women") or Bacchants or Bacchae (women of Bacchus). They captured wild beasts, tore them to pieces, and devoured them. The Maenads practiced Dionysian frenzy and rites of ecstatic liberation; they sang, danced, whirled, and played wild music in the mountains.[345]

Let's put two seemingly unrelated mythic images together. The Greek Maenads are the Egyptian Sphinx and both are the door guardians for Dionysus. The Maenads were not so much the followers of Dionysus as his protectors. They also protected the unprepared from Dionysus, whose vivid, electrifying spiritual presence would dismember their identity and cognitive processes.

The Maenads, like the Greek sphinx, were the testers, the riddlers; they evaluated the supplicants for the Mystery temple of the Elder Horus for their spiritual worthiness and assessed the question: Will they survive this encounter? If they are wild beasts, which is to say, identified with the animal aspect of the human, they will die from the encounter; if they are human, they might survive. Oedipus survived; he "killed" the sphinx by answering its question.[346]

At the same time, the Maenads start preparing the initiate for his frenzied encounter with Dionysus by taking his identity apart, dismembering animal-based ego and body-based selfhood. The Maenads "symbolized the obliteration of personal identity and the liberation from conventional life that came with Dionysus's ecstatic worship." The Dionysian ecstasy, the inspired frenzy, was a "'standing outside oneself' in which the human personality vanished, supposedly replaced by the identity of the god."[347]

It's *Not I, but the Christ in me*—the voluntary substitution of identities, the graduation of the human into the Christ ego in the Dionysian revelation.

It's not the god who is dismembered: *You* are, you who wish to encounter the Elder Horus-Dionysus. You are devoured either way; either you lose consciousness and relapse into the wild beast–animalistic aspect of the human, or you stay awake during your dismemberment, holding fast to your heart—the seat of your human "I"-ness and the only part of Dionysus-Zagreus that was not devoured when he was dismembered. (*Zagreus* was a Greek term, prevalent on Crete, to mean one who catches live animals, a catcher of game.)

Yet, paradoxically, it is Dionysus who is dismembered, whose flesh we eat in an earlier, pre-Christian version of the Eucharist. This is my body, eat of it, the Christ says. This is my blood, drink of it. It is the Communion dinner, where we eat the god, consuming his divine flesh, shred by shred, limb by limb, consuming—*devouring* when the ecstasy fills us—the undying god, and through this, assimilating his essence and ontological reality. Then *we* are the Maenads.

The Eucharistic feast, consuming the god whose flesh and blood are constantly replenished—this is highly similar to the Norse concept of the *Einherjar* in Valhalla feasting every night in Odin's hall on the boar.

The Nordic boar, the Greek ecstatic god, the Christ—can they be the same? Yes, the same large reality seen through different cultural and psychic filters, for the Hindus said that Vishnu's third incarnation was as a boar called Varaha, and we have already established that Vishnu is the Hindu name for Christ. The *Einherjar* who feast daily on the divine "flesh" presumably live constantly in that state of inspired ecstasy and illumination that the Dionysian human votaries aspired to and occasionally achieved. They are Maenads too.

There is yet another nuance to the Dionysian eucharistic feast. It is the feast of the Self, and you are its food. Your fragmentation, all the little selves, the rational world construct known as the ego, all are revealed to be secondary, minor, peripheral in light of the Self, your central planner, spiritual authority, totality.[348]

So come joust with your Self in the guise of the sphinx and suffer the dismemberment of your "relatively subordinate" sense of yourself, that "secondary phenomenon" of identity that arises out of the root of the Self. And in the course of your transformation mysteries, inaugurated for you by your Self, you'll make many discoveries, peer through many veils. You'll see, for example, that even the Maenads are not what they seem.

In actuality, these frenzied, inspired, Dionysian-crazed women are an angelic family called the Seraphim. Their prime manifestation number is 1,080, and they accompanied the resurrected Christ in his ascension from the Mount of Olives.[349]

Part of their commission is to accompany and support all manifestations of the Christ in his Elder Horus guise, which includes through the 1,080 Silver Eggs around the Earth. Their staid mythic guise is the human-faced, lion-bodied sphinx, vigilant temple guardians. Their active guise is as the frenzied Maenads.

Thus before you can enter the temple of the Elder Horus and the Greater Mysteries, you need to pass through the Seraphim's domain, expressed as riddling sphinx, devouring Maenads, or perhaps closer to their own essence, which is a rapidly oscillating vibration, a wavelike, dancing pulse.[350]

So who are the Seraphim? Conventional angelologies are confused as to their identity. The name "Seraphim" is taken to mean the plural of *Seraph,* which means "fiery serpent," and thus the angels of the fire element. This is incorrect. If anything, given their lunar number of 1,080, they "rule" the water element. The Seraphim come into sharper focus when we reveal another of their mythic identities. They are the Nordic Valkyries, the fell women who collect the slain on the battlefield and evaluate their worthiness for inclusion at Valhalla.

Years ago in the earliest days of my training under the auspices of the Ofanim, the Seraphim put their oars into my initiation as well, in a curious way. Prominent in the Arthurian mythos is the act of jousting. Two guys in heavy armor ride horses at each other, level long spears, and try to unseat each other, even if it injures or kills them. We should not take this at face value, despite what we think is historically and probably true. There is an esoteric side to this.

On several occasions I was asked to engage the Seraphim in a joust. This was a visionary experience of course. I would be in meditative focus out in a preassigned landscape site; the Seraphim would appear, one at a time, on a horse, lance fewtered, ready to unseat me. They would charge, I would unseat them, plunge my lance through them, and extract a gold coin, which turned out to be either a nugget of wisdom or a "memory video" of a past life in which I had learned something relevant to present circumstances. Or so I thought.

Another time I experienced my body hacked into a hundred pieces by these same knights, and all the parts dumped in a wicker basket—surely a dismemberment worthy of the Maenads.

The tricky thing about psychic visions is just because you see something doesn't mean you're seeing it accurately or interpreting it appropriately. I got it way wrong about the Seraphim on horses. It was I who got lanced, I whose heart center yielded the gold coins, I who was summarily dismembered.

The jousting was the Seraphim evaluating my worthiness to penetrate a Silver Egg, behold the ecstatic Dionysus, and enter Valhalla to enjoy the ceaseless boar feast, the perpetual Eucharist. That was the Valkyries' commission. Jousting is a way by which the Seraphim as Valkyries can probe you to assess your worthiness, your readiness.

Let's keep in mind from earlier that the Valkyries are *Odins meyar,* "Odin's girls," and *oskmeyjar,* "wish-girls," those who fulfill Odin's wishes just as the Maenads are in effect Dionysus's "wish-girls."[351] Let's put the images together. The Sphinx guards the entrance to the Silver Egg, to Dionysus's presence. The Sphinx is a snapshot, a congealed symbolic interpretation of the reality of the Seraphim, one picture among many possible to indicate what they are and do.

On your way to the Silver Egg and Dionysus (Balder, Bala Brahma, Christ), you encounter and deal with the Sphinx-Seraphim. Their presence is a battlefield; you enter the Sphinx, deal with its question—what part of you is truly the human?—and experience yourself penetrated, slain, chopped up into dozens of parts. You have been "processed" by those god-frenzied Maenads, the storm-riding Valkyries, the Trisagion-intoning Seraphim. *You* are the slain, the dismembered, the wild animal eaten.

This is the price of the ticket of admission to the feast of the *Einherjar,* the little death. For to enter the Silver Egg of the Dionysian Mysteries is virtually the same as to sit in Valhalla among the *Einherjar* (those for whom the truth is *Not I, but the Christ in me*) enjoying the delicious, ecstasy-inducing roasted meat of the boar *Sæhrimnir,* constantly feeding on the ever-resurrected Child of God. Of course, the Seraphim as Valkyries

would also be the servers in Valhalla; they always accompany the Christ during his full epiphany on Earth and in Heaven.

The Ofanim *lead* you to the Christ, like the Star of Bethlehem leading the magi to Nazareth (the inner cave of the heart), while the Seraphim *prepare* you for the Communion, the Eucharistic feast. They serve you and celebrate Christ. They surround the Christ Child in his various guises as Balder, Dionysus, Horus, like a nimbus of flames, searing, purifying, impenetrable save for those ready.

Let's look more closely at the jousting field. Most of my training encounters with the jousting Seraphim took place at an old British hill-fort (elevation 500 feet) called Cadbury Castle, about a dozen miles from Glastonbury. Based on archeological excavations, scholars haltingly entertain the possibility that this was once King Arthur's Celtic Camelot (Camalate, my preferred spelling).[352]

Superimposed on the grassy flat hilltop of Cadbury Castle is a Round Table. This is a geomantic feature reminiscent of King Arthur's legendary Round Table around which the Grail Knights sat in nonhierarchical fashion; it is also suggestive of astrology's circular horoscope with its 12 signs and houses. Picture a circular table perhaps 500 feet across laid upon the landscape. It has 12 equal divisions or wedges, and each represents a constellation in the conventional zodiac.

This Round Table is an interactive geoastrological template. There are 1,080 of these on the Earth, one for each Sphinx and Silver Egg. Thus there are 1,080 Silver Eggs, Sphinxes, and Round Tables; the Sphinx and Round Table will be in the same place, but the Silver Eggs may often be close by but elsewhere. In Glastonbury, the Sphinx and Round Table are at South Cadbury Castle, while the Silver Egg is 14 miles away at Glastonbury Tor.

With the geomantic Round Table, you occupy the different star positions to encounter, assimilate, and maybe transmute their energies in accordance with your own astrological configuration.

This is the geomantic or visionary jousting field, and the Seraphim supervise it. At the *center* of the Round Table sits the Sphinx, or the Seraphim in whatever guise they prefer. Their Sphinx guise, though, indicates the *function* of the Round Table.

The Sphinx faces all 360 degrees of the Round Table at once; wherever you are, that's where its attention is focused. You are always jousting with the Sphinx, whose fewtered lance is the probing, unsettling question—are you a human?

You joust against the Sphinx (you may, as I did, see the Seraphim done up as horsemen with lances) from the different positions, the varying human-animal energy forms, on the Table, measuring your humanness against their angelic lance. You sit in the Scorpio wedge, for example, and encounter its energies; you joust with the question of whether you are human—awake, self-aware—in this context. Potentially, you sit in all 12 positions of this Table, which is also a geomantic map of the 12-petalled outer heart chakra.

You could say, experientially, the entire jousting field is inside the Sphinx; certainly it is entirely within the Sphinx's initiatory purview and supervision. The Sphinx or Seraphim wear the 12-wedged Round Table like a broad collar or ruff. The jousting field is also the alchemical retort for the dissolution process—yours.[353]

You encounter negative aspects of the self and the shadow personality, all the thrown-out parts of the psyche. Geomantically, you joust with these disavowed shadow knights of your fragmented self, courtesy of the Seraphim. You undergo the Dionysian shredding and tearing of the god as a preparation for the Eucharistic feast inside the Silver Egg. It's almost impossible to describe this without it seeming like metaphysical code. The Sphinx and Round Table help you prepare for the experience of the Silver Egg's revelation of the elder Christ. For the younger Christ, you need a Golden Egg. In the Silver Egg, you devour the old god; in the Golden Egg, you birth the new god, but it's Christ either way.

Golden Eggs—You Become the Revelation of God as the Divine Child

With the Golden Egg we encounter the Right Eye of Horus, the Younger Horus. When hatched, the contents of the Golden Egg resemble the traditional Christmas tableau in Christianity: the newborn Christ infant in the manger observed adoringly by the magi. But it also portrays the Egyptian version: the infant Horus on Isis's lap. However, when you use the geomantic temple of the Golden Egg, the scene is inverted: *you* are the newborn divine child on the lap of the Mother.

Interacting with any of the 666 Golden Eggs in the Earth's visionary geography (see table 7-7) facilitates your rebirth as the divine golden child.

The geomantic structure of the Golden Egg temple is different from a Silver Egg. Experientially, the totality of this temple is the infant Horus cradled in the lap of Isis, or the Christ child held against the bosom of Mary. These two elements have a geomantic expression, and the entire structure can often be several miles long. The Golden Egg at Tetford, in Lincolnshire, England, is nine miles long. I'll use this as an example to explain how Golden Eggs work.

Tetford is a tiny, obscure village in central England in Lincolnshire, two miles from the birthplace of Alfred, Lord Tennyson. In recent years, it has been revealed to contain a complex, multi-aspected geomantic temple, which I detailed in *The Galaxy on Earth*. The geomantic Golden Egg has three parts: an egg cup or saucer, the egg itself, and the Madonna embracing it.

If you like, you can construe the Golden Egg as a chakra template, though, technically, it is not as they were described earlier. Given that, the egg

Table 7-7: Golden Egg, the Right Eye of Horus

Planetary Total: 666

Selected Locations:

Vesle Solukletten, Rondane National Park, Norway	Acropolis, Athens, Greece	Bethlehem, Israel
Tetford, Lincolnshire, England	Edfu, Egypt	Burley Hill, Oakham, Rutland, England
Burrowbridge Mump, Burrowbridge, Somerset, England	Mount Holyoke, Hadley, Massachusetts, U.S.	Shrine of Our Lady of Walsingham, Walsingham, England
	Teotihuacan, Mexico	
Goetheanum, Blood Hill, Dornach, Switzerland	Wawel Hill, Cracow, Poland	
	Glastonbury Abbey, Glastonbury, England	

Equivalent Names: Heru-pa-khart, Horus the Younger; Christ Child; Castor the Mortal Twin; White Eye; Sun Eye

cup is the first two chakras marked by a small church in a hamlet called Bag Enderby and Somersby, a few miles away. Ideally, you process overland from Bag Enderby to Somersby in preparation for entering the sacralized domain inside the Golden Egg through the "door" at Somersby.

From Somersby, you can see the Golden Egg like a single pea in an open pod, or as a huge golden sphere of light resting upon several miles' worth of landscape. Inside the egg is the golden child and its next five chakras. Its head or crown is at Tetford. The Madonna aspect is grounded at a hill called Maidenwell, very aptly named, for this is the inexhaustible well of the maiden's love and care for the newborn divine child. Maidenwell is the baptismal fount for the divine child's crown chakra, the site of its perpetual baptizing in the Spirit by its Mother.

To psychic vision, her arms reach down all the way to Bag Enderby, nine miles in a straight line overland, as she completely envelops the Christ child. The benefit to you in sitting in the Maidenwell site above the crown chakra of the landscape golden child is that it will help develop your clairvoyance through stimulating and "baptizing" your crown chakra.

From the Earth's point of view, the benefit to "hatching" a Golden Egg is that it allows a little more of the Christ Child's energy to flow into the world. From our point of view, this temple models, mirrors, and facilitates the birth of the Christ Child within us, the Higher Self expressed as the divine child within. It represents the third phase of initiation begun with the Cosmic Egg and continued with the Silver Egg. The intent is to birth the New Man within the old human.

You find the seed and flame of immutable love inside the Cosmic Egg of the aura. You hatch the Silver Egg of the Elder Christ, then the Golden Egg of the Younger Christ, and you become one with both aspects. You are reborn. "Man internally is a *seed* capable of a definite growth," commented Gurdjieffian scholar and Gospel interpreter Maurice Nicoll some years ago. Man is like a seed capable of an evolution. "As he is, Man is incomplete, unfinished. A man can bring about his own evolution, his own completion, *individually.*"[354] If he wants to.

Again, the geomantic function depends on your perspective. Creating the worlds, the three eggs—Cosmic, Silver, Golden—produce the prototype of the divine and celestial human. He has the

Christ (Horus, Balder, Dionysus) as his innermost essence. We have here then the revelation of God (Brahma, the Higher Self) expressed as the divine child (Christ, Horus, Bala).

God born as the Son of God—it's almost too circular to express it clearly. God born parthenogenetically for the first time as the divine child; not a rebirth, though, for God by definition was never "born," but was always existent. This divine child, the Son of God, God birthing "Himself," will be the heart of the world.

Going up on the path of initiation facilitated by the Earth's geomantic terrain, you crack the Cosmic Egg of your aura, hatch the Silver and Golden Eggs, sprout the seed capable of evolution, and achieve rebirth as the New Man. You behold and you *become* the revelation of God as the divine child, Elder and Younger Christ at the heart of the egg-born world.

The Elder Horus and the Younger Horus, the Elder Christ and the newborn Christ Child, combine to form something new—Adam. Not the first human male, but the pregenderized archetype of the embodied human. Some Qabalists decode this word as meaning the *Aleph* (A) in the blood (DAM), which means, approximately, the point of spiritualized consciousness residing wakefully in a human form. As an equivalent expression for the "*Aleph* in the blood," let's say the Blazing Star in the human body.

How do we get the Adam? It is the composite of the 1,080 Silver Eggs (Elder Horus) and the 666 Golden Eggs (Younger Horus)—1,746, the mustard seed, mentioned earlier. At least two archangels are involved in this birthing of Adam from the eggs. The Archangel Gabriel oversees the Silver Eggs, archetype of the water element; the Archangel Raphael, the Golden Eggs, archetype of the fire element. There is another connection, though it should not be construed reductionistically: Gabriel's total manifestations are 1,080, Raphael's 666, so by gematria and

function each archangel is necessarily associated with the eggs.

What is the geomantic purpose of the golden child? "It is the link with the Solar Logos and the Grail and the myth that exists within the landscape," the Ofanim explain. "The intention is to facilitate human conscious evolution. Conscious cooperation, reciprocal maintenance with Man and Gaia, produces expansion of consciousness in beings on the surface of Gaia and within Gaia."

In terms of their deployment around the planet, you will sometimes find that the locations of Golden Eggs match well the cultural activities undertaken there. Glastonbury Abbey, once one of England's foremost and presumed earliest Christian establishments, was founded on the site of a Golden Egg. Rudolf Steiner's modern Mystery temple and Anthroposophic headquarters, the Goetheanum on a hill in Dornach, Switzerland, is also at a Golden Egg. How fitting, insofar as one of Steiner's chief messages was the importance of grounding the Mystery of Golgotha—his term for the Christ event, from birth to ascension—in modern times and in contemporary formulations.

In the Hall of the Troll King—the Contribution of the Gnomes

The Norse myths say that maggot-like beings called dwarves were generated in the flesh of the proto-giant Ymir and that the gods endowed these beings with reason and set them loose in the world. The reference to maggots is certainly unflattering, but the image of the dwarves crawling out of the skin of the planet-sized Ymir is geomantically apt.

First, who are the dwarves? The name derives from the Old English *dweorg* and Old Norwegian *dvergr*. Norse myth specifically lists the names of 100 of them and sometimes associates them with the black elves or *Svartalfar* who live in *Svartalfaheim*. The short-statured dwarves were well regarded as smiths, excellent stone and gem workers, fashioners of rings, swords, necklaces, shields, hammers, and helmets, treasured and used by the gods. They lived under mountains in deep rocky caverns, seldom ventured above ground, and had a reputation as fierce jewel hoarders.

So who are they? The dwarves are gnomes, elemental spirits of the solid, dense, mineral aspect of the planet's matter. It is appropriate to say they are crawling about the skin of Ymir because their geomantic function is global and they originally were found everywhere on the solid landmass parts of the Earth. Given the spread of human civilization and its attendant technological noise and disruption, the gnomes have tended to retreat to the less populated parts of the planet, especially in northern latitudes. Their geomantic function is interactive with ours. In effect, the gnomes depend on us to transmit angelic instructions for Earth changes and adjustments so that they, the executors of the celestial instructions, can put them into place and ground the higher energies.

Here's a way of picturing it: You're meditating out in the landscape at a place of high numinosity. The angelic realm communicates with you, and to some extent you are aware of what they're transmitting; it might be specific instructions, or perhaps it is a pure energy infusion, a beam of light passing through you into the land. You are like a burning pillar. The gnomes come up to you with dry straw torches, ignite them with your flames, and distribute them throughout the local landscape, planting hundreds of torches with angelic light in minor geomantic nodes.

You as the human are the intermediary between the angelic and elemental worlds. This is a key relationship. In terms of experienced presence, humans are potentially to gnomes as angels are to humans. The gnomes hold us in high respect—awe even—or would like to. For the most part, humans have forgotten all about our "ancient contract" with the earth elementals to hold up our end of maintaining the Earth's geomantic terrain. Unfortunately, the gnomes cannot fulfil their tasks alone; they are dependent on human mediation.[355]

Not many people in Western countries take the idea of contact with gnomes seriously. However, we cannot fulfill our human geomantic tasks without the gnomes. They have something we need to gain entry into the subtle aspects of the Earth's geomantic terrain: Gnome Eggs. Unlike the Cosmic, Silver, and Golden Eggs, which hatch the Christ Child, a Gnome Egg hatches a Grail Knight.

The hatched Gnome Egg provides an interface between the angelic and elemental realms, with the human as the intermediary. Long-term interaction with a Gnome Egg is a necessary part of the Grail Knight training. It's how you develop sensitivity to the elemental aspect of the Earth's energy web. The Gnome Egg does not really hatch anything, or crack open like a Cosmic Egg; rather you gain entrance to it by degrees (as you develop psychic sensitivity) and through invitation (by the gnomes who come to trust you). Afterwards, the Gnome Egg looks the same as before you started, but the door, for you, is now always open.

One thing I learned from this communication and my long-term association with Gnome Eggs is that if you intend to be a Grail Knight—that is, to pursue the mysteries of the Grail through Earth's visionary geography—you need the assistance of the gnomes. They know the terrain; they have the eggs. If you read Malory's *Le Morte d'Arthur*, you'll note many of the Grail Knights had dwarf attendants or almost collegial encounters with dwarves. These weren't human midgets, but gnomes in medieval disguise.

A Gnome Egg to me looks like a huge white golf ball partially submerged in the ground. Huge means perhaps 100 feet high and just as broad. It is translucent and pockmarked like a golf ball when seen close up. Most often the Gnome Egg is set into the ground in a remote or isolated place, away from humans. You enter the Gnome Egg at a gnome's invitation and stand inside a spherical space reminiscent of domes; but with the Gnome Egg, most of the activity and finer structure are underground.

There is an array of tunnels and underground passageways beneath the Gnome Egg, some of which terminate at dragons or dragon eggs and others in what you could only call the Hall of the Gnome Kings. In practical terms, all Gnome Eggs lead to the Hall of the Gnome Kings.[356]

This appears as a long rectangular hall, seemingly made of marble, with double rows of pillars on both sides and a bright blue domed roof overhead. Alcoves contain busts or portraits of former gnome kings, and as you look at one, it turns into a three-dimensional video or hologram of that gnome king's life and adventures. You could spend days living inside those holograms.

The current gnome king sits on a throne amidst a stunning collection of precious gems, the Earth's mineral hoard. The gnomes aren't jewel hoarders; they are responsible for the mineral frequency on the planet. The mass of gems could be construed in some sense as their "control panel." The gems also serve as "eyes" into the dragon realm. As part of your initiation into the domain of the Gnome Egg, the gnome king may give you a gnome sword, which is a way of accessing elemental earth energy later on.

The Gnome Eggs are regional headquarters for gnomes. Think of them as engineering outposts, providing residential and work facilities for the gnomes servicing a specific landscape. They are little eruptions of the gnome world into ours, where gnomes and humans meet. The eggs are dimensional portals by which the gnomes come and go in our world, of which we are oblivious.

The gnomes say they help the Grail Knight gain his "legs," which means an ability to walk wakefully in the elemental world without falling over or being frozen in one spot. Similarly, the gnomes as a group work to animate the legs of the global Albion. The Grail Knight with *legs* has footing and mobility in the elemental realm; he can effectively pass on angelic information, energies, and instructions, and cooperate with the gnomes in their work. When you have legs, you become a player.

Here are two revealing references to Gnome Eggs by other observers:

Norwegian playwright Henrik Ibsen set his play *Peer Gynt* in the Rondane Mountains of south-central Norway in the 1860s. Peer Gynt, out in the Rondane Mountains, is accosted by a green-clad woman who says she is the Dovrë-King's daughter. The Dovrë-King is the King of the mountain Trolls (large gnomes). Peer Gynt follows the green-clad woman to the royal hall of the King of the Dovrë-Trolls and finds a great assembly of troll-courtiers, smaller gnomes, brownies (nature spirits), and imps. The "Old Man of the Dovrë" sits on his throne, crowned, scepter in hand, surrounded by his retinue.[357]

The second description of Gnome Eggs comes from Slovenic geomancer and elemental expert Marko Pogacnik. He describes a "mega-center" nature temple area at the edge of a Moslem cemetery on a hill called Cicin Han in Sarajevo, Bosnia. This type of elemental clustering performs a specialized task, usually for the entire visible landscape or a large portion of a country.[358]

Pogacnik saw a "huge sphere" located just beneath the ground, composed of "innumerable, differently colored facets, and its interior is structured with conical ventricles." The elementals were busy inside like bees, constantly going in, coming out, dispersing across the landscape. "My insight told me that they were distributing impulses essential for the fecundity of the land."[359]

He also recounted his psychic experience of visiting a gnome king's hall, accessed by a long tunnel that started underneath an old oak tree. Pogacnik found himself in a vast subterranean hall, the walls covered in rough rubies, and presided over by an enthroned gnome king and queen, with a "huge crowd" of dwarf miners. It was like being enclosed in the womb of the Earth, he said.[360]

Unbelief, destruction of landscape temples, and demonization are serious affronts to the earth elementals, but the human-gnome relationship, the ancient contract, is repairable. It still has life in it. It is still needed by the Earth and angels.

In an Earth Circle with Three Hands on the Dimmer Switch

It is not too hard to start making amends in that estranged relationship. I had the chance while visiting Peer Gynt country, the land of the Dovrë-King, in the Rondane Mountains of Norway. This is the Gudbrandsdalen Valley. There are lots of gnomes there, and 12 Gnome Eggs, but I noticed the trolls were glum and scarce. I could not remember ever having seen gnomes who were not merry and high-spirited; on another visit to Roros, at the other end of the Rondanes, the gnomes had been almost joyous to welcome our small group to town and were bursting with enthusiasm to show me the geomantic sights.

I asked the Ofanim what the problem with the trolls was. (The trolls are basically large gnomes, but Norwegians portray them as ugly, scary beings.) "They are reflecting the cultural-national fear towards the entities of the Earth realm. If culturally and nationally the Norwegian people have feared the trolls or gnomes, then the gnomes or trolls reflect that within their national

identity. Love from Above is the antidote to fear. Open the doorway through the Star from above through your belly to the gnomes. *Be* as Love from Above. Allow the gnomes to know it's possible that humans need not be afraid of them, then they do not have to fear the humans."

I decided to hold a troll love-in. It was the height of summer, which meant it never got fully dark—nor did you as a visitor, enjoying the novelty of the first fringes of the Midnight Sun, ever particularly feel like sleeping. Who'd want to, when there was this fabulous nonstop party going on outside? Around two A.M., I went outside the hotel and sat on some large rocks overlooking the Rondanes. I connected myself with the Ofanim through my Star and allowed the Blazing Star at my belly to grow very large and bright, like a lighthouse beacon. Then I asked my gnome colleagues to round up their friends, and trolls, and gather round me.

As I started, about 100 gnomes and some trolls sat in crescents around me. I beamed the light of the Star to them, like food. I let the Ofanim transmit Love from Above through me to the assembled gnomes and trolls, and I added, "We love you, gnomes and trolls. We aren't afraid of you. That's silly. You guys are essential to the grid work we do. We need you for this work. All humans aren't like the Norwegians in how they feel about you. We love you."

You could *feel* the elementals absorbing the light and good feelings. By the time I was finished at least a thousand gnomes and trolls were enjoying the light feast, and they seemed much happier than before, then, and in the days after.

Now I'll tell you about the troll-yard. This is in the Porsanger-Halvöya area, at the tip of Scandinavia where Norway, Sweden, and Finland blend together. This is the earth elemental equivalent of our Blue Room. It is their master Gnome Egg for the Earth, the largest and the original. It seems to be perhaps a mile high and almost the

Table 7-8: Gnome Eggs

Planetary Total: 10,660

Selected Locations:

Heritage Foundation trail, Palmyra, Virginia, U.S.	Worlaby, near Tetford, Lincolnshire, England	Rondane Mountains, Norway (12 Eggs)
Eden, New York, U.S.	Hill of Tara, near Dublin, Ireland	Monsignor Patrick Smith Park, Santa Fe, New Mexico, U.S.
Fairy Dell, Hellard's Hill, Wick, near Langport, Somerset, England	Cicin Han, Sarajevo, Bosnia	Truckee, California, U.S.
"Bildare's Egg," near Hanover, New Hampshire, U.S.	Jay Peak, Vermont, U.S.	
	Roros, Norway	

same across. This is where the gnomes and trolls assemble the earth element and all that pertains to solidity and density.

In many respects, this place is like a lumberyard. There are rows of stone slabs, like paving stones or dominos; in some curious way, these are potential gnomes, gnome seeds, or portals for sleeping gnomes. There are thousands of these slabs. When it's time, they get animated and arise from out of their two-dimensional inertia. These stones, as did the gnomes, came from beyond the Earth long ago. Perhaps these stone slabs are the gnomic equivalent of King Arthur's hollow hills. I see gnomes walking out of the stones.

In any event, the troll-yard is where the earth elementals assemble a planet of stone and solidity. In fact, the troll-yard with its connection to the Gnome Eggs is a planet in itself, a planetary dimension perhaps: the planet of matter, solidity, density, earth—the planet's *earth* element expressed as a realm.

There is a chief troll named Gorkiye. He looks like a Viking, round face, beard, horned helmet, a bit fierce. He runs the troll-yard. He has a map of the planet showing the locations of all 10,660 Gnome Eggs (see table 7-8).

The trolls prefer stones, and the inside of stones, more than the gnomes do; to them, the inside of a stone can be a cathedralic space. Gorkiye and his troops originally planted stone seeds that became the Gnome Eggs, like balloons inflating. The Gnome Egg is the expansive interior of this inflated stone seed.

The gnomes and trolls have colleagues in this global work of implementing and maintaining the earth element. They are the Mephibians.[361] "They were commissioned by the Mother-Father God, the Architect of All That Is, to bring the Gnome Eggs to Earth," the Ofanim explain. "We would not call them ETs, but you would. They determined the placement of the Gnome Eggs."

The Mephibians may appear as human-like beings around four feet tall, with dark blue or light black skin and a huge, elaborate headdress three times the size of their head. It looks like an intricate upward-growing webwork of roots cast in silver, yet it also resembles a ritualistic headpiece or crown with dozens of points at different levels. Functionally, the crown seems to be the way the Mephibians stay attuned to the energies of the stars and their effects on the Earth's subterranean mineral element, which, with the gnomes, they oversee.

The Ofanim say of the Mephibians that "their relationship to gnomes today is one of mutual fear. They both fear the same thing: to be bound to conditions they don't like." My gnome friends explain that they fear being pounded into the ground, flattened for lack of angelic light filtered through humans in the course of gnome-human interactions. This light filtration is food to them; it keeps them uplifted, merry, focused, on point, able and enthusiastic to fulfill their geomantic mission. Without it, they fear densification, immobility, suffocation.[362]

We must work closely with the gnomes in restoring and maintaining the Earth's visionary geography. One practical way is with the Earth circle, a personalized meditation spot in the landscape that demonstrates the cooperation among angelic, elemental, and human concerns. When you're ready, the angelic realm hands you a light seed; the gnomes show you where to plant it; and you create a circle on the ground, one inch deep with a diameter two times the distance from your elbow to wrist. You plant the light seed in this circle of earth on the Earth (the "Earth circle" has these two nuances) and allow it to grow into a personalized Tree of Life that offers psychic access.

Ideally, you need to be in a rural environment, because the Earth circle needs to be isolated, protected, and preferably secret; you don't want people interfering with it, even looking at it, or observing you meditating on it. I have had a few in protected countryside locations, and a few in suburban backyards with much less privacy. With the former, I felt comfortable meditating there at any time during the day, while with the latter, only at night.

If you have access to a country setting, the gnomes will indicate the best place for you to create your Earth circle—"best" being a combination of maximum benefit to the local geomantic terrain and your own energies, for the Earth circle equally benefits you and the landscape.

Making an Earth circle is easy. It's based on one body measurement—the distance from your elbow to wrist—which becomes the circle's radius. It must be one inch deep, precisely, and level. The gnomes show you the best place in your local environment for your Earth circle. The light seed given to you from the angels gets planted in the center, and you "water" the circle every day with Love from Above from your Star. You can visit the circle daily and meditate briefly in it, sending it more Love from Above. Let the crystal seed germinate and sprout on its own, but keep feeding it with Love from Above from a distance.

If there is a chance your circle will be discovered, cover it with leaves or grass; try to keep it inconspicuous. The need for secrecy and protection comes from the fact that this circle is a highly personalized energy spot for you, based on *you,* nurtured by you, and for your spiritual benefit. It's precious to you, and you don't want anyone else's energies or thoughts on it, and certainly not their physical body. As you work with your circle more, this will be more evident.

Similarly, don't meditate in your Earth circle during the two weeks of a waning moon cycle during the first year or so of having the circle. Only go during the daylight hours of the two weeks of the waxing moon. Inimical, disruptive energies tend to be active at night, especially during the waning moon, and as the Earth circle puts you in a position of heightened psychic vulnerability, wait until you have some practice with the Earth circle and have perhaps learned some auric protection techniques before exposing yourself.

Over the weeks, you will notice your seed is growing. After a while, it may seem to you that you are meditating inside a huge tree, maybe a hundred feet tall, with broad arching branches and a thick trunk. You may feel deeply, satisfyingly grounded while sitting in your Earth circle; you may find you have surprising psychic access to deep memories and past lives; you may find your awareness can move around to other places on the Earth.

"The Earth circle is a way for you to ground your consciousness within the Earth sphere," the Ofanim told me. "As you create these Earth circles, you harmonize with the Earth and bring your consciousness in line with the Earth and its form. When you harmonize your vibrations with the Earth, then you effectively connect with the subtle energies of the Earth.

"When the Earth was created, the energy matrix of the Earth was implicit in every particle of matter. The Earth's energy grid [its visionary geography] is a manifestation of that energy matrix that was harmonized by those working from the upper levels so as to be able to emphasize the energy aspect of matter. As your consciousness within each particle of your body contains the same energy matrix, then as you evolve consciously, you harmonize with the Earth.

"This has repercussions both for you as an individual via your RNA-DNA encoding and for the planet via its coding. If through your circle you harmonize your consciousness with that circle, you harmonize with the Earth itself. You come to terms with solidity and expansion, energy and extension.

"The light seed is a gift from the angels via the human channel to the elemental Earth. It is necessary to have human intermediaries between the angels and Earth. The elementals are also intermediaries between the Earth and humans, just as angels are intermediaries between humans and the Creator. As the angels wish to communicate with the elementals, it is only possible through humans. The Earth has a need. It is only through the human that the angels may assist the elementals in healing the grid and loving the Earth."

The Earth circle is possibly one of the most practical and beneficial geomantic contributions you can make to the planet. It will feed you and the Earth. It will deepen your conscious understanding of how the Earth's visionary geography works, and it will provide you reliable, responsible ways to participate in that matrix. You will probably feel embedded, implicit, in the Earth.

The Earth circle is an excellent training device whereby you can experience the reality of the geomantic "dimmer switch." For real changes and energy infusions to occur in the Earth's visionary geography, *three* hands must be on the dimmer switch that gradually illuminates the terrain. Humans cannot (and should not try to) single-handedly "activate" geomantic sites. The simultaneous presence of three parties is required: angels, humans, and elementals. Together, these three hands turn the dimmer switch a little, allowing a little more light into an area. Meditating frequently in your Earth circle will sensitize you to this.

If you are planning a pilgrimage or trip to sacred sites, you can prepare yourself by meditating—the Ofanim prefer the term "unifying"—for 30 to 60 minutes every day, or as often as possible, in your Earth circle. This will attune and entrain yourself with the Earth's energy body and potentially amplify both your awareness and ability to contribute positively. When you return from the trip, you can deepen your experience and perhaps expand your conscious recall of subtle or psychic events by unifying further in your Earth circle. The Earth circle tends to heighten and sharpen clairvoyance, psychic recall, and penetration.

If you visited multiple sites on that trip, or if over the years you have, you can link them through your Earth circle, in a way superimposing them all in your circle. This is an act of geomantic digestion and assimilation. Remember, ultimately, all the Earth's sacred sites are but extrapolations of your cosmic nature, your body parts, organs, and systems projected out into the landscape. You can start to reassemble the fragments of your extended global geomantic being by unifying your experiences through your Earth circle.

Taking the Sky Roads with the Queen of the Sylphs

It's hard to talk about experiences with the elemental spirits of Nature without it sounding like a Celtic fairy tale. Of course that's where fairy tales came from: initiate reports of adventures in the elemental world. Like the gnomes, sylphs, the elementals of the air, have their own "world" in the atmosphere, in the realm of air, winds, and all movement through this medium. They live *in* the element of air, mobility, wind, atmosphere, just as the gnomes live *in* solidity.

The sylphs move constantly through a sky network that in many respects mirrors the organization of the gnomes' subterranean tunnel network. There is a corresponding tunnel network in the Earth's atmosphere, and many entrances into this network. I call these entrances Sylph Doorways. There are a great number of these, 1,746 to the ninth power, on the Earth—actually, slightly *above* Earth. That comes to approximately 155 septillion doorways.

"They are a window of perception into another dimension parallel to your own," the Ofanim told me. "If the window looks towards another window, then it goes through other dimensions, psychical through to subtle, so that many phenomena can occur between them."

The first Sylph Doorway I saw and experienced was at the top of a 50-foot tall ash tree in the backyard of my parents' house in Massachusetts. I became aware of it under strange circumstances. At the age of 13, I got knocked unconscious while playing basketball on ice, wearing sneakers. The brazenness of adolescence. Twenty years later the Ofanim helped me remember what happened next.

I circled around my prostrate body, then headed for an octagonal clear glass doorway atop the ash tree. A sylph awaited me there and we departed immediately. It seemed almost instantaneously that we stepped out of another Sylph Doorway at Chalice Well Gardens in Glastonbury, England. Later, when I became professionally associated with the angels and gnomes in the geomantic work, a sylph became part of my regular "invisible" Grail Quest retinue.

What does a sylph look like? It depends on your conceptual base. Like Snow White. Like a fairy queen made of transparent glass or congealed water. Like a whirlwind with eyes inside a crystalline sword filled with spinning discs. The sylphs organize and shepherd the air currents; they move thoughts; clear the air of stagnant energies; facilitate the precipitation of atmospheric weather, such as with hurricanes.

Sylphs move constantly through this sky tunnel network. Picture the blue-white planet, then an equal volume of space on all sides of it, bounded by a membrane at its outermost level. This is the atmosphere and its four levels, the sylphs' domain, extending some 372 miles above the Earth.[363] Picture this space threaded with tubes, with many thousands of transparent octahedral doorways into the tubes, and 24 sky caves, conical cavelike structures in the atmosphere around the planet, each containing large concentrations of sylphs, like a packed sports stadium.[364]

All this is the air grid tended by the sylphs. It's an intricate webwork of doorways, air channels, and sky caves, a spherical basket woven of air threads enveloping the physical Earth. You can see how human thoughts help create the weather. You can also begin to appreciate how long-term human neglect of the Earth's terrestrial geomancy has had dire repercussions in the sky grid.

Originally most of the Earth's major holy sites had a feature I call Blue Dishes under them; later trained geomancers projected Blue Dishes into the visionary geography. A Blue Dish is a flattened parabolic dish made of light and placed like a tea saucer under the "cups" of sacred sites.[365] The idea was the angelic world sent down high consciousness and light vibrations like a gentle rain; humans grounded it, and it was collected in the Blue Dishes for the gnomes to distribute through their realm; but it also *reflected* back up into the atmosphere for the sylphs to distribute in their realm. Just as the angelic light could permeate the entire Earth, thanks to the gnomes, it could also be reflected back to permeate the entirety of the atmospheric space or volume.

I know I've mixed metaphors here, but incoming higher light is like rain and fire, so it can be said to pool and reflect. The important point is that originally the thousands of terrestrial Blue Dishes reflected the angelic light, after it was grounded and transduced by human geomancers *upwards* into the atmosphere to irradiate the sky grid with filtered celestial energies.

This regular circulation of angelic light and energies through the sky grid helped to regulate not only the planet's weather, both global and local, but the quality and mobility of humanity's thoughts and their reciprocal effects on atmospheric conditions.

24 Knights at the Round Table Creating King Arthur

The repairing of the world, achieving Heaven on Earth, is actually why we undertake the geomantic work. It can be done, though it is a formidable task, and will be done. It has in fact been under way for some time, catalyzed in part by the Camalate Centers.

Camelot, a variant spelling, is known to many as the fabled headquarters of King Arthur and his Knights of the Holy Grail. It's mythic; they made a popular musical out of it. Archeologists

grudgingly grant that South Cadbury Castle in Somerset might once for a short while have supported a Camelot-like Celtic king's residence. But that's it. Suggest that the term refers to an initiate's academy that manifested 26 times in different cultures over the course of the Earth's history, always with the same agenda, and you'll quickly lose your audience. It's true, even so. The Camalate Center is a name to describe a physical Mystery training and geomantic maintenance academy that periodically reappears in different cultures to rekindle interest in human interactions with the Earth's visionary geography.

The work of the Camalate Centers has included servicing the Earth's geomythic body, working with the spiritual worlds on implementing galactic and solar schedules, activations, and infusions, bridging the angelic and human kingdoms, sponsoring initiations into the Grail Quest, birthing the Christ consciousness in matter, and providing orientations to the Earth's visionary terrain.

There are at least two long-term efforts of the Camalate Center: to build and operate the Emerald modem; and to awaken all the Albions in the Earth. And a third but variable assignment: to work with the King Arthur representative during times of manifestation. To date, there have been 15 King Arthurs on the Earth.

The Camalate Centers are not geomantic features like the rest on our list, counted out and installed at the start of the Earth. Nor are they of an indeterminate number, such as white lilies or Earth circles, which depend on individuals manifesting or creating them out of their own initiative. In a sense, one Camalate Center was assigned to the Earth as a single geomantic feature, but its location would continually change as it continually reincarnated.

So far, there have been 26 Camalates, each manifesting in a different culture, landmass, or mythic system. Locations of former Camalate

Centers are still geomantically potent, carrying the strong vibration of those earlier spiritual efforts, still feeding the energies into the Earth's circulation (see table 7-9).

What is its purpose? "To encourage people, ruthlessly and without mercy, to uncover and take responsibility for the Star they are," say the Ofanim.

Historically, Camalate has been "the place to which came a lot of people for the purposes of the realization of light, understanding, humility, truth, love, sincerity, spirituality, integrity, and compassion. Camalate is a sacred name from a divine source. It has numerological correspondences, a gematria that forms patterns of light. These represent a reciprocal matrix that surrounds this name so that it takes on for certain people a focus to harmonize the energies of consciousness and take it to the process of individuation. The sacred name, held in the heart or in the center of a sphere of beings, will draw to itself the nature of its generation and spread, like a stone dropped in a pool, creating waves."

We could think of the Camalate Center as the executive arm of the *Ananda-kanda* inner heart chakra, as the dynamic worldly expression of the eight Celestial Cities around Mount Meru. Part of the Center's charge is to ground the eight star and constellation energies that inform the Celestial Cities (see table 5-3). These are key seeds or catalysts dropped into the human and Earth at inception.

Let's put this in perspective. We have an inner and an outer heart chakra, and many geomantic attributions for each. The outer, the *Anahata*, has 12 petals; the inner, the *Ananda-kanda*, has eight. In terms of the Arthurian mysteries, the *outer* expression of Camalate pertained

---

Table 7-9: Camalate Center

Planetary Total: 26

Selected Locations:

Cuzco, Peru

Mycenae, Greece

Troy, Turkey

South Cadbury Castle, Somerset, England

---

to the altruistic, worldly activities of the Round Table of Grail Knights (in the sixth-century A.D. British milieu of the "historical" King Arthur, keeping the land safe against invading Saxons), and the 12 petals pertained to the standard (in the Western astrological system) 12 constellations arrayed on the Sun's ecliptic, the apparent path of the Sun each year through the signs of the zodiac.

The *inner* expression of Camalate pertained to the esoteric activities to do with the eight stars and constellations (again, refer to table 5-3) and their planetary mandate. This might have taken the form of Grail Quest initiations, adventures, and epiphanies on behalf of regional geomantic structures. Sometimes, the world is aware, or wants to be, only of Camalate's outer activities. After all, how many people, truly, will flock to a Mystery center advertising a "ruthless and merciless" immersion in the enigmas and epiphanies of a tiny pinprick of light, all sponsored by invisible, arcane angels?

You have then a Round Table with two levels, or perhaps two tables. The outer has the 12 zodiacal seats for the constellations of the ecliptic, the formal basis for Western astrology and its horoscope. The inner has the eight positions for the Camalate stars and constellations that correspond to the Celestial Cities. Perhaps this should also be the basis for an esoteric astrology.

It's strange, but the Grail Knights come first, Arthur comes later. They create the matrix into which King Arthur is born. The matrix is the completed Round Table, but here I mean the Round Table in a different sense from the landscape jousting field described above. It does have the 12 zodiacal divisions, but here they are operative in a *group* context, for what might be called a Soul

Group. This means individuals join together each to embody an aspect of the whole: a Gemini, a Taurus, a Libra, etc. Each person's responsibility to the whole is to complete the journey, to be thoroughly the energies and consciousness of that sign.

King Arthur and the other characters do not exist in time, even though from time to time their representatives do. "They pertain in time periods when human consciousness has found familiarity with certain archetypal viewpoints for its elucidation," the Ofanim note. There have been 15 periods thus far in human history that resonated with this complete myth system, with different names according to the varying languages and cultures, but in accordance with the same archetypal formula, for Arthur and the Knights of the Round Table are elements of a myth.

It's a myth—not in the pejorative way scholars use this term but in the way archetypes and symbols are bigger than life and perennially relevant. The once and future Arthurian mythos, true once, true again.

Let's look at the big picture. Remember the Big Man of the Cosmos with lots of names—Purusha, Adam Kadmon, P'an Ku, Ymir, Gayomart? This is the vast cosmic Man made of billions of stars, each a point of intelligence, awareness, and experience. Some stars have formed groups—Soul Groups—that represent even greater assemblages of intelligence, awareness, and experience. We know them as constellations. But Purusha's scope of cognition is too big for the human psyche, at least at first. A lot of his awareness needs to be pushed into the background for a while so a human psyche can be grown and manifested.

Your building blocks are four elements in three qualities, giving us 12 variations on a theme, 12 wedges out of Purusha's full consciousness.[366]

The goal is to produce a matrix in which consciousness can experience itself and the world through the 12 different elemental filters—the inert side of Scorpio (water), the light-filled aspect of Aries (fire), the dynamic particulars of Aquarius (air)—then to balance and integrate these to yield a harmonious psyche to negotiate the world.

"The Round Table portrays 12 aspects that need to be developed, the signs or aspects of the astrological journey of each soul from point beginning to point end," the Ofanim state. Implicit in the array of Knights of both genders about the Round Table was the goal of individuation culminating in the birth of the Christ Child, along the lines described earlier regarding Golden Eggs.

The Ray Masters were involved, too. "At each point on the Table, a different Ray Master is concerned, relevant to each astrological sign or position."

The goal of all this, for individual Knights and for the Round Table consortium as a whole, was the metamorphosis of the psyche towards balancing the 12 aspects of the self from the 14 rays. The Camalate Center facilitated and supported this metamorphosis and offered this balanced, integrated, and individuated collective psyche to the world in service.

The personal and collective individuation achieved through a Camalate Center set an example.[367] Even today, you can absorb the achieved energies of individuation, both personal and collective, from visiting the site of a former Camalate Center.

Obviously, the Arthurian Grail Knights didn't have the benefit of Jungian vocabulary, archetypal symbolism, and depth psychology. But the processes and mysteries of transformation were essentially the same, and the requirements of individuation were just as challenging and formidable then as now.

The Round Table is an egalitarian seating arrangement; there is no head of the table, no

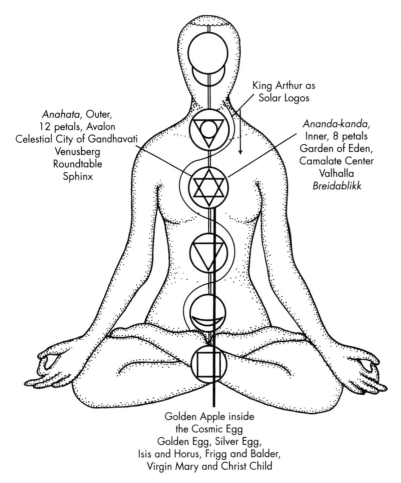

King Arthur as
Solar Logos

Anahata, Outer,
12 petals, Avalon
Celestial City of Gandhavati
Venusberg
Roundtable
Sphinx

Ananda-kanda,
Inner, 8 petals
Garden of Eden,
Camalate Center
Valhalla
Breidablikk

Golden Apple inside
the Cosmic Egg
Golden Egg, Silver Egg,
Isis and Horus, Frigg and Balder,
Virgin Mary and Christ Child

Figure 7-1. The Geomantic Riches of the Heart Chakra

expressed through communication, the solar energy expressed creatively for the benefit of the human, animal, plant, and mineral kingdoms.

King Arthur is the Solar Logos born in the throat chakra manifesting in the center of the Round Table of the heart chakra (see figure 7-1).

In practical terms, you cannot have a King Arthur without a Round Table *first*. Establishing a Camalate Center does not always generate the incarnation of an Arthur representative. There have been 26 Camalates but only 15 Arthurs.[368]

Was there a historical, actual, human male called King Arthur? Yes. Why was he called the "once and future king"? Because he came back—14 times, and will yet again, though not always in the same culture or mythic guise. Yet Arthur is also something that is created—*generated*—out of a Round Table grouping of men and women intent on individuation on behalf of unification—the Grail.

Each Grail Knight, ideally, strives to create the entire Round Table within their own psyche and being, to be all the players, including King Arthur. At the same time, each Knight strives to complete their own individuation so as to manifest the respective part in the whole of the Round Table. When all the parts are complete and in place, the totality can birth King Arthur, in the

hierarchical seating plan. So where does King Arthur sit, and if the Round Table is nonhierarchical, how come he's called King?

Arthur, when he arrives, will sit in the *middle* of the Round Table. He is the expression of the *developed* 12 aspects of the Round Table. He's King because he is the energy of the Sun expressed through communication, the Solar Logos, the Word spoken without being filtered, the Word made manifest. These are not words, but sounds or mantras. Arthur is the element of growth which is governed by higher energies and linked to Gaia. He is the energy of the Sun sense of creating the space, the matrix, and the preconditions for his manifestation. You would have then an Arthur within each of the Knights and an Arthur within the Round Table, as the Sun in the center of the Knights; and you would have the archetypal ideal of King Arthur "above" in the spiritual world as the model.

The Camalate Center assemblage was an action mandala of wholeness, both catalyzing and balancing, an energized template of the Earth's healthiest, most spiritualized cell, an archetype of wholeness and integration at every level.

8 The Sun Temple and the Smithy of King Arthur
Mysteries of the Bull-Slaying, the Pleiades, and Time

Let's start with an image of a smith at his forge.

Deep beneath Mount Etna on Sicily, a still active volcano, once labored Hephaistos, son of Zeus and Hera, master of fire, metal, and smithing. Assisted by three one-eyed giants called Cyclopes, Hephaistos fashions the weaponry of the Olympian gods in his forge, using the tumultuous volcanism of Mount Etna as a perpetual source of fire. Lord of artificers, patron of crafts, and divine artisan, he makes the arrows of Apollo and Artemis, Zeus's thunderbolts, Poseidon's trident, Hades' cap of invisibility, Harmonia's wedding necklace, Demeter's sickle, Aphrodite's girdle, scepters, Olympian thrones, tripods, even the chains to bind Prometheus to the cliffs of Mount Caucasus.

Hephaistos is all about fire and controlling it to shape things. He fabricated the gods' splendid residences and palaces, and on occasion he made shields and armor for humans like Achilles and Aeneas, and the golden breastplate for Heracles. The Latin poet Virgil spoke of the mighty blows upon anvils and the hissing of iron bars that could be heard within the mammoth cave of the forge under Etna.

Hephaistos's anvil was said to rest upon the gigantic head of Typhon, a formidable demon-monster, half-man, half-beast, with 100 heads, numerous wings, and vipers' tails. Typhon was flung there by Zeus in ages past, after which the Olympian god threw Mount Etna itself upon Typhon to keep him permanently imprisoned and pinned down. Some myths say that Etna's volcanic fire was actually the flaming breath of the everlastingly imprisoned Typhon.

Impressions of the Celestial Smith, the Solar Logos— King Arthur

So what does this image mean geomantically? The smith is the Solar Logos, and the volcanic fires of his forge are the Sun. The smith is the tamer, shaper, and artisan of the fires of the Wild Sun God Typhon. The smith is the logos, the spoken Word, in the Sun or fire element. All the weaponry, armor, shields, thrones, jewelry, and other devices Hephaistos fashioned are expressions of the Solar Logos at work, shaping (taming) the Sun energy.

Hephaistos has many mythic equivalencies, including King Arthur, Ray Master Jesus, Mithras, Wayland, Goibhniu, Gofannon, Vulcan (also called Mulciber, "Smelter of Metals"),[369] and so has the Wild Sun God: Agni, Helios, Ra, Sorath, Shamash, Amaterasu, Dazhbog, La, Inti, Kinich Ahau, Surya, Utu, and others. Inner and outer, tamer and tamed, focused energy and raw energy—the relationship between smith and forge is the subject of this chapter and the basis for understanding the next level of geomantic expression—the realm of the Sun temple and the influence of the Pleiades through the throat chakra.

Smiths are the masters of fire. In shamanic cultures, they ranked higher and were regarded as elder to even the most developed shamans. They cooperated with the gods to gain sovereignty over the world, and they were the gods' architect and artisans. Similarly, in Irish tradition, Goibhniu, the smith-god and member of the august godly assembly called the Tuatha de Danann, was charged with making armory for the Tuatha and their leader, Lugh. We find a similar story in the Vedic tradition's artisan god Tvastr (from the root *tvaks*, which means "to form or fashion"). Using his great metal tools, he fashioned Indra's thunderbolts. The Vedas cast him as the epitome of craftsmanship and the earliest born god, capable of assuming any form he wanted.[370]

The smith god Ilmarinen, one of the prime figures in the Finnish saga *Kalevala* and a son of a primeval ancestral personage named Kaleva, forged the Sun, the vault of Heaven, the magic mill called Sampo that grinds out prosperity and on which the Heavens sit, and the golden maid. Ilmarinen is "the great primeval craftsman," "the greatest of the craftsmen," "most accomplished of the craftsmen," and a prodigious creator, the *Kalevala* declares —"For 'twas I who forged the heavens,/And the vault of air I hammered. He was born on a hill of charcoal with a copper hammer in his hands, Ere the air had yet beginning."[371]

Working in his hut, Ilmarinen's forge is filled with red-hot iron, for which reason he was called the inventor and tamer of iron; like the other divine smiths, he taught humanity how to work with ores and make iron objects, and he could forge more things than are found on land or sea, the *Kalevala* claimed.

The Sampo is the Finnish conception of the world mill, an image of the dynamics of the Heaven-Earth relationship expressed in terms of the common hand mill and water mill once commonly used to grind flour in Europe.[372] The unmoving lower stone, upon which the grain sits, represents the Earth; the upper, moving stone is the revolving dome of the Heavens, while the axial point that turns the top wheel represents the Pole Star, the unturning still point in the celestial far North. The Sampo as a whole is "nothing but heaven itself."[373]

From these diverse descriptions of the celestial smith, we can put a picture together of the qualities of the Solar Logos as the *shaper* of raw Sun energy. The smith is the master of fire and iron; he works through singing, chant, and speech as well as the customary smithing tools of hammer, tongs, and anvil; he is the master of generative potency, of increase and well-being through the realms of created life; he created the first humans of both genders or at least the first woman; he shapes wondrous devices for the gods and select mortals; he produced the cosmic mill, the Sampo, with which to grind out prosperity and maintain the health of the Earth and Heaven, and he may have structured Heaven and created the Sun too.

The smith is master of fire—Agni, the Sun, the fire element—so he can make it *function* as the gods require. Here, to make function is the same as shaping fire into serviceable objects and devices, the numerous and diverse products of the smith's forge. He directs the solar fire to function in prescribed ways, as a weapon, a throne, a palace, a chalice, necklace, and the rest. Some of these objects find a place in the Earth's visionary terrain.

On a hill in Os, a village near Roros, in south-central Norway, and on the edge of the Rondane

Mountains (the Earth's primary *Ananda-kanda* chakra—see chapter 7), I saw a large astral chalice filled with light or spiritual water. Large means the size of a two-story house. The light was spilling out over the lip of the chalice into the etheric aspect of the landscape. The chalice, I later understood, is a receptor for the energies of the Solar Logos, and it was facilitating an orderly flow of this precious fertilizing energy of growth and change into the landscape.

But the smith is also master of iron. The *Kalevala* says Ilmarinen was born in response to the origin of iron and an unstaunchable wound from which torrents of blood flowed from the "aged" music god Väinämöinen. Iron arose as the flowing breast milk from three maiden sisters, "fair Daughters of Creation./Mothers of the rust of Iron," created by Ukko, mightiest of creators and "God of realms supernal." The newborn iron feared the "hands of furious Fire," so Ilmarinen arose to negotiate a harmonious relationship between them.[374]

The role of iron in the work of the celestial smith gets attention in other myth systems. The myths of the Yakuts hold that human smiths received knowledge of their trade from the "evil" deity K'daai Maqsin, the Master Smith of Hell, who lives in a house made of iron surrounded by splinters of fire. The Irish smith Goibhniu works in the Mountain of Iron (*Sliabh-an-Iairinn,* east of Lough Allen in County Leitrim, Ireland), and Irish myth also recalls (through the Welsh poets of the *Mabinogion*) an Iron House. Here's the story:

Llassar Llaes Gyfnewid was an enormous, uncompromising, yellowish-red-haired man who walked about Ireland with a great cauldron strapped to his back. His wife, Cymidei Cymeinfoll, was twice his size, and pregnant; their future child was predicted to be born as a fully armed warrior, and they needed lodging and hospitality for a year's gestation. The Welsh god Bendigeidfran (Bran the Blessed) obliged the couple, but after

four months the couple became obnoxious guests and would not leave when asked.

Bendigeidfran assembled all the smiths of Ireland to construct a chamber made entirely of iron. They enticed the unwanted couple into the iron house, then kindled the forges around it until the house grew white-hot and the iron wall was searing white. Even so, Llassar Llaes Gyfnewid burst down the walls and escaped with his wife; later he gave Bendigeidfran the cauldron. It was a magic cauldron, by the way: Put a dead warrior in it at night, and by morning he will be reformed and hale, as good as ever, but without speech.[375]

What on Earth is this story about? I think it must be read backwards. Llassar Llaes Gyfnewid was a celestial smith, like Ilmarinen perhaps, and the iron house was his smithy where he made prodigious objects for the gods. His magic cauldron might have been on the order of Ilmarinen's Sampo because Bendigeidfran was the Welsh name for Brahma, Odin, God, and His other mythic guises, and his geomantic feature is the Crown of the Ancient of Days.

But why all the attention on iron? Let's put aside the obvious physical relevance of iron to smithing and making weapons. Let's think metaphorically. Myths of the divine smith are consistent in saying that one of his functions was to create or give *life* to the first humans. Iron is essential to life; it is found in all the natural kingdoms—mineral, plant, animal, human. In plants, it is essential for chlorophyll, and every plant contains iron in its ash; in humans, it is the cornerstone of hemoglobin, the carrier of oxygen in the blood; without it, there would be no red blood or breathing of air.

Without oxygen to form hemoglobin, we could not breathe or have organic life. Further, chlorophyll and hemoglobin "are so completely attuned to one another that they maintain the air in perfect equilibrium between oxygen and carbon dioxide," so that what the plant extracts from the air, animal respiration gives back.[376] Let's recall Ilmarinen's boast that in the beginning of the world, he hammered the vault of air. As the Solar Logos, the celestial smith "hammers" the air, which is to say, masters the iron principle central to respiration and the maintenance of the air; he *tempers* it in his forge, making it as soft and malleable as bread dough, then shapes it accordingly into useful objects.

So iron, which lives in the blood, is the carrier of the life principle in humans, and blood, in esoteric thought, is the carrier of the human spirituality, the I or Self. Iron "is built right into the central ego organ, the blood, and thereby becomes an instrument not only of the waking soul life, but of the willing ego."[377] We might interpret the Irish Iron House as the blood, prime residence of iron in the human body.

Yet the Iron House, the celestial smith's forge and smithy, is also a place of shamanic initiation, for in archaic cultures, the shaman and smith were allied. In fact, according to research by historian of religions Mircea Eliade, the smith was older, more primal, than the shaman—the shaman's tutor in the mysteries. The Yakut shamanic deity K'daai Maqsin mends the broken or amputated limbs of heroes, he participates in shamanic initiations, and "he tempers their soul as he tempers iron."[378] To temper the soul could be understood here as imparting the knowledge and skill for controlling the Sun within the blood.

British psychic Grace Cooke, in her clairvoyant impressions of the ancient spiritual centers of Britain, reported in 1971 that Wayland's Smithy,[379] a long barrow or Neolithic burial chamber on the Ridgeway in Oxfordshire—a Mithraeum, or Sun temple (see below)—was originally a place of initiation and that Wayland was the "silversmith of souls." Initiates spent time in the Smith gaining "'God-shod feet' or [understanding the mysteries of] the God-guided initiate sometimes symbolized by golden shoes."

Humans were spiritually "re-shod" at Wayland's Smithy "so that they might 'travel' onwards" in their visionary journeys through the landscape. Pilgrims came to the Smithy when their horse had become lame, which meant that their outer, weary worldly self had lost a "shoe" and become unsure of their "way." Here they were renewed, divested of a layer of unproductive worldliness, reshod, succored, ready to seek new tracks "across the 'waylands,' not so much across the earthly as across the heavenly places."[380]

The Ixion Wheel—Where the Celestial Smith or King Arthur Is Born

Where the celestial smith is born is a geomantic clue.

The *Kalevala* tells us that Ilmarinen was born and nurtured on a hill of charcoal, then later sought a suitable place for his smithy. He erected his bellows on a land ridge in a swamp, "a small place in the marshes," where, as it turned out, the original iron was hiding from the fire. The important point here is that the smith is born in a different place from where he works as a smith. This tells us there are two different but related geomantic structures involved. Similarly, Hephaistos was "born" on Earth on the Greek island of Lemnos in the North Aegean Sea, though he plied his smithcraft primarily under Mount Etna in Sicily. You find this with King Arthur, too.

King Arthur was born at Tintagel, a windswept promontory 250 feet above the sea on the western coast of Cornwall in England. The story goes that Merlin arranged a match between Ygerne and King Uther Pendragon, who came to Ygerne disguised as her lawful husband, Duke Gorlois of Cornwall. Perhaps one of the historical Arthurs—presumably the sixth century A.D. Celtic Arthur—was physically born here, but that's beside the geomantic point. Tintagel's once and future purpose is to birth the Arthur within the Grail Knight.

"Tintagel means tints of angels," the Ofanim comment. "It is Arthur's birthplace in the sense that Arthur, in the etheric and astral sphere of the planet, is always present there to be birthed. Arthur is the element of growth that is governed by higher energies and linked to Gaia." It's appropriate for the Arthur myth that the dome over Tintagel represents Megrez, one of the stars in the Big Dipper, a figure also known as Arthur's Wain.

From an esoteric, geomantic viewpoint, what does it mean that Arthur was born at Tintagel? King Arthur, as I suggested in chapter 7, is a vivid expression and incarnation of the Solar Logos, the Word of the Sun made manifest. The Solar Logos in its active phase is the celestial smith, the master of fire and iron and shaper of objects, as we're discovering in this chapter.

Arthur's name itself encodes his function as Solar Logos, and it is meant to be spoken, hieratically, as a chant, an invocation, a declaration: *AR* means growth, the Sun or solar aspect; speaking it produces an attunement to the Solar Logos, the manifestation of the Word in flesh. The second syllable, *THUR*, is the Word or Logos aspect, to do with the change facilitated by the growth.

But there is a third syllable to this name: *HUM*. As the Ofanim explain, "*HUM* or alternatively *HUMG* is about the Earthing of the sword or the direction of Excalibur, the grounding of the insight within. Excalibur is what you would call a mantric sound." So *AR-THUR-HUM* is a sound of the Solar Logos, and the HUM at the end is both the Earthing of the sword, which is Arthur's, and the indication that the Solar Logos is (or wields) a sword of insight.

"Excalibur is a Gnostic word that means insight. It is the point at which human insight is able to perceive the angelic realms," the Ofanim state. Part of the initiation of candidates for

Arthurhood in the Grail mysteries was to be able to claim this sword, by degree, and to receive its point at the heart from Arthur.

The Sampo of course is a rich and complex image, but one of its nuances is immediately geomantic. As the Ofanim explain, when the 14 Rays of the Great Bear are anchored into a dome and there are humans within the radiating extent of that star dome who have activated the Christ in the Buddha Body—meaning, have undergone and assimilated the prime geomantic initiation called the Christed Initiation in the Buddha Body—then the Solar Logos can manifest *through them* at that site.

In fact, it can manifest at more than that one site. The Solar Logos is multilocational. It is movable and not limited by the number of humans fitting the qualifications, only by conscious intent. At the same time, certain locations over the vast life cycle of the Earth have been a primary grounding point for the Solar Logos, for Ilmarinen's Sampo or cosmic mill.

Avebury, the 28-acre stone circle and hamlet in Wiltshire, England, was once the residence of the Solar Logos through the dome over that site; in our time, the Solar Logos is temporarily resident and anchored through the dome (corresponding to alpha Aquarius, Sadalmelik) in Tetford, also in England. Though "an unassuming village in the Lincolnshire Wolds" three hours' drive north of London, Tetford has an astonishing array of geomantic features, making it an Aquarian Mystery temple on the verge of coming into its own.

What is the Solar Logos like, as an experience or a vision? I will give two examples, each expressing aspects of King Arthur.

I was at Ivy Thorn Hill near Glastonbury late one autumn afternoon. The Ofanim had asked me to come here and meditate for an hour, so I presumed they had a "trip" in mind for me. After a while, I found the visionary part of my consciousness—my psychic awareness I suppose—

whizzing briskly through space en route to Megrez. Perhaps like Ilmarinen I had been swept up in a supernatural wind at the top of the great spruce tree and whisked off to Ursa Major. The Big Dipper, after all, is often called Arthur's Wain, so I shouldn't be surprised to encounter Arthur at the end of the journey.

After I "arrived" on Megrez, a man stood before me. He wore a golden crown, his eyes were blue, sparkling wise, friendly; his hair was white, as was his short beard; he pointed a long brilliant sword at my chest, and he held a shield bearing the Pendragon image (a rearing dragon surrounded by a lilac flame) and the image of the Mother of Christ with the Christ Child. In this man's heart I saw a golden Grail chalice and, inside that, the Christ in human form, crowned, smiling.

At the time of this encounter, I was still in the process of sprouting my heart seed (as explained in chapter 7). King Arthur pricked the seed with the tip of his sword, and a blaze of light flashed between sword tip and seed. The seed burst into life and put forth a tiny hylum and roots. Ignition! We have growth and change, courtesy of the Solar Logos, I thought to myself, cheekily. King Arthur's function as Solar Logos to initiate growth and change is implicit in his name, especially when you spell it in Hebrew: *AWR*. This means "light," and its gematria is revealing: *A* (*Aleph*, 1), *W* (*Waw*, 6), *R* (*Raysh*, 200)—162.[381] This number, as mentioned earlier in the book, is the rounded-off expression of phi, the Golden Ratio or Mean, an irrational (infinite) number (1.6180339887 . . .) that expresses the *unequal* division of a line.

This inequality of division is the key to creating a spiral (mathematically described by a series of numbers called the Fibonacci sequence, which includes 144, important below). The spiral is the expression of dynamic movement, expansion, growth. The stasis of pi is broken when the spiral starts unfurling. This is what King Arthur does. His energy incites the Golden Ratio into action.

My second experience was very different and was repeated. I was at Tetford in England on the summer solstice. Again, at the Ofanim's invitation, I was setting up the meditational props for a geomantic visionary experience. I saw a tall conical tower like a midwestern grain silo, set in a desert landscape, pockmarked with dozens or hundreds of hexagonal chambers. Before me was a vertical golden spindle, rotating rapidly in this silo. I became one with the rotating golden spindle; I no longer saw my body or the spindle but felt its rapid rotation. "You are a living solar cell," the Ofanim told me.

The rapidly spinning golden bore was perhaps another cognitive interpretation of the *Kalevala*'s vision of the two grist stones of the Sampo. Outside the bore silo were many layers of bright-green squarish sheaves, paper thin, packed in radiating fans like a carnation. The whole cluster of thin green sheaves formed a kind of global flower, for I realized I was seeing an aspect of the elemental world, the *prima materia* of Nature, the original green matrix for organic life on this planet, the raw material with which the elemental spirits work.

The spinning bore was *fertilizing* this expanse of green sheaves, just the way—I realized years later—the Solar Logos brings growth, expansion, prosperity, and well-being to the land, its plant, mineral, animal, and human life. After all, weren't the ancient kings said to be responsible for the health and well-being of their hegemony, the landmass over which they ruled?

Perhaps one way they secured this sustained fertility was through channeling the Solar Logos into the land; times when they were unable to do this are remembered perhaps as the Wasteland presided over by the Wounded (formerly Rich) Fisher King, on whose behalf King Arthur dispatched his Grail Knights on the Grail quest.

My second experience with this golden spindle was on Mount Orohena on the island of Tahiti in French Polynesia. This 6,700-foot mountain is regaled as the dwelling place of the ancient Polynesian gods and the home of the mountain god Oro. I later suspected it was the site of the Tahitian Eden as well as a stargate, insofar as the Polynesian kings of old sought interment on its slopes, a fact consistent with the clues surrounding the Tetford stargate (see chapter 11).

Near the top of the mountain, I focused my attention under the dome enveloping the entire island. Suddenly I found that I had become (or had entered) the spinning golden bore. Like a golden corkscrew, it was drilling the ancient volcanic island with solar energy, infusing its etheric field and landmass with the Solar Logos.

This continued for perhaps 15 minutes. One intriguing possible result of this infusion of the energies of growth and change was that within a few months (in 1995), the Tahitians at Papeete rioted against the French, partially against that country's continued nuclear tests in a relatively near vicinity of the South Pacific. Normally a politically passive people, this was a rare, even shocking, arousal of Polynesian political sentiment.

Those are impressions of the Solar Logos in action. But what is the Arthur initiation like, the Arthur birth? I first experienced this at Beckery in Glastonbury, though it took me a long time to understand and see even sketchily what I did.

Beckery is a neglected, passed-over tussocky field next to the sewage treatment plant at Glastonbury. It's off the tourist maps. Perhaps that's just as well, for it is arguably one of Glastonbury's most important and complex geomantic sites. Here, among other things, you can birth King Arthur.

Picture a large, white rectangular Grecian temple, perhaps like the Parthenon on the Acropolis. In the center of this white edifice is a deep recess almost like an indoor swimming pool. Inside is a sarcophagus designed to accommodate one human form. You lie down inside this and try to stay awake, which is to say, clairvoyantly aware of what happens. There is a sound like a current or stream that flows from above down into you. The sound is intelligible: *AR-THUR-HUM, AR-THUR-HUM*, over and over. It's like a mantra uttered on high and thrown like a spear into you.

You are the stone out of which Arthur draws the sword, yet you are also the anvil into which the sword is originally inserted. It's the same thing. It's also King Arthur on Megrez shoving a sword through your heart to ignite the seed. It is the Word-Sword, the stream of Solar Logos speech, Arthur syllables of growth and change, quickening your birth from out of the stone, like Mithra, born from a stone. The Arthur current is a sword, yet it creates a sword in you; it turns you into a sword. In a sense, Arthur is the sword in the stone. He doesn't pull the sword out of the stone; he *is* the sword. The sword is the Arthur stream birthed in you.

At Sedona, Arizona, at a site called the Chapel of the Holy Cross, I experienced the Arthur birth a little differently. Instead of a Parthenon-type white temple, the overarching structure was like a glass-domed building. Directly underneath the apex of this roof was a golden cross (rather than a sarcophagus), though its function was the same: You lie in it psychically. Instead of a Word-Sword made of pulses of *AR-THUR-HUM*, I saw the Solar Logos in its form of the golden spindle bore into me like a corkscrew of light. I sensed that the golden cross-sarcophagus was rotating around a flat circle.

I call this geomantic feature an Ixion Wheel, borrowing a vivid image from the Greek myth of Ixion. The Greeks say Ixion was the first human to commit murder of a family member; Zeus forgave Ixion and invited him to Mount Olympus for a purificatory rite, but Ixion used the occasion to

---

Table 8-1: Ixion's Wheel

Planetary Total: 360

Selected Locations:

Beckery, Glastonbury, England	St. Paul's Cathedral, London, England	Mount Orohena, Tahiti, French Polynesia
Banaras, India	Mount Etna, Taormina, Sicily, Italy	*Sliabh an Iairinn* (Mountain of Iron), Lough Allen, County Leitrim, Ireland
Chapel of the Holy Cross, Sedona, Arizona, U.S.	Church of St. Andrew, Aller (Arthur's Village), Somerset, England	Tintagel, Cornwall, England
Teotihuacan, Mexico		
Edfu, Egypt		

Equivalent Names: Ilmarinen's Smithy; the Iron House; Iron Mountain; Forge-City; *Mesnet* (Foundry); Fire Bricks on Agni's Altar; Arthur's Swords; Wheel of the Chariot of the Sun; the Sun's ecliptic; Barque of Ra; Boat of Millions of Years; Tintagel ("tints of angels"); Cattle of the Sun

Names for the Celestial Smith: Hephaistos (Greek), Vulcan (Roman), Wayland (British), Gofannon (Welsh), Goibhniu (Irish), Ilmarinen (Finnish), Tvastr (Vedic), Koshar-wa-Hasis (Canaanite), Horus (Egyptian), Ra (Egyptian), Mithra-Mithras (Persian), King Arthur; Abraxas (Semitic)

---

try to seduce Hera, Zeus's wife and the Queen of the Olympian gods. Zeus punished Ixion by strapping him to a fiery, winged, four-spoked wheel that would revolve and flame forever. The wheel was made by Hephaistos in his smithy. (See table 8-1 for a partial listing of sites with this feature.)

Putting aside the murder and seduction elements in Ixion's story, which may have been a later storyteller's gloss, I see Ixion's Wheel as an initiation chamber for candidates for birthing King Arthur or the Solar Logos within the Round Table of the heart. The key aspect of the Ixion's Wheel feature is that it is a structured *receptacle* for the Solar Logos or Arthur stream. If you're occupying the Ixion seat in this Wheel as the Arthur current comes in, you benefit, and so does the local landscape.

"Each of these Wheels has a different function relative to is location," the Ofanim say. "At Beckery, it is an initiatory wheel to transmute energy vortices and to facilitate the ley line energy

of communication in the human throat chakra. At Sedona, it primarily works with energy from the ley lines structure within the area, transmitting ley energy and making it available to human consciousness to facilitate angelic-human and human-Earth spirit communication."

We could say that the Ixion Wheel as a receptacle is like a *scabbard* for Excalibur. Merlin once chided the young Arthur for allowing the scabbard for his sword to be stolen, counseling his apprentice that the scabbard was far more valuable than the sword. The scabbard is the container, the bounds, the restraints, the control and mastery of the sword. The scabbard is the *tints of angels* surrounding the birth of Arthur—in other words, Tintagel (tints of angels) is the Arthur scabbard and, in turn, another nuance to Ixion's Wheel.

We could also see the tints of angels as the color spectrum of the 14 Ray Masters, all from the Great Bear, including Megrez, Arthur's birthplace, surrounding—nourishing like a placenta—the newborn Arthur blade.

The total number of Ixion's Wheels on Earth is 360, for a precise reason. To make this point, I'll have to draw from several different mythic images.

The Vedas speak of the fire altar of the fire god Agni as having 360 border stones and, inside these, 10,800 bricks arranged in five equal layers. There are also an additional 756 bricks, though the Vedas are not clear why. The 10,800 bricks equal the hours in a year, but this is cosmic time; the Vedas say Prajapati is the Year and that the purpose of building Agni's fire altar is to reconstitute Prajapati, the dismembered god whose body parts became the world. The implication is that Agni's fire altar is a measure of solar time—the cosmic Year—an important concept I'll return to below.

We find an equivalent though outwardly different expression of this in the Greek image of the Cattle of the Sun. Homer says in Book 12 of the *Odyssey* that 350 Cattle of the Sun, owned by the Sun-god Helios, grazed on the slopes of Mount Etna on the island of Thrinacia (the antique name for Sicily). Helios is "overlord of high noon" who "rides high heaven," and his island is "the world's delight, the Sun."[382] Odysseus's men were warned to leave them unharmed and uneaten or face death as punishment. Helios's cattle never die nor does their number ever increase, and the goddesses Phaëthousa and Lampetie, daughters of the Sun god, herd them on his behalf. Homer numbers the Cattle of the Sun grazing on Mount Etna as seven flocks with 50 cattle per flock, or 350.

"'The cattle, the sleek flocks, belong to an awesome master,/Helios, god of the sun who sees all, hears all things,'" Odysseus warns his shipmates.[383] But they didn't heed him, for after a month when their rations ran out, they raided the herd and roasted a fair number of them. Later his shipmates all drowned.

It would have been elegant if Homer had named 360 not 350 Cattle of the Sun, as then the local example would match the global one. None

the less, globally, there are 360 Cattle of the Sun (or fire bricks) grazing the Sun temple just as the cattle of Helios graze Mount Etna, one of the Earth's 144 Sun temples (see below).

And these 360 Cattle of the Sun and 360 fire bricks are the 360 Ixion's Wheels.

The global image is complex but rich: on the outside, the scabbard, or 14 Ray Masters of the Great Bear providing the tints of angels; inside this, the global wheel of 360 Ixion's Wheels, each a place where the Arthur sword is born; in the center of the image, the 144 temples of the Sun God (the same as the *fires* of the forge, the burning furnace of the Solar Logos' smithy). In a larger sense, scabbard, Ixion Wheels, and Sun temple together comprise Ilmarinen's smithy.

The Ixion Wheel is like a mold into which the molten iron is poured to create the sword; the molten iron (or Sun gold) comes from the central fires of Agni. The celestial smith draws off a portion of Sun gold to fill the sword mold. Then the sword is inserted into the solar fire again to temper the metal. You have 360 Arthur swords, each a point of access to (and a product of) the fires. Here Arthur and Arthur sword are equivalent; the sword is Arthur in action.

All of this, too, keep in mind, is your throat chakra expressed outwardly in the landscape.

Each Ixion Wheel is a sword of insight, a point of insight into the Sun temple. Each Ixion Wheel is also an initiation chamber in which a sword of insight may be created in the candidate for Arthurhood. When you picture this globally, you have 360 swords pointing into the fires, for tempering and mastery. The swords give you controlled access into the fires of the furnace, and as they surround the Sun like a wheel of swords, they also can control it.

Each Ixion Wheel provides Grail Knight candidates for Arthurhood the opportunity to temper themselves, to receive the sword-making Arthur current, so as to be able to withstand and survive the immersion in the Sun temple. The smith, as master of the fire—the Solar Logos, the mind and reason in or behind the Sun—prepares you for an encounter with the Wild Sun God. You would not want to go directly into the Sun's domain without first gaining—becoming—a tempered sword under the smith's tutelage.

Remember, this is the same Wild Sun God that Zeus saw fit to throw Mount Etna upon. Metaphorically we could see the 360 fire bricks or swords encircling the Wild Sun God as equivalent to the prodigious weight of Mount Etna on Typhon. Just as that Sicilian volcano holds down the tempestuous Typhon, so do the 360 Ixion Wheels, like the walls of the furnace, restrain the Sun within Earth's geomantic terrain.

This image is applicable and descriptive on the archetypal, galactic, and planetary-geomantic levels. We can think of it as the next generation (the fifth planetary sphere) within the Vacated Space *and* as a composite geomantic structure involving all of the Earth. At the second planetary sphere, that of the Moon (see chapter 5), Soma was allocated equally to the 27 "wives" or *naksatras;* King Soma visited or infiltrated each *naksatra* of 13.3333 degrees.

Now in the fifth planetary sphere of the Sun, the Fire King, Agni, is apportioned equally to 360 wedges of the cosmic sphere. Each of the 360 sword tips touches the Agni's searing flames. Now each of the 27 *naksatra*s overlaps 13.3333 degrees of this cosmic space, or approximately 13 swords. The relationship between Agni and Soma is dynamic and devouring, for the Vedas say Agni as cosmic fire consumes the precious substance of Soma just as the Cattle of the Sun consume the delicious grasses on Mount Etna's slope.

There are many ways to interpret this complex image of Ilmarinen's three-part smithy. One is that it describes the wheel of the Chariot of the Sun, a wheel with 360 spokes. Greek myths tell us that Helios travels east to west across the sky every day in his chariot drawn by four horses. At the end of the solar day, Helios rests in a golden palace in the Hesperides in the farthest West, then he makes his night journey through the Underworld on the stream of Oceanos in a vessel, variously described as a solar barque, golden ferryboat, golden cup, golden bowl, or winged golden beaker, returning to his golden palace in the East by daybreak.

Whatever its true shape, the chariot-cup was forged for Helios by Hephaistos in his smithy. We could reasonably interpret this golden chariot conveyance as the 360 Ixion Wheels that encircle the Sun like a wheel, or as the 360 fire bricks on the outside of Agni's fire altar. Simply put, Helios's Sun chariot has but one wheel of 360 parts, or 360 slender wheels compacted together.

How we describe this depends on our viewpoint. From the smith's point of view, the Sun is the roaring flames of his furnace. He controls and masters the fire by regulating the flow of oxygen and fuel; he uses the fire's intense heat to soften metals, enabling him to shape them into serviceable objects, including swords. The Ray Masters "behind" him provide the scabbard or tints of angels for the swords.

From the Sun's point of view, though, Helios has 360 windows out beyond his own domain of fire. He has 360 stations to visit, to irradiate with fire and light. He can look through all 360 windows at once, or peer through one at a time. If Helios revolves, then his fire-light illuminates one window at a time, until he has illuminated the full circle. If we think of fire as something that can flow, perhaps like molten lava, Helios fills each sword-window with fire as if it were a dry streambed awaiting the spring floods. Then he goes to the next, and next.

In terms of the Earth's geomantic structure, we might think in terms of the fire-light of the 144 Sun temples irradiating the 360 Ixion Wheels on a regular, if not sequential basis, perhaps over the course of a planetary year of time.

The path of Helios's Sun chariot is a wheel through the galaxy. We call this wheel the Sun's ecliptic, its apparent path through the star fields of the galaxy, or more specifically, in Western astrology, "through" the 12 signs of the zodiac. We say "through," but more accurately it is a *juxtaposition;* from a planetary viewpoint, the Sun is framed for a month against each of the signs, but it is not physically "in" that constellation's three-dimensional star field.

But more accurately we are dealing with the 360 degrees of the circle (12 wedges of 30 degrees each, if you prefer), and Helios stops at each for an equal time. His transit of the 360 stations of the Sun makes a solar calendar, a year of traveling. Each of the 360 stations (Cattle, Ixion Wheels, Arthur forges) is a point of insight. In each place, King Arthur is born and expressed; in each, he wields his sword; in each, he speaks as the Solar Logos; in each, he is master of the smithy's fire, or the Sun. The Sun's ecliptic is a solar wheel, a calendar of expected visits to solar stations separated by one degree, a wheel composed of 360 Ixion Wheels.[384]

The Fires of the Forge—the Wild Sun God Typhon, Agni, Apophis, and Others

It's time we looked more closely at the fenced-in fire god, starting with Typhon, whom the Greeks portrayed as a fearsome, dangerous, wild monster.

Typhon was the offspring of Gaia, or Earth—remember, cosmic Earth, not the planet—and Tartarus (an abyssal aspect of Hades' kingdom) and was half-human, half-beast, more massive and formidable than any other of Gaia's progeny. Typhon was taller than the mountains, and his head knocked up against the stars. One of his arms stretched to the sunrise, the other out to the

sunset—in other words, his girth extended to the two horizons.

Typhon's body was covered in wings; his hair was unkempt and streamed down onto his face; his eyes were made of fire, and flames shot forth from his eyes, his nostrils, and his hundred mouths, and he uttered such noisome imprecations that even the gods on occasion fled from Typhon for safety. One hundred serpent or dragon heads sprouted out of his shoulders; from the hips downwards, he had a serpent's torso where two intertwining serpents yelled and hissed constantly. "From the thighs downwards he had huge coils of vipers, which when drawn out, reached to his very head and emitted a loud hissing," recorded the ancient historian of myths, Apollodorus.[385]

Typhon often flung boulders upwards to Heaven, and sometimes he spoke the language of the gods, but at other times he simply bellowed like a bull or barked like a mad dog. Zeus battled Typhon across the Mideast and at last won the fight by throwing Mount Etna upon him. Sicilian folklore still holds that any signs of volcanic activity in Etna are evidence of Typhon restively stirring in his imprisonment.

The Egyptian Apophis, also called Apep, is described as an immense serpent-devil of the mist, darkness, storm, and night who lives in the celestial Nile that flows through Heaven.[386] He perpetually tries to interfere with Ra's passage through the sky fields; occasionally he is successful and an eclipse occurs. Like Typhon, Apophis has a hideous roar that resounds throughout the Underworld. He requires no nourishment, other than to breathe in his own shouts. Though Apophis was a serious threat to Ra, one Egyptian myth said he was actually a previous form of Ra, hence his strength.[387]

We encounter a somewhat less antagonistic Sun figure in the Polynesian myth of La, their name for the Sun, which the demi-god Maui lassoed and tied down to Mount Haleakala, the 10,023-foot volcano on Maui in Hawaii. People had been complaining that the Sun was passing overhead too fast, that the days were too short, that there was no time to dry their bananas. Maui promised to capture the Sun and force it to cross the sky more slowly to benefit Polynesian life.

La was "in form like a man, possessed of fearful energy." He was a divine living creature who shook his golden locks morning and evening before men. He was unapproachable due to the extreme heat he gave off, and nobody before Maui had successfully subdued him or regulated his movements across the sky.[388]

The fierce, tempestuous, even monstrous, aspects of the Sun god we encounter in the portrayals of Typhon and Apophis are only one view of it. The Polynesian La is less demonic but still formidably fierce. Perhaps they are memories of cosmic days of titanic struggles by the gods to subdue the newborn suns of the galaxies. Maui's story seems to describe the inauguration of a Sun temple on a volcano, depicted as a fierce wrestling with the Sun god.

The Vedic presentation of Agni the Fire god is more neutral and perhaps an ultimately more accurate image. Agni, whose name means fire, is the fire of the Sun, the endless, primeval cosmic fire, the lord of ritual sacrifices based on fire. His appearance, though intimidating, is not inherently frightening.

He is the lord of the 49 fires. Agni was born as an all-consuming flame, completely grown but ever youthful. Agni's tongue itself is a flame, and he exhorts the gods to always tell the truth. Agni is all that consumes; he exists to consume Soma, the root of substance. His breath is the fiery exhalation of the Indestructible Person, Purusha, and he sprang originally from that Cosmic Man. He is the mouth of the gods, and through his mouth all the gods take their breath. Agni is the mental fire, the power of illumination, and the

potency of perception and knowledge.[389] Among his many epithets, Agni is *Pasupati*, "Lord of Cattle," linking him with Helios and the Sun Cattle.[390]

It may initially seem confusing that the Vedas also describe a Sun god called Surya. Surya is the Eye of Heaven that sees a long way; he spies the entire world. Surya is also Aditya or Dinakara, the Day-maker. He emits a thousand rays from his body, or he is ray-wreathed with 100,000 rays about his head; he is the rising illuminator who destroys the evil spirits of darkness; he is twelvefold, 12-souled, and his essence is superlative goodness.[391]

We see the beneficent aspects of the Sun god in the Mesopotamian formulation of Shamash (the Sumerian Utu) from the Semitic root *sms,* for Sun. Shamash surveys all living things, sees all countries, understands all languages, illuminates the world. Nothing can be concealed from Shamash's gaze. He regulates the seasons, accompanies travelers, judges the dead in the Underworld, and can even make the dead live again.[392]

The Mesopotamian hero Gilgamesh has to pass through the Sun's gate in the mountain of the western horizon called Mashu. This mountain guards the coming out and going in of Shamash every day by way of scorpion-men whose "aura is frightful, and whose glance is death," their "terrifying mantles of radiance drape the mountains."[393] It's fair to say Mount Mashu, wherever it existed geographically, was a Sun temple, and the epic of Gilgamesh describes in part that hero's penetration of the Sun mysteries through it.

The stories of Agni, La, Helios, Surya, and Shamash are geomantic clues indicating another major feature in the Earth's visionary geography.

Before moving on, let's consider some of the physical qualities of our Sun.

On the physical Earth, we live within the atmosphere and radiational field of this Sun, as do all the other planets in our solar system, as its atmosphere extends beyond Pluto. In fact, the solar influence roars and seethes through the solar system until it reaches a barrier, called the heliopause, somewhere at the edge of the region of interstellar gas. The entire solar system of planets lives within the vast aura of the Sun estimated to be 7.3 billion miles across (the solar system diameter), participating in its spiritual and physical aspects.

Obviously, the Earth as a planet is "ruled" by the Sun as the magnetizing center of the solar system and the source of 99 percent of its mass, but more specifically, the Sun's solar wind (a vigorous flow of protons and electrons) carries "the imprint of its energy and magnetism" while activity on its surface, including periodic explosions such as sunspots, solar flares, coronal mass ejections, and geomagnetic storms, "shapes, distorts, and influences" our planetary environment. "We live inside the atmosphere of a stormy star," and its physical activities—according to a science now called space weather—affect everything on Earth, from biological life to electronic devices, satellites to electric power grids, short-term weather to long-term climate.[394]

A coronal mass ejection, for example, which is the eruption of a huge plasma bubble and electrically charged gas from the Sun's outer atmosphere, can travel from one to five million miles per hour and assume a diameter of 30 million miles, and with a mass equal to 100,000 battleships, creating an impact equivalent to 100,000 hurricanes. A solar flare is a sudden explosive release of built-up magnetic energy with the comparable force of ten million volcanic eruptions in a few minutes. The Sun is described as a "perpetually exploding hydrogen bomb fueled by nuclear fusion," emitting 70,000 horsepower of energy into space for every square yard of surface.[395]

No wonder space weather experts say the Sun "constantly seethes with activity," generating the cosmic equivalent of tornados and hurricanes.

The sunspot cycle is an 11-year event from minimum to maximum to minimum again, with an average of 110 sunspots during the peak, but up to 169 or so have been observed in the most recent solar maximum. There is no precise peak to a sunspot cycle either, only a broadly defined highpoint because the Sun "roils with maximum activity" on either side of that peak for many months.[396]

Notice the vividly descriptive terms "seethes," "roils," and "stormy." What space weather authorities are saying about the Sun's tumultuous physical life is similar to what the ancient Greek mythographers (or psychics) said of hundred-headed Typhon and his wild, flailing, almost uncontrollable existence.

Let's not overlook the Sun's extreme heat either, as the original of Hephaistos's volcanic hot forge under Mount Etna: At its core, it's 29,000,000° F and 10,000° F on the "surface" or photosphere, though the corona, which extends for millions of miles above the photosphere and away from the Sun, reaches temperatures in the millions of degrees.

"In a sense we are actually *in* the outer reaches of the solar corona."[397] Wherever we stand on Earth, we're in the solar wind, which is "howling" past us at a speed of ten protons and electrons per cubic centimeter per 500–700 kilometers/second and at a searing temperature of 200,000 K. Fortunately, the Earth's enveloping magnetic field shields the planet from the full impact of the solar wind, creating a powerful bow shock and long magnetotail around it. That trailing magnetotail is up to 100 planetary radii long, like the long wake behind a speeding motorboat (the Earth), which compresses the water (solar wind) in front.

With this in mind, welcome to the Sun temple of Agni, the sixth of the eight Celestial Cities about Mount Meru. Agni's city is called Tejovati and is in the Southeast with respect to Meru; it is a city of "immeasurably splendid fire, full of divine wonders" in which dwells "the blessed god of fire, shining forth with his own flame."[398] For reasons I will explain below, I call the Fire-Sun Temple of Agni a Mithraeum.

The Mithraeum—inside the Flaming Bull's Head

Here is an impression of part of the picture of the Sun temple. Afterwards I'll comment on the meanings and mythic contexts of some of its elements.

Bear in mind that the Ixion's Wheel creates the smith. That's where the smith is born in you. Here is where the Solar Logos, the Arthur stream, creates a sword in you or, more precisely, makes you into a sword. When you have a sword, when the Solar Logos has penetrated you, then you are in the process of becoming a smith who can master fire and who can withstand meeting the Sun.

All 360 Ixion's Wheels lead into a Sun temple. In some cases, such as at Edfu, Egypt, and Mount Etna, Sicily, both structures are geomantically present. Inside the Ixion's Wheel temple, as described above, I noticed a huge gold bas-relief of a face with sunbeams around it on the wall facing the sarcophagus. In Mayan tradition, the name Kinich Ahau, the equivalent of Helios, Ra, and the rest, means Lord Sun-Face or Sun-eyed Lord, and what I saw was like that. I realized that the name of Arthur itself would allow me to pass into the Sun, so I intoned AR-THUR-HUM over and over like a speaking sword. The Arthur stream had created the sword in me, and in effect the Arthur stream is the sword.

I passed through the Sun face and found myself in a vast golden cave. Before me was a huge flaming golden bull's head, yet I knew that this bull's head was the cave itself and I was seeing it both from the inside and outside. The bull's head was magnificent and a little dreadful. Stars glittered inside its thick neck.

A geometrically patterned netting fitted around its head and neck; it was composed of dozens of squares, each with a number and a Hebrew letter on fire. It was as if the Magic Square of the Sun, a number-letter matrix used in medieval occultism, had been rendered in three dimensions and was wrapped around the bull's head like an electronic keypad in lieu of a door lock. Type in the right numbers—more precisely, speak the right letters—and you can pass through.

I had to laugh: here, unexpectedly was the Beast, that great fearsome monster of biblical misunderstanding. The medieval occultists (and Rudolf Steiner) called it Sorath, the evil Spirit of the Sun, whose name itself, through Hebrew gematria, spells the so-called demonic number 666, which is also the sum of the total of the 36 numbers arranged in six rows in the Magic Square of the Sun.

What's really going on with the Beast and Sorath? Is Sorath a scary, evil Sun spirit? No. "The Beast guards the timeline, and Sorath is one aspect of the Beast," the Ofanim told me later. I'll come back to the timeline in a moment.

Here before me was yet another image of the Fire-giant and Sun god, the flaming Agni. One of Agni's appearances, the Vedas said, was as a bull; the Egyptian Pharaoh had to pass the Bull of Offering before entering Heaven; and one of the Greek accounts said bulls, not horses, pulled Helios's chariot. I realized then that not only does a bull pull the chariot of the Sun, but the bull is the Sun god, and thus the Sun itself pulls the chariot. Geomantically, this means all Ixion's Wheels (the chariot or chariot wheel) lead into the Sun temple (bull or Sun).

I knew my next move was to slay the bull, just as the Persian solar hero Mithra (later the Roman Mithras) kills the bull by slicing open its neck. We need to be subtle here. There is no real bull-slaying, no tauroctony, as the Mithraic scholars like to say. After all, in this dimension, you are the sword itself, and the sword is a degree of insight and penetration, so you penetrate the Beast with your insight. It is true that the bull's blood will flow, but this has to do with the mysteries of time, which I'll return to in a moment.

I recognized the stars in the bull's neck as the Pleiades, the six bright stars and the one faint star of the Seven Sisters, astronomically in the neck of Taurus. I passed into the bull's neck and made for the brightest of these stars, Alcyone.

I saw perhaps a dozen tall crystalline pillars standing before a shallow pale-blue basin made of clear crystal. Inside the basin was a hologram of the galaxy, or multiple galaxies embedded in a geometric matrix. Looking more closely at the figures, I realized these pillars were actually eight-foot-tall humans with very large hairless craniums, as if they had two extra chakras in their heads. They were not speaking, but they were clearly in telepathic communication. They were placing little marbles at points of intersection in the holographic galaxy.

I had seen these beings before. They are Pleiadians, or at least one branch of the family: tall, cerebral, deeply psychic, differently embodied from Earth humans though from the same original stock as us. But what were they doing?

Later the Ofanim helped me understand that the Pleiadians were putting "pearls of longevity" into the star grids of the galaxies. Here's how to conceive of a pearl of longevity: Imagine the tiniest point of light you can, and make it even tinier. Then imagine this infinitesimally minute point of light is shattered into billions of even tinier parts. In the spaces between these particles of light is time. The pearl of longevity is the compression of the spaces between these most minute particles of light into a single spherical container.

To me, they are like time caves. The Pleiadians create a space for life, such as a solar system (a sun with planets requiring its energies of growth and change), and give it a predetermined allotment of cosmic time—a few drops of bull's blood—in which it can fulfill its evolutionary agenda. This time allotment would be on the vast scale as recounted in Vedic time reckonings, such as Days and Years of Brahma, which number in the billions and trillions of Earth years.

I realized there is a difference metaphorically, if not astronomically, between a sun and a star. A star that spawns a family, so to speak—a bevy of planets—becomes a sun that nourishes them. A sun with a family of planets clarifies the function of the Solar Logos (the directing, mastering mind or point of consciousness within the star or sun), which is to impart the energies of growth and change—the *AR* of life, the fires of the forge. The sun acts like the central furnace in a house with many rooms, that is, planets.[399]

Let's review the story of Mithra. He was born from a rock. This is the Arthur candidate emerging as a sword from the stone under the Arthur stream. He was destined to slay the primal Bull of Heaven called Geusha Urvan, the first living creature generated by Ahura Mazda (Ormazd), who also birthed Mithra to maintain watch over the entire moving world. Slaying the bull is the Arthur candidate penetrating the Sun-Beast that guards the timeline. Mithraism holds that once the bull was killed with a dagger stroke to its neck, its blood fertilized the Earth, yielding plants and animals and fecundating everything with life force.

This is letting the Pleiadian energies and timeline into the galaxy on Earth.

Mithraic temples, originally in Persia then later, once they spread, across central Europe, were conceived to be world caves (in likeness of the galaxy conceived of as a cave) in which the god (the Mithraic candidate acting as Mithra) killed the primordial bull. As such the world cave in which the bull-slaying takes places came to be called a Mithraeum. Most often the physical Mithraeum was located in a cave or subterranean crypt.[400]

As mentioned above, Mithra emerging from the rock is the same as King Arthur withdrawing the sword from the stone, for both Mithra and King Arthur are Solar Logos swords—Word Swords. Metaphysical tradition tells us that the spoken word, mantrically empowered, can be like a sword—can *be* a sword.[401]

The Sun is where the Word-Sword originally was whole before it was bestowed upon humanity. The biblical story of David slaying the giant Goliath with a slingshot is actually a veiled metaphysical reminder of this origin. The important part of the story was that David took Goliath's sword and kept it.

The sword of course was the Word-Sword, whole and vital, and Goliath (though the Bible doesn't tell us this) was in fact the Elohim as an angelic group. In other words, initiation into the mysteries and application of the Word-Sword came originally from the Elohim of the Sun (Rudolf Steiner places their prime sphere of activity as within the Sun). Later (now we draw on *Le Morte d'Arthur*), King Solomon, David's son, sends this same sword on the Ship of Time to arrive at Camalate centuries later for the sole use of the Christed Grail Knight Galahad.

You don't always have to kill the giant to get the sword. Sometimes he'll just hand it to you if conditions are right. Not that you could kill an Elohim, or would ever want to. I experienced this at Tintagel one winter's morning. I had spent the previous day at the Ofanim's suggestion meditating inside a stone circle in Cornwall called the Merry Maidens at Land's End. Here 19 stones, each about four feet high, form a perfect circle 78 feet wide. Later the Ofanim commented on the Merry Maidens: "This site involves the feminine aspect, all the coherence of what you may term right-brain activity. This site involves

the powers of clairvoyance, clairsentience, and clairaudience. All are available at this point. These are prerequisites to a fundamental understanding of the energy around this area and also in a wider context."

My time amidst the Merry Maidens must have sharpened my perception a bit because while standing on the windy headlands of Tintagel looking north towards Wales, the 19 Merry Maidens rose out of the Atlantic and made a half circle around the headland like 400-foot-tall Elohim mermaids. I realized among other things that no errant girls had been turned to stone at the Merry Maidens; rather the Elohim use the stones as portals to and from our world.

Here they were again, surrounding me like mammoth living, though diaphanous versions of Botticelli's Venus in the clamshell. One Elohim Maiden handed me a sword (Excalibur, I presumed), with colored lights twinkling throughout the blade and handle. On the sword's pommel were a pearl and a gem. I took the sword, brandished it to the four directions, and bowed to the Elohim. A rainbow arced over the southeastern cove, then the Elohim handed me a bouquet of flowers, or maybe it was another version of the tints of angels.

Sometimes you get the Arthur sword straight through the chest, but other times you get it handed to you, if not on a silver platter, then on a bed of flowers. I remembered the Ofanim's counsel that you gain your sword (insight into the angelic realm) by degrees, so it may seem over the years, you get a lot of swords, but essentially it's always the same sword, just sharper each time. Yet . . . maybe the swords are a little different. Here's why, from the Ofanim:

"We hold the sword above you pointing down your spine. We point the sword towards your heart. It lies in front of you. You have a sword in your right hand. Above, reaching from a cloud, a hand offers you a sword. All these are different perceptions at different levels of different aspects of Excalibur. For instance, the hand holding the sword out of the clouds is the root of the power of Air. When it is held in your right hand, it is the sword of intellect. When it runs down your spine, it is the sword of healing and transmuting, the sushumna before the snake of kundalini arises. When it points to the heart, it is the sword of detachment. We could go on, but we think you get the point of the sword."

The Fisher King got the point of the sword too, right in his groin. He lacked the understanding of its safe use. The Fisher King seriously maimed himself with the legendary (though to most scholars, baffling) Dolorous Stroke.

This was basically a misuse of the sword, a magical working that backfired owing to insufficient knowledge and the nonpresence of the Christ as an initiatory precontext. Only the Christed Grail Knight can wield the Word-Sword of the Sun correctly, safely, and therapeutically— so as to heal the Fisher King. That is the Sun-knowledge transmitted by the Elohim-Goliath to David and then to Galahad.

In a sense Galahad would heal the Wounded Fisher King by a mere word. But of course a mere word can be a mantrically charged one, such as *AR-THUR-HUM*, the sound of the Solar Logos, the master smith working his solar fires. We can picture the Christed Grail Knight speaking like a sun emitting solar flares, an oracular Typhon.

Deepening the link between Sun mysteries and speech is the fact that the human throat chakra, called *Visuddha*, has 16 petals or surrounding vibratory fields described in Tantric texts as of a crimson (blood-like) hue. In the Polynesian myth of La the Sun god, mentioned earlier, he has 16 legs, requiring Maui to tie him down with 16 ropes or one rope with 16 strands. Maui in effect was grounding the solar, speech-generating energies of the *Visuddha* throat chakra

by way of its geomantic correlate at Mount Haleakala, a Mithraeum Sun temple.

Inside the Pleiadian Cave— Bleeding Time and the Elements into the World

Let's return to Mithra and the bull-slaying. The primordial Bull is not slain, though his blood is drawn. Remember this is a metaphor for the flow of time into a defined space, a Pleiadian time cave such as a solar system. The Bull is another expression of the Wild Sun God. Here the Bull's blood equals time, but it also is the fructifying life force of the Solar Logos flowing into that world. We could almost say that solar time is a fructifying nutrient for growth and change.

So in the symbolic gesture of Mithra being born from the Generative Rock, withdrawing himself from this matrix as a Word-Sword, we have a practical way of decoding some aspects of the mysteries of the Sun and speech.

An image of Mithra suggests the time factor. Mithra is depicted as a lion-faced human with a serpent wrapped around him from feet to shoulders; a lion figure appears on his breast. In this guise—"the leontocephalous god of Eternity . . . this god of Time"[402]—he is called the Mithraic Kronos or sometimes the Aion (or Aeon), meaning an age of the universe, a time allotment.[403] In one Roman bas-relief, the Mithraic Kronos is surrounded by the 12 signs of the zodiac, which make an oval or egg shape around him.

In Mithraic theology, the pinnacle of the divine hierarchy and an exalted image of Mithra was Aion, or Boundless Time, depicted as a human monster with a lion's head and serpent-wrapped body. Aion bears a scepter and the bolts of sovereignty, and in each hand he holds "a key as the monarch of the heavens whose portals he opens."[404] This is Mithraic language for what I describe here as the Sun-Beast Sorath as guardian of the time line, which is the same as King Arthur as Solar Logos opening the Pleiadian time cave within the Bull's neck.

There is another useful nuance to the Aion as a time parameter. Let's call to mind again the image just cited of the 12 signs of the Western zodiac forming an oval about lion-headed Mithraic Kronos. Each of these zodiacal signs is an Aion. In Western astrology that is a time period approximately 2,160 years long during which the Sun is said to "reside" in that sign, imparting to everything the quality of filtered light and life from that specific constellation. We could say, loosely, that the 2,160-year period in which the Sun is "in" a zodiacal sign is a time cave or the experience contained within a single drop of Bull's blood.

But an experience of what? C. G. Jung took the Aionic image of the Fishes (for Pisces, the current, but ending, zodiacal Great Age in which we now live) as a deep symbol of the Self or total psychic wholeness in one time-determined phase of cosmic and ontological experience.[405] Following the Jungian line of interpretation, we could say each Aion within the 25,000-year cycle of 12 zodiacal Aions is a slice of the Self. In a sense, we're back with the Round Table.[406]

We might also say the Solar Logos—Mithra, King Arthur—is the complete time cave for an astrological cycle of 12 parts, or 25,000 years consisting of 12 smaller—shorter in duration—time caves, one for each zodiacal sign.

Or perhaps the Sun's time cave is longer than that? How about 180 million years? H. P. Blavatsky in *The Secret Doctrine* cited an authority who claimed "the sun having Alcyone in the Pleiades for the centre of its orbit consumes 180,000,000 of years in completing its revolution."[407] Metaphorically speaking, the Pleiadian bull's head is 180 million years in circumference.

This idea, presented in a metaphysical book in 1888, is not so far-fetched. Astronomers tell us

that the Sun, moving at about 150 miles per second, completes its orbital revolution about the galactic center in about 200 million years.[408]

Or how about a solar time cave that's as long as a *manvantara* of 306,720,000 years; or perhaps all 14 *manvantaras*, giving us a time cave of about 4,320,000,000 years, which is one Day of Brahma. To get a full day of 24 hours, you have to factor in a Night of Brahma, giving us 8,640,000,000 years. That is theoretically plausible from the view of astrophysics, which estimates the age of our physical sun at 4.5 billion years out of a total life span of ten billion years. Even in such a large number, the Sun number of 864 is still implicit, as the diameter of its solar photosphere is 864,400 miles.[409]

The solar time cave is our solar system, and it's all inside the Bull's head.

The diameter of the time cave is how much time we're given to study the face—Lord Sun-Face, as the Mayans would say of Kinich Ahau. The time cave is the duration of a time allotment—a spatial dimension now expressed as time, the time it takes to fill or experience the space—given us to experience the Self's 12 faces. The Pleiadian time cave—the Mithraic bull—allows us to incubate forms, in this case, the different zodiacal faces or glances of the original Self.

Penetrating the Bull, stabbing it in its Pleiadian neck, you allow solar life and fructifying time to flow into the world and landscape. The bull's blood fecundates all of matter. Yet the time cave also establishes a needed limit.

In the *Kalevala*, before Ilmarinen the primeval smith and great craftsman was born, the older god Väinämöinen was seriously wounded in the knee and foot from an axe wound. The blood burst forth from the wound and "flowed freely" in "streaming torrents . . . rushing like a foaming river." He filled seven large boats and eight large tubs with his blood, and still there was more.[410]

How much blood (time) was there in the Sun Väinämöinen? In Vedic time reckoning, 360 Days and Nights of Brahma make one year of Brahma. That's 3,110,400,000,000 Earth years. One hundred of these years is the life span of Brahma, about 311 trillion years. Creating time is a kind of bloodletting.

This episode from the *Kalevala* is an equivalent presentation of the Mithraic Bull and the Pleiadian time cave. Väinämöinen is like the primordial Bull, full to the brim with blood—Boundless Time—but he needs containers or else he'll bleed all over the place, filling boats and tubs, and still have more blood to flow.

He needs a time cave to limit the flow of his time-blood, to contain it, and for that, he needs a great smith like Ilmarinen, the Solar Logos, who can work the forges and master the fire so as to create suitable and multiple containers for the elder god's time-blood. It's paradoxical: You want to stop the flow of blood, yet the blood needs to flow into the world. The solution is to control the flow, and that's the job of the smith, to craft containers to regulate it.

Boundless, eternal Time is too vast, too long, too immeasurable; it will overflow all containers. If you want movement, growth, and change—a Sun chariot that visits all the solar stations—you need a limited, bounded, reduced time allotment. Otherwise, the journey would never be completed as you would be charioteering through infinity. You need a space that takes less than an eternity to travel through to experience the Sun faces. Even more simply, if you want movement, you need time in which to do it.[411]

What are the containers then? Remember the array of devices, objects, tools, thrones, and residences Hephaistos made? I propose an unconventional interpretation. The celestial smith is actually forging what we call the periodic table of elements—the energy antecedents, the fathers and mothers of the elements of material creation. He is also creating constellations of stars.

In the simplist interpretive sense, we could say the celestial smith, as Solar Logos, fashions numerous forms in which the fires of Agni or the Sun can dwell. These forms are constellations and the elements—originally one and the same. He makes 132 forms, the number of elements and constellations for our Earth.

Putting aside the obvious objection that far fewer elements (103) or constellations (88) than this have been discovered yet or described—I'll address this in a moment—we can note that both elements and constellations are three-dimensional forms, a latticework of atoms held together by bonds. The "bonds" among stars are a more metaphorical or spiritual linkage, what we might call affiliations, with the brightest stars forming a kind of celestial Soul Group.

The chemical description of elements is based on electron configuration (the orbital locations of the electrons in an unexcited atom) and its characteristic crystal structure (such as cubic, hexagonal, and six others) and is a precise science.[412] Not so for constellations. Descriptions and perceived forms vary with cultures, and given the staggering number of stars in our galaxy, surely other constellations exist that have not yet been identified and logged onto the lists.[413]

What makes a constellation exist or a new one appear, I propose, is not the cognitive fancies of a stargazer with a mythopoeic mind, but a necessity of planetary creation. Constellations, understood as the macrocosmic expression of the terrestrial periodic table of elements, are required building blocks for a planet's visionary geography, nutrients for an Albion, the localized geomantic expression of the Original Man. At the level of the galaxy, the constellations—at least the 132—are the building blocks in the "psyche" of this Primal Man or Self.

We might call the Cosmic Self or Original Human simply Adam, for the Hebrew gematria for ADM is 1440, or just 144. This number with all its zero amendments (most notably, 144,000, as in Revelation) is of crucial importance.

In chapter 9, we'll see how 132 constellations are the structural essence of a prime geomantic feature called a landscape zodiac. Technically, each zodiac features 144 constellations, but 12 are repeated, leaving us 132 different ones.

Keeping in mind our foundational metaphorical image of the smith, his forge, and the various shapes that he crafts the molten metals to assume, the Solar Logos, as master of the fire and metallurgy, is creating 132 fire-filled forms, putting the Sun-fire into the archetypes or "parents" of the elements of the periodic table. At least metaphorically, we can say there is solar life, Agni's fire, in each of the 103, or more, elements. He does this on behalf of the gods, as special services to individual Olympians, which is to say, he facilitates their sphere of cosmic responsibility by making it, from their viewpoint, more materialized.

I'm not saying our solar system's Sun creates the 132 constellations of the galaxy; in this chapter, we are dealing primarily with the antecedent of that star, with the archetype of the Sun expressed as cosmic fire, the fire-giant Agni. We are dealing with the primordial Vacated Space now at the fifth planetary sphere of being "filled in" with creation and universal manifestation, in this case, with the primal cosmic fires of Agni. Think of it as a kind of flood. Earlier, Soma flooded the Vacated Space with wakefulness, consciousness, substance; now Agni floods the Vacated Space with life, growth, and change, fire that consumes the substance—Soma aflame, wakefulness quickened with solar life and time.

The constellations of the zodiac and the elements of the periodic table are thus containers for Time, for the Bull's blood, for Agni's fire. Each has the mark of the Solar Logos imprinted upon it; each is formed of his consummate craft.

The celestial smith shapes 132 forms for the fire element on behalf of the assembly of gods.

Then in accordance with the Hermetic axiom, "As above, so below" (there's no middle or planet Earth yet), our Sun (as other stars) acts as what astrophysicists call a "nuclear furnace" to create the elements of matter.[414]

Let's put some of the pieces together regarding the Sun. We are dealing with the origins of the etheric body and the etheric level of reality, what is otherwise called the fourth dimension. Time does not exist yet, but the matrix for it does; the clock is built, but it hasn't been set to tick yet. The consonants and vowels of the Word-Sword are the planets (the seven energy levels of the elements) and the constellations (the archetypes of the elements of matter). These form the matrix or clock. The Word-Sword or Generative Rock will be the solar stream, the Word spoken through the Sun that quickens life in this matrix. Arthur is the Solar Logos that will precipitate growth, change, and movement.

Once the Sun is born and mastered, you have the speed of light, which is the requisite for tangibility, visibility, material manifestation, and biological life.

The Vacated Space, and all its hierarchical levels, including galaxy and solar system, has been filled with the Bull's blood, with its nutrient-rich Time. But the clock has not started ticking yet. Time is still a spatial dimension, a time tableau in which everything is present at once, filling the space. Time is not yet linear, moving forward circulating. When the solar clock is ticking and Time is incarnate, then the Sun's life, its volume of blood loss, is measured by the solar constant,[415] and the speed of light becomes the determinant of time in the solar system.

Let's say, metaphorically, the flowing Bull's blood saturates the elements of the solar system with time, like a dark fluid fully staining a blotter. In a sense, this time saturation is an infusion of mortality into the elements. This is *how long* you'll last; this is your burn rate, your half-life—

how long it will take before your solar life force is spent and you die. Perhaps we could think of the solar constant as the timer for solar time. It sets the rate of burn; its ticking measures the half-life of all solar constituents.

Practical Tips for Your Next Visit to a Sun Temple

So what does one do with a Sun temple? Why go to a Mithraeum?

This book, ultimately, is about applied cosmology, showing the practical geomantic uses for human initiation through creative interaction with the Earth's visionary geography. The Earth is a cosmological template awaiting our interaction and offering us edification. In trying to account for the diversity of geomantic structures and their function and effects on consciousness, you need some kind of cosmological model. My attempt to explain the cosmology is meant to contribute to the use of the cosmological template for the growth and expansion of consciousness and for the simultaneous global benefit to the Earth.

The discussions of Earth sites and geomantic functions are an extended hello to your cosmic-spiritual constitution as it has been extrapolated out into the Earth's visionary terrain, which continuously mirrors it for you when you choose to look, offering you the possibility of remembering yourself. Just to say hello, to acknowledge the outer mirroring of your inner anatomy, is a step towards waking up to your cosmic Self in whose spherical body you live (see figure 8-1).

That spherical body, what the medieval alchemists called the *rotundum*, is the Earth in whose galactic "dreambody" or cosmic and human collective unconscious we live. "Our dreambody is part of the entire world's dreambody, yet the world's dreambody is also found within us."[416] Another name for that global dreambody and *rotundum* is Albion, the Primal Man expressed in the context of a planet and its human inhabitants over time.

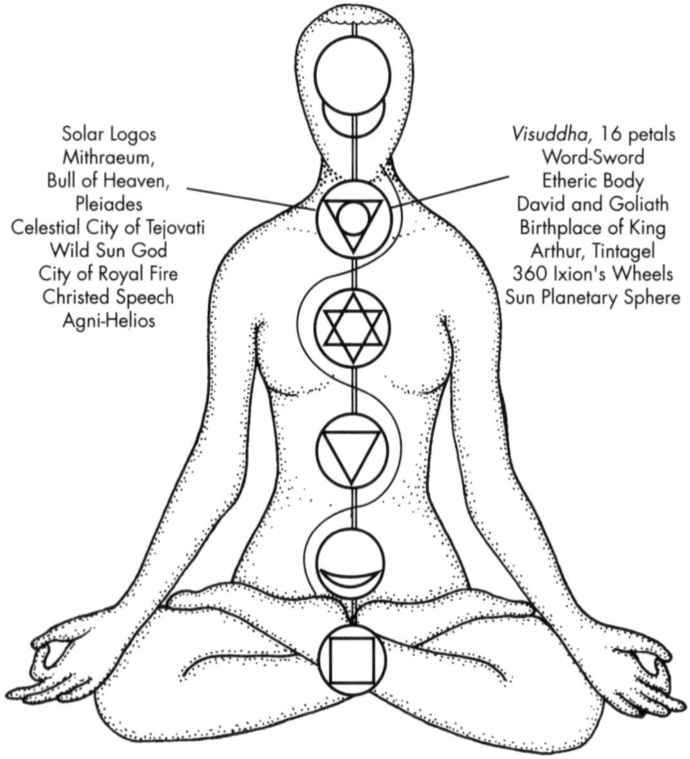

In antique days on Earth, Sun temples were used as places of royal investiture for spiritual kings. Consider Takhti-Sulaiman in Iran. This ruined ancient city, once called City of Royal Fire (its name meant "Throne of Solomon"), was the holiest of all places for Zoroastrians and one of Iran's

Solar Logos
Mithraeum,
Bull of Heaven,
Pleiades
Celestial City of Tejovati
Wild Sun God
City of Royal Fire
Christed Speech
Agni-Helios

Visuddha, 16 petals
Word-Sword
Etheric Body
David and Goliath
Birthplace of King
Arthur, Tintagel
360 Ixion's Wheels
Sun Planetary Sphere

Figure 8-1. The Geomantic Array of the Throat Chakra, Fifth Planetary Sphere

most sacred pre-Islamic sites. In fact, this mountain site in northwest Iran (elevation 7,000 feet) is attributed as Zoroaster's birthplace.

It was the site of one of the Three Sacred Fires described by Zoroaster, and called *Atur Gushnasp*, the Royal Fire (of kings and warriors), located in the northwest; the other two were *Atur Farnbog*, the Fire of the Priests in the south, and *Atur Burzen-Mihr*, Fire of Herdsmen, in the northeast, although archeologists have not determined their exact location.[417]

These three fires were originally created by Ahura-Mazda ("Wise Lord," the One True God for Zoroastrians) for the protection of the world. When the site was active and the sacred fires maintained, kings of the Sassanian Empire (roughly the third to seventh centuries A.D.) made a procession here from their coronation at Ctesiphon for divinely supported investiture in the Royal Fire.

Immersion in the Royal Fire for kingly investiture is not exactly a contemporary theme or necessity for most people—or is it? If we think in spiritual rather than temporal terms, the investiture might be something along the lines of alignment with the Sun within. There is also the chance of having the constellations and archetypes of the elements—the building blocks of the human psyche—activated in you.

A palpable benefit to spending time in a Sun temple would be to tune up, even heal, your etheric body by exposing it to the whole, integrated, and pure energies of its source—the Sun. If you practice mantras, sing, do eurhythmy, or wish to experience an impulse leading to creative speech, immersion in a Sun temple might be a good idea.

If you have been to an Ixion Wheel and had an Arthur sword experience (or however your mind has decoded the energy impact of the site on your consciousness), then it is highly useful to ground this initiation at a Sun temple, to temper your newly made sword in the fires of the solar forge (see table 8-2 for some locations).

A further geomantic application of the Sun temple has to do with assimilation of selves. You may need angelic assistance for this, and it may take more than one visit or one afternoon. One autumn, I "assimilated" for about ten days at Chaco Canyon, principally at the Sun temple at Fajada Butte (also the site of one of the Earth's 13 original dragons: near the visitor's center).

The Earth has a feature called time portals. These are doorways (there are 45) into a dilated experience of time across dimensions and parallel realms. I discovered this feature "inside" Fajada Butte at Chaco Canyon in northwestern New Mexico where in a mystical experience I got to collect and integrate various beings "I" had been in the past into an experiential composite.

The Ofanim showed me that time is something that is more liquid than we presently imagine and that it has a dimensional quality. It is not only linear; it is also in a vertical and horizontal dimension and in various parallels. Picture throwing a stone into a pond; the ripples go out across the surface of the pond and also down into the water; also the air is stimulated above the surface of the pond as the stone hits the water. Any moment in our experience of time equals a potential ripple across dimensions and parallels, up, down, and sideways. So a time portal is a conduit across dimensions and parallels in time.

I was doing other geomantic activities there—it's the dome for Arcturus and it has a landscape zodiac—in conjunction with the Ofanim, but afterwards I understood, thanks to them, that I had also been engaged in an assimilation process. The Ofanim said: "It was a precipitation of your being bodies through time, a consolidation of the wisdom aspect through a condensing of your time body. It was also a memory of entering a time portal at this site in a previous incarnation."

Table 8-2: The Mithraeum, Temple of the Sun God

Planetary Total: 144

Selected Locations:

Rhodes, Greece (dedicated to Helios: Island of the Sun)	Mount Etna, Taormina, Sicily, Italy	Ise, Honshu island, Japan
Wayland's Smithy, Oxfordshire, England	Mycenae, Treasury of Atreus, Greece	Takachiho Gorge, about 50 miles from Mount Takachiho, Miyazaki, Japan (birthplace Amaterasu, Japanese Sun goddess)
Heliopolis, Matariyeh, Cairo suburb, Egypt (Ra's Citadel or City of the Sun)	Babylon (Gate of God and House of the Judge of the World), Iraq	
Fajada Butte, Chaco Canyon, New Mexico, U.S.	Gediminas Hill, Vilnius, Lithuania	St. Michael's Mount (*Dinsul*: Mount of the Sun), Cornwall, England
Angkor Wat (*Baladitya*, "Rising Sun" the primal ancestor), Cambodia	Edfu, Egypt	Takht-i-Sulaiman (City of the Royal Fire), near Tabriz, Iran
	Machu Picchu, Peru	Ise, Shrine of Amaterasu, Honshu Province, Japan
Mount Casius, Syria	Titikala, the Sacred Rock, Island of the Sun, Lake Titicaca, Peru	
Mount Haleakala, Maui, Hawaii, U.S.		Primrose Hill, London, England
	Acrocorinthus, Corinth, Greece	The Plaza, Santa Fe, New Mexico, U.S.

Equivalent Names: Intiwatana or *Intihuatana* (Hitching Post of the Sun, or Sun Fastener); Pearls of Longevity; time caves; *Ame-no-Iwato* (Sky-Rock-Cave); City of the Royal Fire; Los's Furnace and Iron Door (from William Blake—Primrose Hill)

Names for the Sun God: Agni (Vedic), Helios (Greek), Apophis (Egyptian), Typhon (Greek), La (Polynesian), Inti (Incan), Kinich Ahau (Mayan), Surya (Vedic), Utu (Mesopotamian), Sorath (occult Sun Spirit), Shamash (Samas: Babylonian), Amaterasu (Japanese), Dazhbog (Russian)

I had been inside what seemed to me a turquoise igloo or greenhouse, several dimensional layers removed from (or within) the outer Fajada Butte. I was observing (or perhaps participating with) the Pleiadians putting the pearls of longevity into the grid matrix of the Earth, our galaxy, and probably others. As it seemed to me, they were also focusing sword light into a pale-blue crystal basin, which then flushed golden.

According to the Ofanim, during the inhabitation of Chaco Canyon by the Anasazi, what archeologists call a vanished tribe of Native Americans, the portal of time at Chaco was periodically opened, during which occasion the Anasazi had access to other time frames. That is the larger context of what I was participating in. The more "personalized" aspect involved "the process of consolidation of wisdom through your being bodies scattered through time."

Contemplate the vista of the multitude of your past lives arrayed before you. Even though the "you" you were in those many lives is dead, something remains, memories perhaps, something incomplete or unassimilated—the "being bodies scattered through time." In conjunction with your being at a Sun temple (or perhaps specifically the Chaco Canyon one) and angelic assistance from the Ofanim, you can begin to consolidate all the wisdom you gained from these lives into a point of consciousness associated with your present body and all its subtle energy fields or extended being bodies.

Was there really a turquoise igloo? No. "That was a perception of your current psyche of that which is outside time," the Ofanim gently noted. So don't worry about it if your psychic decoding apparatus throws up some unusual or even cognitively jury-rigged imagery. Being there is what's important; seeing things "accurately" is an admirable goal, but not crucial.

As for the sword light flushing the pale-blue crystal basin golden, that was "the communication through your various time bodies [past life being bodies scattered throughout time] into the present assisted by beings you've been in the past." Metaphorically, you're tossing all the golden artifacts you forged in the elemental fires in your past lifetimes back into the Sun furnace to melt into pure, unshaped gold, ready for time use and shaping in a new and current life.

Interdimensional Portals and Aliens in the Earth's Visionary Geography

The ramifications of the information presented in this book about the cosmic antecedents of the Earth's visionary terrain and its mirroring in the human constitution should render moot the questions of whether aliens and ETs exist. Aliens, ETs, and spiritual intelligences at other stages of cosmic evolution are as *embedded* and implicit in the Earth's energy body as they are in the galaxy.

The easiest way to get this concept is through a Pleiadian feature in the Earth's field. The Ofanim call these features interdimensional portals, and there are 60,600 of them on the planet,

each one leading to what we might call a functional field headquarters for the Pleiadians with respect to the Earth. A colleague and I were shown one such at a hill called Hummelfjeld in Os, near Roros, in south-central Norway. Roros is a couple dozen miles to the northeast of the northeastern flank of the Rondane Mountains, already identified here as the Earth's primary *Ananda-kanda*, or inner heart center, and prime patterning template for the Garden of Eden.

We had just walked down a small treeless mountain as part of working with a landscape zodiac amplifier (see chapter 9) with the Ofanim. There was a small, grass-covered mound surrounded by some trees, and my friend suggested I meditate there for a few minutes. He had already checked it out and wanted to compare impressions. At first it seemed to have a high devic, elemental vibration, an impression supported by the dozen or so gnomes standing about like slightly restive doormen. When they had my attention, they gestured for me to follow them. We passed down a lane into the hill then eventually into a vast cavernous space, hundreds of feet across and high.

In the center of this vast, open, yet subterranean space was an ultrasleek alien spacecraft. My mind could not get a fix on its true shape or color, so I had to settle for approximations. The color was a pleasing blend of salmon and lilac, while the shape was something like the sleek rear end of a 1950s Cadillac. I knew I wasn't seeing this with anything even approaching accuracy, but no matter. I concluded that this little tree-girded knoll at the base of Hummelfjeld hill was a portal into another dimension and the parking garage of a spaceship.

Afterwards, I was disoriented, though pleasantly so, for at least an hour. My friend said the Ray Master Saint Germaine was maintaining a lilac flame burning at the portal entrance (where the gnomes had stood) to keep the site cleansed.

The Ofanim debriefed us that night. They told us we had seen and somewhat experienced an interdimensional portal to do with the Pleiades. "It is a doorway to a ship, as you saw. It is peripheral to many zodiacs and has to do with grid maintenance. Its purpose is in relation to the Pleiadian Council of Light. This Council and its many agencies disseminate the transmission of light across dimensions. It is based on several of the planets within the Pleiadian systems. Its members come originally from the Pleiadian planets whose populations then expanded into their quadrants of the system related to the Pleiades."

This is tracking perilously close to *Star Trek*'s galactic Federation, I thought at the time, but then who knows where such ideas come from? The Pleidian Council has 26,000,000,000 members, the Ofanim added, and 14 live on Earth.

A related geomantic feature, though not explicitly involving the Pleiadians or their Council of Light is what I call Heavenly Caves or Og-Min Cave Heavens. This is an arcane feature of the Earth's visionary terrain, one that is primarily referenced in Tibetan writings to do with their Buddhist antecedents, the Bon-po.

Before I explain what the Og-Min Cave Heavens are, in terms of received tradition and esoteric lore, I will first give a flavor of the experience of one.

Mount Kailash is a 22,028-foot peak in the southern Trans-Himalayan Range 800 miles northwest of Lhasa in Tibet. It is Tibet's holiest mountain. Above it is something that may resemble a giant disc-shaped spaceship. Picture a blue disk around 100 miles in diameter situated motionlessly above the peak. Inside are hundreds, perhaps thousands, of caves or spherical niches, each containing a multidimensional being of light. Perhaps they are animate stars or maybe *rishis* or living crystals or maybe something altogether different, formless, and indescribable. On one occasion I saw them as a cluster of about 50 slender crystalline stalks with almond-shaped translucent heads.

One colleague reported that over the course of two years he underwent considerable initiation and training with the Og-Min, whom he accessed through a portal at Cerne Abbas, a hill in Dorset on whose hillside is a huge chalk-etched figure of a human male with an erection, known as the Cerne Abbas Giant. Another colleague, Solara, promulgator of the widely recognized 11:11 activations, discussed with me her experiences with the Og-Min in the mid-1980s and later wrote about them briefly in one of her books.

They are one of myriad "Starry Brotherhoods existing in the cave heavens on higher dimensional octaves," Solara writes. Their cave heavens resemble egg-shaped bubbles in space. At the first level of their starry caverns, there are great caves filled with banks of white candles, Solara says; you may hear chanting here and see robed figures moving slowly about. At an intermediate level, the caves are smaller and have large windows overlooking the star fields. But what do the Og-Min do in their Cave Heavens?

Their function is to maintain the Earth's grid and to maintain a "Golden Beam which keeps this galaxy in position and balance." We're supposed to reconnect with the Og-Min in their starry Cave Heavens because we are all "family," at least on a cosmic level, Solara writes. They can remind us of a higher state of consciousness that is "closer to being Home." Further, contact with the Og-Min can help us "reawaken and reactivate to our fullest potential," enabling us to help the planet's transmutation of matter and our own completion.[418]

To find some cultural context for the Og-Min we turn to the Bon-po. The Bon-po, the original shamanistic inhabitants of Tibet, claimed they came originally from a place or dimension called *Ol-mo lung-ring* in *sTag-gzig*. One text, in describing the Bon-po lineage of royal Bru, says: "As for the gNam-bru, the essence of all Enlightened ones, in the person of an individual divine son named 'Od-zer mDangs-ldan, descended to the place of Bar-lha 'od-gsal from the sphere of 'Og-min stug-po bkod pa, for the sake of sentient beings."

This being then went to the human world and descended at a specific place where he "turned the wheel of Bon for the gods." But he also surveyed the world from the summit of Mount Meru, the Earth's cosmic mountain. The Bon-po texts state that "all the gShen-po [high priests, enlightened emissaries], having hidden the Bon texts, departed, some to the 'Celestial Sphere,' some to solitary places for meditation," and others to Mongolia.[419]

Tibetan Buddhist texts record some information about the Og-Min as well. The four highest "Brahma heavens" in which existence is nonsensory based and formless are known collectively as *Akanishtha* (in Tibetan, Og-Min).[420] The Og-Min heaven is the last outpost of our universe, a transitional state that leads from the mundane to supramundane, Nirvana, and the realm of the Buddhas.[421] The Og-Min live in a state mentally inconceivable to most humans. It is a "pure and holy Realm of Truth." The deities called Devatas are real, holy, divine, and mind-produced, but they do not have an individualized, objective existence.[422]

Admittedly, based on these Tibetan-derived descriptions the Og-Min are hard to understand. The Chinese Taoists also referred to them in a per-

---

Table 8-3: Heavenly Caves—Og-Min Cave Heavens

Planetary Total: 360

Selected Locations:

Mount Kailash, Tibet

Cerne Abbas, Dorset, England

Cathedral Rocks, Sedona, Arizona, U.S.

Mount Holyoke Mountain, Hadley, Massachuetts, U.S.

Tien-Tai Mountain, China

Equivalent Names: Astral *shiens;* Bilasvarga; Akanishtha Heaven; "the Central realm of the Densely-Packed"; starry caverns

---

haps conceptually lighter form. They spoke of astral *shiens,* starry realms or big holes in the universe they call "Heavenly Caves," and said there are 36 of them.[423]

According to Taoist tradition, these Cave Heavens are "openings of the universal high energy . . . energy 'eyes' [or] *shien* islands." The term *shien* refers both to the Caves and the Immortals who lived in them. The 36 Cave Heavens described in Taoist literature are "positive energy spots . . . famous for being the paradise of the *shiens,* the immortal divine beings." One such Cave Heaven is said to be at Tien-Tai Mountain in China, a site known as the Heavenly Terrace.[424] (See table 8-3 for a selected listing of Heavenly Cave sites.)

9 The Starry Heavens All Will Return to the Mighty Limbs of Albion
The Epochal Awakening of the Earth's Primal Man

Our chapter title is an inversion of a somber statement William Blake made in his epic geomantic poem, *Jerusalem: The Emanation of the Giant Albion:* "The Starry Heavens all were fled from the mighty limbs of Albion." Blake wrote that one day a human form appeared in the Sun above "Albion's dark rocks" and declared with "the Voice Divine" that "Albion shall rise again." Even better, Blake has his celestial smith, Los, a guise of the Solar Logos, prophecy that the day will arrive when "all Albion's injuries shall cease, and when we shall/Embrace him, tenfold bright, rising from his tomb in immortality."[425]

First, let's deal with two basics. Who is Albion? What does he look like? As a name, Albion once referred to the White Isle, or England, or to a giant, sired by a sea giant, who then ruled the island. In Blake's mythology, Albion is the name of the Eternal Ancient Man, what Qabala and other mythic systems call the original human template, the cosmos expressed as a human. I've referred to several examples of this throughout the book—a singular cosmic being variously called P'an Ku, Gayomart, Purusha, Ymir, Anthropos, and Adam Kadmon.

In a more general sense, the name might mean *A Light Being In Our Neighborhood.* I don't mean to be cute here, but the Ofanim once suggested this to me when I asked them what the name Albion meant. Anyway, it's accurate, evocative, and certainly easy to remember.

James Joyce had a similar interpretation. His principal, though protean character, in *Finnegans Wake,* is HCE, which translates variously as Howth Castle and Environs, Humphrey Chimpden Earwicker, and Here Comes Everybody. All of Dublin is his body. Howth Castle, a high headland with a castle that "guards" Dublin Bay, is the head of a recumbent landscape giant; downtown Dublin is his abdomen, and his feet are in Phoenix Park. HCE is "a larger Everyman [who] dreams the book of night," explains Harold Bloom in *The Western Canon.* This Everyman "is too huge to have a personality, any more than Albion, the Primordial Man of Blake's epic, is a human character."[426]

In the landscape of Glastonbury, England, I have experienced (interiorly) the body of a huge recumbent figure—some say male, others female—that describes a crescent several miles long across the town landscape, from Wearyall Hill to out past the Tor, curving away through the marshy flatlands called the Levels to his cranium. You can walk this Albion's landscape body in a day, pausing at each energy center, knowing you are walking inside something big, cosmic, portentous.[427]

What does Albion look like? He looks like you. Like me. Like all the humans who ever were on this Earth, male and female, combined in one face. Picture the Earth as a blue-white planet. Now picture a generic human, either androgynous or of no clear gender, and of remarkable flexibility, draped luxuriantly over it, his back to the planet, his face towards the sky, his head touching his feet, meeting somewhere midway across the Earth's sphere.

Inside his body, many thousands of points of light twinkle and blaze. He seems, in fact, to be made of stars. All of the world's physical terrain is contained within his planetwide body. All 85 geomantic features lie within his planet-sized body and are part of his global life. As a character in Vladimir Nabokov's novel *Pnin,* gazing at the stars, says: "I suspect it is really a fluorescent corpse, and we are inside it."[428]

Albion is Gaia's husband and soul, her spiritual half, who remembers and embodies her (and our) celestial origin. He is round, as the ancient Western philosophers said the soul is round, and that the form of the Original Man, the Anthropos, the World Soul, is round, a *rotundum.* It is spherical like the Moon, one authority wrote, and is furnished with eyes on all sides: "His soul was like a glassy spherical vessel, that had eyes before and behind." Commenting on this remark by a medieval philosopher, C. G. Jung says that the "indescribable totality of the psychic or spiritual man" is compounded of consciousness and "the indeterminable extent" of the unconscious, such that the "'total' man is as big as the world, like an Anthropos."[429]

Albion is this world-sized indeterminable extent of conscious and unconscious states—an archive of the totality of *our* human experience in the context of *this* planet. Albion is the planet-sized compendium of humanity over the history of our life and dreams on Earth. Albion is still sleeping, but it is now a light sleep; he twitches

restively, as if in preparation for waking up. He senses a new world, the one awaiting him. He is on the verge of reality.

Whose Stars Are These? Albion on the Earth at Three Levels

Perhaps the easiest way to approach a conceptual understanding of this big concept is to explain that Albion exists at three levels on the Earth. There are 445 Albions (12 in the Albion Plates, 432 in the zodiacs, plus the one global form). There is the single, globe-encompassing Albion, whose limber, back-floating form is draped over the planet, his head touching his feet. Bear in mind, this is a poetic or metaphorical description of a complex planetary totality. Simply put, one physical Earth, one soulful Albion.

The second level of Albion is twelvefold. Recall that earlier in the book I described the 12 equal geometric divisions of the Earth's surface as Albion Plates; the 12 together comprise a dodecahedron, which is one of the five Platonic Solids implicit in the Earth's geomantic form. The totality of energy features within an Albion Plate make up its Albion.

Here we might picture Albion as a generic human, lying upon a pentagonal shaped plate of glass. Picture Earth with 12 pentagons, and on each, a recumbent Albion. Each of the 12 is both different from and the same as the original.

Each is different in that only one of the 12 zodiacal energies highlights all life within that Albion Plate, so that, for example, the Albion Plate over France and the British Isles will carry the Virgo energy, and the one over Australia and New Zealand, the Libra current. They are the same in that most geomantic features within an Albion Plate are replications of the spiritual constitution of the singular, planetary Albion. The intent of this replication was to expose all of the planet at different levels to the same types of energies so that humans did not have to travel too far to experience them.

The third level of Albion is as the totality of what I call a landscape zodiac or terrestrial star map, discussed later in this chapter. There are 432 such zodiacs on Earth, and when completed and activated, each expresses an Albion. The Albion in the landscape in Dublin and Glastonbury is the consummation of a landscape zodiac; what Blake described in London is a zodiac, but he was also describing the singular, planetary Albion that subsumed all the others.

A landscape zodiac is a congeries of stars. Picture 132 constellations and hundreds of individual stars, all crowded into a sphere laid flat on the ground. But what do they add up to? To see, we have to connect the stars like dots.

More properly, in accordance with the old theory of holograms, think of these points of light as the interference pattern, the jumbled incoherent picture of scattered light, midway between the original and the virtual copy. Apply the laser light of consciousness and you produce the copy out of the pattern. The cosmic original is Adam Kadmon; the planetary virtual copy is Albion.

"Albion is the unperfected, unreleased, unawakened Christ of the Earth waiting to fulfill its destiny," the Ofanim comment. "As those souls destined to walk in Albion awaken, so he will awake." Awakening Albion began with the inception of the planet and humanity. Albion has never awakened before on this planet, so when he does—and that's expected to be fairly soon—it will be a planetary precedent.

The previous 15 Arthur incarnations in Earth history and the activities of the 26 Camalate Centers constellated around him contributed towards this time. Albion blinked at the Harmonic Convergence in August 1987. Now with the imminent arrival of the sixteenth King Arthur, "inevitably and inexorably," the Ofanim state, "Albion is almost ready to get up and have his breakfast."

When one Albion stirs and starts to awake, as is the Albion within the Albion Plate overlighting the British Isles and France, the others become involved with this awakening in a process of reciprocal maintenance and are energized. "When Albion awakes, the New Jerusalem will begin to germinate," the Ofanim note. "Within each Yuga, Albion is reborn, but now Albion is about to become *conscious*." In the Hindu time model, there are four Yugas, or Ages, lasting a total of 4,320,000 years; we are currently in the fourth and darkest of these, the Kali Yuga, which lasts 432,000 years.

Before we enjoy that epochal breakfast with the well-rested Albion, much geomantic work still needs to be done, and we need a conceptual framework from which we can begin to contemplate and eventually understand who he is.

Let's start with the concept of landscape zodiacs. Two insightful researchers, a Canadian named Katherine Maltwood in the 1920s and a Britisher named Mary Caine in the 1970s, first brought the idea of a star map on the landscape to public attention in modern times.[430]

Maltwood, studying topographical maps and aerial photographs of Somerset in England, discerned the approximate shapes of the Western zodiacal constellations on the land, their shapes and edges made by hedges, lanes, woods, streams, rhynes, hills, earthworks, and other topographical minutiae of the terrain.[431]

This array of constellations and giant star effigies on the landscape, Maltwood wrote in 1929, was Glastonbury's "temple of the stars" and the original of the fabled Round Table of King Arthur and his Grail Knights. Their mystical sojourns were in fact geomantic forays through the star fields "over the tracks and along the streams that outline their Giant Effigies."

Maltwood had discerned the Arthurian and Grail myth in the landscape. One could make "a complete itinerary and map of the Quest" by plotting out the star forms. Maltwood plotted out the locations of 16 different constellations, most of the 12 on the solar ecliptic (the Sun's annual path) and several outside or inside it, such as Canis Major, Canis Minor, Orion, and Argo Navis.[432]

Later, Mary Caine and others would expand Maltwood's perception of the stars in the landscape, and still others would propose and outline several dozen other landscape zodiacs throughout Britain.[433]

The implication of the zodiac writings of Maltwood, Caine, and others is that in some manner the terrestrial star maps are places for spiritual events. Grail Knights—or more simply, humans interested in revelation—traversed the various landscape nodes hoping to encounter the numinous and gain insights.

Of all the geomantic features described in this book, the landscape zodiac is probably the most widely recognized and discussed. Bear in mind this is only a relative popularity, that is, among Earth Mysteries enthusiasts and researchers. Among the general public, the concept remains unheard of. However, all discussions of landscape zodiacs, however arcane, labor under a fallacy.

The landscape does not have to conform to the conventional outlines of the constellations for there to be a landscape zodiac in a given locality. The suggestion of possible landscape conformities may be valuable, initial clues to the presence of a landscape zodiac, but one must not be too literal in the search for the original pattern. In fact, to expect the landscape to conform, point for point, or even loosely, is also a fallacy and will lead one into dead ends or misattributions.

In a few cases, such as the Glastonbury zodiac, the landscape may "remember" the original imprint of the star map, but in most cases, the conformity is gone, and it does not matter one way or another. But even the Glastonbury zodiac differs considerably from its plotted star positions; it is much larger and has far more constellations than popular belief expects. In the majority of cases, the landscape does not noticeably conform to the star map imprint, though local myths and legends may be valuable clues substantiating the existence of such a star imprint and perhaps its general orientation.

Conceptually, the landscape zodiac is an interactive holographic miniature of an edited version of the galaxy. It contains constellations on both sides of the ecliptic, which is the envisioned annual path of the Sun through the star fields. The 12 signs of Western astrology lie on the ecliptic; the other constellations lie inside it or outside.

Let's establish 13 facts about zodiacs.

First, they are implicit to the Earth's visionary geography and are thus an inherent aspect of the planet's energy anatomy; they are not imprinted, nor are they made by Nature.

Second, there are 432 of them, unequally and asymmetrically distributed across the 12 Albion Plates (see table 9-1). They tend to be on relatively flat areas, allowing for regular and fairly convenient human interaction.

Third, all 432 zodiacs are the same in composition, though they differ radically in size (from one-tenth mile to 108 miles across, based on my current figures, though larger ones presumably exist). There are 72 different sizes with six copies of each size, totalling 432.

Fourth, each zodiac contains 144 constellations consisting of the 12 conventional zodiacal figures presented twice, and 120 other constellations.

Fifth, these 144 constellations are arrayed in two overlapping circles, with 96 in one, 48 in the other; this is 56 more star patterns than recognized by astronomy. The diameter of the circles is equivalent to the Sun's ecliptic.

Sixth, not all 432 zodiacs are "on" at the same time, nor should they be. Globally, their periods of activation and quiescence are predetermined and work like a series of clocks.

Table 9-1: Landscape Zodiacs

Planetary Total: 432

Selected Locations and Physical Ecliptic Diameters:

Boston–Cambridge, Massachusetts, U.S.: 8,720 MY/4.4921212 miles

Northampton, Massachusetts, U.S.: 17,460 MY/ 8.9945454 miles

Eden, New York, U.S.: 220 MY/0.1133625 miles

Foster, Quebec, Canada: 4,440 MY/2.287272 miles

Syracuse, New York, U.S.: 37,600 MY/19.369696 miles

Rochester, New York, U.S.: 9,320 MY/4.801212 miles

Newport, New Hampshire, U.S.: 7,460 MY/3.8430303 miles

Brimfield, Massachusetts, U.S.: 490 MY/0.2524242 miles

South Egremont–Mount Washington, Massachusetts, U.S.: 1,080 MY/0.5563636 miles

Shokan Lake, West Hurley, New York, U.S.: 890 MY/ 0.4584848 miles

Moosehead Lake, Maine, U.S.: 29,820 MY/ 15.361818 miles

Washington, D.C., U.S.: 27,180 MY/14.001818 miles

Mount Balsam Cone, Waynesville, North Carolina, U.S.: 17,460 MY/ 8.9945454 miles

Charlottesville, Virginia, U.S.: 9,990 MY/5.14636363 miles

Kingston-on-Thames, London, England: 8,540 MY/ 4.3993939 miles

Rennes-le-Chateau, France: 10,800 MY/5.5636363 miles

Carnac, France: 42,710 MY/ 22.0021212 miles

Goring-on-Thames, London, England: 27,600 MY/ 14.2181818 miles

Glastonbury, England: 34,860 MY/17.958181 miles

Verdun, France: 126,340 MY/ 65.084242 miles

Hill of Tara (near Dublin), Ireland: 17,460 MY/ 8.99454545 miles

Bilbao, Spain: 7,320 MY/ 3.77090909 miles

Chysauster, Cornwall, England: 7,960 MY/ 4.10060606 miles

Harlech, Wales: 1,800 MY/ 0.9272727 miles

Skipton-Colne-Pendle Hill, Yorkshire, England: 107,460 MY/ 55.358181 miles

Maiden Castle, Dorchester, England: 5,050 MY/ 2.60151515 miles

Rennes, France: 5,370 MY/ 2.7663636 miles

Murtheimne Plain, Ireland: 27,140 MY/13.981212 miles

Eugene, Oregon, U.S.: 34,180 MY/17.607878 miles

San Francisco, California, U.S.: 10,800 MY/ 5.5636363 miles

Chaco Canyon, New Mexico, U.S.: 26,210 MY/ 13.5021212 miles

Santa Fe, New Mexico, U.S.: 18,880 MY/9.7260606 miles

Sedona, Arizona, U.S.: 34,160 MY/17.597575 miles

Monte Alban, Oaxaca, Mexico: 8,290 MY/ 4.270606 miles

Nazca Plain, Peru: 10,800 MY/ 5.5636363 miles

Teotihuacan, Mexico: 6,640 MY/ 3.420606 miles

Palenque, Mexico: 104,000 MY/ 53.575757 miles

Chichen Itza, Mexico: 25,640 MY/13.208484 miles

Rondablikk, Rondane Mountains, Norway: 48,930 MY/25.2063636 miles

Table 9-1 (continued)

Dornach, Switzerland: 13,590 MY/ 7.0009090 miles

The Brocken, Harz Mountains, Germany: 4,620 MY/ 2.380000 miles

Jerusalem, Israel: 18,020 MY/ 9.2830303 miles

Mecca, Saudi Arabia: 14,760 MY/ 7.6036363 miles

Giza, Cairo, Egypt: 17,480 MY/ 9.0048484 miles

Luxor, Egypt: 18,060 MY/ 9.3036363 miles

Baghdad, Iraq: 17,200 MY/ 8.860606 miles

Lhasa, Tibet: 91,240 MY/ 47.002424 miles

Banaras, India: 1,940 MY/ 9.9939393 miles

Little Hartley, Megalong Valley (near Sydney), Australia: 660 MY/0.34000 miles

Troy, Turkey: 46,900 MY/ 24.160606 miles

Mycenae, Greece: 46,900 MY/ 24.160606 miles

Ephesus, Turkey: 28,000 MY/ 14.424242 miles

Cumae, Naples, Italy: 14,500 MY/ 7.4696969 miles

Lincoln, England: 10,050 MY/ 5.17121 miles

Still being researched:

Dublin, Ireland: 14.2 miles

Palm Springs, California, U.S.: 14.2 miles

Silver City, New Mexico, U.S.: 24.5 miles

Alexandria, Egypt: 108 miles

Rome, Italy: 48 miles

Thebes, Greece: 52 miles

Abydos, Egypt: 7 miles

Bimini Island, near Florida, U.S.: 3 miles

NOTE: The diameter of a landscape zodiac is calculated in megalithic yards (MY), a value which is usually rounded off to 2.72 feet. The diameter is given here in miles as well to give one a physical sense of the feature's size. However, each zodiac has an etheric component, which is usually the same size or slightly larger, so the full diameter of a landscape zodiac is roughly double the physical ecliptic.

Seventh, the landscape zodiac is inherently an *interactive* geomantic feature, dependent on the sustained collegial cooperation among humans, elementals, and angels to bring them "on line."

Eighth, the landscape zodiac is an inner spiritual temple that is "built" or illuminated in stages, as the three groups of collaborators progressively activate its parts.

Ninth, of the zodiacs, at most 144 are complete and active in any given time, and 288 are incomplete and inactive.

Tenth, the landscape location of specific stars and constellations in a zodiac is variable and can change in accordance with a geomancer's intent insofar as the geomancer has them implicit within his or her being bodies.

Eleventh, zodiacs will have different astrological energies highlighting their terrain, dependent on which Albion Plate they are in.

Twelfth, landscape zodiacs are well suited for group events on key days, such as Epiphany, Candlemas, Pentecost, Michaelmas, the solstices, and equinoxes.[434]

Thirteenth, it takes 180 years to activate one, which then stays illuminated for 1,080 years. Twenty years after I started working with the Ofanim on zodiacs, only three are minimally illuminated. They have about 160 years to go until "lit."

Life inside a Landscape Zodiac: Reports from Adventurers

Here's an example of what a group can do in a zodiac on one of these spiritually alive days. I was working with a group on the zodiac centered on Northampton, Massachusetts. We had made half a dozen visits to key star points within this nine-mile-wide zodiac over the previous year and assembled on the evening of February 1 to participate with the Ofanim in their Candlemas event. Candlemas, or Imbolc, is one of the classic Celtic solar holidays, a cross-quarter day considered the herald of spring. From the Ofanim's viewpoint, it's a good time to plant your wishes for the coming year as a candle of aspiration.

About 20 of us met in a large house within the zodiac. Earlier in the day, four of us had been with the Ofanim on a nearby mountain, part of the zodiac entrance and the site of one of two domes comprising the temple gates. At midday, the Ofanim had asked that we four each face one of the cardinal directions and ask one of the four primary archangels (Michael, Gabriel, Raphael, Uriel) to be present with us for ten minutes. The event would prepare this zodiac "for the lighting at Candlemas," the Ofanim explained.

Around ten P.M., the members of the group divided up to face the four directions while focussing on their Blazing Star, their bodies surrounded by a pale blue sphere about four feet wide with orange, gold, and amber flames burning on the outside surface. We also participated in the almost palpable Ofanim presence and contributed to their feeling of Love from Above. Finally, each person offered their wishes and programming for the next year to the archangel of their direction, visualizing their aspirations as a candle flame.

While we were doing that, the Ofanim and their archangelic colleagues were "lighting the zodiac." That meant the Light was being poured into this landscape zodiac (co-inhabiting the space with a progressive university town, home of Smith College) from the angelic realm, from the Nefilim through the Elohim to the Serafim (three different angelic families) who were positioned at all the star points in the zodiac. "Then the archangels will energize the respective zodiacs throughout Gaia's being bodies through you and your group."

Was there a particular reason for using this zodiac for Candlemas? "Only that this is where you are now," the Ofanim answered. "Any zodiac would have been equally efficient, though this one has some properties which make it particularly suitable. Candlemas is the beginning of the letting go of the Dove [Holy Spirit] within the phase of the year and the first spark of light in the new year, which dawns tomorrow. This is the first light of spring when many great souls incarnate on this planet to bring the Light in. So there is the possibility for you to program your year in the next few hours before the new light dawns."

Afterwards we shared impressions. One woman said she saw "something like the Northern Lights with pinpoints of light" across the zodiac landscape; she saw our group, as if from above and at a distance "lighting up as a point of light." She saw other similar points of light around the Earth. She gave her candle to the Archangel Uriel and saw many other candles being handed over to the archangelic realm. "I saw all of us under Heaven's spotlight."

Another woman felt uplifted and saw "a golden Buddha baby, laughing, beautiful, surrounded by thousands of points of light. All of Gaia was lit up, inside and out. I felt exhilarated, almost giddy, by the time we finished." A third woman faced East, "which heralds the winds of change, clearing out old energies that are inappropriate. I sensed a huge broom sweeping out the landscape."

The smaller zodiacs also lend themselves wonderfully to group events, but of a different nature. In this case all the participants can be arrayed across the small-diameter zodiac as if it were merely a large meditation hall.

Some of the zodiacs are as small as one-tenth mile across, which means you can encompass a virtual hologram of the galaxy in a physical space so small you could shout across a field to other participants.[435] Over the course of a year, I directed three group "innings" at a very small landscape zodiac in New York state. I had spent many months preparing the site, with frequent visits and collegial infusions of starlight into the template. By prearrangement with the gnomes and Ofanim, I had charted out the approximate locations of the major constellations and meditated at these key sites, allowing the Ofanim to infuse me with angelic light, and through me, the landscape by way of the earth elementals, the gnomes.

I invited a dozen or so people to join me on Pentecost (June 3 that year) out in the landscape zodiac. We made some processions at dawn and midday to key energy features in the zodiac, keeping our attention focused on the Blazing Star within us and allowing this light to infiltrate the landscape. Then we went to the Polaris node; Polaris is the cosmic North Pole, located in Ursa Minor, Avebury's counterpoint in the cosmos.

We attuned to our own Blazing Stars at Polaris, then I led the group around the ecliptic, dropping off a person at one of the larger stars in the constellations. At a prearranged time, everyone spent 30 minutes focusing on their Blazing Stars. I suggested each person collect impressions of the metaphorical or spiritual aspects of the constellation in which they sat.

It was an exhilarating, revelatory event, and everyone sensed the experience's uniqueness and value. Their comments were intriguing and in effect the best empirical "proof" of this geomantic feature, as these excerpts show:

A woman occupying Praesepe (the Beehive) in Cancer said, "Cancer is our mother, and I felt tremendous Goddess energy. I had thoughts of corn, nourishment, and bees, which give the Father Sun energy to Mother Earth who sends up flowers. I became thankful for this energy, so I began pouring this energy back into the Earth. I invited the

gnomes and fairies to visit me. I sensed Creation happening and came back to my body like surfing waves of energy."

A participant at Nunki, the sigma star in Sagittarius, said: "I felt I started this process several days ago, and I felt a stillness come over me this morning. This intensified when I took my position in Sagittarius. I got a good fire going in my star then saw a huge centaur of light standing over the whole zodiac. Much of our animal nature, the unconscious, was rising, being alchemically changed. All the wild things outside us are part of the redemption of Nature through man. The centaur represents our misunderstanding of our wild animal nature. It's time we became one with this.

"I felt I became a hollow statue. I saw points of light where the people sat on the ecliptic. These points formed an arch. I also saw two gyres of light where I was sitting. I felt myself in a crowd of what the Druids would call 'companions,' the wood folk. I went into the prayer posture of hatha yoga and felt a light go from me into the Earth then come back up again in a wave. It's people's attention that will make these images in the landscape live again. I've been working with Druid, Celtic rituals, and Earth energies for 20 years, but I can honestly say I've been waiting that long to do this kind of complete group ritual with the Earth to understand subtle energies."

A man sitting at Giedi (alpha Capricorn) reported: "I saw a circle of light emerge around the ecliptic. I knew the Blazing Star was working. It was magnificent and contained all of us in the fulfillment of a purpose to which we all agreed earlier. My star went nova, and the gnomes lit their torches from my body and amused themselves especially with lighting them off my toes."

Sitting at Sadalsuud (beta Aquarius), a woman observed: "I saw the whole gestalt of elimination. Water is not just fluidity and nurturance, but it purifies and dissolves particulates. There were lots of gnomes taking the firebrands from me. I sensed the angelic realm. There were beams of light, mostly blue rays in this constellation. The angels were feeding these blue rays with water and light. The water was to purify, eliminate. It's the water you use for blessing and baptism."

At Regulus (alpha Leo), a man commented: "I felt a strong heart glow. I saw a lion crouching. I felt I was sitting in a big crater, on a vortex that spun counterclockwise, which to me is the direction of change. There was a lot of Sun imagery. I saw a lion's mane made of the Sun's rays. It's very much male energy seeding the void of space, moving light through darkness. I saw sparks of lightning shooting out orange and red fire. I sat in inside a light column and was aware of a huge, crowned ruler with a fiery sword."

A woman seated next to me at Polaris (alpha Ursa Major) observed: "I saw the feet of a huge bronze Buddha. This bronze-gold Buddha [probably the zodiac's Albion] was lying on his back. There was a multifaceted white stone at his brow chakra, which then became a lotus as it opened. As the lotus opened, it became a circle of angels. As I looked down into this, there was a whirling golden tunnel like moving honey. There were small beings climbing all over this Buddha. I saw the root system of a huge tree, and within that, thousands of people were reaching up with their hands in celebration."

As for myself, I created a light pillar from the ground to the top of the zodiac dome and made it wide enough to include the ecliptic, the people situated around it, and the Blue Dish—several miles across in total. The Ofanim took on angelic form and streamed by the hundreds down the light pillar and out into the zodiac. I was aware of everyone in the group, one at a time, in a kind of continuous lighthouse sweep of faces. Each person waved to me as he or she came into focus, and the Ofanim amplified the star of each.

On another occasion, I assembled a group at the same tiny zodiac, but this time everyone sat within Canis Major, the guardian of the zodiac. I suggested that after they established their Blazing Star, they visualize the Albion of this zodiac as a humanlike being laid out on his back on a table of stars—the half-mile-wide landscape zodiac in which we sat. I encouraged the people to whisper in Albion's ears how it will be when he wakes. Keep in mind the observation quoted earlier that there seemed to be a golden Buddha in the midst of the landscape zodiac. That was a perception of Albion.

One woman commented: "I tried to feel his essence. His body turned to gold, revealing him as a great holographic being. My Star went to his forehead, and I blew something into it. Blood formed in his body. The stars of other people went to his forehead. More blood formed in his body. This circle of people formed a huge window of light around Albion. This work took centuries."

A man said: "I saw Albion's solar plexus. Flames came out of his forehead. I placed my hands on his head. My heart area hurt as I did this, and I felt jabs in my back and a shortness of breath. I sent peace, love, joy to Albion. I told him: You are a spark of the God I AM. I became a cone of energy. I felt all of us were doing parallel healings on Albion, that we generated all the ray colors. When I sent Albion feelings of peace, the pain in my heart subsided. I kept hearing: 'We are a divine spark of the essence.' Everyone held hands around Albion. I saw the stars in everyone on the edge of a disc, or table, that shone brightly."

Another woman participant observed: "I saw Albion as a golden being on a rotating table. The glow from his body concealed the presence of the other people here. I remembered a dream I had last night. I was interacting with disparate parts of myself—teacher, healer, junk collector, homosexual—but I didn't know who I was at the core. The essence of all these pieces is you, Albion, I told him. I felt Albion was listening, speaking back to me, even though he's in a coma. I told him it's okay to wake up. It's safe, things are falling into place."

A woman noted: "I saw Albion as a beautiful being, golden, androgynous. I let the negativities in my mind float off. I reminded Albion of his beauty."

Let's take stock of what we're describing. Rudolf Steiner, the clairvoyant founder of Anthroposophy, made the prescient remark that cosmology equals organology. This may sound ponderous, but it's rivetingly to the point.

Steiner said that the human constitution—physical and subtle bodies—represents the entire cosmos and its angelic hierarchies turned inside out, compacted into a human form. He said that when you die and return to the spiritual worlds, you now behold your body—its generic original, the archetypal human form—all *around* you as the cosmos.

Incarnate, we bear the cosmos within us as our body and its organs and systems; disincarnate, we behold the world again *outside* us, as our cosmic environment. All that is within us was once outside; humankind is woven out of the cosmos, and humans on Earth stand each as a shrunken universe. Each of our internal organs was produced and shaped by cosmic forces, Steiner said, and we bear all the stars, planets, and world-creating angelic hierarchies within us.[436]

Steiner doesn't use the term Albion, but he implies it when he says every organ we bear is "the terrestrial counterpart of a divine-spiritual being." The entire cosmos originally appeared as a "gigantic being," and the whole man is "seen as a gigantic cosmic Being appearing as the sum-total, as the inner-organic, cooperative activity of generations of Gods." We behold "Cosmic Man through human organology," which is why self-knowledge is also cosmic knowledge.[437]

This is why it is worthwhile for us, individually and collectively, to interact with landscape zodiacs. When we array ourselves as a group across a landscape zodiac, or meditate there on our own, we are within the body of that "gigantic cosmic Being" as expressed on the Earth. We are within the cosmic organs of Albion; we are among the smithy-crafted devices and objects of the celestial smith's forge, the archetypes of the periodic table of the elements and the 132 constellations.

The amazing opportunity presented by the zodiacs is that while incarnate we can have an experience otherwise reserved for when we're disincarnate. We can behold, and interact with, our inside world projected outside us in the landscape.

Let's remember the key fact: When we sit or walk within an Albion, we are inside ourselves, in our cosmic original form, extrapolated outside us as a mirror. When we walk the landscape zodiac's ecliptic or through the constellations, we are *walking in Albion*.[438] It's like Isaac Asimov's science fiction story *Fantastic Voyage*, in which scientists travel in a miniature spaceship through a seemingly gigantic human body. In the zodiac, our consciousness is the spaceship, and the star fields of Albion comprise the gigantic human body we travel through.

It is a *reciprocal* activity: The landscape zodiac and its Albion help us recall our original cosmic totality, and our process of recall reconstitutes and gives life to the extrapolated landscape expression of Albion for the planet. Conscious cooperation, reciprocal maintenance with Man and Gaia, produces an expansion of consciousness in beings on the surface of the planet and within Gaia.

When you interact with a landscape zodiac, you are simultaneously activating the zodiac within your psyche. Your being bodies become attuned to this energy pattern, and wherever you go thereafter, such as to other zodiacs, you will have an effect on that external pattern. Knowing you carry the imprint actually amplifies its effect on the new location.

What a Turtle and a Zodiac Dome Have in Common

The ultimate boundary of a landscape zodiac is determined by a zodiac dome. These are like the star domes, but much larger, with a different purpose. There are 432 zodiac domes on the Earth, one for each zodiac, usually about twice the size of the combined diameters of the physical and etheric ecliptics.

For example, the Glastonbury zodiac (physical ecliptic 17.9 miles in diameter) has a zodiac dome that is 79.786091 miles across. That means that overlaying Glastonbury, its zodiac, its star domes, and other geomantic features, and a fair bit of Somerset, is a massive dome nearly 80 miles wide and about 40 miles high at its topmost center.

As with the sizes of the landscape zodiacs, the zodiac domes around the planet vary considerably in size from 0.50365 miles to 289.16164 miles, based on my current smallest and largest zodiac diameter figures. But their number must be added to the 1,746 star domes, giving us 2,178 etheric energy canopies of light of varying sizes. To these we add the 12 Universe Domes, discussed earlier, each overlaying an Albion Plate, for a planetary total of 2,190 domes.

The zodiac dome does not generate a landscape zodiac. It activates and projects a star pattern implicit in the etheric field of a given diameter of physical landscape. The star map is actually blueprinted into the atomic structure of matter composing the Earth as a kind of planetary genetic program, just as, for example, male pattern baldness is genetically imprinted in certain men. The zodiac blueprint is in the Earth's genes, loosely speaking. This same pattern, the Ofanim explain, is similarly blueprinted in the human constitution, though not exactly in a genetic and thus physically quantifiable sense. This trilevel resonance (human, Earth, galaxy) makes it possible for us to interact constructively with a landscape zodiac.

Thus the landscape zodiac, as a virtual galaxy, is somewhat self-contained within the aegis of the zodiac dome, yet there is also a connection above. "Zodiac domes are different from regular star domes as they have a star projection feature like in a planetarium," the Ofanim state. "Each of the zodiac domes has little holes in it, allowing starlight to penetrate to specific points of the Earth. Each star has a relevance. Each pinpoint of light is a thread through space. These threads create an energy matrix in the electric field around the Earth. The electric body of the Earth is resonated by these beams."

Thus in subtle ways the stars in a terrestrial zodiac are connected to the zodiac dome and the actual stars, yet they are still in some respects virtual presences, a self-contained hologram projected and sustained by the dome.

The zodiac domes themselves correspond to star maps, each with different emphases, relevant to a particular star system and orientation. In other words, while domes correspond to individual high magnitude stars, individual zodiac domes correspond to constellations. We could say the dome over the Glastonbury zodiac, for instance, hypothetically corresponds to the constellation Virgo. Again, this is not a matter of archeoastronomical alignment, but hologram copresence: Virgo is represented on Earth through this zodiac dome.

Landscape zodiac work is not something you finish, or should want to, in one day (see table 9-1 for some locations). It takes weeks, years. Your system has to assimilate these strong, possibly unfamiliar energies, and you don't want to overload your physical and being bodies.[439]

Second, what you are doing, potentially, has an energy impact on those living within the territory overlit by the landscape zodiac. Those people have to be able to tolerate and digest these new energies. Remember the dimmer switch analogy. You are turning the knob a few degrees, and though everything now gets a little brighter, this is still a strong light and must be absorbed gradually. Pockets of darkness will resist.

The complete list of landscape zodiacs represents an ultimate design parameter for the Earth, a kind of logarithmic expansion table from the smallest so far discovered (0.11 miles) to the largest (108 miles).[440] We could think of zodiac sizes in terms of sizes among flowers, from bluets to sunflowers. With flowers, each in accordance with its size reflects certain movements of the planet and Sun; it's the same with zodiacs: Their tropism is to do with constellations.

The larger zodiacs have an additional feature the Ofanim describe as a zodiac amplifier. The 360 zodiacs whose physical ecliptic diameter is ten miles or wider each have a zodiac amplifier. Here's how the Ofanim explain this feature:

"Zodiac amplifiers have different parts. They can be either latent or active, and they have different outputs. Some have the potential to broadcast to the whole stellar matrices above, modifying all of those suns thousands of light years away. Some amplifiers do not have this potential. The landscape zodiacs affect the galaxy if the amplifiers are turned on. As above, so below. The light from these stars in the galaxy reaches the Earth equally when the stars on the Earth are active through conscious interface with a zodiac and amplification. The stars below feed back to those that are above."

That is a remarkable prospect. We work on a landscape zodiac, along the lines suggested ear-lier with the group experiences, for example, with the cooperation of the angelic and elemental families, and bring the landscape star map to a point of activation. Then the virtual stars on the landscape start feeding back to the real stars overhead in the galaxy, and the reciprocal exchange begins.

Our experiences in walking the star fields in the 360 zodiacs that have amplifiers then repercuss on the galaxy itself and in some way modify those great stars. Not only is the galaxy, as the *above*, templated around us in multiple copies in the form of landscape zodiacs, but the *below*, when activated, has a positive feedback influence on the original. Then the two systems, the above and below, are in living *reciprocal* exchange, like an open modem link or, better, a chat room.

Let's look at the structure of a zodiac amplifer, based on my experiences of one outside the Rondane Mountains zodiac in south-central Norway. That zodiac, affiliated with the Earth's primary *Ananda-kanda* chakra and original Garden of Eden template, as explained in previous chapters, and known as the Hills of Heaven zodiac, is about 50 miles in diameter (including physical and etheric ecliptics); the zodiac dome enclosing both halves is 111.98891 miles wide. That tells us the three zodiac amplifier features, though outside the ecliptics and situated ten to 50 miles away, are still encompassed by the zodiac dome.

The zodiac amplifier can be conceived as like a three-part tail to the main torso of the zodiac. The three features are set on the Oroboros line that passes through the zodiac, from the double-domed gates (most zodiacs have two intertwined domes as their "front door") out the other end of the zodiac dome. In a sense, the zodiac dome, two zodiac halves, two domes, and amplifier are part of a single chakra template, which when activated can transmit information and light back to the stars above.

We enter the template through chakra six, the brow center, at the double domes; the two zodiac halves are chakras four and five, heart and throat; the three amplifier features are chakras three, two, and one, solar plexus, sacral, and base center; the zodiac dome is chakra seven, the crown. The three zodiac features, when activated, become linked by way of the Blue Dish laid under each by the "grid engineer" or geomancer preparing this large landscape system. Thus three linked Blue Dishes set on the Oroboros line contain the amplifier features; the placement on the Oroboros line enables the three linked Blue Dishes to be in communication with the rest of the system, the two zodiac halves, double domes, and zodiac dome.

When our group installed the Blue Dishes at these three zodiac amplifier sites in August 2000, we made them large enough so their edges would touch, making the three a linked system. That made the Blue Dishes about five to ten miles wide, which, incidentally, is no harder than making them one yard wide. In this zodiac, the edges of the physical and etheric ecliptics are about 35 to 40 miles from Blue Dish Number 3.

In a strange, perhaps amusing, and certainly metaphorical sense, this system reminds me of a turtle. The head is the double-domed entrance; the thick-shelled back corresponds to the two zodiac halves; the three Blue Dishes and their geomantic amplifier features to the turtle's tail. When the zodiac halves are activated and the zodiac amplifier parts have been previously prepared, the tail rises like a humming antenna transmitting the light and information to the galaxy.

For the most part, this is merely a descriptive metaphor to describe something complex and not much like anything in our physical world. Yet. . . .

Long ago the Vedic psychics found the turtle image similarly useful when they referred to Vishnu's second incarnation or avatara as Kurma the Tortoise.

This was way back in the antique days of creation when the gods were proposing to churn the Ocean of Milk for the ambrosia of immortality. They needed something thick and hard to put the churning stick against. The turtle's shell was perfect. Vishnu agreed to help out and turned into a turtle. The gods put Mount Mandara (the churning stick) on his back as he rested at the bottom of the sea, and they churned, using his shell like the bottom millstone in a mill.

Based on my experiences in the Soma temple (refer to chapter 5), I believe the zodiac dome is the same as the Kurma tortoise avatara of Vishnu. In the Soma temple (accessed through several different geomantic sites), I saw the Soma vat in the center of a temple; the curved ceiling was made of many dozens of crystalline windows or facets, which, when penetrated, were revealed to be the faces of gods, looking adoringly down upon the Soma vat.[441]

I'm suggesting here that the gods in the ceiling of the Soma temple are the same as the 144 constellations projected by the zodiac domes and as the Vishnu-Kurma turtle. The turtle's bottom shell corresponds to the landscape zodiac that receives the star projections and Soma-fed star consciousness of the constellation gods. Thus the turtle represents the complete system of zodiac dome (top shell) projecting the starlight of 144 constellations down to the landscape zodiac (bottom shell), the real and virtual stars equally "fed" by Soma.

To be consistent with the turtle image, the inside part between the two shells, where the turtle proper resides (head and internal organs) corresponds to Albion, the Cosmic Man generated by the confluence of real and virtual stars. We might think of Albion as the turtle's innards as the sleeping Vishnu, the unawakened Christ essence residing in the Anthropos projected upon the Earth. The Soma churned from the Ocean of Milk becomes food for consciousness, pineal gland brow chakra nourishment for the soon-to-awaken Albion, the distilled essence of perfect and continuous wakefulness, the food all gods want.

The Turtle's Planetary Anatomy—Organs and Chakras of Albion

The turtle image, a living being of organs and biological processes wedged between two thick carapaces, is also useful in discussing Albion.

Let's start with his head. The issue at this level of geomantic extrapolation is developing conscious cognition for the emerging Cosmic Man expressed upon the Earth, and that is the purview of the constellation Cepheus, the seventh in our eight Camalate and *Ananda-kanda* inner heart chakra constellations.

In star lore, Cepheus was the king of the Ethiopians, husband of Cassiopeia (also a constellation), and the father of Andromeda (another constellation), the maiden exposed sacrificially to a sea monster but rescued by Zeus's son Perseus. Cepheus was one of the 50 Argonauts in Jason's Golden Fleece expedition. Classical star charts assign 19 stars to Cepheus, who is pictured as a standing king with outstretched arms; the star figure, abstractly seen, is a square of four stars with a fifth star on the top like a peaked roof near Polaris.

Though the star myth of Cepheus is scant and not widely known and the constellation itself is inconspicuous, apparently in ancient times (before the fifth century B.C.), Cepheus was highly regarded as the father of the Greek Royal Family; Andromeda was the mother of at least seven named mythic progeny. The Babylonians associated Cepheus with Enlil (the Greek Zeus; and Bel and Baal), who was in charge of one of three heavenly roads; the king of the city-state of Babylon was his Earthly counterpart, the Babylonians con-

tended. According to the Ofanim, Cepheus's contribution to Albion (and us) is conscious cognition. This is a star quality Albion obviously needs to achieve his prophecied awakening.

As a singular global being, Albion has body parts, organs, and chakras. These are large geomantic structures, often subsuming many subsidiary ones. Let's start with one "organ" called the Three Perpetual Choirs; it is sketchily known among Earth Mysteries researchers and Celtic enthusiasts, but for the most part, little is understood as to its true nature or geomantic function.

The primary textual reference is in the ancient Welsh Triads (*Trioedd Ynys Prydein*), an intriguing repository of hints, clues, and enigmas from old Wales. This document speaks of the three *Cyfangan*, which means a harmonious song or an uninterrupted choir. The ninetieth Triad declares that there are "Three Perpetual Harmonies of the Island of Britain," located at the Island of Afallach, Caer Garadawg, and Bangor. At each of these places are assembled 2,400 religious men or saints, and during each of the 24 hours in a day, 100 saints devote themselves "ceaselessly" in prayer and service to God, "without rest for ever."[442] Thus the full system has 7,200 saints singing prayerfully all the time.

Scholars have exercised their imagination in trying to figure out where these three sites lay. The Island of Afallach is easy: That's Glastonbury. For Caer Garadawg, Salisbury, York, and Stonehenge have been proposed; and for Bangor, the assumption is generally accepted that Bangor, Wales, was meant.

John Michell proposes that the three *Cyfangan* are Llantwit Major, on the southeast coast of Glamorgan in Wales, Glastonbury in Somerset, and Stonehenge in Wiltshire. They lie equidistant (38.9 miles apart) on an arc, which is part of an hypothesized circle 126 miles wide, with an ancient pagan site called White-Leaved Oak and Midsummer Hill in Gloucestershire in the middle. White-Leaved Oak, Michell says, sits at the junction of three counties in a valley of the Malvern Hills that is reputedly the oldest geological formation in Britain. White-Leaved Oak has an ancient though vague reputation as a sanctuary and as "a significant point in the sacred geography of archaic Britain."[443]

Michell's deductions and map plottings are astute but mistaken in one respect, for which he cannot be faulted. The Triads themselves are mistaken in assigning the third *Cyfangan* to Bangor. It's not there, according to the Ofanim. Rather it's at Lichfield, north of Birmingham, site of an old cathedral.[444]

Let's start with the basics. The Three Perpetual Choirs are Albion's lungs, and the Choirs of 7,200 saints are singing to Gaia. Here's how the Ofanim put it:

"Over the landscape of England, three heavenly Choirs were established and activated from a divine source. The Choirs are not found anywhere else on Earth. They are reflections of a heavenly model related to three different aspects of consciousness translated to Earth, where they will be revealed later in Man's evolution should he develop along the lines intended for him. The Choirs were more active in the past in their long history. Their activation again is imminent through human consciousness involved in healing. Even so, in the astral body of Gaia, they are still active. The Choirs are singing to the Earth."

What are they singing? The theme music of Albion, which changes in every epoch. Formerly, it had been Faith, Hope, and Charity, but now in our time, these themes are changing to Humanitarianism (Glastonbury Choir), Individuation (Lichfield Choir), and Idealism (Llantwit Major Choir). Obviously we should not take this literally. Rather, we might better think of this as sound patterns or mantras emanating from these places to underlie and catalyze new, desired states of consciousness.

White-Leaved Oak in a sense is a fourth Choir, but at a different level from the three Cyfangan. It is at the center of a 124-mile-wide sphere that encompasses the Three Perpetual Choirs. It is the Blazing Star center-point within the sphere.

Further, White-Leaved Oak is the etheric umbilicus for the Albion of the Virgo Albion Plate, which includes the British Isles and France. That means it is the place in the Virgo Albion's geomythic body equivalent to where the Blazing Star sits in our own individual body, two inches above the belly button and two inches inside. Functionally, this means White-Leaved Oak, as the Virgo Albion's etheric umbilicus, is like Avebury, the Earth's primary umbilicus.

There are 12 etheric umbilicus points on the Earth, one for each Albion Plate. Each is a holographic copy of the prime one (the thirteenth) at Avebury. These are the Dhruva Anchor Points.

What is this umbilicus connected to? Polaris, the Ofanim's "white hole" at the "top" of our galaxy. "The white hole is a beam of light, for Polaris is a bright star," they comment. "White-Leaved Oak is a major point of influence for Britain. It contains implications not only for the immediate locality, but for all of England and its egregor, Grand Britannia, as well as France's, the rooster."

At one level, White-Leaved Oak is the center of a four-part geomantic structure known as the Three Perpetual Choirs that compose the lungs of the planetary Albion. Let's look now at the next level of geomantic expression and see how this site, and others, are organs within an Albion Plate. But even stating only this, we can see how one site, such as White-Leaved Oak, can have a planetary and a regional (Albion Plate) function at the same time.

One of the Earth's 12 Albion Plates takes in all of the British Isles and France, and within or over one-half of this landmass lies an Albion, his

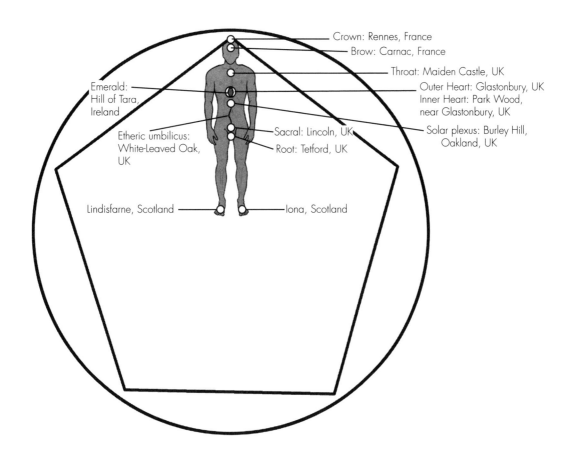

Crown: Rennes, France
Brow: Carnac, France
Throat: Maiden Castle, UK
Emerald: Hill of Tara, Ireland
Outer Heart: Glastonbury, UK
Inner Heart: Park Wood, near Glastonbury, UK
Etheric umbilicus: White-Leaved Oak, UK
Sacral: Lincoln, UK
Root: Tetford, UK
Solar plexus: Burley Hill, Oakland, UK
Lindisfarne, Scotland
Iona, Scotland

9-1. Geomantic Sites in the Virgo Albion of the British Isles and France. Current astrological influence: Virgo. The Albion Plate occupies one-twelfth of the Earth's surface.

head in France, the rest of his torso in the British Isles. The distribution of energy points within his large geomythic body—or in any of the other 11 Albions at this level—as a generic human figure may look distorted, odd, implausible. We must remember that the energy points and their interrelationships in an Albion Plate are based on energy connections, not topography (see figure 9-1 and table 9-2).

Albion fills only half the diameter of the Albion Plate because he is inside the Kav, or Line of Light, which enters only one-half the Vacated Space.

This is easier to understand when we remember that Albion really is a *rotundum*, a spherical being. He is not ultimately linear. Picture Albion as a spherical being filled with many energy centers and bounded by the five geometric sides of the pentagon that is the Albion Plate.

This geomantic feature (both the Albion Plate and the Albion) has nine major chakras (the heart has three parts), 72 minor chakras (such as feet and

---

Table 9-2: Geomantic Features at Major and Minor Chakras in the Virgo Albion

MAJOR:

1. Root Chakra: Tetford, Lincolnshire, England
   Features: Dome, Golden Egg, Silver Egg, Mount Olympus, Tree of Life, Lily, Palladium, Gnome Egg, Dragon, Grail Castle, Stargate, Soma Temple

2. Sacral Chakra: Lincoln, Lincolnshire, England
   Features: Landscape Zodiac, Lucifer Binding Point, Cosmic Egg, Dome

3a. Solar Plexus: Burley Hill, Oakham, Rutland, England
   Features: Mount Olympus, Golden Child, Epiphany Focus

3b. Etheric Umbilicus (not a chakra): White-Leaved Oak, Midsummer Hill, Malverns, England
   Features: Blazing Star for Virgo Albion, Avenue of Trees, Dome

4a. Outer Heart or *Anahata*: Glastonbury, Somerset, England
   Features: Domes, Dragon, Avenue of Trees, Avalon, Cretan Labyrinth, Underworld Entrance, Arc of Developing Consciousness, Pointer's Ball, Grail Castle, Interdimensional Portal, Tree of Life, Soma Temple, Shambhala Doorway, Golden Egg, Silver Egg, Perpetual Choir, Vibrating Stone, Ixion's Wheel, Landscape Zodiac, Mobile Shambhalic Focus

4b. Inner Heart or *Ananda-kanda*: Park Wood, Butleigh, Somerset, England
   Features: Reputed center of the physical ecliptic zodiac

4c. Emerald: Hill of Tara, near Dublin, Ireland
   Features: Dome, Mount Olympus, Palladium, Avalon, Landscape Zodiac, Gnome Egg

5. Throat Chakra: Maiden Castle, Dorchester, Dorset, England
   Features: Hill-fort, Landscape Zodiac, Dome

6. Brow Chakra: Carnac, Brittany, France
   Features: Earth Dome for Sirius, Landscape Zodiac, Standing Stones (*Menhir*), Stone Rows

7. Crown Chakra: Rennes, France
   Features: Landscape Zodiac

MINOR:

1. Left Foot Chakra: Iona Island, Hebrides, Scotland
   Features: Earth Dome for Canopus, Chakra Template

2. Right Foot Chakra: Lindisfarne Island, Scotland

---

hands), and 144,000 sub-minor centers (the Hindus call these *nadis*). All the major centers and some of the minor ones have complex geomantic features. Note the layering of geomantic aspects, such as at Albion's outer heart chakra in Glastonbury where there is a landscape zodiac, which itself has an Albion with a landscape outer heart chakra.

In some cases, geomantic sites that occupy a chakra position within an Albion Plate also fulfill a chakra role for the planetary Albion. Glastonbury England is an example. Within the Virgo Albion, it is the *Anahata* or outer heart center; within the global Albion, it is also the outer heart. But two other sites complete the global heart chakra: The Hills of Heaven landscape zodiac in the Rondane Mountains of Norway is the inner, *Ananda-kanda* heart center, and El Templo del Santa Maria churchyard (El Tule, for short) near Oaxaca in southern Mexico is the Emerald. The three together are the grounding points for Albion's global heart. But that's only at one level.

Increasingly, Earth Mysteries researchers and psychics are publishing claims for planetary chakra identifications. It is less likely that most of these researchers are wrong in their assignment of specific chakras than they are as to the level of the system in which these chakras exist. A site can be a throat chakra within an Albion (Maiden Castle in the Virgo Albion), but not necessarily within the global Albion. The issue of planetary chakras is complex, perhaps the most so of all features.

Let's tally the total number of possible Earth chakras. Every landscape zodiac has an Albion with 81 chakras (9 major, 72 minor), and there are 432 zodiacs on the planet. That totals 34,992 chakras. Next, each of the 12 Albion Plates has 81 chakras; that's 972 more chakras. Then the singular planetary Albion has 81 chakras. The planetary total is 36,045. And none of this counts the 144,000 nadis at all three of these levels of Albions, or the chakra templates.

In fact, it is still more complicated, for each of the seven major chakras for the singular planetary Albion has seven aspects or levels. Here the heart center is treated as a single energy center. That's another 42 chakras to add to the list. If we consider this aspect alone, there are 49 chakras, even of the seven having seven levels, but since one level of these seven is included in the earlier tally of nine major chakras for the planetary Albion, then there are only 42 additional ones. Think of this as an onion with seven skins surrounding the planet; on each onion skin are seven major chakras, except, level to level, they don't always match up.

Our total for Earth chakras is an astonishing 36,097. Frankly, there are probably even more.

"Gaia has chakras on many levels," the Ofanim note, probably understating things. But they are explicit on one matter to do with chakras: Across the surface of the Earth are 7 + 1 places where the chakras in all the levels align. These are called major nodal points, or primary Earth chakras.

Think of the onion skin again. There are seven places only where the same chakra in each skin of the onion lines up to form a column of, for example, the throat center, the throat chakra in seven expressions. The eighth major nodal point corresponds to what the Ofanim call the "extra monadic point," or the Blazing Star. Technically this is not a chakra, though it is located at the junction of the second and third chakras. Everywhere else within the Earth's multiple chakra layers, each layer may have a different chakra corresponding to the same site.[445]

Each country has a major nodal point that focuses energy for that region. But two things must be qualified in this sentence: First, "country" means each of the 72 significant landmass divisions to which an egregor was assigned; and second, these are a subsidiary level of major nodal points, not part of the eight. For the purposes of distinguishing these, let's call them Energy Focusing Nodes.

These 72 Energy Focusing Nodes are actually the same as the global Albion's 72 minor chakras. They are allocated parallel to the distribution of the 72 egregors, which as I explained earlier was originally by landmass subdivisions. For example, in the case of Norway, one of the Earth's 72 significant landmass subdivisions, the egregor is a moose, and the Energy Focusing Node, or minor chakra in the global Albion, is situated in close proximity to its grounding point. Where an egregor is grounded is often equivalent in location and emphasis to a country's national gods or holiest shrines or sometimes its birthplace or origin.

The major energy nodes, or primary Earth chakras, all relay planetary energies, both from the planetary spheres (the seven Heavens) and the actual planets of the solar system, but the minor Earth chakras do not. Rather, they transmit the energies of the angelic realm as focused through what Qabala calls the 72 Names of God, the *Shemhamforesh*. The 72 Names are understood to be God's 72-syllabled complete Name. Each of the 72 minor chakras represents one of the 72 Names (or syllables), which is actually an angel that bears or intones the Name.

Here is one way of picturing these minor chakras: A vertical pillar of light is grounded in the Earth. It resembles a downward-facing arrow or a Shiva lingam; it pulses with light like a pipe full of water. This water or energy fountains out at the pillar's base and flows out into the landscape. The pillar contains a complete major chakra sequence of seven to one, crown to root, the higher energies being stepped down in that order before they reach the ground.

Irish myth gives us a probable Energy Focusing Node for that landmass, one of the original 72, and a vivid description of its function. That place is Uisneach, said to be the exact center of all of Ireland and that country's navel, set at the meeting place of Ireland's five major divisions (Ulster, Leinster, Munster, Connacht; the navel was at the center of the fifth, the Meath of Midhe).

The Stone of Divisions (a large craggy lump of limestone also called the Catstone because it resembles a squatting cat) marks the spot. The Hill of Uisneach, a 602-foot-tall prominence, is visible from great distances away, located 12 miles west of Mullingar in County West Meath; it is also referred to as *Umbilicus Hiberniae*, Navel of Ireland. The grey stone stands on the southwest slope, about 90 feet from the hill's summit.

Irish tradition holds that it was the legendary Mount Killaraus, the site of Stonehenge before it was moved to England, and that it was also known as the Hill of Balor, a one-eyed giant.[446]

The prime ceremony celebrated at Uisneach in ancient Ireland was the Feast or Fire of Bel, the Irish Sun god, celebrated on May 1, known as the Celtic fire festival, Beltaine. Legend says Ireland's first Beltaine bonfires ever were lit on Uisneach, then everywhere else throughout the island.

The Irish landscape itself seems to be organized to support this omphalic function. The topography of Ireland has been likened to a great saucer; the island's center is low in elevation while mountain ridges ring the island along the coastline. This shape is remarkably like an etheric Blue Dish, a physical echo perhaps of the underlying geomantic reality of the entire island.

At the Hill or Uisneach, the glacial erratic, also called the *Umbilicus Hibernia*, marks the center of Midhe, the fifth part of Ireland, once believed to be the meeting place of the mystical and mundane, of the Otherworld dimension that holds the other four sections in balance.

According to one observer, "The numinous energy which pours from the Centre illumines the landscape and animates the very rocks and trees—an 'atmosphere' remarked upon frequently by visitors to Eire [Ireland]."[447] The twin fires lit on the Hill of Uisneach at Beltaine are meant to symbolize the two godly eyes of Eriu, the original goddess of Ireland, and the source of its name. Eriu's eyes survey all of Ireland from the Uisneach prominence in the midst of the Beltaine fires, understood by the ancient Irish to be a spiritualizing force. The Beltaine fire ritual at Uisneach was called *Oenach*, or May Eve great assembly in honor of Eriu, the Irish conception of their land's egregor.[448]

The net of the planet, its geomantic gridwork and geomythic body, is equipped at many levels to receive, ground, and distribute cosmic energies. The Earth chakras ground and represent the sequence of planetary energies (again, both the planetary spheres and the physical planets), but another geomantic feature collects specific planetary energies almost like a rain barrel. These are called Planetary Energy Receptors, and Earth has three: at Easter Island, Mount Ida in Crete, and Mount Meru in the South Pacific.

All three are located on solitary islands: Crete is in the Mediterranean; remote Easter Island, several thousand miles due west of Chile in the Pacific Ocean; Mount Meru on an invisible, unapproachable, and thereby ultra-remote island off the southeast coast of the South Island of New Zealand.

You need some astrological knowledge to understand these receptors. But let's say that over the course of a century different planets will have a strong or pronounced influence on the Earth. During that time, probably a matter of years, the Planetary Energy Receptors are tuned to that specific planet like a radar dish.

Since there are three receptors, the Earth can collect three "flavors" of extraplanetary energy and light: positive, negative, and neutral. These valences are consistent with the three subtle energy channels along the spine (*pingala* [Sun], *ida* [Moon], and *sushumna* [neutral]) and the three Oroboros Lines that do not correspond to the 12 astrological signs.

Crete handles the incoming positive planetary energy, Easter Island the negative, and Mount Meru the neutral. For negative and positive here it's useful to think in astrological terms of the types of energies generated by planetary alignments, such as a square (negative) or a conjunction or trine (positive). The effects on consciousness of these various planetary relationships can be experienced (and thereby interpreted) dualistically, as good, favorable, and positive, or bad, difficult, and negative.

What does a Planetary Energy Receptor look like? Let's take the one at Mount Ida on Crete. This mountain is 8,058 feet high and has two neighboring peaks, almost as tall: Lefka Ori (8,045 feet) and Mount Dicte (7,047 feet). The receptor is like a shallow bowl that rests on the tops of these three peaks. The receptor has a guardian, and we are fortunate that Greek myth remembers his name—Talos—and has even given us a delightful story about him in the geomythic odyssey by Apollonius of Rhodes, *The Argonautica*, the tale of Jason and the Argonauts in search of the Golden Fleece. One of their last stops was Crete.

When Jason and his Argonauts sought safe harbor in the haven of Dicte, they were accosted by the island's guardian, a bronze giant called Talos. He was made all of bronze but had gods' blood, or ichor, in him to give him life. He was invulnerable save for a thin-skinned patch by his ankle. He was spawned of the "brazen race" that sprang from ash trees, long before the era of demigods.

Olympian Zeus had assigned Talos to guard Crete, and Talos did this by running the island's circumference three times daily. Medea, daughter of Helios the Sun god and regaled as a "witch," mesmerized Talos with her baleful glare, causing him to scrape his ankle and cut open his vulnerable spot. He died.[449]

I doubt Medea killed Talos, because he's still there on Crete, running laps around the island every day. Apollonius's story might have referred to an encounter of ancient Greek psychics with Talos and certain negotiations with the formidable protector being—a colleague of mine describes Talos as being the same height as Mount Ida—to allow them to enter his domain. In any event, Talos himself may be responsible for the generation of the receptor dish.

Picture Talos as a blue-white spindle that rotates rapidly, spinning so fast it is difficult to distinguish any of its features. Its very spinning weaves the Planetary Energy Receptor as dish composed of three overlapping concentric circles. Each circle is one of Talos's laps around the island's perimeter. Talos runs at almost the speed of light, and since he is virtually everywhere on the island's perimeter at once, in practical terms the bowl is Talos running. In a functional sense, all of Crete is Talos's planetary energy bowl, which of course reinforces the reason that Zeus assigned him to protect all of Crete, for the entire island, geomantically, is the collector of planetary energies and a sacred precinct.

For instance, if during a particular period, Venus is the most important planet for Earth, then its energies and influences as collected on Earth will be guarded. The guardian carries something of that energy and then protects it.

The myths about the Easter Island Planetary Energy Receptor are less explicit about their protector being. It might be Make-Make.[450]

Make-Make is charged with protecting an island precinct of 64 square miles. In *The Galaxy on Earth,* I proposed that the Easter Island *moai,* the stone heads of gods with long ears of which 887 still remain, their heads facing inland, were probably replicas of Make-Make or the Polynesian equivalent of Talos, and that they were, at least symbolically, tent posts holding down the Planetary Energy Receptor as if it were a giant concave tent. Each *moai* is like a frozen-action still of Make-Make protectively running the perimeter of the island.

These Make-Make statues face into the island, their backs to the sea, because their focus is on the island's Planetary Energy Receptor. The *moai* were thought to once all have a *pukao,* or topknot on their heads, a fat stone disk, and in a sense, all of Easter Island is a *moai* with *pukao,* the topknot here interpreted as the Planetary Energy Receptor and the *moai* as Make-Make, its guardian. In this interpretation, you could say Make-Make wears the island as his topknot, which is also the Planetary Energy Receptor tuned to whatever planet is active. As with Crete, all of Easter Island, geomantically, is the dish to collect planetary light.

Albion has another geomantic feature of a global nature. These are Celestial Body Lights, which exist in 613 locations in connection with dome caps.

Qabala states that there are 613 parts or lights in the human body and that when perfected, a human shines with these 613 lights. Jewish religious belief similarly holds there are 613 *mitzvot,* or holy nonselfish acts understood to be commandments and obligations handed down directly from God through Moses and the Torah; religious Jews are expected to follow these as an act of obedience to God's will. In fact, the gematria of the word Torah in Hebrew implies 613.[451]

Of these 613 "unchangeable" *mitzvot,* 248 are "positive" (meaning they encourage one to do things, such as believe in God) and 365 are "negative" (not to do specified things). Further, the 248 *mitzvot* correspond to the human body's organs, "every one of which is identified with a corresponding *mitzvah,*" while the 365 correspond to the solar days in a year. Yet it's also said that the body is made from 248 limbs and 365 veins.[452]

In Qabalistic interpretation, the 248 lights assume an arcane significance. The soul of the righteous man who in life has performed the 248 positive commandments is attired after death in these 248 lights. There are 248 angels who raise the soul up, associated with the "illuminating vision," and 365 angels who also raise the soul up, but associated with "the vision that does not illuminate." The Qabala also suggests that the 248 lights are not only parts of the body, but wings, and it further insinuates that the 248 are lights of the Shekinah, the feminine presence or aspect of God. The 248 organs are "tools of the hasadim" on the right side of certain divine images; the 365 lights are sinews on the left.[453]

Geomantically, this feature is represented by an array across the Earth's surface of 613 major dome caps (out of the Earth's total of 83,808). Each of these has a specific function corresponding to this Qabalistic anatomical model of bodily lights, the 248 limbs, organs, or wings, and the 365 veins. The 248 lights have an additional geomantic expression by way of the maximum energy expansion potential of a dome. According to the Ofanim, under certain circumstances, a dome can generate 248 dome caps rather than 48. "When each one of the dome caps has the maximum amount of energy matrices coming from it, then this makes the function of the dome caps from the dome total 248."

How Healing the Fisher King Helps to Awaken the Global Albion

This next bit is complex but vital to understanding Albion. It is too multidimensional to talk about other than by poetic insinuation and inference.

The one Albion lies sleeping at the core of the planet. He is like a fetus in the womb of Gaia. He is a spherical being, so he lies as if coiled up in a fat ball inside the Earth. Not the physical Earth with its presumed molten core, but the etheric Earth, the geomythic Earth, the Earth with its complicated, multilayered geomantic form. Each Albion Plate is like a pentagonal window that looks in on Albion. He is a vast being, the size of the planet, only on its inside.

He's inside the Earth, at the heart of its geometric, geomantic energy grid, and as he awakens he will expand like an inflated balloon to fill all the interior space of the Earth. Looking through the planet's surface, as if it were transparent, you will behold this vast spherical, cosmic being, his lips and nose pressing against the topmost glassine surface, his body dense with stars and temples and revelations. He is as big as the Earth; he's the physical Earth turned inside out to reveal its spherical soul; he is another layer of skin, just

below the planetary surface and the surfaces of consciousness.

Look through any Albion Plate and you'll see part of his planet-sized round form. Each Albion Plate is a speculum allowing us to observe Albion in the womb of Earth. Yet go down one of the special tunnels into the Pit of Gaia and inexplicably you'll behold not parts but his entire form, fetal, oroboric, now sleeping fitfully.

These tunnels are viewing platforms from which to observe this sleeping, gestating Albion. I call these features Albion Viewing Chambers, for they provide present-time glimpses of the whole Albion on his journey to wakefulness.

There are 36 points of entrance into the Earth's womb, three per Albion Plate. These are like amniocentesis insertions, cognitive tunnels that open up into the viewing room, like the observation deck in an old surgery theater for teaching new doctors. I presently know of three: Meriden common in England; Litchfield common in Connecticut; and a spot inside the coral reef midway between the islands of Raiatea and Tahaa in French Polynesia.

Some years ago I ventured down the Albion tunnel through Meriden. It was like walking down a long open tunnel to the center of the Earth. More precisely, into a central chamber with a table upon which lay Albion, bound, restrained, wrapped in winding sheets, midway between a cocoon and a mummy. Why was Albion bound? Was he a threat to the Earth? Yes, in a sense.

You have to remember what he represents, what he is. He is colossal; his cosmic reality for the unprepared human can be apocalyptic. His presence can be electrifying. Albion is the projected copy of Adam Kadmon, God's idea of perfect existence expressed as the Original Man. Albion contains the 85-plus geomantic features in the Earth's visionary geography, and he contains the cosmic awareness these features embody and emit. He is potentially fully wakeful in God, and he's here, among us in multiple copies—445 cosmically awake Albions.

He comes to Earth with the matrix of the cosmos and its multiple revelations, then Albion is filled with the fruits of collective human experience since the beginning of this planet. These experiences fill him like wire wrapped around a motor's armature. *This* Albion is what *this* Earth has made of him.

It's said that when you die, first all the daytime events of your life flash before you like a vast video presentation; later, in the spiritual worlds, you remember everything you did in your astral body or dreamtime, and that's mostly stuff— strange, frightening, gorgeous, translucent, demonic—you were never conscious of or even suspected during your life, yet it's still part of you. The global Albion is like this, full of unconscious, transcendent content that will shock us when it is revealed, when Albion awakes.

Just think: For an atheistic, materialistic, reductionist culture such as ours, any real revelation of God—not a *cinema verite* of dogma but real, naked, unmediated, unfiltered presence— can be appalling because it is so inescapably *real*. Albion is God's messenger, message, and revelation, and he's a light being in our neighborhood patiently waiting for our belated, disbelieving acknowledgment.

"Albion is about to become conscious," the Ofanim comment, "When Albion awakens, then the Earth awakens to the new consciousness of Gaia." Further, beings that humanity once thought it had to combat, such as dragons, now become Albion's allies. "In the new myth, Albion does not slay the dragon. He loves it and, through love, transforms it. Then the dragon and Albion become a living being and the Shadow is illumined. Then those who walk in Albion learn to walk among the stars."

My vision of the bound, cocooned Albion at the center of the Earth was in 1990. Since then, Albion has been unbound, his swaddling clothes unwrapped, parts of his glorious celestial form revealed, cleansed, and baptized. Merlin has been healing Albion in preparation for his unique awakening.

When Albion definitively awakes, this will not be some world-shattering, time-ending catastrophe. Rather, we will have *more* time here on Earth; time will pass more slowly because in the light-filled planetary form of Albion we will be existing closer to the speed of light, and as Einstein proposed, time slows down to nil as you approach the speed of light.

Albion is now sleeping very lightly inside the Earth. He awaits his healing, and part of healing Albion is the reintegration of the 13 parts of the Wounded Fisher King. Albion is the original Cosmic Man presented in multiple virtual copies within the zodiacs and Albion Plates of Earth; essentially Albion is the repository of the 81 different Earth chakras, and he is templated in 445 places—individual zodiacs, Albion Plates, within the Earth.

But even when unchained and awake, Albion lacks *mobility*. He has chakras in the arms, legs, palms, and soles, but these are light centers, not agents of mobility. For mobility, he depends on the Fisher King. His 13 parts are the three parts of each arm (upper, lower, wrist) and leg (thigh, calf, foot) and the penis.[454] These are the Fisher King's means of movement—and generation, which is a kind of movement through time by creating new life.

The Fisher King is not templated geomythically as is Albion. He lives in the Grail Castle, which has 144 doors across the planet, and ultimately is of Albion's psychic mobility. The Fisher King is wounded because he cannot use his sword safely, cannot remember his cosmic origins, cannot connect his root chakra with his crown. Technically, those spiritual centers are in Albion, and we must think of these two symbolic figures as overlapped: the Fisher King's flexible limbs superimposed over Albion's spherical body of chakras—like Humpty Dumpty with arms (six parts), legs (six parts), and a penis.

The Wounded Fisher King is healed when he can reclaim his cosmic memory, remember why he is here, where he came from, and why, and move fleetly, agilely, anytime, back and forth along the vast timeline from now back to before the beginning of this cosmos—a mere Day in the life of Brahma, after all. His cosmic memory regained, his wounds are healed, and he is once again the *Rich* Fisher King. This healing through the reclamation of deep cosmic memory has repercussions on the healing and awakening of Albion and his body full of chakras. In effect, the Fisher King becomes Albion's mobility in cosmic recall.

The Fisher King's healing through remembrance is *our* responsibility. It can only happen through frequent trips to the Grail Castle and our retrieval and assimilation of deep memory. Ultimately, it's our psychic mobility Albion needs, and also ultimately, we are all Albion.

"If you have an imprint of an event in your higher being bodies, then that event transmits itself into the body of Gaia, which repercusses on the surface of the Earth," the Ofanim say. "One reason for developing your self nature, for coming to awareness of yourself, for realizing the Star you are, is that this imprint makes an imprint within the body of Gaia and repercusses on the Earth.

"If you are in a particular place where the energies are sympathetic with your blueprint, then there is synchronous reciprocation of vibrations. These will make an impression within the body of Gaia. The more conscious you are of your personal imprint and its part and the imprints that have been graced you, the more these imprints have an effect in the planetary body. It's up to you."

The Ofanim report that currently four out of

13 parts of the Fisher King are in "a state of remembrance." These are the two upper arm parts and the Moon at his brow and the Sun in his solar plexus. This may seem confusing in light of the distinction I just made about chakras (and implicitly, planets) as being Albion's domain, the limbs being the Fisher King's.

Nonetheless, for Albion to be healed, the Ofanim explain, "what needs to take place is the balancing of the Moon at the brow and the Sun in his solar plexus. The silver child [of the Silver Eggs] and the golden child [of the Golden Eggs] in Albion's heart may then walk together under the Sun behind the Sun. The healing in Albion's heart may then illumine the solar plexus, healing Albion's solar plexus so that humanity can move from individual will to *Thy Will Be Done*. This also creates in the light of day the possibility of the angelic kingdom manifesting in the Earth's being bodies at a material level by the year 2020 A.D."

Albion awakening for the first time in the history of this planet means everywhere you walk on the Earth you are walking *in* Albion. His star-filled colossal form is pushing itself up like a tremendous spring bulb through the soil of ordinary perception and daytime waking consciousness. Mother Earth is birthing her own prodigious spiritual soul from within her physical form, pushing out an awesome cosmic landmass in our midst.

Soon Albion will no longer be within the Earth. He is rising like newborn mountains out of the molten Earth, and soon wherever you look into the landscape, you will see more than what was there before: You will see Albion, alive with the galaxy and all its wakeful beings.

This is good, even if it seems monumental in implication. For Albion brings to us a great gift, once ours, but forgotten (just as he was) in the long sleep that has been our cognitive biography for millennia. He brings *AL*, the cocreative power, the seeds of the secret of bringing things into

Table 9-3: Shambhala Doorways

Planetary Total: 1,080

Church of St. Andrew, Aller, Somerset, England	Avenue of Cedars, Glastonbury, England	Mount Kailash, Tibet
Hummellfjell Mountain, Os, near Roros, Norway	South Cadbury Castle, Somerset, England	Merlin's Cave, Tintagel, Cornwall, England
Iao State Park, Maui, Hawaii, U.S.	Merlin's Mound, Marlborough, Wiltshire, England	Merlin's Hill (*Bryn Myrddin*), Carmarthen, Wales
Hunter Peak, Guadalupe Mountains, Texas, U.S.	Blackhill Spring, Tetford, Lincolnshire, England	Bardsey Island, Wales
Chalice Well, Glastonbury, Somerset, England	The Cadmeia, Thebes, Greece	

Equivalent Names (for the doorway and destination): Merlin's Glass House, *Ty Gwydr;* the *Esplumoir;* Merlin's crystal cave; Sukavati; Western Paradise; Buddha-field; Dilmun (Sumerian)

manifestation. *AL* (or *EL*) is one of the 72 Names of God, mentioned earlier.

"You create your own reality. You are as we are, and you have the possibility of *AL* (*EL*). This means you are a cocreator. As in *EL-ohim.* The Elohim as an angelic family are the forms of *AL*, the projections, entities, or forms which are acceptable to conscious perception of this essence. If you have a grain of faith, then you can move mountains. The myths [grim and fearful future scenarios] people are cocreating today could be transformed into a more possible probability of positive expectancy."

To create our own reality with the cocreative power of *AL* is to reclaim and responsibly use the Elohim's sword, this time without the Dolorous Stroke. "You are a cocreator with the Most Almighty Architect of Divine Existence in the Plan of all positive possibilities within this Earth. You either take up each step as your conscious responsibility or you don't. It's up to you."

Cocreation means taking our part in the responsibilities that being human implies, and that includes being open-minded about the future. "There are many expressions of the future. If the future is shaped by past experience, then it is no more than an outliving of the ghosts of the past. If, on the other hand, the past is relinquished and the present acknowledged, then it is possible to make the first step into a conscious future. This is cocreation."

This letting go of the past is both an individual and collective event. The willingness to let go of one's karmic momentum is in itself a preliminary step towards cocreation, a gesture of freely willed action. "You may release your past, let go of who you have been only a moment ago. You may release who you have been yesterday, the day before, last week, and back into the past. There's only one place to let go from, and that's *now.* If you're holding on to some identity, you diminish the possibility of being a cocreator. There is only one step ever to make: that is the *next* step. The Logos is the Word that issues forth in the step that is made in the moment of consciousness that you call now."

Albion is the essence of the Essence within Gaia. Albion is the Light Bearer brought to Earth. "Walking in Albion means walking consciously, step by step, contacting the essence, making an imprint in the energy matrix of the Earth, producing a tangible effect in the consciousness of Gaia that the initiation of the Christ in the Buddha Body may come to be a positive practicality and a recurrent possibility."

Walking in Albion is the same as the Christed Initiation in the Buddha Body, the Earth-based initiation the Ofanim and their colleagues are supporting in this time period. "This is your task as cocreators in the positive possibility."

Merlin's Glass House and How to Get into Shambhala

Our next geomantic feature has to do with a Glass House.

Bardsey, known as *Ynys Enlii* in Welsh and the Island of Twenty Thousand Saints to Christians, lies off the Lleyn Peninsula in northwest Wales at the entrance to Cardigan Bay. The myths say Merlin lies there in an enchanted sleep, or that he disappeared into his mysterious *Ty Gwydr* (Glass House: also called a *wyr*, an underground invisible glass structure); or set off upon the sea in a house of glass; or vanished up a tree (the *Esplumoir*); or was seduced and imprisoned under a stone or in a crystal cave by his duplicitous apprentice, Nimuë or Vivienne.

It turns out Merlin disappeared into the Western Paradise, as it's known in Buddhist parlance, which also calls it *Sukavati* or Shambhala, and his Glass House is known as the Buddha Body, perceivable as a mobile octahedron (eight-faced polygon) and one of the Platonic Solids.

That's our seventh Celestial City, and it's where Merlin went when he vanished and from where he returned when he reappeared. He would disappear into his Glass House and travel to Shambhala, the realm of the spiritual masters and mentors of the Earth. His Glass House on Bardsey Island was a trapdoor to Shambhala. There are 1,080 such trapdoors or Glass Houses

into Shambhala, and it's not only Merlin who can vanish through one. You can, too.[455]

So where is Shambhala? Is it a physical place? It's more or less where Tibetan legend places it, roughly in the Gobi Desert at the base of the Altai Range in Mongolia. It is no more physical than Mount Meru, and in many respects, it's an outpost of that heavenly city on Earth. Shambhala sits under a vast dome and, to borrow the jargon of physics, is phase-shifted out of our reality so we cannot see or touch it or physically interact it with under normal circumstances. Shambhala of course is the original upon which Shangri-la, the secret, but highly desirable Himalayan paradise of immortal youth in James Hilton's *Lost Horizon*, was based.

Can you get there physically? Many would like to, some have tried, a few, like the medieval Prester John, claim they made it, but frankly, it's not necessary to go there physically. Your body probably wouldn't survive the higher light vibration anyway. It's relatively easier to slip through one of the Earth's 1,080 doorways (see table 9-3) and go there in your visionary body.

So what is Shambhala? As one of the eight Celestial Cities, it's known as Suddavati or Sukavati, the City of the King of the Immortals in the West. Many secondary sources do not consider Sukavati and Shambhala to be identical, but as far as I can tell, from empirical evidence, they are the same "place."

It's a grand, opulent city, filled with exquisite fragrances, radiance, wondrous flowers, jeweled trees, rushing water that sounds like music—it is the home of the heavenly and post-human Hierarchy, the world corporate headquarters and central field office for all the spiritual agencies (including the Olympian gods—Mount Olympus being a branch office) working on Earth's behalf. This is the seat of the true government of the world, even more recessed than all the human and human-allied shadow governments and conspiracies.

Sukavati (from the Sanskrit, meaning "the Blissful") is a pure land in the West, one of the most important "Buddhafields" ever recounted in Buddhist lore. One can be reborn in Sukavati in a white lotus and reside there in absolute truth until you reach nirvana. You can derive inordinate happiness there listening to Amitabha proclaim the truth. Amitabha (Boundless Light) is one of the great Buddhas, said to have created Sukavati more as a state of consciousness (a "pure land")

Table 9-4: Golden Pillars
Planetary Total: 228,964
Selected Locations:
Thebes, Greece
Colchis, Georgia, U.S.
Os, near Roros, Norway
Jasna Gora, Poland
Easter Island, Chile
Equivalent Names: Golden Cylinders; *Spartoi* (by Cadmus), the "Sown Men"; Golden-Helmed Seed; Dragon's Teeth; Gegeneis (by Jason and the Argonauts)

than a location, on the basis of his cumulative good karmic merit.

Shambhala has a similarly grand mythic description. The name is Sanskrit and means "the Source of Happiness." It is usually said to have the shape of an eight-petaled lotus blossom set within a rosary of snow mountains that shine with a crystalline light; at its center is Kalapa, its capital. The King of Shambhala sits on a golden throne supported by eight carved lions; all his ministers and all the residents of Shambhala are fantastically healthy and virtually immortal.[456]

On a more esoteric level, it's said that Sanat Kumara is the Lord of the World ruling from Shambhala and is assisted by numerous pupils and adepts. According to Alice Bailey, Shambhala, "the bright center lying far ahead," was founded 18.5 million years ago on Earth in "the higher ethers of the physical plane" and occupying "a definite location in space." It was established to be "an organisation and a headquarters for the mysteries." Shambhala originally had an outpost and templic base in Ibez, South America, then this was shifted to Asia.[457]

That's the high-end version of Shambhala. But

for those of us who aren't highly evolved Himalayan adepts, what function does Shambhala have for us? Based on my experience, I would say it has something to do with initiation.

My first trip to Shambhala was unexpected, though no doubt planned, just not by me. I was meditating at a churchyard in Somerset, just across the Levels from where I lived in Somerset, England. It was the Church of Saint Andrew, about one-half mile from a village called Aller. In a previous chapter, I listed Aller as an Ixion's Wheel; I was about to discover it is also a doorway into Shambhala.

Getting there was like passing through a series of doors, each opened by penetrating a symbolic image. The first was a casket with a golden sphinx on the front by way of a latch. This casket seemed to be set in a grave some dozen feet below the ground. Beneath it was a white marble cubic chamber, perhaps six feet square. A sheathed sword lay on the smooth floor, the carved face of a lion on one wall. I used the sword to probe the lion's brow and found a pearl. Inside the pearl, I now saw a much more living, animated lion holding a blazing torch, and as soon as I locked my attention on that flame, I was gone, and arrived.

I had arrived on very high ground. I guessed it to be 20,000 feet above the plain below. I'm not sure how I traveled down, but I pointed my sword down to the plain and left the craggy snow peaks for a vast luminous dome perhaps one hundred miles in diameter. No, I didn't travel like a modified witch on a sword's point rather than a broomstick; the sword was a symbolic presentation of my brow chakra and its ability (obviously pumped up by outside help this time) to penetrate arcane and subtle dimensions. I arrived more or less at the front gate and was greeted by people who had large Moon crescents on their heads.

Inside the dome, which housed a vast city of light, I found myself at a gorgeous spuming fountain of light overlooking a spacious green lawn and Grecian-style stately buildings, like a regal college campus of porticoed libraries. I visited one of the libraries, examined some books (one of them seemed to be a record of my karma and past lives), then spent time with three pleasant men.

The first looked like William Shakespeare, the second like Benjamin Franklin, and the third looked like himself. Later I learned these were the Ray Masters Saint Germaine and Lady Portia (who had appeared as humans in those guises), and the third was Merlin. I say he looked like himself because I had already seen him on several occasions. I also learned that you need to have one or two Ray Masters sponsoring your visits to Shambhala to get through all the red tape and security checks at the doors. The three of them taught me some interesting things about the Earth grid and the initiations possible through certain geomantic features, and no doubt a lot more I didn't realize at the time.

Afterwards, the Ofanim debriefed me. Both these Ray Masters are working with them at this time on behalf of the Earth's energy matrix. Ray Master Saint Germaine brings the transmutative energy of the Christ, and Ray Master Lady Portia brings the discriminative wisdom of that transmutation. As for Merlin, "We have worked with him since the beginning of your planet, and before. He is a Grand Square Master, which is a magus of high degree."

As for Shambhala, it exists on another plane. "It is not influenced by Earth activity, though symbiotically it is related to Earth with a degree of intercommunication when and where necessary. We showed you a gateway."[458]

And the sword I used to probe the lion's brow chakra? "Shambhala may be accessed through a sword when insight is refined enough and the consciousness has reached the point of communication and sees the patterns that lie behind things," the Ofanim told me. "Then the sword of insight can be used to open the door to Shambhala."

On other occasions I have seen certain objects brought through a Shambhala Doorway to be placed at a geomantic feature such as a zodiac amplifier. Or perhaps I was just tracing the origin of those objects already established at those sites. I'm referring to a feature the Ofanim call Golden Pillars.

There are 228,964 of these around the planet (see table 9-4). Golden cylinders of energy, they are a technology from the future, waiting for the future to come about. Their purpose is to bring Shambhala a bit closer to our physical-human realm as a preparation for our future when human-Shambhala interactions will increase. The pillars tend to be placed at our end of the Shambhala doorways, though sometimes they are used in the zodiac amplifiers.

What do they look like? I first saw these golden cylinders while contemplating the Solar Logos receptor at Os as part of the zodiac amplifier for the Hills of Heaven zodiac in south-central Norway. I dove into the receptor, which resembled a very large chalice filled with light, and immediately emerged in a valley surrounded by abrupt, steep green hills. It looked exactly like a place on Maui in Hawaii called the Iao Needle in Iao State Park, which I knew was a Shambhala doorway. Probably this was my mind giving me by mnemonic shorthand the news that here was another such gateway to Shambhala.

I counted 24 golden cylinders about one hundred feet tall that formed a circle around the Solar Logos receptor. As I studied these pillars, they turned into golden beings, somewhat like generic Egyptian pharoahs, arms crossed at their chests, with full headgear and kingly appurtenances. They seemed to be channeling golden energy into the Solar Logos receptor, and it flowed out over the top onto the Blue Dish, thus into the physical landscape. As I looked more closely, each pillar seemed like a massive face, a blend of human and angelic visages; the faces touched at the cheeks, forming a fence of transcendent faces around the chalice, like a unified gaze, facing outwards.

Shambhala has another effective way of beneficially influencing our world before the time when more direct interactions will be entertained. The Earth's primary sixth chakra is not situated permanently at one site, as are, for the most part, the other chakras. The sixth chakra moves around like a roving divine eye and is called the Mobile Shambhalic Focus. It changes location every 200 years.

There is a 50-year buildup in a new location, then 100 years of full-intensity residence, then a 50-year withdrawal process. It's helpful to think of the Focus as like a dimmer switch that's slowly turned on to full wattage for 50 years, stays there for 100, then is gradually turned down for the last 50 years. It is presently at Glastonbury in England; at other times in the Earth's history, it has been present at Banaras in India, Mount Kailash in Tibet, and Jerusalem in Israel.

The Mobile Shambhalic Focus is the energy and consciousness of the sixth chakra as transmitted from Shambhala. For a community, such as Glastonbury, having the Mobile Shambhalic Focus present, even without knowing it, can be like sitting next to a very high spiritual being. It can be both uplifting and disconcerting, a revelation and almost a nightmare. It would be revealing to write a history of the Earth and its cultures from the vantage point of the chronology of where the Mobile Shambhalic Focus was sited.[459]

In the earliest days of the Earth, the Mobile Shambhalic Focus was used to scour entire landscapes, preparing them for human culture. Hindu lore recounts Vishnu's Discus, also known as the *Sudarsana* or *Chakravarta*. Sudarsana means "fair to see," while the related word *darsata* means "visible, striking the eye, conspicuous, beautiful." Sudarsana symbolized the unbounded power and speed of Vishnu's mind; as it spun, entire worlds were created, upheld, and dissolved; Vishnu also used it to fell ranks of demons and evil-minded beings.

For example, a site in Banaras called the *Manikarnika* (or *Chakrapushkarini Kund,* the "Discus-Lotus Pool" or simply Vishnu's Lotus Pool) was said to have been dug out by Vishnu with his Discus. It was the world's first pool and sacred site, older even than the Ganges. Today that pool is still present as a sacred well near the Manikarnika Ghat, or cremation grounds, along the Ganges in Banaras. All of India, when it was known by its original name, Bharata, was dug out or prepared by Vishnu's Discus, wielded by the first of India's *Chakravartins* (a spiritual king).

Vishnu's Discus is beautiful to see, auspicious to behold; it grants life and light, a "sharp-rimmed battle-discus" and fiery weapon usually represented as a disk with spokes or rays. The Discus always enabled its wielder to be victorious in battle (presumably against agents of the Dark), and if thrown, it would always return to its owner. It blazed with energy and was "effulgent as fire." The world-wheel was a "discus of irresistible force," and the *Chakravartin* a superman.[460]

Tune into the Christ's Yearly Geomantic Epiphany

All of this of course is symbolic and metaphorical. Vishnu's Sudarsana is like a Sun Wheel, though it is more than that; he lives in a rarified dimension that is like our Sun, yet is more than that. It gives us some conceptual footing to approach an Epiphany Focus, a yearly manifestation of Vishnu (Christ) in the Earth's energy matrix. This takes place on January 6, and every year since about 4000 B.C., it has focused on a different grid point. Thus, as of 2004, 6,004 different geomantic nodes around the planet have been irradiated with this sun-like eye of Vishnu.

Each year for a week, the Eye of Vishnu or the Christ Gaze focuses on a specific site, getting ever brighter, peaking in intensity on January 6, then falling off for the next few days. The Christ energy is immediately transmitted through this grid point to all geomantic nodes on the Earth. Recent sites for the Epiphany Focus have included Sedona, Arizona; Rondane Mountains, Norway; Burley Hill, Rutland, England; Mount Temehani in Raiatea, French Polynesia; Bimini Island (directly east off the South Florida coast); Teotihuacan, Mexico; and Santa Fe, New Mexico.

I call it an Epiphany Focus as January 6 is the original birth date of the Christ on Earth and is still observed by Orthodox Christians and followers of Rudolf Steiner. The Greek word *epiphaneia* means "manifestation." On Epiphany, the Christ showed forth (through Jesus) as a revelation of light to the three Magi; that was when "he" was physically present on the Earth.

Unfortunately, nobody publishes the advance listing of Epiphany sites. Sometimes the Ofanim let me know a few months in advance, and I have participated in perhaps a half dozen Epiphany events at the Christ-infused site. However, on a practical geomantic level, if you have the opportunity to visit one of the previously Christ-infused Epiphany sites, you can still gain much benefit.[461]

From the viewpoint of the spiritual and angelic hierarchies, the name of the game in Earth's visionary geography in our time is the Christed Initiation in the Buddha Body.

The Christed Initiation in the Buddha Body is an experience *long* in the preparation. One night the Ofanim helped two colleagues and me to remember an experience from a past life in which we were priests of some sort in a temple located in the capital of Lemuria, today's Honolulu. A kind of sacramental service and energy grounding ritual was under way. "This [presumably millions of years ago] was the beginnings of the implantation of what was to become the seeding of Christ in the Buddha Body," the Ofanim said.

"During the time you have incarnated within, the Christ must be brought within the personal sphere as a direct experience," the Ofanim state. "Steiner acknowledged this as a coming event. We, as your Blazing Star, are part of that experience. We are the beginning of what will be the realization of the Christ within the Buddha Body. The Star is the potential for the Christ to awaken in the Buddha Body. The Christ is the potential for awakening to the Good. The Christ has always had a potential in that Jesus as an individual brought that potential to cosmic reality through a divine drama he was commissioned to enact.

"When the Star goes nova, then the light extends to the outermost limits of the personal sphere into the Buddha Body or Buddhic shell. This is the full realization of the Christ in the Buddha Body. This is when the Star becomes concentrated within itself and is on the outside rather than inside."

No doubt some will be confused by this unexpected confluence of the Christ and Buddha, Vishnu and Shambhala. If the Sudarsana is Vishnu's Discus, and Vishnu is Christ, how come this feature is also called the Mobile Shambhalic Focus? How does Shambhala fit in with the Christ and Vishnu?

Many decades ago, Rudolf Steiner said that in the future Buddhism and Pauline Christianity would start to flow together. His future is our present, and that confluence is starting to happen. Steiner said that one of the first visions people would have when Shambhala "shows itself again" (that is, enters public awareness as a fact) will be

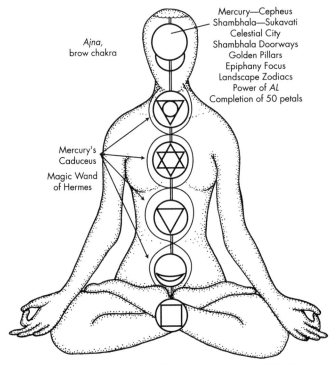

Ajna,
brow chakra

Mercury—Cepheus
Shambhala—Sukavati
Celestial City
Shambhala Doorways
Golden Pillars
Epiphany Focus
Landscape Zodiacs
Power of *AL*
Completion of 50 petals

Mercury's
Caduceus

Magic Wand
of Hermes

Figure 9-2. The Starry Wheels of Albion, the Sixth Level of Manifestation

Christ in his etheric form. Steiner had always maintained that the Christ left a permanent imprint of himself in the Earth's etheric field, and that there was no need for a Second Coming because energetically he had never left. It would just be a matter of that etheric imprint registering in human consciousness as a fact.

That registration started to happen in the mid-twentieth century and increased in prevalence afterwards, as more people became clairvoyant. Now Christianity and Buddhism can start to fuse, and "mankind will rise through normal human faculties into the land of Shambhala." Humanity, Steiner said, "has no other leader than the Christ to take it into the land that oriental writers declare to have vanished. Christ will lead humanity to Shambhala." This will start with a few who will experience "the light-woven, light-gleaming Shambhala . . . teeming with wisdom." This experience will denote "the most momen-

tous turning point" in human evolution.[462]

This may still seem confusing. But you don't have to become a Christian or Buddhist to participate in this. You don't have to be anything. This Initiation, and all avenues of participation in the Earth's visionary geography, does not require belief in any doctrine. It is an empirical, long-term numinous encounter *you* have on *your* terms with a system of energy, consciousness, and symbols that *predates* all doctrines.[463]

It is fitting that Albion's ability to contemplate the Divine Vision be restored at this sixth stage of cosmic manifestation, corresponding to the brow chakra (see figure 9-2). From our embodied viewpoint, the brow is the place of psychic insight, the viewing screen through which we see the subtle world and interpret its pictures.

The *Ajna* (brow) chakra's two petals are like two psychic eyes with which we start to see the visionary geography around us; they also neatly correspond to the two zodiac halves, the physical and etheric—the *BI*, or twoness, of Albion. And in the brow chakra, we complete the Name of 50 petals, the 50-lettered Sanskrit alphabet whose sound shapes have determined the vibratory field of the first six layers of cosmic manifestation and, within the human experience, the first through sixth chakras. Chakras one through six have a total of 50 petals.

Remember, though, that we must see this in a mirror, for we are encountering the stages of cosmic creation from the top down, from God's sequence of manifestation. For us in bodies, the brow and crown chakras seem to be the last two and highest in the developmental sequence of consciousness centers, but in the stages of cosmic creation they are the last two to be expressed.

The easiest way to conceive this is to picture yourself hanging upside down; your rear end and root chakra are closest to Heaven, your crown closest to Earth. Coming into manifestation, especially at the level of the Earth, the crown is the last stage, the one that touches physical matter; leaving matter and the body-based Earth reality, the crown chakra is the last stage on the way out.

An excellent representation of the brow chakra and Albion's point of psychic insight into the divine vision is the caduceus traditionally assigned to Mercury: two snakes intertwined around a vertical pole, their heads facing each other just under the top, which has a single sphere and two wings. This is the *Ajna* chakra, the Third Eye, the place of psychic insight, the single eye of divine seeing the Elohim demonstrated in their guise as one-eyed Cyclopes.

The caduceus is an apt streamlined depiction of the energy circuit of the first six chakras. The *ida* and *pingala* "snakes" or energy currents weave around the *sushumna,* or central channel, passing through each other at the chakras, then terminate their heliacal dance at the *Ajna* and become one. Tantric iconography depicts this blending as a white circle with two luminescent petals.

In the brow center, the yogi gains an experience of oneness with cosmic laws, realizes he is immortal in spirit though in a time-based body, reaches a state of "undifferentiated cosmic awareness" in which all dualities cease, knows that he embodies all the elements in their purest form, and "becomes a divine manifestation."[464] Surely that qualifies as Albion having reclaimed the Divine Vision.

It may also qualify as the foundation for experiencing the Buddha Body, which is Merlin's Glass House, his means of transportation to Shambhala. "Mercury is the God of Wisdom, and

as such is associated with the Buddha," explains astrologer Alan Oken; in general terms, Buddha and Christ are generic terms that signify "one who has been enlightened by divine wisdom (*budhi*)." Oken refers to Mercury as the "Light of the Messenger."[465]

The caduceus is also known as Hermes' rod or the magic wand of Mercury. Here we can usefully correlate the Ofanim's description of the "cocreative power of *AL,*" associated with the brow center; *AL* wielded appropriately can be like a magic wand, capable of generating new, more positive realities. Further, insofar as the *ida-pingala* energy dialectic of lunar and solar currents terminates and blends at the brow, this is also the place of neutrality, of nondialectical detachment, a place free from the opposites, a place of creative equilibrium between opposing forces.

There is great cocreative power in this neutrality; in fact, it is probably the necessary foundation from which *AL* can be effectively wielded to shape reality. From a psychic point of view, it is certainly a prerequisite for relatively clear seeing, which means seeing that is only minimally filtered and conditioned by one's emotional life and partial view of the world in the lower five chakras. The caduceus's correlation with healing is also apt here in light of the need to heal the Wounded Fisher King.

Again, it's probably easiest to conceive of the caduceus of the Mercury sphere in terms of direction. From the direction of incarnated humans seeking illumination within matter, we climb the caduceus or interior chakra tree to get some clear views at the brow chakra, including a vision of Albion. All of this helps us wake up and remember and prepares us for an even more exalted knowingness we will experience through the crown.

From the direction of manifesting a cosmos (and its reflection on Earth), Albion (as Adam Kadmon) is now equipped with six planetary spheres, six Heavenly levels, six chakras, and lots of starry wheels (landscape zodiacs and all the other light-filled geomantic features). With the emergence of Albion's brow center, he is equipped for the divine vision. The brow center is the completion, the fiftieth, the Pentecost; it is all 50 of the Argonauts rowing, all facets of the five Platonic Solids generated and nested in place. Albion is ready for the world.

10 The Crown of Elohim
Albion Lands with His Head on the Earth

At last we come to the realm of the visible, the tangible and touchable. Stones. In circles, rows, stacks, standing alone. Hill-forts. Earthworks. Artificial caves above the ground. Megalithic structures upon the land.

In the realm of the megalithic, we have the momentous interface of spirit and matter, paradoxically the fastest vibrations—light and sound—meeting the slowest, the slow-moving density of stone. Albion, vast cosmic being full of stars and spiritual temples and celestial insights, touches down upon the physical Earth, his head crowned with megalithic structures, most of them designed and implemented by the Elohim. I call this level of Earth's visionary geography the Crown of Elohim, a circlet of star-filled stones and hollow hills.

To me, the majesty of the vision reinforces an insight that I hope has been building in the reader's awareness throughout this book. The Earth's energy matrix, its visionary geography, is a vast consciousness-generating machine. The geomantic features described in *The Emerald Modem* are all dedicated to manifesting, supporting, and amplifying human consciousness in the context of biological bodies on a physical planet. Not only has the Earth's energy grid made biological life possible; it has made conscious life possible and viable. It's a globally distributed system that reflects and nurtures our awareness and provides the exhilarating possibility of fully remembering our deep cosmic origins.

As you interact with the Earth's visionary geography, you start to realize that you are helping to birth a cosmic being on the planet. Yet this vast being is also your Self, your original complex cosmic essence, turned inside out to be an interactive visionary terrain. You walk through yourself, in Albion, visiting the numerous geomantic features, and reconstitute your Self and illuminate and birth the Albion templated across the Earth. Both awakenings happen together. As you walk through Gaia's soul, her Albion, you reconstitute your own soul in a context of matter.

Here's another take on it: The cosmos is the externalized organs and systems of a vast singular being called Adam Kadmon. As a physical human, you turn Adam Kadmon inside out and condense it into an organic human body. You now bear the cosmos and spiritual worlds inside you, *as* you. You find yourself on a planet whose spiritual essence is this same cosmic architecture of Adam Kadmon, which is the same as your own spiritual essence and body. You walk in Albion, the star-filled soul of Gaia, and find yourself distributed across it.

Stone Circles—Contributing to the Global Morning-Glory Effect

Stone circles have always intrigued me. I confess I have never believed the standard theories of their creation as put forward by archeology. Those accounts always seemed to me too narrow in scope, too constricting, too atheistic.

In essence, archeologists contend that primitive humans somehow amazingly figured out how to array stones in ovals and rough circles with some kind of mathematical precision and astronomical alignments, though for what purpose, we have no earthly idea; it might have been "ceremonial." They erected these stones in such a clever way that, for the most part, they never fell over. That was all in the enigmatic, undocumented, savage past, and anyway, it doesn't matter today.

However, things might not be that way. Based on information from the Ofanim and my own research, I propose a radically different picture.

Stone circles were designed and implemented from the top down for our benefit. Largely, this feature is not as active as it once was. Many of the original stone circles have disappeared or been distorted; those that remain are mostly museum pieces from an indecipherable megalithic past. Let's try to put some kind of a picture together of how it probably once was.

In the original design of the Earth, 1,746 stone circles were designed and installed around the Earth. It is quite likely that a majority of them were placed in the landmass we now know as the British Isles, for, long ago, that was the epicenter of the world civilization known as Hyperborea. That was the first Albion Plate in which significant original geomantic activation took place, just as today it is the prime site for the newest phenomenon in Earth Mysteries, crop circles, especially in Wiltshire, the English county that

includes Avebury, Earth's umbilicus. As William Blake presciently (but not jingoistically) declared in his poem *Jerusalem*: "All things Begin & End in Albion's Ancient Druid Rocky Shore."

While 1,746 stone circles were originally installed, more were added later. According to the Ofanim, some of these additions were imitations of the originals, others were imitations of the imitations, and still others were added to balance the effect of the imitations. The implication is that 1,746 circles were sufficient to the task, and the original geomantic engineers (including the Ofanim) would have preferred no more be added, as it only threw off the energy balance. Since that long ago time when the stone circles were installed, many have been destroyed, though still a fair number of the originals and imitations remain. An estimated 900 are in the U.K. alone; many other European nations have extant stone circles as well.

Why stone? "Stone is slow-moving consciousness," the Ofanim note. "In a circle this means longevity. The vibration lasts there for a long time. A fly may only have 24 hours to live, but a stone may have taken 24 million years to grow." At a material level, there is a manifestation that is a stone, but beyond that, the manifestation is not a stone but a wave form. Each stone in the circle maintains its own wave form, and the circle as an entirety maintains the total wave form manifesting through it.

Sound is a limited frequency, with very specific and limited wavelengths within the full wavelength spectrum of light. Obviously, sound travels much more slowly than light (at 1,125 feet/second), and the spectrum of hearable sound for humans is limited, ranging from infrasonic (16 Hz) to ultrasonic (20 kHz).

A circle or rough oval is perhaps the most appropriate form to contain sound. Sound waves spread out like ripples on a pond from their point of origin and spread out in three dimensions with crests and troughs. If you blow into a recorder—let's say you are one of those ancient Sunday morning pipers later turned to stone at a circle—and produce a note, this vibrates the air and sets up a standing wave, which is a stationary pattern of air. Multiply this by the number of stones in the circle—typically a dozen to almost 100—and you get a complex, interactive series of standing waves bounded by the stone perimeter.

A friend of mine, a stone sculptor, thinking about this subject, said she had a vision in which a sound shape or acoustic form that was a type of spiritual being entered each of the stones, the kind used in the old circles. If left outside the stone, the sound would spread out to fill the world and would become so dispersed as to be ineffective. It is, instead, concentrated in the stone, a bit like a dam (the geometry of the circle) holding in a great reservoir of water.

This is perhaps why many myths of stone circles say the stones originated from dancing or singing maidens being turned to stone as punishment for sporting on the Sabbath. To understand the curious myths of maidens turned to stone, perhaps we need to invert it: Spiritual sound beings (maidens) *enter* our world through stone. In the realm of stone and other earthworks from the megalithic era, we have the palpable meeting of spirit and matter, spirit in this case shaping matter as stone.

We find another intriguing interface of spirit and matter in the much-remarked faces in the stones of Avebury stone circle in Wiltshire. Researcher Terence Meaden has documented that of Avebury's 184 extant stones (including the main and subsidiary circles), at least 60 have clearly discernible facial features on them, mostly females facing left. They look less as if they were carved than as if they emerged from inside the stone as a kind of soul essence or animate spirit.

Differences during the day of sunlight and shadow tend to highlight these stone faces. This is a "novel art-form," Meaden says, "a species of sun-guided mobile sculpture—by which the movement of sun and shade over subtly engraved stones brings the stones to life, seeming to animate them like spirits."[466]

On a recent visit to Avebury, I sat in a car in the parking lot on a late winter's afternoon and observed some of the protean faces in the stones. Just among the half-dozen stones visible from where I sat I saw images of a polar bear, a Madonna and child, and a female Ganesh (Hindu elephant god and a form of the Ofanim).

Later the Ofanim commented: "The faces are the characters in the stones as consciousness is being moved in them over time. These faces were not carved. They are due more to the fact that people have worked with these stones. A priest may have been given a stone to look after like a domestic animal. Then that stone would become the embodiment of that priest. This is a phenomenon that happens when sites have been activated and maintained over reasonably long periods, more than four human life spans [288 years]; then the stones will have faces."

Dancing maidens turned to stones, stones holding wave forms, and priestly faces emerging in the stones are a few aspects of the *programmability* of old stones. In other words, this was all intentional. Each stone was originally programmed to *do* something, *be* something, *transmit* something, and to keep doing it for a very long time, reckoned in the millions of years. There is a standing stone near a sacred mountain in India, the Ofanim told me, that has the effect of balancing all the human chakras at every level when you merely lean against it. The Men-an-Tol in Cornwall, a stone hollowed out like a doughnut, was believed to produce fertility in barren women who crawled through it.

Each stone contains knowledge that we can access once we align our being bodies with the energies of the stones. I experienced this firsthand in the stone rows in Carnac in Brittany, France. Out of its several thousand standing stones, I focused on a few in the Kerlescan section to see what they might contain. Here are my impressions from that investigative session:

I look down the row from two capstones and see a series of yellow archways, one for each stone, like a sliced bread loaf or a necklace of yellow cells around me. At each stone there is a yellow archway; the entire row is a tightly packed vertebral axis of yellow archways. I stand before each stone, enter it in vision, absorb the yellow arch, which adds another layer or membrane to my being bodies. It's as if the first two capstones are the Sun and the 42 stones in the row are shells of resonance, sound waves packed tightly together.

I thread my attention through this yellow row, in sequence. Possibly, back in Hyperborean days, one actually entered each stone, physically, or in the light body, and absorbed its wave form at an atomic and preatomic level as a vibrational essence. Now I project myself in my thought body into each stone and its yellow crystal cave. One after another is like moving through a sequence of sound chambers or vibrational showers. At each stone, the yellow gets subtler, faster, suffused with more light.

I stand inside a crystal cave in each stone that reflects a yellow pressure, a presence, an echo. Maybe this is a way to restructure one's DNA or brain cells. As you move into each stone you dematerialize past the atomic level. The sound frequency reforms you in a new acoustic template. It's like moving by membranes through a yellow human head, and, as I stand before the last stone, I feel as if reconstituted into a whole yellow Sun, completing the transmission.

On another occasion I had two more insights into the old stones, this time as I stood before one of the huge sarsens in the original circle. Some of these stones are ten to 12 feet tall and weigh more

than 40 tons. You get the uncanny sensation that these are not natural stones, not of this Earth, as if poured molten from out of the ethers and left to congeal in queer, asymmetric ways. Archeologists estimate the age of most of them at Avebury as being 25 million years old.

I stood very close to this stone's rough and pockmarked surface as if peering through a window. I saw Elohim inside—or in another dimension connected to this stone. They are giant, luminous, white human figures in light, summoning stones out of the very air, setting them into the ground effortlessly. Behind the Elohim, I saw troops of humans arriving, entering life through these illuminated stone doors, as if born from Eden to Earth through Avebury.

Another sarsen was like a portal. Thousands of beings that look like Hindu divine beings, probably the Gandharvas (celestial musicians), trooped out of the stone, six abreast, seemingly endlessly, onto the flat field of Avebury. These heavenly musicians, attired in bright yellow, all played flutes. They paraded down a long mountain road from a celestial palace high on a mountain and passed through the stones into the physical space bounded by the circle of stones at Avebury.

Let's establish some basics about stones. First, where did they come from? Some were quarried from the Earth, others manifested out of the ethers. Who designed and placed the circles? The Elohim in their quasi-human form as giants, as well as the Hyperboreans with assistance by Merlin and guidance by the Ofanim. When? For the most part, before Time began on the planet, so it is ironically impossible to say how long ago, but certainly starting before Hyperborea and continuing through Lemuria, which gives us as a minimum 18 million years ago (based on H. P. Blavatsky's Lemuria dates).[467]

I once tried to get an exact date out of the Ofanim. They pleaded paradox. "This would be pointless. There was a different type of spatial, temporal relation then. Just accept it that time has not always been. It was devised to teach. When its lessons have been learned, then it will be removed. When the stones were placed in Hyperborea, there were sequential temporal shifts but not in any way similar to what you call time."

Identifying Nine Geomantic Functions of Stone Circles and Rows

The central practical question is what did the stones *do?* See table 10-1 for a summation of their functions.

First, they created permanent Blue Dishes. Each stone circle, energetically, is like a Blue Dish, a big shallow tea saucer slid under the stones and extending considerably beyond their perimeter. During Hyperborea, which was the time of the Earth's visionary geography in its pure and whole expression, the planet's surface was interlinked with many blue bowls "to receive the Light that was able to generate consciousness," as the Ofanim put it.

There were blue bowls under many other megalithic and subtle energetic structures as well, creating what I call the morning-glory effect. Picture a pristine planet floriated in morning-glory blooms, each a Blue Dish. All the stones in the original stone circles were programmed to collectively generate a long-lasting Blue Dish at that site. These Blue Dishes ranged in diameter, depending on the width of the stone circle, up to ten miles in radius. As the Ofanim indicated, each blue bowl acted like a radar dish, attuned to celestial light. Globally, the 1,746 stone circle-generated Blue Dishes acted somewhat like today's spread-array radar dishes.

The number of stones in a given circle was important in terms of the acoustic effect that circle generated. If we think, somewhat metaphorically, of each stone as a musical instrument, or perhaps the same one tuned to many different pitches, the full array of these tones or sounds (and their multiple harmonics) created a complex, three-dimensional wave-form shape, a cymatic structure.[468] In many respects it's like a crop circle image, a sound and light sculpture. Many of today's crop circle images actually illustrate the sonic fields originally generated at the stone circles as a gesture of the coming revelation of many of the mysteries of the relations of Heaven and Earth. To the extent a stone circle is

---

Table 10-1: What the Stone Circles and Rows Could Do

1. Generate long-lasting Blue Dishes to create a global morning-glory effect.
2. Provide a sonic frequency diet for the planet as counterbalance to domes.
3. Amplify incoming cosmic sounds, tones, vibrations, and energies.
4. Function as astronomical calendars, star locators, and eclipse predictors.
5. Align Grail Knights with the Cosmic Feminine, Divine Mother, and Christ.
6. Balance the Sun and Moon energies and consciousness at all levels.
7. Create and ground light temples such as Grail Castles at selected sites.
8. Support and amplify all human psychic faculties.
9. Institute and maintain the Time function and cycle on the Earth.

still whole and preserved, its "crop circle" sonic field is still there.

Now think of this in global terms, as a calendar or clockwork mechanism. The stone circles, each with its cymatic, three-dimensional sound shape, would be like a planetary organ with 1,746 keys. In accordance with a celestial schedule (probably discernible through astrology), one or more stone circles would be sounded, and their sound, amplitude, and wave forms would be amplified, as if the organist were playing with the pedals down.

Structurally at each stone circle, then, you would have the physical stones, a large shallow Blue Dish up to 20 miles in diameter, and the complex three-dimensional wave form inside it. Again, just picture one of today's complex crop circle images, which though two-dimensional, tend to be geometric, symmetric, and elegant; now inflate it so it has a third dimension of height and volume. It sits like a jewel or crown in the center of the Blue Dish blazing in the landscape like a fabulous morning-glory blossom, the stones like the stamen of a flower.

A second function was that the total array of stone circles gave the Earth a kind of sonic diet, a balance (in sound frequencies) to the distribution of light frequency and star magnitudes represented by the 1,746 domes. Think of sound as a nutrient, and think of the great diversity of sounds on the Earth as a kind of acoustic ecology, with niches and specialized environments. The various tones and harmonics of the stone circles continuously "fed" the Earth with these cosmic sounds.

Third, the stones in some cases acted as amplifiers for subtle cosmic sounds. This was accomplished by the joint action of the stones in a circle and a surrounding outer ditch. This function was especially present at Avebury stone circle, perhaps the most important, as it is Earth's umbilicus. This complex stone circle has many geomantic functions, but to explain any of them we need to understand its megalithic architecture.

The amplification feature concerned the use of 72 original sarsens placed on the inside edge of the deep ditch that surrounds the 28.5 acre site. These are the gigantic, ten to 12 foot tall, multiton stones that I described as looking as if congealed out of the ethers.

The original plan for Avebury called for 72 of these sarsens to be placed in a circle, just on the inside of a deep ditch or ring. That ditch is four-fifths of a mile long, completely encircling Avebury, created by the Elohim who dug out an estimated 200,000 tons of rock to form a bank today about 14 to 18 feet tall from the bottom of the trench. Based on partial excavations, archeologists propose that the ditch originally was 50 feet deep, measured from the top of the bank.

These 72 sarsens were manifested out of the ethers by the Elohim and placed in a rough circle 400 megalithic yards wide (1,088 feet). This was done before any humans incarnated. One of the functions was to manifest 12 rays of the Ray Masters into the six worlds.[469] This would be a global effect throughout these six dimensions as they pertained to Earth and would remain in effect even after some of the stones were gone.

The amplifier effect has to do with the ditch. Here it's useful to think in terms of the now outmoded phonograph record. The ditch is the groove in the LP, the needle is you walking the ditch attuned to your Blazing Star, and the amplifiers are the 72 stones, which broadcast celestial "music" throughout the circle. Remember that Avebury is the site of Earth's own Blazing Star, so when at Avebury your attention is on your Star, the effect is multiplied many times over in potency because of this resonance. As the Ofanim quaintly put it, "If you play the record with the needle of your spirit, then you hear some hi-fi sounds."[470]

It may seem that you are walking in the current of a woman's voice, as the sound continuously circles the stones. The voice leads you to the body, though it's too big, too cosmic, to see—yet you feel you walk inside it, or flow through it, like a corpuscle. In *Looking for Arthur*, I described the sensation as follows: "With each step, I feel in deeper resonance with something truly beyond this Earth and yet of this Earth, indwelling, lawfully, mercifully resident. The feeling is monumentally feminine, a soft river of silent flowing light."[471]

After human incarnation began, the Blazing Star was grounded at Avebury—the name suggests it was buried—and 22 more stones were added, completing the pattern at 94. These 22 stones were quarried on Earth, though not nearby. They were installed to "enclose the energy of the ascended hierarchy [Ray Masters] in a different formation to help activate the original umbilicus at a later date," the Ofanim said. Once humanity was grounded on Earth (in some odd way, through Avebury), the planetary geomantic mixture could be enriched with these additional stones.

The original Avebury plan called for a double stone row leading out of the circle into the landscape. Today remnants of that stone row are known collectively as the West Kennet Avenue, a 1.5-mile sinuous walkway about 50 feet wide. It terminates (or starts) at the northeast causeway in the ditch and passes across an open field. Only 27 of an estimated 100 stones remain in the avenue, spaced at 80-foot intervals. Traces remain of a second row, called the Beckhampton Avenue, leaving Avebury through the West causeway, 45 degrees from the West Kennet Avenue. Based on excavations and estimates, this double row was 1.25 miles long, consisting of 200 stones spaced 48 to 51 feet apart.

The function of the stone rows was to channel energy; these rows were matched with henges and rings, some without stone circles. If Avebury is a big amplifier, playing cosmic hi-fi sounds on its "record player," then the stone avenue focuses that beam of sound and light and channels it out into the landscape. Changing metaphors, if Avebury, or any stone circle, is like a dam, then the stone row is the controlled spillway that funnels "water" as needed into the river below, which then distributes the water through its own network of tributaries.

Archeologists catalogue about 683 stone rows of different types as being extant in the British Isles and Brittany. These types include avenues, long double and long single stone rows, multiple rows, rows with four to six stones or only three stones. Though Carnac in France is one of the most famous multiple stone rows, at least nine multiple rows exist in Northern Scotland, ranging from four to 18 rows in a single formation; some multiple rows are parallel, others splayed, others erratically fanlike.[472]

Fourth function: Stone circles can have archeoastronomical functions. Archeologists have already documented this to some extent, beginning with Gerald Hawkins's insights on Stonehenge in the 1960s. Since then, other stone circles have been revealed to have astronomical correlates in their design. A university astronomer, Hawkins demonstrated that each significant stone in the array aligns with at least one other point to an extreme position of the Sun or Moon (summer and winter solstices) and that the enigmatic "aubrey holes" in some stones were used as eclipse predictors, attuned to the 56-year eclipse cycle.[473]

Hawkins was right on the mark with his astronomical research. According to the Ofanim, "Stonehenge is a table to disclose all pertinent astrological and astronomical information pertinent to Britain." There are more than enough stones there today for Stonehenge to still fulfill its original astronomical function, the Ofanim note. However, that resumption of function is unlikely.

A fifth function of stone circles is ceremonial, religious, and initiatory. These rites had to do with alignments with the Cosmic Mother, the Feminine, and Christ. Stonehenge, the Ofanim explain, was a temple to the Goddess. It was a solstice temple primarily, though it was used at each equinox and solstice, which means at least four times a year.

During the time of the Celtic King Arthur and the Grail Knights—it's more precise to say that particular "Arthur wave," because it lasted more than one human lifetime—the Knights were gathered by Merlin and Arthur and stood before the 12 main stones of the circle. Each Knight was aligned and energized and put before the Goddess in a ritual for joining themselves as men with the Feminine. This is the fifth function of a stone circle, though not all circles performed this.

"The stones held the Earth magic of the Mother, each aligned by Merlin to the 12 constellations of the zodiac," the Ofanim state. "Each stone was rooted in Earth, dug into the Mother Earth below to bless the Goddess above. Each stone was attuned to the Spirit-Masculine quality above in each constellation. Each Knight was thereby attuned above and below to Heaven and Earth in a ritual to greet his feminine, to unlock the doors through the circle to the unconscious."

This fairly complicated alignment became unnecessary after the physical incarnation of the Christ on Earth. Then the Christ spirit was freely available in the planetary ethers. So it is unlikely that Stonehenge will ever be used this way again, or in any way; things have changed. "The potential through the Christ now is more accessible generally without such complex Earth rituals. It was one of the first events to hold heart integration, the male and female, for the birth of the Christ Child within that allowed Christ to then come in matter as Jesus."

A sixth function of the stone circles is to balance the Sun and Moon at all levels. This is best understood in alchemical terms, as a balancing out of all polar opposites in the personal, collective, and planetary levels. You have, for example: the inner masculine (Sun) and outer feminine (Moon); the inner feminine and outer masculine; the physical effects of the physical Sun and Moon; the time cycles of the day and year (Sun) and month (Moon); the equinoxes and solstices; day and night cycles; the Mithraea (Sun) and Soma (Moon) temples, the finite and immortal, substance and fire, consciousness and speech, time and space.[474]

The stone circles' seventh function is to ground light temples, somewhat like tent posts holding down a billowing tent. This function is demonstrable at Castle Rigg, a stone circle in Keswick in England's Lake District. This pear-shaped circle of 38 extant stones (archeologists believe it once had 42; the Ofanim say 39) about three to five feet tall is set on a bare level stretch on Chestnut Hill about 1.5 miles from the town.

The meaning of the site's name is straightforward: The circle is the rigging up to the light castle, in this case, a Grail Castle. "The rigging is all you have to work on to connect with the castle of light," the Ofanim note.

Let's consider some aspects of the stone's energy structure. There is of course the large radiating Blue Dish underlying the site. Next are the 39 original stones of this circle (one is missing), which are the rigging; they create and ground the light temple, and they are also the bottom rungs of the ladder *up* to the castle. In between the stone circle and the Grail Castle is a complex geometric shape created by the wave forms of the 39 stones. It resembles an icosahedron of light, a Platonic Solid with 20 equilateral triangles. The Grail Castle sits on top of this light structure, like a ship bobbing on the sea.

When you spend time inside the Castle Rigg stone circle, your own "rigging" or psychic apparatus gets activated, enabling you to climb the rigging. The rigging helps you shift cognitive dimensions, moving you into the fourth dimension—the "above"—where the light castle resides.

If you're lucky, the curtains might momentarily part, revealing an ancient vista. I had occasion one summer to spend about a week meditating three times a day (sunrise, midday, sunset) at Castle Rigg at the invitation of the Ofanim. Geomantic reality is multilayered: At Castle Rigg, you have the physical hill, its vista, and the 38 stones; in the next layer you have the dome overhead, the Blue Dish underneath, the geometric light form in and above the circle, the Grail Castle above it; behind that—or *before* that, in time—I saw a sleek, silvery-blue, otherworldly temple in the same place.

"The Castle Rigg temple was originally conceived in UR," the Ofanim told me. "It was then implemented by the Chaldeans later. As you saw, there was an earlier temple at this spot before the stones were sited, the one you saw. It was a Pleiadian temple." The UR the Ofanim alluded to is the famous if enigmatic UR of the Chaldees, mentioned in the Bible. Apparently long ago there were many such civilizations, designated by just two letters (such as UR, MU, and ON), that existed at different levels of reality on the planet. Based on the Ofanim's clue, it appears that the Chaldeans of UR were deeply involved in Earth's geomancy.

An eighth function is that in some cases they are programmed to facilitate and amplify all human clairvoyant and psychic faculties, to attune one to the Feminine, and to activate all right-brain activities. The Merry Maidens stone circle at Lands End (four miles from Penzance) in Cornwall, England, is a prime example of this function. This circle has 19 stones (each about four feet high, spaced 12 feet apart) on the perimeter of what archeologists call a perfect circle, which is 78 feet wide. About one-quarter mile away are two standing stones called the Pipers:

One is 15 feet tall; the other, 317 feet away, stands 13.6 feet tall. Cornish belief links these two with the Maidens.[475]

I spent a couple hours meditating inside the Merry Maidens circle one winter's morning. The 19 stones became beacons of light that seemed to transmit laser beams from around the circle straight to the pineal gland in my brain. My physical body seemed to fall away, crumbling from the impact of light. My remaining light body, from the neck below, was a solid cone of purple, with a gold head and silver crown, and a gold-silver caduceus with a white-light shaft rising from the end was topped by a crown; the rest of my body was now underground; my pineal gland was a white sphere at the center of the circle.

My colleague reported these impressions: "I saw a clear, transparent dome over the stone circle and a huge white angel circling the Merry Maidens. The maidens lay face down above us on top of the dome, which was divided into 19 sections. I saw an aura around each stone, maroon-purple in color; then the stones turned golden. Gold rings of light floated up from out of the center of the circle. These were caught by the maidens and tossed out into the landscape. I was shown a connection. If you go into the Earth in a straight line, you'll come out somewhere on the opposite side of the planet. The effects of our meditation here are felt in direct correspondence to this line."

According to the Ofanim, our meditations at the Merry Maidens (there were five of us) were coincident with an activation of "an important aspect" of the Earth grid. The straight line my colleague perceived was real: "This site has an access point through the Earth and repercusses at many points throughout the grid matrix, predominantly increasing awareness and helping the Earth detoxify at an organic level without major cataclysm."

The primary function of the Merry Maidens is to help manifest the psychic faculties through accessing the Feminine. "The powers of clairvoyance, clairsentience, and clairaudience are available here. These are prerequisites to a fundamental understanding of the energy around this area, and also in a wider context. This is to do with the feminine aspect, intuitive coherence, and the right brain."

The Ofanim explained that each of the 19 Maidens is a representative of a phenomenon or aspect of the Goddess. The 19 Merry Maidens are the principal aspects of those, and each one represents a phylum or group of aspects out of a total "Mothership" of 94 features. Each stone is an amplifier of these aspects.[476]

A ninth function of stone circles and rows is to ground the Time mechanism for the entire Earth. This is the prime purpose of the huge stone rows of Carnac in Brittany, France, sometimes referred to as the "Army of Stones," as the several thousand stones in rows are said to have been invading pagan Roman soldiers turned to stone by the French Saint Cornely. At least 3,846 standing stones are still arrayed in sets of parallel rows (at least ten sets identified) that march across five miles of French landscape just outside the resort town of Carnac on the Gulf of Morbihan in northwest France.[477]

To understand the role of Carnac's stones with respect to Earth time, you need to appreciate its overall geomantic structure first. The stone rows stretch out across five miles of terrain; the dome over this area is 15.598 miles wide and is the Earth's dome for Sirius; the landscape zodiac here is 44 miles wide, including the physical and etheric ecliptics; its zodiac dome is 97 miles wide; and the entire site is the brow chakra of the Albion of the Virgo Albion Plate.

The Ofanim say that in Hyperborea the structure was much simpler, involving only 365 stones, created with the involvement of the Elohim, Merlin, and certain beings from Sirius. The stones marked the minor nodal points within the cranium of Albion, and they created the cycle of

Time on Earth, one stone per day of the year. Even today, those remaining of these 365 stones are the most energized of all the thousands of Carnac's standing stones; many can be found in the Kerlescan array.

More stones were added later to diffuse the energy over the cranial structure of Albion due to certain functions within the beings now incarnated under that Albion Plate. Human evolution, and advances or alterations in human consciousness, necessitated an enrichment of the mixture generated and sustained by the Carnac stones. Thus, in the second Lemurian epoch, 2,176 more stones were added, bringing the total to 2,541. When was this? Let's say less than 18,000,000 years ago, which, as stated earlier, H. P. Blavatsky gives as a rough starting point for the Lemurian world culture.

It's important to remember that the stones were placed in rows, rather than circles, to follow the cranial energy routes of Albion in accordance with how his "head" was geomantically templated across the Carnac landscape. You can get a visceral sense of this by examining an acupuncture map for the human cranium; you'll note that at least 12 important acupuncture meridians cross the cranium from the ears up to the crown as if in more or less parallel rows.

During the "final Atlantean period," another 666 stones were added "for further alteration of the cranial rhythms within this Albion," the Ofanim note.[478] This brings the total to 3,207. Presumably the other 2,000 or so stones were added still later, possibly not under guidance by the Ofanim or Elohim, as was the case with other physical geomantic features.

The Sirius dome over Carnac was put there "to ground the Mind of the beings of Sirius. It was necessary to transform the input into the brain or cranium of Albion." The Carnac stone row structure today is "intact," the Ofanim state, "but it is largely unsupported by human consciousness."

In other words, even though the Carnac stone rows ground the energies of Sirius and funnel them through the rows in such a way as to establish the Earth's Time mechanism for our benefit, the ultimate health and well-being of this geomantic tool require our active and continuous involvement. This feature, like all others in the Earth's energy matrix, is interactive and reciprocal: It needs our conscious input as nutritive feedback to keep it running optimally.

If you feel motivated to help support global consciousness (and gain some personal benefit as well) by interfacing with the Virgo Albion, I suggest going first to Maiden Castle in Dorchester, Dorset, England. I discuss this below under Light Corrective Centers, but going there first will be a useful, possibly necessary, preparation for Carnac. That was my sequence.[479]

A point of clarification. Carnac is a unique array and function because it is under the auspices of the planet's only Sirius dome. The cranium and brow chakras of the planet's other 11 Albions do not have this stone row array, nor do they need it. It's handled globally at Carnac.

Across the British Isles and Europe, you can still encounter very tall single standing stones or *menhir*, typically ten to 25 feet tall and weighing hundreds of tons. At Locmariaquer, near Carnac, Le Grand Menhir Brise now lies on the ground, broken into four pieces; if standing, it would tower 67 feet and weigh 300 tons. The *menhir* still upright at Le Manio in the Carnac rows is 16 feet tall.

Here are a few other examples: The Devil's Arrows in a field near Boroughbridge in Yorkshire are three massive stones, 18, 21, and 22.5 feet tall. The Rudston monolith in Rudston, Humberside, stands 25 feet tall but may once have been 28 feet high and is England's tallest. The Blind Fiddler (10 feet 9 inches) stands near Catchall, Cornwall, in an area with other solitary stones. Harold's Stones, in Trelleck, Monmouthshire, consist of three standing stones, the tallest being 12 feet, roughly in a straight line. The menhir of the Champ-Dolent near Ille-et-Vilaine in Brittany is 30 feet tall.[480]

While the height and weight of some of these megaliths is impressive, if not astounding, size and girth are not essential for their function. Scale is not important, the Ofanim say. "The external form does not necessarily relate to the energy matrix of the stone." The solitary *menhirs* at Carnac function like acupuncture needles within the structure of the landscape Albion's head, and attune his minor meridians. The huge *menhir* at Locmariaquer attunes the energy from a dome cap to a minor *nadi*, or landscape energy line. The Ofanim say that the Hyperboreans (Pleiadians) placed 2,430 *menhirs* on the Earth.

If you've ever had an acupuncture treatment, you already have a bodily sense of what this effect might be like on a global scale. If you haven't, I'll try to suggest its qualities. You lie on a padded table in your underwear; you're relaxed; the acupuncturist has inserted anywhere from a dozen to four dozen tiny fish-bone-sized needles in the topmost layer of your skin, all over the front or back of your body. You are barely aware of them. Yet you can sense energy zipping around in your body. This is *qi*, your vital life-force energy, moving around, opening up the meridians. After the session is over, the needles come out, and you feel fantastic: deeply relaxed, mellow, glowing, as if without bones or even the memory of agitation or dis-ease.

Acupuncture regulates the body's flow of *qi* through its many meridians as a way to balance the body and maintain health. Its chief application, ideally, is as a preventive measure. You keep the body's subtle energy in balance to prevent the physical system from getting ill, and you do this at the first signs of energy imbalance. *Qi* can get stuck, move too fast, too slow, be too hot or too cold, too damp or too dry.

Pretend you're a planet. You have a physical body, which is all of nature, the mineral, plant, animal, and human kingdoms of life. You have a subtle energy circulation system, the Oroboros and dome lines. The 2,430 *menhirs* are like acupuncture needles permanently inserted into your planetary skin, continuously regulating the flow of *qi* through your 15 Oroboros lines, your 1,746 dome lines and your 83,808 dome cap lines—all the *nadis* of your planetary body.

Chinese acupuncture calls an acupuncture treatment point, where the needle is inserted, a *qi hole*, a place where the life force wells up when one is healthy. We might usefully think of dome caps as Earth's *qi* holes or wells; you insert the *menhir* in the *qi* hole to bring the energy to the surface so as to move it along the line.

While acupuncture needles are never left in our body for longer than an hour and each treatment may call for needle placements in different points, that's not practical on a planetary level. The Hyperboreans inserted the huge stones once and forever, it seems, so that the Earth, for as long as this system was intact, received a permanent stimulation of its *qi* holes. Perhaps the system of 2,430 stones was timed to activate according to a celestial or astronomic schedule, like intermittently blinking lights on a Christmas tree.

In any event, one wonders how the Earth has been coping these many centuries with many of the 2,430 original needle-stones now broken or removed.

The Tuatha in Their *Sidhes*— the Function of Hill-Forts and Otherworld Castles

Irish myth speaks of the Tuatha de Danann, Ireland's old gods, the Followers of the Goddess Danu, gathering in their *sidhes* (pronounced shays) or Otherworld dwellings accessed through hollow hills, barrows, and mounds.

Once the Tuatha lived above ground, but later they retreated to the inside of mounds and became known as the *aes sidhe*, "the people of the hills." Most popular among these people is the banshee (from *bean sidhe*, "woman of the *sidhe*," thought to be a death messenger). Each of the main Tuatha was given a sidhe by the Dagda, their chief: Lir got *Sidhe Fionnachaidh* (near Newtown Hamilton in County Armagh), Aonghus Og got *Brugh na Boinne* (Newgrange, near Dublin), and at least five others are specified. In practical terms, this allotment of sidhes to the Tuatha meant these were the places you could reasonably expect an audience with—a vision of—the respective deity.

Geomantically, what kind of feature is a sidhe? Variable. As Western culture increasingly disbelieved in the Otherworld in the last millennium, the Tuatha got downgraded to fairies, and their *sidhes* became regarded as fairy mounds. Today the term *sidhe* refers to an ancient hillock used for burial, a tumulus or artificially raised hill, or a round, flat-topped man-made barrow. Hundreds of sidhes are cited in Irish myth, but some were situated in what archeologists call hillforts, even though this term, geomantically, is misleading.

Hill-forts are usually flat, grassy hilltops fortified with and enclosed by several steep ramparts. The enclosed area is generally small, normally not more than one-half acre. Archeologists presume the hill-forts were built by "prehistoric man" to protect livestock and families, as early military fortifications equipped with tactical defensive advantages such as view and difficulty of access.[481]

Some 2,000 hill-forts have been identified in Britain, some of which retain very old and enigmatic names, such as the Wrekin, Old Sarum, and Maiden Castle. Maiden Castle is situated just outside the city of Dorchester in Dorset. Its ramparts are immense, consisting of two knolls that rise 15 feet above an intervening "saddle"; the enclosed grassy oblong hilltop is about 7.4 acres and features the remains of a huge burial mound 1,620 long by 81 feet wide; the inner circumference is 1.5 miles. Archeologists propose that the entire site was constructed before 3000 B.C., but they aren't sure of its specific use.

A few clarifications before we go further. First, the ditch that is the trough between ramparts is different from the encircling ring-ditch around stone circles. In almost no cases has evidence of stone circles been found at ramparted hill-forts. Stone circles have ring-ditches, but these were *dug*. In contrast, the ring-ditches or ramparts at true hill-forts were *manifested* and have a different function.

Second, there were only 1,080 true hill-forts in the original energy template for Earth, so some of the 2,000 hill-forts are not true ones, geomantically speaking. If the so-called hill-fort does not have a rampart, it may be a hill-fort in archeological terms, but it is not an example of the geomantic feature I'm introducing here. The Ofanim call this feature a *light corrective center;* the ramparts and ditch are essential to their construction. Obviously about half of the identified hill-forts are imitations of the original design—we saw this with stone circles—or they were once literally defense fortifications on hilltops.

The temple structures were never physical or overtly visible; as with Castle Rigg, the *castle* at Maiden Castle, or Segsbury Castle on the Ridgeway in Wiltshire and Oxfordshire, is above, or beyond, in another dimension. At Castle Rigg the castle is a Grail Castle; at Barbury Castle, a Soma Temple; at Maiden Castle, a landscape zodiac; at South Cadbury Castle in Somerset, it's King Arthur's Round Table.[482]

So what is a light corrective center? "These are receptacles for energy to come in from various places, such as stars of various types," the Ofanim say. "Let's say if you have the right equipment, you can play a record. If you imagine these features upon the Earth, then each will be able to be played by different beings or energetics stimulated by different beings. The hill-forts were produced by matter manipulated through wave energy. Their function has been one of enhancing energy topically. There have been many etheric and interdimensional features or temples over many of these so-called hill-forts."

Each of these 1,080 light corrective centers has its own history, and none ever had stones in circles, rows, or on their own, the Ofanim note. They have energy matrices that correspond to the five Platonic Solids or other complex solids. For example, at Figsbury Rings in Wiltshire, the energy structure is a dodecahedron; at Liddington Castle on the Ridgeway, it's a cube with a Mount Olympus. "These are models of perfection seeded within the Mind of His Most Highest Cosmic Architect. They are mirrors of each other, Man and the Platonic Solids."

How were they made? It sounds a little fantastic for our contemporary limited view of what's possible or how the Earth got organized originally, but the Ofanim explain it this way: "Like a pebble in a still pool, a jewel was fragmented at each of these places [the 1,080 light corrective center sites]. The energy field set up a wave motion in the superficial part of the Earth's etheric field, which physically manifested as rings that previously looked like boils."

Let's decode and expand this information. Some years ago, during a long visit to England and many megalithic sites, I dreamed of the formation of one of these light corrective centers. In the dream it was called Blookey Hole. An Emerald, or a fragment of one, was set on a stand in the center of the landmass designated to be a light corrective center. Using the Ofanim's still pool image, it was as if this Emerald fragment was perpetually falling into the etheric waters just above or beyond the physical hill, creating a boil on the Earth.

Picture boiling water: You have numerous dome-like half-bubbles roiling on the water's surface before they pop. It's as if the rounded roof of the bubble folds down to the sides, leaving a crown or a structure with only a periphery. The inside is empty. If you've ever seen a close-up of a milk drop striking a flat surface and splashing upwards, it forms an elegant white crown around the now empty center where the drop originally dropped. This is a variation on a boil.

When the domed boil pops and folds down, you get a ramparted effect. Blookey Hole seemed like a cave aboveground, with the ramparts forming high walls. The Emerald fragment, still present at the hill-forts, keeps sending out the wave form that generated the boil that turned into a ramparted hill-fort. The sequence would have been this: Emerald fragment placed, wave form generated, still pool of the ethers reshaped into a boil, the boil reshapes the physical landmass, the boil top and sides fold down to form ramparts, and these have a Platonic Solid and one or more galaxy-on-Earth temples present.[483]

Unlike the stone circles, incidentally, light corrective centers are not always circular, oval, or even obviously symmetrical. The hill-fort of Hambledon Hill in Dorset, enclosing 24.5 acres and with two sets of ramparts, looks like a long dog biscuit twisted in the middle. Beacon Hill hill-fort in Hampshire (12 acres, two ramparts) looks like an hourglass with a fat midriff. Viewing it through an aerial photograph, you can almost discern the quivering wobble set in motion by the wave form generated by the Emerald fragment in its center.

The majority of these light corrective centers seem to be in the British Isles (including Ireland); if you were to see the system as a whole, it would be a variety of geometric shapes of different colors set on many bare hilltops.

Since many of these sites are still functional, you can visit them with reasonable expectations of intriguing mystical experiences. Obviously, if they are mirrors of the five Platonic Solids implicit in the human spiritual-physical makeup, then merely being at a hill-fort that presents a light matrix version of a Platonic Solid is beneficial to your energy constitution, notably the chakras.

Let's take Maiden Castle. What is the castle there? I mentioned there is a landscape zodiac on the grassy playing field of the enclosed area; that measures 5.2 miles, including the physical and etheric ecliptics. Maiden Castle, as mentioned in chapter 9, is the throat chakra for the Virgo Albion Plate. But the castle there is a Castle of the Maidens, as its name suggests and veils.

Visualize standing in the center of an englobing sphere of 94 crystalline facets or windows; each is the face of a different feminine deity, or 94 aspects of the Cosmic Mother. If the stone circle called Merry Maidens represents the 19 aspects or phyla of the cosmic Feminine, this is the point of origin, the full warehouse. At Maiden Castle you stand within a tetrahedron (a Platonic Solid with four equal triangular facets), and inside that you are surrounded by a sphere with 94 motherly faces, a House of the Mother, with 94 ways of knowing and clairvoyant faculties, a family of Merry Maidens—the Castle of the Maidens.

The Ofanim explain that Maiden Castle is the Mother of the Merry Maidens, or the Mother behind the Mother. "The maiden is the representative of Gaia. Beyond being a handmaiden, it is more like an archetypal representative of the planetary being, like a hologram of Gaia. Maiden Castle is the entrance to the womb of the Mother. The Mother is also the guardian of Gaia as well as being the archetypal image for her, just as Demeter and Persephone are in the Underworld."

The three ditches and ridges at Maiden Castle represent the three aspects of the Goddess, virgin, mother, and crone, while the hill-fort is so comparatively large because it's "the grounding of the Mothership." The tetrahedron corresponds to the fire element, which is appropriate for the Mother. "Is not the function of the Mother love and warmth? The love and caring of the Mother for Her children is compassion, which is pure fire." That fire is expressed through the four-sided pyramid called the tetrahedron, Platonic Solid of the fire element.

There's a marvelous and surprising secret implicit in the 94 aspects of the Mothership. Ninety-four is an awkward number; it does not have a whole number square root, nor does it have well-remarked symbolic aspects. Mathematically, it's the product of 72 plus 22, the number of stones at Avebury, Earth's umbilicus, and another grounding point for aspects of the Mothership. Here is the surprise: 94 is the gematria (number equivalent of the letters) for *Madim,* Hebrew for Mars—*MDYM,* or *Mem* (40), *Dallet* (4), *Yod* (10), and *Mem* (40), or 94.

So you wonder: Is the Mothership based on Mars or does it work through the Mars sphere?[484]

Quoits, Tumuli, Barrows, and Cyclopean Cities of Stone

You will encounter several other types of stoneworks and earthworks out in the megalithic landscape of the British Isles and Northern Europe. The nomenclature for these structures is various, depending on the host culture, sometimes overlapping, and at times confusing. Let's start with quoits.

A quoit, also known as a cromlech (Breton) or dolmen (French), is a rough stone monument that usually involves two upright stones, or orthostats, topped by a single horizontal capstone, although there are examples of three orthostats topped by two capstones or roofing slabs. Quoits as we find them today are uncovered stacked stones, resembling small caves suitable for no more than two people. Archeologists presume they were once covered by earth, but perhaps they were not.

A stacked quoit, the Ofanim note, is "another energy device or doorway into the Summer Country or Shambhala." In other words, you could meditate inside a stacked quoit and have the possibility of ascending in awareness and dimensional participation into the realm of Avalon, the astral plane, or Shambhala.

A tumulus is essentially a larger version of the aboveground cave, but decidedly covered by earth, making it an earthen mound with a front entrance. Tumuli mark minor dome caps, the Ofanim explain. "They were implanted later than the first stones [as in stone circles and single standing stones], but before the second Lemurian phase," which was towards the end of the phase of installing earthworks inspired by angelic designers. Their shape "pertains to the function of craniums."

A third, related megalithic structure is the barrow, which combines features of the quoit and tumulus, but adds another: chambers. A barrow typically has a long central passage, with several chambers on both sides, terminating in a central open chamber that is more or less circular. The structure, usually rectangular or trapezoidal, is reminiscent of a spinal column, the side chambers being vertebrae, with a cranium at the top, represented by the central chamber at the terminus. The existence of the long spine-like entrance to the central chamber has led archeologists to use the terms passage-grave and gallery-grave to characterize barrows.

Barrows proliferate throughout the British Isles like dandelions on a spring lawn.[485] Archeologists report 1,000 barrows within a ten-mile radius of the Stonehenge stone circle in Wiltshire, England. These barrows were situated so as to be mostly visible from Stonehenge and clearly to form "a major component of the ritual landscape."[486] Archeologists also state that in the four-county complex called Wessex (including Wiltshire), there are 4,000 barrows.[487] Ireland has 505 identified wedge-tombs, which are barrows with a gallery that diminishes in height from the western to eastern end. Most archeologists assume the barrows were used for burial purposes and that their construction dates back to the Neolithic period (New Stone Age, circa 5000–2500 B.C.).

According to the Ofanim, barrows were used for burials, but they were also earlier used to enhance consciousness in the living. As they were intelligently sited on dome lines or within dome caps, they were able to collect or draw off energy from larger geomantic reservoirs, such as dome caps, domes, hill-forts, single stones, stone circles, or zodiacs—"structures we had inspired."

Just as the ancient Celtic kings wanted burial on hillsides such as Bluestone Heath in Lincolnshire because it was the site of a stargate, thus ensuring, they thought, more likely passage into the desired spiritual realms after death, so the recently deceased wanted placement in barrows. Proximity to heightened consciousness by placement in a geomantically numinous area presumably would give the souls of the dead extra and perhaps needed "lift-off" for their after-death ascent into the Summer Country or the stars.

For the living, the cranium shape of the tumulus or central chamber of the barrow could have the effect of squeezing the etheric body off from the dense physical, facilitating visionary experiences and clairvoyance. The result would be an induced near-death experience (NDE) in which the participant would gain information about their life and soul purpose, and it would also be a kind of induced out-of-body experience (OOBE) involving the astral body and its perceptual apparatus.

Both psychic experiences, the NDE and OOBE, are now a fairly familiar part of our contemporary metaphysical scene, and the possible use of barrows and earthen mounds to produce the same experience indicates the longevity of the endeavor. Barrows and tumuli theoretically can still be used for this purpose; it would be interesting to use a barrow for a conscious dying ritual as well.

I once sat inside a stone-lined, earth-covered tumulus at Carnac in France. The place is called the Kercado tumulus, situated on a lane that leads to a chateau near Kerlescan. In midwinter, I noticed that it was ten degrees warmer inside than outside. The interior wall consisted of eight broad, vertical stones set adjacent to one another. Energetically, it was like a direction selector: Choose a stone and walk through it to somewhere else.

The dynamics of the chamber amplify your psychic ability to see into other dimensions. Ideally, when fitted out properly and in correct working order, it should work as a sensory deprivation chamber; again, it's another aid to meditative focus. I saw through one stone: a long stone-lined avenue leading to a yellow light. I walked along this avenue for a while but got lost several times, or else diverted into a labyrinth of corridors and side tunnels. Then I saw the tumulus, its chamber, and the multiple subtle avenues through the stones from above. The tumulus was a switching station to shift you from the physical world in your body to the astral world in your visionary form. I saw the avenues leading up into the Summer Country, to Avalon.

The barrows, though prodigiously implanted across the ancient landscape, were not part of the original Blue Room megalithic-geomantic template. "These are not of our origin," the Ofanim state. "We did not inspire their building; others did at another time. They were not necessary. Many times in the course of history Man has built things which are a distraction rather than in line with the main theme. These 'caves' are an example of distracted behavior."

Even if the Neolithic geomantic designers added earthworks that were technically unrequired by the Earth energy template, their desire to do so suggests a widespread earnest effort to stay in close contact with the spiritual worlds and to use whatever means possible to maintain and deepen that link. Aerial photographs of multiple barrows in a field or near a larger geomantic structure, such as Stonehenge, convey an impression of spiritual excitement, like a multitude of tents and caravans parked as close as possible to a festival site like a geomantic Woodstock.[488]

If the barrows were tent sites pitched close to the geomantic festivals at the stone circles or dome caps, the Cyclopean Cities were interactive megalithic television.

Throughout the world today we find evidence of former colossal stone buildings, of massive stones fitted together with an engineer's precision. At places like Baalbek in Lebanon, Ggantija in Gozo in Malta, Lalibela in Ethiopia, Sacsaywayman in Cuzco, Peru, we can still marvel at remnants of these stone colossi. A careful reading of world myths yields many more examples of stone cities now mostly gone though vaguely recalled in story, such as Mycenae and Tiryns in Greece, Jericho in Israel, Great Zimbabwe in Africa, and Tiahuanaco in Bolivia.

I use the term Cyclopean City to describe colossal stone structures that myth and legend say were made overnight by the angels or gods according to a celestial plan at a very early period of Earth history, such as before the Flood. The stones don't seem to be quarried or derived from the local landscape, they are fitted perfectly together without mortar, and it is impossible for conventional engineering and consensus reality to imagine how they were moved. Often there is one key superhuman figure who directs the work, such as Perseus, Lalibela, Amphion, Brutus, or the Cyclopes, among many examples.

The term cyclopean is used by archeologists to refer to the stonework. Cyclopean technique means using huge, irregular boulders, carefully fitted together without mortar to create a massive wall with an uneven face. But it's also defined as randomly shaped rock walls built out of large stone, presumably by the legendary one-eyed giants, the Cyclopes. The term further denotes huge, gigantic, rough, massive, of or relating to the Cyclopes. The walls are typically massive, 15 to 30 feet thick, made of huge stone blocks, crudely shaped, though sometimes they are well-finished blocks. At Ollantaytambo, Peru, and Tiahuanaco, Bolivia, the cyclopean walls are made from tight-fitting polygonal stone blocks each weighing many tons (see table 10-2 for selected locations).

The world's mythic record offers intriguing clues about these stone cities. The Celtic god Lugh (or Lud) surrounded *Troia Nova*, the New Troy (the antecedent of London) built by Brutus on the River Thames, with lofty walls and towers constructed with extraordinary skill, calling it *Kaerlud,* Lud's City *(Lud's dun)*.[489]

Both Homer and Apollodorus tell us that the human king Laomedon engaged the gods Apollo and Poseidon to build broad city walls for him at Ilium (Troy, in today's Turkey); they labored for a full year. Poseidon boasts that their walls were massive, made of well-cut stone, rendering Ilium impregnable. Homer spoke of Troy's great walls, gates, and rings of stone. Euripides wrote "the Cyclopes built well/cramping stone on stone with plumb and mallet"[490] at Mycenae "where/the stone walls built by the giants invade the sky."[491]

In Bolivia, according to Aymara Indians, the megalithic complex at Tiahuanaco (or Tiwanaku) was built at the beginning of time by the founder god Viracocha and his followers, who caused the massive stones to be carried through the air to the sound of a trumpet. When the invading Spaniards arrived in the sixteenth century, the Indians told

Table 10-2: Cyclopean Cities

Planetary Total: 6,300

Selected Locations:

Mycenae, Greece	Trepuco, Menorca	Temple of Solomon, Jerusalem, Israel
Thebes, Greece: the Cadmeia	Talati de Dalt, Menorca	Acropolis, Athens (fortified by Agrolas and Hyperbios), Greece
Troy, Turkey	Filitosa, Corsica	
Sacsaywayman, Cuzco, Peru	Knossos, Crete	
Baalbek, Lebanon	The Heraeum (Argive Heraion), Argos, Greece	Temple of Apollo, Cumae acropolis, Naples (built by Daedalus), Italy
Tiahuanaco (Tiwanaku), Bolivia		
Puma Punku, near Tiahuanaco, Bolivia	Lalibela, Ethiopia	London, England: Lud's City, Trinovantum, built by Brutus
Tiryns, near Mycenae, Greece	Great Zimbabwe, Republic of Zimbabwe	
Ollantaytambo, Peru	Egyptian Labyrinth, Lake Moeris-Arsinoe, Egypt (per Herodotus)	*Palatkwapi,* "Red House," (Hopi Red City of the South)
Hagar Qim, Malta		
Ggantija, Gozo	Jericho, Israel	

Equivalent Names: Stone Cities; *talayot* ("Watchtowers," a round cyclopean tower in Menorca); *Kaerlud,* Lud's City (London)

them the stone marvels sprang from the ground in a single night, built after the Flood by unknown giants.

At Baalbek, "city of Baal," in Lebanon, you can see a few stones of the former Cyclopean City. The Roman Jupiter temple has the largest blocks of any known "man-made" structure, with three colossal stones called the Trilithon, which weigh an estimated 1,500 tons. Arab legend says Baalbek's first citadel was built before the Flood, then rebuilt by giants; another source says Lebanon's first city was Byblos, founded by the god Ouranus, who designed cyclopean structures and made stones move as if they were alive.

Or there's Lalibela in Ethiopia, the site of 11 linked, rock-hewn churches set into the ground, sculpted out of solid volcanic rock. These stone churches are linked by underground tunnels and mazes and exhibit many grottoes, courtyards, and caverns. Legend says the complex was built in one night by angels equipped with masonry tools; legend also says angels carried the human Lalibela to Heaven where God instructed him in the construction details.

The amusing fact about Cyclopean Cities is that we can best understand them if we take the myths about their creation to be literally true. They *were* built overnight by giants, the Cyclopes, who were the Elohim in human disguise.

According to the Ofanim, the Cyclopean Cities were dimensional matrices, both formed and formless, interfacing in the third dimension. The Cities fed into human and planetary reality possibilities to go beyond the state of affairs as they were then.

The Elohim helped to build the Cities, but they were assisted by the Hyperboreans, the Ofanim, the Archangel Metatron, and many of the 104 Time Lords who rule time and are particularly concerned with the fourth dimension.

Even though very few of these cities are left in the physical plane, they are still on the planet as memories and imprints in the light field. Were they built in a single night? Probably. "Imagine clicking your fingers and 30 tons of stones fit together because they are in alignment with the preexisting structure that exists in the light field there," the Ofanim remark.

Here is a composite visionary impression of the inside of a Cyclopean City. I drew upon the energy fields of Sacsaywaman, Mycenae, and Lalibela:

Some of the shapes were squares and rectangles, and the Cities had roofs of stone. You sit inside a massive stone box, whose walls are colossal stones each weighing many tons. Once you focus on this stone environment, the stones disappear, turn into apertures, first yellowish, then transparent, windows into other realities of all permutations—parallel, alternate, elsewhere, "what if," contingent, conditional, possible.

To put it in contemporary media terms, it's like being in a square room whose walls are televisions. You look into the stones, and each reveals a different vista, a different reality. Through some, you can see mock-ups of the future; through others, comparable scenarios on other planets, stars, or galaxies, and how those situations played out; in still others, you can play with outcomes, mold reality according to different inputs and variables. In all the windows, the Elohim are the stage managers, the view masters, and you watch the manifold forms of *AL,* of which the Elohim are the consummate expression.

The Cyclopean Cities were "what if" workshops for the multiple forms of *AL,* the cocreative energy that builds and changes reality. I quipped above that the effect was like interactive satellite TV: You can change the channel (stone window) and interact with the programming (play out alternate endings). Say you're a king, high priest, master shaman, tribal leader, prophet, and you need celestial input, differing views, alternate scenarios on a major course of action. You can get the information you need for making your decision here; in the movie theater for the forms of *AL,* you have many choices for how to use *AL.*

I know this sounds wild; maybe I should sell the idea to a science fiction writer. But consider this:

Psychic Kurt Leland in *Otherwhere,* his marvelous topography of aspects of the astral, after-death world, describes "Alternate *Is* Worlds" and "Alternate *Will Be* Worlds." The Alternate Is Worlds exist as workshops to study the extrapolations of *past* conditions or unfulfilled wishes or crucial decisions or turning points to see how they would have played out in a parallel reality. In the Alternate Will Be Worlds you can extrapolate *future* results of taking actions now, such as major career moves, relationship changes, and the like.

On the Earth we usually have access only to the present, Leland notes. "While you can recall the past and anticipate the future, you're largely unable to experience the future or the past as if it were the present." In nonphysical reality, "past, present, and future all coexist simultaneously," and you can "easily experience the past or future as if it were the present."[492]

The 6,300 original Cyclopean Cities on the Earth made that after-death experience of a changed past or alternate future experienceable while still in the present as a living human. As I suggested above, the possibilities were more extensive and adventurous than merely replaying the past or mocking-up the future. The stones were like flat screen TVs, and, using the satellite TV metaphor, you had *many* channels (realities, contexts, and dimensions) to choose from, with programming from all over the galaxy, all part of a fourth-dimensional workshop—or from a viewpoint of detached amusement, a 4D funhouse.

Inside the Knight of the Green Chapel's Underworld Abode

In the fourteenth-century heroic saga *Sir Gawain and the Green Knight,* we encounter another aspect of the *sidhe.* It can be an entrance to the Underworld.

Sir Gawain, a valiant or perhaps foolhardy knight among King Arthur's Knights at Camalate, accepts the challenge of a strange visitor to the court to chop off his head. A year later, Gawain must visit the Green Knight and suffer at least one axe stroke without flinching. Nobody at Camalate knows who the Green Knight is, or what country he came from, but he is strange and scary. He is clad all in green, taller than all other men, awesome, fierce, handsome, giant, and he has a monstrous axe. The Knights figure he's a phantom from Fairyland. When Gawain chops his head off, the Green Knight picks it up, laughs, and says, unperturbed, he'd see Gawain in a year to return the chop, then walks off nonchalantly.

The Green Knight's chapel, Gawain discovers after many adventures en route a year later, is a "hillock of sorts, a smooth-surfaced barrow on a slope beside a stream." The barrow is overgrown with great patches of grass, has a large hole at either end, permitting entry, and is hollow on the inside. This is the Green Chapel, the "rough dwelling" of the "Fiend himself," Gawain states, "a hideous oratory . . . a chapel of mischance . . . the most evil place I ever entered."[493]

We shouldn't be surprised at Gawain's fulminations. Nobody likes the Lord of Death, whether he's called the Green Knight, Yama, Hades, CuRoi, or Donn. Just as the Gawain poet identified the Green Knight's Underworld entrance at a barrow, so other mythic traditions have similarly provided geographic clues (see table 10-3). Here are a few examples:

According to Sophocles, a rocky hill near Colonus is an Underworld entrance, and the Erinyes (or Furies, Underworld death goddesses) had a grove there. Apollodorus tells us that Hercules descended to the Underworld through an entrance at Taenarum in Greece and that at Hermione, facing the island of Hydra in Greece, there is a chasm that communicates with the infernal regions. Pausanias states that Troezen, also in Greece, is an exit from the Underworld once used by both Heracles and Dionysus and that once this site had temple altars to the death gods.

In Ireland, the Dead journeyed to the Skellig Rocks off the Kelly coast on their way to *Tech Duinn,* the House of Donn, or Lord of Death. At Knockfierna, in Ireland, you pass through a cleft in a rock to enter Donn's realm. Hawaiians say that at Kahakaloa on Maui there is an entrance to the Pit of Milu, Milu being the Polynesian Lord of Death; another entrance is at the head of the Waipio Valley on the big island of Hawaii, and ghostly processions were once seen marching down the Mahiki Road to enter the *Lua-o-Milu,* or Cave of Milu.

The Well of Souls *(Bir el-Arweh)* under the Dome of the Rock in Jerusalem is a cavern in which sometimes you can hear the voices of the Dead, their cries mingled with the rushing of the rivers of Paradise. At Bag Enderby, a tiny English hamlet in the village next to the birthplace of Alfred, Lord Tennyson, you can stand before the old stone church and see the great closed gates of Hell.

Is the Underworld Hell? Not really. Many of the world's myths about such a place have characterized it that way, and the Judeo-Christian milieu has propagated the infernal, dismal, frightful nuance to this realm, but in Vedic literature, the place is known as Samayamani, our eighth Celestial City, located in the cosmic South and presided over by Lord Yama.

It's true, Yama is scary, probably a lot more so than the Celtic Green Knight. In the Tibetan

Table 10-3: Underworld Entrances

Planetary Total: 1,746

Selected Locations:

Cumae, near Naples, Italy	Bag Enderby, Lincolnshire, England	Well of Souls, Dome of the Rock, Mount Moriah, Jerusalem, Israel
Eleusis, near Athens, Greece	Acropolis, Athens, Greece	Lundy Island, Bristol Channel, England
Colonus, near Athens, Greece	Skellig Rocks, Kelly, Ireland	Beare Peninsula, Beare, Ireland
Afrasiab, Samarkand, Uzbekistan	Knockfierna, Ireland	Raz, Brittany, France (Bay of Souls)
Taenarum, Laconia, Greece	Kahakaloa, Maui, Hawaii, U.S.	The Tor, Glastonbury, Somerset, England
Troezen, Greece	Waipio Valley, Island of Hawaii, U.S.	Tomb of the Patriarchs, Hebron, Israel
Hermione, Argolis, Greece	Uaimh Chruachan (*Cruachain*), County Roscommon, Ireland	
Abydos, Egypt		
Mount Damavand, Iran		
Mount Holyoke, Hadley, Massaachusetts, U.S.	Lough Derg (St. Patrick's Purgatory), County Donegal, Ireland	
Garaband, Spain		

Equivalent Names: Tech Duinn (House of Donn); Hades' Palace; Judgment Halls of the *Duat;* Hall of Maat; Celestial City of Samyamani; Green Chapel, or Chapel of the Green Knight; Cave of Machpelah; Amenti (Egyptian); Cave of the Eumenides; *Lua-o-Milu* (Pit or Cave of Milu: Hawaiian); Annwn (Celtic); Xibalba (Mayan); Mictlan (Mictlantecuhtli's Realm: Mexican); Cinvat Bridge (Bridge of the Requiter: Persian)

depiction of the Wheel of Life, showing the six realms of dependent creation (including ours), Yama's frightening face glowers over the top of this vast wheel. His teeth are sharpened, he has three eyes and all glare, and he has skulls in his hair. He rides a black buffalo and carries a mace, a noose to seize victims, two ferocious dogs, each with four eyes, and a Bird of Doom.

Yama is a red god dressed all in green, or he has a dark-green complexion and dresses in red. He's the Green Knight, and he sits on the *Vicara-bhu*, the Throne of Deliberation in the Halls of the Dead. His domain, Samyamani, means "City of Bondage"; *Chitra-gupta* (Manifold Secret) is Yama's register of the dead; Yamaduta is his messenger who, like the Greek Charon, guides the souls of the dead through the Land of the Dead to Yama.

In Vedic and Hindu lore, Yama is the Binder, Restrainer, Curber, Lord of Death, Judge of the Dead, and chief of the Ancestors. The Gate of the South is here as both the Way of the Dead and the Way of the Ancestors, an unusual, but intriguing linkage. Yama's father is Vaivasvata, said to be the King of the Ancestors, the embodiment of ancestral law, morality, righteousness, and conduct, and he's the Chief of the Ancestors because he was the *first man to die*. Vedic myth blurs the distinction as to whether it was Yama or Vaivasvata who was the first to die, and perhaps they are the same being with two functions.[494]

Judaic lore holds that Adam, the first human to die, became supervisor of the Cave of Machpelah in the vicinity of Paradise.[495] The soul after death must pass through seven portals before arriving in Arabot, the highest heaven, Judaic lore says, and Adam, blamed for creating death from sinfulness, lords it over the first created humans. Adam, and Yama/Vaivasvata, as the first man to die, is perfectly positioned to act as Chief of the Ancestors because he was the first of the lineage.

We need to keep something important in mind here. The Underworld as the eighth Celestial City to be considered is also the *last phase* in cosmic creation. From the Supreme Being's viewpoint, it is the First and Last heaven, the jumping off point for biological incarnation for humans and a physically manifest Earth.

There is no physical death yet because we, as spirits in this last stage, are but on the verge of bodily form on a planet. If there is death, it is a dying to the spiritual world and a birthing into the manifest matter-based world. Of course, from our vantage point now as embodied humans, the Underworld, to the extent we credit it with experiential reality, is the after-death place, and since we are collectively well advanced in the cycle of births and rebirths, there are many souls in the Underworld because a lot of dying has occurred on Earth since the swinging door into Gaia's physical playground was opened.

A second clarification is that the Underworld is not inside the Earth. Myths have often depicted the Underworld as a Hell region in the bowels of the planet. The Underworld is inside the Earth but not the planet. We must remember the Earth originally referred to the totality of cosmic space filled with matter; from the viewpoint of the higher spiritual realms, the Underworld is the lower astral plane, deep inside cosmic Earth. As embodied humans, though, the Underworld is if anything *above* the planet Earth but *within* the cosmic Earth.[496]

A third important distinction is that as a name, Adam does not refer to the first human male, or even to the first androgynous human. It is a code, written in Qabala, that must be read through gematria. Adam is ADM, which is *Aleph* (1), *Dallet* (4), and *Mem* (40), or 1440 in total. What does 1440 mean, or, dropping the superfluous final "0," what does 144 mean?

According to Qabalist Carlo Suares, it means the *Aleph* immersed in the blood *(DAM)*.[497] It can also be stated this way: the Blazing Star *(Aleph)* buried in the human body. The Gnostics put it a little grimly, but meant the same, when they referred to the living spiritual spark of divine light trapped in the darkness of matter. It's the Blazing Star in the blood, the *Aleph* in the *DAM*, the possibility of spiritual illumination and Christed initiation in the human body.

What does it mean that Adam is grounded at the Cave of Machpelah? Let's work it from the opposite direction, from that of a human entering the Underworld. We find excellent examples of this incursion into the Underworld in the literature and phenomena of the near-death experience (NDE). Most NDE reports include a vivid description of what is called the Life Review.

It seems to have two aspects or phases. All the events of your present life vividly pass before you as if you are watching a holographic video, and you review them from a moral perspective, evaluating your actions and their effects on other people. According to the illuminating experience of NDEr Ned Dougherty, this Life Review seems to occur in a specific otherworldly place.

Dougherty describes this place as a "magnificent ethereal structure" resembling an amphitheater made of a "brilliant, crystal-like substance that radiated multicolored waves of energy throughout its form." The amphitheater was as large as a sports stadium, he said, suspended in the void of space the way you would imagine a space station to float in empty space, and it was filled with thousands of spiritual beings, all of them observing him at the very center.

He next found himself inside a shimmering crystalline sphere that descended upon him. Inside it he underwent his Life Review, with all the scenes, moments, and minutiae of his present life present to relive and reexperience him. Meanwhile, the thousands of spiritual beings in the amphitheater observed this and supported Dougherty in the performance of his Life Review, "communicating, by musical sounds, feelings of goodwill to me." These beings sent Dougherty "feelings of love," encouragement, support, even cheers. "You are part of us, and we are part of you," they informed him.[498]

You don't have to be dead or nearly dead to experience the Life Review in this celestial amphitheater. On several occasions I found myself in an equivalent place, at the center of an amphitheater or on the stage before a large, attentive, and supportive audience. I was both accounting for myself and instructing the viewers. Several of the Elohim were present, and it seemed I was both debriefing them and receiving counseling on the particularities of my reported experiences.

The key to making sense of this Underworld tableau is Dougherty's quoted statement that the thousands of spiritual beings in the amphitheater seats were part of him and he was part of them. How can that be? It can be because these observing souls are the totality of lives an individual has ever had, the thousands of fragments of his one being, his total Self, arrayed before him, offering support and awaiting revelation. The NDEr is the latest explorer on their behalf, the most recent fragment of the Self set out to learn something new about life. In this sense, the NDE Life Review is a debriefing outside of time.

Think of this Underworld amphitheater as a karma arena. Say you have had 10,000 different lives, on Earth, Mars, the Pleiades, the Andromeda Galaxy, and other places too strange to even remember because they can't be humanly conceptualized. All these thousands of different incarnations still live; they are an adoring archive, an educational resource, well-wishing cheerleaders, a Castle of Maidens awaiting their final delivery in a moment of apocalyptic unity.

They are all the beings you have been, good, bad, indifferent, angelic, beastly, illuminated, thick as bricks, male, female, mother, father, son, daughter, wife, and husband—a dizzying concatenation of permutations, outcomes, debts, and obligations. This is the *Adam-ship,* the assembly and grounding of the full panoply of all our selves throughout time and space.

Your array of 10,000 previous incarnations are truly the Judges of the Dead, but the judging is more of an observation and evaluation, not a justification for punishment, hellfire, and brimstone as we might tend to think. Free will means at the end of the day *you* judge *your*self. In biblical terms, this is the obligation of being granted the chance to eat—to *know*—of the Tree of the Knowledge of Good and Evil. Your choice, your results, your responsibility.

Another Snapshot of Adam Wandering through the Underworld

Let's reverse perspectives and approach it from Albion's viewpoint. Albion, as the total expression of the two halves of the zodiac, is a generic cosmic summation of all possibilities. Albion is pure, complete, somewhat theoretical. He needs to be individualized, set in motion into a finite slice and taste of time. He needs to have horoscopic individuality, his own unique slot in space-time.

Think of the karma arena or Life Review amphitheater as a four-dimensional living horoscope. A horoscope is an astrologer's map of the planetary influences on an individual over a lifetime. You have a specific fixation of planetary influences at birth, which remains a baseline, but over the course of biological life, the planetary and stellar influences are dynamic, changing daily in short- and long-term cycles and permutations, squeezing, seducing, irritating your psyche in ever new configurations of influence, energy, and consciousness.

It is a dance, the dance of life, the dance of the blood in Adam that makes him real, visible, in the world, a player. The karma arena is a life-planning workshop, a horoscope permutation laboratory. What variation in the array of energies, pressures, and influences shall we try next to achieve a particular result? A new individuality is planned to embody these influences; it's like stamping soft clay with a three-dimensional imprint of a unique horoscopic moment, a template that soul will bear throughout life like a full-body tattoo.

Let us create yet another copy of ourselves, the 10,000 spirits in the amphitheater declare, and send him or her forth into the world with this set of variables to experience life. Each life is a new and unique horoscope, another snapshot of Adam wandering through the Underworld.

It's all a commotion in the blood, in the suddenly alive and interacting Adam, no more a hypothetical construct of the cosmos, but real, set in motion, let loose on the horoscopic playing field, individualized in a space-time bubble. The *DAM*, or blood, of Adam, the Blazing Star or *Aleph* in the blood, is the etheric counterpart of our own individualized blood chemistry, our unique DNA fingerprint, its molecular configurations reflecting our karma and horoscope.

In the Underworld, known to the Egyptians as the *Duat*, things exist midway between the purely spiritual and the physically observable in an "invisible yet dynamic state of metamorphosis and transformation." *Duat*, the term usually translated as Underworld, actually means "place

of morning twilight," a point of transition from night to day, darkness to light, but this is only one of at least three interpretations of the Egyptian Underworld concept.[499]

The Underworld also is *amentet*, "the hidden place," personified by the "Lady of the West," a goddess who receives the setting Sun; and it is *neterkhert*, "the divine under place," as in under the stars, in a lower dimension, one closer to the manifest level of physical existence. The Underworld, as the Egyptians saw it, did not have an exact physical location, even though there might be points of access in the material world; rather its location is "psychic and mythographical," and one encounters it "whenever one approaches the borders of normal sense-based consciousness."[500]

Everything in the *Duat* is upside down, turned inside out, topsy-turvy, the mirror opposite of physical, worldly life, confusing, disorienting, dreamlike. Choose your metaphor: the quantum sea of uncollapsed possibilities, or the myriad seeds of the Dreamtime, the protean formative prephysical reality. Or the roiling Six Realms of Yama's Wheel of Life, the wild samsaric phantasmagoria of gods, antigods, the dead, animals, humans, and the hell-bent. The Six Realms play out their destinies in 12 possible permutations, what Buddhism calls dependent origination, giving us an Underworld of at least 72 realms.

Think of it as Yama's funhouse, with Yama as guide and judge. He's the guide because it's his realm; he's charged with its supervision. Yama is the Vedic visage of the Egyptian Anubis, the jackal-headed psychopomp of the Underworld. Who better to guide souls through the *Duat* than the Dog of Sirius, for the Dog is the guardian of the dwelling of the stars, and now that the zodiacal wheel has been set to spin, churning out myriads of incarnational scenarios, the Dog as Anubis guides our Underworld journey, as the *Upawet*, Opener of the Way.

Yama in all his guises shares in the dance of the horoscope.[501] But who is the Lord of the

Dance? It is the star Arcturus, the alpha star in the constellation Boötes, the Ox Driver and Shepherd. Arcturus, our galaxy's fourth brightest star and the eighth of the stars of Camalate and the *Anandakanda* inner heart chakra.[502]

Arcturus, the Ofanim comment, "is a gateway between nothing and something, the source of the possibility of Light, one reflection." In terms of the eight aspects of Camalate, Arcturus represents "the collective cultural experience of this Earth," and in our model of chakras and planetary spheres, it corresponds with the seventh chakra and the planetary sphere of Mars (see figure 10-1).[503]

The crown chakra is a gateway, too, as widely attested by the world's spiritual traditions. Some religious systems, such as the Tibetan, emphasize the importance in conscious dying of leaving the body through the crown chakra. In dying, the life-force energy and consciousness progressively withdraw from the first six chakras, leaving one, ideally, focused and aware within the crown, a bit like being on the roof of a burning building, awaiting a helicopter rescue. But here the "helicopter" is the momentum that will lift you off the crown into the Underworld, the first rung in the ladder up through the spiritual worlds.

Given this, if you are facing death, from old age or illness, it could be beneficial to spend time meditating at an Underworld entrance. Similarly, if you have sustained an NDE and wish to deepen your experience, or reclaim more of it, it could be useful to spend time collecting yourself at such a place.

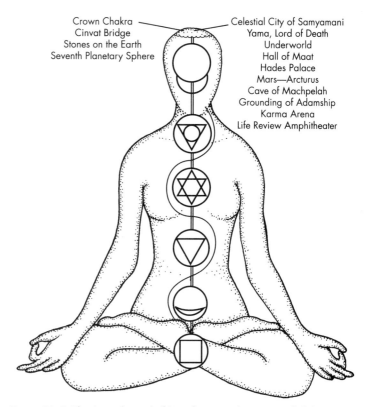

Crown Chakra
Cinvat Bridge
Stones on the Earth
Seventh Planetary Sphere

Celestial City of Samyamani
Yama, Lord of Death
Underworld
Hall of Maat
Hades Palace
Mars—Arcturus
Cave of Machpelah
Grounding of Adamship
Karma Arena
Life Review Amphitheater

Figure 10–1. The Seventh Level of Manifestation, the Crown of Elohim

Further, if you want access to your Life Plan (the correlate to the NDE or after-death experience of the Life Review), depending on your psychic abilities, you may be able to gain insight by meditating at an Underworld entrance. Bear in mind that the entrance is merely that: a doorway to a place or level of experience. Earth's 1,746 Underworld entrances all lead to the one same place.[504]

Avenues of Trees: Walkways into Other Worlds

Earth's geomantic designers brought the realm of spirit even further into matter than stone in the form of living trees, notably oaks and cedars. In parts of England there are traces even today of once grand tree-lined processionals across the landscape, terminating in many cases at a hill or sacred site. The point seems to have been to show that biological life, a tree, could be a geomantic temple as well, and like the stones be a carrier of the Crown of Elohim template.

The Ofanim prefer to call these avenues energy funnels and have informed me there are 2,864,000,224 such features on the Earth. Each funnel leads to a subtle plane temple, though all the temples are not the same. The energy funnels were part of the Earth's original geomantic design as energy features with the potential to channel or funnel light into the grid matrix.

Geomancers, recognizing the preexistent energy funnel templates, often planted living trees (such as oaks or cedars) to mark the spot and size of the funnels and to activate the potential of the energy funnel at that spot. Sometimes stones were used, such as with the baffling underwater megalithic avenue in the Caribbean called the Bimini Road. That was (and still is) an energy funnel.

According to the Ofanim, some 150,000 years ago, just before the landmass including Bimini sank under the waves but after the sinking of Atlantis, the Bimini Road was aboveground, and trees had been planted behind the stones. The light temple at the terminus of the Bimini Road grounded energy from the star Arcturus (in the heel of Boötes, the Shepherd) at Bimini.

Thus the human activation was made in coordination with the energy features already seeded at a site. When Joseph of Arimathea, known to the Ofanim as a master geomancer, came to Glastonbury, England, in the time of Jesus Christ, he activated the energy funnel that leads up to the Tor (a conical, pyramidal shaped hillock in the center of town) as marked then by an avenue of 144 oak trees, 72 on either side of the funnel.

At present, I know of four such avenues of trees: the oak processional leading to the Tor in Glastonbury; another at White-Leaved Oak in the Malverns; the Kingweston Cedar Walk near Kingweston, near Glastonbury, leading to Copley Wood; and the Avenue of Cedars between Butleigh and Glastonbury. In the case of the two oak processionals, each of which originally had 144 oaks, almost no living oaks remain, while of the 94 cedars in the cedar processionals, some still survive to mark the course of the walkways.

In Glastonbury even today people remember the oak processional. It started at a point called Stonedown, a presumed former Druidic site, perhaps one-quarter mile from the slopes of the Tor at two now dead oak trees known locally as Gog and Magog. When extant, two rows of trees about 30 feet apart and each with 72 oak trees marched in a straight line to the base of the Tor.

Lionel Smithett Lewis, a former Vicar of Glastonbury, writing in 1922, noted that though most of the remaining oaks in the avenue were "shamefully cut down" around 1906 by a farmer who sold the wood to timber merchants, five immense oaks, plus Gog and Magog, still remained. One of the felled oak trees was 11 feet in diameter and had 2,000 season rings, Rev. Lewis said. He cited an earlier antiquarian who proposed that the name Glastonbury derived from *Glastan-byrie* (Hill of Oaks) in reference to the defunct avenue.[505]

One of the first places I visited when I lived in Glastonbury was Gog and Magog. They were grand though sadly derelict trees, but they marked the spot. I realized that even if the physical trees were gone, the avenue of oaks still stood. It was an energy avenue, a road of light, across the landscape to the Tor. Where Gog and Magog each stand, there is also a pillar of light around 40 feet high, sheathing the trees so that they stand within this light column. A massive double door connects the two pillars; it can swing open when required. When it does, you can see the broad avenue of light, perhaps 30 feet wide, marked by the light-body equivalent of the physical oak trees.

While standing at the Gog-Magog gates, I saw a ritual processional from a vanished age, probably far older even than Celtic days. Hundreds of men and women stood by the trees and observed several regal or priestly figures walking along the avenue towards the Tor. They were escorting a younger man robed in white with a green waistband; he seemed to be an apprentice to them, though one advanced in his training.

I learned from the Ofanim that the Avenue of Oaks was designed to escort initiates to the first level of the labyrinth on Glastonbury Tor. "The Oaks of Avalon were made sacred by Joseph of Arimathea accompanied by the Christ in his thought body," the Ofanim said. "Each plant, animal, each living entity, has an energy field. Joseph and the Christ were able to increase, through their being, the etheric or auric possibilities of those trees at that time."

Further along the processional, several dome-line energy vortices cross. "They form a pattern whereby humans ready for initiation would have been helped to be balanced by the vortices they crossed on their way to the places of initiation," the Ofanim explain. "Glastonbury was a center for learning, a place of true education. The Qabala was integral to the tradition practiced there."[506]

So as the initiates processed through the Avenue of Oaks, a miniature Tree of Life of three pillars, they walked in a river of amplified spiritual light and Christ-being as emanated from the trees on both sides, all designed to help them concentrate their attention inward in preparation for initiatory experiences and epiphanies at the Tor. The Avenue of Oaks predated Joseph's arrival, but when he came to Glastonbury, he illuminated the trees with Christ light. As a master geomancer working with the Ofanim, "Joseph was in touch with a living reality over the surface of the Earth on which he worked with love," say the Ofanim.

Of the cedar avenues, the one known locally as Kingweston Cedar Walk, starts near the Somerset village of Somerset and heads towards Copley Wood and Worley Hill, which I identified earlier as the site of a Cosmic Egg. The Avenue of Cedars outside Glastonbury is much more prominent in local folklore, and owing to the flat land, it is visible from a fair distance as a serene promenade of dark green cedars in two parallel rows that start from around Park rhyne and process to the edge of Butleigh. In some parts of the Avenue, you can recline on the rich, open, green but uncut lawn between the trees and view Glastonbury Tor.

The last time I counted the trees, there were 68 standing, spaced about 80 feet apart in each row, the two rows being about 150 feet apart. The entire avenue, which to the nongeomantic eye resembled a grand bridle path on a country estate, stretched about 3,800 feet. The Ofanim told me that originally the avenue had 94 cedar trees, the number honoring the Mothership whose number is 94. In a sense the Avenue of Cedars was a linear version of the Merry Maidens and Maiden Castle, a display of the 94 aspects of the Mother Goddess.

As with Gog and Magog in the Oaks of Avalon processional, here there is also an astral double-door sealing off the ritual entrance to the cedar avenue. In my experience, presentation of one's Grail Knight sword is sufficient bona fides to get the massive doors to swing open. The gates open, and you see before you a brilliantly lit, long arched hall, made as if of milky glass and translucent columns. You can see the 94 cedars and light columns in the same place. At the end of this passageway is another double gate, this one of gold. The sword is the key, and the gates again swing open, revealing a vaulted circular chamber imbued with a strong though indefinable feminine presence—the Mothership.

Inside this vaulted chamber are at least nine pillars spaced evenly around the perimeter. Each emanates a different colored light; before each stands a woman, a priestess of some type, in floor-length robes, hooded, pale faces with ruby red lips. I wonder if these are Morgan le Fay's famous eight sisters with whom she once ruled all of Avalon. The priestess by the red column beckons me, and as I walk past her column, the vaulted chamber disappears and I stand before a red globe on a marble pedestal set at the height of my chest. Behind her are two marble pillars, and through them I see into another dimension.

Afterwards the Ofanim debriefed me on my little outing. "The Avenue of Cedars is a connection through to another Shambhala doorway, as on the Tor. The beings you saw are here at one level to protect, but at another level, they are initiatory. These beings use the cedar trees as access points." Even so, I suspected there was another aspect to this Avenue of Cedars that I had not quite seen yet.

It is often asked in Glastonbury why the Avenue of Cedars stops short of Glastonbury. The question assumes that its termination is at the Glastonbury end. It isn't. This avenue leads you away from Glastonbury to a majestic temple at its other end. On another occasion I had a more detailed view of the vaulted chamber temple with the nine chromatic pillars and priestesses, or perhaps what I saw co-occupied the same psychic space but in another dimension.

You walk up the Avenue of Cedars, away from Glastonbury. Its energy matrix helps you concentrate your focus and prepares you to shift dimensions. At the terminus of the avenue is a Pleiadian temple. It partially resembles the White House in Washington, D.C., though it stretches out farther on both sides from a central domed chamber. The structure is also similar to the original Pleiadian temple at Castle Rigg, placed there before the stones were erected.

Inside the building, the primary color scheme seems to be bluish silver. At first glance, as you walk down the two wings from the central domed chamber, it resembles an art gallery. What look like paintings hang on the walls, but you realize this is really an archive of holograms, more of a library. In the central domed area, there are rings painted on the floor. When you stand in the center of this, you seem to be immediately translated to another place.

It is somewhere in the Pleiades, possibly a planet associated with the star Alcyone; it is a pale olive-green landscape outside this different white marble temple you stand in. You realize you were just shifted from one otherwordly temple to another, or perhaps to one metaphysically recessed within the other. This temple is presided over by a towering golden griffin, a seemingly mythic though spiritual being, which as I mentioned earlier derives from the Pleiades.

You might think, based on what I described, that this site is either an interdimensional portal, which leads to the Pleiadian Council of Light, or a stargate to somewhere in the Pleiades. It is neither. Discovery of this temple puts us in the context of Hyperborea, of a time even before the Earth grid was fully or maybe even partially installed, when various ETs and "aliens" instrumental in establishing the Earth grid "walked" the Earth and maintained outposts to their home system, be it Pleiades, Sirius, Arcturus, or other destination.

The Kingweston Cedar Walk that leads towards Copley Wood terminates at the base of the wood and Worley Hill at another dimensional temple for the Great Bear. This one presents itself with minarets and a dark-blue hue. In either case, the 94 trees in the cedar avenue build up the cognitive charge that enables one to leap, perceptually, into the rarefied dimension where the ET temples reside. The cedar avenue is a linear consciousness accelerator, a straight-line version of the circular Merry Maidens, with a light temple at the end. . . .

So now we have reviewed 82 of 85 geomantic features of the Earth's visionary geography. We are about to return to our starting point, the Cube of Space, or Emerald, of the Lord of Light, the Light Bearer, whose life and deeds we'll now learn.

Part Three

Activating the Emerald Modem—The New Jerusalem on Earth

11 Reconceiving the Lord of Light
The One Who Holds the Emerald

The Lord of Light and Light Bearer is Lucifer, the most maligned and misunderstood angelic being in Judeo-Christian civilization.

For us to get anywhere in understanding and participating in Earth's visionary geography, we have to get past this formidable bugbear of Lucifer in our path. There is no way around it, because the Emerald is his. The Emerald is our Heart within the Heart, the essence of the Earth's spiritual body, from the crown of the Lord of Light. It is Lucifer's Emerald.

The Light Bearer's Many Lives and Pejoratives

I mentioned in the introduction that biblical cartography says that in Eden there are two trees. The Tree of the Knowledge of Good and Evil forms an outer hedge around Eden; the Tree of Life, so vast it would take a person 500 years to walk the diameter of its trunk, sits inside the hedge. Lucifer as the double-valenced Lord of Light is the outer tree, as I'll explain below, and the Emerald is the precious inner tree. It is the same as the paradise seed crystals brought with every dome to Earth; it is the same as the Cube of Space or Jerusalem archetype.

It is the same as the Emerald in the chest of every human, the Heart within the Heart. So if we want to experience—to *be*, to *have*—the Tree of Life, we must come to terms with the outer Tree of the Knowledge of Good and Evil. It is a two-step process. This chapter will present guidelines on that first step.

Earlier I mentioned that Jerusalem, as the cosmic archetype, is the Foundation of Venus, Morning and Evening Star. Anciently Venus was known as Lucifer or Phosphorus, so Jerusalem (secretly) means the Foundation of Lucifer.

We have to deal with Lucifer and re-reveal his light and mission to our compromised understanding. Lucifer is the theological Shadow we have devoted lifetimes to suppressing, the Tree of which we wanted only half, the knowledge of Good. Yet Lucifer is the high celestial redeemer being who "fell" solely on our behalf, and he awaits our recognition and reaffirmation to reverse his fortunes.

Yes, it's shocking, but it is also liberating and is an unavoidable task.

Judeo-Christian culture has blinded us to the true nature of this high celestial being (regarded as God's chief archangel and cherub), his history and relationship with humanity, and his role in Earth's visionary topography.

I say "high celestial being" because according

to conventional Judeo-Christian belief, Lucifer started out that way. Then everything went wrong, and he got demonized.

According to Jewish sources, Lucifer was God's chief archangel and cherub; on the third day of Creation, he "walked in Eden amid blazing jewels, his body a-fire" with the light of precious stones, all set in pure gold. These jewels included carnelian, topaz, diamond, beryl, onyx, jasper, sapphire, carbuncle, and Emerald. God had made Lucifer Guardian of All Nations. He was *Lucem ferre*, from the Latin for "bringer or bearer of light."

He also had something to do with the planet Venus, the "last proud star to defy sunrise." Lucifer was *Helel ben Shahar*, Venus (*Helel*), Son of the Dawn (*Shahar*), Lord of Light, the Shining One, Dawn Bringer, Light Giver, and Light Bringer—Lucifer, the Morning Star.[507] But it meant the first morning of self-aware consciousness.

Then, the story goes, Lucifer's pride got the better of him. He wanted to enthrone himself on Mount Saphon, the Mountain of the North, also called Mount of Assembly or Mount of God, and thereby be God's equal. God wanted Lucifer to serve the newly created humanity, but instead he organized a revolt of the angels against God's intentions. It's said of Satan ("the Opposer," his name is used interchangeably for Lucifer in Christian theology) that he foresaw that the Earth would be populated with God-worshippers, and he wanted that worship for himself. He went into competition for the worship of humans and used all his wiles to secure that worship attention.[508]

God curtailed Lucifer's ambitions and cast him out of Heaven to the Bottomless Pit of Sheol, along with his fellow rebellious angels. As he fell from grace he was said to shine like lightning but was reduced to ashes on impact; only his spirit flutters blindly and ceaselessly in the deep gloom of Sheol. "How art thou fallen from heaven, O Lucifer, son of the morning," wrote Isaiah (14:12).

Once imprisoned in Sheol, whether as ashes, spirit, or full-bodied, Lucifer became identified with Satan, the Adversary or Devil, also known as the Prince of Darkness and Prince of the Power of Air.[509] Satan's deeds represent Lucifer's doings after the Fall. The Judeo-Christian belief holds that, as Satan, Lucifer was able to interfere with human affairs and oppose God and the angelic hierarchy. Satan was the Serpent in the Garden of Eden who tempted Eve to eat the forbidden apple of the Tree of the Knowledge of Good and Evil, thereby precipitating the expulsion from Paradise.[510]

Dante Alighieri codified the medieval view of Lucifer in his thirteenth-century "Inferno," one of three parts in his *Divine Comedy*. In Dante's cosmography of Hell, Lucifer resides below the Ninth Circle of Hell, frozen in ice. Dante calls him both Satan and Lucifer and calls him the "foul creature" and "Emperor of the Universe of Pain." Dante refers to "the shaggy flank of the Great Worm of Evil/which bores through the world," to this "gross Fiend and Image of all Evil," who even now eons later is "pinched and prisoned in the ice-pack still."[511]

The English poet John Milton contributed to the Western cultural demonizing myth of Lucifer in his *Paradise Lost*. To Milton, Lucifer was the "infernal Serpent" who "set himself in Glory above his Peers." He opposed the Throne of God, instilled war in Heaven, and was eventually "Hurl'd headlong flaming from the Ethereal Skie/With hideous ruine and combustion down/To bottomless perdition, there to dwell." He was bound in "adamantine chains and penal Fire" where he was condemned to "rowling in the fiery Gulfe." Lucifer couldn't die, but he couldn't be released either, Milton said.[512]

The Lucifer portrait received another dark stroke through Johann Wolfgang von Goethe's unforgettable arch-demon Mephistopheles in *Faust*. Goethe's Mephistopheles is the honey-tongued persuader, the forked-tongue promiser, the ambivalent Prince of Lies and Prince of Light. He offers Faust, who is a frustrated metaphysician stuck in his quest to penetrate life's secrets, all knowledge in exchange for his soul. It's the classic Devil's bargain as the West sees it. "I am part of that part which was the Absolute,/A part of that darkness which gave birth to light,/The arrogant light," says Mephistopheles.[513]

We may never read Dante, Milton, or Goethe; we may never consciously think about Lucifer; but these views are already in us as deep conditionings. In effect, for many, they keep one's attention off the subject altogether, having quarantined Lucifer and his Fall as an "off-limits, no trespassing" topic. Another name for this "no-fly zone" is the Shadow or the unconscious.

The Shadow is a psychic closet into which we toss unwanted things; we lock the closet and hope we never have to open the door again; in fact, we do our best to forget that the closet even exists. It becomes a dark, dangerous place, a zone we never set foot in if we are wise. But what we push into the shadows only grows darker in our perception; if Lucifer was an ambitious, overweening fallen angel, as Satan he is now the Devil, God's enemy and surely ours.

It's time to be courageous regarding Lucifer. It's time to tell the truth. In the late 1970s, British psychic and visionary David Spangler wrote of the coming Luciferic initiation. Lucifer "comes to give us the final gift of wholeness. If we accept it, then he is free and we are free," Spangler explained. That act of accepting is the Luciferic initiation, he said, something that many people will start facing in the days ahead (he wrote this in 1977) and must get through because it is an initiation into the Aquarian astrological Age. "Lucifer prepares man in all ways for the experience of Christhood," Spangler said.[514]

In a similar vein, though earlier, Wellesley Tudor Pole, an English initiate intimately familiar with the Earth's energy body, wrote in 1966 that Lucifer was not cast out of Heaven for malfeasance or disobedience. Rather he "descended into our midst of his free will and to his own sacrifice. He can only rise out of our darkness when we are ready and able to rise with him." As such we should appreciate Lucifer as "a colleague" and wish him success in "his mission among men, and for his triumphant return whence he came."[515]

Another Lucifer Biography— Prometheus, Stealer of the Gods' Fire

Unarguably, Lucifer, even his name, is a charged, volatile topic in the West. But how was this celestial being perceived in cultures in which the concept of a Fall into demonization was not a cultural or theological feature? What might a more neutral biography of Lucifer yield? What else has he been called?

The Greeks knew Lucifer as Prometheus the Titan. His name means "forethought," "one who thinks ahead," or "he who knows in advance." Prometheus was accused of stealing the fire of the gods and awarding it to humanity against the gods' wishes. Prometheus's punishment ordered by Zeus was to be chained to a pillar at Mount Caucasus where each day Zeus's eagle ate his liver; it grew back overnight.

Prometheus rebelled *for us*. His fate is bound up with humanity's, his bond with humans. "More than any other god, he intercedes for mankind," says scholar and mythographer Carl Kerenyi. As a god, he suffers "injustice, torment, and humiliation—the hallmarks of human existence." Prometheus was our "divine advocate, precursor or ancestor of the human race [who] alone confronted the celestial gods."[516]

Zeus, the chief of all the gods on Mount

Olympus, had decided, despite Prometheus's entreaty, not to award the "the unwearying fire" to humanity. Prometheus took matters in hand and stole the gods' fire, stuffing it in a hollow fennel stalk or narthex tube and giving it to the humans. This defiance angered Zeus when he saw the gods' fire now burning within humans. Hephaistos, the smith god of Olympus, bound Prometheus; later, Heracles would unbind him.[517]

Prometheus bewails his cruel, unfair fate, to be punished for his "man-loving disposition," his "excessive love for Man," as Aeschylus wrote in *Prometheus Bound*. Prometheus didn't fear the gods' anger "but gave honors to mortals beyond what was just," gave them "the secret spring of fire that filled the narthex stem." He speaks of "the goodwill of my gift."[518]

In the Greek view, Prometheus wanted to aid the nascent humanity by giving them the gift of the gods' fire, did it in defiance of Zeus, and was punished grievously. The Christian view of Lucifer is that God asked him to serve Adam (symbolic of nascent humanity), and he refused; for this, he was thrown into Hell by God. It's the same being and same story but each has a different valence and emphasis.

The Greeks say Prometheus defied the gods to willingly aid humanity; the Christians that Lucifer defied God by refusing to aid humanity. Prometheus was never demonized; in fact, he was eventually unchained. Lucifer was demonized seemingly for eternity, and nobody will unbind him. Which story is accurate?

Perhaps we should clarify the nature of the "unwearying fire" in the narthex tube. This is code for the Emerald. The narthex tube, at one level, is the channel for subtle energies called *sushumna*, running from groin to crown, that links the seven human chakras; it is also the outer casing of the Emerald, whose vast, unfathomable, overwhelming interior light is certainly Zeus's

fire. Fire means cognition, the fire of consciousness, of heightened awareness.

Let's add to this a certain unique freedom of consciousness to choose; we know it today as free will, but very few are free to exercise their will as it was intended. The unwearying fire gave us a certain stance of self-awareness: We became aware that we are aware. Consciousness became self-reflexive, self-referential. The choice of course was the classic good and evil, to love God willingly or to scorn Him willingly: our choice. The moral universe was ours. The first taste of the juice from that apple was shocking. The enormity of the awareness, the scope of the consequences, the deliriousness of the freedom.

Prometheus explains that he deserves credit for having given humans all their arts and knowledge. Before the gift of the fire, which made possible the acquisition of these "arts," humanity had eyes but couldn't see, ears but couldn't hear, and they handled their lives "in bewilderment and confusion." In other words, they had no clairvoyance, or the possibility of it; their higher spiritual faculties were dark and unawakened; they were dumb and mute in the cosmos. They were "witless" before the gift of fire, but "masters of their minds" after.[519]

Did Prometheus "steal" the unwearying fire? No. Did Lucifer "rebel"? No.

According to the Ofanim, Lucifer proposed that humanity be given the Emerald, and the Supreme Being approved and commissioned this gift, even applauding Lucifer for his daring. God went so far as to change reality to make this possible, relocating the Emerald from its position in between two Sefirot on the Tree of Life (between Geburah, the fifth Sefira, and Chesed, the fourth) into a single Sefira, Chesed. Lucifer gave humanity the Emerald; God moved the Emerald into Chesed; Prometheus stole the fire; Lucifer fell to Earth—it's the same event.

The fact that the Emerald given to humanity

came from among the precious jewels in Lucifer's crown is the basis for Kerenyi's prescient remark about Prometheus's bond with humans. Of course there would be a strong bond: Our Emerald is Lucifer's. But it's more than possession of property; we carry the essence of Lucifer inside us, as the planet wears it outside. A little bit of Lucifer "fell" into incarnation with each human born with an Emerald. That's why his suffering is existential; his existence is now tied up, on loan, to us. His "suffering" is our not knowing this, our not making good on the gift, our denial the gift ever happened, our demonization of the gift-giver.

Now let's clarify something Lucifer is not. Lucifer is not Mephistopheles.[520] Mephistopheles has sunk deep roots into the Western psyche, and nearly everyone assumes he is a clever, scary, and dangerous version of the Devil. The logic is that Satan in the Garden of Eden used his subtle arts to hoodwink Eve into eating the apple; Mephistopheles used his consummate arts of persuasion to get Faust to surrender his soul to his keeping after death. However, metaphysical investigation breaks the seemingly direct logic train.

Satan in the Garden was not a serpent, and he didn't persuade Eve of anything. The Supreme Being commissioned the offering of the choice to human souls prior to the phylogenetic advent of incarnation, before the first ones ever. Lucifer offered part of his own essence to humans, the Emerald from his crown. We could take it or leave it. We took it. It would not cost us our souls; rather, it would cost Lucifer his soul until we mastered the Emerald and its ramifications.

Later myths confused the dragon that guards the golden apples of wisdom with Lucifer, transforming him into a beguiling serpent. The golden apple part is correct: They embody higher divine knowledge, the fruits of spiritual attainment. Knowledge of the scope and implications of the choice for good and evil came of a golden apple, but it was not a deceiving ser-

pent who offered us the opportunity. It was a free being offering freedom.

The Lucifer issue is paramount in the healing of the planet because it is implicit in the Earth's overall geomythic body. To interact fully and usefully with the Earth's visionary geography and aid its healing and ours we must get through this theological doorway of the "fallen" Lucifer and his sullied Cube of Space. We must, if we want to use the Emerald modem, Lucifer's "stolen fire."

Lucifer Binding Sites—the Geomantic Meaning of Mount Caucasus

Now let's see the geomantic aspect of Prometheus-Lucifer. Mount Caucasus refers to a peak in the Caucasus range in southwestern Russia, between the Black and Caspian Seas, and is a literal indication of how and where Lucifer was bound and chained on Earth. This feature is called a Lucifer Binding Site, and the planet has 3,496 of them (see table 11-1).

It is not quite accurate to call it exclusively a binding site, for at these sites, Lucifer is arriving in glory, being bound, and being unbound. It is a time tableau, a fourth-dimensional quality best appreciated by considering it in the course of the planet's life and by viewing the planet as a whole, with Lucifer coming, staying, and going, continuously and simultaneously.

For example, Lucifer is arriving in glory at the El Tule tree in the churchyard of El Templo del Santa Maria near Oaxaca (Harmonic Convergence, 1987); he is still bound in agony at the Dome of the Rock in Jerusalem and Gediminas Hill in Vilnius, Lithuania; and he is being released from Steep Hill which is crowned by the eleventh-century Lincoln Cathedral (officially known as the Cathedral Church of the Blessed Virgin Mary) in Lincolnshire, England (since August 2001). This is

Table 11-1: Lucifer Binding Sites

Planetary Total: 3,496

Selected Locations:

Lincoln Cathedral, Lincoln, England: Jerusalem

Brocken, Harz Mountains, Germany

Chichen Itza, Mexico: Tollan

Citamparam, India

Dome of the Rock, Jerusalem, Israel: Mount Caucasus

Gediminas Hill, Vilnius, Lithuania: Mount Caucasus

Lalish, near Mosul, Iraq (Yezidi holy site for Peacock Angel): Tollan

El Tule Churchyard, near Oaxaca, Mexico: Tollan

Temple of the Quetzal Butterfly, Teotihuacan, Mexico: Tollan

Tiahuanaco, Bolivia: Mount Caucasus

Oraibi, Hopi Third Mesa, Arizona, U.S.: Tollan

Heliopolis, Egypt (near Cairo): Nut's "Lower Mansion"

Cholula, Mexico (chief center of Quetzalcoatl cult)

Mount Damavand, Iran: Mount Causcasus

Cova da Iria, Fatima, Portugal: Mount Caucasus

Equivalent Names: Mount Caucasus; Bottomless Pit; *Sheol;* Below the Ninth Ring of Hell; Jerusalem; Tollan; *Het-shenat* (shrine to Sky Goddess Nut); the Isle of Lyngvi in Lake Amvartsnir

Three Types of Sites: Tollan (Lucifer arriving in glory from his celestial origin); Mount Caucasus (Lucifer being bound in chains to the Earth); and Jerusalem (Lucifer unbound, establishing his Foundation on the Earth). Locations without attribution are still being researched.

only four out of the 3,496 Lucifer sites. A grand theological-geomantic drama is continuously played out in slow motion around the planet.

Thus to refer to these sites only as a Lucifer Binding Site or a Mount Caucasus reflects only one of three aspects of Lucifer's planetary reality. We might with equal justification call these sites Jerusalem or Tollan after Lucifer's and Quetzalcoatl's point of origin in the Venus sphere. He may be bound on Mount Caucasus, but when he arrives in glory or when he has been released, his point of origin becomes his place of destination, and the Lucifer Binding Site becomes instead a Jerusalem, a Foundation of Lucifer on planet Earth.

Let's say when he arrives, he is fresh from Tollan (see below, under Quetzalcoatl) still exuding its celestial glories, and such a site could be called a Tollan; when he is unbound and free to establish his reality on the Earth, that is, within the Earth's visionary geography, then such a site

is a Jerusalem, a Foundation of Lucifer (see table 11-2).

Let's see how all this plays out in a real-life geomantic setting. On August 18, 2001, a colleague and I led a small group through the initial stages of unbinding Lucifer at Lincoln Cathedral, which is about three hours north of London by car. We hadn't expected to unbind Lucifer; in fact, at the time, we didn't know that Lucifer Binding Sites existed.

We were walking down the central axis of Lincoln Cathedral, practicing a certain dynamic meditative image given to us by the Ofanim. A few months earlier we had visited Salisbury Cathedral in Wiltshire and had meditatively walked the central axis until we reached the midpoint of the cathedral. There the Ofanim and the Archangel Michael had amplified our image a hundredfold to fill the building and beyond. You give a penny and they match it with a hundred

Table 11-2: The Three Types of Lucifer Binding Sites—the Time Tableau of the Lord of Light on Earth

Tollan: *Lucifer Arriving*	**Mount Caucasus:** *Lucifer Bound*	**Jerusalem:** *Lucifer Unbound*
Phanes, Revelation of Light	Lucifer's Fall	The Emerald as inverted Cube of Space
The Astral Light	Prometheus's punishment	The Emerald as modem
Great Magical Agent	Sophia's exile	Foundation of Lucifer
Quetzalcoatl, Plumed Serpent	Sophia Prunikos, Sophia the Whore	Heart within the Heart
Precious Twin		Venus sphere
Geb-Nut Relationship	Sheol, Bottomless Pit	Eros, Linking Heaven and Earth
Mother of the stars and gods	Satan, the Infernal Serpent	
Protogonos, First-Born	God's Adversary	*Malak Tawus*, Peacock Angel
Lord of the Eastern Light	The Shadow	Lucifer's commission achieved
Glorious in Eden	Tezcatlipoca, Smoking Mirror	Robe of Glory restored
Son of the Dawn	Lucifer's commission repudiated	Loki-Fenrir unbound at Ragnarok
Light Bearer, Light Bringer	Robe of Glory buried	
Morning Star	Loki the Trickster	
Sidereal Virgin	Fenrir the Wolf	
Mysterium Magnum	Bevarasp	
Lucifer's commission undertaken	Zohak (Dahak, Azidahaka)	
Epiphany of the Robe of Glory		

dollars. The church felt deeply grounded and elevated, and we, too, felt remarkably uplifted.

So we figured we'd do the same at Lincoln Cathedral. Except it wasn't working. By the time we reached the center point, our image was distorted, wobbly, ineffectual, enervated, chaotic, and decidedly unamplified. Both the Ofanim and the Archangel Michael were present with us, but they seemed unable to do anything with our vitiated image. I interpreted the failure of this image to work here as a symptom of a geomantic problem, and we set about trying to figure out the origin of the problem. We walked the entire central length of the cathedral and along both sides. The problem was rooted in a small enclosed space between the central axis point under the central, tallest steeple (the cathedral has three steeples, two over the main entrance) and the choir.

We stood before this enclosed area, which was about ten feet wide. I saw a flattened black head like the top of an octopus under the stone floor, the vast weight of the cathedral having hammered it into the ground. Whatever was down there was enraged, disturbed, and had been for a long time. I thought of the account of King Solomon imprisoning all the demons beneath Temple Mount in Jerusalem as a prerequisite for building the First Temple of Jerusalem. Maybe there was something similar going on here. I also remembered a remark the Ofanim made some years before; it hadn't made much sense at the time, but it did now.

We left the church and went for a cup of tea. I was far enough away from the cathedral to be unaffected by its disturbing vibrations, and I could finally see what was going on. There was indeed a being—a very large, formidable one— buried underneath the thousands of tons of stone. It was Lucifer in the Pit.

His color, or energy signature, was a dark rich royal blue, and attuning to this color with my crown chakra enabled me to participate in his energy field. The spirit of this energy is freedom. "Why have you forsaken me?" I heard Lucifer cry out from under the stone, the weight of a Gothic cathedral on his celestial head. It's ironic: Christ was crucified on the Earth but ascended in glory to Heaven; Lucifer was crucified on the Earth but was buried in ignominy under the ground, in matter. Please free me, he moaned. Lucifer still awaited his ascension. He was full of disappointment, grief, anger, isolation, vituperation, like Prometheus scorning the young upstart god Zeus who failed to reward the Titan's loyalty.

We deployed the members of the group around the outside of the cathedral to hold supportive energy for us as we sought to release Lucifer. Specifically, they would create a Blue Dish to set under the cathedral as a foundation for incoming supportive angelic energies. My colleague would stand at the front of the church, just outside the massive doors, and practice the dynamic image the Ofanim gave us. He mentioned that he sensed another being caught between the worlds, incarcerated along with Lucifer.

I made for the far end of the cathedral grounds and sat down on a grassy patch next to the fence that abutted the street. Just as I started to work, an ambulance raced past, sirens sounding, as if synchronizing with our activities—paramedic geomancers, if you will, servicing a very distressed patient.

Somewhat like a physician examining a patient before taking any action, I surveyed the scene under the cathedral. An alien being resembling an immense black octopus sat on top of Lucifer as a jailer and warden. The octopus prevented most psychics from perceiving what was beneath it—the bound Lucifer—by throwing off angry, frightening, intimidating energy at passersby so people hurried away without penetrating this offensive shield. No doubt this unpleasant being was largely responsible for the interference with the Ofanim image.

However, no being of this nature works alone, without outside help. High above the cathedral and in another dimension were 12 alien "motherships," each with a device that sent a light beam down to the octopus and Lucifer. The effect was to tether Lucifer like a tent from above; each of the beams was like a guy-line and post hammered into the ground to keep him fastened to the Earth. A thirteenth ship positioned above the 12 orchestrated the tie-down, and it too had a light beam control device that regulated the 12 lower light beams.

I wasn't surprised to see interference by what we would commonly describe as extraterrestrial intelligences (ETs), or aliens, for short. As I mentioned in chapter 2, a consortium of friendly ETs worked cooperatively to produce the Earth and its visionary geography; just as many unfriendly ETs sought to undermine this work and have since the time of the Blue Room found various clever and effective ways to interfere, distort, and to an extent commandeer the energies of the Earth grid to serve their own agenda.

What's their agenda? To keep humans from achieving their innate freedom, free will, and full spectrum of awareness—from penetrating their Emerald. Keeping Lucifer bound and the public oblivious to the fact serves that agenda. Even so, their negative agenda is permitted and in a sense commissioned by the Supreme Being to achieve a deeper, subtler purpose for us.

It was time to get to work. I neutralized the 13 alien control devices, shutting off their beams. This was equivalent to psychically cutting the tethers. The octopus-being, now unanchored, popped out and was taken away. Beneath it the heavy lid of a massive sepulcher was thrown open, and a slow-moving freight elevator seemed to rise up from deep within the Earth, from the Pit. Hundreds of demonic, inimical beings flew out in a wrenching purgation. Surrounding this open pit with the slowly rising elevator stood dozens of archangels as tall as the cathedral. Thousands of Ofanim occupied the space behind and above them. The cathedral was now suffused with angelic presence.

Finally, borne upwards by the freight elevator, came Lucifer in dark blue. He had hundreds of wings, but they were cramped against his body from centuries of confinement in a tight space. He slowly stood up and allowed his multiple wings to flex and extend. He looked magnificent. Then he turned bright red.

It was as if he suddenly became a different being. Thousands of devils flew out around him, and Lucifer turned into Satan just as Western culture has portrayed him. Horned, disfigured, menacing, subhuman, scabrous, scary. What have I done, I thought. You can't put the genie back into the bottle. Then I laughed. Of course. They're two aspects of the same being.

The blue Lucifer and the red Satan started to merge, as if glued at the back, and they began to turn slowly like a barber's pole. There was the demonic red Satan, then came the lovely blue Lucifer, then the Satan again, the dark and light sides, appearing over and over. For a moment I sensed them merge into a single, two-valenced being, angelic and demonic at once, beautiful and ugly, alluring and repulsive. Then I realized I was observing a living expression of the Tree of the Knowledge of Good and Evil, the tree in Eden that caused all the fuss.

This gets at another aspect of Lucifer's bold deed. He modeled for us what it's like to experience the polarity of the knowledge of good and evil from a vantage point of freedom in consciousness. Lucifer shows us what it's like from a position of neutrality in consciousness, that is, freedom to choose good or evil, to know you can choose, to know you must, moment to moment. To know through experience what good feels like and what evil feels like, to be the good angel and the bad demon. Lucifer is the Logos in his highest aspect, and the Adversary in his lowest aspect, both of which are reflected in the human Ego, or the I-consciousness operating out of freedom.

The simplest statement we can make about what Lucifer gave humanity is this: He gave us our self-consciousness, our awareness of ourselves as individual egos, individual seats of cognition and activity, with the free will to choose our actions and the awareness of the consequences of our deeds. Lucifer gave us the possibility of self-awareness leading to individuated consciousness as an alternative to unitive consciousness in which each of "us" is inextricably part of the unified whole of consciousness.

Freedom after all is very expensive, and painful: The price is living knowledge of this tree. Most of us want only the bright side; we don't want to know about Satan or the Shadow. The experience of this excruciating polarity is God's gift of freedom to humanity. We can be good, or we can be bad: It's up to us.

Yes, Lucifer was in the Garden of Eden, but he wasn't the serpent. He was Old Adam himself. The pre-genderized archetypal human, both Adam and Eve. The apple was the knowledge of duality, and Lucifer, through his free will and on behalf of Adam (us), took a bite and savored the bittersweet taste. There was no expulsion, no Fall, no plummeting from grace. It was, the essence of Lucifer as Prometheus: foreknowledge of life in duality. Only later did a serpent appear in the

Garden, as a contrived scapegoat. The part of duality we didn't like we used to create Satan, the *bête noire* in the closet of the psyche.

The daringness of the plan takes your breath away when you think of it. The Supreme Being was sufficiently confident in His creation—humanity—that He felt confident agreeing to Lucifer's proposal to give us free will, that is, independent full-spectrum cognition through the gift of the Emerald. We were allowed to be angels or demons, our choice. This is an awesome onto-logical freedom, and Lucifer modeled it for us on the runway of a new planet. The Greeks could handle it, the Christians couldn't. Prometheus rebelled but was never demonized, and was res-cued and redeemed by a human hero. Lucifer was dumped in the Pit forever, the Christians hoped, and with no further discussion.

It's the no further discussion part that has been the problem. Lucifer buried, Satan sup-pressed, the subject of the Devil avoided at all costs—all you do is create an enormous Shadow the mere approach of whose penumbra seems apocalyptic to the daytime psyche. Knowledge of one half of our free will choice got buried with the institution of Christianity. But what you don't acknowledge in the daytime visits you at night, and the Shadow—Lucifer demonized as Satan—has been attacking us from the corners of the darkness for centuries.

Now the Shadow has grown so demonic, so fearsome, so destabilizing, that we not only do not confront it, we do our best to convince ourselves of its unreality. Now we project the Shadow out-side and blame everyone else for it, entirely forget-ful that this grim shadow play is autobiography.

This refusal to acknowledge the existence of a Shadow side to the individual and collective psyche allows higher dimensional beings to con-trol humans through their unconscious and the hierarchies of power built on it. So the effort is to keep humans from approaching this issue. Satan and demons are posted on the front gate to scare away anybody who inquires. Satan becomes the warden of the Shadow, and everything is off lim-its because it is demonic. It becomes too scary, too shocking to psychic balance, to approach this repressed area, the Pit within us. Unacknowl-edged, the Pit can now manipulate us from the inside, from the place where we're not looking.

At a certain collective level, we gave the aliens permission to lock in the octopus control-being and Lucifer's sepulcher with 13 light beams. This is why only living humans can undo the permission, cancel the agreements, and unbind him. If you can choose freely, you cannot be controlled, and your freedom is the envy of the galaxy, as is your planet. That's what is at stake with the Lucifer Binding Sites. That's why there are angels and demons involved, helping and hin-dering, in the refurbishing of the Earth's visionary geography.

From this perspective, it is unnerving to con-sider what we have done to the Lord of Light over the centuries. Lucifer made the daring sacrifice of part of his being, undertook the fall into incarna-tion of his precious Emerald. Then he was repudi-ated, invalidated, reviled, spat upon, crucified, demonized, bound, chained, ignored, and vilified for life. Not only do we not speak of the mad-woman in the attic; we no longer acknowledge there is an attic.

There is yet another aspect to our Lucifer revulsion. He is our scapegoat. We do not forgive him for the sin of sundering our unity with God. Individuality is a fall from grace, a separation into two. Lucifer bringing forth the Light as a majestic, magnificent revelation moved it outward into vis-ibility as form. Adam Kadmon, God's idea of per-fect existence expressed as the prototypal Human, was modeled for us by Lucifer, our Old Adam. Form inherently individualizes. Now there are two things: object and ground, manifestation and context, light and source, Lucifer and God.

Here is the origin of all the difficulty with selfhood and the spirit of independence that is Lucifer. He individualizes the Light. Here is the source of the erotic temptation by the Astral Light, referred to by Blavatsky and Levi. We want it, and we don't want it. We desire it, but we can't stand the consequences, the "sin," the karma, the responsibility. We must account for our use of this freedom. Lucifer is the Fall, and it's his goddam fault. He is the reason we are not in heaven with the Supreme Being, why we are each the wandering whore, Sophia, miserable in the Lower Worlds made of our own desolation. So we whine.

Our repudiation of Lucifer, our unwillingness to accept the karmic responsibility of incarnation, started to spread outward through the worlds of creation. It informed our attitude towards substance, towards our body and planet—our inner and outer environment made of light densified into substance. So we brought matter along with us in our fall into oblivion. If there was a Fall, it was not Lucifer's original departure from Eden, but our subsequent refusal to acknowledge his gift and its consequences.

To accept Lucifer's gift and to honor his bold execution of his plan is to unbind him, within ourselves and in the Earth. It is to acknowledge the Emerald. Then we get to use the modem, our point of connection to a multiplicity of places, planes, states of awareness. What's our way back, how do we pull off this rapprochement with the Lord of Light so we can freely use the Emerald modem?

The Christed Initiation in the Buddha Body. It's the new geomantic spiritual experience introduced by the Ofanim and the Archangel Michael. It's how the Flesh is made Word again, how matter becomes light, how despicable Satan becomes lovely Lucifer, how the Cube of Space gets illuminated, how the Emerald modem gets switched on, how we dial up the cosmos from here.

The unbinding of Lucifer on the planet and within the heart of humanity is an event of signif-icance that extends beyond the Earth. Much of the celestial hierarchy is watching this process with keen interest, as the Ofanim note:

"When Lucifer comes back, He comes to gather all of you. He comes to complete his part in the plan. He comes returned to his position as Lord of Light. He begins the return with those he brought down. The Lord of Light has made many attempts in the past to reunite with the Absolute. Always through Man's unknowing and unforgiving he has remained tied to the material plane. Ever since the Elohim came to Earth he has been tied here. Now we open the door for Lucifer to be forgiven, to find his rightful place at the right hand of the Absolute where he was shining brighter and more brilliant than the most infinite source of light you can imagine—10,000 times brighter than the brightest star."

The Elohim, colleagues in this work, offer this positive long-term view and give us another angle on Lucifer's bright side:

"Lucifer comes and is part of each creative ascendant thought or image or when Man is involved in anything towards that which is of beauty and of light. Then Lucifer is present in that. This touches that which is beautiful within yourself and that which touches the most beautiful in all of Man. The Son of Man [the Christ] knew the beautiful and the highest. He was not seduced by it and therefore made it possible at this time to release Lucifer from his earthly connections and for him to be restored in his rightful place."[521]

Back in Lincoln Cathedral, the event over, there was a gaping hole in the center of the etheric version of the cathedral. You could peer down into the Pit if you liked, but nothing was down there anymore. The wild woman had come down from the attic and was having tea with us in the parlor. Appropriately, above the front door of the cathedral is a frieze carved in stone. We hadn't noticed it when we first entered the building. A holy figure, perhaps Jesus or a saint, stands triumphantly amidst a group of people, his foot holding down a demon. Like a signature of a magical working, the frieze declares for those who see it: Here, again, the Church has subdued a demon. Later in the day, after we debriefed the group on the different aspects of the event, there was emotional processing. People were sad, in tears, in shock; in the ensuing days, a few people got colds as their bodies processed the energies. The magnitude of the event, and its ramifications, quietly crept up on all of us.

We had all recovered a little of our long-surrendered freedom; we had all sampled the collective and individual Shadow. We are all transmuting the poison of our unexpiated pain into wisdom and light, and, in a provisional sense, we were doing the same for the planet. That's how geomancy works: Whatever you do under angelic supervision at a sacred site benefits the site and yourself (and the planet) in equal measure.

The geomantic task of unbinding Lucifer at the hundreds of Mount Caucasuses around the Earth is a daunting one, and not likely to be completed soon. "This is an ongoing situation like time-lapse photography," the Ofanim note. "One event appears to be stationary, but each moment these things are taking place to a greater or a lesser extent. Lucifer is still being bound and unbound. In some places, all three functions are happening at once, at other places, only one, or at others, two at one time. It is part of the potential development for human consciousness to release that which is bound."

How many of the 3,496 Lucifer binding sites will have to be worked on to reasonably free Lucifer for the planet? "We don't know how this will go. It's like gambling. The odds are favorable, but when you gamble, you don't know how the dice will fall. Each Lucifer Binding Site involves the other places—they are interconnected. At Lincoln, it is very possible that through releasing

something in terms of structure and form it will repercuss in many places."

The unbinding of Lucifer at Lincoln Cathedral in August 2001 was like letting some air out of an overfilled tire to prevent it from exploding with further use. It was an emergency safety measure, a precaution, but it was also an overture. Lucifer can be unbound at a Mount Caucasus only if there are people willing to unbind him in themselves. This is a slow, difficult, and painful process. But cognitive freedom would not be so galactically desirable if it were easily had.

Forgiving the Supreme Being for Killing the Kings of Edom

When Lucifer was released from Lincoln Cathedral, even when he slowly ascended from the Pit on what looked like a freight elevator, he was accompanied by other beings that had been incarcerated along with him. Theological history remembers them, if sketchily, as the Kings of Edom.

Biblical history tells us eight kings reigned over the land of Edom before the Israelites under King David established their presence and rule in that area.[522] That is the outer history of the Kings of Edom. It may be true, and may not. But Qabala instructs us that "a deeply concealed mystery" is to be encountered in the "allegory" of the Kings of Edom.[523]

One of the old texts of Qabala states that "the kings of ancient time were dead, and their crowns were found no more; and the earth was desolate." Edom was the kingdom of the "destroyed world" in which "seven kings had died and their possessions had been broken up." In this allegory, Israel, more of a state of reality rather than a country and a people, was the "restored world" formed out of the destroyed one.[524] It was the second human generation after the first failed.

The "Kings of Edom" refers to the aborted first generation of Earth humans.

It's shocking to discover that as a species we have forebears that nobody ever speaks of. I'm not referring to the supposed human descent from apes. Rather, we have a somewhat aberrant first generation, progeny of Cains and Liliths who disturbed creation, upset the planet, and so startled even the Supreme Being that after a while He put them down.[525]

The Kings were prodigies of body and spirit. Their time was before most of the Earth's energy grid was installed; it was between Polaria and Hyperborea. It was the Wild West of the planet. No laws, no limitations, no sheriff. Certainly there were more than eight kings, for this number is Qabalistically symbolic; it was a lineage and they were many upon the Earth, and for a time it was theirs.

Arising in the "freight elevator" with Lucifer, they seemed about ten feet tall; they were broad, thick, large, so full of celestial light that their chakras created an energy field about them that made it seem the Edomites wore thick armor. They were slightly monstrous from today's perspective, and a little scary; the men were bearded and fierce-eyed, their physiognomies a strange, unsettling mix of primitive and celestial, demonic and angelic—Conan the Barbarian meets Planet of the Apes.

They were crowned in token of their connection with the Supreme Being, who had created them and let them flourish on Earth, but their crowns were slightly askew. You could see the divine wildness, the feral freedom in them; in contrast, we are tame, leashed house dogs today.

One of the Edomite Kings, using the term generically, was Lilith, the so-called demonic, rebellious first wife of Adam. God supposedly created her out of filth and sediment rather than pure dust, as he had used for Adam. The legend has it that she demanded equal power and stature with Adam, who refused; she left the Garden of Eden and refused to return even after God sent three angels to persuade her. Lilith's punishment for noncooperation was to lose one hundred babies every day; her retribution was to threaten pregnant and nursing mothers to whom she would appear as a demon with a woman's face, with long lustrous black hair and wings, and glowing eyes, her torso ending in a serpent's tail.[526]

In a sense, Lucifer was their mentor, guardian, and chaperone. The Edomites were the first recipients of Lucifer's daring gift and the first to embody his plan for human cognitive freedom within a biological form. He was responsible for them; it was his ass on the line if they got out of hand. Which they did. As the Bible suggests, this first race of humans overran the Earth; they became degenerate; they were unbalanced; they abused their powers; they were not a suitable "helpmeet" to Adam who should be appreciated as the Edenic archetype of humanity, before incarnation.

When the Bible says God had to find Adam a second wife because Lilith was too unruly to be domesticated, it means the Kings of Edom were unable to incarnate the Adamic archetype of spirituality. We must interpret the Adam and Lilith relationship in broader, subtler terms than the standard literal ones. The resume of Lilith gives us a fair portrait of the general nature of the Edomites.

God got sick of His first creation, according to Genesis. "Yahweh saw that the wickedness of man was great on the earth, and that the thoughts in his heart fashioned nothing but wickedness all day long. Yahweh regretted having made man on the Earth, and his heart grieved." He got rid of the Edomites with what is remembered as the Deluge, the great Flood, after which humanity started afresh with the new generation shepherded by Noah, who had a covenant with the Supreme Being not to destroy the human race again.[527]

The Edomites were removed from the Earth, but did they die? Not exactly. Legend says Lilith didn't die because she left Adam and the Garden of Eden before the Fall and its consequence of biological death. When the Supreme Being repudiated His own first attempt to create viable biological human beings, he "buried" the Edomites in the Earth along with Lucifer, their sponsor. In other words, the Edomites were thrown into the Pit at the Lucifer Binding Sites, and there they have remained ever since, stuck between the dimensions, unreleased.

Like Lilith, the Edomites were too wild for the Earth. They were planetary housebreakers, party animals in the extreme. They had freedom, but not the balance in consciousness needed to wield it with wisdom. The Edomite excesses in fact partly account for why Lucifer had to be bound or chained in the first place. Not only was he responsible for this first brood of humans bearing his modification, but the Edomites embodied some of his essence and energy, so, if they were punished and removed from the Earth as viable creatures, so must a part of him be.

Some limitations and diminutions had to be put in place; the Mount Caucasus sites at which a hologram of Lucifer and the Kings of Edom was enchained and buried would accomplish that necessary, God-ordained limitation. In that respect, a Lucifer Binding Site by definition is a place of limitation and diminishment, a Pit into which was placed a portion of the energy and essence of Lucifer and his first co-progeny, the Edomites, or first humans.

If the full human expression as the Edomites had to be severely curtailed, and even buried from the surface of the Earth and human memory, so did Lucifer. Lucifer's full being was apportioned out among 3,496 sites on Earth, so each Lucifer Binding Site holds 1/3496th part of his essence—at least, that essence which is expressible or relevant to our planetary context.

Seen this way, it is easy to appreciate Lucifer's voluntary sacrifice into fragmentation. Imagine that you were once loved by God, then sliced into thousands of parts, bound, spat upon, denied, and forgotten by all those whom you tried to serve. You cannot be whole again until the ones you tried to serve give you back to yourself by finding you within them.

Today when we access a Lucifer Binding Site, part of the grief and sadness we experience comes from the Kings of Edom as well as Lucifer. When we open the sepulcher lid and peer into the Pit, we see not only the blue-winged chief angel of God's presence, but our family's abortions from the deep past. They were so much more than we are presently today, yet they were unbalanced; we are for the moment seemingly much less than they, yet potentially fully balanced. We are the second attempt at getting humans right. We are the corrected generation. Even so, though we may be oblivious of it, we carry their phylogenetic memories of the pain of limitation and incarceration.

Probably the main reason Lilith got demonized and was said to roam at night on the edges of our rational, domesticated world is the fact that the Kings of Edom were enchained in the next dimension along with Lucifer. It's as if we hear their cries from across the threshhold, they unnerve us, and we demonize them. Granted, we would probably find the Edomites highly intimidating were we to encounter this primordial and chthonic version of our own humanity.[528]

Why were the progeny of the Edomites so wild, rebellious, and dangerous to the Earth and anathema to God? Why were they the embodiment of unbalanced forces? Qabala offers a complex explanation to do with the generation of seven of the Sefirot and how the down-flowing Light shattered the vessels. This happened in the Second World, called Emanation, and led to the existence of death.

We need to remember that the Sefirot, or primordial vessels of Light, were the backbone of the prototype of Adam, the archetype of ideal, pure humanity. Each of these seven Sefirot were Kings, according to Qabalistic theory. The Sefirot are "spiritual extensions from the Infinite, employed to create the world." But these were disunited and disordered, and when the "infinitely pure Light" flowed through them, "they broke and descended below."[529] In effect, the energy architecture for the bodies, minds, and spirits of the seed of Edom meant they began incarnation with this unbalanced, shattered spiritual condition.[530]

Qabala asserts that Nature and all its destructive forces and imperfect aspects today are the consequence of the shattering of the Primordial Kings. Similarly, their shattering is the origin of evil and its negative hierarchy of "damaging agents," the *Sitra ahara,* or Other Side. "The Creator only fashioned an incomplete source so that evil might come into existence to test man."[531]

Qabalists assert this was the intention of the Supreme Being, that this apocalyptic shattering of the Sefirot that led to the creation of evil was no accident. Or was it? Was the Supreme Being taken by surprise?[532]

If you ask Carl Jung, he would say yes, God didn't see that one coming. In his profound meditation on God's consciousness, *Answer to Job,* Jung proposed that insofar as God is the totality of all opposites, God (Yahweh) is as much unconscious as He is conscious. The proof, Jung suggested, is found in the travails of Job. God accepted a wager from Satan that the Devil could break Job's faith. Yahweh wanted to see if Job still liked him even if he ruined his life and covered his body with boils. It was Satan's idea, of course. Yahweh's behavior from a human point of view is intolerable, that of an unconscious being "who can project his shadow side and remain unconscious at man's expense."[533]

Job's suffering and his bold petition to Yahweh, the source of his suffering, to ameliorate that suffering force Yahweh to become conscious of the effects of his unconscious actions. In an elegant irony, Satan becomes the "godfather of man as a spiritual

being," enabling Job to see God's backside and the "abysmal world of 'shards.'" Job, through Satan's machinations, has been elevated to a "superior knowledge of God which God himself did not possess," namely, an awareness that Yahweh is a bewildering totality of opposite states, both persecutor and helper, benefactor and scourge.[534]

Hebrew tradition asserts that humans may not see the back of God, only the front, and sometimes only the profile; this is usually taken to mean God never turns His back on Man, but here Jung gives it a twist. Where else would God store His *Sitra ahara,* the husks of the shattered Sefirot, but behind Him?

Yahweh regrets having created humans, yet, being omniscient, surely He would have foreseen the consequences? Yahweh wants humans to be conscious, yet His own unconsciousness strives to prevent that from happening. When Job learns something new about Yahweh, this has an effect on the deity, for then, as Jung observes, "God must also learn to know himself."

Jung's provocative view is corroborated by the Ofanim. Yes, remarkably, we do have the right to ask God for retribution for past mistakes and screw-ups.

"The Supreme Being was trying to make beings in material form. He didn't get it quite right. The Kings of Edom are buried at the Lucifer sites, so the geomantic work there is about repairing part of what should not have been. It's partly about retribution. Let's say the Supreme Being made humans in His image. Humans can bring retribution to the Supreme Being that He may be able to feel more complete, as humans feel more complete within themselves."

An aspect of freedom for human consciousness involves "challenging the Supreme Being on what mistakes have been made," the Ofanim note. "This is not blame, but retribution. You cannot blame the Supreme Being for your own shadow. Retribution needs to happen before completion. Retribution has to do with settling accounts that need to be settled before things can move on, before consciousness and Albion awaken. When humans awake, then Albion awakens, and Lucifer is free to take up his rightful place next to God within the Self. Then retribution is complete."

It's an arresting thought to consider ourselves forgiving the Supreme Being. Forgiveness in the human realm is not usually between humans and divinity. But it is for us to forgive the Supreme Being for having issued this limitation of our own ancestral being by imprisoning the Kings of Edom, for having generated and loosed evil into the world, for having made mistakes in creating the Kings of Edom that led to their excess and wildness that led to His limiting them and thereby limiting us, their descendants.

In a broad sense, we are paying for the excesses of our phylogenetic parents in how we endure the seeming limitations of human life on this planet. The Kings of Edom were real cutups, so now our wings are clipped. From a certain vantage point you could see the Earth's visionary geography as a terrain of limitation. This is how the Supreme Being instituted restraints on the second generation of humanity—Noah's brood—by limiting the scope of possible activity.

Of course, this is a relative concept. From Lucifer's point of view, anything slower than the speed of light is technically a limitation of the full scope of consciousness, a fall into diminution. As it is for us when we remember. In a sense, the Lucifer Binding Sites and their correlates, stargates (discussed below), are key elements in the Earth's grid of limitation. These two features are now in the process of being undone (the former) and activated (the latter), lessening the limitation and restoring more of what the Edomites presumably had but abused.

Some of the structurally inherent features of the Earth's energy grid were of course already in place at the time of the Edomite kings (e.g., domes, dome lines, Oroboros lines, landscape zodiacs), but others (e.g., eggs, stargates, dragons, Lucifer Binding Sites, and many others) were added later because they afforded more discretion as to placement and quantity.

The intent was to tie things down a little more securely, to align human consciousness (and the body and the planet) more firmly and directly with the galactic template in accordance with the "laws" of Heaven. I said "seeming limitations" because though we are as a species initially more limited than the Edomites, we have every opportunity and "excellent odds" to achieve full awakening here and make the limitations in effect nonexistent.

In many respects the Earth's visionary geography embodies a theological allegory, all the stages of the Fall of Man and our redemption and restoration. Perhaps the largest statement we can make about it is that it's a liturgy in geomantic script of our origins and destiny. Think of the 85 different geomantic features as ensemble members in this cosmodrama enacted on the Earth stage. Seen from the right vantage point, we can behold the intricate vastness of Creation and our embedded place within it, and why it all is this way. "It is a Road of Life he has traveled by his own free will, exhausting every capacity for good or evil, that he may know himself at last as a finite part of infinity."[535]

Settling accounts with Yahweh is not a question of revenge against an incompetent deity. Rather, it is the conscious recognition of the history of the project to create humans. Of our freedom to participate in this apparently unique process of creating humans this way for this context at this time. Of our freedom—the invitation—to digest the mind-spinning paradox of God's inner antimony, this and its opposite, the Garden of Eden and the *Sitra ahara,* Eve and Lilith, Adam and the Kings.

It's our right to be debriefed on the setup and to critique the plan. Then we are in a suitably informed position to start cocreating the next phase, which is to consciously and wisely use the Emerald modem to link up across space-time.

Lucifer and Christ Comprise the Cosmic Robe of Glory

One element needs to be added to the emerging reconceived portrait of Lucifer in his true nature and function. The Christ.

The key that opens this door is the Christ-Lucifer connection as described by Austrian spiritual scientist and clairvoyant, Rudolf Steiner (1861–1925).

The identity and function of Lucifer were of foremost concern in Steiner's philosophy. In the bulk of his published material, he modeled a schism between Lucifer—representing psychic inflation, expansion off the Earth, and spiritual flight—and Ahriman, who represented gravity, the densification of spirit into matter. This schism was mediated and transcended by the Christ, who was thereby more or less at odds with both Lucifer and Ahriman. But in his earlier writings before 1909, Steiner had proposed a bolder, more inclusive model of Lucifer and Christ: cosmic brothers. Lucifer bears the Light, but Christ is the Light; thus Lucifer is the Christophor, the Christ-Bringer. Another phrase from early Christianity also suggests this relationship: *Christus verus Luciferus*, which means "Christ is the true Light-Bearer."

Early on, Steiner says Christ is Lucifer—they are two aspects of the same being. To call Lucifer the Christophor is to say he is the vesture of the Logos, or Christ. Lucifer bears (and wears) the body that is the Light of the Christ.

Steiner explains that before the Mystery of Golgotha (the crucifixion and resurrection of the Christ on Golgotha—when the Christ energy was grounded on Earth through Jesus), Christ was the upper cosmic god and Lucifer the lower inner god within human consciousness. Initiates had visions of Lucifer within the realm of their soul and beheld the Christ through the outer sensory world. Christ and Lucifer had since ancient times and by divine decree dwelled naturally side by side.[536]

Thus the relationship between Lucifer and Christ is close and collegial. Lucifer becomes the guide to the soul, the psychopomp, in our inner journey to penetrate the mystery and reality of the Christ within us. Lucifer will guide us to the "safety of a luminous spiritual life," while Christ leads us to "inner warmth of soul." Their union would herald the essential kernel of a new spiritual stream that needs to flow through the world. Steiner foresaw an eventual marriage of these two worlds, Lucifer and Christ, as they "unite themselves in love," as an agape of Logos (Christ) and Light-Bearer (Lucifer).[537]

So Christ went inward, Lucifer outward. Lucifer provided the form, Christ the substance. Lucifer's influence would help us comprehend the world, while the Christ's would continuously strengthen us from within. Lucifer in fact would fortify us with the spiritual vitality, intellectual independence, and cognitive freedom necessary to describe and understand the Christ. Lucifer is the "Spirit of independent cognition, wisdom-inwoven," that which lifts into the full light of consciousness what would otherwise remain in the unconscious. It is the Spirit through which we can comprehend what "Christ has wrought." Thus Lucifer "blazons the way" for Christ.[538]

Steiner says that when Lucifer fell from Heaven a precious stone was loosened from his crown and fell to Earth. That stone became the vessel with which the Christ took the Last Supper and received his blood when it flowed on the Cross. It was later made into the Holy Grail as a means for "those who wish to come to a true understanding of the Christ principle."

We now know that "stone" from Lucifer's crown as the Emerald.

One of the foremost goals of spiritual evolution since Golgotha, Steiner said, is to "receive this precious stone in its transformed character" as the Grail. It is to comprehend the cross of the Christ in the star of Lucifer. That star had shone throughout early human evolution until it fell from Lucifer's crown, for the star of Lucifer and the precious stone from Lucifer's crown were the same.[539]

With these final pieces laid out before us, let's finish the portrait of the reconceived Lord of Light with a key bit of information from the Ofanim.

The Lord of Light is formed out of the stellar interface, the stars being the body of Lucifer, the body of Light. Lucifer as the stellar interface connects one star with the next. Lucifer's cosmic body is the patterns of light made by the billions of stars in this matrix. Thus Lucifer births the stars from out of his body, and, reciprocally, the star-birthing process reveals the extent and form of that body. The Logos, or Christ, is all the spaces between the points of light, or stars. As the Ofanim explain, "The Logos is the Word manifest. The Logos is an empty space between things."[540]

So Lucifer is the body of stars and the matrix of their connection, and Christ is the space between the stars. Together Lucifer and Christ, Light-Bearer and Light, comprise what I call the Robe of Glory, expanding the term's scope somewhat. (Theologically, the Robe of Glory is a term used to denote Christ's purple robe or his auric field, but my usage here intends a broader reference.) The Robe of Glory is the Logos (Christ) and Eros (Lucifer) as a singular influence. The Robe of Glory is a way of conceiving of the galaxy as a single being with two aspects, the Light and the form that Light takes—all the stars and the spaces between them.[541]

Just picture it: You're standing outside somewhere in the country, away from city lights, and above you are the twinkling stars and the gaps between them. Imagine that all the stars have little lines connecting them up. This matrix of interconnection is Lucifer. All the dark spaces in between are the Christ. If you pretend you are the Earth for a moment, with 360-degree vision, then you are wearing the Robe of Glory; it is wrapped spectacularly around you.

Now we can understand why Zeus had Hephaistos, specifically of all the Olympian gods, undertake the chaining of Prometheus. Hephaistos, as the bearer of the Christ energy and consciousness (as Master Jesus, Ray Master No. 6), was already implicit in the Robe of Glory comprising Lucifer and Christ. Hephaistos did in fact bind Prometheus (Lucifer) to Mount Caucasus, but this tableau of an Olympian god chaining a Titan also shows us the close working relationship of Christ and Lucifer. Chaining Prometheus grounds Lucifer's energy on Earth.

Hephaistos in his smithy at Mount Etna creates the stellar matrix that is Lucifer's body. It isn't so much that Hephaistos did the binding, tying down the god, as that he forged the bonds in the stellar matrix that connects the Christ and Lucifer. After all, you need the empty spaces to allow the light to fill out Space itself; otherwise, you would have a tiny, compact pile of ropy threads, which is to say, intense but undistributed light.

Explaining that this deed was not of his own devising but Zeus's, Hephaistos tells Prometheus, "Yet I shall nail you in bonds of indissoluble bronze on this crag far from men." Even so, Hephaistos tells him, "I groan for your sufferings."[542]

Opening the First of Lucifer's Many Stargates

The Robe of Glory has a geomantic aspect that affects the entire planet.

Once you make contact with a Lucifer Binding Site and start to interact with the energies present, this opens the door to a second key aspect of Lucifer's presence on Earth. This aspect is called a stargate.[543]

A stargate is a means of physically and almost instantaneously moving from a point on Earth to a specific star or constellation. "They are like doorways to access the energetic phenomena of these star systems," say the Ofanim. There are stargates for individual stars (1,080) and for constellations (2.2 million), with some duplication (see table 11-3). In the case of the star stargates, you "go" to the named star, or presumably a planet or system within its sphere of influence; with the constellation stargates, you go to the umbilicus star in each star system, the star from which the collective energy field of the constellation was birthed.

I earlier described domes that also pertain to individual stars. Domes impart the experiential essence of a specific star, but stargates *take you* to that star, so such sites are literally a gate to the stars, a dimensional portal. A total of 1,746 different stars are represented by domes, but only 32 stars have stargates. However, these 32 have 32 stargate copies each. The star stargate network is a matrix of 32 squared, plus an additional 56 stargates located off planet, for 56 different stars. This gives us a total of 88 star destinations for the stargates.

There are also 2,200,000 stargates that go to constellations. With 8,333 duplicate stargates for each of 264 constellations, that comes to 2,199,912. The remaining 88 stargates (completing the planetary total of 2,200,000) remain incomplete and only partially assembled.[544]

If we didn't have the idea from popular science fiction movies and writings, the idea of a travel gate to the stars would produce incredulity or even incomprehension. It probably still does. The stargate feature, like the Lucifer Binding Sites, is one of the earliest geomantic features of

---

Table 11-3: Stargates

Planetary Total: 1,080 for single stars, 2,200,000 for constellations

Single Star Stargates: 32 different stars, 32 copies of each = 1,024; an additional 56 located off-planet, for 56 different stars

Constellation Stargates: 264 different constellations; 8,333 copies of each; 2,199,912 on the Earth; 88 incomplete

Stargate Diameter: Ranges from 3 feet to 40 miles, but average width is 30 yards; originally measured in megalithic yards (1 MY = 2.72 feet); the constellation stargates have the larger diameters.

Selected Locations:

Bluestone Heath Road, Tetford, England (8 Stargates: Stars: Sirius, Canopus, Arcturus, Pleiades; Constellations: Great Bear, Cepheus, Cygnus, Orion)

Vinstra, Norway, for the constellation Corona Borealis: 2 overlapping stargates

Bermuda Triangle, Atlantic Ocean: 2 overlapping stargates (dysfunctional)

Gobi Desert, Mongolia: 40 miles diameter, largest on planet

Mount Orohena, Tahiti, French Polynesia

Devil's Sea, between Iwo Jima and Marcus Island, Japan: 2 overlapping stargates

Devil's Tower, Devil's Tower National Monument, Wyoming, U.S.

the Earth's visionary geography. Stargates have also been a well-kept secret. The Ofanim spent 18 years preparing us for the revelation of the stargates, indicating that much preliminary work and preparation were required first. "For many thousands of years the appearance of the stargates here was not seen, and it was only partially recognized as an energetic feature."[545]

Let's have a look at some aspects of the stargates before we discuss their significance in the cosmodrama of Lucifer on Earth, as part of his Robe of Glory.

The first stargate the Ofanim revealed to our small group is located just outside the village of Tetford in Lincolnshire, England. In *The Galaxy on Earth,* I explained that this unassuming English village, about 20 miles east of the city of Lincoln, has many important geomantic features and is coming into its own as an Aquarian Mystery initiation and geomancy training center. The village sits in the center of a topological bowl surrounded and rimmed by mostly treeless hills; one of these hills is called Bluestone Heath, and a road runs along the top for some ten miles.

The Tetford stargate is a large, complex feature with many dimensions. To start with, there are eight stargates arranged in a particular pattern; this is the only place on Earth where these eight stars and constellations are represented together as adjoining stargates, the Ofanim say.

Specifically, they are: Orion, Pleiades (seven stars within Taurus), Cepheus (a constellation), Sirius (a star in Canis Major), Canopus (a star within Argo Navis), Cygnus (a constellation), the Great Bear, and Arcturus (a star within Boötes). These eight stars and constellations represent the eight elements in Camalate; they correspond to the eight vibrational aspects of the Earth's inner heart chakra, the *Ananda-kanda*; and they are directly associated with the eight Celestial Cities of Mount Meru, as described earlier in this book.

In this first aspect of the Tetford stargate

array we find three important elements: First, eight essential stars and constellations are represented; second, these are arrayed in a model of seven solar systems and 54 planets about the Great Bear in a shape that looks like an unequal cross of eight circles; third, each circle also designates a sun that organizes a solar system.

The 54 planets within these seven solar systems are arrayed variously, as five, six, seven, or eight planets per solar system. Each solar system is contained within a circle that represents the central sun or star of that system. The central circle in this unequal cross of circles represents the Great Bear and contains 12 smaller circles that represent both planets and 12 rays (five master rays and seven cosmic rays) that originate in the Great Bear.

This design implies that one of the eight stars or constellations in this array oversees a specific solar system, including ours, and that the Great Bear is the "Mother" of the array of seven solar systems, not overseeing an individual one but being the cohering center for these seven. Each of the Great Bear's seven major stars (which form the Big Dipper and are the home of the Ray Masters) is associated with one of the seven solar systems overseen by the Great Bear.

Seen from above, through clairvoyant vision, the eight stargates look like large transparent domed greenhouses, each abutting its neighbor. Seen from in front at ground level, the array resembles a vast wooden cargo ship, bearing eight enormous translucent vats as its prime freight. At the same time, the stargate array also brings to mind the image of the Judaic Merkabah,[546] God's Throne Chariot, the conveyance of the Supreme Being as described by Ezekiel, or as I joked at the time, a bit staggered by the enormity of the sight, the Supreme Being's Bentley with which, as the Yezidis (an ethnic-religious group in Iraq) said, he toured the universes for 30,000 years before creating anything, waving royally to the void.

There is a place on Bluestone Heath Road

where you can stand at the "front door" or prow of this ten-mile-long stargate ship. You gain the impression that this is a vast wooden cargo ship whose prow has been carved into a dragon's head and that flaying out like huge sails on either side of the ship are the dragon's wings. It turns out the stargate array here rests on the back of a blue dragon. The dragon is the ship on which the cargo of the stargates rests.

The dragon's tongue extended for at least a mile from its mouth, out across the Tetford landscape as if in search of something. "It is searching for the holy substance," the Ofanim note, and that is Soma, the liquid of immortality, which is its food (refer to chapter 5).

Is this stargate array really some kind of boat? There is a vehicle within this temple that at one time was interpreted as a boat. It was something to get the soul or vital essence towards the Ocean of Consciousness. You could call it something between a boat and a Merkabah. Proximity to the vehicle that will transport you to the Ocean of Consciousness explains why the ancient Celtic kings asked to be buried in Bluestone Heath hill at Tetford.

Inside the hold of the ship, which is to say, inside the dragon, are 217 rooms that are like libraries or data streams related to the stargates at the Tetford array. Each room has a different function and is occupied by intelligences projected here either through the stargates or from other dimensions. Some rooms are used to adjust the energies of the stargate.

These rooms are connected by light tendrils or subtle tunnels to other locations in the greater Tetford landscape, including the Gnome Egg a few miles away. The gnomes, or elemental spirits of the earth element, have the responsibility of primary maintenance of this geomantic feature but depend on humans for input and suggestions as to the broader picture and site operation. Obviously, if the existence of the Earth's many stargates has

been unknown until recent times, the gnomes have been in the dark as to instructions.

As our geomancy workshop demonstrated, humans pass on information from the angelic realm to the elemental kingdom, chiefly the gnomes, so they can maintain the site. "The dragon extends its tongue to seek the holy substance that is no longer available for its awakening," say the Ofanim. "The gnomes don't know how to feed it, so they need instruction in what to gather from the golden tubes to feed the dragon to enable the 'food' to enter the rooms underneath to awaken the dragon and the stargates. The golden tubes are receptacles from this which is above to that which is below to bring down the golden light to Earth."

Above the stargates in the "cargo hold" of the dragon ship there appears to be a celestial being seated on a golden throne or standing before it. This being appears to be the chariot driver. In Merkabah mysticism, this is the Ancient of Days, the charioteer. Also present on top of the dragon ship is the Archangel Michael with sword and shield upraised, one in each hand. He seems to be standing underneath the Throne of God (even though, paradoxically, this seems to reside on the top of the ship as well). Perhaps the Throne is in the position of the crow's nest above the ship's deck.

According to the Ofanim, "The driver is the Architect of All That Is, the Mother-Father God. The Ancient of Days is a manifestation of an aspect of this Architect, like a hologram of the being of the Architect transmitted into the seven dimensions. Sometimes this being is also known as *OM*, the sound, and that is also a manifestation of the Architect within the seven dimensions."

Numerous lines of light connect the dragon ship vertically to the underside of the Throne. "These lines of light can be enhanced," the Ofanim explain. "You can put your attention on what is above and below and breathe to this. This will bring awareness to this aspect of the feature. There will be a response immediately as the lines come from underneath the Throne of the Architect of All that Is."

When the Archangel Michael raised his sword and shield and officially activated the connection of Throne to dragon ship of stargates, it appeared to rain golden yellow light, as if light of a high and rare order were flowing down from the Throne into the stargates. This had the effect of turning the stargates "on."

How did Michael turn on the stargates? "The sword is light coming in from the sixth dimension and is something to which consciousness can be brought," the Ofanim say. "The activation of the sword is achieved through the crystal upon its hilt. When this is done, it can activate the stargates. Michael's shield bounces the energy from the activated sword through the stargates; it is positioned at the opposite end of the feature to the sword to bounce the energy through the stargates. The Archangel Michael will facilitate all activities to do with the sword and shield if you ask him."

The rain of golden-yellow light had a thick consistency suggestive of honey. I mentioned earlier that one of the earliest names for Britain (its second name) was Island of Honey. The "honey" in this metaphor would be, depending on how you put it, the sweetness of the divine nectar or God's grace or the Supreme Being's benevolence flowing from above to below. Britain was truly the Island of Honey at one point long ago when all its stargates were "on" and working; in fact, "Britain" was probably a metaphor for all of the Earth, for the stargates are distributed more or less uniformly across the planet.

This fact gives the expression "Land of Milk and Honey" a suddenly exciting and refreshed nuance: a land geomantically prepared, activated, and maintained, into which celestial light and the sweetness of consciousness perpetually flow for the spiritual nourishment of all living creatures and the planet. When the stargate network was open and operating, the "honey" of God's attention flowed perpetually from above to below, nourishing it.

Even the dragon's breath mirrors this continuous flow: The endless cycle of inhalation and exhalation, the coming and going of the Holy Spirit through the dragon's breath, represents the continuous downward flow of grace, insight, and wisdom from the highest spheres into this geomantic feature. The dragon's exhalation cycle in fact represents the perpetual influx and outflux, from above to below and back to above again, divine to human to Earth and around again.

Like the rest of Earth's geomantic features, the stargates must be maintained, or else entropy prevails. The Bermuda Triangle in the Atlantic Ocean is a vivid example of what happens when two adjacent stargates start to malfunction; they create an aberrated transport field in which people, ships, and planes are transported not to stars or constellations but to a parallel dimension. The Devil's Sea between Iwo Jima and Marcus Island near Japan is another example of a distorted stargate system. There are in fact 48 places around the Earth (including these two) where there are abnormalities of function in the stargates due to lack of conscious human attention to them.

You can see how far we as a culture are behind the curve. Not only are we failing to maintain this and other geomantic features, we don't even know they exist. How are stargates maintained? By regular human interaction. Can you imagine a day when people routinely went through the stargates? Apparently that kind of regular use is required to curtail stargate entropy.

The Paradox of the Stargate's Fifth-Dimensional Now-Ledge

Is it true that you can go through a stargate to the actual star? I think so, but the ability to travel this way is gained by degree. The body (and the psyche, too) needs to gradually acclimate itself to this kind of transportation.

The Ofanim had suggested our group invoke the Archangel Michael and to expect a response from underneath the Throne. This was how it happened. The Archangel Michael activated the stargates and the honeyed rain of grace fell from above. I took that auspicious confluence of celestial attention to try out the Pleiades stargate. I wasn't sure which of the stargates was for the Pleiades, but I set my intention to be at that one. Somehow I found it.

Outside it looked like a white, crystalline dome-like celestial enclave or a huge curved vat of light. Inside it looked like a train station very early in the morning. When the Archangel Michael did his thing and the golden lines of light rained down in response, the stargates changed appearance and resembled a bishop's mitre with four golden strips quartering the domed roof with squares of red in between them. Later the Ofanim would say that was "phenomena related to the opening of the gates, but to understand what this was would mean you would have to understand the construction and material content of the gates." Inside the gate, there was a very bright light at the top of the domed greenhouse-type ceiling, while the space below was open, wide, and empty.

I didn't sense any motion or translocation, but in an eyeblink I was somewhere else or perhaps the "train station" turned itself inside out to be its counterpart somewhere in the Pleiades. I was surrounded by Pleiadians. They looked like humans only their heads were much bigger, more bulbous, their craniums bulging as if their head space accommodates a couple more chakras than we have. They seemed to have no hair on their heads, either. Several Pleiadians looked at me in surprise; perhaps nobody from Earth had been through that portal in some time. Several women in green cloaks clustered around me, studying me

with curiosity. I wondered if they somehow knew me.

Later I asked the Ofanim if I had actually gone to the Pleiades. I knew my body hadn't, but part of my awareness had certainly registered a different reality. "Primary delta stream. When you connect with the energy through a stargate, the first part of that energy is described this way. Then, given more access, more of your materiality can pass through the gate, giving you more access to what's on the other side. You can revisit the experience, and through accessing the experience later, more of you can pass through and you can experience more."

How about the dragon as ship and foundation for the stargate array? Not every stargate array has a host blue dragon. In fact, the Ofanim point out that Tetford's arrangement of eight stargates atop a blue dragon is unique for Earth at this time. The reason has to do with the astrological dawning of the Aquarian Age and Tetford's heightened role in that new matrix of energies.[547]

One would logically think the blue dragon represents an aspect of Draco, the constellation of the dragon that circles the Pole Star. It doesn't. "What you call a blue dragon is part of the appearance within the landscape of the energy body that clothes the energy feature," the Ofanim note. In other words, it's a blue dragon for metaphorical purposes.

"Many things are presented to consciousness that are implicit to consciousness," they continue. You know it as long as you don't look at it, because it's implicit in our consciousness; once you try to see it, some confusion arises as to exactly how it looks. "This is an example of a primary moving force that, interpreted by consciousness, is expressed as a dragon. Draco was labeled after this primary phenomenon in consciousness, not the other way round." Draco itself, even the archetype of a dragon or energy serpent, is from the Ofanim's viewpoint still a metaphor for a more sublime, less quantifiable reality.

In some respects, it's easy to understand what a dragon is. Take a line of light and induce a vibration in it. The line will wiggle. There's your dragon. How do you induce a vibration in a line of light? You "slay" it with a sword; you introduce a focused energy, symbolized by a sword, and transform and awaken the static line of light into the wiggling dragon of light.

When the stargate network was fully operational in the time when Britain (and the Earth) was the Island of Honey, the Earth was riddled with pinpricks. Straight beams of light rayed out from two million points (technically, 2,201,080) around the Earth, each beam of light a transport beam connecting a stargate on Earth with a star or constellation in the galaxy. The Earth was so brilliant with these light beams and surface pinpricks it was as if it harbored a vast sun within itself, raying out in these millions of directions all across the galaxy. This was the scintillating Robe of Glory as described earlier, the Christ-Lucifer interface.

The Earth's stargate network was a way of anchoring a new planet in space-time so that it was perpetually connected to 352 different places (32 stars on Earth, 56 off-planet, 264 constellations on Earth). Two-way traffic through these light beams connected the stargates and their galactic destinations. Humans and extraterrestrials came and returned. Beings of all types, including human, traveled effortlessly through this vast interconnected body of cosmic light.

In effect, the system was (and remains) fifth dimensional: It gives space a fourth-dimensional or time aspect so that being here and there in two different points in space can be simultaneous. The fourth dimension of course is time, as typified by time-lapse photography or what mathematicians call phase shift topology. You watch a flower bud, blossom, droop, and dry up in a matter of seconds; its entire life cycle is compressed into a brief moment of viewable time.

In the fifth dimension, places on Earth are also places in the galaxy at the same time and over time; if you can imagine a time-lapse photography aspect to two different places being in the same place, that gives you a sense of the fifth dimension. You're here at a stargate on Earth, such as on Bluestone Heath Road; you pass through one and you're in, say, the Pleiades, and at some point you'll be coming back. The possibility of coming back exists, and with it the ease of two-way traffic linking the two sites, here and the Pleiades.

In effect, you are in both places over the spectrum of time. In the visual example cited above (the millions of light beams raying out from the pinpricks on the Earth's surface), the connection between 2,201,080 heres and 2,201,080 theres has the effect of putting the heres and theres in the same place: Pleiades stargate here, Pleiades the actual star there, and the light beam connecting both.

There's another twist to this complexity. The fifth dimension is what we call knowledge, the Ofanim note, but they mean it as now-ledge, a point of entry. "Time is indeed the fourth dimension with all its aspects, future, past, and present. The access point to this time dimension is through the now-ledge. Bluestone Heath Road with its stargate array is a now-ledge. It is like a ledge from which you enter the now, and from there you enter the fifth dimension."

The stargate network on Earth starts to reawaken after and as Lucifer and the Kings of Edom start to get unbound at the Lucifer Binding Sites. We could say when Lucifer was bound in the 3,496 sites, he was stripped naked of his celestial glory; that glory is the stargate network, a magnificent robe of light. As Lucifer regains himself, reincorporates his fragments, becomes himself again, he can start to put on the robe of light once more as is his right. Presumably, with each unbinding, a little more of the stargate network will become visible.

That robe of light, the Robe of Glory, is the stargate network on Earth. But it is also much more. It is the panoply of stars in the galaxy. Lucifer is the lord of that light.

What does being Lord of Light entail? Lucifer is the pivot point between unitive consciousness and individuative consciousness, between the fathomless Ocean of Consciousness and its fragmentation into billions of points of light, each a different viewpoint. Lucifer is the one who is aware of this arc between the unitive and individuative, and he maintains the arc. He knows all the different states and levels of consciousness this differentiation produced: He has full star knowledge because he is larger, older, antecedent to it.

Lucifer exists before the stars; he is the source of their differentiated light and thus of their existence; he is the Lord of their light, and his Robe of Glory comprises the multitudes of stars that are the bodies of the gods.

In effect, he is the same as the Robe of Glory, which he wears, yet he is more, too. He is the summation of all the star knowledge and states of awareness, and he is the awareness that is aware of being that summation, which is a step beyond merely knowing the totality. Knowing you know it, being aware that you know it, makes all the difference. This is the Norse Fenrir Wolf, his mouth open so wide the upper jaw scrapes Heaven. This is another way of seeing Lucifer's Robe of Glory, his Eros function as the pivot point linking the domains of Earth and Heaven, the planet and the galaxy, humanity and God.

Lucifer's consciousness—ours, too, through the Emerald within each of us—is the diversity of the stars encompassed and embodied in one vast multidimensional being. As more of Lucifer's reality gets released on Earth, through unbinding him at the sites, more of the stars in the stargate network get activated and thus more of the stars in his Robe of Glory "come online," and more types of consciousness can enter the Earth and human experience. We start becoming more galactic in our frames of reference.

Why are there stargates on Earth? "Man is not just from the Earth," the Ofanim say. "He is also from the stars. For consciousness to be integrated with the evolutionary program, the stargates are a constant reminder of the inheritance that lies in the mirror of the Supreme Being in the form of Man."

As Lucifer is unbound, "so his body begins to be freed, and he becomes more whole again," the Ofanim comment. "As these aspects of Lucifer are unbound in different places, so the body of Lucifer begins to be whole again. When this occurs, Lucifer takes on his true form; then many possibilities begin to unfold." Why? Because that which has been repressed is now free. Therefore, out of that potential unleashed in consciousness is the possibility of a new understanding from different star systems as the unfolding of the Luciferic-stellar interface takes place.

The vision of the Luciferic-stellar interface, the Robe of Glory consisting of the stars of Lucifer and the Christ Light, is spectacular, something to be approached in stages in a kind of serial cognition. We can start coming closer to it by climbing a conceptual scaffolding of different names and evoked qualities.

One of the more helpful conceptual descriptions comes from Mazdean cosmology, an early pre-Islamic branch of Iranian mysticism. That tradition uses the term *Xvarnah* for what I refer to as the Robe of Glory.

Xvarnah is "the celestial Light of Glory, the 'fire of victory,'" which is primarily the property of high celestial beings called Yazatas. Henry Corbin, a renowned scholar of Iranian mysticism, says that the Glory was visible as the nimbus or flaming halo, the *Aura Gloriae,* surrounding the heads of ancient princes, saints, Buddhas, and the Christ, but it is more than that. It is the power that is and weaves together the existence of a Light being, the preexistent Soul itself before the advent of any body. It is the soul of every being of Light, the aura of a star as a celestial being, a "figure of eternal Time."[548]

Corbin calls the Light of Glory the "all-luminous substance, the pure luminescence" given to all celestial beings at their conception, the "Energy of sacral light" which organizes their beings and gives them lasting coherence. *Xvarnah* is not only the primordial constitutive light, but it is the energy in operation since the beginning of existence and creation. It is the "victorial fire," the "radiation everlasting," the "perdurable radiance," the "astral incandescence"; it is the light of the dawn of spiritual stars who are "pure spiritual entities of light." It is Glory, Destiny, and the Soul itself.[549]

Corbin also speaks of a "landscape of *Xvarnah*," a visionary geography haloed with the Light of Glory, of earthly landscapes restored to their paradisal purity by an infusion of *Xvarnah*. Even this visionary terrain, this enhaloed Earth, is a projection of the Soul, which is the Light of Glory, Corbin adds.

Through the images of Mazdean cosmology, Corbin evokes for us a planetary terrain after unbinding Lucifer and opening the stargates. The *Xvarnah* imagined by the soul transfigures the Earth into a heavenly Earth, "a glorious landscape, symbolizing with the paradisal landscape of the beyond."[550]

Lucifer's Revelation of Light as Phanes and Eros

Through another strain of early Greek philosophical insight we get another panorama of Lucifer as a cosmic spectacle of original Light. Here he is Phanes, the Revealer, the Lord of Light with all his *Xvarnah* intact.

According to Orphic myth, Phanes burst forth from the Silver Egg, a primordial cosmic container, and his light shone in the four directions and set the world whirling into life. When the egg split in two, the two halves forming Heaven and Earth, there stood Phanes, a figure of shining light, golden-winged, double-sexed, with four eyes and the heads of numerous animals growing out of his sides, ready to create the race of gods unaided, "bearing within himself the honored seed of the gods."[551]

As Phanes emerged from the Egg "the whole universe shone forth by the light of Fire—the most glorious of elements." Phanes presided over Heaven as if he were seated on a mountain range and from there "in secret shines over the boundless Aeon," observed Clement of Alexandria, an early Church father and Christian theologian. Phanes "created Heaven with forethought for his children" so that they might have their own seat and habitation, and founded for the immortals "an imperishable mansion," commented Lucius Lactantius, a fourth-century Christian theologian.[552]

One of the Orphic Hymns (from roughly the seventh century B.C.) characterized Phanes as "the glory of the sky," the "shining flower," and the "mighty first-begotten." He was glorious in his golden wings, and from him the race of gods and mortals, the Sun, stars, even the dwelling of the gods sprang.[553]

Sceptered Phanes was the author of the sensible world, the world that could be seen, sensed, that was *visible*. He was also the limit and boundary of the intelligible Light. Insofar as he makes things *visible* (illuminates the rest of creation), Phanes was sometimes called Light itself. Phanes alone started the process of creation and manifestation, the Orphics maintained, and Heaven and Earth were separated and the myriad seeds were differentiated into life and stars; Phanes had to stand between the two realms and hold them together.

Here Phanes assumed another of his names and functions, Eros, or Love. Love was the necessary principle of union that secured the marriage of the sundered Heaven and Earth, making it possible to birth the younger gods and, eventually, humanity. The primordial egg split in half, but Eros held the parts and all the contents together. "Life springs from Love, and so Love has to be there before life in order to provide the vital force which will mingle or marry two beings that further beings may be produced."[554]

Eros, the demiurge commissioned by God to unfold the world, would "give impulse and rhythm to the great dance of creation when 'the Morning Stars sang together.'"[555] This is a refreshingly different perspective of the Lord of Light from the failed celestial being who fell from Heaven in disgrace. It takes us one step closer to appreciating his true or original essence and role in the cosmos.

It's useful to note that the Ofanim describe the Emerald as the *source* of Love and Light, the experience of which transcends our conventions of space-time, which in turn frames the identity of the experiencer. "When a human begins to awaken to other humans, when the Love in you meets the Love in someone else, then the Emerald awakens." The identification of the Emerald and Emerald-bearer as Eros accounts for this attribution of the source of Light and *Love* to Lucifer. It also gives us an intriguing clue about the inseparability of visibility (Light) and Love (Eros).

In the Orphic model of the cosmogony, we have a primordial androgynous being, a subcreator or demiurge initially containing the seeds of all creation, birthing the world of Light in all its differentiation and thereby separating Heaven and Earth. Yet this same being—variously called Phanes, Protogonos, Eros, Love, *Lucifer*—remains in place, linking the two realms. And he gave us the means to do the same: the Emerald.

For now the Emerald is equivalent to the Emerald-bearer. The Emerald is the Cube of Space, initially containing Heaven and Earth within its volumetric sealing of space; the 45-degree tilt that converts Cube of Space to Emerald also establishes the link or marriage between Heaven and Earth. Lucifer, in his guise as Phanes, Protogonos, and Eros, is the *embodiment* of that link.

The identification of Lucifer as Eros makes this startling conclusion possible: Eros is the Emerald modem connection between Earth and Heaven.

Eros binding Heaven and Earth is the Emerald modem in action. It is a cosmic function performed by Lucifer. Through his gift of the Emerald to us, we can perform it, too; in fact, we can participate in this *hieros gamos* of the realms. The Emerald's modem function is activated in this linking function; linked, we can communicate across the ten dimensions of Heaven and Earth.

Heaven and Earth are separated; this is an aspect of the Fall. We are here on Earth in bodies; Heaven is out there in light. How do we stay connected? Eros's Emerald maintains our connection, keeping us grounded at both ends, feet and head, so to speak, to our source and our destiny. Lucifer (as Eros) *is* the Emerald modem link between the world of substance and the world of origin. And Lucifer (as Phanes) is the revelation of Light *as* the world of substance.

The aspect of Lucifer that is Phanes, the revealer of light, the light itself, finds brilliant support in the perceptions of H. P. Blavatsky. She was not taken in by the Western theological demonization of Lucifer into Satan and found it remarkable (and dismaying) that culture had deconstructed the "universal soul and Pleroma, the *vehicle of Light* and the receptacle of all the forms, a force spread throughout the whole Universe" into a vile, seductive, dangerous Devil.

To her, Lucifer was the Astral Light that informed and made the stars. This Astral Light is the *Akasa*, the universal soul and matrix, the *Mysterium Magnum* and "Sidereal Virgin," which births everything that exists by way of differentiation, Blavatsky explained. It is the cause of existence; it fills the infinity of Space; it is Space itself filled with pure, virginal, visible light.

"But in antiquity and *reality,* Lucifer, or *Luciferus,* is the name of the angelic Entity presiding over the *light of truth* as over the light of day," she wrote. The Astral Light has two valences: It may be God and Devil at once, angel and dragon, just as Lucifer is divine and terrestrial, Holy Ghost and Satan. This of course is in accordance with the Orphic descriptions of the androgynous, double-aspected Phanes who was not one, not another, but both at once.

Both Lucifer and Satan, Light-Bearer and "the Red Fiery Dragon"—which is to say, both valences of this prime angelic being—are in us because this single being is our mind itself: "our tempter and Redeemer, our intelligent liberator and Saviour from pure animalism." In Blavatsky's view, Lucifer is the essence of our self-awareness, a perception that matches with the Greek concept of the gods' unwearying fire bestowed by Prometheus. The Astral Light, "the manifested effects of the two who are one, guided and attracted by ourselves, is the *Karma* of humanity," Blavatsky adds.[556]

Lucifer as the embodiment of the Astral Light, of visible, revealed light, can also be interpreted as the embodiment of the Fall *into* that Light, into the vast realm of Earth characterized by light traveling just *under* the speed of light. It sounds paradoxical, but at the exact "speed" of light, there is no light or time or motion. That is the Pleroma, or Heaven. The created worlds of Earth are the vehicles for speeds *less* than the full speed of light, from a little to a lot. Lucifer's Fall was a speeding violation for going *slower* than light speed.

All the seeds of stars, planets, gods, humans, and living creatures contained within Phanes' Silver Egg comprise the Light of which Lucifer is Lord and Bearer. Lucifer contains this prodigy of Light, so therefore he is its Lord. He is Lord of Light not out of ambition, but because this is how the Supreme Being made him: He is the container of the light and the means by which the world is visible.

His appointed task is to bear and *bare* the Light, to be reservoir and epiphany. Lucifer is the Lord of Light because the Light he holds births the stars, which is to say, generates the multiplicity of gods. They are beholden to Lucifer for their Light and are subsequent to him in the sequence of creation (see table 11-4).

Lucifer Returns in Harmonic Glory to His Tree of Life

We've already started our rapprochement with the Lord of Light, even though we didn't realize it at the time and he was using another name. It was the much-publicized, much-ridiculed Harmonic Convergence of August 1987. The Lord of Light's name for that event was Quetzalcoatl, the Plumed Serpent.

According to the Zapotec Indians of Mexico, the Tree of Life was planted by their god, Quetzalcoatl. It was both an actual tree and an energy imprint left in the same place. In his last incarnation as Ce Acatl 900 years ago, he reconvened his ancient Confederation of the Tree in his capacity as Lord of the Dawn and vowed, when he died, to one day return to his Tree and Zapotecs.

According to the Toltecs and Aztecs, Quetzalcoatl was one of four sons of Ometeotl, who created the cosmos and rules over its cycles. Ometeotl (two god) was a bisexual god whose principle was duality; he occupied Omeyocan, "Place of Duality," above the highest sphere of the Central Mexican model of 13 Heavens. In his guise as Ometeotl and with his consort, Omecihuatl, the two were the eternal progenitors,

Table 11-4: Nine Cultural Guises of Lucifer

Judeo-Christian: Light Bearer, Lord of Light, Son of Dawn, the fallen Satan (Islamic: Iblis)

Greek: Prometheus, a Titan ("Fore-Thought")

Mesoamerican: Quetzalcoatl, the Plumed Serpent

Orphic: Phanes, the Revealer (Protogonos ["First-Born"], Eros [Love])

Egyptian: Nut, Goddess of the Celestial Vault

Gnostic: Sophia, Goddess of Eternal Wisdom

Norse: Loki (Trickster God) and Fenrir, Wolf of Ragnarok

Yezidis: *Malak Tawus,* the Peacock Angel

Hopi: Pahana, the Lost White Brother, and Maasaw, Guardian of the Earth

Note: The Norse and Hopi mythopoeic conception divides Lucifer's complex nature into two beings, seemingly different, but ultimately the same.

the root of ultimate reality, dispatching to the Earth the souls of those seeking birth.

Quetzalcoatl, their "son," was the manifestation of their wisdom. In one Mayan depiction, he sits on the Jaguar Throne, holding the staff of fertility and wearing the spiral-shell jewel of life; the "flowering blood of sacrifice" flowed from his shinbones; and a hummingbird hovered about his crown, symbolizing resurrection and nectar-imbibing. His mission was to establish communication between Heaven and Earth, to unite humanity with Ometeotl.[557]

Quetzalcoatl came from the mythic homeland of the gods of high civilization known as Tollan, the Land of the Sun, where he was king. One of his prime cosmic temples was the Morning Star, the ancient name for the planet Venus. His celestial residence was Tollan (or Tulan, both Mayan words), whose name is translated as "Place of Cattail Reeds" or "Place of Rushes." At some point Quetzalcoatl voluntarily left Tollan, or was banished after having been deceived by another god into committing unsuitable sexual actions, or was dethroned by his enemy, Tezcatlipoca, who destroyed the Celestial City.[558]

His heart soared into the sky and became the

Morning Star, or Venus; the Mexicans used to say Quetzalcoatl died when Venus became visible, which is why they called him "Lord of the Dawn" and "Lord of the Eastern Light."[559]

The myths further say that Quetzalcoatl created humanity and opposed the enemies of the Light, chiefly Tezcatlipoca (Smoking Mirror).[560]

The myths show these two beings as perpetually in conflict, dethroning each other. Tezcatlipoca was believed to be omnipresent, causing discord and conflict everywhere and making humans evil. He was a destroyer and bringer of misfortune, yet he also assisted Quetzalcoatl in the creation of the world and its peoples. A kind of cultural benefactor, he also gave humanity the gifts of understanding and intelligence, and he could read their most interior thoughts.

The Zapotecs prophesied that Tezcatlipoca would reign for 900 years to be finally overthrown by Quetzalcoatl, and the Tree of Life would blossom with "fruit" never seen before in all of creation—the new spirit of humankind.

The Zapotecs claim Quetzalcoatl buried his heart under the El Tule tree in the nondescript courtyard of a country church called El Templo del Santa Maria, ten miles east of Oaxaca. This tree, at the time of the Harmonic Convergence, was a massive, stout cedar, 131 feet tall, 138 feet in girth, and said to be 2,000 years old. It was ground zero for the Convergence and Quetzalcoatl's long-awaited return. Ironically, he returned for millions around the world who were not at the El Tule tree and had never heard of it or Quetzalcoatl.[561] I witnessed his return:

The tree burst into billions of tiny sparks of light, sent shimmering and radiant out through the leaves and around the planet, to implant within individual human hearts a vision of peace, love, and harmony. These sparks would touch the heart of every human on Earth, "touching their minds, their souls, with a new awareness, a new glory." The tree, incidentally, glowed with "an ever brightening aura, green in color, like transparent jade"—or Emerald.[562]

Quetzalcoatl did return to his Tree near Oaxaca, and his uncovered heart did burst into billions of points of light. Obviously this was a Lucifer Binding Site, but the kind where he could be witnessed arriving in glory and *Xvarnah*.

At dawn on August 17, 1987, the Lord of Light came back, and the impact of that event is still being assimilated by people around the world. It was an event long in preparation, from even before the appearance of the first humans in the planetary milieu (and continental location) called Lemuria.[563]

As part of the Blue Room team's work to implement the Earth's visionary terrain, high celestial beings periodically came to Earth to activate and prime certain features. At one early point, prior to the first human incarnations, Lucifer as Lord of Light came to Earth, accompanied by the Ofanim, Elohim, a number of archangels, some Pleiadians, Sirians, and representatives from various galactic stations, and a Ray Master called Santanda who bore the Christ impulse (and who would later incarnate as Master Jesus). This collaboration between Lucifer

and the Christ energy and its prime bearer is a hallmark of his cosmic function.

They "arrived" at an energy enclosure set over the site now known as Tierra del Fuego, at the southernmost tip of Argentina. The energy enclosure was the first dome on the planet (it's still there). It, too, was a Lucifer Binding Site.

So at the Harmonic Convergence in Mexico, Lucifer towered over the landscape, a majestic, glorious angel. From his Emerald heart, he sent green rays out over the landscape and the entire planet. He planted a copy of his Emerald at the El Tule tree; eons later it would be remembered as Quetzalcoatl's heart buried under the tree.

"Within each of the people involved in this event, Lucifer was activating the Heart within the Heart, or Emerald," the Ofanim explain. In other words, whether in human form or any other, participants were *grounding* the Emerald on behalf of the planet just as Lucifer was establishing a hologram of his own Emerald in the Earth and activating it. You can see the key geomantic principle of *As above, so below, and in the middle, too* perfectly exemplified in this tableau from the planet's vast past.

This first single dome presence was a prerequisite for all the domes being implanted later. The first dome was visited by Lucifer in his full manifestation on his first visit to Gaia. Here he made a commitment to Earth and thereby to the humanity that would reside here. It was necessary for this to happen before the implantation of the first domes over the surface of the Earth.

The Ofanim say that Lucifer's first step towards matter, also described as the Fall, occurred synchronously and coincidentally on other planets, as part of conscious evolution.

So it made geomantic sense for Lucifer on his first return to Earth to revisit the prime copy of his Emerald, held in trust by planet and humanity. Which he did, magnificently plumed in Elohim, the multicolored feathers of the glorious and divine quetzal bird. As he approached his Emerald, it took on the appearance of a green pomegranate stuffed with tiny seeds of light. As he touched his own Emerald, which had turned crystalline white, its light seeds were released in a Big Bang dispersal across the globe.[564]

Let's decode a little of the myth. Lucifer (Quetzalcoatl) came from his Celestial City, Jerusalem (Tollan), under the auspices of the Supreme Being (Ometeotl) to reenergize his Emerald (Heart) at the place where he grounded (buried) it. This unassuming Mexican churchyard near Oaxaca is actually one of the Earth's three prime Heart chakra sites, being the Emerald, or in-between space, to the *Anahata* (outer) at Glastonbury, England, and the *Ananda-kanda* (inner) at the Rondane Mountains in central Norway. Ground zero for the world Harmonic Convergence was Lucifer's own Emerald on Earth; we might say as well that it took place in Jerusalem, Lucifer's own Celestial City.

The event's high point seemed to be August 17, but things had begun building on August 14 and continued on the downward curve of the parabola until August 24. During that momentous week, the Ofanim explain, "under the direction of His Most Highly Evolved Conscious Architect of the Cosmic Plane, [the Mesoamerican Ometeotl]

within which the ether fields of Earth reside began work on opening receptive areas of the material plane to a new source of cosmic energy. This was focused through Lord Lucifer at El Tule."

Lucifer "illumined the astral sphere around the planet and infused this into those who had any degree of receptivity at an astral or higher mental level illumination of a specific type. This coincided or converged with the opening of doorways on a material plane that will activate the Earth's grid in a new way. The El Tule tree formed the link between the etheric, astral, and physical levels."

I said above that Lucifer's return to his Heart or Emerald at the El Tule tree had lasting ramifications still unassimilated by many. It was a psychically shocking event even to be reminded of the existence of this dual-natured being.

The Emerald of every human registered the impact of his return; every Emerald thereafter vibrated faster even though most people were unaware of it. And that quickened vibration started to shake loose the "heat tiles" of denial insulating the daytime psyche against the destructive gravitational pull of the Shadow as we started to make our reentry into the fullness of our Earth incarnation, and as we started to get ready for the next phase, when the Emerald modem is on.

12 Ragnarok in Slow Motion
The Transfiguration of Planetary Reality

It was a wild, windy, rainy summer solstice in 1985, one of the first days of the slow-motion apocalypse in which our planetary reality would be transfigured. I was perched under a nearly blown-out umbrella with several friends atop a small grassy prominence called Balham Hill near Chiselborough in Somerset. The Ofanim called it Mort Hill, as in *mors*, mortality, death, mortification, and as things turned out, getting thoroughly, mortifyingly wet.

We had barely learned that the Earth has a geometric grid, and now the Ofanim were beginning to change it on us. Apparently it had all been long planned. The wind was blowing so hard and the rain driving so furiously that I almost could not hear my friends speaking less than a foot from my ear. Writing down notes on a soggy pad with a runny ball-point was almost amusing, when it wasn't frustrating the journalist in me. The Ofanim had invited us to witness and, to a small extent, participate in the awakening of an Earth grid point.

Dozens of Ofanim and Seraphim formed a luminous coronet around the hill, a bright lilac flame burning in its midst. They asked us to breath as Love from Above to our Blazing Stars within the big lilac flame and to allow this image to sink into the hill for the benefit of its energy template. They invoked and blessed the four elements and their spirits. As the event proceeded, we saw Mort Hill as a node of intersection within a matrix of lines of light crisscrossing the Earth; numerous other nodes were part of this planetary web, and all were being tended by angels who supervised lilac flames burning upon them.

After about 30 minutes it was over, and as soon as the Ofanim and Seraphim departed, the rain stopped, and within ten minutes the sky started to clear and the midday sun came out from behind innocent-looking cumulous towers. It was typical of the Ofanim: Over the years they had demonstrated a penchant for designer weather, tailored to suit the geomantic occasion.

"We are aware of what you call weather," the Ofanim remarked. "Water is consciousness on a material plane, as close as can be. It is also truth. Water is light. Water contains consciousness, and consciousness is light. We brought the pure element of change, fresh air on a material plane, a wind spiral, which, through playing with the water element, created a spectacular event." The Wagnerian weather display served for a bravura demonstration of a new act in the planetary opera.

The Ofanim explained that they, with the Archangel Michael, the Seraphim, and other angelic colleagues, were "consciously activating certain Earth energies" in a specific section of the planetary grid system. "Mort Hill is a nodal point. The Earth energy here has been closed for many years. It has now been activated. We are pleased that you were all there to witness its activation and the beginning of that portion of the conscious activation of the grid system."

But the activation of Mort Hill was only the prelude. "The Earth grid is a phenomenon with multiple dimensions confirmed by various agencies throughout its evolution. Changes are happening now within its original structure." It had to do with the Platonic Solids, which compose the Earth's grid configuration. All five are part of it, like Chinese boxes, one inside the other, with the dodecahedron on the outside. This is where (and how) we have the 12 Albion Plates across the Earth's surface.

Some of the Platonic Solids within the Earth grid have been relatively inactive in recent centuries, the Ofanim said. Now they are starting to be reactivated. "The forms of the Platonic Solids are in a process of change from one to another. The astrological attributions of each Solid simultaneously change. This change happens about every 2,160 years. You witnessed a little of the seeding of this activation today. One of the first events of this time on your planet experimentally happened today at Mort Hill."

The geomantic logic was unassailable. Here is a hill whose geomantic design supports transformation through radical change, almost mortification. It is a temple for Scorpionic death and transmutation mysteries, for the mythic encounter with Mortdred, King Arthur's bastard son who eventually ruined all of Camalate. Of course, that's just the outer story, not what really happened. But at Mort Hill you can encounter your *dread of mort*, of death and transformation. You can run from it or embrace it or, perhaps as a middle ground, sit on a windy, water-soaked hilltop and watch the change happen all around you.

The *mort* that the Ofanim and their colleagues were activating would have an impact on the entire planet. It would be as momentous and shocking and wonderful and outrageous as the bodily changes one undergoes at puberty. But it would be more than a fairly regular, once-every-2,160-year kind of change. The Earth started on a process of profound morphological change such as it has never undergone before. The structural blueprint for Earth, designed in the spiritual worlds and executed from the Blue Room before Hyperborea, moved on to phase two.

The End of the World Will Be Accomplished through the Changing Earth Grid

Let's be honest: All of us at some level are worried about the Apocalypse. We're like the Hobbits of Hobbiton before the Ring ever came to Bilbo or Frodo, for whom Sauron, Mordor, and their even darker antecedents were but a vaguely disturbing rumor at the far edges of their comfortable social world.

In our world, the dread of mort wears a different guise from Sauron's, but Tolkien's metaphor is apt. There is John of Patmos's grim End-Days scenario in Revelation. Contemporary religious fundamentalists have taken his prophecies literally, foreseeing an elitist Rapture in which Jesus saves the righteous and all else are left on Earth for a grim Tribulation and takeover by the Antichrist.[565] Or the Christ will make his long-expected Second Coming and rebalance the world.

Edgar Cayce and many psychics since have foreseen tumultuous Earth changes, sudden, violent landmass reconfigurations, the sinking of islands, sweeping physical alterations to the surface as to make Earth unrecognizable.[566] Or the Earth may be gearing up for a Pole shift, evidenced by the increase in the Schumann resonance or planetary "heartbeat" from 7.8 to 8.6 cycles per second as noted in the 1990s, with a corresponding drop in the Earth's magnetic field of about five percent per 100 years, so that it is 38 percent lower today than 2,000 years ago.[567]

Others worry about cataclysmic comets and crashing asteroids or the catastrophic consequences of the return of the twelfth planet called Marduk, whose 3,600-year orbit way out beyond Pluto is about to bring it close to Earth again.[568] The Mayan calendar, and the world whose time it clocks, is scheduled to end on December 21, 2012, when all manner of apocalyptic events might occur. Also on that date our Sun at the winter solstice will make a rare alignment with the galactic center, facilitating a chance for "spiritual renewal for humanity."[569]

What should we most fear? A vengeful God? Aberrant celestial bodies? Maybe the Earth itself, "the most ambitious mass murderer in the galaxy," who, one journalist observed, explodes at least one volcano every day, among other human-killing natural disasters. Earth's "pleasant, cloudy face should be slapped onto a WANTED! poster, and soon: This lunatic is out to get us."[570]

While we're considering humanity's mockups for the end of the world, why not go to the source, the Norse prophecy of Ragnarok? This term is usually interpreted as "twilight of the gods," but more accurately as "final destiny of the gods." It's the Norse foretelling of the shape and sound of the final end to things. The scenario makes an excellent disaster movie script, and it is strikingly graphic.

There will be a world fire, the Fimbulwinter, in which Surtr will burn up the planet; the Midgard Serpent will arise from its oceanic sleep and whip up the seas to drown the land; the Fenrir wolf will break its chains and devour the Sun, darkening the world. The World Tree Yggdrasil will shake, the rainbow bridge Bifrost

will collapse, the giants will fight the gods on the battlefield *Vigridr*. Most of the deities, including Odin and Thor, previously presumed immortal and invincible, will fall in furious battle scenes that will rival if not surpass Homer's *Iliad*. But a few gods, including Balder (the Norse Christ), will survive and regroup on the plain called *Idavollr*, the former site of Asgard, and a new world and humanity will arise.

I had occasion recently to sit under Yggdrasil in south-central Norway, surveying the future battlefield, as it were. This is one of the exciting and empirically valuable things about geomyths: You can clairvoyantly update old prophecies by finding their geomantic grounding points and having a fresh look. Yggdrasil is a real geomantic fixture on the Earth, and it can easily be visited by those willing to travel to a miniscule hamlet called Rondablikk in Norway.

I sat on a hill and observed Yggdrasil. Technically, I was inside its trunk, as it measures almost five miles in diameter and I was virtually in its very center. Even so, I saw the vast, towering tree and Nidhoggr, one of the Earth's 13 dragons, coiled majestically underneath it. The Ragnarok prediction gives Nidhoggr 50:50 odds for surviving the Apocalypse. I saw a white humanlike figure on a horse, which was slowly turning in a circle as if on a slow-moving carousel. One arm was upraised, brandishing a mighty, flame-licked sword.

The Norse poets said that Surtr (Old Norwegian for "the Black One") would appear with a flaming sword, so splendid bright it would outshine the Sun itself; Surtr would ride in the vanguard, just ahead of the raging fires (Surtr's Fire), whirl his flaming blade, and fling fire in all directions until everything is burned to ashes. But something similar is said of the Kalki Avatar.

This is the Vedic futuristic scenario in which Vishnu undertakes his tenth and ultimate incarnation. Kalki will sit on a massive white horse holding aloft a sword that blazes like a comet. He will appear at the end of the Age of Strife, or what the Buddhists call the Battle of Shambhala, punish the evildoers, assuage the virtuous, and generally reestablish a golden age upon the ashes of the old, incinerated world. The Kalki Avatar, as Vishnu's tenth "Descent," will pervade and fill the world with Vishnu's presence. Insofar as the Vedic Vishnu is equivalent to the Christian Christ, this is a potentially pleasing prospect.

I say potentially pleasing because we are still, most of us and for the most part, paralyzed by fear in the midst of the End Days disaster mockup of our future. Psychologically and culturally, we are still scared silly of what's coming.

But what is coming? Is Gaia a massmurdering lunatic out to get us? Jungian depth psychology teaches us that whatever we repress, suppress, or generally stuff into the closet of the subconscious remains there as our Shadow. The more we resist it, the more strenuously we deny its reality or that it is ours, the stronger and scarier it gets. Eventually the bogeyman in the closet becomes the unstoppable monster that destroys the world. We become so riveted in fear we forget the monster is us.

It's useful to use this psychological model when we think about the Earth. If we fear a lunatic Earth bent on destroying us, that is a gauge of how alienated we are from our rightful and, in fact, reciprocally dependent relationship with Earth. We need the Earth to maintain us physically, but She needs us to maintain her spiritually. The Earth as a sentient planetary being in the cosmos needs us to awaken her soul, Albion, so that She may be complete as a planet in the solar system. Pollyannish? It might seem so, but think of it in terms of feedback.

In this book I have briefly outlined 85 geomantic features of what I call the Galaxy on Earth, an array of geomantic structures and templates that make higher human consciousness possible.

These features require a regular cooperative infusion of angelic, elemental, and human energy and consciousness to keep them optimally functioning. They are highly sensitive and responsive to human input, or the lack of it. In a sense we have collectively been oblivious of this geomantic feedback system and polluting it with our own cast-off negativities. We've been doing this for a very long time. The Earth's grid system has become toxic and clogged, and it needs a cleansing.

Think of physical detoxification. Natural medicine practitioners routinely recommend ways to help the body purge itself of accumulated toxic material and unprocessed colonic residue. The end result is always better health and well-being, and improved cellular and organic functioning. When the detoxification is over, you feel great. But there is a bump in the middle of the cleanout called the Herxheimer reaction, named after an Austrian dermatologist who characterized it in 1895.

The term refers to a temporary worsening or intensification of symptoms under the influence of treatment. The undesirable bacteria and pathogenic organisms in your system are dying off faster than your liver and intestines can neutralize them and remove the toxic debris and byproducts safely from the body. Technically, the Herxheimer reaction, though unpleasant, is positive feedback that your detoxification program is successful. The worsening of symptoms—typically, cold or flu-like aches, pains, headaches, nausea, chills—is commensurate with bacterial die-off in the body's cells; it's the short-term cost of discomfort for long-term health gains. At its worst, you may feel you're dying.

Let's apply the detoxification concept to the planet. Our Earth is going through an angelically supervised detoxification program. As a planetary body, it is experiencing a Herxheimer reaction. This may sound strange, but often conflict and wars are expressions of a planetary Herxheimer reaction. The dreadful purge of Bosnia and Kosovo during the 1990s can be seen as a radical detoxification of toxic human thought-forms (poisonous tribal and ethnic hatreds), a kind of scorched-Earth treatment of negative aspects of the Slavic folk soul.

The revelation of the Shadow is never pretty. It is not suitable for postcards or television ads. It can be terrifying but ultimately salutary. A Tarot image vividly illustrates this. It's usually called the Lightning-Struck Tower. It shows a bolt of lightning searing through a stone tower; people are jumping out the windows for safety as this light and energy from above rips through the most solid expression of matter, stone, and all it contains. This is Surtr's Fire, Kalki's cometary sword, Christ's Second Coming—Ragnarok.

I say "angelically supervised" because Surtr's Fire is actually a controlled slow burn. It's Ragnarok in slow motion. It's a fast-burn apocalypse if you disbelieve in the spiritual worlds or in rationality, purpose, and intention in the cosmos and on Earth. But it's a slow-burn revelation of the entirety of the spiritual hierarchy if you accept the possibility that it has been planned out, well controlled, and for our good. It could be the chance for all of us to witness divinity in the Earth.

Many had a taste of this in the first International Earth Day in April 1990. Though this observance started in 1970, in 1990 it went international with an estimated 200 million people in 141 countries participating. Some may have experienced an unaccountable grief and upwelling of tears that day. "Earth was preparing to be remembered by human consciousness for the first time in a long time," the Ofanim told me. "The feeling for those already attuned to Gaia was the experience of immense grief at her oncoming thought-forms."

Those onrushing thought-forms are the Shadow contents of humanity projected and dumped upon Gaia, now awaiting imminent acknowledgment. "As you are aware, the Earth is in the process of detoxifying herself," the Ofanim note. "You know by now we are dealing in the realm of multiple probability. We have a number of probabilities, one of which would be to shift the axis of the Earth. The Earth is about to shed its skin. Gaia will cleanse herself. We will assist her in this cleansing or birthing process."

The Ofanim explained that they are "attempting through the grid where possible to stabilize as many of these detoxifying impulses as is feasible to prevent much loss of life because this is necessary for the future conscious evolution of mankind. Through us, people can focus some energy at nodal points to prevent too much loss of life. Through us, people can learn the means of harmonizing personal and planetary energies.

"The time the Earth now faces is unprecedented in Earth's history. It is coincident with an event that happened on another planet many, many years ago when life was destroyed and many developing spirits who were emerging again into the universality of consciousness were deprived wrongly of their opportunity. We are redressing that balance. Those who have already chosen, the ones that begin to remember, will not be removed. They will have the opportunity this time to fulfill their destiny. Those who haven't chosen will be unprepared. We will lose them this time. They will return later."

Apparently, we are at the same pivotal moment that our deep ancestors faced many millennia ago on the now extinct planet Maldek. Traces of its former wholeness exist now in the form of the asteroid belt between Jupiter and Mars.[571] It exploded because the humanity living on it failed to cross the threshold of initiation and destroyed its own world. It failed to harmonize personal human energies with those of the planet. The spiritual hierarchy is determined that this won't happen again on Earth, the replacement planet for Maldek and its people.

Getting in Bed with the Fenrir Wolf: We're All Little Red Riding Hood

Let's bring this all back to Mort Hill, where it all started. In addition to an angelically facilitated global detoxification through the Earth's thousands of nodal points, the geometric structure of the Earth grid itself is morphing into a new shape. The Greek geometer Archimedes (287–212 B.C.) demonstrated that the five Platonic Solids can naturally morph or transfigure into only 13 new shapes. Johannes Kepler (1571–1630) later described and illustrated these in his *Harmonices Mundi,* although they remain known as the 13 Archimedean Solids.

These 13 Solids are called semiregular polyhedra, which means they have regular geometric faces of more than one type, but identical vertices; they also all fit perfectly into a sphere. A dodecahedron, one of the five Platonic Solids, has 12 equal-sized pentagons; these are faces of the same type. An Archimedean Solid may have pentagons and triangles as part of its geometric appearance.

In 1985, the Ofanim said the spiritual hierarchy had not yet decided which shape the Earth grid would eventually morph into; it was still experimental then. In 2002, they announced it had been decided: an icosidodecahedron, one of the Archimedean Solids, a combination of the dodecahedron and icosahedron. This complex polyhedron has 32 faces (some pentagons, some triangles), 60 edges, and 30 vertices (see figure 12-1). It is more than just a superimposition of the two Platonic Solids, which the now "old" Earth grid exhibits. It is more like melting the two Platonic Solids and regrowing a new crystalline shape out of their combined essence called the icosidodecahedron. This is the new shape of Earth, now being "grown."

With this in mind, it is fairly easy to conceive of how the prolifically prophesied and variously

modeled Earth changes can happen. The geometric shape of our planetary reality is undergoing a morphological change. The old, classical grid remains, but a new one is growing out of it. Where the new edges and vertices of the icosidodecahedron are popping out of the old Platonic Solids grid, major fracture areas are being created for Earth reality; these will likely manifest in multiple ways, through changes in the weather and climate, geopolitical upset, geological turbulence, psychological edginess. As planetary reality gets set at a new energy level, our sense of the world will be in turmoil.

Volcanoes may erupt, earthquakes may be generated, strange weather patterns may prevail, wars engaged in, genocides enacted, apparitions of the Virgin Mary recorded, UFO and alien encounters or abductions experienced, crop circles manifested, sacred site group activations undertaken, spontaneous psychic activities arising, a seeming proliferation of evil. There will be many signs on the Earth, signaling the departure of the old, heralding the shapes of the new. It will be a real circus on planet Earth.

All of this is part of the Apocalypse, but whether it's a catastrophe that seems to end the world or what J. R. R. Tolkien called a eucatastrophe, a tumultuous though ultimately benign and positive turnabout, depends on you. Which do you prefer? Metaphorically speaking, the Fenrir wolf is already untied. The Lucifer secret is out of the bag. He has been unchained at a few sites. The reality of his Emerald is now being confirmed, individual by individual. We're all Little Red Riding Hood in bed with the big bad wolf. It's a shocking, pivotal moment. Will he eat us? Or will we joyously recreate the world with him?

The Fenrir wolf, also known by the Norse mythographers as the ambivalent trickster god Loki or his son, was bound in chains by the Aesir of Asgard on the isle of Lyngvi in Lake Amsvartnir. He was bound so securely that he would only gain

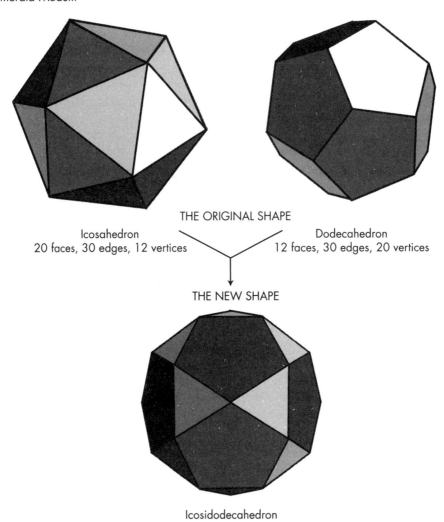

THE ORIGINAL SHAPE

Icosahedron
20 faces, 30 edges, 12 vertices

Dodecahedron
12 faces, 30 edges, 20 vertices

THE NEW SHAPE

Icosidodecahedron
32 faces, 60 edges, 30 vertices

Figure 12-1. The Change in the Earth's Geometric Grid Shape

his freedom when the world ended, when Ragnarok started. Ragnarok has started, and the Fenrir wolf is already starting to be unbound at selected geomantic equivalents to Lyngvi Island.[572]

These are Lucifer Binding Sites, and the Fenrir wolf coming unbound is another guise for our outcast Lord of Light and Light-Bearer, Lucifer.

The information and alternate views of Lucifer in chapter 11 got us started in this crucial reappraisal of the Lord of Light. We've started to haul him out of the Pit of human revilement into the light of a day of reconsideration, possibly of forgiveness. We should forgive Lucifer, forgive the Lucifer in ourselves, because he has something we want. The Emerald. Yes, we all already have an Emerald, given to us courtesy of Lucifer, but he has the original, and for us to use our own Emerald is a tacit acknowledgment of our benefactor.

Can we do it? Fearlessly unbind the Fenrir wolf and forgive him?

The logic is unassailable, and the teleology is inevitable. Wake up to the Earth's subtle anatomy, its galaxy template and visionary geography, and you discover how it mirrors your own spiritual constitution. Then you discover the key to it all, which is the Emerald, and then you learn whose Emerald it is, that the Emerald sits in your chest and surrounds the Earth and is Lucifer's heart, and at present Lucifer, thanks to us, stands in the Shadow of humanity.

Can you handle this? That's the theological—the existential—revelation about human life on this planet that all of us must address at this time. Your individualized process of handling that is Ragnarok in slow motion. Forgive the Light-Bearer. Forgive the Lucifer in yourself. And move on. Help the Light-Bearer and yourself return to your rightful position of glory and sovereignty at the right hand of the Supreme Being. You'll be helping the Earth do the same because the Earth is inside Lucifer's heart, and the redemption of Lucifer is the redemption of our planet—it's the same event.

Don't wait for the year 2012. Don't hold your breath and hope we will squeak by unnoticed by the agencies and energies that rule reality, as the world did with the projected trauma of Y2K, now virtually forgotten. The year 2012 is already upon us; it started in 1985 when the Earth grid started to morph.

On that day at Mort Hill in June 1985, the Ofanim and their colleagues introduced a new energy into a circuit that up till then had been functioning poorly. "Only the old grid system is presently a reality," they commented in 1985. "The old grid will carry on to a degree even if the anchoring of the new dynamic doesn't completely take form. The new pattern that emerges is free of some of the constraints of domes and dome lines, which have locked the growth spiral on Earth into a particular pattern for a particular period.

"Now it becomes more open. We are looking at a multidimensional field, a hologram of possibilities, a new grid structure emerging from the potential seeding from the beginning, from the source. When enough of these grid points are empowered and cognized, then the Earth will automatically detoxify. Gaia will be freed. Everything changes."

Where the new sacred sites will be in this transfigured planetary grid system is still uncertain, still open to development and experimentation. Many more of the original sites will be activated in the coming decades, "facilitated by the Archangel Michael, as He brings the Supramundane Light to the subtle body of Gaia," the Ofanim note. It won't be over in 2012. "There is much to be done over the next 50 years before the next phase is completed."

Turning On the Emerald Modem and Dialing Up the Cosmos

Part of that "much" that needs to be done is that more people need to become familiar with the Earth grid or the planet's visionary geography so that they can participate as cocreators with the angelic realm in bringing life to the many sites that need attention. At the same time, more people need to start conceptualizing the transfigured geometric reality and dealing with the implications at all levels, social, geological, and psychological.

Unfortunately, in the course of recent human development, we have paved over the Galaxy on Earth with artificial constructs and a synthetic, unnatural, atheistic culture. We have progressed as a global civilization largely oblivious to the fact that the Earth's visionary geography continuously creates and sustains our biological and cognitive-existential reality, every second of every day. We live amidst the galaxy on Earth, but we do so asleep to our subtle environment. We even deny the possibility that the Earth has a spiritual aspect. We barely acknowledge our own.

Bear in mind that in between the reactivation of the original template and the full emergence of the new grid the planetary Albion will awaken. That in itself will have profound effects on the collective psyche and unconscious of humanity. In a sense, the entire planet will become a Mort Hill, a morthouse for the transfiguration of reality, inner and outer, personal and planetary. The galaxy on Earth will become a workshop for voluntary mortification, a mortuary for outmoded thought-forms and the emergence of new, relevant ones.

In this new Gaian morthouse, the Emerald will emerge as a crucial tool for reestablishing our innate connection with one another, the Earth, and the galaxy.

The Emerald is the once and future Jerusalem, the key to the Earth's visionary geography, the summation of the geomantic plans of the Blue Room, and the ticket of admission to the New Jerusalem of the Earth's transfigured reality. How could it be otherwise, when Lucifer is the foundation of Jerusalem?

We all carry that foundation within us in the form of the Emerald, the electromagnetic doorway between the inner and outer heart chakras, the miniaturized Cube of Space, our modem link to all humanity and the cosmos. The Earth's entire grid structure is in a sense one Emerald, which is the same as the Emerald we all carry. All the domes brought fragments of this one Emerald as a seed of paradise, and fragments of this one jewel were used to generate the light-corrective centers or henge-rings throughout Britain. All the Emeralds one encounters in the geomantic landscape are a reflection of the Grail Knight's own Emerald being used to bring the new energy into the grid system.

Everyone on Earth has an Emerald. There is not a human who lives on Earth (now or ever) who does not have an Emerald, though very few are aware of it or choose to use it. You could walk down the street and see the Emerald sparkling in the chest of everyone you observe, a two-inch double-terminated green crystal to the right of the sternum and starting at the third rib down. The world's most powerful modem, with the fastest baud rate conceivable, given free to all humans, sits unused, factory fresh, warrantied, turned off, inside our chests.

Consider your own. Try to remember it once every hour for a day. Take it out of your chest and handle it. Visualize a two-inch-long, six-sided Emerald in your hand. Study it. Appreciate it. You could expand it to the size of a house and set it upright in a Blue Dish out in the landscape like a piece of outdoor sculpture. Visualize the Earth with thousands of such landscape-emplaced Emeralds, sparkling in their Blue Dishes, a light as fiercely real as God burning inside, each a modem connection with everyone on the planet and with the cosmos itself.

John of Patmos envisioned this, though he worded his vision differently. In Revelation he spoke of the companions of the Lamb or Christ. "Next in my vision I saw Mount Zion, and standing on it a Lamb who had with him a hundred and forty-four thousand people, all with his name and his Father's name written on their foreheads." These 144,000 were singing a new hymn before the Throne of God, and only they could learn it because they had been "redeemed from the world," had "kept their virginity," and never lied.

This passage, elegant and mystical as it is, has caused no end of grief through literalist and elitist interpretation, especially so in our times by religious fundamentalists and New Age evangelists alike. John's criteria for the 144,000 are actually much like those given for Grail Knights: "Redeemed from the world" means they have remembered their spiritual origins and are not slaves to the material appearance of things, not atheists; "virginity" means the Virgin Sophia, the pure soul, washed clean of defilements, spiritually chaste, the psychic apparatus or chakras cleansed and functional; "never lying" means never betraying your true spiritual self for expediency, never denying the Christ.

And the number 144,000? Let's say it's an absolute break-even minimum on God's wish list for the opening of the Emeralds around the planet. "If I can only get a mere 144,000, we can make it through this," God says on Earth's behalf.

Everyone has an Emerald, but not everyone is ready to use it. "It is like a tiny homing device pretuned to your requested purpose," the Ofanim explain. "You must realize the number 144,000 is specific, and at this time no more than that are likely to awaken spontaneously. Certain humans have for karmic reasons more or less possibility of connecting the Emerald within the heart than others. The 144,000 are possibilities or probabilities within the biophysical base of certain humans for activation within the heart of the heart. Let us put it like this. Everybody has a nose, but can you imagine each of them smelling the same thing at the same time? Not very likely."

So visit the Jerusalem while you walk down the street. As the Ofanim suggest, "Open your hearts. Each person you meet is a doorway or facet within the Emerald within the heart. See the reflections. Do not envisage them as external. See within the facets of the Emerald the reflections of who you are."

A sure way to make that experience likely and easy is to approach the Emerald from your Blazing Star. "The Emerald is purely in the etheric. The Emerald is the manifestation of the Star in the emotional body or etheric body of recognition. Concentrate on talking from your Star. See what happens in the Emerald. Trust your Star. First, place your attention in your Star. Then through your Star see the Emerald. Know that the Emerald only exists if the Star is given attention. If you talk from the Star, then the recognition and corroboration you seek will be thrown into the Emerald. If you do not, then the corroboration will not exist and the people you meet will be external to your heart."

The Ofanim demonstrated this once. It was when I was living with a few colleagues in the Ofanim work in England. One evening the Ofanim "visited," but before they became discernible, they put something in our living room. First we saw a large Blazing Star. Then it flashed and became a Blue Dish 20 feet across. Then set in the center of this Blue Dish was an Emerald two stories high, brilliant, adamant. The Archangel Michael towered above this Emerald, seemingly with four heads, one facing into each cardinal direction, and with four arms and four swords.

"Michael will touch the Emerald within each of you, if you wish," the Ofanim said. We wished. The swords came down through our heads into the Emerald within our chests, and they burst into blinding light. Then I asked a silly question: What's the significance of the Blue Dish with an Emerald in our room? "These things are gifts. Be grateful, don't worry, be happy. Wouldn't you like an imprint of an effulgent Emerald primed by Lord Michael in the middle of your living room with a blue sapphire bowl brought by an order of angels not even known about by most people?" Their logic was unassailable, and I nodded yes.

Picture it: thousands, even millions, of Emeralds around the planet, these portable, two-inch-long, high baud-rate modems, flashing brilliant green, dialing up, their Internet protocols established, putting users online. The very process of dialing up brings the Earth and its thousands of sacred sites and its Emerald along with us, puts Gaia online, too. What's our online home page? Freedom. Freedom to know, to experience, to choose, to be good or bad, awake or asleep. The freedom to fulfill the Light-Bearer's bold plan, for each of us to be a lovely little Lucifer, free, daring, individualized, yet fully connected with the Source.

We have to appreciate that the structure of reality itself was altered to make it possible for each of us to have this little Emerald modem in the chest. Before Lucifer's plan was approved by the Supreme Being, the Emerald existed elsewhere on the Tree of Life or Cube of Space. It was on a path of connection between two spheres of light called "Strength of the Lion" in Tarot language.

When Lucifer got the green light for the project of human cognitive freedom, the Emerald was moved down to Chesed, the fourth Sefirot on the Tree, but in our reality, it was the first Sefirot. So when Lucifer gave us the Emerald, it was simultaneously *relocated* within the spiritual structure of the cosmos—a big deal, surely, done on our behalf with a large lien on Lucifer as surety.

It may seem a little confusing. How many Emeralds are there? Lucifer has one. Gaia has one. All of us have one. And there are a bunch in the landscape, projected by grid engineers, and more in the domes. Plus there is the big one at El Tule in southern Mexico where Lucifer himself projected his Emerald and to which he returned as Lord Quetzalcoatl, the Plumed Serpent, in August 1987.

"We refer to the One Emerald which was Lucifer's gift to Earth, which was the birthing of the Emerald in the consciousness of Man," the Ofanim explain. "The Emerald is a unified field expressed synchronously with all the grid engineer tries. All attempts are made to project the Emerald to stimulate this process, move everything closer to the unified field where all Emeralds are one, to where Lucifer's gift is comprehended. When that occurs, there is only one Emerald."

So there are three awakenings for us through the Emerald. To know that we have an Emerald. To know how we got it, and at what price. To learn how to use it and accept our responsibility to start using it.

Throughout this book, we've been discovering and describing the planet-sized cosmic being

of light, Albion, a hologram of Adam Kadmon and Lucifer. This vast cosmic human who lies upon the Earth, who is the soul of Gaia, is also a mirror of our own spiritual constitution and a map of our cosmic origins, and this human colossus has a marvelous modem connection to its source and maker, as do we. The green light has come on in Albion's chest.

The Emerald modem is blinking, ready for use. It blinked on at the Harmonic Convergence in 1987 when millions of people received the Luciferic initiation within their Emeralds and when the Lord of Light returned triumphantly to the original site of his own projected Emerald at El Tule. It's been a vast drama within the planetary body of Albion, yet it's our human drama, too.

The Emerald is inside this planet-sized cosmic being, and he is inside the Emerald. The Emerald is inside our body, and we are all inside the planetary Emerald. The Earth is inside a single planet-size Emerald, and that is inside Lucifer. The Emerald is inside Lucifer as his heart, and yet Lucifer is inside the Emerald, which is the very Cube of Space, the structure of reality, God's being.

Jerusalem, the original foundation of Lucifer, was this extrapolation of the cosmic human and the Emerald onto and into the Earth. It was the gift of spiritual freedom. The New Jerusalem is the redemption of Lucifer and the rededication of the global temple foundations and the turning on of the Emerald modem. It will be the reaffirmation and expression of our spiritual freedom.

For the first time in the history of the planet, Gaia's Albion will awaken, the global Emerald modem will be on, and we'll all be online—if we wish—with the galaxy, as Jerusalem morphs into New Jerusalem, like a child becoming a teenager, like a troubled sleeper awaking to a fresh new world, to the enthusiastic cheers of 144,000 people with their Emerald modems blinking green.

Endnotes

1. Louis Ginzberg, *The Legends of the Jews, I* (Philadelphia: The Jewish Publication Society of America, 1909): 70.

2. Jeremy Naydler, *Temple of the Cosmos: The Ancient Egyptian Experience of the Sacred* (Rochester, VT: Inner Traditions, 1996): 13.

3. Ibid.

4. Ibid., 14.

5. Martin Gray, *Places of Peace and Power Occasional Newsletter* 9 (March 15, 2002), at: www.sacredsites.com.

6. "Ecopsychology holds that there is a synergistic interplay between planetary and personal well-being," comments social historian Theodore Roszak, who pioneered this bridge discipline in the 1990s. Another approach, called Earth literacy, inspired by the writings of Thomas Berry, "seeks to support, link up, and assist in the self-education of the growing community of people participating in the Great Work of creating a benign human presence on planet Earth." Theodore Roszak, "Ecopsychology: Eight Principles" (Hayward, CA: Ecopsychology Institute, 1998): published at: http://ecopsychology.athabascau.ca/Final/Intro.htm. Earth Literacy Webpage statement, 2002, published at: www.spiritualecology.org/earthlpu.html.

7. Carl Kerenyi, *Eleusis: Archetypal Image of Mother and Daughter*, trans. Ralph Mannheim (Princeton, NJ: Princeton University Press, 1967): 10–12.

8. *The Mahabharata 2: The Book of the Assembly Hall*, Vol. 2, trans. and ed. J. A. B. van Buitenen (Chicago: University of Chicago Press, 1975): 388–390.

9. John Michell, *The New View over Atlantis* (London: Thames and Hudson, 1983): 83–86, 212.

10. Nigel Pennick, *The Ancient Science of Geomancy: Man in Harmony with the Earth* (London: Thames and Hudson, 1979): 7–10.

11. Ngawang Zangpo, *Sacred Ground: Jamgon Kongtrul on "Pilgrimage and Sacred Geography"* (Ithaca, NY: Snow Lion Publications, 2001): 174.

12. Kiiko Matsumoto and Stephen Birch, *Five Elements and Ten Stems* (Brookline, MA: Paradigm Publications, 1983): 14, 201–209.

13. This expert further states that the stems and branches connect vertically and diagonally to create 60 subchannels, which are polarized to either yin (female, passive, cool) or yang (male, active, hot) qualities; these subchannels interweave through 36,000 energy points in the body. Ni, Hua-Ching, *The Taoist Inner View of the Universe and the Immortal Realm* (Malibu, CA: Shrine of the Eternal Breath of Tao, 1979): 132, 147.

14. William S. Becker and Bethe Hagens, "The Rings of Gaia," in *The Power of Place: Sacred Ground in Natural & Human Environments*, ed. James A. Swan (Wheaton, IL: Quest Books, 1991): 259.

15. David Hatcher Childress, "Mapping the World Grid," in *Anti-Gravity and the World Grid*, ed. David Hatcher Childress (Stelle, IL: Adventures Unlimited Press, 1987): 5.

16. Regarding the epistemological basis for my model of the Galaxy on Earth and its particulars, I refer readers to my previous book, *The Galaxy on*

Earth: A Traveler's Guide to the Planet's Visionary Geography (Hampton Roads, 2002), where I address this in detail. For this book, I will say that the information, models, and concepts presented here derive from 20 years of field investigation, my own clairvoyant research, technical conversations with a few key psychic colleagues, standard scholarship, and a 20-year dialogue with a family of angels called the Ofanim who have been instrumental, as part of a consortium of spiritual beings, in creating, implementing, and maintaining the Earth's visionary geography. For information on some of the more personal aspects of this "dialogue"—it was as much an apprenticeship as it was a conversation—see my books *What's Beyond That Star* (Clairview Books, 2002) and *Looking for Arthur: A Once and Future Travelogue* (Station Hill Openings/Barrytown, 1997).

17. Mesocosm is a word scholars sometimes use to indicate the middle or mesocosmic position in this relationship between the above and the below. Scholar Robert Levy, for example, uses the term "structured mesocosm" to describe the organization of the Nepalese city Bhaktapur in the Kathmandu Valley. The former capital of Nepal, it is a prime example of "an archaic city" in which its layout mirrors a cosmic model, Levy argues. It is organized as a "minutely divided and interrelated sacralized space," he states. The city's design is symbolic, based on a yantra, a magical diagram or mandala with nine protective deities positioned in the eight cardinal directions and the center, and shrines marking those sites. Levy's sources told him a similar sacred mandala was templated on the religious geography of the whole Kathmandu Valley. Robert L. Levy, *Mesocosm: Hinduism and the Organization of a Traditional Newar City in Nepal* (Berkeley: University of California Press, 1990): 153–156.

18. Gershom Scholem, *Major Trends in Jewish Mysticism* (New York: Schocken Books, 1946): 265, 279. Gershom Scholem, *On the Kabbalah and Its Symbolism*, trans. Ralph Mannheim (New York: Schocken Books, 1965): 115, 128, 162, 202.

19. Mircea Eliade, *A History of Religious Ideas, Vol. 1: From the Stone Age to the Eleusinian Mysteries* (Chicago: University of Chicago Press, 1978): 224.

20. C. G. Jung, *The Archetypes and the Collective Unconscious*. Second Edition, Bollingen Series XX, trans. R. F. C. Hull (Princeton, NJ: Princeton University Press, 1969): 308.

21. At the risk of confusing things, I must mention that the ancient folk name for Britain was also Albion. This is not quite the way Blake used the name, although there is a connection. The geomantic presentation of Albion occurs on several levels—local, regional, and global. Thus it is accurate to say there is a landscape expression of Albion that encompasses all of Britain, and it is both the same as and different from the singular Albion that Blake evokes.

22. We find traces of the memory of this geomythic presence in unlikely places, such as Jonathan Swift's eighteenth-century classic, *Gulliver's Travels*. Lemuel Gulliver was shipwrecked upon the land of the diminutive Lilliputians who strapped him, fearsome giant that he was, with ropes and pegs to the ground. Waking at daylight from his near death at sea, Gulliver was astonished to find himself bound to the ground while 40 six-inch-tall humans clambered over him. Even his head and long hair were strapped to the ground. Gulliver roared so loudly "that they all ran back in fright; and some of them, as I was afterwards told, were hurt with the falls they got by leaping from my sides upon the ground." Even so, he lay there "in great uneasiness: at length, struggling to get loose." Jonathan Swift, *Gulliver's Travels* (New York: Harper & Brothers Publishers, 1950): 6.

23. In James Joyce's *Finnegans Wake*, Albion is cast as the ubiquitous and polymorphic HCE—Humphrey Chimpden Earwicker, Howth Castle and Environs, Humme the Cheapener, Esquire, Haveth Childers Everywhere, Here Comes Everybody, all indications of the *Ur*-hero's "universality and his role as the great progenitor," as Joseph Campbell noted. HCE is a citizen of Dublin and a world wanderer, father and abandoner of civilizations, twentieth-century hod carrier and renowned Irish hero Fionn mac Cumhaill (Finn MacCool), and Dublin itself—that's one of the places they buried him, out near Phoenix Park. The hillocks nearby at Castle Knock, local legend says, are the upturned toes of the giant lying on his back upon the land, his belly is the city of Dublin itself, and the headland of Howth Castle, overlooking Dublin Bay, is popularly regarded as the cranium of this recumbent giant. Finnegan's form is the landscape itself such that we may still

behold him, Leviathan-like, outlined in the contours of the Dublin landscape. Much of Joyce's "dreamlike saga of guilt-stained, evolving humanity" is the extended wake for the fallen, deceased, and soon-to-be resurrected Finnegan, as if, in Joyce's view, all of Western culture parties before "the fallen Finnegan's all-suffusing, all-feeding, slumberous presence." All of us are at Finnegan's wake, all of us fell with him, all of us are like maggot sons and daughters breeding, living, and quarreling in the "body of the gigantic sleeper . . . the foundation substance of the old World Father." Joseph Campbell and Henry Morton Robinson, *A Skeleton Key to* Finnegans Wake (New York: Penguin Books, 1944): 3, 6–7, 36, 37, 39, 40.

24. William Blake, "Jerusalem: The Emanation of the Giant Albion," in *Blake: Complete Writings*, ed. Geoffrey Keynes (London: Oxford University Press, 1972): 649.

25. Richard Wagner, *Parsifal: Music Drama in Three Acts,* trans. Stewart Robb (New York: G. Schirmer, 1962): 4.

26. Uriel's name means "Fire of God," and he presides over Tartarus, the deepest layer of the Underworld, and holds its keys; he buried Adam and Abel (the first slain human) in Paradise; the archangel of salvation, he will warn Noah about the imminent Flood and advise building the Ark, and give humanity, through Merlin, the Qabala, the map and access keys of the Four Worlds.

27. Raphael, whose name means "God Has Healed" or "the One Who Heals," is the Regent of the Sun, the source of Time, and lair of the Beast; he is the guardian of the Tree of Life, the guide to souls in Sheol (the Underworld), the one who will equip Solomon with the magic ring sufficient to quell the demons so he can build the Temple of Jerusalem. Raphael will heal the Earth and humanity as needed.

28. Michael, whose name means "Who Is Like God," is the captain of the celestial army, leader of the heavenly host, ruler of Arabot, the Seventh Heaven; he holds the keys to the kingdom of Heaven and its relations with Earth (i.e., geomancy); he is the Prince of Light who "slays" (activates) the dragon. Michael will always be a prime "player" in matters of the Earth's visionary geography, especially when he is Regent of the archangels, a rotating responsibility every 268 years. Then his possible manifestations will mul-

tiply from 9,400 to infinite (as they are today, at the opposite end of the time continuum from the Blue Room).

29. The traditional interpretation of the name "Hyperboreans," which is found almost exclusively in a few ancient Greek texts and poems, is "People of the North Wind" or "People beyond the North Wind," the Wind being Boreas, known to the Greeks as the North Wind. The place "beyond" was traditionally attributed to the far North, including or perhaps beyond the British Isles, closer to the Arctic Circle.

30. There are more than 85, but how many more I do not presently know. I am currently researching eight more features, which brings the total to 93.

31. Hermann Hesse, *The Glass Bead Game (Magister Ludi)* (New York: Henry Holt and Company, [1943], 1990): 15, 38–40.

32. Karl Kerenyi, *Goddesses of Sun and Moon,* trans. Murray Stein (Dallas: Spring Publications, 1979): 6.

33. The existence of Lemuria of course is denied and ridiculed by establishment historians and uncritically accepted by mystics and new-agers; for here, let's say this term refers to an epoch of life on the Earth whose earliest days were some 18 million years ago and whose demise was more recent, perhaps within the past 200,000 years, perhaps much earlier.

34. Curiously, the movie *Chain Reaction* (1996) intuits some of the efficiencies of hydrogen as an energy source. In that film, the scientists successfully extract an unlimited, low-cost energy from hydrogen; the U.S. government commandeers the technology and its scientists to keep the breakthrough from the public.

35. Bode's Law was formulated and popularized by Johann E. Bode (1747–1826), a German astronomer and director of the Berlin Observatory in 1772. It is a way of describing the spacing of planets in the solar system such that their distance from the Sun is based on a mathematical relationship. Bode's Law is a mathematical series in which 4 is added to the series 0, 3, 6, 12, 24, 48, 96, 192, 384, and 768. Each of these is obtained by doubling the previous number; then 4 is added to each number and the sum is divided by 10. The result gives the approximate distances, expressed as astronomical units (AU), of the planets from the Sun. The law applies to all the planets except

Neptune and Pluto. Of particular interest to the Maldek scenario is this statement: "There is no major planet at a distance corresponding to the 2.8 position [between Mars and Jupiter], and a search for the 'missing planet' was actually organized." Mars is 1.524 AU, Jupiter 5.203 AU, and the missing planet, Maldek, would be in between them at 2.8 AU. George A. Abell, *Exploration of the Universe*, Second Edition (New York: Holt, Rinehart and Winston, 1969): 326.

36. Herodotus, *The Histories*, trans. Robin Waterfield (New York: Oxford University Press, 1998): 239–240, 245–246 (Book IV, 13, 33–36).

37. Apollodorus, *The Library*, vol. 1, trans. Sir James George Frazer (Cambridge, MA: Harvard University Press, 1921): 33, 221, 231.

38. Pindar, "Pythian X," *The Odes of Pindar*, trans. C.M. Bowra (New York: Penguin Books, 1969): 22–23.

39. A Greek astronomer named Meton (fifth century B.C.) noted that 235 lunar months were equal to 19 solar years, such that after one 19-year cycle the full moon would occur on the same calendar date again. This cyclicity became known as the "Year of Meton."

40. Pausanias, *Guide to Greece, Vol. 1, Central Greece*, trans. Peter Levi (New York: Penguin Books, 1971): 416.

41. Diodorus Siculus, *Library of History*, Book II, trans. C. H. Oldfather (Cambridge, MA: Harvard University Press/Loeb Library, 1935): 55, 56.

42. H. P. Blavatsky, *The Secret Doctrine, Vol. II: Anthropogenesis* (Pasadena, CA: Theosophical University Press, 1977): 11.

43. Sophocles, *Women of Trachis*, trans. C. K. Williams and Gregory W. Dickerson (New York: Oxford University Press, 1978): 61.

44. C. K. Williams and Gregory W. Dickerson, "Introduction," in Sophocles, *Women of Trachis*, trans. C. K. Williams and Gregory W. Dickerson (New York: Oxford University Press, 1978): 8–9.

45. As Maui, he summoned up whole islands and tied down the Sun on Mount Haleakala. As Cuchulainn, Merlin was a prodigy of battle and magical feats, defending the fabled Brown Bull of Cuailnge. As Saint Columba, Merlin cleansed the planet's grid connection with the star Canopus. As Padmasambhava, he drove all the demons and denizens of the Night out of Tibet so that the Buddha Dharma could take root there. As John, he testified to the Christ incarnation and foretold a planetary future of epiphany and apocalypse. As Merlin, he locked up Saturn or Cronos in the Islands of Ogygia and made Time possible on Earth.

46. Merlin's connection to the Mother as the Mer-Line stares us forthrightly in the face in the meaning of his Greek name. Heracles means "Hera's glory" or "the glorious gift of Hera." Hera, Queen of Heaven, "Goddess of the Golden Chair," whose arms "shone white as ivory," as Homer says, is the "wife" of Zeus (Heracles's father), the Greek version of the World Mother, Heracles' *Mer*.

47. The Tibetans recognized the connection of Merlin and fire for their term for the vital principle of the element of fire is, transliterated, *me-rlun*. Their word for the pranic essence or the vital principle of the element of earth is similar: *rlun*. In fact, the root of Merlin's name is implicated in the other two elements in Tibetan philosophy as well: for water, as *chu-rlun*, and for air, as *rlun-gi-rlun*. See: Lama Anagarika Govinda, *Foundations of Tibetan Mysticism* (York Beach, ME: Samuel Weiser, 1969): 182.

48. For further information on the Ofanim, especially from an experiential viewpoint, see my *Looking for Arthur: A Once and Future Travelogue* (Barrytown, 1996), *What's Beyond That Star* (Clairview Books, 2002), and part one of *The Galaxy on Earth* (Hampton Roads, 2002).

49. Constance Victoria Briggs, *The Encyclopedia of Angels* (New York: Penguin Putnam/ Plume, 1997): 201–202.

50. Regarding the specificity of the numbers cited, for their manifestations the math is 6 angels each with 144 major manifestations, and each of these has 6 to the 6th minor manifestations = 40,310,784. For their galactic reach, the Ofanim said, "Think of a line of zeros extending around your planet—that would give you a partial understanding of how many galaxies we are involved with." Calculated at a "0" in 12-point Palatino, this is 144 per 12 inches; 760,320/mile X 24,902 miles (Earth's circumference) = 18,723,488,640 galaxies. On the matter of their age, the Ofanim say they have lived One Week of Brahma, based on the Vedic time reckoning system. One Day of Brahma is equal to 14 *Manvantaras*, each of which is 306,000,000 human years. That amounts to 4,284,000,000 years/day X 7 days (one week)

= 29,988,000,000 years. Brahma is said to live 100 Years (311 trillion human years), then enter a period of sleep and quiescence known as the Night of Brahma.

51. The Ofanim have inspired the image of the jovial elephant god Ganesh, regarded as the Lord of Overcoming Obstacles, and one of India's most popular deities. Just as the elephant, the largest of animals, pushes its way confidently through the thickest parts of the jungle, so Ganesh overcomes obstacles on humanity's behalf, making paths for travelers. Of interest here is that he's considered the god of sciences and skills, especially writing, and was the first scribe. The gigantic Hindu epic, the *Mahabharata,* was dictated by Ganesh (the Ofanim) to its presumed author, the sage Vyasa.

52. The Elohim were the first giants, but not the only ones. Later in planetary history, a second angelic family, lower on the angelic hierarchical tree, called the Nefilim, also took human incarnation as giants. They were the "fallen angels" criticized for finding the women of Earth comely. One of the Nefilim's contributions was the creation of the Polynesian soul group; see *The Galaxy on Earth* (Hampton Roads, 2002), "Mount Temehani, Raiatea, Society Islands," for more on this.

53. A giantess named Sunsuna was credited with building Ggantija (Giant's Grotto) on Gozo (near Malta in the Mediterranean) in one night. Virgil wrote of three Cyclopes (Thunderclap, Anvilfire, and Flash) toiling with Hephaistos, the Greek fire god, in his forge underneath volcanic Etna. Virgil called them "the brotherhood of Etna." The Greeks knew the Elohim as the Titans, the gods before the Olympian pantheon. The Greeks thought of the Titans and their mates, the Titanesses, as gigantic beings who ruled the world in a primitive antique age. They were produced by Uranus (Sky) and Ge (Earth). Later, Zeus and his Olympian gods waged a ten-year battle called the Gigantomachy against the Titans, after which they were "exiled" to Tartarus along with their chief, Kronos, Zeus's father.

54. Alexander Russell, *Aristocrats of the South Seas* (London: Robert Hale Limited, 1961): 126, 128, 182.

55. Medieval alchemists had at least 50 synonyms for the *prima materia,* which for them was the basis of the entire alchemical process by which through a transmutation process the basic starting substance was transformed into the Philosopher's Stone, the highest attainment in consciousness. The *prima materia* was known variously as chaos, the mother of all the elements and created things filling all of etheric space, the black fecund Earth, and the lapis (stone).

56. Harold Courlander, *The Fourth World of the Hopis* (New York: Fawcett/Crown, 1972): 285.

57. F. H. Cushing, "Outlines of Zuni Creation Myths," *Thirteenth Annual Report* (Washington, DC: Bureau of Ethnology, 1896): 325–447.

58. Alf Hornborg, "Environmentalism, Ethnicity, and Sacred Places," *Canadian Review of Sociology and Anthropology* 31 (2000): 245–267.

59. Hessdalen, near Roros in central Norway, is a site renowned for its physical UFO sightings and unusual light phenomena usually in the form of fast-moving, pulsating, colored (often yellow) spheres, sometimes observed daily. The fastest sphere to date was clocked as moving at 8,500 mph. Hessdalen has been studied by UFO buffs and scientists for decades now. The light phenomena began in 1981 and exhibited high activity, often 15 to 20 sightings per week, until 1984; since then, sightings have tapered off to 20 per year. See: www.hessdalen.org for reports and information.

60. Kevin Townley, *The Cube of Space: Container of Creation* (Boulder, CO: Archive Press, 1993): 2.

61. Leonora Leet, *The Secret Doctrine of the Kabbalah: Rediscovering the Key to Hebraic Sacred Science* (Rochester, VT: Inner Traditions, 1999): 258.

62. L. Gordon Plummer, *The Mathematics of the Cosmic Mind: A Study in Mathematical Symbolism* (Wheaton, IL: Theosophical Publishing House, 1970): 29.

63. David Allen Pulse, *New Dimensions for the Cube of Space: The Path of Initiation Revealed by the Tarot upon the Qabalistic Cube* (York Beach, ME: Samuel Weiser, 2000): 3–4.

64. The reference to Plato in this term comes from the fact that he is one of the earliest writers to describe them. The subject of the Solids was not a major aspect of Platonic philosophy. Evidence now exists that knowledge of the Solids was prevalent among the Pythagorean Mystery schools, the ancient Egyptians, and much earlier European neolithic cultures. In Plato's *Timaeus,*

he describes the Earth as if seen from space as being like a sphere onto which were sewn a dozen equal-sized patches. Plato was describing the dodecahedron (made of 12 equal pentagons), which is a prime aspect of the Earth's grid.

65. In all of Nature there are only five such figures. All other regular volumes or solids are only variations on these five. The faces are triangles, squares, or pentagons and no other shapes, these being the most economical expressions of space. In fact, mathematicians know that three-dimensional space can be divided only into five equal divisions.

66. Michael S. Schneider, *A Beginner's Guide to Constructing the Universe: The Mathematical Archetypes of Nature, Art, and Science* (New York: HarperPerennial, 1994): 82.

67. There are certain intriguing symbolic aspects to the Platonic Solids too that reinforce the idea of God geometrizing, communicating with us through geometric shapes. Here are just a few examples, by way of teasers: The sum of the faces of all five Solids is 50, corresponding to Pentecost ("the fiftieth," and the clairvoyant experience and miraculous speech of the 12 Apostles of Christ) and the 50 Gates of Binah (in Qabala). The sum of the plane angles in the cube is 2,160, the number of years in which the Sun resides in one astrological sign; the diameter of the Moon is 2,160 miles. The length of years in terms of Earth days of the planet Venus is a variation on this: 216. (Venus is central to the mysteries of the Earth's unfolding.) The sum of the plane angles for all five solids is 14,400; the number 144 and its variations (varying amounts of additional zeros) is a key number in the Earth's visionary-mathematical matrix as well as the Jerusalem archetype.

68. Robert Lawlor, *Sacred Geometry: Philosophy and Practice* (London: Thames and Hudson, 1982): 96.

69. Carlo Suares, *The Qabala Trilogy* (Boston, MA: Shambhala, 1985): 461–463.

70. Nekhama Schoenburg, *The Unifying Factor: A Review of Kabbalah* (Northvale, NJ: Jason Aronson, 1996): 125.

71. The literal meaning of Sefira is "counting." In fact, Qabala calls the Sefirot primordial numbers, by which it means "metaphysical principles or stages in God's creation." They are "living numerical beings and the hidden 'depth' and

'dimension' to all things." Sanford L. Drob, *Symbols of the Kabbalah: Philosophical and Psychological Perspectives* (Northvale, NJ: Jason Aronson, 2000): 155–160.

72. Atziluth is the most rarified of the Four Worlds. It is the World of Emanations, nearness, divine glory, essences, archetypes, and lights, of the Originator, the unseen radiance that permeates the three lower worlds. The root of the word *Atziluth* means "to stand near," which means Atziluth is close to the Absolute, just a little separated from it. The World of Emanations is said to stand within the boundary of the divine and to be the repository of Light from a preexistent source. This realm contains Heaven's cosmic purpose, the complete scheme of all possible worlds, the potentiality of everything that will one day be called forth, and "the perfect image of the likeness of God." It is "the perfect and unchanging realm of Eternity that precedes Creation." Z'ev ben Shimon Halevi, *A Kabbalistic Universe* (York Beach, ME: Samuel Weiser, 1977): 63. —*Kabbalah and Exodus* (York Beach, ME: Samuel Weiser, 1988): 17.

73. Beriah (or Briyah) is the World of Creation, the archangels, and pure spirit. It is the domain of the highest angels, the Throne, and the Merkabah (God's Chariot). It is the realm in which the biblical Elohim created the world, in which manifestation in the sevenfold realm of time and space (the seven days of Creation) unfolded from the divine plan. In Beriah, the intensity and quality of the Endless Light from Atziluth are transformed. Beriah is a lower counterpart of Atziluth, a realm created in its likeness, now one step removed from the infinite.

74. Yezirah is the World of Formation, the angelic world, the astral seedbed of the physical world, the reservoir of forms and shapes, physical reality's chromosomes and gene pool, and the discrete but invisible aspects of reality.

75. Assiyah is the World of Making, of expression and action, the physical, manifest, natural world, of the human, animal, and plant kingdoms. In this realm, the tendencies and energies of the previous three Worlds are projected into material actualities. We live in the world of Assiyah.

76. Sometimes Qabalists refer to this sequence of stages as Jacob's Ladder. In his famous vision, the Hebrew patriarch saw myriad

angels ascending and descending on this ladder from the highest heavens to Earth. Alternatively, you could picture the Four Worlds as a series of four cubes, one inside the next, each one bigger, encompassing the smaller, previous one, like a cube with a triple echo.

77. The name Zeus (the Roman Jupiter) is cognate with the Sanskrit *dyaus div,* which means "Sky," and the Latin *dies,* which means "Day." Sky and Day imply the existence of higher mind, of far-seeing awareness; Zeus's domain is "the open heaven of air and cloud," Homer wrote; from there, Zeus views the wide world. He is prescient, mighty, the fulfiller of tight-knit designs. Zeus's familiar weapon, the thunderbolt, is actually a reference to his primal generative potency. The legendary Mount Olympus and the Norse Asgard are projections out of Zeus's Atziluthic World.

78. Poseidon (the Roman Neptune) was also known as Earth-Shaker. Poseidon's lot, Homer attested, was to "abide forever in the grey sea water." The Sea that he presided over was the Great Mother's Sea of ether, the wave-vibratory stratum of Earth (the greater cosmos), Merlin's *Mer.* Esoterically, "water" always means the etheric realm as well as higher consciousness states attainable in this level. Poseidon lives in a cavern deep in the deep sea, said Homer, and he drives his great chariot out over the waves to shake the islands.

79. Appropriately one of Hades' epithets was Plouton (Pluto), which means "the Rich One," which was translated into Latin for the Roman pantheon as *Dis* (from dives, "rich"). In Hades' Underworld the primary element is cosmic fire, the higher lights in action and differentiation. As his lot, Hades received "the dark mist at the world's-end," said Homer. But Hades' realm is a rich one because it contains the abundance of forms, ideas, "genes," seeds, and the fire of life for physical reality; it is the astral world, the fertile realm of stars. It is rich in the way a pomegranate is rich with seeds; that's why Hades gave Persephone a pomegranate seed to secure her presence in his realm after he "abducted" her from the higher worlds. Hades' realm is only the Underworld from the vantage point of Zeus or Poseidon; for us, it is clearly the Upperworld, accessed above the crown chakra. Homer, *Iliad,* trans. Robert Fitzgerald (Garden City, NY: Anchor Press/Doubleday, 1974): 355.

80. Leonard R. Glotzer, *The Fundamentals of Jewish Mysticism: The Book of Creation and Its Commentaries* (Northvale, NJ: Jason Aronson, 1992): xvii, xviii.

81. Carlo Suares, *The Qabala Trilogy* (Boston, MA: Shambhala, 1985): 40, 50, 63, 67, 229, 409, 415.

82. Z'ev ben Shimon Halevi, *Kabbalah and Exodus* (York Beach, ME: Samuel Weiser, 1988): 13.

83. Louis Ginzberg, *The Legends of the Jews, I* (Philadelphia: Jewish Publication Society of America, 1909): 5.

84. David Allen Pulse, *New Dimensions for the Cube of Space: The Path of Initiation Revealed by the Tarot upon the Qabalistic Cube* (York Beach, ME: Samuel Weiser, 2000): 3.

85. John Michell, *The Dimensions of Paradise: The Proportions and Symbolic Numbers of Ancient Cosmology* (New York: Harper & Row, 1988): 11,14,15,16.

86. He was specific about the design of the New Jerusalem: It was perfectly square, measuring 12,000 furlongs in length, breadth, and height—a cube, in other words. It had 12 gates, three in each cardinal direction, presided over by an angel and on each of which was written the name of one of the 12 Tribes of Israel; the city walls rested on 12 foundation stones, each of which featured a different precious gem and the name of one of the 12 Apostles. The city wall was 144 cubits high and made of diamond, while the city itself was "of pure gold, like polished glass."

87. The city had no temple, "since the Lord God Almighty and the Lamb [the Christ] were themselves the temple." The New Jerusalem was illuminated from within by the "radiant glory of God" while the Christ was "a lighted torch" for it. Never during the day would the city's gates be closed in this city of "God-with-them." Sickness and death will be no more, because with the advent of the New Jerusalem "the world of the past has gone."

88. Some suggest that the New Jerusalem might descend upon the old one, or that perhaps it is already there, implicit in the ancient city's design. Geomantic studies by John Michell led him to propose that the physical city's ground plan is a mirror image of the blueprints of the First and Second Temple of Solomon, as if the archetype of the heavenly Jerusalem had somehow been etched upon the landscape and then

embodied in the design of the physical city of Jerusalem. The city as a whole itself is the prophesied Temple, Michell contends, a world sanctuary open to all religions and beliefs—"the pattern of a greater temple that accommodates all twelve tribes." [John Michell, *The Temple at Jerusalem: A Revelation* (York Beach, ME: Samuel Weiser, 2000): 61, 65.] Others suggest that the New Jerusalem will descend upon the Tor, a truncated pyramidal green hill in mystical Glastonbury in Somerset, England. This prophecy has gained the status of a new age shibboleth, yet the angelic hierarchy states that it is nonetheless a likelihood, planned for long ago with preparations set in place 2,000 years ago by Joseph of Arimathea, a master geomancer and colleague of Jesus, who came to Glastonbury to establish the first apostolic Christian church in England. On Easter morning in 1985 on Glastonbury Tor, I saw that "beautiful walled city" hovering motionlessly like a promise from the future over that Celtic hill. We need to be subtle in interpreting major prophecies such as the siting of the New Jerusalem; it seems more metaphysically sensible to propose that Glastonbury is scheduled to be a prime portal, or open doorway, within the Earth's visionary geography into the higher dimensional overlay of the New Jerusalem temple. Think of it as a prime grounding point for this higher plane archetype of cosmic order. As this book unfolds, it will become clear that ultimately it doesn't matter too much where the New Jerusalem descends because everyone will have—already has—full access.

89. The Bible has 60 different names for this ancient holy city, including Zion, Jebus, the City of David, and Ir Ha-Kodesh (The Holy City). An Egyptian text from the eighteenth century B.C. refers to it as Urushalimum; a fourteenth-century B.C. text has it as Urusalim; Assyrian texts called it Urusilimmu, later shortened to Urusalim to mean, approximately, City of Salim (Peace). An early Biblical reference had it as City of Salem, from Shalem, a reference to Melchizedek, its first king.

90. Martin Lev, *The Traveler's Key to Jerusalem: A Guide to the Sacred Places of Jerusalem* (New York: Alfred A. Knopf, 1989): 9–10.

91. We find a similar dual reference in the Ugaritic deities, Sahr and Salim (*shr w slm*) whose names mean Dawn and Dusk; their epithet (*ilm n'mm wjsmm*) meant "Gracious and Merciful Gods." Similarly, Salim is the Western Semitic (Syrian) god of Evening, linked with Sar, the god of Dawn. The pre-Islamic Palmyrans of the Syrian desert venerated the planet Venus as both the morning and evening star as the dual deity Arsu and Azizos, the "compassionate" gods. *Funk & Wagnalls Standard Dictionary of Folklore, Mythology and Legend,* Volume Two, ed. Maria Leach (New York: Funk & Wagnalls, 1950): 749.

92. Ramana Maharshi, *The Spiritual Teaching of Ramana Maharshi* (Boston: Shambhala, 1972): 106–107.

93. In recent years, especially since the Harmonic Convergence of 1987, some writers have construed the number 144,000 as the basis for a spiritual elitism. It isn't. It's more of a mathematical minimum, a statistical projection, a threshold. Potentially every human could (and one day will) stand on Mount Zion. "The number 144,000 is specific, and at this time not more than that number of people are likely to awaken spontaneously," comment the Ofanim.

94. Yoga describes the *nadis* as minute nerve fibers for the transmission of prana, or subtle life force energy, through the body. The nadis (the name means "motion," from the root *nad*), like the meridians of acupuncture, exist somewhere between the physical and the etheric. They are sometimes called Yoga-*Nadis*; however, the term can encompass gross channels for prana as well, what conventional science would term nerve channels. One Tantric source says there are 72,000 *nadis*; another says 300,000; a third, 350,000.

95. Paradoxically, despite the Ofanim's caution earlier, you may enter the Emerald safely. Think of it in terms of layers or degrees of Light, as provisions enabling you to get your feet wet, to test the waters before you swim. You can enter it like a cathedral, except it is hexagonal, green, and vast.

96. Later in the book I will discuss the 12 Tribes in more detail, but for now I will say it is not particularly a Jewish concept, but rather a geometrical one to do with the deployment of Earth's original incarnational human stream (the 144,000 at the start of planetary habitation) through the Earth's 12 equal divisions of space, called Albion plates. Each Tribe was assigned a plate.

97. We see a two-dimensional expression of this as the eight petals of the Ananda-kanda inner heart chakra, the foundation of the Jerusalem citadel-archetype, the eight Celestial Cities about Mount Meru, Hinduism's cosmic mountain, and, intriguingly, the eight aspects of the Camalate Center, the underpinning of the Arthurian Grail Mysteries, explained later in the book.

98. Kevin Townley, *The Cube of Space: Container of Creation* (Boulder, CO: Archive Press, 1993): 63.

99. The Buddha Body is a concept and experiential reality that will be referred to throughout this book as part of a new angelically sponsored initiation for humans in the context of the Earth's visionary geography.

100. The Ofanim state that when the decision was made to give humans the Emerald, its placement in ultimate reality was shifted. Previously it had been on a path (the energy stream of a letter: the path linking Geburah and Chesed on the two-dimensional Tree of Life model), then it was relocated to Chesed, a Sefira or planetary sphere. Functionally, Chesed, though the fourth Sefira, would be the top of the experiential Tree of Life for humans, situated at the crown chakra place.

101. Qabalist Carlo Suares offers this exercise as a way of becoming familiar with the planets' array within the Cube of Space. Picture yourself standing within the Cube of Space, facing East, he says. The side of the Cube in front of you is East for Mars; the one behind you is West for the Sun; below you is Jupiter; above your head is Saturn; to your right, South, is Mercury; to your left, North, is Venus; and inside the Cube, where you stand, is the Moon. Carlo Suares, *The Qabala Trilogy* (Boston, MA: Shambhala, 1985): 507.

102. To put this in perspective, there are a sextillion possible permutations of 22 letters—that's 10 to the twenty-first power, or 1,124,000,727,777,607,680,000 different names for stars. Aryeh Kaplan, *Sefer Yetzirah: The Book of Creation* (York Beach, ME: Samuel Weiser, 1990): 193.

103. Logres may derive from the Welsh word *Lloegr*, which means England in that tongue. In the Grail myths, Logres indicates not only the land of England, or all of the British Isles, it is also the condition of humanity and planet that is divested of the services of the Holy Grail. It is a state of consciousness. The opposite of Logres is Sarras, the city of the Grail. So Logres indicates a condition of Fall, of expulsion from paradise, a state of infirmity.

104. There are many variations on the story even in the Western spiritual and mythic traditions, including the Celtic. The Grail is a magical dish, a cornucopia, a prodigiously fruitful *cor benoit* or "blessed horn" that immediately grants the wishes of everyone for food and drink. Grail Knights feast happily and endlessly in a Grail castle that never runs out of refreshments; the Knights never age or die and always have exactly what they want right at hand. The Fisher King's magical dish, deep bowl with handles, chalice, or drinking vessel—or the *Dysgl of Rhydderch*, the Welsh christened it—always produces whatever food one desires.

105. Lama Anagarika Govinda, quoted in Anna Morduch, *The Sovereign Adventure: The Grail of Mankind* (Cambridge, UK: James Clarke, 1970): 180–181.

106. Henri-Charles Puech, "The Concept of Redemption in Manichaeism," in *The Mystic Vision: Papers from the Eranos Yearbook*, ed. Joseph Campbell, Bollingen Series XXX, (Princeton: Princeton University Press, 1968): 261.

107. One account said Galahad, a Grail Knight of equal stature to Parsifal, perceived the Grail at Sarras then died. Nobody knows the location of Sarras, but in earlier times some said it was near Jerusalem, others that it was in Britain. Supposedly, the Roman god Mars was worshipped there; one text attributed to Merlin said a pagan giant named Alchendic ruled there. In his survey of Grail literature, Arthur Edward Waite collated some of the key references to Sarras: After Lancelot beheld the Grail, it was removed to the Spiritual City of Sarras; Sarras is a spiritual place "on the confines of Egypt"; in Sarras, there is a "Great Cohort of Angels"; three of the Grail Knights, Parsifal, Bors, and Galahad, are conveyed by the Ship of Solomon to "a place in the East, named Sarras"; its aged king is named Evalach; there is a building in Sarras called the Spiritual Palace; the Grail originally came from Heaven above into the city of Sarras. Arthur Edward Waite, *The Holy Grail: The Galahad Quest in the Arthurian Literature* (New Hyde Park, NY: University Books, 1961): 57, 78, 85, 99, 177, 178, 197.

108. The Ofanim state: "Sarras is an ancient word. It is the same forwards and backwards. It was part of a ritual device and holds a magic square. The Grail was earthed in a sense through this name in ritual. Amongst a particular group, there was a mutual agreement as to a particular place to ground their individual experiences of the Grail."

109. In the vicinity of the oracle of Trophonius at Lebadeia in classical Greece, there were two springs. Those consulting the oracle had to choose which to drink from: One was the spring of forgetfulness (Lethe), the other the spring of memory (Mnemosyne). The Grail Castle is the opposite of an oubliette: The latter is a place of deep forgetting, but the former is one of deep remembering—Mnemosyne.

110. Now Titurel's Grail Castle would properly contain the Grail. The structure would be tall, circular, topped with a grand cupola, and surrounded by 22 chapels forming an octagon. At every second chapel there would be an octagonal bell tower topped by a white crystal cross and a golden eagle. The towers surrounded the central cupola, which was red-gold and blue enamel. Inside this central domed enclosure, the Sun and Moon were to be depicted against a blue enameled sky of stars on the ceiling; under this would be a miniature replica of the entire Grail Castle, and inside this, the Holy Grail.

111. *The Mahabharata: 1—The Book of the Beginning, Vol. 1*, trans. J. A. B. van Buitenen (Chicago: University of Chicago Press, 1973): 149.

112. The celestial Lanka is not to be confused with the landmass and country called Sri Lanka. Lanka is a city of the gods set atop a mountain called Trikuta that may or may not have some topographical reference to the country of Sri Lanka in terms of being an ancient name for a holy site. The *Ramayana* places Lanka 800 miles south of the southern tip of India, a far greater distance than the island of Sri Lanka is presently situated.

113. *Ramayana*, retold by Krishna Dharma (Badger, CA: Torchlight Publishing, 2000): 213–14.

114. *The Mahabharata: 2—The Book of the Assembly Hall*, Vol. 2, trans. and ed. J. A. B. van Buitenen (Chicago: University of Chicago Press, 1975): 49.

115. Let's look at Vishnu for a moment. Vishnu is the pervader and preserver of the universe, which his name reflects. It derives from the root *vislr*, which means "to spread in all directions," thus to pervade. But it may also, or alternatively, derive from *vis* (as in *visnati*, "to spread," or *visati*, "to enter") and from *visli* (in *vivesti*, "to surround"). Vishnu is the inner cohesion that holds everything together; he dwells in everything, owns everything, and thereby defeats the powers of entropy and destruction. He is the centripetal tendency, the center towards which everything spins and gravitates. [Alain Danielou, *The Myths and Gods of India* (Rochester, VT: Inner Traditions, 1991): 149.] Vishnu is also the principle of duration, of perpetual or eternal life, which is fitting for the Rich Fisher King attributions of superintending a cauldron that regenerates the dead. As a principle, Vishnu is the source and plan of life, the repository of all prototypes yet to be manifested in the world. We could think of him as the universal intellect, the king of the sphere of mental creation and world planning. When Vishnu sleeps, the universe dissolves and reverts back to its original formless state, the causal ocean; what remains of the former state of manifestation is the coiled cosmic serpent, Sesa-Ananta, whose name means "Remainder." Sesa-Ananta floats on top of the primordial waters, and Vishnu rests upon him, being known now as Narayana, "Moving on the Waters." According to Hindu tradition, Vishnu periodically makes "descents" (*avataras*) into the world to save humankind from suffering and evil deeds and to restore the world's goodness, as in his guise as Rama, Krishna, and Buddha, but earlier, as the fish, tortoise, boar, and man-lion, to help manifest the forms and structures of the world.

116. W. J. Wilkins, *Hindu Mythology: Vedic and Puranic*, second edition (New Delhi, India: Rupa & Company, 1882, 1975): 141.

117. W. Norman Brown, *Man in the Universe: Some Continuities in Indian Thought* (Berkeley: University of California Press, 1970): 80.

118. *The Mahabharata: 1—The Book of the Beginning, Vol. 1*, trans. J. A. B. van Buitenen (Chicago: University of Chicago Press, 1973): 21.

119. Richard L. Thompson, *Mysteries of the Sacred Universe: The Cosmology of the Bhagavata Purana* (Alachua, FL: Govardhan Hill Publishing, 2000): 169.

120. Michael Jordan, *Encyclopedia of Gods* (New York: Facts on File, 1993): 76.

121. Gwendolyn Leick, *A Dictionary of Ancient Near Eastern Mythology* (London: Routledge, 1991): 37, 40–41.

122. "In general it [the term *me*] would seem to denote a set of rules and regulations assigned to each cosmic entity and cultural phenomenon for the purpose of keeping it operating forever in accordance with the plans laid down by the deities creating it." Samuel Noah Kramer, *History Begins at Sumer: Thirty-Nine Firsts in Recorded History* (Philadelphia: University of Pennsylvania Press, 1956): 79.

123. Samuel Noah Kramer, *Sumerian Mythology: A Study of Spiritual and Literary Achievement in the Third Millennium B.C.*, rev. ed., (Philadelphia: University of Pennsylvania Press, 1961): 62–63.

124. This of course is an area for potentially fruitful research once one's intellectual parameters have widened a bit to accept the possibility that a Flood myth probably recounts the location of a Grail Castle. Based on the great number of Flood myths among different peoples and tribes around the world, here are some Grail Castle possibilities: Mount Gerania, Greece; Mount Nisur (ancient Assyria); Mount Tendong, near Darjeeling, India; Mounts Amuyao and Kalawitan, Philippines; Mount Lakimola, Timor; Mount Tauga, Papua New Guinea; Toamarama, Raiatea, French Polynesia; Mounts Baker and Rainier, Washington; Mount Shasta, California; Mount Jefferson, Oregon; Mount Colhuacan, Mexico; Tiahuanaco, Bolivia. These sites, and others not listed here, have common mythic attributions: They were high points immune from the flood waters; a primogenitive human couple survived there and repopulated the world. The presence of these mythic attributions in itself is not a guarantee that a Grail Castle is present, but it certainly indicates the place is worth investigating along those lines. One needs to be careful about the exact location cited. In Raiatea, there is a Grail Castle, but it's not in the lagoon on a two-foot-high mound called Toamarama as the myth says, but on (above, actually) the island's highest point, Mount Temehani. But since Raiatea is a small island, the error in location accounts for only a dozen or so miles. For a useful summary of world Flood myths, see: "Flood Stories from around the World," Mark Isaak (January 1, 2001), at www.talkorigins.org/faqs/flood-myths.html.

125. Mircea Eliade, *Patterns in Comparative Religion*, trans. Rosemary Sheed (Lincoln, NE: University of Nebraska Press, 1996): 206.

126. Sadly appropriate to the psychically wounded condition of Anfortas is the somewhat unbalanced Grail Maiden, Kundry. She is both Anfortas's helper and opponent. In Wagner's opera *Parsifal*, Kundry is in league with Klingsor and, disguised as a beautiful siren, distracts Parsifal when he visits Klingsor's magic garden. She has been miserable ever since she laughed at the Christ on the cross on Golgotha. Wagner also blames Kundry for having betrayed Anfortas into allowing his sacred spear to be stolen by Klingsor. In Kundry we see how the woundedness of not remembering distorts the psychic process by which the soul should be able to reclaim its deep memory. Kundry, as the intuitive or psychic aspect, is just as wounded (and some might say corrupted or at least compromised) as Anfortas.

127. By Christ, here I refer to the Cosmic Christ, not his incarnation through Jesus as Jesus Christ in historical times. I refer to the Christ as a cosmic fact, as Rudolf Steiner would say, the Son of the Supreme Being. The Greek philosophical concept of Logos, as the Reason-Speech principle of reality, evokes some of the Rich Fisher King's attributes as upholder of *rta* and the divine laws, or *mes*. For the Greek philosopher Heraclitus, for example, the Logos meant the world-principle and world-process, the rationality of the universe, which implied a knowability by the human mind and spirit. The concept of Logos also describes a pervasive *connectivity* among all created things; that connection is rational, that is, it serves a purpose, was intentionally instituted, and can be understood. The term also connotes the primal Word by which creation began. In the beginning was the Word (Logos), and the Logos was with God and was God, the Fourth Gospel states. Further, the Apostle John identified Jesus Christ as the Logos made flesh.

128. Henri-Charles Puech, "The Concept of Redemption in Manichaeism," in *The Mystic Vision: Papers from the Eranos Yearbook*, ed. Joseph Campbell, Bollingen Series XXX, (Princeton: Princeton University Press, 1968): 263.

129. Henry Corbin, *The Man of Light in Iranian Sufism* (Boulder, CO: Shambhala, 1978): 40, 41.

130. Ibid., 8, 11, 59, 60.

131. Alain Danielou, *The Myths and Gods of India* (Rochester, VT: Inner Traditions, 1991): 261.

132. The Greek version is of course far less spectacular in terms of special effects and amazing gods and scary demons, but the location of the events is probably the same as in the *Ramayana*: a Grail Castle. A beautiful celestial woman, Helen (Zeus's daughter), is abducted by Paris, son of Priam, King of Troy, and held hostage at a citadel (Troy); her husband, Menelaus, raises a vast army that besieges Troy and eventually reclaims her. Her nonhuman celestial identity is clearly stated by Homer, but most scholars and interpreters somehow ignore or dismiss this fact, even though it is the key to the myth. She's another expression of Sita.

133. Arthur Avalon, *The Serpent Power* (New York: Dover Publications, 1974): 347, 351.

134. See Book XVII, Chapters 5–7, Sir Thomas Malory, *Le Morte d'Arthur*, vol. 2, ed. Janet Cowen (New York: Penguin Books, 1969). Malory records a variation on the Anfortas saga in which Pelles is the Maimed King. One day while hunting in a wood he came across Solomon's Ship of Time, boarded it, found the sword, and drew it out. "So therewith entered a spear wherewith he was smit him through both the thighs, and never sith might he be healed, ne nought shall tofore we come to him." Despite the difficult early English, we can see that Pelles was spiritually unqualified to claim the Giant's sword, which is to say, wield the world-creating (or destroying) power of kundalini on his own. So he incapacitated himself in his creative center, "thighs" being a euphemism for the root chakra.

135. Unfortunately, I have been unable to confirm this allegation, at least in English. I encountered a single reference to it, translated poorly from the German, on a website related to Heidelberg.

136. I thank Erica Jong for drawing my attention to Heidelberg and its Holy Mountain. In *Fear of Flying*, she briefly recounts some of the legends of the Holy Mountain, how the Nazis appropriated it during World War II, and how once it had been the site of a shrine to the Nordic high god, Odin, then later, one dedicated to the Christ. "The ground was sacred," writes Jong. It is likely that the Nazis, since they had a partial understanding of the Earth's visionary geography (which they used for perverted purposes), took over Holy Mountain so as to use the dragon energies as part of the geomantic control program for Europe whereby they occupied important sacred sites. See: Erica Jong, *Fear of Flying* (New York: Holt, Rineheart and Winston, 1973): 70–71.

137. Alain Danielou, *Yoga: Mastering the Secrets of Matter and the Universe* (Inner Traditions, Rochester, VT, 1991): 141.

138. Arthur Avalon, *The Serpent Power* (New York: Dover Publications, 1974): 337, 346, 351.

139. Ibid., 354.

140. *Beowulf: The Donaldson Translation, Backgrounds and Sources,* criticism and editing by Joseph F. Tuso (New York: W. W. Norton, 1975): 42–49.

141. Jan Knappert, *The Aquarian Dictionary to African Mythology* (Wellingborough, England: Aquarian Press/Thorsons, 1990): 75–76.

142. *The Saga of the Volsungs,* trans. Jesse L. Byock (New York: Penguin Books, 1999): 57, 59, 64, 66.

143. African myth recounts a similar tale. Aido-Hwedo is the Fon-Benin name for the cosmic serpent and primordial creative force that existed even before Mawu-Lisa, their name for the Supreme Being. However, Aido-Hwedo is the faithful servant of Mawu-Lisa, sustaining the universe's original designated shape. He carries Mawu-Lisa in his mouth through the universe. Once the world was created, Aido-Hwedo "coiled himself around and beneath it; he continues to hold everything in its place, assuring regularity." Further, like Draco and the Midgard Serpent, he revolves around the Earth, which causes the movements of the stars. See: Harold Scheub, *A Dictionary of African Mythology: The Mythmaker as Storyteller* (New York: Oxford University Press, 2000): 8.

144. Alain Danielou, *The Myths and Gods of India* (Rochester, VT: Inner Traditions, 1991): 316–317.

145. Robert Lawlor, *Voices of the First Day: Awakening in the Aboriginal Dreamtime* (Rochester, VT: Inner Traditions, 1991): 115.

146. Arthur Avalon, *The Serpent Power* (New York: Dover Publications, 1974): 110, 113.

147. *Classical Hindu Mythology: A Reader in the Sanskrit Puranas,* ed. Cornelia Dimmitt and J. A. B. van Buitenen (Philadelphia: Temple University Press, 1978): 304.

148. Mircea Eliade, *A History of Religious Ideas, Vol. 1, From the Stone Age to the Eleusinian Mysteries* (Chicago: University of Chicago Press, 1978): 206, 207.

149. You find a similar story with the Babylonian king-hero Marduk. He splits open the skull of Tiamat, the behemoth water dragon, then breaks her in two like a dried fish. One half of Tiamat (from *tiamtum*, "Sea") will thereafter roof the celestial vault, the other will surface the Earth; her breasts will be the planet's mountains, her spittle will form the clouds, and the Tigris and Euphrates Rivers will flow from Tiamat's eyes. In latter days, Marduk's royal emblem would be the *Mushussu*, a composite image of dragon and snake. We see the same story retold around the world in different cultural guises. Saint George slays the dragon at Silene in Libya; he also overpowers a dragon at Nevsehir in Turkey; Saint Martha overcomes the dragon Tarasque at Tarascon on the River Rhone near Avignon in southern France with a jar of holy water and a crucifix; Cadmus kills the Dragon of Ares by the spring at Thebes; Saint Michael (a euphemism for the Archangel Michael) slays the formidable Dragon of Heaven; in Colchis (now the Republic of Georgia), Jason of the Argonauts slays another dragon of Ares.

150. Mike Dixon-Kennedy, *Encyclopedia of Russian & Slavic Myth and Legend* (Santa Barbara: ABC-CLIO, 1998): 98–99.

151. *The Mahabharata: 1—The Book of the Beginning, Vol. 1*, trans. and ed. J. A. B. van Buitenen (Chicago: University of Chicago Press, 1973): 92–93

152. Margaret and James Stutley, *Harper's Dictionary of Hinduism: Its Mythology, Folklore, Philosophy, Literature, and History* (San Francisco: Harper & Row, 1977): 13, 276.

153. Alain Danielou, *The Myths and Gods of India* (Rochester, VT: Inner Traditions, 1991): 163.

154. Switching mythic language, in the Judeo-Christian cosmogony, the realm closest to God is Arabot, the Seventh Heaven. Appropriately, the Archangel Michael, one of whose prime attributes is dragon-slayer, presides over this Heaven. From Arabot, he "slays" the great dragon-beast Sesa-Ananta, which is to say, he grounds and activates it, performs a sacrificial bloodletting so that the worlds below may be quickened with the fecund blood-water of the cosmic serpent. Arabot is

likened to a vast plain, a bank of endless cloud, or the surface of a vast sea, usually understood to be the Cosmic Sea. The Seventh Heaven exists "on the borders of the Full Sea, crowded with an innumerable array of angels." It is the most divine part of all creation because it is the closest to God. Gustav Davidson, *A Dictionary of Angels* (New York: Free Press, 1967): 194.

155. Gershom Scholem, *Major Trends in Jewish Mysticism* (New York: Schocken Books, [1946] 1995): 260–261.

156. In demonstration of this, in 1989, Columbia University researchers used a supercomputer to calculate pi to 480 million decimal points, a vast number that if printed would be 600 miles long.

157. John Allen Paulos, *Beyond Numeracy: Ruminations of a Numbers Man* (New York: Alfred A. Knopf, 1991): 178–179, 205.

158. It's the basis for the well-known Fibonacci sequence of numbers (1, 2, 3, 5, 8, 13, 21, 34, 55, 89, 144 . . .) which is generated by adding the previous digit in the sequence (5) with the current one (8) to get the next one (13). This number sequence can be plotted geometrically as aspects of an unfolding spiral; in fact, the Fibonacci numbers are a map or coordinate system that describes and creates the spiral.

159. The Rg Veda says enigmatically that when Vrtra's waters were finally released, they rushed into the world like the bellowing of cows. The Goddess Kundalini is likened to "the indistinct hum of swarms of love-mad bees," and let's not forget the popular notion of the dragon's deafening roar.

160. Gershom Scholem, *On the Kabbalah and Its Symbolism*, trans. Ralph Mannheim (New York: Schocken Books [1965], 1996): 166, 167, 168.

161. Aryeh Kaplan, *Sefer Yetzirah: The Book of Creation* (York Beach, ME: Samuel Weiser, 1990): 108, 109, 117.

162. Arthur Avalon, *The Serpent Power* (New York: Dover Publications, 1974): 165, 225, 227.

163. The root chakra has four petals; second chakra, six; third, ten; fourth, 12; fifth, 16; sixth, two, for a total of 50. In effect, the first six chakras, in terms of their vibratory petals or fields, are a foundation and ladder to the crown, which has 1,000 petals, just as Sesa-Ananta has 1,000 heads or 1,000 Naga offspring. This is the mirror image of saying Sesa-Ananta as Goddess

Kundalini is the *source* of the sound-letter matrix that creates reality, and it is also yet another demonstration of Her *oroboric* nature, the beginning and end of things. She is the origin of Jacob's Ladder or the 72 Names and its destination; ultimately it is not a straight but a circular ladder.

164. *The Mahabharata: 1—The Book of the Beginning, Vol. 1,* trans. and ed. J. A. B. van Buitenen, (Chicago: University of Chicago Press, 1973): 103, 121.

165. Ibid., 389.

166. For a full geomantic treatment of these sites, and others, see: Richard Leviton, *The Galaxy on Earth: A Traveler's Guide to the Planet's Visionary Geography* (Charlottesville, VA: Hampton Roads, 2002).

167. Arthur Avalon, *The Serpent Power* (New York: Dover Publications, 1974): 110.

168. Mary Scott, *Kundalini in the Physical World* (New York: Arkana/Penguin Group, 1983): 148.

169. Snorri Sturluson, *The Prose Edda*, trans. Jean I. Young (Berkeley: University of California Press, 1954): 56, 78, 87.

170. Harish Johari, *Chakras: Energy Centers of Transformation* (Rochester, VT: Destiny Books, 1987): 53, 89.

171. *The Mahabharata: 1—The Book of the Beginning, Vol. 1,* trans. and ed. J. A. B. van Buitenen (Chicago: University of Chicago Press, 1973): 74.

172. Rahu, whose name means "The Grasper or Seizer," is regarded as the cause of eclipses and the ruler of meteors. He's also called Abhrapisaca, "Sky Demon," on account of his constant attempts to devour the Sun and Moon in revenge for their bad treatment of him.

173. Bepin Behari, *Myths and Symbols of Vedic Astrology*, ed. David Frawley (Salt Lake City, UT: Passage Press, 1990): 111.

174. Stella Kramrisch, *The Presence of Siva* (Princeton, NJ: Princeton University Press, 1981): 16.

175. Harish Johari, *Chakras: Energy Centers of Transformation* (Rochester, VT: Destiny Books, 1987): 55.

176. Arthur Avalon, *The Serpent Power* (New York: Dover Publications, 1974): 358.

177. Roberto Calasso, *Ka: Stories of the Mind and Gods of India* (New York: Vintage Books/ Random House, 1998): 253–259.

178. Ibid.

179. The Vedas are fulsome in their characterizations of Soma: It is the sacrificial, consumable substance; the water of youth, health and strength; the ever-victorious warrior; the lunar plant, the juice of the Moon, the luminous and celestial herb, the king of herbs, the Moon itself; it is the Milk of Heaven that the gods eat steadily for 14 days every month (from the full to the new moon), reducing its substance; it is the wealth of the gods; the support of the sky, the one who arranges the days, who clothes himself in a garment that touches the sky and fills space, who dispels darkness, whose drops are like waves in the water, who swells up to be an ocean, who is the lord of nourishment, the celestial vessel in the fortress of the gods, the golden well in the sky. Alfred Hillebrandt, *Vedic Mythology, Vol. 1,* trans. Sreeramula Rajeswara Sarma (Delhi, India: Motilal Banarsidass [1891], 1980): 185–216.

180. Frank Herbert, author of the *Dune* series, understood this. The desert planet Arrakis, the third planet in the Canopus system, says Herbert, is in effect a Soma planet, the source of Soma for the universe. The spice melange, as Paul Atreides discovers, is the sandworm, *Shai-hulud,* just as the dragon is the source of Soma in the Vedic story. "Arrakis, the one source in the universe of melange, the prolonger of life, the giver of health. . . . It's like life—it presents a different face each time you take it." Significantly, a saturation by melange caused a mutation in humans to become the members of the Spacing Guild who fold space to transport ships around the universe. In other words, the spice enhanced consciousness, enabling it to transcend space-time and the stars, just as the dragon precedes the stars (gods) who depend on the Soma for their immortality. Thus if that's where your consciousness is, of course you can fold space because you are antecedent and therefore senior to the stars and their array in and as space-time. Frank Herbert, *Dune* (Philadelphia: Chilton Book Company, 1965): 53.

181. Soma reveals "the fullness of life, the sense of a limitless freedom . . . the feeling of community with the gods, even of belonging to the divine world . . . the possession of almost unsuspected physical and spiritual powers . . . the revelation of a full and beatific existence, in communion with the gods." Mircea Eliade, *A History of Religious Ideas, Vol. 1: From the Stone Age to the Eleusinian*

Mysteries, trans. Willard R. Trask. (Chicago: University of Chicago Press, 1978): 210–212.

182. Daksa is one of the six Adityas, sons of Aditi, the Vedic goddess of space, cosmic energy, and force. The Adityas personify aspects of cosmic nature and the range of phenomenal reality. Their number is also given sometimes as seven and 12, but in essence they represent aspects of Light and are sometimes collectively described as the Sun, but here the Sun is not our solar system's star but something of a broader nature, such as the great central sun of the galaxy perhaps, as referred to in esoteric writings.

183. *The Mahabharata: 1—The Book of the Beginning, Vol. 1,* trans. and ed. J. A. B. van Buitenen (Chicago: University of Chicago Press, 1973): 148.

184. S. Balakrishna, Ph.D., "Names of Stars from the Period of Vedas" (January 1998), p. 23, at: www.geocities.com/vijayabalak/stars/nakshathra. html.

185. Soma drives around the cosmos in his three-wheeled Moon chariot; it has ten horses (possibly a reference to the ten dimensions of space) and two drivers (possibly a reference to Rahu and Ketu). Soma as the Moon (Vedic Candra) rules the world of the stars and has lots of epithets: Lord of Constellations, the Luminous Drop, Crown of Siva, Lord of the Lotus, Drawn by White Horses, Having Cool Rays. When the Ocean of Milk was churned, the Moon sprang forth and spread a cool light with its thousands of rays.

186. The number is both irrational (which means "not expressible as the ratio of two whole numbers and hence not having a repetitive decimal expansion") and transcendental ("not the root of any algebraic equation"). An English mathematician named John Napier stunned the Western world in 1624 with the publication of his *Arithmetica logarithmica,* a series of number tables that presented the logarithms to base 10 of all numbers from 1 to 20,000 and from 90,000 to 100,000, and all of this up to 14 decimal points. Later that century, a Dutch mathematician filled in the list of logarithms from 20,000 to 90,000, but Napier was credited with the invention of logarithms. For many years, this was the basis of computational mathematics, until the slide rule, then calculators, replaced it, but the logarithmic process is still vital to mathematics. John Allen Paulos, *Beyond Numeracy: Ruminations of a Numbers Man* (New York: Alfred A. Knopf, 1991): 65.

187. Of particular interest to us here is that at least three physical phenomena follow a logarithmic scale: the Richter scale of measuring earthquakes; the decibel scale of loudness; and the brightness scale of stellar magnitudes. Eli Maor, *e: The Story of a Number* (Princeton, NJ: Princeton University Press, 1994): 26, 27, 113.

188. He reported that the purest demonstration of the mathematical value of the MY was at Avebury stone circle in Wiltshire, that Avebury might be the geometer's touchstone. "We consider that because of its size and the fact we know its geometry, Avebury provides the best site for determining, from a single site in England, the value of the megalithic yard." Avebury provides the "most accurately determined value" of the MY in England, namely 2.722 feet. A. Thom and A. S. Thom, *Megalithic Remains in Britain and Brittany* (Oxford, UK: Clarendon Press/Oxford University Press, 1978): 30, 38.

189. Stella Kramrisch, *The Presence of Siva* (Princeton, NJ: Princeton University Press, 1981): 27, 28.

190. One story has them born from Brahma and suckled by Vac. She is the divinity of Speech and Sound, the basis of the mantras or sacred syllables, the Divine Word; she is Mother of the Vedas and mantras, of the Fragrances (Gandharvas) and Water-Nymphs (Apsaras); consort of Prajapati, Lord of Progeny; and sometimes is equated with the body of the cosmos itself. Vac is the vehicle of knowledge that enters into the seers to give power and intelligence. Appropriately, King Soma too is regarded as Lord of Speech, such that "the voices and songs of the celestial and terrestrial singers . . . were inspired by his drink." As Vacaspati, all eloquence is attributed to him. Alfred Hillebrandt, *Vedic Mythology, Vol. 1,* trans. Sreeramula Rajeswara Sarma (Delhi, India: Motilal Banarsidass, 1980): 225.

191. Visvavasu, for example, plays the seven-stringed lute with exquisite refinement for 42,000 dancing Gandharvas. Their connection to music is even indicated by the term, *gandharvavidya,* "knowledge of music," and refers to a specific musical note.

192. Alfred Hillebrandt, *Vedic Mythology, Vol. 1,* trans. Sreeramula Rajeswara Sarma (Delhi, India: Motilal Banarsidass, 1980): 249.

193. E. Washburn Hopkins, *Epic Mythology* (Delhi, India: Motilal Banarsidass, 1974): 160.

194. The Apsaras were made beautiful and voluptuous to tempt the sages and ascetics from their austerities and spiritual focus so they would not gain so much saintliness that they would rival the gods. They can change their shape at will, appearing in any guise, although they favor water birds. On Earth, they tend to haunt fig trees, inside which people could sometimes hear their lutes and cymbals; the Apsaras, though wives to the Gandharvas, were said to be promiscuous and could drive humans mad with their otherworldly charms.

195. When heroes die in battle, thousands of Apsaras hover about them, each seeking his soul; they place the dead heroes on "divine cars with loud sounds of song and instruments, played in the sky" yet which are audible on the Earth. Indian legend holds that some 16,000 Apsaras were once born on Earth and they still remain here to dance and sing at weddings. E. Washburn Hopkins, *Epic Mythology* (Delhi, India: Motilal Banarsidass, 1974): 163.

196. A crore is an ancient Indian unit of measurement for indicating very large quantities. One crore = 10 to the 7th power, or 10,000,000.

197. Botanists explain that the distribution of petals on a sunflower head (and nearly all plants) is based on the Golden Mean and is called phyllotaxis. They are arrayed around the central stalk in such a way as to maximize their exposure to sunlight without competing with the other leaves' exposure.

198. As mentioned earlier, the goddess of the *Svadisthana* chakra is Rahini Shakti, shown in Tantric imagery as two-headed to represent the "split energy" in this center as well as the sundered Svarbhanu, the cosmic dragon cut into Rahu and Ketu. Rahini is seated on a double lotus (another dualistic image), dressed in celestial raiment and ornaments like the queen of the Apsaras, "and Her mind is exalted with the drinking of ambrosia [Soma]." Arthur Avalon, *The Serpent Power* (New York: Dover Publications, 1974): 362.

199. In some respects the domes, as intense light canopies, summoned the mountains up out of the flat land, especially the ones that would be volcanos. The volcanos were like eczema, boils on the surface of the Earth enabling detoxifica-tion. The toxins came to the surface of the planetary "skin," broke through, and oozed out, just like a pimple on the face. Thus the dome created the possibility, through the volcano, of enabling detoxification of toxic astral substance from out of the planet as well as the obvious manifest substance of lava. Further, the domes, being so hot, brought up water from deep in the Earth to just under the surface to cool the land. Hot above, cool below; light above, water below. This explains why dowsers often remark on the coincidence of conspicuous underground water at sacred sites; they even use the term "water domes." The cool water rose to cool the land and formed a mirror image in physical substance of the light canopy above. Dowsers have also noted water lines and aquastats not only under sacred or megalithic sites, but often under specific parts, such as beneath cathedral altars.

200. The dome caps represent either minor magnitude stars or planets associated with the major dome stars, and in varying combinations per individual dome.

201. The dome caps represent minor stars and planets associated with the major star of the dome. Functionally, we could say the dome caps are held in place, "gravitationally," within the star-dome's energy field the same way planets in our solar system are held in their orbits by the gravitational field of the sun. However, a solar system, by definition, has only one sun, so where do the other minor suns come from in the dome-dome cap array? A plausible model is to say that the major dome star holds in its gravitational field 12 other smaller magnitude (minor) suns from 12 other solar systems; those minor suns, in turn, hold a number of planets in their gravitational field. The Earth dome-dome cap model only represents a maximum of 48 such minor suns and planets, whereas the original galactic array has more planets than that in a given major star gravitational field array. We could call these solar system clusters. It's also important to remember that in the galaxy, the array of 12 minor suns and associated planets "about" a major high magnitude star is in three dimensions, compared to the Earth dome-dome cap array which is laid out like a lace doily over the landscape. Three dimensional here means the given stars and planets in the solar system cluster are likely separated by many light years, so we might better picture this as 48 points

of light arrayed throughout the volume of a transparent sphere.

202. That number comes to 155,704,904,729,922,094,596,797,248. That is the total number of manifestations possible in all universes at this time for the angelic family of Elohim.

203. Here's the math: 33 trillion dragon eggs will combine in units of 48 to produce 692,352,720,200 stars; these can then manifest equally in the 1,746 aspects or categories, giving us 396,536,494 stars per aspect. Then the 692 billion stars get assigned a place within one of the 27 *naksatra* wedges of space. The full number is 19,033,751,758.076176. This is based on dividing 33,232,930,569,601, the total number of postulated cosmic dragon eggs, by 1,746, the prime number of the Elohim.

204. Their manifestation package is calculated as follows, according to the Ofanim: They have 48 times 23 major manifestations, which comes to 1,104. Each of the 48 manifestations has 1,500 subsidiary aspects (72,000), and the 23 manifestations each have 2,630 aspects (60,490). Total Hashmallim manifestations are 4,355,280,000. Their role as Apsaras in comprising the 48 dome cap matrix of a dome is of course fitting in light of their primary manifestation package which is 48.

205. What do we know about the Hashmallim as an order of angels? Their name means "brilliant ones" and is based on the name of their chief or prince, Hashmal. The Hashmallim (also known to Western angelologies as Dominions, Dominations, or Kuriotetes) are said to surround the Throne of God as the fire-speaking angels. They are the channels of mercy and the source of heavenly order and of the perfect (that is, rational) cause and effect of actions. They are charged with merging the spiritual and physical worlds and are not known to communicate with humans. They regulate the activities of angels in all the spiritual and physical worlds, and as a token of this oversight task, they are shown holding a scepter and orb. Angels of leadership and wisdom, ministers of God's justice to the cosmos, through them God's majesty manifests. They are said to receive their instructions from the Thrones (the Ofanim) who dwell in the presence of God. As angels of pure goodness and humility, the Thrones are so named because God's power that emanates out to all aspects of creation initially rests upon them as a king sits on a throne. The Hashmallim inhabit, according to the Zohar, "an inner, supernal sphere, hidden and veiled, in which the mysteries of the celestial letters of the Holy Name are suspended." This reference is especially relevant in light of the Hashmallim's involvement (as Apsaras) with the 48 letters of Sanskrit as the expressions of the vibratory fields or petals surrounding the chakras. Gustav Davidson, *A Dictionary of Angels, Including the Fallen Angels* (New York: Free Press, 1967): 136.

206. Rudolf Steiner remarks: "We look back upon the stars, no longer seeing them shine, but seeing instead the Hierarchies, the Spiritual Beings who have merely their reflection in the stars." See: Rudolf Steiner, *Man and the World of Stars*, trans. D. S. Osmond (New York: Anthroposophic Press, 1963): 32.

207. Among the names for these curving influences are the Persian dome, Adamic dome, dome of Noah, dome of Abraham, Moses, Mohammed, Christ, Bahman, of which there are four, the major Bahmanian dome, the red, white, and perfect Bahmanian domes. Bahman in Persian spirituality is the first archangel of six who collectively are called the Amesha Spentas (or Amshashpands), Six Immortal Holy Ones who emanated from Ormazd (Ahura-Mazda) to be this deity's attendants. Each Amesha represents a fundamental quality, such as truth or wisdom, and each protects a basic aspect of creation, such as the elements fire, water, and earth. Henry Corbin, *The Voyage and the Messenger: Iran and Philosophy,* trans. Joseph Rowe (Berkeley: North Atlantic Books, 1998): 185, 188, 190.

208. Ibid., 198, 203.

209. Norbert C. Brockman, *Encyclopedia of Sacred Places* (New York: Oxford University Press, 1997): 99.

210. William Dalrymple, *From the Holy Mountain: A Journey in the Shadow of Byzantium* (London: Flamingo/Harper Collins, 1998): 40.

211. The Ofanim state that each dome was equipped with a Paradise seed crystal, capable of producing paradisal conditions within the dome. They also state that for the most part, this opportunity was not taken advantage of by humanity over the life of this planet. What is this seed? It's the Emerald or Cube of Space, as explained earlier in the book; it is also the Edenic Tree of Life. It contains the 32 Paths of Wisdom, as explained in

Qabala, consisting of the 22 letters of the Hebrew alphabet and the 10 Sefirot or dimensions of reality. This is often referred to in summary form as *LEV* (32), the Heart; we already know that the Emerald is the Heart within the Heart, so this metaphysical equation is fitting. It is also geomantically fitting. If you activate the Emerald (Paradise crystal seed) in a dome, you have access to the original Tree of Life in Eden and its ability to explain, create, and change reality. You are literally in the *heart* of things then.

On a technical level, the Emerald within the dome is the same as the height of the dome: picture a double-terminated six-sided Emerald placed vertically, so that one tip touches the inside top center of the dome, the other the ground. If the dome is, for example, 2.7 miles wide, then the Emerald will be about half that high and proportionally wide. It's there as a potential, a light seed for us to activate by interacting with it through our own Emerald. Multiply this possibility by 1746 and you may get a sense of the astounding planetary potential for a transformed world should we activate or "sprout" all of these Paradise crystals.

212. Jeremy Naydler, *Temple of the Cosmos: The Ancient Egyptian Experience of the Sacred* (Rochester, VT: Inner Traditions,1996): 92.

213. H. P. Blavatsky gives the figure as 18,618,728 years ago (from 1888, when she wrote) when the *Manvantara* Vaivasvata survived the Deluge and reinstated a new generation of human beings on Earth. This figure, as explained in chapter 3, is an expression of the Grail King inaugurating a new cycle of human development on Earth. Blavatsky says she got the number from ancient Hindu sources. The evolution of the first physical human, Blavatsky maintains, took place in Lemuria 18 million years ago. Since dating monumental events such as the three Dome Presences is inherently difficult and relativistic, her date of 18 million years ago is plausible and credible enough to give us some frame of time reference, however approximate, for the third Dome Presence, the *Zep Tepi*, and the onset of the Lemurian age, based on the now sunken Pacific continent of the same name. See: H. P. Blavatsky, *The Secret Doctrine, Vol. 2: Anthropogenesis* (Pasadena, CA: Theosophical University Press, 1977): 46, 69.

214. For a full description of Avebury's mythic and geomantic terrain, see: Richard Leviton, *The Galaxy on Earth: A Traveler's Guide to the Planet's Visionary Geography* (Charlottesville, VA: Hampton Roads, 2002): 104–112.

215. Let's take a moment to broaden the nuances of this phrase, planetary spheres. In the Western Mystery tradition, these spheres are metaphors for experiential planes and conditions of consciousness and not physical objects in space. "The course of evolution of the human spirit may be conceived as a going out and a return through seven principal conditions," designated by the names of planets. Each is a specific type of consciousness to be experienced, "the sum total of bodies of expression and perception." In this metaphorical interpretation, then, the planetary sphere of Mercury, for example, deals with "intuitive mind and faith—'unmanifest knowledge'" while the Sun is "pure spirit." Gareth Knight, *The Secret Tradition in Arthurian Legend* (Wellingborough, UK: Aquarian Press/Thorsons Publishing Group, 1983): 130–133.

216. He overlooks creation, helps it evolve; he preserves and supports it; he veils the embodiment in illusion; he destroys it, burning it up; and he provides grace, release, and salvation. He is *Sudalaiyadi*, the Dancer of the Burning Ground, because at the core of the universe and of all consciousness, nothing survives his searing flames, and all illusion and ignorance are but ashes.

217. Shiva and Parvati dancing in the *vastu*—there are many nuances to this. This pairing neatly demonstrates the inherent dialectical nature of the Soma Temple, the cutting up of Svarbhanu into two parts, Rahu and Ketu and all its ramifications, even the way dome caps spin left or right. The intertwining of Shiva and Parvati dramatizes the dynamic double helix relationship of the Canopus and Sirius lines, Earth's *ida* and *pingala* currents, as they enter the planet and ground, perpetually entwined. It also represents the duality in Sirius itself, for Shiva and Parvati both hail from Sirius (Rudra as the Archer), yet even to conceive of them as definitively separate beings is, ultimately, illusionary.

218. *The Tree of Life: Chayyim Vital's Introduction to the Kabbalah of Isaac Luria, The Palace of Adam Kadmon*, trans. Donald Wilder Menzi and Zwe Padeh (Northvale, NJ: Jason Aronson, 1999): 14, 15, 25, 34, 71, 367, 372.

219. This tenuous tube of light by which the "Light from the Emanator descends to the

emanated being" is the means by which Emanator and emanated are united, where the Creator and its created beings (everything in the Alef) can meet. Rabbi Moses C. Luzzatto, *General Principles of the Kabbalah*, trans. The Research Centre of Kabbalah (New York: Samuel Weiser/ Press of the Research Centre of Kabbalah, 1970): 137–40.

220. Stella Kramrisch, *The Presence of Siva* (Princeton, NJ: Princeton University Press, 1981): 158, 159.

221. Illuminating the dim worlds with the light of absolute reality, Shiva let out "thunderous laughter," the mantric sound *AUM*, the syllables of the Word resounding from the pillar. His titanic revelation of his essence to the gods completed, Shiva became *Sthanu*, the motionless, self-contained ascetic pillar. Stella Kramrisch, *The Presence of Siva* (Princeton, NJ: Princeton University Press, 1981): 158, 159.

222. Later Qabalists found it cognitively convenient to model the 40 Sefirot (and the ten, as well), as a more complex abstract model with three parallel pillars and multiple connecting lines (32 paths per Tree), both vertical and horizontal, and a few diagonal. This is an abstract model and does not correspond to how the energies actually descend.

223. Dion Fortune, *The Mystical Qabalah* (London: Ernest Benn, 1957): 41, 42, 48, 56. Fortune says, "The angle of the Lightning Flash, which is used to indicate the course of the emanations upon the Tree, slopes downwards to the right across the glyph. . . ." Also: "It will be observed that the line which indicates the successive development of the Sephiroth zigzags from side to side of the glyph and has been aptly named the Lightning Flash in consequence."

224. Hermann Kern, quoted in Helmut Jaskolski, *The Labyrinth: Symbol of Fear, Rebirth, and Liberation* (Boston: Shambhala, 1997): 77–78.

225. For a full description of the geomantic aspects of the Clingman's Dome-type labyrinth and the Cretan labyrinth, see my book *The Galaxy on Earth: A Traveler's Guide to the Planet's Visionary Geography*: 174–179 (Clingman's Dome) and 399–406 (Mount Ida).

226. Each chakra template is basically a unit of 50 chakra parts. We can think of these either as the 50 vibratory petals surrounding the chakras or as each chakra having seven aspects. In any case,

mention of 50 immediately puts us in the symbolic realm and meaning of the other fifties mentioned earlier: the 50 Gates of Binah, 50 Gates of Understanding, the 50 geometric faces of the five Platonic Solids, the Pentecost (Fiftieth), the 50 Argonauts, the 50 letters of Sanskrit which comprise what Hinduism calls Shiva's Garland—the complete mantric soundscape of the chakra hierarchy and planetary spheres.

227. British geomantic researcher Peter Dawkins describes several such urban chakra templates, including ones in Washington, D.C., running along the Mall from the Lincoln Memorial to the Supreme Court building; Berlin running alongside the River Spree; Stein-am-Rhein, also in Germany; Edinburgh, Scotland, where the template is demarcated by the famous Royal Mile from Cannon Gate Kirk to Saint Margaret's Chapel. Towns, cities, and other settled landscapes can be designed as "large-scale temples containing complete chakra systems," Dawkins says. "When done with full consciousness the town chakras have been carefully placed in the natural environment with chakras naturally occuring in the landscape." Peter Dawkins, *Zoence—The Science of Life: Discovering the Sacred Spaces of Your Life* (York Beach, ME: Samuel Weiser, 1998): 87.

228. Diana L. Eck, *Banaras: City of Light* (Princeton, NJ: Princeton University Press, 1982): 29.

229. Ibid., 111.

230. My premise is that Osiris is an expression of the totality of light, the Egyptian Zeus, out of whose fullness the 14 Ray Masters (Olympians) were generated. I know historians and Egyptologists assume Osiris was a physically embodied pharaoh, but I don't agree with that interpretation.

231. On the way, his retinue would spend seven years at Harlech on the northwest Welsh coast where they would be continually feasted and entertained by the Hospitality of the Noble Head, as the old poets put it; they could expect 80 years of the same at Gwales, an island off the southwest coast where Bran's head "will be as good company for you as it ever was when it was on me." The 80-year blissful residence at Gwales was afterwards known as the Assembly of the Noble Head. Bran's seven retainers were not aware of "spending a more pleasurable nor lovelier time than that ever" at Gwales. It was a

moment outside of time as the Head's presence was as much a comfort to them as when Bran had been with them. "And of all the grief they had witnessed and experienced, they had no memory of it or of any sorrow in the world." "Branwen, Daughter of Llyr," in *The Mabinogi and Other Medieval Welsh Tales*, trans. Patrick K. Ford (Berkeley: University of California Press, 1977): 70–71.

232. "The Greater Holy Assembly," in *The Kabbalah Unveiled*, trans. S. L. Macgregor Mathers (York Beach, ME: Samuel Weiser, 1968): 115–118, 127.

233. The exciting part here is that there is not one Head, but three. Like the Gorgons, the Ancient of Days has three heads, one above the other, but also one within the other, the Qabalists say. One head is concealed wisdom, covered and not disclosed; one is the supernal head, which is the most ancient and holy one; and the third is the Head of All Heads, the head which is not really a head and what it contains is beyond the contents of the first two heads. "That part of the emanated being which is in closest affinity with the Origin" is the Head. Rabbi Yehuda L. Ashlag, *The Kabbalah: A Study of the Ten Luminous Emanations,* trans. Rabbi Levi I. Krakovsky (Jerusalem: Research Centre of Kabbalah. 1969): 108.

234. Gareth Knight, *A Practical Guide to Qabalistic Symbolism, Vol. I* (Cheltenham, England: Helios Book Service, 1976): 73.

235. There is a highly useful impression of this face in the movie *Mission to Mars* (2000) in which on Mars's surface astronauts encounter an ancient generic female face seemingly of marble and looking upwards. It had been buried under a mountain of earth and stone until a radio signal from the astronaut's monitoring device caused it to be revealed.

236. The mask of the Gorgon Medusa showed up in the Palladium. This has been described as a magical statue of Pallas Athena capable of preserving the inviolability of any citadel in which it resided. The myths say Athena had a sister who accidentally got killed by the goddess in a youthful game. To honor her fallen sibling, Athena carved a statue in her likeness and included the aegis in it, with the terrible face of the Gorgon Medusa at its center, with snakes for hair and petrifying eyes. The matter of the aegis is a bit confusing, as it is said to have been the prop-

erty of both Zeus and his daughter, Pallas Athena. At some point, Zeus threw it down from Heaven to the citadel at Troy, and there it remained.

237. Appropriately you get 72 faces of the Ancient of Days, 12 big ones, 60 smaller ones, looking in benignly on our world, 72 being the *Shemhamforesh*, Qabala's word for the 72 Names of God made from three-letter permutations of the divine Name, *YHVH.*

238. Ngawang Zangpo, *Sacred Ground: Jamgon Kongtrul on "Pilgrimage and Sacred Geography"* (Ithaca, NY: Snow Lion Publications, 2001): 32, 33, 35, 47, 48, 49.

239. The Greeks say the lily was created when Hera spilled a few drops of her breast milk upon the Earth. For the Christians, the lily stood for pure, virginal love, favored by the Archangel Gabriel, Angel of the Annunciation, and it has been the preferred flower of many saints. In Jesus's Sermon on the Mount, he praised the "lilies of the field" that toil not, intending it presumably as a metaphor for the blossoming of those with perfect faith. It creates a welcome home away from home for visiting angelic orders and joins the two realms of humans and angels.

240. Rudolf Steiner, *The Festivals and Their Meaning: Christmas, Easter, Ascension and Pentecost, Michaelmas* (London: Rudolf Steiner Press, 1981): 341.

241. For more on the Archangel Michael's mission, see the works of Rudolf Steiner such as *The Archangel Michael: His Mission and Ours* (Herndon, VA: Anthroposophic Press, 1994). See also: Bernard Nesfield-Cookson, *Michael and the Two-Horned Beast* (London: Temple Lodge Press, 2000). For a summary of some aspects of Steiner's view of Michael, see my book *The Imagination of Pentecost: Rudolf Steiner and Contemporary Spirituality* (Hudson, NY: Anthroposophic Press, 1994).

242. Henry Corbin, *The Man of Light in Iranian Sufism*, trans. Nancy Pearson (Boulder CO: Shambhala, 1978): 52–53.

243. Ibid.

244. This metaphor has some utility in conceptualizing the Earth grid. The armature is that part of an electric generator, dynamo, or motor in which electrical energy is produced. Typically there is a core of soft iron wound with insulated wires to produce an electromagnetic field in response to an incoming electric current. The

armature is the main, revolving, current-carrying winding that acts as an induced electromagnet. The coiled armature reacts with the stationary bar magnet creating its magnetic field. When the armature rotates between the newly established poles of the bar magnet, this generates the electromotive force, which is the purpose of the motor. A device called a commutator in the motor directs or changes the flow of the primary electrical current from the generator; as the armature rotates, this generates the electromotive force. In the Earth grid context, the planetary wrappings of the Oroboros Lines nested in the five Platonic Solids are the armature; the Sirius and Canopus umbilical lines at Avebury would be the commutator; the flow of cosmic awareness in many of its differentiations flowing through the Earth's energy matrix would be the "electromotive force" and thus the "purpose" of the planetary energy grid. See: Richard Leviton, "Ley Lines and the Meaning of Adam," in *Anti-Gravity and the World Grid*, ed. David Hatcher Childress (Stelle, IL: Adventures Unlimited Press, 1987): 139–197.

245. The credit for describing and naming this feature goes to the late but fabulous Earth matrix visionary Gino Gennaro. In 1979, he self-published a small book (out of print) describing some of the key features of the Earth's visionary terrain, including dragons, domes (he called these "celestial Grails or floating chapels"), and the Vibrating Stones. Gennaro said these "twelve specially vibrating stones" were placed on the planetary meridians (Oroboros Lines) to create a global calendar subject to cyclic sequential activation so that, in all, the Earth would emit 12 musical notes through these stones and their sites. See: Gino Gennaro, *The Phenomena of Avalon: The Story of This Planet as Recounted by the Fairies* (London: Cronos Publications, 1979): 57.

246. Supposedly the Edenic Adam placed the stone in its original position—the geomantic planetary node later called Mecca. During the Flood, the stone was hidden for safety in Abu Qubays, a nearby mountain; when Abraham built (or rebuilt—Adam is credited with constructing the first Ka-aba or House of God) the Ka-aba, Gabriel brought the stone back to Mecca. In 940 A.D., even after the stone had cracked, it was still deeply impressive to visitors: One traveler said it was of "an intense white color on its external side. Its blackness is said to be due—and God knows

best—to the touches and kisses it has received from the pagan Arabs and to [their] smearing it with blood." Cyril Glasse, *The Concise Encyclopedia of Islam* (San Francisco, CA: HarperSan Francisco, 1989): 77. F. E. Peters, *The Hajj: The Muslim Pilgrimage to Mecca and the Holy Places* (Princeton, NJ: Princeton University Press, 1994): 63–64.

247. The concept of humanity originating in another galaxy was suggested and graphically portrayed in the Brian de Palma film *Mission to Mars* (2000). The enigmatic Face on Mars (in the film, a mountain-sized carving of a feminine human-like face) was actually the housing for the last spaceship of an alien race who had otherwise left the inhospitable planet, made that way by meteorite bombardment. One astronaut volunteers to go with the alien race, and one of the last scenes in the film is of that ship speeding towards another galaxy, presumably the home of the "Martians" who, the film implies, were humanity's progenitors. In other words, humanity originated in another galaxy, the movie says. Movies of course are not history or even accurate metaphysics, but they can on occasion suggest or reflect new edges of thought or belief awakening or moving in Western culture.

248. The term "reciprocal maintenance" describes the interdependency among levels, realms, or dimensions of existence. The angelic world "above" us maintains the human; humanity (ideally) maintains the elemental kingdom "below" us. And we reciprocally maintain the angelic world by providing them with "angel food," purified, awakened human consciousness; the elemental kingdom maintains us with the "food" of a healthy, flourishing etheric energy mesh underlying the natural world. The term "sympathetic resonance" has a similar meaning: different physical objects vibrating at or maintaining a light frequency level that is in accord or "sympathy" with others, keeping them in continuous communication despite distance (as in Bell's theorem of nonlocality).

249. For more on the geomancy of Delphi, its Vibrating Stone, and myths, see Richard Leviton, *The Galaxy on Earth: A Traveler's Guide to the Planet's Visionary Geography*, 203–210.

250. Robert Graves and Raphael Patai, *Hebrew Myths: The Book of Genesis* (New York: Greenwich House/Arlington House, 1983): 57.

251. The breastplate itself was a square tablet or pouch of gold mixed with linen or wool worn on the priest's chest. The semiprecious jewels were set in the breastplate, engraved with the names of the 12 Tribes in Hebrew. Inside the pouch or the overall apronlike garment the priest wore, called the ephod, was the Urim and Tummim, an enigmatic esoteric device believed to be used to divine the future and produce oracular answers. Its exact nature, origin, and function, even the origin of the words themselves, have remained uncertain, though it has been associated with the Tribe of Levi as its ritual device or emblem.

252. Pangaia (or Pangaea) is a term used by both plate tectonics geologists and mystics to describe a postulated original single supercontinent in the earliest days of the Earth. The geological theory proposes that several giant continents (Gondwanaland, including Africa, India, Antarctica, Australia, New Guinea, New Zealand; Laurentia, including North America; Baltica, including most of Europe) collided and fused, forming a single massive landmass called Pangaea. See: Donald L. Blanchard, "The Formation of Pangaea: The Making of a Supercontinent," at: http://webspinners.com/dlblanc/tectonic/pangea.shtml.

253. Similarly, Bharata is India's egregor, and also that country's original name. You find clues to a landmass's egregor when you can find its earliest or original name, such as: Cymru (Wales); Prydein (England); Alba (Scotland). Sometimes, as with Bharata and Eriu, the country's name is the egregor's name.

254. Randy Lee Eickhoff, *The Sorrows* (New York: Forge/Tom Doherty Associates, 2000): 244.

255. Knowledge of a country's egregor helps one understand a people's behavior and characteristics; it also accounts for the prevalence of imagery, such as the American eagle or England's matron in national representations, heraldry, publications, or propaganda. On the white magic side of things, it is rumored that during World War II, English initiates called on England's egregor to psychically protect the island against invasion and excessive air attacks. Yet on the other hand it is rumored that the sixteenth-century English magus, astrologer, Qabalist, and adviser to Queen Elizabeth, John Dee, used magic of some kind to control the tutelary spirits (egregors) of certain nations according to the Queen's geopolitical

goals. Dennis William Hauck, *The Emerald Tablet: Alchemy for Personal Transformation* (New York: Penguin Compass, 1999): 25.

256. Willy Schrödter, *Commentaries on the Occult Philosophy of Agrippa* (York Beach, ME: Samuel Weiser, 2000): 127–129.

257. J. J. Hurtak, *The Book of Knowledge: The Keys of Enoch* (Los Gatos, CA: Academy for Future Science, 1977): 48, 49.

258. Rudolf Steiner developed the idea of the overshadowing Folk-Soul, though he did not use the term "egregor," but it seems defensible to say it would be an equivalent term. A Folk-Spirit does not have a form that can be externally perceived the way a physical human can be seen, "but is nevertheless an absolutely real being." He talked of "Folk-Spirits" who belonged to the order of archangels and who expressed what a specific nation was in essence, that the life of a people or folk was the "mission" of the presiding Folk Soul or Spirit. The Folk-Spirits direct the etheric body of humans living in their area of concern and "work in upon man and draw him into their own activity." Steiner also noted the different qualities of etheric auras over various geographical regions or even countries, how the one over Switzerland was notedly different from that over Norway or Denmark, for example. And that these areas "preserve throughout long periods a fundamental tone [and] they have something which continues throughout long ages." If a people migrate from that area, then the etheric aura changes in accordance. The human etheric body is "embedded in the folk's etheric body," and the Folk-Spirit's etheric body is "reflected in the folk temperament" as expressed by individuals living in that area. Germany and Holland originally had the same Folk-Soul, but a separation occurred; Spain and Portugal also once shared the same Folk-Soul, "formed one motherfolk" (which makes sense since the Iberian Peninsula is geographically one landmass, not two). The Folk-Souls (or nation egregors) had roles to play in world history, implementing changes and movements in the folk in accordance with recondite plans for human evolution held by beings that Steiner called Spirits of the Age. Rudolf Steiner, *The Mission of Folk-Souls* (London: Anthroposophical Publishing Company, 1929): 4, 9, 10, 16, 18, 38.

259. In a simplified sense, the old Roman notion of a *genius loci* (the "begetter") or spirit

guardian of a place is an apt equivalent term for egregors. The *genius* of a place could encompass a household, temple, group of people (Romans), a city (Rome), a province (Noricum), the Romans believed. All such localities had their own resident *genius*, or begetting and protecting spirit. The *genius loci* for the smaller space divisions would correspond to the subsidiary egregors and landscape angels reporting to the chief one for a landmass.

260. Z'ev ben Shimon Halevi, *A Kabbalistic Universe* (York Beach, ME: Samuel Weiser, 1977): 7, 8.

261. Polaris lies almost exactly on the Earth's axis of rotation, were you to draw a straight line indicating the alignment of Earth with this star. It's about 1 degree 14 minutes from the exact galactic North Pole, and it keeps getting closer; by 2095 A.D., it will be only 26 minutes 30 seconds from it.

262. This neatly confirms an equivalent statement though in different terms made earlier in this book: The Blazing Star, as the Ofanim, expressed as the star in the belly, at Avebury, or as Polaris (Dhruva), is the route to the Christ (Vishnu), aptly expressed in the image of the Star of Bethlehem guiding the Magi to the Christ. A variation in the Dhruva story has the holy sage Narada appear before the five-year-old, bearing his cymbals and tamboura and singing the glory of God. Narada gave Dhruva guidance in achieving his meeting with Vishnu. The elegance here is that Narada is a Ray Master, also known as Nada (Sound: Ray No. 3), and once as Mary Magdalene, the consort of Ray Master Jesus (Ray No. 6), the bearer of the Christ who, let us not forget, is the Word (the primal sound utterance). So of course Narada would be Dhruva's guide.

263. The Pole Star also has its bodily location around the belly button (*hara* or *dantian*), according to esoteric acupuncture. In Chinese nomenclature, acupoints around the abdomen at least were named after the Pole Star, indicating the ancient Chinese "chose to relate an area in the abdomen to the polar region of the heavens." Evidence exists that the ancient Chinese described the body's acupoints in accordance with a cosmological model using the vocabulary of astronomy and star names. "The Chinese envisioned a microcosmic universe in the body that mirrored the universe itself," and in this model the Pole Star was the "central coordinate" and other key stars were attributed to the region of the abdomen. Acupoint names in the abdomen also testify to its being the prime source of the body's vital energy and a regulator of many key rhythms known as the Ten Stems and 12 Celestial Branches. Kiiko Matsumoto and Stephen Birch, *Hara Diagnosis: Reflections on the Sea* (Brookline, MA: Paradigm Publications, 1988): 71, 75, 76.

264. "Bhagavata Purana," quoted in Giorgio de Santillana and Hertha von Dechend, *Hamlet's Mill: An Essay on Myth and the Frame of Time* (Boston: David R. Godine, 1977): 138.

265. Similarly, in Arab cosmography, the Pole Star (*Kotb*) was seen as the axle of an upper movable millstone that passes through the lower fixed one, the mill-iron. The sphere of heaven was conceived as a turning millstone perpetually grinding the "grain" of stars in the mill of the galaxy, as it were, with the Pole Star as the axle bearing in which the lower mill-iron turned.

266. "Bhagavata Purana," quoted in Richard L. Thompson, *Mysteries of the Sacred Universe: The Cosmology of the Bhagavata Purana* (Alachua, FL: Govardhan Hill Publishing, 2000): 17; and Richard L. Thompson, op. cit., 204.

267. In *The Galaxy on Earth*, I called this a Universe Dome Merudanda or Atlas Pillar. More research has yielded a more refined interpretation of this figure. The column, or Merudanda feature, is still there, but the function of the feature seems better described by referring to its task of *anchoring* the energy of Polaris. I use the Vedic star name Dhruva because the mythology of that star's pivot function is more pronounced in the Vedas than in the Western star lore and its ontological identity as a star god or celestial being implicit.

268. One of the peculiarities of the Earth's energy body is that it is not always geographically symmetrical and "rational." Alignments, at least today, are not always geographically rational or linear, but energetic. This means several parts of a geomantic unity may be in diverse locations such that if you "connected the dots" you would get a strange, lopsided figure. Yet the energy relationships are intact and primary. A partial explanation for this seeming divergence between alignment and symmetry may be the age of the planet and the way the physical planet has drifted somewhat in alignment with its energy body.

Chiropractors use the term "subluxation" to suggest a deviation in alignment of a vertebra from the spinal column; borrowing this term, I would propose the physical Earth is subluxated from its energy body, leading to strange geomantic deformities and of course a nearly global forgetting of the geomantic aspect of the planet.

269. The Germanic notion of the Atlas Pillar was the Irminsul, which is Old Saxon for "huge pillar" and possibly "pillar of the god Irmin," though no actual god of that description has been satisfactorily identified by mythographers. Here the sense of Irminsul is of the order of an *axis mundi* (world axis or cosmic pillar), a line of spiritual connection between the Earth and Heaven. At the Externsteine, a group of five towering limestone spires in northern Germany and regarded a prime holy site for that country, the Irminsul was said to once stand, until the Emperor Charlemagne (742–814 A.D.) cut it down to convert the heathen site.

270. "Culhwch and Olwen," in *The Mabinogi and Other Medieval Welsh Tales*, trans. Patrick K. Ford (Berkeley: University of California Press, 1977): 119–157.

271. Symbolically, the bull (one of Shiva's forms, as Nandin) stands for the Sun's generative force, male procreative strength, expressed in animal form as untamed strength bordering on the brutal when attacking; the Bull Apis was an incarnation of Osiris; Yahweh is the Bull of Israel, embodying Yahweh's might; Agni, the Hindu fire god, was called "the Mighty Bull"; the bull was considered the exhalation of Aditi, the all-embracing; the bull was the first created animal in Iranian thought; to the Romans, the bull was an attribute of Jupiter (Zeus); in Sumeria, Gudibir was the "Bull of Light" and Enlil was the "savage bull of the Earth and Sky." The boar is both a solar and lunar deity, exemplifying both masculine and feminine principles; as an animal, it is an aggressive, raging, ferocious type of energy, even to the extent that one scholar calls it "primarily a symbol of unreined savagery and the rule of diabolical forces." For the Celts, the sacrificial fire was called Boar of the Woods, its huge head representing preservation from danger, the vitality of the life force; Druids often called themselves Boars; the Egyptians saw the boar as an evil aspect of Seth; for the Hindus, it was Varahi, Vishnu's third incarnation, and also Vajravrahi,

the goddess of dawn and the Queen of Heaven; Iranian myth spoke of the "shining boar;" for the Norse, the bristles of goddess Freyr's boar, Gulliburstin, were the Sun's rays, and she rode it like a horse. The goat is interpreted as signifying masculinity, abundant vitality, virility, and creative energy; it can mean the devilish, lewdness, copulatory predilection, or a focus of blame, as in scapegoat (Hebrew-Christian), but for the Hindus it is the preferred animal of Agni who rides one and is favored by various goddesses such as the Greek Artemis and Pallas Athena; the goat is the source of nourishment, abundance, protection, and preservation, having sustained the infant Zeus. J. C. Cooper, *An Illustrated Encyclopedia of Traditional Symbols* (New York: Thames and Hudson, 1978): 22, 26–27, 74. Hans Biedermann, *Dictionary of Symbolism: Cultural Icons and the Meanings Behind Them*, trans. James Hulbert (New York: Meridian/Penguin, 1994): 45.

272. Rabbi Moses C. Luzzatto, *General Principles of the Kabbalah*, trans. The Research Centre of Kabbalah (New York: Samuel Weiser Press of the Research Centre of Kabbalah, 1970): 65.

273. Homer, *Odyssey*, trans. Robert Fitzgerald (New York: Farrar, Straus, and Giroux, 1998): Book VI:45–55, 100.

274. "Enki and the World Order," quoted in Samuel Noah Kramer, *History Begins at Sumer: Thirty-Nine Firsts in Recorded History* (Philadelphia: University of Pennsylvania Press, 1956): 93.

275. Ibid., 91, 92, 93, 291, 360.

276. The Japanese call it the Floating Bridge of Heaven that connected Heaven to Earth and down which the gods came when they first arrived on Earth. The two creator gods, Izanagi and Izanami, were said to have stood on this bridge when they stirred the etheric soup below to summon up the eight islands of Japan. The bridge belongs to the dance-goddess Uzume, who is married to the God of the Paths, the bridge's guardian, though he seems not to be named. Together, Uzume and this guardian would seem to comprise the Japanese equivalent of the Norse Heimdall. The Floating Bridge of Heaven (sometimes referred to as a rainbow bridge called Niji) is grounded on Earth at Mount Takachiho in Miyazaki Prefecture, in Japan, according to Japanese lore. This is a dome-shaped mountain (1,574 meters high) near Kirishima and Ebino and

is considered a sacred peak in Japan. You find a vestige of the Rainbow Bridge in the Greek god Iris, whose name means rainbow. She was Zeus's messenger, often dispatched from Olympus down to the human realm. In Iris we might see Bifrost condensed into a single mobile figure that connects the gods to Earth.

277. Jeremy Black and Anthony Green, *Gods, Demons, and Symbols of Ancient Mesopotamia: An Illustrated Dictionary* (Austin: University of Texas Press, 1992): 106, 130.

278. "Gilgamesh," in *Myths from Mesopotamia: Creation, the Flood, Gilgamesh, and Others,* ed. and trans. Stephanie Dalley (New York: Oxford University Press, 1989): 63, 71, 73, 323, 330.

279. Indra's realm is also called *Devapura* ("City of the Gods") and *Pusabhasa* ("Sun-Splendour"). The palace itself is called *Puskaramalini* and is described as a movable structure five leagues high, 100 leagues wide, and 150 leagues long. It is abundant with fragrant flowers, lotuses, thrones, holy trees, innumerable saints and gods, the sacred grove Nandana, a great store of celestial chariots, and 100 subsidiary palaces. Access to Amaravati is not only difficult, invisible to the sinful, but even the road to it is not easy of access, called the "path of the stars." The Vedic sensibility paints a younger, lusher Indra than old Greek Zeus. Indra is always 25 years old in appearance. Indescribably beautiful, he has yellow eyes and beard, wears golden chains, red bracelets, a diadem, white robes, and garlands that never collect dust. Two nymphs constantly fan him, and he is attended by 100 divine youths and singers, a white umbrella with a gold handle held over him. Indra is the god of 100 powers, lord of the Third Heaven, owner of the magical conch *Devadatta* and the bow *Ayudha*, and wielder of the world-destroying thunderbolt which instantly can split the head of a recalcitrant witness into 100 pieces.

280. *Classical Hindu Mythology: A Reader in the Sanskrit Puranas,* ed. and trans. Cornelia Dimmitt and J. A. B. van Buitenen (Philadelphia: Temple University Press, 1978): 53.

281. E. Washburn Hopkins, *Epic Mythology* (Dehli India: Motilal Banarsidass, 1974): 122–141.

282. It can still be indirect. My favorite color is blue, which is a ray, but the first Ray Master I worked with was Saint Germaine of the lilac ray. For information on relationships between color, color healing, and the Ray Masters, see: Irene Dalichow and Mike Booth, *Aura-Soma: Healing through Color, Plant, and Crystal Energy* (Carlsbad, CA: Hay House, 1996). See also: www.aura-soma.net.

283. Similarly, in the *Iliad*, it seems the Greek and Trojan heroes are the favorites of the various Olympian gods and that those gods orchestrated the ten-year conflict and managed—some would say manipulated—the battles and outcomes on an almost hourly basis. The story reconfigures along intriguing new lines if you think of the activities as initiation-directed, set in a geomantic temple (Troy has many key features), and guided by Ray Masters. The favorites of the gods become seen now as initiation proteges, ultimately under the sponsorship and aegis of the seven stars of the Great Bear.

284. Arthur Avalon, *The Serpent Power* (New York: Dover Publications, 1974): 113, 370.

285. Hathor was the Lady of the Pillar, depicted variously as a woman with cow's horns, as an actual cow, or as a woman with a cow headdress. The number of hidden and secret chambers at the Dendera temple "suggests a mystery cult" in Hathor's honor, and her worship as "Hathor of the Roses" seems to have been "essentially joyous." Certain crypts were clearly reserved for "secret rites of the goddess," and at least one was reserved as treasure room for a reputed huge necklace of Hathor, consisting of a collar and four totems. Margaret A. Murray, *Egyptian Temples* (Mineola, NY: Dover Publications, [1931], 2002): 53, 54, 56, 59, 61.

286. Glastonbury lore has it that this site, a long finger of land raised perhaps ten feet above ground level, 30 feet wide, extending perhaps a half-mile, was once known as the Golden Coffin or Bridge of the Sun, derived from *Pointes Baal* (or Bel, the Celtic name for the Sun-god). A sign at the site calls it *Pontis Vallum*, "the fort of the bridge," stating it once defended the Isles of Avalon from the mainland. Local maps call it Ponter's Ball.

287. Tomas, *The Promise of Power: Reflections on the Toltec Warrior's Dialogue from the Collected Works of Carlos Castaneda* (Charlottesville, VA: Hampton Roads, 1995): 388.

288. Whatever the explanation, once you're seated inside the tumulus, you turn around in

yourself and face the walls and the etheric aspect of the stones around you. Then you walk through one of them. I looked "through" one of the stones and saw a long stone avenue leading into a yellow light. Then for a moment I was observing this from a distance, and it seemed this tumulus and avenue were tunnels out of the physical world into Avalon or what the Celts called the Summer Country.

289. Lewis Carroll evokes the sensation of leaving the physical world and its cognitive parameters through a Pointer's Ball in the first chapter of *Alice's Adventures in Wonderland* called "Down the Rabbit-Hole." Alice follows an enigmatic White Rabbit who popped down a large rabbit-hole under a hedge. She felt she was falling down a very deep well, for the rabbit-hole seemed like a straight tunnel. "Either the well was very deep, or she fell very slowly, for she had plenty of time as she went down to look about her," Carroll writes. As she kept falling, Alice worried she would hit the center of the Earth, or even fall right through the Earth. She didn't; she landed in Wonderland, which is a fair term for the "train station" of the astral. Lewis Carroll, *The Complete Works of Lewis Carroll* (London: Nonesuch Press, 1939): 16, 17.

290. *The Prose Edda of Snorri Sturluson,* trans. Jean I. Young (Berkeley: University of California Press, 1984): 98.

291. The golden apples of the Garden of the Hesperides, explains an Irish adventurer in an old mythological story called "The Fate of the Children of Tuirenn," are the most rare and beautiful of fruits, "the size of a one-month-old infant." Burnished gold in color, they taste like honey. "They heal all wounds and malignant disease when eaten, and they can be eaten forever as one bite takes no substance away from them." See: "The Fate of the Children of Tuirenn," in Randy Lee Eickhoff, *The Sorrows* (New York: Forge/Tom Doherty Associates, 2000): 70.

292. One walker in Avalon reported encountering the legendary Fairy Queen of the Maze here, and he was given a golden apple with two silver leaves by his guide, a griffin, to eat as a preliminary "sacrament" before "entering the City of Revelation" atop the Tor. "The griffin warned me that the power of the fruit would enable me to view the surrounding environment with the full sight of the dragon's dimension," he commented

later of his expedition to Avalon. Gino Gennaro, *The Phenomena of Avalon: The Story of This Planet as Recounted by the Fairies* (London: Cronos Publications, 1979): 27, 31.

293. "Merddin's Avallenau," quoted in Mary Caine, *The Glastonbury Zodiac: Key to the Mysteries of Britain* (Torquay, UK: Grael Communications, 1978): 197, 198.

294. But it might also be the eponymous Teutonic goddess Ursa or Hörsel, after whom the mountain was named. This deity is also sometimes equated with the Teutonic Moon goddess Holda and later with the Christian saint, Ursula, who "legitimized" the pagan goddess. German poets used to envision Holda "sailing over the deep blue of the heavens in her silver boat," followed by a great company of maidens in the form of stars. As part of her nightly pilgrimage, she was believed to enter certain hills and be temporarily resident there, such as at the "sister" hill to the Venusberg called Ercildoune or Hill of Ursula in the south of Scotland. Lewis Spence, *Hero Tales and Legends of the Rhine* (New York: Dover Publications, 1995): 77, 78.

295. Vayu is always pictured as a man of white light riding a deer, and white flowers are his favorite. As a celestial being, Vayu is also shown as a formidable warrior with a broad chest and wearing war raiment, carrying a sharp spear and other weapons of gold. Or he is an antelope with 1,000 eyes to indicate his swiftness of movement and omniscience. Or he rides a golden chariot drawn by 1,000 horses or a chariot pulled by three deer.

296. The Egyptian counterpart appears to be the Field of A'aru (also called *Sekhet-Aaru,* or Field of Reeds, but sometimes simply Aar or Aal), a post-death paradisal realm, part of Amenti, the Underworld, situated in the West; it was near water and blessed with breezes, as the ancient texts say. Osiris and his retinue dwelled in A'aru, which was divided into 15 regions, each presided over by a god. Within the Field of Reeds was *Sekhet-hetep,* the Field of Offerings, where the souls resident obtained their celestial food.

297. Homer, *Odyssey,* trans. Robert Fagles (New York: Viking/Penguin Group, 1996): 230–231.

298. Calliope ("fair voice") inspires epic poetry; Clio ("renown," the proclaimer), history; Euterpe ("gladness," giver of pleasure), flute-playing; Terpsichore ("joy in the dance," the

whirler), lyric poetry and dance; Erato ("lovely"), lyric and erotic poetry and songs; Melpomene ("singing"), tragedy; Thalia ("abundance, good cheer," the flourishing), comedy; Polyhymnia ("many songs"), mime or religious poetry and sound; and Urania ("heavenly"), astronomy.

299. The Muses, Hesiod wrote, who claimed they taught him the art of poetry on Mount Helicon when he was a sheep herder, are Zeus's nine daughters, born on Mount Pieria of "harmonious mind, carefree maidens whose hearts yearn for song." Their lovely voices extol the laws and wisdom of the immortals and "thrilled" the heart of Zeus; they inspire the speech of kings such that they pour "sweet dew" on their tongues so that words flow effortlessly, "honey-sweet." The Muses soothe human troubles and make mortals forget their cares. Hesiod, *Theogony*, trans. Apostolos N. Athanassakis (Baltimore: Johns Hopkins University Press, 1983): 14–15.

300. C. Kerenyi, *The Gods of the Greeks* (New York: Thames & Hudson, 1980): 104–105.

301. Harish Johari, *Chakras* (Rochester, VT: Destiny Books, 1987): 66.

302. Ibid., 68.

303. Traditionally, a griffin is described as having a lion's body, an eagle's head, a bird's wings, and an eagle's claws. It was widely represented in Persian art; the Assyrians referred to a similar creature they called a 'krub; Apollo rode a griffin; and Alexander the Great was said to have harnessed two griffins to his throne and flown with them for seven days into the heavens until being turned back by an angel.

304. According to the genealogies in Greek myths, Zeus plus the Titaness Pluto produced Tantalus. Tantalus plus Dione (a daughter of the Titan Atlas and the Oceanid Pleione = a daughter of the Pleiades; this couple produced seven daughters, known as the Pleiades), produced Pelops, father of Atreus, father of Agamemnon (father of Orestes, Electra, and Iphigeneia) and Menelaus. In this one family lineage going back to celestial parentage we witness a great portion of Greek tragedy as well as a main factor in the Trojan War. Agamemnon sacrifices his daughter, Iphigeneia, to please the gods to provide wind so his ships and those of his brother, Menelaus, can make it to Troy to reclaim Menelaus's abducted wife, Helen.

305. I experienced this firsthand as part of my encounter with the griffin at the Sanctuary near Avebury. This being, who appeared to me as a standing winged lion perhaps ten feet tall, conducted me into a pale-green-olivish landscape, which the Ofanim later identified as a planet within the Pleiades system. Since the Pleiadians, as Hyperboreans, were, with some other star families, instrumental in the earliest installation of the Earth's visionary geography (refer back to chapter 2 and the Blue Room discussion), it makes sense they would have "brought" and left some of their key devices, objects, and assistants including griffins.

306. I call it the Glastonbury Tor Griffin Gold Reserve, but this is not quite accurate topographically. It is situated in a valley at the base of the land rise that culminates in the Tor. There is a lovely green curving slope behind the sections of Glastonbury called Paradise and Stone Down and facing another part called Gog and Magog (the vestiges of two ancient oak trees with those names). At the base of this long gentle slope (it goes about 150 feet down to ground level) and inside the hill, you will find the Griffin Gold Reserve. When I say "inside the hill," I mean inside its etheric or subtle counterpart.

307. This fact goes a long way towards accounting for the intense interest of alien intelligences in the affairs of this planet through what we popularly call UFO visitations. It also puts the following statement by the Ofanim in relief: "There are on this planet many, many different types of beings, probably a greater variety at different states of evolution than anywhere else in the conceptual universe."

308. There are, for example, eight physical attainments. You can become as small as an atom, have no weight, become immensely large, be very heavy, be transported anywhere, have your wishes fulfilled, control all creatures and elements, have lordship over all things. These suprahuman powers are acquired through mastery of yoga, which includes breath, energy, and mind control. Further, the adept gains such "bodily perfections" of appearance, charm, strength, and firmness that "his body acquires such divine beauty that god, man, and beast are charmed." If you reread some of the very old myths, such as *Mahabharata, Ramayana,* and the Irish sagas of Cuchulainn and other heroes in this light, their otherwise unbelievable physical exploits start to seem plausible. There are also 30 subsidiary

attainments, equally formidable. You gain mental control, knowledge of previous births, the ability to read minds; can be invisible; know things at a distance; understand death, the celestial spheres, and heavenly worlds; be free of hunger and thirst; perceive supernatural beings; come and go from your body; levitate—and there are still more spiritual attainments that deliver you into an enlightened state. Alain Danielou, *Yoga: Mastering the Secrets of Matter and the Universe* (Rochester, VT: Inner Traditions International, 1991): 153–155.

309. As one writer on sacred sites commented, referring to Mount Kataragama in Sri Lanka, "the very place remains *connected* [italics added] through living myths or legends that happen in principio, i.e, not at a unique unrepeatable moment in past history, but always in the eternal here-and-now." Patrick Harrigan, "Kailasa to Kataragama: Sacred Geography in the Cult of Skanda-Murukan," *Journal of the Institute of Asian Studies* 15:2 (March 1998): 33–52.

310. The *Kalpa* or *Kalpataru* is described in Tantra as the celestial wishing-tree or wish-fulfilling tree, one of the trees in Indra's heavens, and credited with granting whatever one wishes for through its agency. Sometimes it bestows even more than the supplicant asks for, the yogic texts say.

311. Arthur Avalon, *The Serpent Power* (New York: Dover Publications, 1974): 383.

312. *Ginnungagap* means the "cup of illusion," the abyss of the great deep, or the shoreless, yawning gulf that has no end or beginning. In esoteric parlance this connotes the "'World's Matrix,' the primordial living space." It is the cup that contains the universe, hence the name, cup of illusion. H. P. Blavatsky, *The Theosophical Glossary* (Los Angeles: Theosophy Company, [1892], 1990): 128. *Ginnungagap* also means, loosely interpreted, the void filled with magical and creative powers. It's where life began and where the world and all its aspects were created out of the primordial giant, Ymir, which formed when sparks from Muspelheim fell onto the ice of *Ginnungagap* to generate Ymir's body.

313. Let's remember the Ofanim characterized Eden as an empty space in which Creation could unfold. This is similar to the Norse conception of the cosmic void called *Ginnungagap*. Snorri Sturluson records the names of 11 rivers that flow out of Hvergelmir (the Elivagar rivers): Svöl (Cool), Gunnthra (Battle-defiant), Fjörm (the

one in a hurry), Fimbulthul (Loud-bubbling), Slid (Fearsome), Hrid (Storming), Sylgr (Devourer), Ylgr (She-wolf), Vid (Broad), Leipt (Fast-as-lightning), and Gjöll (Loud noise).

314. The Greek equivalent are the Moirai, the Fates, or daughters of Nyx (Night), three females who weave the destiny of humans. Their names are Clotho (the spinner), Lachesis (the drawing of lots), and Atropos (inevitable).

315. "So in the greatest church of London (whether it were Paul's or not the French book maketh no mention)," wrote Sir Thomas Malory of the young Arthur's Sword in the Stone trial. According to the Ofanim, the London site was the place now occupied by Saint Paul's Cathedral on Ludgate Hill. Arthur's Stone was a great stone like marble, four foot square, next to the high altar, and on it a steel anvil one foot high with the sword stuck through it. The first known structure on this site was built in approximately 604 A.D., a presumed wooden church to honor the consecration of Mellitus, bishop of the East Saxons, by Saint Augustine of Canterbury. A total of five churches have been successively built there since 604 A.D. Sir Thomas Malory, *Le Morte d'Arthur*, vol. 1, ed. Janet Cowen (New York: Penguin Books, 1969): 15, 16.

316. June G. Bletzer, *The Donning International Encyclopedic Psychic Dictionary* (Norfolk, VA: Donning Company, 1986): 261.

317. C. G. Jung, *Answer to Job*, trans. R. F. C. Hull (Princeton, NJ: Princeton University Press, 2002): 86.

318. In later Germanic myth, Frigg was often equated with Venus who was understood as the Latin equivalent such that *dies Veneris* (Latin) melded into the Old High German *friatac* and the Old English *frigedaeg*, to eventually become Friday, the sixth named day of the Western week. The Balder-Venus insinuation is furthered by the fact that the Norse name his "wife" as Nanna, a deity inadequately characterized by Norse mythographers. Scholars tend to associate her (due to similarity in name) with the Sumerian Inanna, Nannar (Babylonian Ishtar), and Nana, mother of the Phrygian dying god, Attis, all of whom have Venus connotations.

319. Lom is a beautiful and arresting site, a large tourist town at the apex of a triangle made by the River Otta curving round it and the Jotunheim (of mythic fame: home of the Jotunn,

Frost Giants) behind it. In fact, 90 percent of the Lom municipality is covered by glaciers and mountains. Lom has an invigorating ambiance, combining the market savvy of a tourist town with an unspecific but definite sparkle of numinosity set in a pristine environment.

320. Jesus is quoted as having made the comment that the Kingdom of Heaven "is like unto a merchant man seeking goodly pearls, who, when he found one pearl of great price, went and sold all that he had and bought it" (Matthew 13:45–6). The expression "pearl of great price" has come to signify the high desirability of practicing a spiritual life that leads to the experience of the Kingdom of Heaven, and its high cost. Paradoxically, it often seems the closer you get to obtaining this pearl, the more it costs. Proximity raises the price. But the term has an inner, developmental meaning, too, according to the Ofanim: "When enough insight is gathered within the sixth chakra, then the drop or wish-fulfilling gem falls from the pineal gland to the pituitary and the pearl of great price is born."

321. This is Rudolf Steiner's term for the entire planetary initiation and Mystery event of the Christ incarnation, baptism, transfiguration, crucifixion, resurrection, and ascension, the externalization of the entirety of previous Mystery initiations.

322. In biblical tradition, this was the furnished second-story chamber in which Jesus and his Apostles took the Last Supper, the night before his arrest. However, some Christian mystics have construed this in a more metaphysical sense to connote the upper, as in higher dimensional or subtler realm-based, aspects of consciousness, in the crown chakra or above, in which one silently, perhaps even nonverbally, encounters God. As part of his design for Chalice Well in Glastonbury, Wellesley Tudor Pole allocated the second floor of one of the buildings (the Little Saint Michael Hostel, he called it in 1959) to be known as the Upper Room. This would be a place for inner-plane spiritual contacts, revelations of the Grail mysteries, and other sublime events in consciousness. See his chapter "The Upper Room," in Wellesley Tudor Pole and Rosamond Lehmann, *A Man Seen Afar* (Sudbury: Neville Spearman, 1965).

323. E. A. Wallis Budge, *The Gods of the Egyptians*, vol. 2 (New York: Dover Publications, 1969): 202.

324. The Chinese say that in the beginning was a huge egg containing chaos; all the polarities were jumbled together inside that single egg. The Egyptians recognized a Mundane Egg that came from the mouth of the unmade, eternal deity Kneph; they also record that Ptah was a godly potter who shaped the Cosmic Egg on his wheel and that Seb and his consort, Nut, produced the Cosmic Egg at Heliopolis out of which they birthed the Sun-God Ra. The Egg of Babylon hatched Ishtar and fell from Heaven into the Euphrates. The Pelasgian Greeks say Eurynome, the Goddess of All Things, took the form of a dove and, brooding on the waves of the cosmic sea, laid the Universal Egg; Ophion (or Boreas), the cosmic serpent, entwined it seven times until it hatched and out came all of Creation.

325. G. de Purucker, *Fountain-Source of Occultism*, ed. Grace F. Knoche (Pasadena, CA: Theosophical University Press, 1974): 114.

326. Arthur Avalon, *The Serpent Power* (New York: Dover Publications, 1974): 334.

327. Willy Schrödter, *History of Energy Transference: Exploring the Foundations of Modern Healing* (York Beach, ME: Samuel Weiser, 1999): 95.

328. Manly Hall, *Man: The Grand Symbol of the Mysteries* (Los Angeles: Philosophical Research Society, 1972): 76, 77.

329. Ibid.

330. Humans are "in essence bubbles of luminescent energy; each of us is wrapped in a cocoon," he explained. We are "egglike luminous creatures." The luminous body around the human is "a cocoon that gives us the appearance of giant luminous eggs." Some of the luminous eggs Castaneda reported seeing were oblong "blobs of white light, seven feet high by four feet wide. Yet he also stated that the "egglike shape is an external cocoon, a shell of luminosity" that contains a core of "concentric circles of yellowish luminosity, the color of a candle's flame." The luminosity of the eggs in fact emanates from this brilliant "mesmeric" core, and the eggshell must be broken from the inside to liberate that inner being, which Castaneda suggested was the true human identity, the "other self" and "totality of oneself." Carlos Castaneda, *The Fire from Within* (London: Century Publishing, 1984): 10, 50, 115, 220. —*The Eagle's Gift* (New York: Simon and Schuster, 1981): 24, 46, 223.

331. David Adams Leeming, with Margaret Adams Leeming, *A Dictionary of Creation Myths* (New York: Oxford University Press, 1994): 49.

332. The first human couple, Askar (male) and Embla (female), emerged from his armpits, while the Frost Giants grew from between his toes. The gods created Midgard, or Middle Earth, from Ymir's corpse after he died; his flesh became the Earth, his blood the seas, lakes, and rivers; the mountains were made from his bones; rocks, pebbles, and boulders came from Ymir's teeth; the grass, trees, and vegetation formed from his hair; and his cranium became the arching dome of the Heavens and his brain the passing clouds. Yggdrasil grew from him. Finally, the gods used Ymir's prodigious eyebrows to form a protective perimeter around Midgard to keep out the Frost Giants. Like P'an Ku, Ymir's sacrificial body birthed the entirety of our world out of the icy Cosmic Egg.

333. His multiple heads formed the sky, his feet became the Earth, his navel the air; from his limbs came mortal beings. Purusha was understood to be the physical manifestation of Brahma, and, after floating for 1,000 years on the cosmic ocean, he shattered the golden Cosmic Egg.

334. Patricia Turner and Charles Russell Coulter, *Dictionary of Ancient Deities* (New York: Oxford University Press, 2000): 392–393.

335. God's height is 236 myriad thousand leagues, or 236,000 myriad parasangs; from His right arm to left is 77 myriads; from left to right eyeball, 30 myriads; from His throne to His head 118, and from throne to feet, also 118 myriad parasangs. Yet it's said the height of His soles measures 30 million parasangs. A parasang is three miles, and a myriad is 10,000 miles, so to say God is 236,000 myriad parasangs high means He is thus 7,008,000,000 miles tall.

336. Gershom Scholem, *Major Trends in Jewish Mysticism* (New York: Schocken Books, 1946): 64.

337. Robert B. Clarke, *The Four Gold Keys: Dreams, Transformation of the Soul, and the Western Mystery Tradition* (Charlottesville, VA: Hampton Roads, 2002): 25.

338. The number 666 is traditionally associated with the Sun, although Christian interpretation has sullied the waters, giving it a negative, demonic gloss as the "Number of the Beast." In medieval magic and occultism, the Magic Square of the Sun consisted of six rows of numbers, each of which totalled 111; the sum of the six rows totalled 666. This was understood as representing or encoding some aspects of the active power of the Sun, especially as the numbers were co-expressed as Hebrew letters, thereby yielding a pronunciation, invocatory table. 666 represents the cosmic yang, or active, "male," rational principle of "unbridled solar power." John Michell, *The Dimensions of Paradise: The Proportions and Symbolic Numbers of Ancient Cosmology* (San Francisco: Harper & Row, 1988): 185–193.

339. The number 1,080 is considered a lunar, yin, "female," passive, watery number, hence the attribution of Horus' Left Eye to the Moon. This number is actually the radius of our Moon in miles, while silver, the metal traditionally associated with the Moon, has an atomic weight of 108. The pentagon (five-sided figure with equal sides), which is taken to be the geometric image of this principle, has angles of 108 degrees between its five sides. The number 1,080 also denotes the Holy Spirit, the Earth Spirit, the inspirational, intuitive side of the mind. Thanks to John Michell for this analysis. John Michell, *The Dimensions of Paradise: The Proportions and Symbolic Numbers of Ancient Cosmology* (San Francisco: Harper & Row, 1988): 180–184.

340. He was *Hor-sa-iset* (Son of Isis); *Horu-Sema-Tawy*, "The Horus, Uniter of the Two Lands" of Upper and Lower Egypt, which means the southern and northern halves, respectively. One of Horus's oldest names was simply *Har*, "the High" or "the Far-Off," a usage found in hieroglyphs dating back to 3000 B.C. Horus, the manifestation of the living king, his falcon wings outstretched, was the protector of all Egypt and its pharaohs. Sometimes he was depicted as a winged Sun disk that scouted the land for demons and enemies of the Pharaoh. Horus was Lord of the Sky and God of the East, which is why he was personified as the rising sun.

341. Here are more epithets and qualities attributed to Horus drawn from the legend of Horus of Behutet (Edfu), the Winged Disk, as recorded on the temple walls at Edfu in Egypt: Horus flew up to the horizon as a great winged disk; he attacked his enemies with great force; he shone with diverse colors; his palace is called Sweet Life and Lord of the District which is Cleansed; he cut off the head of Egypt's enemy;

he smites all of Egypt's enemies (forces of darkness, enemies of the Light typified by Seth's crocodiles and hippopotamuses); he is in the form of a man of mighty strength; his face is that of a hawk; he wears the Red Crown and the White Crown; he is the master fighter; he stands with his blacksmiths, the mesneti, with his metal lance, dagger, mace, and chains; he lights up the Two Lands by the splendour of his Eyes; he is the great hawk who flies through Heaven, Earth, and the Duat (Osiris's Underworld). E. A. Wallis Budge, *Legends of the Egyptian Gods* (New York: Dover Publications, [1912] 1994): 56–95, 189.

342. The number 1,746, the sum of 666 and 1,080, represents the number of fusion and balance between the fiery, active, positive male aspect and the watery, passive, negative female aspect. By way of Greek gematria, 1,746 is called the "grain of mustard seed" in Western mystery tradition because though the smallest of seeds, from it sprang the universal tree and all the living things that inhabit it. This is another way of saying the *Hiranyagarbha*, the golden seed, germ, or embryo from which *Bala Brahma*, the golden divine child, son of Brahma, is born. Again, through Greek gematria, 1,746 refers to the fertilized seed, the Universal Spirit, the primal germ, the Hidden Spirit, Treasure of Jesus, Jerusalem, Glory of the God of Israel, Divinity of Spirit, Chalice of Jesus, Son of Virgin Mary, and others. Again, thanks to John Michell for this analysis. John Michell, *The Dimensions of Paradise: The Proportions and Symbolic Numbers of Ancient Cosmology* (San Francisco: Harper & Row, 1988): 193–194.

343. The Greeks left us with a vivid alternative description of the hatching or birth of Horus the Elder. Dionysus was born in the Cadmeia, the ancient citadel-temple established by Cadmus, the founder of ancient Thebes in Greece. His mother, Semele (sometimes interpreted to mean Moon), was impregnated by Zeus in the form of a lightning flash while she lay in the Cadmeia. She died, then in the same moment Dionysus was born. Thereafter, Thebes was renowned throughout classical Greece as the preeminent Dionysian mystery center, and Euripides deepened that reputation through his tragedy *The Bacchae.* This city lacks initiation in my mysteries, Dionysus (the Roman Bacchus; the Greek Horus) declares in that play, and he vows to vindicate his mother's death by revealing his godhead to all of Thebes, despite the resistance of its king. He declares that he taught his whirling dances, drove his women deliriously mad with intoxicated frenzy (the Maenads), and established his mysteries and rites "that I might be revealed on earth for what I am: a god." A "consummate god, most terrible, and yet most gentle, to mankind," he adds. *The Bacchae,* trans. William Arrowsmith, in *Euripides V, The Complete Greek Tragedies,* ed. David Grene and Richmond Lattimore (Chicago: University of Chicago Press, 1959): 156, 193.

344. E. A. Wallis Budge, *Legends of the Egyptian Gods* (New York: Dover Publications, [1912] 1994): 88, 89.

345. They wore fawn skins, carried flaming torches and *thyrsoi* (*thyrsus*: a staff wrapped in grapevines or ivy stems and crowned with pine cones). The Maenads triumphally accompanied Dionysus when he shifted Mystery centers from Lydia to Greece, and usually when he "arrived" at any new votive site. Dionysus's arrival can be seen here as the hatching of a Silver Egg at the new location, each site becoming a new shrine. In one account, Dionysus-Zagreus was torn limb from limb, utterly to pieces, by the Titans, who then devoured all of him except for his heart, which Pallas Athena rescued and returned to Semele to eat. Thus Dionysus was conceived afresh, just like the Egyptian phoenix that would incinerate itself then reshape itself afresh and whole from the ashes.

346. The theme of a riddle test is present in the film *Mission to Mars* (2000). The astronauts must complete a DNA model depicting the human being to be allowed entry into the Face on Mars temple. The logic of the test is that only humans (and in this case, scientifically advanced ones, knowledgeable in the human genome) could answer this question. It's the Theban sphinx's question again: Are you human? Prove it by your self-awareness and recognition of what makes a human human.

347. David Sacks, *A Dictionary of the Ancient Greek World* (New York: Oxford University Press, 1995): 84, 136.

348. The Self is not knowable, not in the way that we, in our ego-based personalities, know something. C. G. Jung said it was a "hypothetical summation," a symbolic indication of an "indescribable totality." The Self organizes our

everyday reality, sending us messages in the form of synchronicities and meaningful correspondences; it orchestrates our change, even when we don't want it. It's our "unknown and unknowable partner," and we realize, eventually, that our ego, our everyday-world personality, is but "a relatively subordinate executor of an unconsciously prespecified plan." Edward C. Whitmont, *The Symbolic Quest: Basic Concepts of Analytical Psychology* (Princeton, NJ: Princeton University Press, 1991): 216–221.

349. Their full manifestation package is 1,080 to the third power = 1,259,712,000.

350. The first time a colleague and I experienced the Seraphim "in conversation," my friend commented: "These Seraphim sound like drunken elves, the way their voices ride a roller coaster up and down the octave." Of themselves, the Seraphim comment: "We only come in this way because our vibration is one that oscillates, and this is a means for you to see and experience the energy oscillation that is the nature of our sphere. Each human has access within a part of their higher being bodies to at least two Seraphim, but some who are more developed may have access to many more, to 1,080 in all. When the Master Christ was on Earth, he had 1,080 Seraphim accompanying him in constant presence."

351. Their Celtic name is the Morrigan, a trio of furious war goddesses named Morrigna, Badb, and Macha. The Irish word and its variations, Morrighan, Mor-Riogain, Morrigu, mean approximately "great queen or phantom queen." She doesn't fight in battles but affects the combatants psychologically by way of her (or their) frightful appearance; she can shape-shift into a crow, fish, or animal form and is said to live in the cave of Cruachain in Roscommon County, Ireland. The Morrigan is considered an ally of the Irish high gods, or enlightened beings, called Tuatha de Danann. She challenged and obstructed the Irish hero Cuchulainn continuously, finally appearing as a death omen in the form of a hooded crow perched on his shoulder, signaling her readiness to scavenge his corpse.

352. These scholars were inspired in part by a reference by the British antiquarian John Leland in 1542 who declared: "At the very south end of the church of South Cadbyri standeth Camallate, sometime a famous town or castle. The people can tell nothing there but they have heard say Arthur much resorted to Camallate." The more mythologically minded favor the old Celtic folktales that Arthur and his knights still lie sleeping inside the hollow hill or cave of Cadbury Castle awaiting the trumpets that will sound the time for their revival and Arthur's return to Britain. Or that on certain occasions the knights gallop out of the hill and down Arthur's Hunting Causeway, advance, if ghostly, maneuvers for Arthur's return. Locally, in the sixteenth century, people called the hill Arthur's Palace. Leslie Alcock, *'By South Cadbury Is That Camelot . . .' The Excavation of Cadbury Castle, 1966–1970* (London: Thames and Hudson, 1972): 11.

353. In C. G. Jung's depth psychology interpretation of alchemy, this stage is the *nigredo*. It's a disassembling process; you take yourself apart; you experience psychological dismemberment. You undergo the *separatio* or *solutio*, the separation of the primal elements of the psyche. You isolate the black *prima materia*, separating out the male and female elements, the polarities of the personality. Jung identified the *prima materia* with the primal Self, "which contains all the archetypal potential and all the dynamic oppositions necessary to achieve the goal both of the opus [the alchemical term for the "Great Work"] and of individuation." The *nigredo* is black because it is primal, without light, the original unilluminated chaos, and it can symbolize the depression or melancholy that "commonly begins the process of self-examination and brings people into [depth] analysis." Anthony Stevens, *Ariadne's Clue: A Guide to the Symbols of Humankind* (Princeton, NJ: Princeton University Press, 1998): 237, 238.

354. Maurice Nicoll, *The New Man: An Interpretation of Some Parables and Miracles of Christ* (New York: Penguin Books, 1967): 5.

355. What ancient contract? From the gnomes' point of view, humans in essence are each miniature expressions of Ymir out of whose skin they originally crawled into the world. As Ymir, our scope of consciousness and identity once included all of the angelic and elemental realms. When we stepped into matter to inhabit the physical world, there was a three-way split in our being. The angelic part went above, the elemental part went below, and we condensed ourselves into our human forms, gradually forgetting that the angels above and the elementals below

(around us) were once part of who we are, equal parts of our original cosmic being. Where once there had been one Human, now there were angels, elementals, and human beings in bodies.

The angelic side remembers Heaven; the elemental side remembers Earth or Nature; and we are in the middle, forgetting, even denying, both. Humans projected the gnomes and other elementals out into the world to help maintain it. We asked them to specialize in the transformation of Earth energies on our behalf, to help maintain the energetic parameters suitable for conscious evolution. Some years ago one of my gnome colleagues explained it this way:

"You looked outside yourself for the world. You forgot the mirror that showed you how you contain the entire world. We are an aspect of your memory, at large in the world you created. We remember. We remember for you. That is our part of the ancient contract. We are part of your body. As you reclaim yourself, you remember us and we rejoin you in your body of light."

356. Norse myth recounts that the dwarves (gnomes) were ruled by a king variously known as Andvari, Alberich, Elbegast, Gondemar, Laurin, or Oberon. He lived in a magnificent underground palace studded with precious gems.

357. The Dovrë-King discusses the quality of life in his hall, the pitfalls of Christian culture, and says "we troll-folk, my son, are less black than we're painted," meaning less fearsome, frightening, and infernal. Musicians play harps, and the younger trolls "tread the Dovrë-hall's floor." As things progress, Peer Gynt falls out of resonance and understanding with the trolls, and they start regarding him as a threat. The Dovrë-King tells him, "It's easy to slip in here, but the Dovrë-King's gate doesn't open outwards." Peer Gynt is attacked by the troll-imps, and he is only rescued when bells sound in the mountains, causing the trolls to take flight amidst shrieks and an uproar of yells. Then the troll palace collapses and everything disappears and Peer Gynt is once more in the Rondane Mountains, but it's nighttime and he's lost and confused. Henrik Ibsen, *Peer Gynt*, trans. William and Charles Archer (New York: Heritage Press, 1957): 74–98.

358. Marko Pogacnik, *Nature Spirits and Elemental Beings: Working with the Intelligence in Nature* (Forres, Scotland: Findhorn Press, 1995): 188–191.

359. Marko Pogacnik, *Earth Changes, Human Destiny: Coping and Attuning with the Help of the Revelation of Saint John* (Forres, Scotland: Findhorn Press, 2000): 50, 51.

360. He observed a "deeply rooted relationship" between the elementals of an area and the "'higher' spiritual-soul level of the landscape," that the elementals, in effect led by the dwarves or gnomes, would build up a nature temple area in accordance with preexisting "cosmograms" or divine plans, as long as humans helped. But when landscapes were severely altered or destroyed, and their nature temple areas neglected and ruined, "the suppression of the structure of a landscape temple would cause great suffering among the elementals." Marko Pogacnik, *Nature Spirits and Elemental Beings: Working with the Intelligence in Nature* (Forres, Scotland: Findhorn Press, 1995): 94.

361. I have not yet found any other references to the Mephibians. This information comes directly from the Ofanim.

362. The gnomes are "the light-filled preservers of world-understanding within the earth," Rudolf Steiner wrote. They are a compendium of understanding and have direct perception of what happens in the world; they are the bearers of the ideas of the universe. They actually hate and distrust the earthly element and are constantly trying to tear themselves free from it. The "earthly threatens them with a continual danger," that if they "grow too strongly together with the earth" it will force them into amphibian forms. For them, wandering about inside the body of the planet, "the whole earth-body is primarily a hollow space through which they can pass." They "penetrate everywhere," through rocks, metals, chalk, gems—nothing hinders them. Instead, they perceive a space in which they have an inner experience of, for example, gold, mercury, or tin. "Everything in the universe is revealed to them; as though in a mirror they experience everything which is outside in the universe." Rudolf Steiner, *Man as Symphony of the Creative Word*, trans. Judith Compton-Burnett (London: Rudolf Steiner Press, 1970): 121–123, 149–150.

363. Meteorologists divide the Earth's atmosphere, or blanket of enveloping air, into four levels: 1) troposphere, from the planet's surface to five to nine miles high; 2) stratosphere, for the next 22 to 26 miles, up to 31 miles above the

Earth; 3) mesosphere, for the next 22 miles, extends up to 53 miles above the Earth; and 4) the thermosphere, which extends another 319 miles, to 372 miles above the planet.

364. Page Bryant described something possibly similar or identical to these "sky caves," a subtle atmospheric feature she called a "synthesizer vortex" or "atmospheric vortex." These are "originating points of weather fronts . . . located above certain areas of the Earth." There are 16 of them. These features sustain the Earth's electromagnetic balance between the North and South magnetic poles, and they originate the weather, such as the one over Vancouver, British Columbia, which, Bryant writes, "generates what will become high- and low-pressure systems that pass over the continent." Page Bryant, *Terravision: A Traveler's Guide to the Living Planet Earth* (New York: Ballantine Books, 1991): 45.

365. The Blue Dish is created from the energy field of the Ofanim perceived as a single point of blazing light at the center of the being of the geomancer. Through concentration, the Star goes supernova or explodes, generating in its place a pale blue sphere; the bottom half of the sphere is "sliced off" from the whole, and, slightly flattened out to more resemble a shallow tea saucer than a half sphere, it is placed under a landscape feature to be a collection dish for cosmic and angelic energies. It also enables energy and information from the Earth site to be reflected upwards to the celestial and/or cosmic equivalent of this site. In other words, the Blue Dish is a means for reciprocal interaction between a physical site and its cosmic antecedent. The dish can be of any size, though typically they would have diameters of one-half to several miles, even up to ten or 20 miles when required. Long ago the planet was floriated with thousands of Blue Dishes, a pristine global condition I like to call "morning glory planet" as the multiple Blue Dishes, seen from above, resemble freshly opened blue morning glories. Today, in the early twenty-first century, the Earth is greatly in need of having its Blue Dishes redone; most of the many thousands of geomantic sites are lacking in functional Blue Dishes due to the fact they have not been renewed for many millennia.

366. The four elements of course are fire, air, water, and earth, but in their subtler, archetypal formations first, then later in their gross, tangible aspects as we know them. Their subtler aspects in a sense are the lives and experiences of the respective nature spirits, such as the gnomes (earth) and sylphs (air), a few details of whose collective lives we have visited already in this chapter. The qualities are what the Vedas called the three *gunas: sattva, rajas,* and *tamas*—three fundamental dispositions of matter pertaining to light, activity, and inactivity, respectively. Western astrology uses the more abstract terms cardinal, mutable, and fixed signs, respectively. You get a Round Table of 12 qualities (each element expressed through the three *gunas*).

367. Individuation is a central term in Jungian thought. C. G. Jung defined it as a task of "integrating the unconscious, in bringing together 'conscious' and 'unconscious.'" It is "a process or course of development arising out of the conflict between the two fundamental psychic facts." These two facts are the coexistence of the "rational" conscious and "chaotic" unconscious as aspects of the human psyche, a relationship subject to "open conflict and open collaboration at once." C. G. Jung, *Symbols of Transformation,* trans. R. F. C. Hull, Bollingen Series XX (Princeton, NJ: Princeton University Press, 1976): 301. *—The Archetypes and the Collective Unconscious,* Second Edition, Bollingen Series XX, trans. R. F. C. Hull, (Princeton, NJ: Princeton University Press, 1980): 288–289.

368. Celtic myth recalls him as the heroic if tragically fated king of the Britons who unified the Celts against the invading Saxons in the sixth century A.D. Hundreds of books and novels have been written about his deeds and the deeds of those around him; it is a saga of fights, betrayals, epiphanies, and wonder. He established Camalate, created the Round Table, sponsored the Grail Quest, was deceived and seduced by his aunt Morgause, and mortally wounded in combat with his bastard son, Mordred, in the Battle of Camlann, after which Arthur was ferried into Avalon and the hollow hills by his sister, Morgan, and two others, there to await some future time when his services were needed

369. The Egyptian Horus is also depicted as a smith, as at Edfu, but this is a confusing picture. In Edfu along the River Nile, Horus, son of Osiris and Isis, was known as the "lord of the forge-city," and Edfu itself was a *mesnet,* or foundry, where ore was smelted and weapons forged. Horus first

established himself in Egypt as a godly blacksmith at Edfu, the site also of where Horus defeated his arch enemy, Apophis (Apep), the Egyptian equivalent of the Greek Typhon. Horus's followers and assistants were called *mesniti*, meaning workers in metals, or blacksmiths. They made and brandished spears of celestial iron with which to kill the demonic hippopotamuses, enemies of Ra the Sun god. The *mesniti* would ceremonially bring forth a metal image of Horus as the god of the rising Sun in imitation of how he originally emerged from the cosmic foundry. Edfu was also regaled as the place where the great Sun disk was first made such that when the doors of the Edfu *mesnet* were opened, the Sun disk would rise. Technically, Horus is not the Solar Logos, but the Logos itself, Christ. Usually the smith, as presented in mythic images as Solar Logos, works on behalf of the Christ, but in Horus the two identities have been blended.

370. This shape-shifting ability was the basis of his prodigies of craftsmanship. Tvastr made the original sacrificial ladle and the Soma chalice of the gods, from which copies were later produced. The Vedas credit him with forming Heaven and Earth and thus being their proper ruler, "responsible for their increase and well-being." Further, Tvastr "the Shaper" was the fashioner of the embryo, supporter of the seminal germ, surrounded by *gnas*, "who are the recipients of his generative energy"; thus he was called Garbhapati, Lord of the Womb. The Shaper or "Form Fashioner" always carries an iron axe; he bestowed long life and prosperity, gave generative potency, and shaped all forms, human and animal. (Hephaistos was said to have created Pandora, the first woman.) Tvastr is even credited with creating Agni, the god of fire; his associates or "grandchildren," the celestial craftsmen, were known as the *Ribhus* (the Vedic equivalent of Horus's *mesniti*). Margaret and James Stutley, *Harper's Dictionary of Hinduism: Its Mythology, Folklore, Philosophy, Literature, and History* (San Francisco: Harper & Row, 1977): 306–307.

371. *Kalevala: The Land of the Heroes*, trans. W. F. Kirby (London: J. M. Dent & Sons/ Everyman's Library, 1907): 83, 84, 98, 100.

372. Alby Stone, "The Cosmic Mill," *At the Edge*, 1993, republished at: www.indigogroup.co.uk/edge.

373. Giorgio de Santillana and Hertha von Dechend, *Hamlet's Mill: An Essay on Myth and the Frame of Time* (Boston: David R. Godine, 1977): 111.

374. *Kalevala: The Land of the Heroes*, trans. W. F. Kirby (London: J. M. Dent & Sons/ Everyman's Library, 1907): 79, 80.

375. "Branwen, Daugher of Llyr," in *The Mabinogi and Other Medieval Welsh Tales*, trans. Patrick K. Ford (Berkeley: University of California Press, 1977): 57–72.

376. Wilhelm Pelikan, *The Secrets of Metals*, trans. Charlotte Lebensart (Hudon, NY: Anthroposophic Press, 1973): 75.

377. Ibid., 63.

378. Mircea Eliade, *The Forge and the Crucible*, Second Edition, trans. Stephen Corrin (Chicago: University of Chicago Press, 1978): 82.

379. Set amidst a clump of beech trees, Wayland's Smithy is a trapezoidal earth and chalk mound 185 feet long and 43 feet wide at the south end, with six gigantic sarsen stones (the tallest is ten feet high) arranged in a line at the south end and entrance. From these stones extends a passage 20 feet long, with opposing chambers on either side and a central covered chamber at the end. Archeologists claim the long barrow was built between 3700 and 3400 B.C. As one of the many visible (and nontangible) temples along the Ridgeway, Wayland's Smithy is about ten miles overland from Avebury. As late as 1758, the local folklore still maintained that an invisible smith lived in the Smithy and would reshoe a traveler's horse for a penny.

380. Grace and Ivan Cooke, *The Light in Britain* (New Lands, UK: White Eagle Publishing Trust, 1971): 29–33.

381. Carlo Suares, "The Cipher of Genesis," in *The Qabala Trilogy* (Boston, MA: Shambhala, 1985): 78–80.

382. Homer, *Odyssey*, trans. Robert Fitzgerald (New York: Farrar, Straus, and Giroux, 1998): 213, 218.

383. Homer, *Odyssey*, trans. Robert Fagles (New York: Viking Penguin, 1996): 281.

384. We find an equivalent image for Helios's Sun chariot in the Egyptian description of Ra's Barque of the Sun or Boat of Millions of Years. Ra to the Egyptians was the god of the Sun, and, in the terminology of this book, Ra can be understood as another expression of the Solar Logos or smith, master of the fire. During the daylight hours, Ra travels across the sky in his barque called *mandjet* (or *matet*, "becoming strong"); in

the evening he sails on his *meseket* (or *semktet*, "becoming weak") in the Underworld.

Ra as the Sun set in the Field of Offerings (or Field of Rest), then rose in the Field of Reeds, but the theology of Heliopolis, an Egyptian Sun temple center, said that the Pharaoh as a divine and solar hero, in order to reach the Field of Offerings after his death, had to fight the guardian of the Field, the Bull of Offering. This is a suggestive clue about the true nature of the Sun god and the reason for calling the Sun temple a Mithraeum.

Throughout his Night journey, however, Apophis, the Wild Sun God, tries to devour Ra every day, waiting for him on Bakhu, the western-most mountain of the horizon. Ra is most vulnerable as his barque slides past the western horizon and enters the Night. Apophis is said to hypnotize all the occupants of the Sun boat—this included the Ennead, or nine gods of Heliopolis—with his malevolent stare, except for Seth who subdues Apophis. Seth arguably is an Egyptian description of Zeus working through the Great Bear, which brings us back to the sword's scabbard.

385. Apollodorus, *The Library*, vol. 1. trans. Sir James George Frazer (Cambridge, MA: Harvard University Press, 1921): 49.

386. Patricia Turner and Charles Russell Coulter, *Dictionary of Ancient Deities* (New York: Oxford University Press, 2000): 63.

387. Similarly, Ra and Horus have aspects in common. Ra was often depicted as a human male with a falcon's head, or that of a hawk; when equated with Horus, he was called *Re-Horakhty*, the Horizon Dweller. Horus we have already identified as the Egyptian perception of the Christ, yet some of Horus's aspects blurred into that of the celestial smith, or Solar Logos, who is the executive, more incarnate, aspect of the Christ. Again we cannot be too literal in our definitions.

388. Maui climbed Mount Haleakala equipped with 15 strands of rope. He met his grandmother on the upper slopes, and she gave him the sixteenth rope. As the Sun, La, first started to climb up over the horizon of the mountain, Maui snared it with the first of his 16 ropes. Then he used the other ropes to tie down the other 15 legs of the Sun. In a variation of this story, Maui used his ropes to lasso the Sun and then break off its rays; alternatively, Maui used snares to tie down La's feet, knees, hips, waist, arms, and neck; in a third variation, he snares the

writhing, resisting La with a net. Once he had La pinned down, Maui began to beat him with a magic stone club, or with an enchanted jawbone. La's hot red blood turned to volcanic stone. Even though Maui was burned and blistered from such close contact with the Sun, he got the better of La who agreed to travel slower for six months of the year, during the dry season, to make life better for the Polynesians. W. D. Westervelt, *Legends of Maui: A Demigod of Polynesia and of His Mother, Hina* (Honolulu: Hawaiian Gazette, 1910): 40–55.

389. He is red all over, has seven arms, three legs, three or seven heads that spout red flames, a huge mouth, seven tongues (each with a name), and bright gleaming hair. His seven arms span the continents; seven rays are emitted from his body; his seven arms are rays of light. He rides a ram, though he has a golden chariot drawn by red horses (he is thereby called *Rohitasva*, "Having red horses"), and the seven winds are his chariot wheels; he carries an axe, torch, fan, and spoon, one of each in each of his seven arms. Sometimes he has a flaming spear; in his fiercer aspect, he has iron tusks and roars like a bull.

390. Agni bestows wealth; he is life, the enjoyer, the maker of gold, among his many epithets. Agni is also known as the All-Pervader (*Vaisvanara*), the Burner (*Dahana*), Gleaming to Heaven's Door (*Svargadvarasprsa*), Lord of the House (*Grhapati*), and Roarer (*Rudra*). He is also the All-Knowing, Invoker, Ruler, Knower, Support, Purifier, Slayer of Evil Spirits, Son of Self, Lord of Devotion, Lightning, and Existence. References exist to Agni as Lord of Cattle (Cattle of the Sun) and Roarer; these ally him with aspects already presented for Helios and Typhon, respectively.

391. He was born of the eye of Purusha. His chariot is drawn by a horse called Etasa, or by seven red horses. He has been depicted in Vedic art as a stallion, bird, vulture, or bull; he is both shining and black, and his temple was called "House of the Judge of the Land." Surya is *Karma-sakshi*, the witness of the deeds of the world, and sees all that happens below through his heavenly eye. His epithets include Stimulator (*Savitar*), Benefactor (*Pushan*), Distributor of Wealth (*Bhaga*), Father of Humanity (*Vivasvat*), Friend (*Mitra*). Surya has his own capital residence called *Vivasvati*, the Sun-city, from the praise name, *Vivasvat*, which also means "Owner of Rays."

392. He is Lord of Judgment, lawgiver, father of truth and justice. He defends the world against moral disorder, evil, and entropy, and he inspires rectitude and oracular prophecy. Sometimes he was depicted as an old bearded man with sunbeams streaming out from his shoulders or as seated on a throne dispensing rulings, judging mortals in the daytime, the dead during the night. Shamash's temple was called *e-Babbar*, meaning "White House"; his chief sanctuary was at Babylon, in today's Iraq. His charioteer is Bunene, and he has two gatekeepers—some texts call them scorpion-men—who open the gates of Heaven in the morning for him as he begins his daily journey across the sky. At the end of the day, he enters through a vast door in the western mountains and travels through the Earth during the night until morning.

393. *Mashu* means "twins" and was conceived to be a mountain at the edge of the world, where the Sun rises. It was also called *Mashi*, which means "Sunset Hill," and it was said to be a tremendous peak, its foundations in Arallu, the Underworld, reaching up all the way to Heaven and dividing the land of the living from the western land of the dead. Gilgamesh makes it past the scorpion-men, whose heads reach the clouds, enters Mashu, and proceeds through a dark tunnel 12 leagues long, until he reaches the Garden of the Sun, an enchanted garden full of the Sun's rays—his original goal, as he had hoped to gain immortality there. Apparently even to pass through the mountain's inaccessible tract in complete and dense darkness for 12 leagues was an impressive feat; the scorpion-men told Gilgamesh nobody before him had ever done it. "Gilgamesh," in *Myths from Mesopotamia*, ed. and trans. Stephanie Dalley (New York: Oxford University Press, 1989): 96, 97.

394. Michael J. Carlowicz and Ramon E. Lopez, *Storms from the Sun: The Emerging Science of Space Weather* (Washington, DC: Joseph Henry Press, 2002): 8.

395. Guy L. Playfair and Scott Hill, *The Cycles of Heaven* (New York: Avon, 1979): 33.

396. Michael J. Carlowicz and Ramon E. Lopez, *Storms from the Sun: The Emerging Science of Space Weather* (Washington, DC: Joseph Henry Press, 2002): 8, 13, 76.

397. James B. Kaler, *Stars* (New York: Scientific American Library, 1992): 116-117.

398. *Classical Hindu Mythology: A Reader in the Sanskrit Puranas*, ed. and trans. Cornelia Dimmitt and J. A. B. van Buitenen (Philadelphia: Temple University Press, 1978): 53.

399. We find another example of the Pleiadian time cave for the Sun in the Japanese myth of their Sun goddess Amaterasu. She had been "out" in the world, but after her celestial brother Susanowo, an unruly storm god, committed atrocities against her, Amaterasu retreated to a cave and sealed herself in there in seclusion, taking the light of the world with her. There was no alternation of day and night, and the world was dark. Eight myriads of gods entreated her at the mouth of the cave called *Ame-no-Iwato* (Sky-Rock-Cave) to return her illumination to the world. They finally lured her out with a mirror, a necklace, bird song, and a riotous music-dance performance, banking on her curiosity and vanity. The gods had made a number of tools, bellows, and forges and welded stars together to form the mirror, as well as jewels and musical instruments. Finally Amaterasu peeped forth from her rock cavern, saw herself in the mirror, and overcome by her own beauty, stepped out of the cave to approach the mirror. Then the gods roped off the cave door so she couldn't retreat. Once more "the world became golden with her presence" as she dwelled in the Plain of High Heaven as she was meant to. Afterwards in Japanese mythology she was described as *Amaterasu-o-Mikami*, queen of the *kami*, or animated vital forces of Nature, and was especially honored at her temple at Ise in Japan as the Rising Sun, prime ancestor of the Japanese emperor and patron of the royal family, and the source of spiritual power. Amaterasu gave her son the three sacred treasures (the mirror, a sword, and the jewels) and sent him down to earth to rule Japan with these talismans. Now the holiest Shinto shrine in Japan, the Ise complex includes 200 buildings. F. Hadland Davis, *Myths and Legends of Japan* (New York, Dover Publications, [1913], 1992): 27–28.

400. The depiction of Mithra occupied the Vedic, Persian, and Roman imagination, and his name underwent slight semantic changes from Mitra (Babylonian and Vedic) to Mithra (Persian) to Mithras (Roman). He had many of the same qualities as the other Sun gods, such as Shamash and Surya. He has 10,000 eyes (one account says this is because the stars became his eyes) and

1,000 ears; he sees and hears everything and never sleeps; he is the guardian of the laws by which the universe is maintained and kept fruitful, and he is the protector of truth and supporter of justice. Like the other Sun gods, Mithra is the "lord of wide pastures," the one who renders them fertile. He wears a red Phrygian cap and carries a torch and dagger as he emerges from the Generative Rock, as the Mithraic mysteries called it.

401. According to English metaphysical writer Trevor Ravenscroft, "the human word is also a sword which proceeds out of the mouth of man." This "Word-Sword," alluded to in Wolfram von Eschenbach's thirteenth-century esoteric tract, *Parzival*, has "grown old, atrophied, shattered, and lost its power," Ravenscroft says, yet by discovering the original source of its power (in *Parzival*, it's called the Well of Kunneware, source of the magical sword-restorative spring), the Word-Sword can be renewed, its broken pieces fit together again into a whole blade. Eschenbach noted that the Word-Sword, when reforged, has the signs of the constellations engraved on the blade. This is to my mind but a subtle variation on the idea of the sword's scabbard made of the energies of the Ray Masters who helped create the constellations. The shattered constellation-imprinted Word-Sword, Ravenscroft proposed, is the human being. The magic spell that welds together the fragments of the blade is "the Love of Christ, the Word made flesh." In humans has been implanted "the creative principle (Word) of the Universe" made manifest in our "tremendous faculty of speech." Trevor Ravenscroft, *The Spear of Destiny: The Occult Power Behind the Spear Which Pierced the Side of Christ* (York Beach, ME: Samuel Weiser, 1982): 181, 182.

402. Franz Cumont, *The Mysteries of Mithra*, trans. Thomas J. McCormack (New York: Dover Publications [1903], 1956): 223, 224.

403. This can be confusing. In one interpretation, an Aeon is a Platonic Year, of 2,160 years of Earth time, one zodiacal age, such as Pisces or Aquarius. In the Gnostic system, there were 30 Aeons living in the Pleroma, a divine state beyond or before the manifestation of reality and creation. The Mithraic sense seems to be more general, more universally metaphorical or representative of an apportionment of time. However, Hellenistic Gnosticism spoke of seven or 12 Aeons or worlds,

and in some systems within this, up to 365 heavens or spaces were described. In its singular form, Aeon meant "the world," as in saying "this world" as opposed to the coming world or Aeon. The word might have derived in essence from the Hebrew *olam* and Aramaic *alma* which originally meant "eternity," then later "world." The plural *almaya* came to mean "worlds" and "beings" in a superhuman sense. Later the word became even more personified in New Testament conceptualizations that attributed gods or rulers to an Aeon. Hans Jonas, *The Gnostic Religion: The Message of the Alien God and the Beginnings of Christianity* (Boston: Beacon Press, 1963): 52, 54.

404. Franz Cumont, *The Mysteries of Mithra*, trans. Thomas J. McCormack (New York: Dover Publications [1903], 1956): 107.

405. His writings on that theme were pursuant to "the change of psychic condition within the 'Christian aeon'" because the "Pisces aeon is the synchronistic concomitant of two thousand years of Christian development." C. G. Jung, *Aion: Researches into the Phenomenology of the Self*, Second Edition, trans. R. F. C. Hull, Bollingen Series XX (Princeton, NJ: Princeton University Press, 1959): ix.

406. Theosophical theology maintains that the Higher Self, or simply the Self, which is the divine life of the *Manvantara*—the Rich Fisher King for this vast cycle of Brahma; refer back to chapter 3—was the first being created by the Absolute. Or: "The Lord of the Eternity (the Aeon) is the first God." Or: "The Christ-soul now completes its spiral ascent through the 12 departments of human experience, whose cyclic progression corresponds with the Twelve signs of the Zodiac." G. A. Gaskell, *Dictionary of All Scriptures and Myths* (New York: Julian Press, 1960): 29.

407. H. P. Blavatsky, *The Secret Doctrine: The Synthesis of Science, Religion, and Philosophy, Vol. 1: Cosmogenesis* (Pasadena, CA: Theosophical University Press [1888], 1977): 501.

408. Another esoteric source says the Sun revolves around the Milky Way every 206 million years, and since the solar system was created 4.5 billion years ago (the approximate age of our Sun, according to astrophysicists), the Sun has made 22 "Great Cycle Orbits" around "the Great Central Sun of the Milky Way." The 22nd is the turnaround Orbit, as it "completes the time cycle in

which our entire solar system is to remain in its present state of evolution." As the Aquarian Age begins, we, as a solar system, begin a new Orbit, presumably the 23rd, and "move into a new vibration where no expression below the fourth dimension can continue to exist." Joseph Whitfield, *The Treasure of El Dorado* (Roanoke, VA: Treasure Publications, 1986): 78, 79.

409. The number 864 is a "foundation number" with a "strong, solar character," comments John Michell, and it has clear associations with the measurement of planetary time, from the 86,400 seconds in a 24-hour day to the 8,640,000,000 years in a Day and Night of Brahma. The Semitic Sun-deity Abraxas, whose name through Greek gematria spells 365, was the ruler of the solar year of 365 days, but the gematria of his throne is 864. John Michell, *The Dimensions of Paradise: The Proportions and Symbolic Numbers of Ancient Cosmology* (San Francisco: Harper & Row, 1988): 171.

410. The only remedy was iron, which did not yet exist. Words of the origin of iron would staunch the wound and undo the evil that precipitated the bleeding. "Is there no one in this household,/Who can cure the wounds of iron?" Väinämöinen asks, in great pain and misery. First, iron was born from the breast milk of the three maidens, daughters of Creation and Ukko; then Ilmarinen, the great primeval smith, was born to master the iron and the fire. *Kalevala: The Land of the Heroes*, trans. W. F. Kirby (London: J. M. Dent & Sons/Everyman's Library, 1907): 75, 76.

411. The *Atharva Veda*, an ancient text, combines the concepts of solar time, movement, and fecundation in one masterful sentence: "Time, the steed, *runs* with seven reins (rays), thousand-eyed, ageless, rich in *seed* [italics added]." Then it tells us how to relate to this majestic energy-consciousness field: "The seers, thinking holy thoughts, mount him, all the beings (worlds) are his wheels." Time, the first god, "hastens onward" riding with seven wheels, and "immortality is his axle," carrying all these beings and worlds, the text says. "Atharva Veda 19:53," quoted in W. Norman Brown, *Man in the Universe: Some Continuities in Indian Thought* (Berkeley: University of California Press, 1970): 71–72.

412. The crystal structure description pertains to the atomic arrangement of atoms of an element when in its solid state. There are eight structures described: cubic; cubic body-centered; cubic face-centered; hexagonal; monoclinic; orthorhombic; rhombohedral; and tetragonal. The electron configuration model proposes electrons exist in seven energy levels (formerly called shells), each level having a specific maximum number of electrons, as follows: 1) 2; 2) 8; 3) 18; 4) 32; 5) 50; 6) 72; 7) 98. That totals 280. Chemists qualify this by saying the last three energy levels are theoretical and not filled, or not yet observed to be filled. It is interesting to note (in terms of the Hermetic correspondence across levels of reality) that the fourth energy level accommodates 32 electrons; 32 is *LEV* in Hebrew gematria, which means Heart and also signifies the number of paths and Sefiroth on the Tree of Life; the fourth level of the aura and the fourth chakra of course is the heart chakra.

413. It would be an intriguing project to map the chemical forms of the elements onto the constellation forms to find correspondences and even mythic, starlore names for the elements, but, granting first the validity of the correspondence, this would be inherently inaccurate or at least incomplete, given the variation in interpretations of constellation forms and the number of stars included. However, the precision of chemistry might actually tease out better constellation maps once the likely correspondences were made.

414. Astrophysicists tell us that more than 60 of the elements known on Earth have been identified in the solar spectrum, and probably many more are present there as well but cannot be detected (do not produce spectral lines) in the observable spectrum. The spectrum of the solar photosphere is a continuous spectrum of absorption lines such that tens of thousands of absorption lines in our Sun have been catalogued by scientists. These spectral absorption lines are generated by or indicative of the chemical elements composing the Sun, such as hydrogen, helium, oxygen, carbon, nitrogen, nickel, chromium, silicon, and iron.

415. The solar constant is a term astrophysicists use to calculate how much of the Sun dies each day in its natural process of emitting heat and light. If the Earth had no atmosphere to deflect the incoming solar radiation, sunlight would burn on Earth at the rate of 1.94 calories per square centimeter per minute; another way of putting it is that solar energy reaches the Earth's

outer atmosphere at the continuous rate of 1.35 kilowatts/square meter. Generally, the solar constant means the average rate at which radiant solar energy is received from the Sun by the Earth. The solar constant is also expressed as 1336.1 Wm2 (Wm means watts per square meter), based on the mean value of daily averages as collected by six different satellites between 1978 and 1998.

416. Arnold Mindell, *Working with the Dreaming Body* (New York: Routledge & Kegan Paul, 1985): 79.

417. Zoroastrians recognized three grades of sacred fires, in accordance with different sectors of society. The basic, humble fire of the household was called *Atash Dadgah*; *Adur Aduran*, the second grade, was the "fire of fires," suitable for fire temples; the third, arcane grade, was the *Atash Bahram*, "fire of victory," suitable for kings and royalty. Even though these three grades of sacred fire might be physical, Zoroastrian thought on fire held it to be primarily metaphysical, more of a universal fire, a condition of the universe. Fire also pertained to intellectual, inner, and spiritual illumination, the fire-light that ignited the mind to understand and be enlightened.

418. Solara, *The Star-Borne: A Remembrance for the Awakened Ones* (Charlottesville, VA: Star-Borne Unlimited, 1989): 187–188.

419. *The Treasury of Good Sayings: A Tibetan History of Bon*, ed. and trans. Samten G. Karmay, London Oriental Series, vol. 26 (New York: Oxford University Press, 1972): 5, 6.

420. The term *Og-Min* variously means "thickly-formed," "densely packed realm," or "the Central realm of the Densely Packed." This term means "the seed of all universal forces and things which are densely packed together therein." This densely packed realm is Og-Min, or literally "No-Down," meaning the realm in which and from which there is no fall; the Og-Min can, if they wish, voluntarily reenter the human incarnational stream under a kind of short-term service contract. *The Tibetan Book of the Dead*, comp. and ed. W. Y. Evans-Wentz (New York: Oxford University Press, 1960): 107, note 3.

421. One of the Tibetan models of the universe is of an onion with 15 layers, all cohering to Mount Meru. These layers also include the 33 Heavens ruled by Indra and those under the sway of Mara, the lord of the desire realm. Then, as an apex over all this, is the final heaven called "The Supreme" which in Tibetan is written as Og-Min. *The Tibetan Book of the Dead,* comp. and ed. W. Y. Evans-Wentz (New York: Oxford University Press, 1960): 62.

422. "They are the concentrated rays or manifestations of the Sambhoga-Kaya, the Bodhic Body of Perfect Endowment, the first reflex of the Dharma-Kaya (Divine Body of Truth), of those Enlightened Ones of the Akanishtha [the Highest Paradise] Realm." *Tibetan Yoga and Secret Doctrines,* ed. W. Y. Evans-Wentz (New York: Oxford University Press, 1967): 12, 44, 94 (note 3), 238 (note 1), 250 (note 2), 262 (note 3), 264 (note 1).

423. These are the paradise realms of the *shiens* who are divine immortal beings. A Chinese text from the ninth century A.D., entitled "The Report Concerning the Cave Heavens and Lands of Happiness in Famous Mountains," cites ten Cave Heavens and 36 "small cave heavens," all accessible through the mountains of China. But they warned that travelers who entered these caves might return to worldly life and find centuries of Earth time had passed. The Hindu tradition refers to Bilasvarga, a subterranean heaven that sounds similar to the Taoist formulation of Heavenly Caves. In Bilasvarga, you have no sense of time, and the scenery is gorgeous, captivating, and seductive. Richard L. Thompson, *Mysteries of the Sacred Universe: The Cosmology of the Bhagavata Purana* (Alachua, FL: Govardhan Hill Publishing, 2000): 295–296.

424. The astral *shiens* have crystalline bodies and total freedom, and work in accord with the cosmic blueprint for evolution. Taoist traditions hold that the *shiens* were humanity's first teachers, and in the case of Tibet, they cleansed the land of its original unwholesome inhabitants (said to be demons), prepared it for higher spiritual life, and brought and buried high teachings for future discovery. Ni, Hua-Ching, *The Taoist Inner View of the Universe and the Immortal Realm* (Malibu, CA: Shrine of the Eternal Breath of Tao, 1979): 12, 46, 47, 64.

425. William Blake, "Jerusalem: The Emanation of the Giant Albion," in *Blake: Complete Writings, with Variant Readings,* ed. Geoffrey Keynes (London: Oxford University Press, 1972): 626, 653, 709.

426. Harold Bloom, *The Western Canon: The Books and Schools of the Ages* (New York: Riverhead Books, 1995): 393.

427. The shadow of Albion lies over all of England's holy centers, commented Anthony Roberts, the late expert on Glastonbury's geomantic terrain, "symbolizing the power of them all through the body of a giant whose lineaments are shaped by the contours of the living earth itself." Anthony Roberts, *Sowers of Thunder: Giants in Myth and History* (London: Rider & Company, 1978): 165.

428. Vladimir Nabokov, *Pnin* (New York: Quality Paperback Book Club, 1993): 166.

429. C. G. Jung, *The Archetypes and the Collective Unconscious,* Second Edition, Bollingen Series XX, trans. R. F. C. Hull (Princeton, NJ: Princeton University Press, 1980): 294, 308.

430. Around 1580, John Dee, court astrologer to Queen Elizabeth, geomancer, Qabalist, and angelic communicant, referred somewhat obliquely to stars in the landscape around Glastonbury. Dee said, "The starres which agree with their reproductions on the ground do lye onlie on the celestial path of the Sonne, moon, and planets," but most people failed to understand him, and the subject of Earth stars lay quiescent for centuries. John Dee, quoted in John Michell, *The New View over Atlantis* (New York: Thames and Hudson, 1983): 21.

431. To her, the remarkable landscape shapes occupying a roughly circular area about ten miles across explained Somerset's rich mythic overlay, why this area was known as "Merlin's secret" and "a heavenly sanctuary on Earth."

432. K. E. Maltwood, *A Guide to Glastonbury's Temple of the Stars* (Cambridge, UK: James Clarke, 1964): 6, 7.

433. Who made the zodiac? According to Mary Caine, "It was made by Nature in the first place, and continued by man." She suggests the ancient Chaldeans may have had a hand in its elaboration, and that the terrestrial zodiac's "continuous development embraces all the ages of man down to the present day" and that there is no reason to think its evolution will not continue far into the future. Why was it made? It was prepared as "the source of all religious teachings" for the "salvation of mankind," Caine writes. Mary Caine, *The Glastonbury Zodiac* (Torquay, UK: Grael Communications, 1978): 36–38.

434. Epiphany (when the Christ focuses his attention on a selected grid point) is January 6; Candlemas (also called Oimelc or Imbolc, dedicated to the Irish goddess Brighid), February 2; Pentecost is a variable date, 50 days after Easter, which puts it in mid-May to early June usually; Michaelmas (for the Archangel Michael), September 29. These are days in which the angelic and archangelic families, in conjunction with the Ray Masters, the Christ, and the Solar and Cosmic Logos, concentrate their attention on the Earth and/or specific geomantic sites. In other words, on these days, you can count on their presence and participation in your geomantically focused activities.

435. I once jokingly referred to such small landscape zodiacs as *zodiac theme parks* and envisioned how they could be developed into interactive astrological and Grail Quest facilities, a cosmic mysteries Disneyland.

436. The "spirit-seed of the human physical body is, so to speak, a universe of vast magnitude." Before incarnation, the "cosmic human germ" of the physical body is immense, occupying the cosmos; the process of incarnation contracts and condenses it to a human-body size. Yet "he feels his soul nature spread out far across this cosmos. This cosmos is actually nothing else than his future physical body expanded to a universe." After death, "the whole universe may be designated as our inner being," and our inner nature is revealed to us "as if it were a world of stars." Rudolf Steiner, *Man and the World of Stars,* trans. D. S. Osmond (New York: Anthroposophic Press, 1963): 2, 14. Rudolf Steiner, *Philosophy, Cosmology, and Religion* (Spring Valley, NY: Anthroposophic Press, 1984): 87.

437. Rudolf Steiner, *True and False Paths in Spiritual Investigation* (London: Rudolf Steiner Press, 1985): 202, 217.

438. This is the conceptual framework for astrology, the correspondence of celestial bodies with the human. Astrology says, though many people don't understand what it means, that, for example, Taurus "rules" the neck, Pisces the feet, Leo the heart, and so forth. It's more useful to think in terms of Taurus, Pisces, and Leo as the celestial energies that form and sustain those organs, on both the cosmic and human physical level. You just have to add one more step to the landscape zodiac: Start the wheel turning, the wheel being the zodiac. In other words, set it in motion in time, then astrology becomes the predictive science to chart the changing dynamics of

this celestial-terrestrial correspondence. In a zodiac theme park, based on the smallest landscape zodiacs, you could give experiential demonstrations of the conceptual and predictive aspects of astrology, and with a little training in psychic sensitivity, people could walk through their horoscopes and experience their makeup.

439. In working with a landscape zodiac, from the viewpoint of turning it on, you must start with Canis Major, the Greater Dog, outside the ecliptic. As many mythologies attest, the hound is the guardian of the goddess's temple (Hecate's dogs) or the fierce companion of the death god (Cerberus with Hades) or the solar hero (Cabal with King Arthur). You must first befriend the Dog, and anyway, the Dog is the home of Sirius and he (it) is the Guardian of the *Vastospati*, the vast star dwelling of Shiva, as we saw in chapter 5.

Then you move on to Ursa Major, the Greater Bear, home of the Ray Masters; next Aquarius, chief constellation of our new astrological age; then Pisces, the icon of the departing age; then the rest of the ecliptic constellations, and the others inside and outside of this line in the physical ecliptic.

440. I say logarithmic because originally the zodiacs were designed in accordance with megalithic yards (MY), scaled up by ten. Glastonbury zodiac, for example, is 3486 MY x 10 = 34,860 MY. The MY is very close to the mathematical value for e, 2.7182818284. . . , the base of natural logarithms. 2.71 . . . rounded off is 2.72, which is also the rounded-off accepted value for MY. My assumption is that the range of 72 zodiac sizes is somehow a function of or describable in terms of e.

441. The tortoise has a symbolically important function in many Hindu temples. In one old document, India, in its semantic guise as Bharata (its original name), is shown resting on the back of a giant eastward-facing tortoise; the constellations and countries of the world are arrayed around it. An image of the tortoise is often placed in the base of Hindu altars to signify it as the source of all things.

442. *Trioedd Ynys Prydein: The Welsh Triads,* ed. and trans. Rachel Bromwich (Cardiff, Wales: University of Wales Press, 1978): 217–218.

443. John Michell, *The Dimensions of Paradise: The Proportions and Symbolic Numbers*

of Ancient Cosmology (San Francisco: Harper & Row, 1988): 91–94.

444. Michell's plotting of a great circle with White-Leaved Oak in the center is correct, and it helps us pinpoint the third choir. The Ofanim explain that Llantwit Major and Glastonbury sit adjacent at the southwestern end of the circle, while the third Choir at Lichfield sits at the opposite side of the circle. The diameters of each Perpetual Choir intersect the White-Leaved Oak circumference in two places; those diameters are each one-third of the White-Leaved Oak diameter. Michell cites the radius as 63 miles, but arguably on the topographic map it could be 62.5; I find the numbers more mystically suggestive with a 62-mile radius, for each Choir has a radius of 20.666666 miles; the three radii together are just slightly *less* than the radius of the White-Leaved Oak circle, at 61.999998 miles.

445. Let's put the numbers and distribution complexity aside for a moment and get an angelic perspective on Earth chakras. "Picture tiny flowers all over the Earth," the Ofanim suggest. "Some form larger flowers; some of these form even larger flowers. Chakras are like this, flowing into one another, flowers opening as part of other flowers. Each is independent plus interdependent, similar and dissimilar."

446. I have not yet come across any mythic references to a stone circle at Balor's Hill, later called the Hill of Uisneach. However, Balor is represented in Irish myth as an evil giant of the Fomorians, a race of giants, and these I identify with the Elohim in their role as megalithic engineers in giant human form and as colleagues with Merlin in the stoneworks projects around the Earth. So at least the Elohim are associated with Uisneach; the name of Stonehenge as "Giant's Dance" may not have been used in ancient Ireland, which would account for it not appearing in the Irish myths.

447. C. Austin, "Mide," 2001, published at: www.celtic-connection.com; Toby D. Griffen, "The Navel of Ireland. A Sacred Geography," [no date], published at: www.geocities.com/~dubricius/naval.pdf.

448. In light of this geomantic knowledge, it is a shame that Ireland has been kept divided into two parts. Putting aside the political and religious issues involved, this severing of a significant portion of Ireland from its integral whole landmass seriously disturbs the land, its egregor, and its

geomantic energy flow. At the same time the fact that Ireland is a clearly defined landmass—an island—with its own language and myths provides us an excellent laboratory for studying the relationship of myth and landscape in the context of a country's egregor, Energy Focusing Node, and other features at this level.

449. Apollonius of Rhodes, *The Voyage of Argo: The Argonautica,* trans. E. V. Rieu (New York: Penguin Books, 1971): 191–192.

450. He was the Hawaiian patron god of the Bird Cult, credited with having driven the birds to a sequestered island to protect them from those who would steal their eggs. As a deity, his public image may also have grown out of the Tahitian description of *Matu-'u-ta'u-ta'ua,* a giant bird that swallows humans, perhaps an equivalently aggressive protector function to Talos's tendency to hurl boulders at intruders.

451. Technically, the gematria of Torah is 611, even though the Torah provides 613 commandments. The additional two come from two commandments that God, rather than Moses, delivered directly to the Jews, and thus precede the existence of the Torah. 613 also spells *ET Ha-OR,* "The Light," understood in this context to mean the light of the Torah, or 613 *mitzvot.*

452. In the case of the biblical Abraham, the gematria of his name spells 248, making him, according to Rabbi Benjamin Blech, "the paradigm of perfection with regard to fulfillment of God's will" because "the organs of his entire body proclaimed the greatness of God." Rabbi Benjamin Blech, *The Secrets of Hebrew Words* (Northvale, NJ: Jason Aronson, 1991): 175.

453. *The Zohar: Parashat Pinhas,* vol. I, trans. and ed. Dr. Philip S. Berg (New York: Research Centre of Kabbalah, 1986): 93, 95, 177, 178, 179.

454. Anatomically, the mobile Fisher King accounts for 126 of the human body's 206 bones. These 126 are called appendicular and pertain to the limbs. The upper extremities have 64 bones: arms and shoulders, 10; wrists, 16; hands, 38; the lower extremities have 62 bones: legs and hips, 10; ankles, 14; feet, 38. Among the remaining 80 axial bones, the head has 29 and the trunk 51 bones.

455. When Wellesley Tudor Pole lived at Little St. Michael's at Chalice Well in Glastonbury, he had a Merlin's trapdoor virtually out his front door. It lies at the top end of the garden, just over the wall, in a nondescript little cleft in the land. In 1965 he reported in a letter to a friend that he had been visited by an ethereal colleague who had arrived in Glastonbury after having participated in the Wesak festival (the Buddhist May Full Moon ceremony) "in that strange far-off Tibetan valley: one that has its own peculiar connections with Avalon and the vale between the Tor and Chalice Hill." That vale is a Shambhala doorway. *My Dear Alexias: Letters from Wellesley Tudor Pole to Rosamond Lehmann,* ed. Elizabeth Gaythorpe (Jersey, Channel Islands, UK: Neville Spearman, 1979): 127.

456. Among other treasures, Shambhala guards the Kalachakra, the "Wheel of Time" teachings, arcane instructions on the nature of reality. The Bon of Tibet claim that Shambhala is their fabulous eternal city and home of the gods, Olmolungring. Edwin Bernbaum, Ph.D., *The Way to Shambhala* (Los Angeles: Jeremy P. Tarcher, 1989): 6–12.

457. From Shambhala now pours the "first Ray of Will and Power" into the world; only twice before in the history of the world (in Lemuria, then Atlantis) has this powerful catalytic energy been released into the human world. This "little known divine energy now streams" out of Shambhala and, Bailey says, underlies the present world crisis (she wrote this in 1939); few will argue that the world today in the early twenty-first century is not in crisis. Shambhala "is a phase of sensitive awareness wherein there is acute and dynamic response to divine purpose." This purpose, Bailey adds, is to produce "certain racial and momentous changes" in human consciousness sufficient to completely alter our attitude to life and to bring about a mass initiation into "the Mystery of the Ages, into that which has been hid from the beginning." Alice A. Bailey, *The Externalisation of the Hierarchy* (New York: Lucis Publishing Company, 1957): 107. Alice A. Bailey, *The Rays and the Initiations, Vol. V: A Treatise on the Seven Rays* (New York: Lucis Publishing Company, 1960): 276. *Ponder on This: From the Writings of the Tibetan Teacher (Djwhal Khul),* compiled by a student (Lynwood, South Africa: Trulit Publishers, [no date]): 371–374.

458. These gateways are located in the Earth's energy matrix with respect to domes, their placement related to the unfolding of the dome

cap phi spiral from the dome. They appear where two dome caps intersect at a point of critical enlargement of the spirallic pattern, where the phi spiral seems to unfold more rapidly or with a greater arc, which is about two-thirds from the dome center in terms of the phi spiral's total unfoldment. This may sound too technical; let's simplify it by saying at a Shambhala gateway you will be under the influence of two overlapping dome caps and their spirallic lines from a nearby dome.

459. As Alice Bailey stated (note 457), the Shambhalic light stirs things up in our world; but it can also lead to wonderful outbreaks of spiritual light. Unless you are privy to angelic schedules of activations and influences, at any given time period in Earth culture, you won't know if you're under the Focus or not. "The energy of Shambhala is, however, so new and strange, that it is hard for human beings to know it for what it is—the demonstration of the Will of God in a new and potent livingness." *Ponder on This: From the Writings of the Tibetan Teacher (Djwhal Khul)*, compiled by a student (Lynwood, South Africa: Trulit Publishers [no date]): 372.

460. Vishnu used it to cut Svarbhanu the cosmic dragon in half, creating the head (Rahu) and tail (Ketu). In one battle, Vishnu summoned his "enemy-burning discus," which appeared in the sky "in a blaze of light matching the sun's, with its razor-sharp circular edge." It was "terrible, invincible, supreme . . . [a] fiercely blazing, terror-spreading weapon," a "raging" discus that "shone like a roaring fire," according to the *Mahabharata*. The *Chakravartins* were universal kings, world monarchs, primordial spiritual kings, Buddha-like figures who could turn and revolve the wheel, setting it in motion, using it to pacify the world. "The sun-wheel as the Chakravartin's symbol indicates that this universal shepherd-king is as it were the sun—the life-giver and universal eye," as scholar Heinrich Zimmer pointed out. *The Mahabharata: 1—The Book of the Beginning*, trans. and ed. J. A. B. van Buitenen (Chicago: University of Chicago Press, 1973): 75, 76. Heinrich Zimmer, *Philosophies of India*, Bollingen Series XXVI, ed. Joseph Campbell (Princeton, NJ: Princeton University Press, 1951): 128–129, 135, 192, 212.

461. If you can spend the first week of January (January 3–9) at such a site, this is ideal.

These are excellent conditions for practicing the ten stages in the Christed Initiation in the Buddha Body. The energy from the past Epiphany Focus will still be there in the etheric field of that site to enrich you.

462. Rudolf Steiner, *The Reappearance of the Christ in the Etheric* (Spring Valley, NY: Anthroposophic Press, 1983): 87, 88. Rudolf Steiner, *The True Nature of the Second Coming* (London: Rudolf Steiner Press, 1971): 78–81.

463. Ultimately, the Grail, for example, is not a Christian or a Celtic symbol; it is a divine symbol, an archetype, brought here from previous planets similarly organized as Earth because it *works* and corresponds to structures and processes of human consciousness. Ultimately, the Grail and the other symbols and temple structures on the Earth were "thought up" in the spiritual worlds as aids for our conscious development, as points of awareness within human bodies.

464. Harish Johari, *Chakras* (Rochester, VT: Destiny Books, 1987): 80.

465. Alan Oken, *Alan Oken's Complete Astrology*, rev. ed. (New York: Bantam Books, 1988): 189.

466. Terence Meaden, *The Secrets of the Avebury Stones: Britain's Greatest Megalithic Temple* (London: Souvenir Press, 1999): 7, 9, 147.

467. H. P. Blavatsky, *The Secret Doctrine: The Synthesis of Science, Religion, and Philosophy, Vol. 2: Anthropogenesis* (Pasadena, CA: Theosophical University Press, 1977 [1888]): 46.

468. The term cymatics was coined by Swiss researcher Hans Jenny, who documented the effects of vibrations and directed sounds, tones, and music on liquid and solid matter (sand, powders). He showed that geometric shapes arose in selected media in response to specific tones, notes, chords, and other sounds, convincingly demonstrating the age-old metaphysical principle that sound creates and sustains shapes. As Jenny said, his experiments "revealed a characteristic phenomenology of vibrational effects and wave phenomena with typical structural patterns and dynamics (cymatics)." Hans Jenny, *Cymatics*, vol. 2 (Basel, Switzerland: Basilius Presse AG, 1974): 7.

469. The Six Worlds is a concept from Buddhism that describes six overlapping realms of being or dimensions, including the human, ani-

mal, the realm of the Dead (called "hungry ghosts"), the Hell realm, and the Gods and the Asuras (antigods). Recall that earlier I mentioned that for some time two of the 14 Ray Masters were not overtly manifest on the Earth, while 12 were active. The intent here was to permeate the six adjacent realms of being with 12 rays.

470. The encircling ditch appears to be only minimally used for stone circles, based on the 900 or so extant, though given the fact that some ditches are very shallow and many stones have been removed or destroyed, it's possible there were originally many more. At those circles which have a surrounding ditch, presumably the same sonic effect as at Avebury will be produced. Other stone circles with ditches include Stonehenge; Arbor Low, Middleton, Derbyshire; Ring of Brodgar, Orkneys (30 feet wide by ten feet deep); Stenness, Orkneys (19 feet wide, six feet deep).

471. Richard Leviton, *Looking for Arthur: A Once and Future Travelogue* (Barrytown, NY: Barrytown, Ltd., 1997): 609–610.

472. The average length of the long single stone rows on Dartmoor in England is 600 feet; the 174 stones in the Down Tor row on Dartmoor steadily increase in height over the 1,145 feet they span, terminating in a stone circle on a hillside called Sheep's Tor. Aubrey Burl, *From Carnac to Callanish: The Prehistoric Stone Rows and Avenues of Britain, Ireland, and Brittany* (New Haven, CT: Yale University Press, 1993): 4, 19, 128.

473. Overall, Stonehenge was a "sophisticated and brilliantly conceived astronomical observatory" in operation for 400 years starting in 1900 B.C., Hawkins commented. "In form the monument is an ingenious computing machine" with the huge stones placed in precise astronomic alignment, a feat which required of its creators "an absolutely extraordinary blending of theoretical planning abilities with practical building skills." Gerald S. Hawkins, *Stonehenge Decoded* (Garden City, NY: Doubleday & Company, 1965): 115.

474. This balancing of the Sun and Moon function is still operative, the Ofanim note, but only in partial activation. There are fewer original stone circles than the original energy matrix called for (1,746), and energy and consciousness conditions on the planet have changed since those formative days.

475. The Merry Maidens circle is sometimes referred to as the Dawn's Men, a possible corrup-

tion of *Dawns Myin* or *Dans Maen*, or "the stone dance," in reference to the folk belief that the stones are petrified girls, turned to stone as punishment for dancing on Sunday. They were enticed into dancing by two pipers, also petrified, standing one-quarter mile away. Cornish belief says the revelers, both dancing maidens and pipers, were turned to stone by a sudden lightning flash out of a clear sky. But maybe something of their dance remains.

Archeologist T. C. Lethbridge, one of the early British pioneers in Earth Mysteries research, reported that when he dowsed the stones with a pendulum he sensed them rocking and swaying and emitting undefined electrical impulses. When he put one hand on a Merry Maiden stone, his other holding the dowsing pendulum, Lethbridge "received a strong tingling sensation like an electric shock"; his pendulum gyrated almost horizontally (very unusual for dowsing), and "the huge, heavy stone felt as if it were rocking wildly." John Michell, *The Traveler's Key to Sacred England* (New York: Alfred A. Knopf, 1988): 190. Janet and Colin Bord, *Mysterious Britain: Ancient Secrets of the United Kingdom and Ireland* (London: Paladin/Granada, 1974): 7.

476. Note that the 94 total aspects of the Cosmic Mother correspond in number to the 94 Avebury stones, which ground, amplify, and distribute the Mother qualities as "played" and released into the world in the groove or ditch encircling the site, as mentioned. They also correspond to the 47 Golden Apples plus 47 Griffin Gold Reserves (94), which together comprise implicit and explicit wisdom.

477. There are three principal rows accounting for 2,683 stones: the Menec alignment of 1,069 stones in 12 parallel avenues; the Kermario, which has ten rows with a total of 1,029 stones, runs for 3,700 feet and is 100 yards wide; and Kerlescan, which has 514 stones in 13 parallel rows; a fourth postulated row, its stones now removed, vandalized, or ruined, is Le Petite Menec. According to archeologist Aubrey Burl, these rows are "unevenly spaced, not straight, angling and twisting against each other" and are composite settings, "enlarged bit by bit over the years." Aubrey Burl, *From Carnac to Callanish: The Prehistoric Stone Rows and Avenues of Britain, Ireland, and Brittany* (New Haven, CT: Yale University Press, 1993): 135, 136.

478. I do not presently have a reliable date for this period, or for any of the Atlantean epoch. Plato gives a date of something more recent than 10,000 B.C., and many scholars sympathetic to the possibility of an Atlantean continent and civilization concur. However, the Ofanim suggest that nearly all our time frames and speculations about when things happened are remarkably conservative and thus inaccurate. Frank Alper, a well-regarded psychic channeler in the 1980s, proposed a date of 89,000 B.C. for the approximate beginnings of Atlantean civilization; he also gives the date of 77,777 B.C. for the sinking of Atlantis. See: Rev. Dr. Frank Alper, *Exploring Atlantis,* vol. 1 (Farmingdale, NY: Coleman Publishing, 1982): 2. However, the Ofanim recently revealed that Bimini Island, near Florida, sank around 150,000 years ago, and that that was *after* the sinking of the Atlantean continent.

479. The purpose of my visit to Carnac—I was there for two weeks—was to "associate [my] being bodies with the brain of Albion for the mission of working in Albion," the Ofanim told me. "The Maidens at Maiden Castle and the Merry Maidens made you receptive, open to receive, attuning your being bodies like a radio. Then you went to Carnac to 'receive' the brain of Albion. Albion's brain awakens. Sirius is aligned with Gaia."

480. Many of these prodigious single standing stones appear to reside in Brittany. Research in 1880 indicated there were 6,192 standing stones in France, of which 4,747 were in Brittany, and 3,450 of these in Morbihan, the Carnac area. The 15 tallest menhirs in all of France were in Brittany, and ranged from 24.6 to 67.3 feet tall, with an average height for most of about 30 feet. John Michell, *Megalithomania: Artists, Antiquarians, and Archeologists at the Old Stone Monuments* (London: Thames and Hudson, 1982): 81.

481. "The enclosure was a 'burgh,' a 'dun,' a 'caer,' 'urbs antiqua,' 'veterum castrum,' almost always implying a fortified permanent settlement." A. H. A. Hogg, *A Guide to the Hill-Forts of Britain* (London: Paladin/Granada, 1975): 17.

482. This 500-foot-high hill-fort occupies 18 acres and a commanding view and was known as the hollow hill in which King Arthur and his retired Grail Knights of Camalate were sleeping. As the sixteenth-century antiquarian John Leland noted, at the south end of the church of South Cadbury stands "Camallate, sumtyme a famouse toun or castelle" to which Arthur "much resortid." John Leland, quoted in Janet and Colin Bord, *A Guide to Ancient Sites in Britain* (London: Paladin/Granada, 1978): 31

483. Obviously, these "boils" would have been made in the very early, literally formative days of the planet when the Earth was like malleable soft clay. "As old as Eggardon hill" is a folk saying in Dorset, the home of a 20-acre hill-fort at Askerwell, and this saying aptly captures the extreme antiquity of this geomantic feature.

484. In August 1996 scientists announced that an examination of a Martian meteorite revealed evidence of organic compounds suggestive of the presence of microorganisms. The Nakhla Meteorite, discovered in 2000 and said to be 1.2 billion years old, indicates ancient Martian oceans had a mineral composition comparable to Earth's. In fact, to date, 12 meteorites from Mars have been identified; 11 are younger than 1.3 billion years, but the one discovered in 1996, called ALH 84001, is estimated to be 4.5 billion years old. The evidence from all 12 meteorites is thought to be "strong evidence pointing to primitive bacterial life on Mars." Dr. David R. Williams, NASA Goddard Space Flight Center, "Life on Mars?" December 10, 2002, published at: www.nssdc.gsfc.nasa/planetary/marslife.html.

485. The barrows we find today throughout the British Isles are usually covered by earth, or show clear evidence of once having been completely encased in earth, even if much of that has since fallen away. Sometimes they are made entirely of stone and are called cairns. Of the 650 round barrows at Dartmoor in England, nearly all are the cairn type. They range in length from 65 to 400 feet; their width is usually one-half to one-quarter their length; their height varies from three to seven feet on average; and in most cases, the "business end" or front doorway is eastward.

486. Sally Exon, Vince Gaffney, Ann Woodward, and Ron Yorston, *Stonehenge Landscapes: Journeys through Real and Imagined Worlds* (Oxford, UK: Archaeopress, 2002), 45.

487. Leslie V. Grinsell, *Barrows in England and Wales* (Aylesbury, UK: Shire Publications, 1979): 20.

488. An uncertain though intriguing link to uranium and plutonium exists with the placement of megaliths in general. According to French

archeologist Roger Joussaume, "There are many areas in the world where megaliths exist, and they correspond to sites where uranium is found. Where no megaliths exist, no one has yet found the grey gold." The only exception is Denmark, which has thousands of megaliths but no uranium, though there is some 186 miles away from the border. Roger Joussaume, *Dolmens for the Dead: Megalith-Building throughout the World* (London: Guild Publishing, 1988): 21–22.

489. Geoffrey of Monmouth, *The History of the Kings of Britain*, trans. Lewis Thorpe (New York: Penguin Books, 1966): 73–74.

490. Euripides, *Heracles,* trans. William Arrowsmith, in *Euripides II: The Complete Greek Tragedies*, ed. David Grene and Richmond Lattimore (Chicago: University of Chicago Press, 1958): 95.

491. Euripides, *The Trojan Women*, trans. Richmond Lattimore, in *Euripides III: The Complete Greek Tragedies*, ed. David Grene and Richmond Lattimore (Chicago: University of Chicago Press, 1956): 165.

492. Kurt Leland, *Otherwhere: A Field Guide to Nonphysical Reality for the Out-of-Body Traveler* (Charlottesville, VA: Hampton Roads, 2001): 150.

493. *Sir Gawain and the Green Knight*, trans. Brian Stone (New York: Penguin Books, 1959): 103.

494. You find the same story in the Persian-Uzbeki myth of Afrasiab, the Alive King of the Dead. According to myths preserved at Samarkand in Uzbekistan, Afrasiab, after whom the core of the ancient city was originally named, was once human; he lived for 2,000 years under the tutelage of the Goddess Anakhita and had many adventures and initiations. Then Anakhita made him Alive King of the Dead at Samarkand since he understood the secret of immortality and could guide humans in their transition from life to afterdeath.

495. In physical terms, it is believed that the massive Tomb of the Patriarchs, a temple in Hebron, about 15 miles south of Jerusalem, is the actual site of the biblical Cave of Machpelah, which is thought to lie under the huge stone building, itself 2,000 years old. Today, over 300,000 people annually visit Ma'arat HaMachpelah in Hebron, Israel's second holiest site after the Temple Mount.

496. It's also vital not to confuse Underworld entrances with portals into the hollow of the planet, the *sipapuni,* as discussed earlier. These are physical if hidden entrances to a physical realm, and while that may literally be under our world, it is a parallel physical human civilization and not the Underworld, or lower astral realm.

497. Carlo Suares, "The Cipher of Genesis," in *The Qabala Trilogy* (Boston: Shambhala, 1985): 91.

498. Ned Dougherty, *Fast Lane to Heaven: Celestial Encounters That Changed My Life* (Charlottesville, VA: Hampton Roads, 2001): 30–33.

499. Jeremy Naydler, *Temple of the Cosmos: The Ancient Egyptian Experience of the Sacred* (Rochester, VT: Inner Traditions, 1996): 215.

500. Ibid., 215–216, 221.

501. Yama as Judge of the Dead does not condemn us for our misguided life deeds; rather, he "only holds up the mirror of conscience, in which every being pronounces his own judgment," in the Halls of Maat or the karma arena. According to Tibetan Buddhist belief, Yama is an emanation of an exalted spiritual being called Amitabha Bodhisattva who descends into the Underworld out of compassion for created, existent beings and helps them "transform suffering into a cleansing fire" so they can "rise to better forms of existence." Lama Anagarika Govinda, *Foundations of Tibetan Mysticism* (York Beach, ME: Samuel Weiser, 1969): 239.

502. It is 37 light years from Earth. Its diameter is 20 million miles, which is about 25 times bigger than our Sun, and its luminosity is 115 times that of our Sun. One of this star's remarkable facts is that it has the largest annual proper motion of all first magnitude stars, excepting one; its large and fast apparent motion brings the star ever closer to the Earth (traveling at three miles per second) since it first became visible to the naked eye some 500,000 years ago, although after a few more thousand years its approach velocity will diminish to zero and Arcturus will start to recede from our view.

Arcturus appears to be moving a lot faster than our Sun, which merely goes with the stream of galactic traffic. Astronomers explain this apparent rapid motion as due to the fact that it moves "in a highly inclined orbit around the center of the galaxy and is presently cutting through the galactic plane." Robert Burnham Jr., *Burnham's Celestial Handbook, Vol. 1, Andromeda-Cetus* (New York: Dover Publications, 1978): 302–303.

503. The dome for Arcturus is located at Chaco Canyon in New Mexico, and the widely remarked Sun Dagger atop Fajada Butte in Chaco (a dagger of light penetrates a ridged spiral petroglyph at the solstices) was made by beings from Arcturus. The Sun Dagger signifies "the point outside time, the point of timelessness through which one perceives all time." Thus Chaco is a gateway on Earth in the same sense that Arcturus is in the galaxy.

504. In ancient times, such as classical Greece, this kind of voluntary immersion in the Underworld was part of the Mysteries practiced at Eleusis, 12 miles from Athens. The actual details of the Mystery initiation at Eleusis were not recorded—they were mysteries after all, reserved for the illumination of the initiated—but they seemed to involve an epiphany of Persephone, the Queen of the Underworld and Hades' consort.

505. Rev. Lewis speculated that possibly the oak avenue stood when Joseph of Arimathea landed in Glastonbury and was greeted by King Arviragus, and that possibly his landing place had been here at the head of the oak processional, which was at sea level. "The sea must have come up to just below the oaks, and it would have been a very possible landing place," he proposed. Local legend has it that Joseph of Arimathea, after landing, planted an oak in memory of the occasion and it was afterwards known as the Oak of Avalon. Lionel Smithett Lewis, *St. Joseph of Arimathea at Glastonbury* (Cambridge, UK: James Clarke, 1922): 29–32.

506. In Qabala's two-dimensional model of the Tree of Life—this is the one traditionally used in popular texts—three parallel pillars are posited. Two represent opposite energies; the one in the middle is the balance between them. Often these two contrary pillars are called Boaz and Jachin, but according to the Ofanim, they might as well be called Gog and Magog, or anima and animus. The Avenue of Oaks mirrors this schematic, with the avenue of light between the trees representing the central balancing pillar in the Tree of Life model.

507. Robert Graves and Raphael Patai, *Hebrew Myths: The Book of Genesis* (New York: Greenwich House/Arlington House, 1983): 57–59.

508. Lucifer's alleged rebellion is clearly illustrated in his Islamic guise as Iblis, also called *Shaytan* (an early form of Satan) in the Quran.

Iblis is a spirit of fire and refused to follow God's commandment to bow before and serve humans, mere creatures of earth (clay). Iblis was outraged that God would ask him to prostrate himself before such a lowly creature as Man. "The essence of his sin was rebellion against God provoked by pride." Jeffrey Burton Russell, *Lucifer: The Devil in the Middle Ages* (Ithaca, NY: Cornell University Press, 1984): 55.

509. The Air reference is apt, because the Heart chakra, of which the Emerald is the esoteric, in-between zone (refer to chapter 2), is the chakra of the Air element. For the theological tradition to retain this attribution of Satan as Prince of the Power of Air is a long-lived remnant of the original knowledge of Lucifer as Lord of the Heart. Satan is also equated with Sammael, a Seraphim of ambivalent reputation; with the Islamic Iblis; and the Zoroastrian Ahaitin or Angra Mainyu, the opponent of the solar god, Ahura Mazda. His other epithets include Prince of Lies, Father of the Lie, Prince of Evil, Prince of Evil Spirits, and Keeper of Hell.

510. Even Satan began pure. He was said to be 12-winged, originally called *ha-Satan,* the chief of the Seraphim, wearing the nine hierarchic orders of angels "as a garment, transcending all in glory and knowledge," according to Pope Saint Gregory the Great (540–604). Nor would he be "evil" forever. According to church fathers and apologists Jerome, Gregory of Nyssa, Origen, Ambrosiaster, and others, one day Satan would be reinstated in his "pristine splendor and original rank." In the meantime he had a job to do as the Devil.

Gustav Davidson, *A Dictionary of Angels, Including the Fallen Angels* (New York: The Free Press, 1967): 261.

511. He has three heads, and their chins jut above the ice; each mouth is eating a human being, and each face is a different color. He is repulsive to behold, says Dante, noting "the shaggy coat of the king demon." Lucifer has two wings under each of the three heads, but they are like bat's wings. The frantic flapping of these wings creates three winds merging as one great storm, which freezes all of Cocytus, the Underworld river along which Charon ferries the souls of the dead. Dante and his guide, Virgil, climb out of Hell by gripping Lucifer's hair and using it like a rope ladder. Arriving aboveground

again, they see Lucifer's legs projecting into the air, upside down, his torso and head buried, as if he hasn't moved since he was propelled from Heaven headfirst. Dante Alighieri, Canto XXXIV, "The Inferno," in *The Divine Comedy*, trans. John Ciardi (New York: W. W. Norton, 1977): 178–180.

512. His eyes are baleful, his dungeon horrible, and on all sides of him great fires burn like a furnace, Milton wrote. He has no hope, only endless torture in his "Prison ordain'd/In utter darkness." Why does everyone hate him so? Because through his fall from grace and his revolt with the Rebel Angels, he was responsible for humanity's first disobedience to God and for the introduction of physical death. How changed he is now, said Milton, compared to his earliest days, where in "the Happy Realms of Light/Cloth'd with transcendent brightness didst [he] out-shine/Myriads though bright." John Milton, *Paradise Lost* (New York: Collier Books/Crowell Collier, 1962): (Book 1, lines 26–115), 16–18.

513. "Though I am not all-knowing, much is known to me!" he declares. Mephistopheles has been called Destroyer, Liar, God of Flies—which of these titles accurately describes you, Faust queries him. He offers to stay with Faust and "profitably" pass his time with beguiling arts such that in one hour, Faust's senses will experience more than in all the previous years of his life combined. Here's the key exchange, the contract: He promises Faust that if he'll take Mephistopheles "as a mate" and go through life with him, he will agree to "be your comrade to the grave." He will serve Faust in all circumstances, without rest during his life if Faust does the same for him when they stand together "in the beyond," after death. In other words, Faust must surrender his soul to servitude on behalf of Mephistopheles after his physical death. Johann Wolfgang von Goethe, *Faust: A Tragedy*, trans. Alice Raphael (New York: Heritage Press, 1930): 46, 49, 55, 56, 57.

514. "He is aptly named the Morning Star because it is his light that heralds for man the dawn of a greater consciousness." Lucifer, Spangler commented, is "a great and mighty planetary consciousness" who bears the light of wisdom. Lucifer's task, said Spangler, was to give humans energies to strengthen their inner being such that the "light of the microcosmic world would be kindled" and burn more brightly than ever. David

Spangler, *Reflections on the Christ* (Forres, Scotland: The Findhorn Foundation, 1977): 26, 32.

515. *My Dear Alexias: Letters from Wellesley Tudor Pole to Rosamond Lehmann*, ed. Elizabeth Gaythorpe (Jersey, Channel Islands, UK: Neville Spearman, 1979): 154.

516. Carl Kerenyi, *Prometheus: Archetypal Image of Human Existence*, trans. Ralph Mannheim (Princeton, NJ: Princeton University Press, 1963): 3, 45.

517. Perhaps the mythic Mount Caucasus is Mount Damavand in Iran, which has a very similar myth attributed to it (it is a Lucifer Binding Site). The culture hero Faridu (also called Fredun, Faridun, and Thraetona) forcibly binds a demonic being with three heads, three mouths, and six eyes, variously called Bevarasp, Azidahaka, Azdahak, Dahak, and Zohak, to a rock, with mighty chains and nails driven into his hands, and leaves him there to perish in agony. Dahak was bound and chained on top of Mount Damavand under the hot sun and with no shelter. His chains cut into his flesh, and he was consumed with thirst; but one day in the future he would escape his binds and generate a massive surge of evil into the world, the old Persian texts, such as the *Bundahisn* and the *Shah-Nama*, or *Epic of Kings*, tell us.

518. Aeschylus, *Prometheus Bound*, trans. David Grene (Chicago: University of Chicago Press, 1942): 139, 140, 143, 148, 155, 172.

519. Ibid., 155.

520. Mephistopheles is of a different order of being, and one that in fact is opposed to the human mastery of free will. They are probably of the more advanced orders of demons, but a convenient and more familiar term for them is gurus. They are astral gurus, or guru-beings, who offer to take away your pain, your not-knowing, your seeming inability to get what you want, in exchange for your soul. They work through physically incarnate humans who assume the guise of gurus, authoritative teachers, mentors, spiritual counselors, and the like. These are the true snakes in the Garden, for when you sign the contract, this gives them permission to cord themselves through your entire energy body, entering through your crown chakra and growing downwards through all your major and minor chakras like a carrot thrusting through pliable soil. You're stuck with the guru-being until you cancel the contract, and that

could be many lifetimes into the future. This is how you sell your soul to the Devil. You get knowledge, like Faust, or solace, potency, power, worship, adoration, at the cost of your spiritual freedom. You are no longer free; you are no longer yourself. Guru-beings like Mephistopheles don't give you freedom; they take yours away.

521. The comments by the Ofanim are culled from material gathered from conversations with them during the years 1984–2002. The Elohim's quoted remarks date from June 8, 1986.

522. Also known as Seir, or Mount Seir, the Edomite land was about 40 miles wide and 100 miles long, between the Dead Sea and Gulf of Aqabah. The Kings were known as Bela, Jobab, Husham, Hadad, Samlab, Saul, Baal-hanan, and Hadar. David conquered the eight kings of Edom and put his own garrisons throughout their land, but after the Temple of Jerusalem was destroyed in 586 B.C. by the Babylonians, the Edomites rejoiced at their losses and began reclaiming Palestine.

523. The Kings of Edom who reigned over Israel before there was a king, according to the Qabala, is a reference to a time of unbalanced forces and psychic instability, while Israel itself (not the country) allegorizes "a type of the condition of the worlds which came into existence subsequently to the later period when equilibrium had become established." H. P. Blavatsky, *The Theosophical Glossary* (Los Angeles: Theosophy Company, 1990 [1892]): 110.

524. "The Book of Concealed Mystery," in *The Kabbalah Unveiled*, trans. S. L. MacGregor Mathers (York Beach, ME: Samuel Weiser, 1968): 43, 48.

525. They are called Kings because on the abstract, archetypal level, they represent the seven Sefirot and their ultimately unbalanced condition used in this first creation (Chesed to Malkuth).

526. One version of the myth of Lilith says Adam too left Eden, had intercourse with Lilith, and populated the world with demon offspring at the rate of 100 per day, presumably the Edomites, and including Cain, the first murderer. Lilith is also accused of being the bride of the demon Sammael (Satan). Associated with uncleanliness and evil, she is perpetually trying to ensnare humans. It's said that once the prophet Elijah forced Lilith to reveal the 17 different names she used in her different disguises as she performed her evil deeds among humans. Another source gave 27 names; another said she commands 480 legions of demons and that she is the Princess of Screeching, roaming the night like an owl. Further, Lilith is the Mother and Queen of the *Shedim* (Pourers Forth) and *Muquishim* (Ensnarers), and her daughters are known as *Lilins,* a type of devil. Shedim (or Siddim) is Hebrew for "nature spirits" or "elementals," but it also seems to denote demons; they are the same as the *Afrits* in modern Egypt and the Djinns of Persia and India. Some sources claim Lilith was the Queen of Sheba, King Solomon's consort; others that as a demon she disturbed Solomon's Torah studies, making the Hebrew letters fly up off the pages. She was regarded as a temptress-succubus, eliciting night sex from sleeping men. In fact, Lilith was associated primarily with the night, and Babylonian demonesses were called *lilitu,* female night spirits, presumably after her.

527. The Hopis of North America forward a similar myth. They say that our present world and reality are called *Tuwaqachi*, the Fourth World, which means "World Complete." It was created by Sotuknang after He destroyed the Third World, called *Kuskurza* (an untranslatable ancient term). This World was destroyed when the humans started using their reproductive powers in wicked ways, misused their creative energies for magic, conflict, and warfare, and generally forgot to praise the Supreme Being and His creation. They were unable to conform to the plan of Creation and instead became preoccupied with their own terrestrial intrigues. Spider Woman, having been warned by Sotuknang of the coming Deluge, instructed selected humans to prepare for the flood; she sealed them up in hollow reeds that floated on top of the floodwaters until they subsided. All their large proud cities were now at the bottom of the seas. The Hopi version differs from the Judaic in that the Hopis posit four Worlds, not two: The first was paradisal but was destroyed by fire sent by Sotuknang; the second was destroyed again by its maker by a sudden pole reversal that turned the planet to ice; the third was overturned by water. See: Frank Waters, *Book of the Hopi* (New York: Penguin Books/Viking Penguin, 1977): 3–20.

528. We don't, and the Edomites remain in the collective Shadow, passingly referred to by various names, such as Djinn, mentioned previ-

ously. The Djinn are known to Islamic cultures as invisible, illusion-casting species who are centuries old, can travel anywhere, manifest instantly, and live in the desert. They are intermediate spirits, between angels and humans. The Quran says they are an ancient species created before humans from smokeless fire. They lack bodies but can assume any guise they choose. Since they are made of fire, when they manifest, their eyes appear to flame and are set vertically in their head.

529. Rabbi Moses C. Luzzatto, *General Principles of the Kabbalah* (New York: The Press of the Research Centre of Kabbalah/Samuel Weiser, 1970): 24–27.

530. The Vedic tradition talks of antigods and Asuras, and these are probably equivalent to the Judaic formulation of the Kings of Edom. The antigods are older than the gods (but both were progeny of Prajapati, Lord of Creatures); the antigods struggle with each other for dominion of the worlds. Originally, the Earth, its forests, mountains, and oceans were ruled by powerful *genii* called *daitya,* but these were later overcome and killed by Vishnu. The antigods delighted in the play of life energies through the senses, in all that drew humans away from the path of gaining full consciousness. Their name says it all: Asura, meaning "delight" *(ra)* in "life" *(asu).* According to the *Mahabharata,* India's vast epic saga, the Asuras multiplied and became proud, vain, quarrelsome, and shameless; they were liars and preferred to exercise their power at night. "They infringed the law, neglected the sacrifices, did not visit the holy places to cleanse themselves from sin." They tortured living creatures, generated confusion, and challenged the gods. They were animated by passion and rage as the "Divine Law had disappeared from them." One of the many types of Asuras described in Vedic tradition are the *nivata-kavacas,* "wearers of impenetrable armor," which matches an aspect of my perception of the Edomite Kings. Another is *dasyus,* "barbarians," which also matches a nuance described in the text. Alain Danielou, *The Myths and Gods of India* (Rochester, VT: Inner Traditions, 1991): 139–143.

Early Vedic references to Asuras portray them as lords, leaders of a fighting force, wielding a magical power called *maya,* and of an uncertain status between human and gods. They are godless enemies of the gods whom the gods' leader, Indra, slays with his vajra weapon, a kind of thunderbolt, in a cataclysmic battle between the gods and Asuras on the Earth in primordial days. The Asuras have coverings of different colors, use metal nets, roam the word at will assuming large or small shapes, and are the demonic enemies of Agni, the Fire god. See: Edward Hale Wash, *Asura in Early Vedic Religion* (Delhi, India: Motilal Banarsidass, 1986).

531. Rabbi Moses C. Luzzatto, *General Principles of the Kabbalah* (New York: The Press of the Research Centre of Kabbalah/Samuel Weiser, 1970): 153.

532. Certainly the gods were, if not by the Kings of Edom then by the Frost Giants, as evidenced in Norse myth. The Aesir, or gods of Asgard, were so intimidated by the threat of the Frost Giants overrunning Asgard, that they commissioned one of their own to build a fortress-type wall around it, a job which remained incomplete due to political wranglings among the gods. The Hoarfrost Giants, or *Hrimbursar,* were created by Ymir, the original Man, who also created the Giants. The Frost Giants grew out of Ymir's toes, but all of them, save one, Bergelmir and his mate, were drowned in a deluge of blood that flooded the entire world when the chief god, Odin, so ordered it. Bergelmir founded a second race of Frost Giants, and they lived in Jotunheim.

533. C. G. Jung, *Answer to Job,* Fiftieth Anniversary Edition, trans. R. F. C. Hull (Princeton, NJ: Princeton University Press, 2002): 10.

534. Ibid., 10, 11, 15, 19, 20–21, 29.

535. Frank Waters, *Book of the Hopi* (New York: Penguin Books/Viking Penguin, 1977): 26.

536. The Luciferic impulse had impregnated the human etheric body for eons, and Luciferic spiritual currents perpetually streamed into it. This was the primordial light out of which the etheric body of the human (and planet) was originally formed. Humans experienced these Luciferic currents as the inwardmost aspect of their being. By the time of the Mystery of Golgotha, this stream had become exhausted, and Lucifer became invisible to humans. Golgotha marked a complete reversal of the roles and placements of Christ and Lucifer. Christ penetrated the Earth, becoming an inner spiritual reality to the clairvoyants on the planet, while Lucifer, ascending, shone forth as a cosmic god. Christ became

apparent within human soul life as an indwelling reality, while Lucifer assumed ever greater radiance in the outer world. In the future, Steiner said early in the twentieth century, Christ will be increasingly realized by way of inner meditation, while Lucifer will be perceived when one directs one's spiritual gaze outwards into the cosmos.

537. Rudolf Steiner, *The East in the Light of the West* (Blauvelt, NY: Spiritual Science Library, 1986): 6–7, 97–99, 118–125, 130–132, 136–137. See also: Richard Leviton, *The Imagination of Pentecost: Rudolf Steiner and Contemporary Spirituality* (Hudson, NY: Anthroposophic Press, 1994): 330–335.

538. Rudolf Steiner, *The Deed of Christ, and the Opposing Powers Lucifer, Ahriman, Mephistopheles, Asuras* (North Vancouver, BC, Canada: Steiner Book Centre, 1954): 18.

539. Rudolf Steiner, *The East in the Light of the West* (Blauvelt, NY: Spiritual Science Library, 1986): 3–6.

540. You get a clear picture of Lucifer as a divine being full of stars through the Egyptian myth of Nut, the Sky Goddess, her body packed with stars. Nut is most often shown as a female stretched over the sky, her body forming an arc like a rainbow, her outstretched hands touching the Earth at one horizon, her feet grounded at the other. In fact, her body arches over all of the Earth, touching down in the four cardinal directions. She is clothed in stars, planets, and celestial lights, although more precisely, these comprise her body. She is the Goddess of the Celestial Vault, Mother and Guardian of all. Nut's epithets included the Great Deep, the Starry One, Cow Goddess, Mother of the Gods, Mother of the Sun, Protector of the Dead, and Mystery of the Heavens. Nut is *Khabewes*, "One with a Thousand Souls," in which "souls" is understood to mean star gods, whom she birthed. She is Great Protector, Grand Horizon, Mother of the Gods. She—Lucifer—is the Mighty One who gave birth to all the gods, stars, and planets. The figure of Nut obviously blends aspects of Lucifer and the Great Mother, the Mother aspect of God.

541. It's said of Tezcatlipoca, the dark opponent of Quetzalcoatl, that he descended to the Earth on a spider's web or a rope of cobweb. This is an intriguingly suggestive reference to the stellar matrix comprising Lucifer and the Christ, which in general terms could be likened to a spider's web.

542. Aeschylus, *Prometheus Bound*, trans. David Grene (Chicago: University of Chicago Press, 1942): 139, 141.

543. This term today already carries a certain amount of cultural baggage and preconception. But the popular science fiction series called *Stargate SG-1* (shown on the SciFi channel on cable and based on the original movie from 1994), with its wormhole portal to other planets, is close to what I mean by a stargate in geomantic terms.

544. It's intriguing to note that 49 of these still incomplete stargates sit, higher dimensionally, in the space between the Tigris and Euphrates rivers, a 125-mile stretch roughly between Baghdad and Basra, Iraq. The remainder of the incomplete stargates are in the Gobi Desert in Mongolia. These 88 incomplete stargates have not yet been assigned constellation destinations.

545. Once you have seen and experienced a stargate, you can use this information to help pinpoint likely prospects for other stargates, such as the Devil's Tower in Wyoming, that anomalous bare-stone cone of a peak that rises 1,267 feet above the Belle Fourche River, which was a centerpiece in Steven Spielberg's film *Close Encounters of the Third Kind*. Here is the stargate clue: Five different tribes of Native Americans relate essentially the same story about seven young girls chased by a grizzly bear until they hid on a low rock and prayed to the Supreme Being for help. Immediately, the rock began to rise and grow upwards; soon it was the peak known as *Mato Tipila*, "Grizzly Bear Lodge." It continued to grow upwards until soon it had reached the starfields of the galaxy and the girls became the seven stars of the Pleiades. A rock growing vertically to become a mountain that goes all the way into the galaxy to where the Pleiades will be is in my interpretation a stargate *to* the Pleiades, semantically cloaked in Indian legend-telling. To say the mountain grew all the way to the Pleiades (many light years distant from Earth) is to say the mountain transported the girls there and is a conduit to the Seven Sisters of the Pleiades.

546. The concept of the Merkabah (also spelled Merkavah) was developed in the first chapter of Ezekiel, in which he describes a monumental vision by the River Chebar of the divine chariot. This vision has often been foolishly interpreted to mean UFOs and ET ships appearing overhead, but its reality is far more subtle and

exalted than that type of apparition. In Merkabah mysticism the Merkabah is taken to be synonymous with what's called the *Shi'ur Komah,* the mystical shape of the Godhead—in other words, God's size and shape, His height and stature, as well as the details of His *Kavod,* or celestial Glory. In Ezekiel's description of the "Chariot of Yahweh," or Merkabah, he describes a magnificent chariot with a driver, wheels of fire and angelic faces, the four Holy Beasts (angelic animals with human faces and multiple wings), a human-like being shining like bronze and made of fire seated on a sapphire throne, and much more. See: Gershom Scholem, *On the Mystical Shape of the Godhead: Basic Concepts in the Kabbalah,* trans. Joachim Neugroschel (New York: Schocken Books, 1991): 20–47.

547. Again, I refer the reader to the chapter on Tetford in *The Galaxy on Earth.* Tetford has an energy feature called a dome, which corresponds to the alpha star in the constellation Aquarius; the nearby city of Lincoln has a dome that represents Aquarius's beta star. Thus between the two sites, much of the Aquarian energy is being grounded for the planet at this time.

548. Henry Corbin, "Cyclical Time in Mazdaism and Ismailism," in *Man and Time: Papers from the Eranos Yearbooks,* Bollingen Series XXX.3, trans. Ralph Mannheim and R. F. C. Hull (Princeton, NJ: Princeton University Press, 1983): 139–140.

549. Henry Corbin, *Spiritual Body and Celestial Earth: From Mazdean Iran to Shi'ite Iran,* Bollingen Series XCI.2, trans. Nancy Pearson. (Princeton, NJ: Princeton University Press, 1977): 13–16, 44, 45, 125.

550. Ibid., 29, 31.

551. W. K. C. Guthrie, *Orpheus and Greek Religion: A Study of the Orphic Movement* (Princeton, NJ: Princeton University Press, 1993): 75, 76, 80, 95.

552. G. A. Gaskell, *Dictionary of All Scriptures and Myths* (New York: Julian Press, 1960): 242–243.

553. Barbara C. Sproul, *Primal Myths: Creation Myths around the World* (San Francisco: HarperSanFrancisco, 1979): 169.

554. W. K. C. Guthrie, *Orpheus and Greek Religion: A Study of the Orphic Movement* (Princeton, NJ: Princeton University Press, 1993): 100, 101, 223.

555. Jane Ellen Harrison, *Prolegomena to the Study of Greek Religion* (Princeton, NJ: Princeton University Press, 1991): 626, 650, 656.

556. H. P. Blavatsky, *The Secret Doctrine: The Synthesis of Science, Religion, and Philosophy, Vol. 2: Anthropogenesis* (Pasadena, CA: Theosophical University Press, 1977): 511–513.

557. Martin Brennan, *The Hidden Maya* (Santa Fe, NM: Bear and Company, 1998): 68–69.

558. One myth says at the end of his career as king, Quetzalcoatl immolated himself, and the ashes, rising upwards, turned into birds with gorgeous plumage—phoenix-like quetzal birds perhaps. In one Mayan document, he is shown "descending on a celestial cord through a fleshy opening in a sky band decorated with Venus glyphs in a scene that refers to his rebirth with divine attributes." His slow descent along this cord, archeoastronomers suggest, might be an imitation of the slow descent of the Morning Star phase. See: Susan Milbrath, *Star Gods of the Maya: Astronomy in Art, Folklore, and Calendars* (Austin, TX: University of Texas Press, 1999): 183.

559. They also said when he died, he was invisible for four days, then wandered for eight days in the Underworld, then when the Morning Star appeared again, he was resurrected and regained his throne. In effect, Quetzalcoatl was the Venus god. Based on Mayan art, calendrics, and cosmology, Venus, the "sun passer" and "great star" *(nima ch'umil),* was to them the most important planet, and recording the planet's changing horizon positions was common. Lewis Spence, *The Myths of Mexico and Peru* (London: George G. Harrap, 1913): 79–80.

560. He was the Smoking Mirror, Lord of the Surface of the Earth, Lord of the Nine Hells, god of death and destruction, Black God of the North, ruler of the past world.

561. Credit for popularizing the otherwise obscure Zapotec myth that fueled the global Harmonic Convergence goes to Tony Shearer who in 1971 published a series of Zapotec prophecies in *Lord of the Dawn.* He envisioned Quetzalcoatl's return to his tree as he came from the East like the Morning Star. Thunder would roll in the sky, the heavens would grow dark with heavy rain, and bright blue lightning would illuminate the Valley of Oaxaca. It would happen on August 16, 1987, Shearer wrote.

562. Tony Shearer, *Lord of the Dawn:*

Quetzalcoatl, the Plumed Serpent of Mexico (Happy Camp, CA: Naturegraph Publishers, 1971): 134, 189.

563. H. P. Blavatsky, *The Secret Doctrine: The Synthesis of Science, Religion, and Philosophy, Vol. 2: Anthropogenesis* (Pasadena, CA: Theosophical University Press, 1977): 46.

564. For a full descriptive, firsthand report of these events, see "The Lord of the Tree Returns: A Perspective on the Harmonic Convergence," Richard Leviton, *Life Times* 5 (1988): 84–91.

565. Tim LeHaye and Jerry B. Jenkins, *Left Behind: A Novel of the Earth's Last Days* (Wheaton, IL: Tyndale House, 1995): 194.

566. Gordon-Michael Scallion, *Notes from the Cosmos: A Futurist's Insights into the World of Dream Prophecy and Intuition* (W. Chesterfield, NH: Matrix Institute, 1997): 170.

567. Gregg S. Braden, *Awakening to Zero Point: The Collective Initiation* (Questa, NM: Sacred Spaces, Ancient Wisdom, 1994): 52, 53, 67.

568. Zecharia Sitchin, *The Twelfth Planet* (Santa Fe, NM: Bear and Company, 1991): 224.

569. John Major Jenkins, *Galactic Alignment: The Transformation of Consciousness According to Mayan, Egyptian, and Vedic Traditions* (Rochester, VT: Inner Traditions, 2002): 2.

570. Tom Bissell, "A Comet's Tale: On the Science of Apocalypse," *Harper's* 306:1833 (February 2003): 33–47.

571. This belt contains an estimated 40,000 asteroids larger than 0.5 mile across, although the total estimated mass of all the asteroids is less than 1/1000th the mass of the Earth; the total estimated combined diameter of all the asteroid rock would measure about 810 to 930 miles across, which is less than one-third the diameter of the Moon. NASA astronomers are not yet willing to admit the possibility that an exploded planet created the asteroid belt, although laypeople are suspecting it might be possible.

572. We find another illuminating nuance to Lucifer's multivalent character in the Norse mythic characterization of Loki and his offspring, Fenrir the Wolf.

Loki, companion, servant, and nemesis to the Aesir, the gods of Asgard, and particularly of Thor (the Norse Zeus), is the song of the Wing Giant called Farbauti and Laufey ("Leafy Isle"), his wife. Farbauti is sometimes understood to be the same as Bergelmir, the sole survivor of the Flood, thus making Loki a deity of extreme antique origin. Loki is also sometimes said to be the son of the great giant Fornjotnr (the same as the Norse primordial prototype of humanity and all creation, Ymir, equivalent to the Qabalistic Adam Kadmon).

Loki is pure ambivalence: He is a doer of good and evil; he helps and hinders the gods; he is Thor's traveling companion throughout the nine worlds, and he is Thor's enemy under other circumstances. He is the trickster, the thief, the cunning one, the sky traveler, the schemer, the deceiver. Once the embodiment of fire and the spirit of life and having endowed humanity with the power of motion and circulation, Loki becomes seen as the personification of mischief and evil. He stands for the seductive beauty by which evil parades through the phenomenal world. He is selfish and malevolent, ultimately seeking only his own good, according to the Norse sagas.

He starts out as a god, Thor's peer, possibly his brother, then becomes a confusing amalgam of god and devil, "and ends being held in general detestation as an exact counterpart of the mediaeval Lucifer, the prince of lies, 'the originator of deceit, and the backbiter' of the Aesir [the gods of Asgard]."

On one occasion Loki traveled to Jarnvid in the Iron Wood, a land of "foul witches," according to the Norse sagas, and ate the heart of the witch Gulveig. Later he married the giantess Angrboda ("Anguish-Boding") and produced three formidable offspring: the Midgard Serpent (which encircles the planet), Hel (the mistress of Niflheim, the Underworld and Land of the Dead), and Fenrir (a wolf of prodigious size).

Loki bestows boons and disasters. Loki is responsible for the birth of Sleipnir, Odin's magical eight-legged steed, yet he also causes the death of Odin's precious son, the beautiful Balder (the Norse Christ). For Odin, this act is unforgivable, and the gods set out to capture and bind Loki as a punishment. The gods are shocked that Loki's machinations led to the first death of a god.

It is against the laws of Asgard to commit murder, so they have to settle for binding Loki and removing him from the world of action. The gods capture him using Loki's owning fishing net, then bind him to a rock inside a dim cavern. They tie him down to three slabs of rocks using the entrails of his slain children to hold him fast. They place a venomous snake above him so that venom will drip down onto his face continuously, filling him with anguish and torment.

Loki's faithful wife, Sigyn, holds a wooden bowl over his face so as to collect the poison; when it's full, she empties this fermenting bowl of poison into a rock basin. Meanwhile, Loki shudders and writhes in misery, and the entire Earth quakes with his torment. He knows he cannot escape—until Ragnarok, the cataclysmic End Times known as the Twilight of the Gods when a necessity higher even than that of Thor or Odin will release him at last.

Clearly the binding of Loki reminds us of the binding of Prometheus, although whether Loki performed deeds commendable to the world of humans is unclear, if in doubt. However, the saga of his progeny, Fenrir, reveals more of how the Nordic mythic mind construed Loki's transgressions. The wolf Fenrir, who is bound and punished in similar circumstances to his father, is another aspect of Loki. It would be missing the point of the symbolism to think of Loki and Fenrir as two separate beings.

The trouble with Fenrir was he was simply too big. Every day he grew larger, his strength increased, and his voracity burgeoned. His contin-ually increasing size threatened the stability of the gods; by sheer size Fenrir would command and possibly destroy the nine worlds. The gods used two types of fetters in succession, but these failed to contain Fenrir. Then the dwarves (the Norse name for gnomes) of Svartheim created a magical fetter, a kind of super-strong silken cord; they attached the cord to a boulder known as Gjoll which they pounded into the Earth for a depth of one mile; then they held it fast with a vast rock called Thviti. Then they inserted a sword in Fenrir's open mouth such that that point held the upper jaw open, the hilt pressed against the lower.

Fenrir's howls of misery were so great, and the blood and foam that dribbled out of his mouth so prodigious, that it created the River Von, the river of fury and expectation. There Fenrir would remain, bound and in agony, on the Isle of Lyngvi in Lake Amsvartnir until the end of time—until Ragnarok. Then the same cosmic necessity that would release his father, Loki, would unbind Fenrir, and he would join Loki in the great battle against the gods of Asgard. It was predicted that at Ragnarok, Fenrir would burst his chains and, with every moment, his colossal size would assume even greater proportions such that his open jaws would embrace all the space between the Earth and Heaven.

Index

About the Author

Richard Leviton is the author of ten books, including, most recently, *The Galaxy on Earth: A Traveler's Guide to the Planet's Visionary Geography* (Hampton Roads, 2002) and *What's Beyond That Star: A Chronicle of Geomythic Adventure* (Clairview Books, 2002). He regularly conducts workshops and field trips on the subject of myth, sacred sites, and landscape spirituality. He lives in Santa Fe, New Mexico, where he is the director of the Blue Room Consortium, which he describes as a "cosmic mysteries think tank" to do with Earth energies, mapping, and interactions. He may be contacted at blaise@hrpub.com.

Hampton Roads Publishing Company

. . . for the evolving human spirit

Hampton Roads Publishing Company
publishes books on a variety of subjects,
including metaphysics, health,
visionary fiction, and other related topics.

For a copy of our latest catalog, call toll-free
(800) 766-8009, or send your name and address to:

Hampton Roads Publishing Company, Inc.
1125 Stoney Ridge Road
Charlottesville, VA 22902

e-mail: hrpc@hrpub.com
www.hrpub.com